Nobody's Home

NOBODY'S HOME

Speech, Self, and Place in American Fiction from Hawthorne to DeLillo

ARNOLD WEINSTEIN

New York   Oxford
OXFORD UNIVERSITY PRESS
1993

Oxford University Press

Oxford   New York   Toronto
Delhi   Bombay   Calcutta   Madras   Karachi
Kuala Lumpur   Singapore   Hong Kong   Tokyo
Nairobi   Dar es Salaam   Cape Town
Melbourne   Auckland   Madrid

and associated companies in
Berlin   Ibadan

Copyright © 1993 by Oxford University Press, Inc.

Published by Oxford University Press, Inc.,
200 Madison Avenue, New York, New York 10016

Oxford is a registered trademark of Oxford University Press

Library of Congress Cataloging-in-Publication Data
Weinstein, Arnold L.
Nobody's home : speech, self, and place in American fiction
from Hawthorne to DeLillo / Arnold Weinstein.
p.   cm.   Includes bibliographical references (p.   ) and index.
ISBN 0-19-507493-9 — ISBN 0-19-508022-X (pbk.)
1. American fiction—History and criticism.
2. Self in literature.   3. Language and culture—United States.
4. Freedom of speech in literature.   5. Speech in literature.
6. Home in literature.   I. Title.
PS374.S44W45   1993   813.009—dc20   92-22792

The following essays appeared either in journals or books, and I am grateful for permission to reprint them in altered form: "Hawthorne's 'Wakefield' and the Art of Self-Possession" appeared in *The Scope of Words*, ed. Peter Baker (N.Y.: Peter Lang, 1991), reprinted with permission of Peter Lang. "Fiction as Greatness: The Case of *Gatsby*" appeared in *NOVEL: A Forum on Fiction*, vol. 19, no. 1, Fall 1985. Copyright. NOVEL Corp. © 1987. Reprinted with permission. "Fusion and Confusion in *Light in August*" appeared in *The Faulkner Journal*, vol. 1, no. 2, Spring 1986. Reprinted with permission of *The Faulkner Journal* and the University of Akron. Portions of W. H. Auden's "Musée des Beaux Arts" are reprinted from *W. H. Auden: Collected Poems* by W. H. Auden, ed. Edward Mendelson. Copyright 1940 and renewed 1968 by W. H. Auden. Reprinted by permission of Random House, Inc.

2 4 6 8 9 7 5 3 1

Printed in the United States of America
on acid-free paper

To my mother, and to the memory of my father

Preface

This book has been taking shape for some ten years now, and I can accurately pinpoint its origin: my stint as Fulbright professor of American literature at Stockholm University in 1982–83. At that point I had the challenging experience of teaching American fiction to Swedish university students, and although my notions of what is "American" had been percolating ever since my student days in Paris, I found that this particular venture, namely, looking at American texts "from outside in," triggered a process of reflection and self-definition that was to have real consequences.

I had, of course, worked with American literature ever since my college and graduate school days, when I had the privilege of being exposed to a host of formidable Americanists: Laurence Holland, Lawrance Thompson, Perry Miller, Harry Levin, Kenneth Lynn, Albert Gelpi. But my job at Stockholm University caused me to rethink more than my American syllabus; it shed unexpected light on my practice as a comparatist, and it forced me to see the "Americanness" of my work with European narrative, most especially concerning the origins of my cardinal belief in the freedom and maneuvering room made available to us in language and literature. This belief fuels much of what I do: reading, speaking, teaching, writing. When I realized that none of my mentors had emphasized this cluster of issues and concerns, I was led to think still further back, to the core of convictions — many of them doubtless myths, fantasies, and constructs but no less operational for all that — that has animated my thinking as long as I can remember. Stated most simply, *language as freedom* — in all the complex guises it may assume — emerges as the bedrock of American life and literature, present to me in my daily life and no less present in the fictions I read. I realized that my best work has always somehow been done in the service of those beliefs, not on any ideological grounds but rather as a way of quickening my responses and insights, a way of lifting me, critically and sympathetically, into whatever texts I was reading. I realized, ultimately, that I had been working with American themes all my life, and that now it was time to test them against the actual corpus of American fiction.

Nobody's Home is the result of these realizations. It is a very personal book in the sense that I have presented my beliefs as explicit principles for the ordering of these American materials. Yet I have consistently felt that the pieces miraculously fell into place as I wrote, that no pushing, shoving, or special pleading was necessary to enlist these varied fictions in the American design that I had in mind. I certainly understood that the keenest and liveliest view that I was likely to attain on these very different books derived from my notion of freedom of speech and self-making, but that this bias — if bias it be — strengthened rather than weakened my case, indeed, was part of my subject. It had always seemed to me that the major American texts exhibited a kind of uncanny family resemblance, and I felt that a sufficiently supple criticism could be true both to the hue and coloration of individual texts and historical moments as well as to the gathering family portrait.

It is obvious that this kind of a study goes rather breezily against the grain of most critical work being done today. My view of American fiction may be thought "unhistorical" by some readers, and my concern with mapping the career of the "self" may be considered either naive or reactionary by others. But I have been sustained by the certainty that I had a story to tell, one comprised of close-grained analyses of significant American novels, but a composite story nonetheless. This tale is ultimately about American ingenuity and resources, about a peculiar form of energy and passion that seems especially at home in this country. This is hardly a scientific thesis, nor is it the kind of argument that is easily documentable by direct testimony. On the other hand, it is not likely to be invalidated by the counterargument that American culture is unfree, that the self is a myth, or that the particulars of race, class, gender, and other determinants "actually" govern our lives — which they may, perhaps. But we live in and out of many prisons, from birth to death, and the business of fiction, as I see it, is with our desires, our flights, our reprieves, our lifelong resistance to the coercions that do us in. We are both inmates and builders; we make selves and homes. There is nothing escapist or irresponsible in this view of literature. The most serious gifts we can receive from art and literature have to do with this pursuit of freedom. From Hawthorne to DeLillo, American fiction speaks to us about the desire to be free and shows us how that struggle is played out in particular precincts and at particular moments across the centuries. Literature itself, when viewed in this way, is transformed from a mere document to a resource, from a simple record of the past to a rich repertory of the future.

In Stockholm in 1982–83 I began to formulate this view of American letters and to understand my own work in the light of these principles. A decade later, at a time when Americanness seems a more vexed and problematic notion than ever, I would like to think that *Nobody's Home* amplifies our sense of how some of our greatest writers have wrestled with the determinisms that hound both life and art. These performances, I would argue, do us proud.

Block Island, R.I.   A.W.
July 1992

Acknowledgments

A number of people have helped me in the making of this book in terms of specific readings, the larger thesis at hand, and the design of the gathering argument. It gives me pleasure to acknowledge these debts.

My twin brother, Philip, has long been a source and sounding board for my ideas about literature; his particular views on Faulkner and O'Connor, as well as his general sense of what reading and writing portend, are at play in *Nobody's Home*, and his presence in my mind doubtless influences some of these essays, especially my meditation on "twinning" in Twain. My thinking about American literature in general is indebted to the work and example of Laurence Holland, whose influence started in 1961 and still continues. More particularly, in writing and revising these chapters over the past few years, I have benefited enormously from the assessments and suggestions offered by James Cox, Donald Kartiganer, and David Minter; their response to my work, although not uncritical, had a kind of generosity that is rare in the academy. Their appraisals of this book at various stages did much to keep this enterprise afloat.

I have also been assisted by others. Thomas D'Evelyn helped me to see the ramifications of my argument in ways that I could not have managed alone. Elizabeth Maguire of Oxford University Press was unfailingly judicious and insightful in her advice to me about converting a sprawling manuscript into a book. To Susan Chang and Henry Krawitz, also of Oxford University Press, I also owe a debt of thanks for their prompt, warm, and professional assistance. To Dan Reed—artist, critic, and friend—I am grateful (once again) for the translation of my thought into his image. The genesis of this book, as I indicated in the preface, goes back to Stockholm, but the hard work of research and writing took place at my home institution, Brown University, and I am happy to acknowledge the research and editorial assistance I received from Ellen Douglass, Leanora Olivia, and Heidi Schultz. Ineke Van Dongen and Jean Sheldon have provided invaluable (and often overtime) services in the preparation of this manuscript, and these gifts of labor have meant a great deal to me.

My final acknowledgment is more personal and more profound. It may be that each of us is, in some ways, Nobody, but I have had great good luck in the Homes where I have lived. This book is dedicated to my parents, who gave me the love and support that account for much that is good in my life. As for my wife, Ann, and my children, Catherine and Alexander, they constitute both the ground and the horizon of a great deal of my life and work. Above all, I have come to understand that my concern with self, speech, and the making of a family is dependent on the family that has made me.

Contents

V THE AMERICAN POSTMODERNISTS AND
FREEDOM OF SPEECH

Nobody's Home

Introduction: Self-Making and Freedom of Speech

This book is about freedom. More pointedly it is about language as the field in which this freedom is deployed: language as human speech and gesture as well as language as the medium of literature. Our maneuvering room, our ability to resist the forces that coerce us, and above all our capacity to *make* — a self, a world — are profoundly verbal operations. And it follows that our literature is always, willy-nilly, performing a double mission: to tell stories about freedom and to make us free.

These views fly in the face of contemporary thought. We have learned that our culture and history bind us in ways beyond our control. The individual as free agent is a tarnished notion, a fully discredited and perhaps dangerous myth. And to posit language as the very arena of freedom would seem to be even more quixotic, since our post-Saussurean knowledge has made it amply clear that language is a differential system, an impersonal but culturally inflected code that always speaks both more and less than "we" intend or know. This modern reversal of authority stares us in the face in Heidegger's formulation: "Man acts as though he were the shaper and master of language, while in fact language remains the master of man. When this relation of dominance gets inverted, man hits upon strange maneuvers."[1] What meaning can freedom of speech have within these frameworks?

I have come to understand these constraints with ever greater clarity over time. But I have also come to understand something else, something perhaps deeper and more vital than this doctrine of impersonality and anonymity, of empowered ideology and decentered subjects — namely, that the basic energies of our lives are spent in the service of freedom and self-making. I am not speaking about politics. Our everyday gestures — working, entering relationships, speaking to others, thinking about one's life — share a common purpose: to make or maintain a self. To be sure, we know how much censorship and bad faith are possible in this scheme, how much terrorism and artifice may come into play in this project of self-fashioning. But the forming of self is an extraordinarily deep-seated need, and its significance is only heightened by these threatening and disabling factors. Stated most simply, it is because we

3

know the environment is both real and all-powerful, because we know that our identity is somehow a construct, that this elemental drama of self-making is so important.

I also see more clearly as time goes by that my interest in literature has invariably been focused on this issue of freedom and self-making. My earlier books on vision and response, self-enactment, and the relationship theme stemmed from this view of human freedom and self-fashioning; central to all of them is a belief that literature is a privileged arena for exhibiting these issues. The question I have avoided thus far is: *Why* do I believe this? Where does this belief come from? Using precisely the environmental logic that undercuts individual doing, I have come to understand my own posture as cultural, as an American premise: I am "conditioned" to believe in freedom. And with this understanding there follows another, very momentous one: the stubborn premise that conditions my life is an old premise, visible in the Declaration of Independence and in the works of writers from Thoreau and Whitman to Coover and Morrison. American literature reflects and refracts precisely these living beliefs, and its major item of business—despite its "knowledge" that these matters are in some sense impossible—is freedom of speech and self-making. Wallace Stevens expressed it perfectly:

> From this the poem springs: that we live in a place
> That is not our own, and much more, nor ourselves
> And hard it is, in spite of blazoned days.[2]

From this the poem springs. From this knowledge of place and self as fictions we create. And what we create is precisely place and self.

The purpose of this study, therefore, is to illuminate—across a time span ranging from Hawthorne to DeLillo—a persistent, indigenous, and intriguing feature of American fiction: the freedom of speech. Freedom is construed here in multiple ways: the quest for moral and political freedom; the freedom to "make" a self that transcends the constraints of social and economic origin; and the effort to move beyond those laws, restrictions, and codes that govern or repress human potential. These are common, perhaps mythical, assumptions about American culture, and they inform our national identity in countless ways, ranging from a personal sense of human possibilities to the image of the United States held by other nations, from the time of Tocqueville to our own day. It is hardly surprising that the American novel would tell us about these matters, and influential critics of American literature such as Richard Chase, Quentin Anderson, Richard Poirier, Tony Tanner, and Hugh Kenner have focused on the drama of individualism and the tension between freedom and constraint that inform the American scene.

Why, then, call such a study *Nobody's Home*? The answer to this question contains the central thesis of my book: America's gift to the world—the atomic self of free-enterprise fame—comes across as something of a ghost in the major fictions of the past two centuries. "Nobody's Home" is to be understood as "Nobody Is Home," as a formula for the empty shell called self; but it also means "The Home of Nobody": America as the ghost land, the home that ghosts build to become real. Needless to say, I am not talking about specters or phantoms in the gothic sense of the term; I am using the word "Nobody" to signify: (1) the subject who experiences self as unreal, who appears spectral or "fictive" both inwardly and outwardly (Wakefield, Bartleby, Gatsby, Darl Bundren, Coover's Nixon, Morrison's Beloved, DeLillo's Oswald); and (2) the subject who is denied status or selfhood by the culture (Uncle Tom and Topsy, Joe Christmas, O'Connor's Displaced Person, again Beloved). American fiction is insistently drawn to the theme of Nobody, and the plight of Nobody — to become "real" or "recognized" or "equal" — is passionate stuff, encompassing both existential and social crises of great moment, illuminating the varieties of American alienation and inner doubt, but also radiating outward, like Melville's Drummond light, to illuminate the great cultural and social forces that deny our humanity.

"Home," the second focal point of my book, is also to be grasped in a multiple sense: the immediate setting that is personalized, lived in, and "made," but also and no less crucially the larger human nexus, the family that one lives in, that one both inherits and "makes." American fiction is obsessed with this situational drama: the "home scenarios" of rented quarters and law office in "Wakefield" and "Bartleby," the mutilation fables of unmaking and making the family in *Uncle Tom's Cabin*, *Puddn'head Wilson*, *As I Lay Dying*, *Light in August*, "A Good Man Is Hard to Find," informing the story of the fathers and daughters of *Second Skin* and Hawkes's Alaska book, of Jack Gladney's brood in *White Noise*, and the racist severances of *Beloved*. These are all Humpty-Dumpty stories describing fissured subjects and torn-apart families; in every case the narrative seeks ways to bind what has been sundered, to reconstruct or reconceive what has been dismantled or denied. "Home" is also the textual container itself, the word-world that is designed, before our eyes, to make possible a type of maneuvering room that can be fashioned in no other way. American fictions are wonderfully shrewd in this sense, capable of converting verbal space into living space.

These texts all explore the premise of *Nobody's Home*, and they pit the resources of art against the stresses and coercions that visit self and home. Known as "romance," as "fabulation," the American novel has always seemed different from its British or European counterpart, less a record of manners than a magic script in its own right. But this is no simple matter of writerly solutions for cultural problems. Looked at closely, this script, like all textual utterance, often seems to have a mind of its own: it "produces" the necessary structures of self and home, but it also makes visible, writes large in its systemic way, the meshes and traps that give the lie to unitary, integral lives. The divisions of race, class, and gender are not to be dismissed as mirages; the still deeper divisions, including the suspicion that nothingness is primal, that Nobody lurks within all selves, that our forms of being are culturally produced, prove to be stubborn and intransigent facts of life. Hence the value of fiction: to record fissure while imagining integrity, to denote division while connoting linkage, to render — even to construct — Nobody's Home.

To discover how that magic script works is the goal of this study. The two central themes that crisscross these texts are the making of the self and the making of the world. These are curious matters. Both self and world can be bracketed, taken apart, and reassembled in American fiction, something less conceivable in the literature of other cultures where the environment and the subject are more immovable, more historically pinned down. Not that history and culture do not exist, or exist as curtains to be lifted; on the contrary, they condition human life from cradle to grave. But they are thought in America to be alterable. Here is where freedom of speech enters: not merely the constitutional right to public utterance of one's beliefs, but the enormous spectrum of enabling language acts that may become constitutive of self and world. The subject in American literature resembles Lévi-Strauss's *bricoleur*, in that he or she is endlessly in pursuit of the bits and pieces with which to make an identity or, better yet, to remake an identity, to fashion, in Hawkes's term, that "second skin" as a way of living other, elsewhere, and again. And the writer of American fiction has intuited that all declarations are at some level "independent," capable of spawning multiple meanings, blessed with indeterminacy, usable in some real tactical way as a means of making one's mark, building one's home. Language is called on to constitute new vistas, to restore broken connections, and to hint at unavowed linkages and twinnings; and this demiurgic activity is located both in the individual and in the text as a way of making a figure of one's life and also of "speaking" the environment. Hence, we shall see in all these American texts signs so luminous that they create a kind of Morse code, an actual spectacle of "signing," as if each letter could suddenly speak, or could speak many tongues. We find in American fiction a parade of semiotic projects in which "markers" are strewn everywhere, overturning our conventions of center and margin, bombarding us with "language" from the strangest corners, issuing in a view of literature as both dismantling and re-combinant.

Freedom of speech has a clear moral and political significance for Americans, and the larger purpose of this study is to show that the novelist takes such ethical values most seriously *as writer*, as the maker of a verbal domain. In examining the exploits of language, we shall see that there is a persistent war under way that pits the signifying potential of words against the great recognizable enemies of freedom: time and space, the coercions of war and death, the prejudices of class, race, and gender. These are the powerful forces that produce Nobody, and the American writer is truly picking up the gauntlet in his or her bid for freedom. How can it be done? It is a question not of neologisms or private idioms but rather of projective strategies, of narrative gambits that create, as mirrors do, virtual spaces and new territories in which to live. Even in its most ludic and fantastic phases American literature calls on the verbal for special service in life saving and life making. All the texts studied herein draw their power from this calculated fusion of verbal and moral energies, this wrestling with the fixed meanings that dog both lives and texts; and all of them are committed to the making of a writerly reprieve from contingency. It is this oddly heroic language that constitutes something of the special nature of American fiction over the past century and a half.

Semiosis is common to all literature, not merely that of the United States. Joyce, Borges, Robbe-Grillet, Kundera, and Calvino, to name just a few modern writers, have produced texts with the same anarchic power as the American materials under discussion. And it is tolerably obvious that other American authors could have been included here. The presence of Henry James will be everywhere felt in this study, even though he is specifically mentioned only a handful of times. As for later writers, Thomas Pynchon's absence is a glaring one, and it could be reasonably maintained that Ralph Ellison's *Invisible Man* displays virtually every feature of my American argument. Even more obvious is the fact that there exists enormous variety in the literary output of a country during two centuries, and it would be naive to posit some kind of secret tradition that unifies all this material. But this book is more than just a series of essays on American writers. The common threads are real, and the wide-angled view of American letters that emerges is intended as an alternative to the historicist work that now dominates the critical scene. It is possible to respect the specificity of single writers and historical moments while still aiming for a larger view that would illuminate common ground as well as cultural difference. *Nobody's Home* is admittedly a large proposition, but the driving force behind its thesis is that American letters have displayed some obsessively repetitive patterns over the past two centuries, and that the apparently distinct ventures of specific texts—each endowed with its own coloration and reflecting its particular moment—nonetheless share, when seen through my lens, common cause. The mythic project of self-enactment fuels, however variously, the figures of American fiction: Wakefield, Gatsby, Joe Christmas, Catherine Bourne, Coover's Nixon, DeLillo's Oswald. And the grandmother's fateful cry to the Misfit, "Why you're one of my babies. You're one of my own children!" is the theme song of the severed American family, reaching back to the broken slave families of Stowe and Twain, replayed in Morrison's slave elegy, extending to the libidinal echo chambers of Faulkner's Bundrens, Hawkes's fathers and daughters, DeLillo's rendition of the Gladney clan in their environmental trap.

My study moves along roughly chronological lines, and I begin with two of the most riddling texts in the American canon: Hawthorne's "Wakefield" and Melville's "Bartleby the Scrivener," a pair of mediations about the enigma of self, each infused with a peculiar desire for portraiture and lodgings, for turning Nobody into Somebody, for making a Home. Already in Melville's "tale of Wall Street" the existential proves to be inseparable from the social. In Part II, entitled "Masters and Slaves," I examine the racial and political dimensions of Nobody's Home by fashioning another diptych, *Uncle Tom's Cabin* and *Pudd'nhead Wilson*, so as to assess the modalities of power in culture and writing: didacticism versus play, the search for freedom through the law and the text, families made, unmade, and remade. At this juncture in my book chronology takes something of a beating, because the next odd couple is Sherwood Anderson and Flannery O'Connor, yoked together in an analysis of Americana as modernist venture. In *Winesburg, Ohio* and O'Connor's short stories the local is shot through with signs and sights of another realm, and Ohio and Georgia turn out to be at once cultural bases and launch pads. Each of these "bridge" figures—one leading into, the other leading out of modernism—has put together a bold narrative language that is more "active" than we had realized, for its words gesticulate and "sign" and "count" and thus point us beyond.

My book then moves beyond pairings to look at the great trio of American modernists who have stamped the fiction of our century: Fitzgerald, Faulkner, and Hemingway. *The Great Gatsby* is the central American fable of my study, and Fitzgerald's "Mr. Nobody from Nowhere" must take honors in any discussion of the power of fiction and desire to make a world and a self. I have allowed myself the luxury of delving into two Faulkner texts, *As I Lay Dying* and *Light in August*, not only because Faulkner is (for me) at the core of American fiction but also because these two novels richly illustrate the diverse strands of my argument: Darl Bundren and Joe Christmas are two harrowing versions of Nobody, and Home ranges in these two fictions from the traveling coffin that survives flood and fire to the mangerlike hut where Lena's baby is born and the family is made anew. With Hemingway I have taken a chance and selected the posthumously published, suspiciously edited *Garden of Eden* because it can be read as a strange summa for the literary corpus we thought we knew. In this account of the war between two rival forms of self-enactment—the woman's project of sex change and the male's commitment to writing—correspondent Hemingway makes his most complex and provocative statement about the nature of his life and art.

In Part V I move into the fiction of the past several decades, focusing on those writers and works that may be tomorrow's classics. My medley of authors—Hawkes, Coover, Morrison, and DeLillo—may seem at first glance militantly unconnected, but we shall see a replay of familiar issues in a new light. The story of racial oppression and family mutilation, already seen in Stowe, Twain, and Faulkner, is reconceived in *Beloved*; the colonizing enterprise of selfhood, teasing in "Wakefield" and "Bartleby," emblematic in *Gatsby*, is presented in racial and gender terms in Morrison, mythically in Hawkes's Uncle Jake, and politically in Coover's Nixon and DeLillo's Oswald; above all, the contemporary work displays a fascination with language itself: as libidinal undercurrent and alchemical force in Hawkes, as manic cultural carnival and imperialist design in Coover, as *écriture féminine* in Morrison's text of amnesia and "thick blood," as mix of pure violence and white noise in DeLillo's fictions. Positioned in the larger literary and cultural landscape of the earlier books, seen against the vistas generated by American fiction from Hawthorne and Melville on through Faulkner and the rest, these postmodern texts acquire a surprising resonance and pathos. The most severe critique of postmodernism is that it constitutes navel gazing, that it may be verbally fascinating but is otherwise "exhausted," with no moral or political bite to it. By closing my book with these four contemporary figures I want to challenge that weary view by emphasizing the passion of this material—social, sexual, political—and thus place it within the continuum of American fiction.

A further word is in order about the assumptions of this book. To posit the large twin theses of self-making and freedom of speech as the central story of American fiction for two centuries may seem unacceptably generalist and naive to some of the historicist critics working on American fiction today. As a comparatist accustomed to the pleasures of linkage and diachronic pattern, I have attempted to highlight the astonishing common ground that these narratives display, even though each text has a tonality and an agenda of its own. Morrison returns us to Faulkner and to Stowe and Twain; DeLillo and Hawkes make common cause with Fitzgerald and Hawthorne. What we call lamely the "tradition" is a living force field, a charged terrain of energies that are to be found, not surprisingly, formed and deformed and reformed in the strangest places. So this is a book of echoes and refrains, and I can only hope that it gives in the reading the same heady sense of leitmotif and melodic pattern that I experienced in the writing of it. I believe that these novels, taken together, tell us something enduring about our myths and our reality, something that we could not see if we studied them singly, something that emerges because they are so profoundly in tandem with one another. And I have particularly wanted to link the work of some of the most exciting contemporary writers to the great canonical texts of the past, for all of the noise that is made about rupture and the "new" tends to obfuscate our vision, to blur our sense of what is vital and continuous in our culture and our art. I fully acknowledge that I am guided by my own taste in choosing the contemporary materials, and that I have bypassed a number of major midcentury texts, but my rationale consists in taking a substantial close-up look at some of today's most interesting work to discover just how forcefully the band is still playing on. There is, however, nothing static in this view of continuity, nothing fixed and set; on the contrary, it is only by seeing the pattern and hearing the echoes that we can truly measure (and savor) the sea changes that have been wrought by cultural moment and writerly temperament.

Reading literature as the arena where self-making and freedom of speech take place stems from my conviction that art records truths about our lives that are to be found nowhere else. I believe that art is at once personal and capacious, subjective and environmental, that it reaches us to recognize both our own dance and the place where we live. That is why I have spent a considerable amount of time with each novel or story under examination: the fullness of these texts — whether it be the seemingly sparse "Wakefield" or the panoramic *Public Burning* — warrants our settling in for a while. These books (and, by extension, these chapters) are, as the figure of my title suggests, "homes" — homes, in the last analysis, for the most free-floating Nobody of all, the reader, who enters these precincts and then leaves. Those entrances and exits, the transactions that take place inside, make life different for each of us, make each of us different from what we were. That, too, is self-making and freedom of speech.

I

OUTCASTS OF
THE UNIVERSE

1

Hawthorne's "Wakefield" and the Art of Self-Possession

To ground a view of the self in American letters on Hawthorne's slight, wispy story "Wakefield" may seem to be a foolhardy enterprise. This odd parable of a man walking out on his wife after ten years of marriage, then settling down in a flat one block away in order to survey — for some twenty years — the effect he is having, finally to return to his hearth, is a distinct oddball in the Hawthorne corpus, a kind of radiant metaphoric narrative for which no sure key is provided.[1] Mainstream Hawthorne criticism has, by and large, regarded "Wakefield" as either minor or flawed, and we are therefore justified in looking abroad, in the direction of Borges, for the revisionist reading that begins to take the measure of this strange tale. Borges, it will be recalled, singles out "Wakefield" for his highest praise, rating it above *The Scarlet Letter* and savoring in it the modernist concerns with identity and enigma that we associate with Gide, Kafka, and Pirandello. Written in 1834, at the very outset of Hawthorne's career, "Wakefield" seems leaner and tougher than the more famous novels and tales that followed; unburdened by curses, witches, Puritans, fauns, unpardonable sins, or any other stock accouterments of romance, "Wakefield" is stark and bare. Its riddling emptiness is what we note, and its mechanistic plot seems to prefigure Ionesco and Robbe-Grillet as well as Kafka and Borges. This tale of a man who walks out of his marriage hints at an exodus of still larger proportions, and Hawthorne's conclusion spells it out for us with considerable clarity: "Amid the seeming confusion of our mysterious world, individuals are so nicely adjusted to a system, and systems to one another and to a whole, that, by stepping aside for a moment, a man exposes himself to a fearful risk of losing his place forever. Like Wakefield, he may become, as it were, the Outcast of the Universe."[2] This moral, put forth with fanfare, advertises the nineteenth-century Hawthorne, for the adventures of twentieth-century wanderers such as Kafka's K or Joyce's Bloom are rarely capped in such a fulsome way. Borges makes no secret of his modernist disdain for Hawthorne's moralizing tendency, but in "Wakefield" matters are murkier than they appear, and we may begin to wonder just how well the label fits. We are cautioned early in the story that "a pervading spirit and a moral" will be provided, "even should we fail to find them, done up neatly, and condensed into the final sentence" (290–91). The moral is properly dished up for us, yes, but it seems to come in brackets, as if daring us to trust it.

There can be little doubt that Borges—whatever strictures he had about Hawthorne's moralizing—found this moral to his liking. John Wright has spelled out the mileage that the Argentinian writer was to get out of Hawthorne's summation:

> An "Outcast of the Universe" is already No Man—the same No Man figure, in fact, that haunts Borges' fiction. He has grasped Hawthorne's fascination with the enigma of identity, personal and authorial alike, and he read "Wakefield" as a parable depicting the slow unconscious processes of loss (or gain) of No Man's (or Everyman's) name, place and power of action. In "The Immortal," "The Circular Ruins," and "Borges and Myself," Borges has written of this No Man figure from a point of view more nearly within the character.[3]

But let us ask a simple question: Is Wakefield indeed an Outcast of the Universe? Is this moral the right one for this character? Despite the narrator's dark predictions—"Stay, Wakefield! Would you go to the sole home that is left you? Then step into your grave!" (298)—Wakefield returns to his wife and home. Recrossing his threshold, a bit stiff-legged but with the same "crafty smile," Wakefield broadcasts his peculiar independence, his odd freedom of motion and of motive, his weird act of closure that defies interpretation. The narrator dutifully coerces these opaque gestures into moral and figure, but they do not stick. Wakefield completes his design, but we are in the dark; the most striking feature of Hawthorne's story is the impenetrability of its central figure.

At the beginning of the story Hawthorne tells us flatly that Wakefield left his wife and home for twenty years "without the shadow of a reason for such self-banishment" (290). We may travel around him all we want, label him outcast or Wandering Jew or urban victim, but this is so much name calling; it does not take us one step closer to his motive. In this Wakefield we have an enigma that is radically different from standard nineteenth-century mysteries: no heinous secret, no missing letters or corpses, no ghosts, not even any romance. Just an exit and a vigil and a return—without explanation.

This is, of course, not quite true. Hawthorne does offer some particulars. Wakefield is a creature of habit, possessed of a certain "sluggishness," "intellectual but not actively so," given to "long and lazy musings" but without the rigor to pursue them; "imagination," Hawthorne tells us, "made no part of Wakefield's gifts," and he is essentially posited, at least in the eyes of his friends, as a No Man well before his strange adventure. We read also in a memorable phrase of a "quiet selfishness that has rusted into his inactive mind"—"rusted" beautifully conveys the mechanical passivity of the figure— and we note his peculiar vanity, his "disposition to craft," all of which his good wife can only call "a little strangeness," a strangeness then modified and undercut by Hawthorne as "indefinable and perhaps nonexistent" (291). This is cunning narration, and it delights in withdrawing or eroding what it has appeared to offer. Not many nineteenth-century heroes are characterized in such a fashion: pedestrian, almost phlegmatic, marked by nothing except a noteworthy smile (about which more later). Wakefield is the utter opposite of Hawthorne's usual gallery of types. Next to the famous trio of *The Scarlet Letter* or the boldly defined figures of the other novels or Young Goodman Brown or Robin or Giovanni or Hooper or Aylmer or Ethan Brand — all of whom are vibrant, even if stock, figures — Wakefield is amazingly limited, blurred, nondescript, mediocre. And, perhaps for all these reasons, he commits his astonishing geste, becomes "as remarkable a freak as may be found in the whole list of human oddities" (290) as mysteriously and inexplicably as if he were programmed to do so by an alien power beyond his control or even understanding.

Hence the story is the most open-ended piece Hawthorne ever wrote, for his central character is as inscrutable as Camus's Meursault or Robbe-Grillet's compulsive but empty figures. To be sure, Hawthorne "tracks" his man, registers his pulse rate, has him weep and wail, but he steers entirely clear of any "mental event": much circling and sniffing, but no going inside. If we think here of other Hawthorne figures and the amount of scrutiny they receive, we easily measure Wakefield's "flatness." Or we have only to consider John Marcher of James's "Beast in the Jungle," another absentee from experience, to gauge just how rich and complex the psychic landscape might be for such a figure.[4] Why is Wakefield a blank? Why does he do what he does? The void at the heart of this story is its most audacious feature, and much of the criticism written on it is an effort to fill the void, to find precisely that "pervading spirit and moral" even if one is obliged to fabricate it oneself.

It is devilishly hard not to see Hawthorne himself as this No Man figure, and the epithet "Outcast of the Universe" may be thought to translate into cosmic terms the well-known solitude of Hawthorne's character. Writing, we know, was for Hawthorne one way to "open up intercourse with the world," and marriage to Sophia Peabody was doubtless another act of integration of Nobody into the human community. The fate of Wakefield, then, might stand as a dark portrait of what Hawthorne — without literature, without Sophia — might have become.[5] But if Wakefield's isolation is recognizably Hawthornian, what is one to make of his other traits: sluggish, unimaginative, mediocre. Above all, to account for Wakefield by naming him Hawthorne is to close the story backward rather than to open it forward. This little tale is not static portraiture; things happen in it, and we need to look more closely at those happenings. One way of sizing up these events is to place oneself at eye level in the text, and the moment we do so we are struck by the powerful and controlling voice of the narrator. This figure, equipped with Hawthorne's familiar bonhomie, invites us into the story, urges us to join in the fabulation, to participate in the telling and elucidation of the riddle. But the connection between narrator and Wakefield is not altogether congenial, and in certain passages we may wonder if Wakefield's strange odyssey is not ascribable entirely to narrational whimsy (or tyranny). In the very first sentence the narrator flexes his muscles by inventing a name for his man, "let us call him Wakefield," showing us something about who is active and who is passive in the tale. And there is something peculiarly marionettelike about the motions of the character, seen especially in the encounter (staged by the narrator) between Wakefield and his wife after ten years' separation ("Now for a scene!" [295]), leaving the reader to feel that some sort of power play is at work here.[6] In this light the story appears suspiciously ordered and symmetrical (Wakefield leaves in autumn, he returns in autumn, and so on), and we may indeed feel there is something of an experiment in narrational power here, a kind of game played by the narrator involving the naming and positioning of his pawn, Wakefield, perhaps even a daydream. Of course the result of such a reading is to displace the rationale of the events onto the narrator, to centralize his gestures as the core of the story.

But the nagging question remains: Why does Wakefield do what he does? The narrator could bully him in countless ways, but there is something about Wakefield's particular trajectory that speaks of Wakefield, not of the narrator. Any man could leave a wife after ten years of marriage, but only this one needs to set up residence in the next street for twenty years to carry out the project. And thus we are led to what must be the central relationship of the text, not that between Hawthorne and Wakefield, or the narrator and Wakefield, but between the man and his wife. There, if anywhere, one should find the hidden reason for his conduct. Why does a man abandon a woman, spy on her for two decades, and then return?

One answer might be because he wants to, because hurting her pleases him. That hurt may range from the teasing and "quizzing" which is a manifest part of Wakefield's makeup (his "crafty smile" bears witness to his trickster tendencies) to altogether darker, more sadistic feelings. His wife becomes ill shortly after (because?) he leaves, and even though he suspects she may be dying, he "still lingers away from his wife's bedside, pleading with his conscience that she must not be disturbed at such a juncture. If aught else restrains him, he does not know it" (295). The last line is diabolical and once again opens the door for the critics. Frederick Crews's ground-breaking Freudian study of Hawthorne, *The Sins of the Fathers*, made it possible for subsequent Hawthorne readers to see the latent sexual and oedipal energies that fuel so many of these pristine stories.[7] The genteel Hawthorne is exposed as harboring intense, unresolved feelings of cruelty, incestuous longing, and other assorted libidinal impulses which account for the lines and compulsions of his work. Hence, the Reverend Hooper adopts his infamous black veil to avoid marriage (among other things); Beatrice's sensuous beauty expresses a kind of threatening sexuality that Hawthorne needs to make literally toxic; Aylmer's dream of removing Georgiana's birthmark is, as dreams are wont to be, executed in strikingly sexual terms: "But the deeper went the knife, the deeper sank the Hand, until at length its tiny grasp appeared to have caught hold of Georgiana's heart" (767). In light of this critical orientation, Wakefield's exodus may be thought to be an anxious one, the response of a beleaguered man whose "matrimonial affections," we are told, "never violent, were sobered into a calm habitual sentiment." As Deborah and Michael West, following in Crews's footsteps, have written: "Wakefield's baffled fascination with his wife's behavior suggests an inability to categorize it as either virginal or lascivious," and they go on to characterize his desire to "control" his wife in terms of "scopophilia" and "radical fears of impotence."[8] Even if one is unable to credit quite this much libidinal turmoil within the poor man, it would seem impossible to dismiss the sadism charge; after all, we see, if nothing else, an elaborate and quite nasty hoax played by the husband on the wife.

Or do we? Herbert Perluck has argued that Wakefield's geste is a sublime, albeit comic, experiment in loving.[9] Everything can be made to speak *for* Wakefield instead of against him. Hence, Hawthorne's description of the good wife's recovery—"Her heart is sad, perhaps but quiet; and let him return soon or late, it will never be feverish for him again. Such ideas glimmer through the mist of Wakefield's mind, and render him indistinctly conscious that an almost unpassable gulf divides his hired apartment from his former home" (295)—is read as a tender double recognition of the nature of love: Mrs. Wakefield's apprehension of her husband's crisis, the bittersweet acknowledgment that love is found (only) on the far side of separation. "Feverish" would then connote sickly hunger (like that of Giovanni toward Beatrice in "Rappaccini's Daughter"), and it is all to the good that Mrs. Wakefield is now beyond such selfish affections. In short, the argument goes, we have here a story of remarkable tact and generosity, a discovery of mutuality rather than its loss. In this light the Wakefields' entente is comparable, in its conflation of spectating, absenteeism, and love, to the pas de deux executed by John Marcher and May Bartram in "The Beast in the Jungle."

On balance this generous reading is no more fanciful (and much more appealing) than the fear-of-impotence explanation, and it begins to make the proper argument for the *value of absence* in the story. Wakefield leaves his wife, we now gather, in order to find her. At the very least we have moved closer to the matter of the story, namely, that it hinges on Wakefield's bizarre itinerary, his exit-vigil-reentry scheme. This must be the kernel of the piece, and there is nothing wrong with refining such behavior into an exalted love story. Certainly the Wakefields' conjugal arrangements acquire more interest in this version than if the husband had remained at home. And, ultimately, separations and gulfs may indeed be avenues as well as impediments to love, especially for the sluggish, unimaginative Wakefield, "the man in London surest to perform nothing today which should be remembered tomorrow" (291). Indeed, nothing in his marriage so becomes him—or it—as the leaving of it. Except perhaps the return.

But was it to save his marriage that Wakefield left? Was it to gauge and deepen the impact he could make on the good woman? Hawthorne tells us that Wakefield is displeased by "the inadequate sensation which he conceives to have produced in the bosom of Mrs. Wakefield" (294), but let us focus instead on the sensations within *his* bosom. We know that Wakefield remains, although absent, faithful to his wife, that he is "figuratively . . . always beside his wife and at his hearth, yet must never feel the warmth of the one nor the affection of the other" (296–97). Yet he maintains his vigil for twenty long years. Why? Hawthorne has told us that Wakefield "was likely to be the most constant [of all husbands], because a certain sluggishness would keep his heart at rest, wherever it might be placed" (291), but do inertia and complacency suffice as explanations? Can this behavior be mere "sluggishness"? Hawthorne himself coerced these events into a figure by calling his protagonist the Outcast of the Universe, but it is high time to reconceive these matters, to reexamine the trajectory of this bizarre figure. We will then see a different "figure" altogether, a strange voyager no less heroic and compelling in his own oddball way than Odysseus, no less exemplary in his urban station drama than Leopold Bloom. Great things are in play here, for the story is showing us something elemental, indeed massive, about the motive behind Wakefield's pilgrimage. "Figuratively . . . beside his wife and at his hearth," Hawthorne writes, and it is imperative that we begin to open up this mystery of figuration, of absence and presence, for therein lies the story's deepest claim to our interest. Notwithstanding the narrator's assertions, the story's central truth is that Wakefield can feel the warmth of his hearth and the affection of his wife *only* when he is separated from them. And that is just the beginning. Wife and hearth are not the ultimate target of Wakefield's longing. The central relationship in this tale is that of Wakefield to himself. The elaborate figural drama that he has played out is nothing less than a strategic net for capturing the form of his own life. The figure he is bent on appropriating is himself.

Literary self-portraiture, from Montaigne and Shakespeare on through Rousseau, Dostoyevski, Proust, and Beckett, is so characterized by the language of plenitude—Hamlet's doubts and Molloy's dismantling use the discourse of plenitude, the "I" that inventories its estate—that we are unaccustomed to figural, spatial, mute gambits like those of Wakefield. Yet it is arguable that no other text in Western literature maps out the topography of self with as much purity and poetry as the nine-page "Wakefield" does. This brief tale not only prefigures the entire epic project of self-recovery that Proust undertook in his many-volumed *Recherche*, but has a kind of metaphysical elegance and intellectual audacity that make us wonder if Borges himself did not write it one day in order to rival Proust in some Pierre Menard fashion, or to add to his own forking narratives about time and identity. These are large claims for a small fiction, and it is time to substantiate them.

Passer outre may sound more like Rimbaud than Hawthorne, but there is high adventure in Hawthorne's story of an interrupted marriage. The allegedly "sluggish" Wakefield experiences passion for the first time. The morning after his exit habit guides him back to his own door, where he seems to "wake" up, and we read that "he hurries away, breathless with agitation hitherto unfelt" (294). He is astonished that no one has seen him, and rather than carping on his egotism, as the narrator does, one should assess the liberation that is unfurling here. Unseen by others, he is free to see and make himself anew. There is an aura of great excitement about these events. Wakefield, fearing pursuit, elevates himself to "lord and master"; his escape is indeed "wonderful," because his life is becoming filled with wonder. This night is "magic," and it has produced a "transformation," "a great moral change," even though the narrator insists, "But this is a secret from himself" (294). Secret? Why then the exaltation? Wakefield returns "home" with a "glad" heart and a "dizzy" brain. Now emboldened and embarked, he buys a full disguise: wig, clothes from the Jew.[10] "It is accomplished. Wakefield is another man," says the narrator (294).

One would be closer to the mark in saying that he has gotten a purchase on himself by donning a disguise. He does not want to be someone else, or he would leave altogether. Rather, he absents and alters himself to find himself. This peculiar form of retrieval is a retrieval of one's peculiar form, and it constitutes no mean feat. It is for Wakefield something of a *carnaval*, not so much a release through mask as a front-row seat at the show he has been missing up to now, the greatest show on earth; he is the both the performance and the audience, and he enjoys it with unaccustomed keenness.

What Wakefield is savoring is *presence*. It is what he has never known. "No Man" is a state of being that Hawthorne acutely understood. The central ghost of Hawthorne's work, far from being the specters and goblins and other accoutrements of romance that we see lurking everywhere in his writing, is the self. Writing is called on to open up an intercourse with the world, not because the world seems out of reach, but because oneself is unreal. Hawthorne was obsessed with the notion of his own insubstantiality, his ghostliness, his secret identity as Nobody. Over and over in the *American Notebooks* we see the seeds of stories about inauthenticity, about entrapment within roles. Consider the following, which is a veritable blueprint for "The Beast in the Jungle": "Two persons expecting some occurrence, and watching for the two principal actors in it, and to find that the occurrence is even passing, and that they themselves are the two actors."[11] Or consider this view of being cut off from the real: "A man tries to be happy in love; he cannot sincerely give his heart, and the affair seems all a dream. In domestic life, the same; in politics, a seeming patriot; but still he is sincere, and all seems like a theatre" (618). Perhaps this is what the "sluggishness" looks like on the inside. It is as if one were living in a permanent haze, a gauzy world with nothing vital in it, nothing searing, nothing that cuts through. One's own interior muddle, the originary falseness that is indwelling and precedes all else, is consistently assessed as a perceptual affair, an unwanted fate of histrionics: "Insincerity in a man's own heart must make all his enjoyments, all that concerns him, unreal; so that his whole life must seem like a merely dramatic representation. And this would be the case, even though he were surrounded by true-hearted relatives and friends" (619). Here is the dreamworld that Hawthorne knew so much about, but it has little to do with romance, and, strictly speaking, there is nothing oneiric about it. Instead it is the muted, muffled experience of factitiousness, inauthenticity, consciousness as cocooned in mist and shrouded in weightless forms. Such characters are to be found everywhere in Hawthorne's writing, from the manic Clifford Pyncheon, always precarious, teetering, permanently out of sync with the world, even to the apparently more purposive types, such as Dimmesdale, caught here in the erosive undoing of his sham, much like a man sinking in quicksand: "It is the unspeakable misery of a life so false as his, that it steals the pith and substance out of whatever realities there are around us, and which were meant by Heaven to be the spirit's joy and nutriment."[12] To such people, Hawthorne wrote in another *Notebook* entry, condemned to "misery," the universe becomes "an unsubstantial mockery" (623).

So it is against this backdrop of *mauvaise foi* and lapsed identity that little Wakefield scores his ecstatic breakthrough, his spectacular and specular victory of self-possession. A block away from his former lodgings, surveying the gap he has left, Wakefield is at long last recuperating his form, coming into his estate. Witness to the shape of his life, he finally possesses it. But "witness" will not do; seeing is transformed into having. Wakefield's giddiness is the experience of self-enactment. He is made real by dint of observing his own absence, the vacancy he has "crafted," which is the very shape of life, a shape he could not see as long as he lived it. Like one who can believe in his body only by seeing its imprint, Wakefield thrives on his *trace*, feeds on it, lives through it. Hero of self-possession, Wakefield remains awake, appropriates his past and keeps covenant with his life by making it an effigy and himself a walking shadow. But this shade is full — of himself.

The crafty Wakefield who watches over his vacated roost exposes the pure mechanics of Hawthornian doubt and desire. Critics have noted Wakefield's resemblance to the "observer" type that Hawthorne made famous in creations such as Chillingworth, Aylmer, Ethan Brand, and Coverdale. The traditional view of this nefarious figure is that he is condemned for his coldness, that scrutiny of another's heart is sinful where there is no sympathy or love. Crews has properly challenged the coldness assessment by asserting that the "relationship of investigator to investigated, of tormentor to tormented, is a kind of mock-marriage, a substitute for more normal sexual feeling in both parties."[13] But in its workings the case of Wakefield displays the fascinating hidden economy of the model. The energies involved may be sexual, but the relationship itself is more "homing" than has been acknowledged, more masturbatory than exploitative. The marriage at hand is a marriage of one. In subsequent texts, indeed in most of his writings, Hawthorne "externalizes" his scheme, sets up duets instead of solos, moves from the amoeba to more complex arrangements. But one is tempted to say that the chemistry and the true nature of the project remain the same: observation as a means of self-realization, as a route toward presence.

Once we as readers see how much libidinal energy there is in observation, we may better grasp the other displacements and taboos of Hawthorne's work. Hence *The Scarlet Letter* remains in our minds as not only static, a series of tableaux, but essentially atomistic, a grouping that is forever forced, so that Hawthorne speaks endlessly of illicit connection while we see three closed, virtually hermetic figures. Sexual intercourse seems terrifying to Hawthorne, and he ducks it wherever he can. Who can imagine the actual lovemaking between Hester and Dimmesdale? Hester bravely claims for it "a consecration of its own," but it is narratively — because imaginatively — off limits to Hawthorne. The case for sexual malaise made by Crews was made earlier still by Lawrence and Fiedler, and everyone knows the fear and trembling that voluptuous creatures such as Zenobia, Miriam, and Beatrice inspire. But it has not been sufficiently noted how the sexual theme serves as a cover for the identity quest. The woman may indeed be sexually devouring, but the man is surprisingly often his own libidinal target.

"The Minister's Black Veil" might be thought of as paradigmatic of this game of desire and displacement. We must understand the powerful logic that links Hooper's donning the veil and his breaking off the engagement. Much like Wakefield in disguise, but even more formidably unknowable and incognito, Hooper alters his appearance, puts on the mask, puts aside his erotic life, all in order to devote himself to his true calling: the crafting of himself as absence to others, as impenetrable, as unseen. The enigmatic Wakefield and the veiled Hooper are cloaked in mystery, but we cannot fail to sense the same mechanisms at work here, the private course toward self-enactment depicted in terms of community riddle, the personal gratification at the expense of others' understanding, the making of an identity in purely figural terms. It will be objected that Hooper is obsessed with his moral agenda, unlike the sluggish Wakefield. But the mechanics of these tales speak; the tale overpowers the teller, and we are struck by the pattern of exit, mask, and enigma.

It is a pattern we encounter often in Hawthorne. "Lady Eleanor's Mantle" is a parallel example of figural identity eroding social relations. Perhaps what we are encountering is the behavioral pattern of allegory itself, the intrusive and disruptive force with which it supplants human connections and flaunts its forbidding autonomy. The infamous "A" of *The Scarlet Letter* is doubtless the best known of these devices, and for more than a century Hawthorne criticism has dealt much with the subjects of romance, symbol, and allegory. Hawthorne seems enamored of these inflation devices, these machines for huffing and puffing, for hinting at more than they can say, for positing a spiritual realm beyond the tangible one, for inaugurating commence between the real and the imaginary. But it is possible to feel that there is a psychic economy at work here as well, a terrible fear of a thinness approaching nothingness, and it is to this dread of emptiness that we owe the carnival of masks and masquerades. We understand this fear to be at once personal and cultural—personal in that Hawthorne was gripped by a sense of unreality all his life, but cultural in that our early American literature had precious little stock of its own, was to be derived from a social landscape without shadow or echo. Hawthorne's views on this quandary, like those of James after him, have had considerable success in shaping our sense of the deficitary conditions facing the nineteenth-century American writer.

But it would appear that the threat of hollowness stemmed more from Hawthorne's temperament than from any cultural dilemma, and his full-dress operatic fictions rarely succeed in entirely camouflaging the suspected emptiness that subtends them. That is why he seems a tease to so many readers: one senses that he is tactical throughout, hawking visions to cover the bareness, dressing up the self. All too often the closer he gets to identity—portraiture by means of "A" or a veil or a mantle or a birthmark—the more slippery his fabrications become. And there is no small irony here. He seems to have backed into the discovery that signs have a dazzling potency of their own, can be used not only for window dressing but for endless Rube Goldberg semiotic contraptions. "Keep 'em guessing" certainly applies as much to him as it does to Joyce.

That is why one returns to "Wakefield." There seems to be no need for romance here, no accoutrements or props or icons. So brief that there is little room for capital letters, other than the heralded Outcast of the Universe, "Wakefield" squarely presents itself as enigma, as a riddle that Hawthorne refrains from explicating. To be sure, the narrator coerces the protagonist into a moral and speaks darkly of Wakefield's severance from systems, but the sluggish little man himself seems impervious to such strictures. He has made good on a great adventure and he knows it. He has traveled far, rather as Thoreau was said to have traveled a great deal in Concord. He is an altered man ten years "out," and Hawthorne does justice to his metamorphosis:

> Amid the throng of a London street we distinguish a man, now waxing elderly, with few characteristics to attract careless observers, yet bearing, in his whole aspect, the handwriting of no common fate, for such as have the skill to read it. He is meager; his low and narrow forehead is deeply wrinkled; his eyes, small and lustreless, sometimes wander apprehensively about him, but oftener seem to look inward. He bends his head, and moves with an indescribable obliquity of gait, as if unwilling to display his full front to the world. Watch him long enough to see what we have described, and you will allow that circumstances — which often produce remarkable men from nature's ordinary handiwork — have produced one such here. (295–96)

This zoom shot encapsulates much of the tale's narrative strategy: close observation from the outside which staunchly refuses to move inward. The familiar "reading" trope is introduced here as a kind of blatant self-conscious provocation to the reader's powers of analysis, so that Wakefield now appears to us as a noteworthy hieroglyph, one who displays the "handwriting" of nature for us to read, if we can. But the external description keeps us at our distance. Yet one thing is clear: if the narrator stays "out," it is startlingly evident that Wakefield himself has gone "in." The wrinkles on the brow, the obliquity of gait, the eyes that look inward all announce the voyage he has made. No less ravaged than Ethan Brand or Roger Chillingworth, he has set up his lodging and practice "within," in a place much farther from his initial home than we might think.

We may be able to gauge the distance he has traveled if we consider the no less fascinating pilgrimage of Chillingworth in *The Scarlet Letter*. What the doctor found is expressed by his excitement and rapture at finding it, a very precise experience of *ecstasy*, that is, of moving from the place. Wakefield's passion is of the sort that Chillingworth experiences as he finally "moves into" Dimmesdale:

> After a brief pause, the physician turned away.
> But with what a wild look of wonder, joy, and horror! With what a ghastly rapture, as it were, too mighty to be expressed only by the eye and features, and therefore bursting forth through the whole ugliness of his figure and making itself even riotously manifest by the extravagant gestures with which he threw up his arms toward the ceiling, and stamped his foot on the floor. Had a man seen old Roger Chillingworth, at that moment of his ecstasy, he would have had no need to ask how Satan comports himself, when a precious human soul is lost to heaven, and won into his kingdom.
> But what distinguished the physician's ecstasy from Satan's was the trait of wonder in it! (102)

Once we see past the Puritan frame and the satanic allusions, we are struck by the properly ecstatic view of knowledge put forth here. This passage figures forth a possession scenario of extraordinary power and splendor, a scenario that offers much food for thought. It can hardly be accidental that the posture of Chillingworth is the posture of the novelist, the man who studies others, seeks to know what is inside them, is even obliged to go inside them if he is to render them in his fictions. This kind of "breaking and entering" is central to Hawthorne. But we need merely graft this scene onto "Wakefield" to recognize that the raptures of possession may not require a couple at all, that the well-nigh sexual pleasure of moving in might also be, for the ghostly Hawthorne, a solitary drama, a self-embrace.

Unlike the torturers Chillingworth, Brand, and company, Wakefield has made his way, with an "indescribable obliquity of gait," into himself, not another, or better, into himself *as another*.[14] Nineteenth-century fiction is filled with dark doubles; one thinks of Poe, Dostoyevski, Twain, Conrad, and Stevenson. But their pairings seem downright melodramatic in comparison to what Hawthorne has wrought in "Wakefield." Literalists all, they have real-life doubles: William Wilson, Twain's twins, Gentleman Brown, Jekyll-Hyde. Wakefield is different; his is the story of a man in search of his own form, who can find it only by turning, as it were, inside out, or outside in, depending on one's perspective. The astounding modernity of Hawthorne's tale lies in its prescient awareness that the self is Other unto itself, that it is the dark side of the moon, that it operates beyond the scrutiny of consciousness. Hawthorne's version of fissured being looks beyond Freud all the way to Lacan's theories of the sundered psyche. Unlike other nineteenth-century writers, he is wonderfully aware of how unapproachable the secret Other/self is, how cunning one must be to glimpse it, to hear its discourse, to corral it and bring it into view. His solution in "Wakefield" is draconian: only when one's life is vacated, transformed into dumb play, into effigy, does it become visible. While we are "in" it, we are as sluggish as Wakefield, for there is, properly speaking, nothing for us to see. How can the I/eye see itself? And if we could see it, "we" would be in the way, blocking the picture. It comes to life only when we leave, and the austere law of such transactions in that we must die to live, must exit if we are to enter. Wakefield has said no to his world, perhaps not "in thunder," as Melville prescribed, but no nonetheless, and he has in his peculiar fashion carried out the full charge of selfhood so famously ascribed to Hawthorne by the author of *Moby-Dick*: "For all men who say *yes*, lie; and all men who say *no* — why they are in the happy condition of judicious, unencumbered travelers in Europe; they cross the frontiers into Eternity with nothing but a carpet-bag — that is to say, the Ego."[15]

Wakefield left home one fine day, as Ishmael left for the sea, as Dante left for the dark wood. Young Goodman Brown and Robin Molineux also left "home"; but only Wakefield left it to find it. His project is at heart, despite striking differences in tone, scope, and psychology, akin to Proust's famed *Recherche*; each protagonist is learning to possess his own life. Proust's Marcel is quite prepared to regard Others as the stage props and furnishings that give shape to his private itinerary, and his hunger to appropriate his own "form"

entails an exit from life that is reminiscent of Wakefield's. One may even
recall that the Marcel of the beginning of that long novel is a listless, indeed a
"sluggish," man who has been shut off from his own reach. The ecstatic
experience of the madeleine is not so very unlike "the agitation hitherto unfelt"
that Wakefield registers as he moves into his second life.

Lawrence reported, with considerable malice, that "Hawthorne's wife said
she 'never saw him in time,' which doesn't mean she saw him too late."[16] But
Lawrence may have had it backward. The meager Wakefield is endowed with
an imperial appetite, and he has, at least for himself, stopped the clock, sealed
his life off from the accidents and erosions of time or event, and who is to say
that he does not thereby both have his cake and eat it? What does it matter
that Mrs. Wakefield has become a "portly female, considerably in the wane of
life," with "the placid mien of settled widowhood" (296)? She is so only in the
eyes of the narrator, but surely not in the gaze of her husband. His vision,
like his lodgings, is within, and she is no less well preserved than the lovers on
Keats's Grecian urn. Our narrator may indeed stipulate that Wakefield, on
his momentous return, "ascends the steps — heavily! — for twenty years have
stiffened his legs since he came down — but he knows it not" (298), but Wakefield is far the craftier of the two, as he completes his imaginative odyssey and
effects his special fusion of realms, reenters the real with his small carpetbag
of Ego.

It is hard to think that Hawthorne did not have the figure of Rip Van
Winkle somewhere in the back of his mind when he fashioned Wakefield, but
the contrast is instructive. Irving's protagonist passively undergoes his fate,
whereas Hawthorne's little man is out to best nature, to play out his life as the
nineteenth-century Invisible Man. And he succeeds. Admittedly he becomes a
bit of a ghost, but that is the price of stopping time, and who is to say that his
spectral second life was not fiery and passional in its own way? Thus we come
full circle, from the Hawthorne of the sins of the fathers and the return of the
repressed to the Hawthorne who robs the past of its power and turns it into
the object of his experiment. Unlike that of the participants in "Doctor Heidegger's Experiment," however, Wakefield's retreat and retrieval is neither
produced by a magic potion nor of brief duration; after all, he has given his
best years to the enterprise, and we are entitled to surmise that he has gotten
them back as well. We have here the Borgesian Hawthorne, the man bent on
possession of fullness — whether it be the spatializing encyclopedic memory of
Funes, the potent attributes of the Zahir, the all-containing Book in the Library, or the epiphanic vision of the God's Script — and it is no great step from
Wakefield's "indescribable obliquity of gait" to that more sustained looping we
see in "The Garden of Forking Paths." Each text is a meditation about time
and the figure of one's life, but whereas the twentieth-century writer lards his
story with metacommentary, we must be somewhat more agile to perceive and
assess the stakes of "Wakefield." That they are high stakes, even absolute
stakes, should by now be obvious, and once we reject the narrator's doomsday
reading of events, we can discern in the adventure of Wakefield Hawthorne's
staggering effort to break out of the parameters that ordinarily govern life:
time, identity, even consciousness. This brief tale has the resonance of Kafka's

parables, but whereas Kafka deals with sacrifice, paralysis, and stifled longings, Hawthorne explodes the determinist prison by imploding it.

Hawthorne's nineteenth-century story is an uncanny guide to the future.
The phlegmatic Wakefield, with his crafty smile, is a quester in the bureaucratic tradition of Flaubert's Bouvard and Pécuchet and Kafka's Joseph K,
for he shares their mediocrity and limitations and, like them, lives in a secular
world. But, unlike them, he completes his Inventory, wins his Trial, comes
into his Castle, and returns home with his trophy, namely, his life. But he is
further still our contemporary. With bold and simple strokes Hawthorne has
given us a fable of Faustian reach in a modern era. The sluggish Wakefield
lives twice, becomes, in every sense of the word, "proprietor" of his life. The
changes of clothing and apartment may seem materialist, but the venture is
spiritual, and he lives out every writer's dream: to *see* life, to espy its shape, to
possess its elusive core. And his way of doing this is strangely contemporary,
as if he were the living emblem of our own computer age with its technology
for self-imaging: he clones himself, he presses the "duplicate" button, he
makes himself visible to his consciousness. Wakefield's desire to possess the
entirety of himself is truly heady, not so much anal retentive as cerebral
retentive, and his homing venture bears a strange resemblance to the human
hunger for storage and retrieval that our current age of electronic information
gratifies ever more prodigiously. The intellectual pretensions of such a program are real, and we may think of his project in terms close to McLuhan's
theory of media and technology: they extend the whereabouts and the reach
of the human brain. The actual spawning of an immediate replica is beyond
the powers of flesh, however, so Wakefield must settle for second best: he can
make himself visible by making himself absent; he can see his life by seeing
the *trace* it leaves. Here, arguably, is his price, his end of the Faustian bargain.
But the fate of being an eternal witness to life was one that Hawthorne found
congenial; indeed he found it to be an altogether active role. Above all, *pace*
the narrator, Hawthorne's story about the art and craft of self-possession is,
for once, going to be a happy story, a story that skirts but transcends alienation, for this witness is also actor, and this exile returns home. In so doing he
offers a vivid contrast to the shipwrecked figures of the nineteenth century, the
mariners and Ahabs, the swan of Baudelaire and the expatriates of Conrad. In
the manner of Leopold Bloom, who returns after a day of peregrination that
has seemed an eon, so does Wakefield return to his Ithaca. But unlike all
of them, and doubtless wearing his crafty smile for that reason, he has never
left it.

Nineteenth-century American literature is a gallery teeming with larger-
than-life portraits of imperial selves. One thinks of Ahab, Hester, Huck, and
many others. One thinks especially of the enormous self-making venture in
Whitman's work. What is to be gained by adding Wakefield to this group?

The freedom of the American writer I have said is demiurgic because it is
called on to create, or at least to alter, both person and place. In "Wakefield"
and in its companion piece, Melville's "Bartleby," we encounter the zero degree
of fiction. Each of these texts, in different ways, is purgative, performs an act
of purification and cleansing that is reminiscent of Descartes's tabula rasa.

The sluggish Wakefield and the pallid Bartleby resist interpretation, flaunt their thinness, their emptiness, their existence as puppets, their status as Nobody. Bartleby is yet to come for us, but about Wakefield this much can now be said: his story speaks of the birth of fiction. He makes us realize how arduous that labor is, how difficult it is to see a life. And the stark economy of the piece heightens its eloquence, because we have believed that Others may be ungraspable but at least we could know ourselves. That is the myth that is exploded in Hawthorne's text. The self is on the far side of things. Writers and nonwriters may use "I" all day long, but the convention can no longer be innocent for us. His "second life" is life as literature. And even though he is mum about his motives, his odyssey is wildly significant, for it is fueled by the greatest hunger known to civilized humans, namely, to possess their lives, to become real to themselves. "Wakefield" is the ur-narrative of this study because it sets forth the fundamental dynamics of American fiction with great purity: to break free of constraint, to stop time, to own one's life. By telling this story in almost autistic fashion, Hawthorne has made it all the more echoing and mythic. Later texts will bring in the imprisoning particulars of determinism: money, gender, race, death. "Wakefield" is uncluttered, has the purity of a parable. Insubstantial as a shadow, it will cast its shadow on all that follows.

Thus, Wakefield inaugurates a special American parade. He is bent on self-fashioning, and he announces Tom Driscoll, Jay Gatsby, Joe Christmas, Catherine Bourne, Coover's Nixon, and a host of memorably driven characters, also questing after their origins and inventing their form, flaunting their malleability, their status as artistic material unto themselves. Whereas there is something frenzied and manic about most of these figures, Wakefield remains in our minds an inscrutable but pedestrian mummer, an unpretentious little man with a visionary project. The figural drama of his life is achingly clean, and he seems to have been vouchsafed a look into the beyond — into his own beyond, into himself — and to have come home with it. He has moved stealthily into and out of deep waters, and he seems to know the things we do not know: our identity, our relations, the shape we are living. But, sphinxlike, he smiles and we guess.

2

Melville: Knowing Bartleby

Hawthorne's story of the crafty Wakefield and his scheme of self-possession goes a long way toward positing the nineteenth-century self as riddle, indeed as construct. Hawthorne's own sense of ghostliness, his acute understanding of what it means to be Nobody, may seem surprisingly modernist to us. But there is a line of spectral figures in the fiction of the last century—Wakefield, Poe's Man of the Crowd, and Bartleby, to name the best known—whose antics not only call into question the conventions of the novel (how does one "plot" a figure who is trying to be real?) but also reveal some of the demiurgic energies that go into the fashioning of a self. Poe's man, it will be remembered, is relentlessly tracked by the narrator throughout the streets of London at all hours of the day and night, only to be apotheosized as a new urban species, a "man of the crowd" who has no "private" bearings at all, who exists solely (and vampirishly) as a function of the city populace.

Among this set of enigmatic *pantins*, Bartleby, it will readily be acknowledged, takes the honors. In the doings and denyings of the scrivener, Melville is visibly reflecting on the very notion of self—as it exists in literature in the form of character, and as it exists on Wall Street in the form of alienated labor. But the most striking feature of Melville's tale is the amazing hermeneutical energy that can be generated by the slack Bartleby. The *empty* scrivener is a conduit for discourses of plenitude, encompassing a spectrum of interpretive ventures: Bartleby as Christ, Bartleby as artist, Bartleby as conscience, Bartleby as mirror. The central device for triggering this bout of investigations and speculations is of course the narrator, the musing, mystified lawyer whom Bartleby continues, so to speak, to "inhabit" long after he has physically vacated the premises. Bartleby has left his mark, his *trace*, both on and in the lawyer, and the purpose of the story is to interpret that script, to make sense of this estranged figure, this outsider who has somehow, insidiously, gotten "inside." But knowing Bartleby is no easy matter. Wall Street specter, "a bit of wreck in the mid-Atlantic," prince of denial, Bartleby is pure negativity, and his vacuumlike emptiness not only gives rise to a maelstrom of forces; it also undercuts "fullness," exposes it for sham, for masquerade. In short, Bartleby's entry onto the scene proves to be utterly corrosive, for it reveals as factitious and fictitious many of the givens of the nineteenth-century realist scheme. The big questions that frame the life story—who? what? where? why?—become unanswerable here; they malfunction.

There are several instances in Melville's tale when the Sphinx looks right at the narrator—and the reader—and speaks. One of these occurs when Bartleby ceases writing altogether, this being a step beyond the cessation of comparing the copies, and the narrator asks yet again, "Why?" This time there is an answer: "Do you not see the reason for yourself?"[1] It is an unsettling answer, a strange moment when the story and its protagonist turn 180 degrees, from scrutinized object to scrutinizing subject. "Do you not see the reason for yourself?" Our narrator (understandably) does not. Instead he glances around, notices that Bartleby's "eyes looked dull and glazed," and thereupon provides an explanation for the work stoppage: impaired vision. Whose vision is impaired? Needless to say, the narrator's explanation promptly sinks, since Bartleby, true to form, continues his negational calvary independent of any ocular problems. But the reader, if not the narrator, has been buttonholed by that interrogation—"Do you not see the reason for yourself?"—and must come up short. Most of us do not see the reason for ourselves.

At a still more definitive juncture of the story, Bartleby again takes the initiative and speaks. Once again the narrator is discomfited, and for good reason. Bartleby pronounces judgment, and we *know* there can be no reprieve: "I know you" (669), he ominously tells the narrator, thereby dramatically countering the narrator's own thrice-made, Peter-like denial of the scrivener, underscoring both the spiritual and the epistemological challenge at hand.[2] What can it mean to *know* a person? Then comes proclamation number two. When the narrator unctuously explains that the Tombs prison is not so bad after all, Bartleby utters his last living words: "I know where I am" (669).

Such cryptic declarations would hardly be noteworthy, except that they constitute virtually the entire prose record of Bartleby's utterances, once we discount the litany of "I would prefer not to" which is his almost unvarying response to all questions put to him. Most striking of all, however, is the unqualified certainty of these final remarks. "I know you" and "I know where I am" might seem banal enough in most fictions, but in this case they have an oracular dimension. It is no exaggeration to say that Melville's entire story hinges on those two issues as they are directed—and this is crucial—to Bartleby. "Who is Bartleby?" is the echoing enigma of the narrative, and the narrator has not yet, now long after Bartleby's demise, arrived at an answer.

The second pronouncement—"I know where I am"—seems on the face of it more humdrum and situational, less existential than the first. But only on the face of it. Here, too, Bartleby enunciates certainties where there has been absolute doubt, and it seems fair to say that as much of the narrative deals with *where* Bartleby is as with *who* Bartleby is. Not that the scrivener does not know where he is; but rather, he ruptures the lawyer's every notion about "where," as if his true mission in the story were to reconceive "where," to invert and to juggle what had been fixed and stationary, to confound with missionary zeal all notions of work place and living place. Melville's tale is insistently environmental. Ghost that he may be, Bartleby occupies space. Even ghosts have their coordinates, their latitude and longitude, and Melville's story of the scrivener thereby acquires an eerie parallel with Hawthorne's "Wakefield" in that each piece is fueled by a territorial imperative. Both stories flirt with the utter blankness of self, and in each case we are witness to a profoundly *scenic* drama, as if the empty self/player could achieve definition in only one way: by illuminating the stage, by taking measure of the set. Thus, it will be seen that Bartleby's two brief dicta—"I know you" and "I know where I am"—address the central mysteries of Melville's tale, and much like the earlier assault—"Do you not see the reason for yourself?"—they remind us how little *we* know about these basic matters.

And a fruitful enigma it has proved to be. Much of the "Bartleby industry" has been taken up with filling this vacuum, and a good deal of this activity has had a "charades" dimension to it, as if the scrivener were a well-known dignitary in disguise. The roll call includes Thoreau, Hawthorne, Emerson, acquaintances of Melville, and, ineluctably, Melville himself in a kind of psychic self-portrait as alienated writer. A rather different sort of inquiry has focused on Bartleby's behavior rather than his identity in an attempt to move from the textualized symptoms back to the disease that causes them. Dan McCall, in his sane and judicious study *The Silence of Bartleby*, has reviewed these diagnostic forays—analyses ranging from autism to Bergsonian automatisms, from psychological double of the lawyer to stranger in the city, from alienated worker to woman—only to conclude that the subject at hand both fits and eludes all these appellations.[3] The common thread in each of these readings is of course Bartleby's strange blankness and anonymity, and in some sense all speculation about Bartleby is, willy-nilly, a meditation about identity, about the processes of depersonalization that (must have) produced the scrivener.[4]

Complementing these person-based interpretations is the crucial body of work that examines the scrivener contextually, as the victim or product of systemic social arrangements—the boss, the office, the market, the city—that either ignore or destroy selfhood. Here we move into a wider critical arena, and our judgment of Bartleby shades into an appraisal of the society and the order that contain him. The Bartleby phenomenon, in short, has challenged the critics in a very special way, namely, to explain why a man becomes anonymous and unreachable; and the array of answers suggested over the years constitutes virtually a discourse on self and identity as seen through the lenses of psychology and the social sciences.

Yet it is hard to avoid the disquieting feeling that all these theories are like radii moving out from an empty center, from a void which Melville has purposely left undefined and blank. We as critics are *guessing*; Bartleby *knows*. For each of Bartleby's certitudes Melville uses the word "know," but we can easily discern two very different types of knowledge at work here, what the French call *savoir* and *connaître*. Bartleby blithely commands both modes, but we are baffled on each front. We are radically in the dark as to why he does what he does—nous ne savons pas pourquoi; nous ne le connaissons point—and the story's haunting power, for it has haunted the lawyer into becoming a narrator, derives from this refusal to explain. Let us consider the first instance of the Bartleby refusal in order to gauge its strange generative power. Holding out his hand sideways with the requisite copy for Bartleby to take and check, the lawyer is stupefied by the scrivener's phrase:

> "Prefer not to" echoed I, rising in high excitement, and crossing the room with a stride. "What do you mean? Are you moon-struck? I want you to help me compare this sheet here — take it," and thrust it toward him.
> "I would prefer not to," said he.
> I looked at him steadfastly. His face was leanly composed; his grey eye dimly calm. Not a wrinkle of agitation rippled him. Had there been the least uneasiness, anger, impatience or impertinence in his manner; in other words, had there been anything ordinarily human about him, doubtless I should have violently dismissed him from the premises. But as it was, I should have as soon thought of turning my pale plaster-of-paris bust of Cicero out of doors. (643–44)

This passage is a veritable adventure in negativity, in self-consuming assertions swept up in denial or erasure. "Not a wrinkle of agitation rippled him," we read, and as we negotiate the remarkable maritime metaphor, we simultaneously negate it, see it as a plenitude that is illusory, that denotes what Bartleby is not. And the other busy terms of the description — uneasiness, anger, impatience, impertinence — are likewise foils for the absentee portrait. Bartleby is "leanly composed," and we wonder if "composed" isn't a charged notion here, a kind of avowal that this is no living being but rather a construct; hence, he already displays resemblance with the plaster of paris bust. The "grey eye dimly calm" (dimly?!) reinforces (if that is not putting it too strongly) the sepia character of the description, is a good base for the colorless, affectless portrait. Cicero is not invoked in vain, for there is a powerful rhetoric at play here, the rhetoric of negativity and denial, and it performs the classic job of rhetoric: it moves, indeed enrages, its audience. "Nature abhors a vacuum" turns out to be the first law of narrativity. Bartleby's blankness is tantamount to a dismantling of the whole enterprise of character, and we (lawyer, reader, perhaps even Melville) will not have it.

Melville critics sort themselves out by the way they respond to this blankness. It is really a version of the bottle being half full or half empty. American criticism of the tale has been, for the most part, essentialist, aimed at explicating Bartleby's antics, positing depth and mystery behind the pasteboard mask.[5] But what about "half empty"? Isn't this the true threat that Bartleby poses: that the human subject is — not transformed into, but inherently — marionette, construct, blank surface? Here is the seamy underside of Emersonian ebullience, and Francine Puk is not wrong to see in "Bartleby" a satire of Emerson's "Insist on yourself: never imitate," for the entire project of self-reliance goes quietly up in smoke when the self is dissolved.[6] But the boldest critical response to these matters comes from the deconstruction camp: Bartleby's "incurable disorder," far from being a flaw or symptom of psychological or social arrangements, is itself the grand truth of the story, the nihilist mirror held up to nature. Hence Thomas Joswick suggestively echoes Roland Barthes in referring to the scrivener's antics as "a kind of zero degree of intentionality, a blankness to which the lawyer must give a 'coloring' in order to protect his own vanity against the suggestion that self is a nothing, a transitory appearance in a repeated disorder."[7] Noting the imagery of Joswick's prose, however, we detect additional and more powerful echoes, Melvillean this time, which unmistakably link the mystery of "Bartleby" to the project of *Moby-Dick*.

Is Bartleby not that "Albino man" who "so peculiarly repels and often shocks the eye, as that he is loathed by his own kith and kin"?[8] The inscrutable scrivener who defies interpretation and reference comes to us virtually spawned out of the most famous chapter in all of Melville, "The Whiteness of the Whale." There it is remarked that "the one visible quality in the aspect of the dead which most appalls the gazer, is the marble pallor lingering there as if indeed that pallor were as much the badge of consternation in the other world, as of mortal trepidation here" (997). The gray-eyed, pallid Bartleby is forecast here, and we sense that he, ghoul-like, is close to the living dead, that he brings news of that "other world," a realm allied not only to death but also to art, a place where visages are "composed" of marble or plaster of paris rather than flesh, where whatever flesh there is may be transformed into the inanimate, into a pillar of salt or a cadaver. But the deepest tie with Bartleby is to be found in the whiteness itself, in the extraordinary meditation on blankness that Melville penned in his whaling story; it is worth quoting in full the final words of that chapter, for they shed more light than any other passage in Melville on the scandal of corrosion that we call interpretation:

> Is it that by its indefiniteness it shadows forth the heartless voids and immensities of the universe, and thus stabs us from behind with the thought of annihilation, when beholding the white depths of the milky way? Or is it, that as in essence whiteness is not so much a color as the visible absence of color, and at the same time the concrete of all colors; is it for these reasons that there is such a dumb blankness, full of meaning, in a wide landscape of snow—a colorless, all-color of atheism from which we shrink? And when we consider that other theory of the natural philosophers, that all other earthly hues—every stately or lovely emblazoning—the sweet tinges of sunset skies and woods; yea, and the gilded velvets of butterflies, and the butterfly cheeks of young girls; all these are but subtile deceits, not actually inherent in substances, but only laid on from without; so that all deified Nature absolutely paints like the harlot, whose allurements cover nothing but the charnel-house within; and when we proceed further, and consider that the mystical cosmetic which produces every one of her hues, the great principle of light, for ever remains white or colorless in itself, and if operating without medium upon matter, would touch all objects, even tulips and roses, with its own blank tinge—pondering all this, the palsied universe lies before us like a leper; and like wilful travelers in Lapland, who refuse to wear colored and coloring glasses upon their eyes, so the wretched infidel gazes himself blind at the monumental white shroud that wraps all the prospect around him. And of all these things the Albino whale was the symbol. Wonder ye then at the fiery hunt? (1001)

In what may be the noblest passage in American literature, Melville takes full measure of both the seen and unseen worlds, and he goes on to chart the dread commerce between them. Acting on the fearsome principle that whereas "this visible world seems formed in love, the invisible spheres were formed in fright" (1000), Melville in effect reconceptualizes Pascal's famous cri de coeur, "Le silence éternel des espaces infinis m'effraie," turning seventeenth-century metaphysical plight into an immense nineteenth-century perceptual panorama. Pascal is among the first of the moderns to realize that the immeasurable strikes terror in us, but for him the awesome spectacle itself—the infinite spaces, the vistas that outrun our perception—is indubitably real. For Melville, at critical moments in his fictions the rich material scheme dissolves into mirage at best, fraud at worst, and his genius consists in imagining, richly and materially, the threat and horror of these discoveries in which a kind of medieval sensibility, a maniacally accelerated version of memento mori, eats away, before our eyes, the corporeal envelope to reveal its endless vanity. Like an allegory of long ago, the "velvets of butterflies" become the "butterfly cheeks of young girls," then to finish as the decked-out harlot "whose allurements cover nothing but the charnel-house within." Yet the spectacle of decomposition itself is upbeat in comparison to the alternative scenario that Melville is at pains to render, a scenario that supplants the life-death cycle with a "strike-through-the-mask" drama yielding blankness, nothingness, a vacuum instead of a process or a cycle.

Writing several decades before the impressionists established light as a constitutive force, Melville grasps the enormous stakes involved in such a perceptual and artistic scheme. Light *makes*; but is that not tantamount to saying that it also *undoes*, for we come to understand that the world "before light," before Genesis, is sovereignly blank. The extended painterly conceit of whiteness as both the "absence" and the "concrete" of color introduces the staggering notion that the manifold carnival world that our senses perceive is an elaborate sham, that "blankness" is all, is there before color, and that the richness of the material scheme is a "subtle deceit," "laid on from without." Light, the "mystical cosmetic," gives us rainbow effects, but they are only effects, a material screen that we take to be the thing-in-itself. And that is not the worst of it. Light itself is colorless, and if it were to operate, "*without medium* upon matter" (emphasis added), it would cast a "blank tinge" on the world, robbing it not only of color but, one feels, of life and body as well.

Melville is not a painter. As a writer, however, he has remained true to the "derealizing" quality of light, for he has understood that thought and imagination are nothing but the mind's light, the mind's illumination of the world. Like Ahab, Melville strikes through the mask, on to the nothingness that *is*. The reader of Melville's most interesting work is initiated into the principles of light, becomes heir to a vision of pure corrosiveness, comes to understand that vision *is* pure corrosiveness, endless peeling away. Not only does our "palsied universe" then "lie before us like a leper," but we too are enroute to becoming leprous, our material substance in a state of limitless dissolution, being eaten away from within, by our own vision self-cannibalized.

And that is the point: vision cannibalizes. The fearful taboo encountered in *Typee* has become a perceptual principle. Not the vision of the senses, which always operates "*with* medium upon matter," but the imagination, which moves through and beyond the material envelope on toward the endless vistas without boundary or stopping point. The voyage itself, the trajectory, and even the energies of the tracking imagination are the "fiery hunt," but the target itself is white, spectral, colorless. We have only to replace the albino whale with the figure of Bartleby to grasp how steadfast Melville has been in his quest. "Bartleby" closes in on the mystery of *Moby-Dick*, reduces it to a pure meditation on the blankness of the subject, a wrestling with the ineffable and the impalpable which foreshadows not only *Lord Jim* and "Heart of Darkness" but also modernist ventures such as Beckett's *Innommable* and the fictions of Borges and Calvino.

But the purity of "Bartleby" is purchased at a high price. Like vast quantities of bones and water that simmer for days on end to produce a small amount of stock, "Bartleby" offers the pleasures of distillation, but much has disappeared in the refining process. The great whale that splendidly flaunts its materiality (as well as its immateriality) in *Moby-Dick* is nowhere to be found. The vividness and flavor of the *Pequod* and its crew, of an imagination that loves surfaces as much as depths, of a verbal enterprise that draws upon the Bible, the almanach, and Shakespeare—all this has been subject to leprosy in "Bartleby," pretty much dematerialized out of existence, leaving a few remnants named Turkey and Nippers, and leaving us largely trapped within the narrow walls of the lawyer's office, moving ever further into blankness. The vista from "Bartleby" back to *Moby-Dick* allows a sighting on the Melville curve and sharpens our appreciation for the miraculous equilibrium of the whaling book, its strategic counterpoise of factual ballast and metaphysical fantasy, its capacity for total assent, total belief, even the belief in blankness. Nothing is derealized in Melville's masterpiece; everything enjoys its peculiar authority and shimmering presence. The generative style effortlessly conjures "as if" perspectives, produces more and more meaning, to culminate in a spectacle of surplus and plenty.

In "Bartleby," however, there lurks the Mephistophelean spirit, "der Geist der stets verneint," and Melville seems determined to see how far in the direction of denial he can go, to drain the cup to its very dregs, if dregs there be, in his fiery hunt for nothing. The result is the most leprous character in fiction, one who starts as a "motionless young man" and continues to *lessen* in front of our very eyes, whose liturgical "I would prefer not to" is uttered in the mildest of tones, always gently, "flutelike," even "mildly cadaverous," who comes as an "apparition," "like a very ghost," who "noiselessly slid[es] into view" or "slid[es] aside," a being in the process of disappearance, one who becomes a ghost, a spirit that literally (and stubbornly) haunts the lawyer's precincts and finishes its days as the "silent man" before he finally sleeps "with kings and counselors."

The most insubstantial of creatures, he has no visible intake or substance. At the beginning, "as if long famishing for something to copy, he seemed to gorge himself on my documents" (642). But this diet, all the more noteworthy in Melville's comedy of humors and digestion, moves predictably from the waferlike ginger nuts to its final preferred delicacy, Nothing (despite the ministrations of the Grub-man), so that, unlike other material creatures, resembling no one so much as Kafka's Hunger Artist, Bartleby "lives without dining" at the close, he too never having found "die Speise die [ihm] geschmeckt hätte." The scrivener ingests less and less into his body, and he expresses less and less as well. Nancy Blake has drawn attention to the splendid phrase "he seemed to gorge himself on my documents," and has suggested that the scrivener manifests the kind of confusion between words and things that we find in schizophrenics.[9] But Melville makes us consider the matter both ways. The material world is becoming "linguified," but one might also say that the verbal world is becoming materialized, thingified into something one might eat. To see language as "activist," as energized player in the story, is to see a panorama of slippage and transformation. "I like to be stationary," Bartleby declares, and Blake suggests "stationery" as a plausible double. "I am not particular," Bartleby declares, and we realize that he also means "not individual." "The man you allude to is nothing to me," says the narrator, Peter-like. But maybe he really is "nothing" (and what is "nothing"?), and maybe the three-letter word "m-a-n" that we can allude to is no more human than other candidates we can allude to: Cicero's statue or Lot's wife or the Virginia man who was struck by lightning and only seemed to be leaning at his warm, open window. Loss of self is an occupational hazard, not only under the regime of nineteenth-century capitalism, but within the precincts of a writerly text that taps the semiotic and anarchic potential of its materials.

"Bartleby" would seem the end stop of a meditation on the mystery of character — character exposed as an empty envelope, a shell that can never be anything but hollow. Nonetheless, Melville's fascination with the contours of character and the limits of self was so goading that he endeavored, in *The Confidence Man*, arguably the most iconoclastic fiction he wrote, to go further still, to take the fiery hunt beyond individuation altogether. *The Confidence Man*, appropriately subtitled *His Masquerade*, measures just how far the corrosive vision can be taken, as if the enigma of motive were finally put aside, jettisoned, in favor of the charade of appearances. This picaresque extravaganza, with its cast of swindlers, straight men, and gulls, bears witness to a world so elusive and indecipherable that all self-presentation comes to be seen as an elaborate hoax perpetrated by the subject, an exercise in theater known as the confidence game. And yet Melville will not quite play the total cynic, and more than once he explains the performances in terms of genuine complexity rather than inauthentic deceit, suggesting that the self might be a more various and paradoxical entity than we suspect. The consistent and coherent character is simply not to be found in nature, even though the novelist who is true to the chameleonlike qualities of his subject courts certain censure:

> That fiction, where every character can, by reason of its consistency, be comprehended at a glance, either exhibits but sections of character, making them appear for wholes, or else is very untrue to reality; while, on the other hand, that author who draws a character, even though to the common view incongruous in its parts, as the flying-squirrel, and at different periods, as much at variance with itself as the caterpillar is with the butterfly into which it changes, may yet, in so doing, be not false but faithful to the facts.[10]

Self is unitary, whereas being is multiple; to know another is akin to wrestling with Proteus, and even then, one never sees everything. Melville puts the thought in a sweet mathematical figure: "What are you? What am I? Nobody knows who anybody is. The data which life furnishes, toward forming a true estimate of any being, are as insufficient to that end as in geometry one side given would be to determine the triangle" (1047). It is a way of announcing that you can't get there from here, even though "you" and "here" and "there" are all real. Much starts to happen, semiotically, in a text of pure appearances. We begin to have, in linguistic terms, a parade of signifiers. A fiction in which nothing is reliable—that is, a fiction that unmoors its language, unties its statement from truth criteria—is a liberated fiction, an arrangement of words poised to make good on its indwelling powers of signification because it has given up on the unifying "larger view." The centrifugal yoke, the centering pressures of cogency, have been thrown off; and one's utterances travel unimpeded, indeed prancing, to the circumference. In the boldest metaphor of the book Melville returns to his meditation on light and vision. He shows that the original character is free of origin, outward bound, to be located on the far side of his verbal productions, to be understood as a luminous lens: "The original character, essentially such, is like a revolving Drummond light, raying away from itself all round it—everything is lit by it, everything starts up to it (mark how it is with Hamlet), so that, in certain minds, there follows upon the adequate conception of such a character, an effect, in its way, akin to that which in Genesis attends upon the beginning of things" (1098). This view of the subject inaugurates the peculiar epistemology of *The Confidence Man*; the self may be "essential," may even have integrity, but these qualities are operational rather than demonstrable or even apprehendable. The narrative restraints of personality and identity are thereby transcended, and we have in their stead an occulted but demiurgic source of power, a generative but unreachable origin. Above all, we are to note that such a character, unknowable in himself, makes known. It is this dual feature of the Drummond light that most warrants our attention, for it is the key to *knowing* in Melville: the blank, unplumbable character is peculiarly luminous in that he reflects and refracts the environment in which he appears. We shall return in due time to the case of the scrivener, to gauge how brilliantly Melville has actualized his concept of the "original character," but it is worth our while to remain for a bit with *The Confidence Man* in order to measure the spectacular anarchic potential of such an *ars poetica*.

The Drummond light fiction is prismatic, radiating energy outward; we may think of it as a semiotic machine, disseminating signs that are not referable to a clear origin. *Lying* could be a particularly apt form of expression for the "original character," because lying constitutes a peculiarly free exercise of language—language unconstrained by reference. The confidence game is such an exercise. So too, Melville seems to be hinting, is literature. At one point we hear of "games in which every player plays fair, and not a player but shall win," to which it is objected: "Now you hardly mean that; because games in which all may win, such games remain as yet in this world uninvented, I think" (898). *The Confidence Man* is Melville's Rube Goldberg literary machine, the perpetual motion text that spews signs endlessly, swapping unity and closure for multiplicity and freedom. We are free to label these signs "appearances," but once we do, there is a temptation to look for "realities" which the appearances do or do not match. That is a game that has losers as well as winners. But if we assent to Melville's egalitarian scheme, enjoy the signs for their generative power (including the power to generate feeling), we move closer toward an appreciation of the Drummond light world. People can lie, but can words? In that direction lies the game which all may win. We know that Joyce and other modernists played the game with zest, but so, at least in *The Confidence Man*, did Melville.[11]

This emancipated text revels in bouts of "freed-up" language, contains perpetual motion chapter heads such as "worth the consideration of those to whom it may prove worth considering" (913), ushers in scenes where the words strut and fret for themselves, busily and gaily overthrowing (they are democrats) the hierarchy of fiction's rules, celebrating their own anarchic signifying power. Consider, as an exemplary passage, the shaving sequence between Frank Goodman and William Cream, the barber, an exchange that treats, in vaudeville fashion, the cracked status of the sign. This encounter hinges on the barber's material sign, "No trust," which Frank seeks to challenge. The scene is too long to permit full quotation, but a few examples will show just how "evolved" Melville's slapstick presentation is:

> "But, as a supposition — you would have confidence in me, wouldn't you?"
> "Why — yes, yes."
> "Then why that sign?"
> "Ah, sir, all people ain't like you," was the smooth reply, at the same time, as if smoothly to close the debate, beginning smoothly to apply the lather. . . . (1085)

The slippage in evidence here, the maneuvering room granted to "smooth," betokens a new order of things, a writerly world that rejoices in its internal puns and harmonies and then rewards them by assigning them narrative duties. A moment later, to William's comment "Very true, sir; and upon my honor, sir, you talk very well. But the lather is getting a little cold, sir," Frank again responds *poetically* and completes the rhyme: "Better cold lather, barber, than a cold heart. Why that cold sign?" This outburst closes with Frank pressing William on the score of his putative treatment of a stranger, a man with his face averted: "Being in a signal sense a stranger, would you, for that, signally set him down for a knave?" (1086). All of the sign systems are now in play: face to character, sign to behavior, signal to outcome, word to referent. There is something inebriating here, a kind of superior ludic spirit that may annihilate human priorities (such as sincerity, cogency, belief) but does so with considerable verve, and seems to stick its tongue out at the reader as well, as if to say: "*This* is the reality of literature; this is the game which all win."

One has only to compare this shaving scene to its grisly counterpart in "Benito Cereno" to measure the propriety of the former against the anarchy of the latter. "Benito Cereno" is in its own dreadful way every bit as much about "play" as *The Confidence Man*, but it does not countenance such play in its language; to be sure, there are endless ironies and loaded metaphors in "Cereno," but all remain in the service (pressed into the service, one wants to say) of character and event. There is none of the slippage we see here, the encroachment of a verbal, linguistic order that invades the text, somewhat like a computer virus that has its own agenda, or—to use a simile closer in spirit to Melville—somewhat like an outbreak, a mutiny, in which the "tools" of the writer (his *words*) usurp authority, go on holiday, have it their way, take over the ship.

Melville is not Joyce. It is generally felt that he tacked his abrupt ending onto *The Confidence Man*—"Something further may follow of this Masquerade"—not only out of illness and fatigue but also out of distaste for his subject, a distaste so great that no amount of verbal dexterity and Drummond lighting could sweeten its flavor. It is nonetheless a prophetic text that shows us what kind of mileage could be gotten out of a view of self radically unsayable and transformative. It at once announces the pyrotechnics of modernism and adumbrates the decentered, anarchic strain in American letters, evincing a strange passion for verbal clout, for egalitarian word arrangements, for enlisting the semiotic potency of language as a writerly form of American "can-do-ism," even when all avenues for doing seem closed. Twain, Anderson, Fitzgerald, Faulkner, and the postmodernists were all to continue the masquerade that Melville inaugurates, to assert the freedom of speech as the writer's first and last inalienable right.

The narrative extremism of *The Confidence Man* sharpens our sense of just how much resonance the notion of character still has in "Bartleby"; the scrivener is arguably as enigmatic as any figure on that Mississippi steamboat, but he is neither disguised nor prey to transformation. Ghostly, empty, inscrutable, he remains nonetheless a single figure of great pathos, and as such he fuels a powerful dynamic, becomes effectively the genuine article, the "original character" who functions like a Drummond light, "raying away from itself all round it—everything is lit by it, everything starts up to it . . . so that, in certain minds, there follows upon the adequate conception of such a character, an effect, in its way, akin to that which in Genesis attends upon the beginning of things." We note, first of all, just how hard it is to actualize this formula, since the entire dynamic of the tale of the scrivener hinges on the radical difficulty of forming an adequate conception of Bartleby. Melville's feat is to have thwarted such a conception, to have stupefied his narrator, to have given us a sphinxlike Bartleby. Twice this character pronounces his sibylline truths—"I know you" and "I know where I am"—but the bulk of his repertory consists in the notorious refrain "I would prefer not to." And thereupon ensues the miracle. Sphinxes are generative. The riddling character provokes "an effect, in its way, akin to that which in Genesis attends upon the beginning of things." Let there be fiction. The machine works. The light shines.

Bartleby as original character? Melville remarked in *The Confidence Man* that there are many "odd" characters in fiction, picked up by the novelist in town at the "man-show" where he "goes for his stock," but that an "original character" is almost an impossibility, "almost as much of a prodigy there [in fiction], as in real history is a new law-giver, a revolutionary philosopher, or the founder of a new religion" (1097). What Melville neglects to state here, although it is writ large in the conception at hand, is that whereas the *odd* character is to be picked up in town, the *original* character mystifies and moves us precisely because he is *without origin*.

There we have it: the man without origin. The lawyer, he tells us, could easily have written the biography, or "complete life," of other scriveners he has known, but "of Bartleby nothing of that sort can be done. I believe that no materials exist for a full and satisfactory biography of the man. It is an irreparable loss to literature. Bartleby was one of those beings of whom nothing is ascertainable, except from the original sources, and in his case, those are very small" (635). Melville's tale of the copyist is, we realize, a parable about the status of origins and originals. We come to understand as well that biography may require "original sources," whereas the situation for literature is entirely "reparable" in that it converts loss into gain by transforming lack into plenitude. The missing documents that might have grounded Bartleby are unnecessary, just so many dead letters, since the actual work of the story is to be akin to Genesis, to making something from nothing. How is this "originating" done? How can it be done without "original sources"? We can hardly fail to see that Melville displays an unmistakable reverence, perhaps even a nostalgia, for originals in this story, as if they were an Edenic guarantor of presence and authenticity. Thus, the text seems to oppose the creating of documents to the copying of documents. We recall that the lawyer speaks portentously of his "original business," that he resents Nippers's intrusive efforts to go "beyond" copying and thereby encroach on his own domain, "the original drawing up of legal documents" (639).

Hence, when the Wall Street Lucifer says "non serviam," and it comes out as "I have given up copying," we sense that large things are in play. Some critics have argued that we must sharply distinguish between a *writer* and a *scrivener*, that the former is creative whereas the latter is, to use Dan McCall's term, only a "nineteenth-century xerox machine."[12] Thus, the argument goes, Melville's plight is not to be confused with Bartleby's. But the force of the deconstructionist view comes precisely from its collapsing of this distinction, since it regards *all writing* — from poetry to plagiarism — as copy, as a version of something always already in existence. The sincerest author, like the lowliest copyist, is doomed to being a "gentleman forger." Writing can never deliver presence. "I have given up copying," Bartleby says, and we hear the plaint of all writers here, the indictment of language and literature as *copy*, much like the famous critique leveled by Plato against the poets, namely, that language is sundered from things, that it trafficks in copies and replicas and effigies.

Much of the controversy over the famous "sequel" in "Bartleby," the putative stint in the Dead Letter Office, hinges also on this thorny issue of origins and ends, the communication chain that is meant to unite sender and receiver but manifestly fails to do so. Lewis H. Miller, Jr., has plausibly argued that "Bartleby exhibits a growing recognition of the futility of all linguistic acts to bridge the gap between one isolate self and another."[13] But why stop there?

Régis Durand, in his "Cadre de la fiction," cites Derrida's locus classicus, "*Tout graphème est d'essence testamentaire*," and goes on to interpret the famous scene of undelivered letters, "Sometimes from out the folded paper the pale clerk takes a ring—the finger it was meant for, perhaps, molders in the grave," as a textbook illustration of *différance* itself: "La lettre, par l'effet de retard, de ratage, qu'est la mort inscrite en elle, provoque la rupture, la désintégration: le doigt pourrit qui devait recevoir l'anneau."[14] The breakdown in communication that Melville's story describes begins to look disturbingly inevitable, the secret rule rather than the apparent exception, and perhaps this is the "incurable disorder" that the scrivener introduces into the world.

Delivered wholly without fanfare, the pale scrivener's act of refusal has genuinely apocalyptic implications; his bland work stoppage reminds one of Ibsen's project to "torpedo the ark," for it rocks the foundations of all commerce. Melville has cunningly positioned his rebel in a law office, the very place where the word is taken for the deed, where the "deed" signifies title not action, where "rich men's bonds" have replaced other "bonds"; here is the game that men have played forever, ever since words displaced things and labor became alien. In Bartleby's refusal a very old cultural contract is being breached. Preferring not to copy, then preferring not to speak, Bartleby is Melville's "original character." No less inscrutable than the evil (severed) head of Babo in "Benito Cereno," Bartleby, too, confronts his onlookers, meets, "unabashed, the gaze" of his fellows.[15] Like the Drummond light, however, his meaning is projected outward, not inward, and the very blankness of self becomes in Melville's hands radiant and epiphanic in its illumination of the scene. "I know you," he says, but we cannot know him. "I know where I am," he says, and we must understand that these are related truths, that the pallid Bartleby lights up the law office, that the haunted house is to be inventoried by its ghost. Through Bartleby we see.

Using his light, we see a world in ruins. Bartleby is indeed "a sort of innocent and transformed Marius brooding among the ruins of Carthage!" (651). He stands "mute and solitary," "like the last column of some ruined temple," and we must see that "mute" and "solitary" are clues here, indices of the ruin, of what has failed. Bartleby enters the premises of the lawyer—in all senses of the word: his office, his thinking, his self—and we see those precincts for the madhouse they are. Bartleby's refusal makes even more visible their assent. Their work is pure busyness, a charade of redundant inscriptions and hollow forms. In his never-ending efforts to attain the appearance of respectability, the lawyer wants his forgers to be gentlemen; but the unruliness of his subjects, the play of humors and affect, makes his entire operation—absurdly synchronized and orchestrated by the morning and afternoon schemes—palpably full of sound and fury for us, a cacophonous comedy of errors. The elaborate corralling of Turkey and Nippers, the ritualized dehumanization of the players as evidenced in the distribution of screens and walls, the utter mindlessness of the labor itself, all conspire to produce a kind of human comedy that would have satisfied even Bergson. Comedy lies in the interface between the human and the mechanical, claimed the philosopher. Turkey's matutinal docility and afternoon fire, Nippers's morning hiss and later calm,

Ginger Nut's capricious erranding, the lawyer's ceaseless efforts at marshaling these volatile forces into decorum and cost-effectiveness paint for us a picture of manic energies and precarious order that prefigures the bureaucratic fantasies of Kafka, the minimalist, creatural poetry of Ionesco, and above all the explosive, surreal antics of Chaplin and the Marx brothers. To this consort comes Bartleby, and there can no longer be any pretense that the machine is working, that there could ever be a purpose for the capers and chains located between the narrow walls. The world of business depicted in "Bartleby," the arrangements that are put into place by mid-nineteenth-century capitalism, the choreography of life in the office, comes to us as a grotesque parade of mechanical toys, of sentient humans coerced into the forms of abstract labor, a burlesque of teetering, careening figures from whom the veil of decorum and purposiveness has been lifted. "Do you not see the reason for yourself?"

The mechanization of man was a comic formula for Bergson, but Marx, Melville's contemporary, saw it differently. Mechanized labor in which the worker became a cipher, routinized activity in which the worker lost all sense of purpose, these forms of alienation were to be found in offices as well as on assembly lines. The functionalist ethos, the measure of a human being as determined by how much he or she makes (copies, parts, dollars), and the reification of the self as cog-in-the-machine or member-of-the-team: these features of the workplace have not changed appreciably since Melville's day. The advent of photocopying machines and computers has, if anything, augmented and exacerbated our sense of toiling in a paper world, working at an unbridgeable distance from things themselves.

To all of this Bartleby says, "I would prefer not to." He refuses to *function*. He rejects function as the measure of the human. Here, too, his blankness highlights the others' madness. His absence of motive makes us realize how little we know about the others' motives, *why*, for instance, Turkey blots and beams after lunch, or Nippers hissingly struggles with his desk in the mornings. Why they are the grotesques they are is of no interest to the lawyer: their lives, their being, are material to him only insofar as they affect productivity. The Drummond-light Bartleby exposes the office as nothing less than a regulated asylum, the workplace as a place of screens and walls. Compartmentalization and commodification reign; no one knows anyone. Much of the most insightful critical work on the social dimensions of "Bartleby" — from Louise Barnett's ground-breaking study of Marxian alienation to Patricia Barber's provocative fantasia of *Miss* Bartleby and Allan Silver's learned account of "helping and helplessness" in employer-employee relations over the past centuries — benefits precisely from the spectacle that has been lit up by the Drummond light.[16]

Is all this not what Bartleby knows? "I know you," he tells the lawyer; "I know where I am." He knows the narrator to be the largest tool of all, and he knows the place — the office or the Tombs, it matters not — to be a place for copying and measuring, not for living. This spectral Lucifer of the workplace is not content simply to issue and to reissue his *non serviam*; he takes the final apocalyptic step — like "a new law-giver, a revolutionizing philosopher, or the founder of a new religion"—he *lives at the office*, and it is quickly seen to be his "hermitage." It is the ultimate affront, the ultimate confusion of realms. Palely and sublimely transcending the alienations of both language and labor, the silent scrivener asserts living as the business of humans. It is hard to imagine a more eloquent or biting critique of the machine/man ethos. To make the workplace a home, to prefer living over working, to be the man who "*was always there*" is to make the ultimate humanist geste. In no other way could Melville so illuminate the encroachment of culture on the human subject. There at the office on Sundays and every night—eating, dressing, sleeping there—Bartleby breaks all the decorous rules, becomes indeed the spirit of the place, the genius loci, by giving his life to it, by investing it with life. Bartleby haunts the premises like a ghost, a bad smell, a bad conscience, an incubus. He cannot be separated from it, since the narrative itself actualizes him over and against all removals. This maniacal insistence on *living there* turns Wall Street upside down; upheaval and revolution are not far away: "And he now persists in haunting the building generally, sitting upon the banisters of the stairs by day, and sleeping in the entry by night. Every body is concerned; clients are leaving the offices; some fears are entertained of a mob . . . " (666). Like a prophetic image announcing the plight of the homeless which would not become visible for more than a century, "Bartleby" rays outward into our time. The lawyer's proprietary questions—"What earthly right have you to stay here? Do you pay any rent? Do you pay my taxes? Or is this property yours" (660)—are just as logical and just as mad today as they were in Melville's time.

"I would prefer not to" is a special assertion of human priorities and human dignity, a last-ditch defense of the self in terms of negation, a negation that engenders presence, a desperate reworking of Goethe's "der Geist der stets verneint" in such a way that only through denial—*verneinen*—can the spirit—*Geist*—be saved. *Geist* is to be understood as "human spirit" in its widest, most social acceptation. We cannot pin down or trace back Bartleby, but his great act in the story is eerily domestic: he chooses to live where others are paid to work. The Drummond-light character fulfills his mission doubly: he rays outward to make us see the office as Bedlam, and he then sets up camp there, to live. Such a strategy on Melville's part has an uncanny parallel with the territorial project of identity in Hawthorne's "Wakefield," for each author has faced up to the nothingness of the human enterprise—the self as riddle, knowledge as impossible—and devised an environmental fable, a homing tale, as if to show that the pattern we make is always real, is what counts, even if we ourselves are ghosts and our currency is copy. Melville's fiction, like Hawthorne's, is from beginning to end about "real estate," and we realize that narrative itself is called on to chart and to create the *trace* of human life.

It is tempting to close my consideration of "Bartleby" on this note, but there is more that needs to be said. The blank, Christlike Bartleby who visits Wall Street (the way the plague "visited" Thebes) and ends up at the Tombs, surrounded by "murderers and thieves," does not tell his own story. His uncanny behavior does trigger our understanding, and he alone seems to know whom he is dealing with and where he is; but his life and death come to us by way of Melville's remarkable narrator, and that mediation, much analyzed by critics, deserves some final remarks.

To indict the narrator is both necessary and facile. True, he is a philistine, a safe, prudent man "cheaply purchas[ing] a delicious self-approval" by befriending Bartleby, "lay[ing] up in [his] soul what will eventually prove a sweet morsel for [his] conscience" (647). True, too, he denies Bartleby three times, unmistakably resembling Peter in his denial of Christ, and perhaps most damning of all, he never remotely fathoms *why* Bartleby acts as he does. Hence, he never suspects the idiocy and inhumanity of his own scheme. These are heavy liabilities for any narrator, and Melville has not let this one off easily.

Yet for all that, those critics who have read "Bartleby" as a strange love story are not wrong. Patricia Barber deserves honors for her fascinating revision of the tale, in which she shifts genders to give us "Miss Bartleby," and her conclusion is apt: "By imagining the story of Miss Bartleby, we realize that the story of the lawyer and Bartleby — for all its oddity, dry humor, and stuffy rhetoric — is essentially a love story, a story about a man who is confined in an office setting that forbids intimacy and who comes to love a person he cannot save."[17] Even that does not quite say it all, because the very presence of the story is the most eloquent index of Bartleby's power. The story of the scrivener haunts its readers because it haunts its narrator, and it haunts its narrator because he knows that he has encountered in Bartleby something beyond the pale. We cannot fail to see the narrator's concern, dismay, and compassion; his response to the Bartleby phenomenon is short on understanding but long on suffering and pity, and it is thereby properly cathartic. And although he cannot see the relevance of "Ye should love one another" to the operation of his business, he does take it to heart in his dealings with the strange scrivener "billeted" upon him "for some mysterious purpose of an all-wise Providence." His "mission in this world," as he sees it, is to furnish Bartleby "with office-room for such period as [he] may see fit to remain" (662); it is a dim recognition that we must house the homeless, even in the workplace, that "living" counts, even though it has no clear monetary coefficient.

Above all, the narrator's mission, notwithstanding his own view of the matter, is to furnish Bartleby with human interest, to invest this ghostly apparition with feeling and compassion. Bartleby himself has no affect whatsoever; with his automatic "I would prefer not to" he may seem to be the quintessential machine of the story. What sentiment this tale has comes from the narrator, and that is what distinguishes "Bartleby" so sharply from *The Confidence Man*. In his parable on masquerade, Melville has either given up on or lost any concern with human love. Intellectually and linguistically bracing, *The Confidence Man* is a cold experiment, a willed parade of appearances and speculations. The confidence game is played throughout, but it is played rather than believed in or felt deeply. The narrator in "Bartleby" — bigoted and blinded though he is — is genuinely "invested" in the fate of his scrivener. He cannot see directly the Drummond light any better than we can, but the dead Bartleby lives on in his memory and in his story. He does not penetrate any mystery or save any lives, but he explores as best he can, keeps covenant, to the best of his lights.

All the more reason, then, to attend to the tale the lawyer delivers himself of, for it is unlike the documents he copies, just as the feeling he has for the elusive Bartleby is unlike his regulatory concern for his other workers. Instead, we are witness to the mystery of human connection, and that enduring bond, unlike the bonds he customarily deals in, survives the wreckages he describes, whether in mid-Atlantic or on Wall Street. As remembering, narrating voice, he is ineluctably a saver of lives, a maker of lives. His storytelling, like all storytelling, is inherently generative. It is here that the deconstructionist view of language as "after the fact," as sundered from presence, proves false. Narration is akin to Genesis; it is a rejection of closure, a denial of death, an engendering of presence, a preferring and a conferring of life.

But even language is ultimately less than empathy and love. The lawyer's fellow feeling constitutes the very medium of the story, and it speaks for the deepest values that Melville had in mind. Only through such feeling does the ghost of the Other—and the Other is always ghost, whether he be named Bartleby or not—become real, and only in this way can dead letters become living ones, uniting speaker and hearer, writer and public, through the office of literature.

II

MASTERS AND SLAVES

3

Stowe: Ghosting in
Uncle Tom's Cabin

Stowe's epochal novel has become a *point de repère* for rethinking the American literary canon, and in the vigorous debate over the so-called American Renaissance in the middle of the nineteenth century, scholars of many stripes — most especially feminists, but revisionists of other allegiances as well — have made us understand that the neglect of *Uncle Tom's Cabin* in American studies has been anything but benign. The all-male team of Emerson, Thoreau, Hawthorne, Melville, and Whitman has occupied center stage in part because the critical lenses of a whole generation of literary historians, fashioned by the tenets of modernism and New Criticism, have made it virtually impossible to see and to evaluate Stowe's monumental book. Selling three hundred thousand copies in its first year of print, its author greeted famously by Lincoln as "the little lady who made this big war," *Uncle Tom's Cabin* illustrates to perfection the literary risks of popularity and success. Awesomely influential in its own day, Stowe's book has been written off in a later time as propaganda, sentimental trash, sappy, devoid of art, a sell-out to domesticity and religion, stereotypical in its characters, compromised even in its moral heart by the racial condescension that bathes its view of black and white.

It is against these claims, either asserted stridently or understood silently, that the revisionist critics have been tilting, arguing quite persuasively that Stowe's style, rationale, and success must be seen for what they are (rather than what they are not): a mode of writing and a burning subject that were profoundly inscribed in nineteenth-century American culture. Jane Tompkins puts the case succinctly: "*Uncle Tom's Cabin* retells the culture's central religious myth, the story of the crucifixion, in terms of the nation's greatest political conflict — slavery — and of its most cherished social beliefs — the sanctity of motherhood and the family."[1] Tompkins's discussion of the sentimental tradition in American letters, its crucial connections with domesticity and religion, its positioning of women at the heart of things, helps us to rediscover the force of Stowe's novel and to see in it the potent medicine its contemporaries saw: a displacement of power from government and court and factory to the kitchen, a rendition of the realist agenda of slavery, practical politics and

47

the business as usual of living and dying in choral fashion, measured against the backdrop of the divine and the dictates of spirit. Far from being a utopian retreat, such art is aggressively political, seeking change and conversion by means of feeling rather than logic. If we have been reluctant to consider such work "art" at all, it is because we have been conditioned by the aesthetics of modernism: indirection, psychological nuance, narrative complexity, structural experiment, obsessive concern with language itself. But recent work in American literature has suggested that other critical models may afford us a better entry to much of this material. Sacvan Bercovitch has demonstrated the significance of the "jeremiad" in American literature, an exhortative form that blends public and private, social and spiritual; and Philip Fisher has shown how the dictates of modernism, valuing complex form over direct expression, have blinded us to the power of apparently "plain" and obviously popular writers such as Stowe and Dreiser.[2]

To be sure, not all is rosy in Stowe criticism. *Uncle Tom's Cabin* may be an unqualified indictment of the slave system, but its views of blacks, and even of the black family, have been the subject of heated debate ever since its publication. The white reading public obviously divided along predictable lines in the nineteenth century, but there was real controversy among early black readers, and from Frederick Douglass in the 1850s to writers such as Richard Wright and James Baldwin a good century later, the book's presentation of blacks as mentally inferior types, either sentimentalized or minstrelized, has stuck in people's throats. Moreover, the crucial distinction that Stowe makes between full-blooded blacks and mulattoes — the former being servile and crude, the latter (owing, no doubt, to the white male blood in them) being more fully "humanized" — introduces serious ambiguities and blind spots in a program that calls itself enlightened.[3]

But even if one quarrels with Stowe's discriminations and formulas, there can be little argument that *Uncle Tom's Cabin* is a singularly powerful and moving novel, a text whose force seems artless and unplanned but imperious nonetheless. As we know, the author spoke of its writing in quasi-hypnotic terms, claiming ultimately that "God wrote it." The fastidious Henry James also regarded it as strong, despite its primitiveness, "as if a fish, a wonderful 'leaping' fish, had simply flown through the air," and Edmund Wilson's influential retrospect in *Patriotic Gore* uses terms such as "eruptive force" and refers to characters as projecting "themselves out of the void."[4] We seem to have a test case here of a book that, although aesthetically crude and ideologically tendentious, is somehow undeniably successful. Anthony Burgess, writing in the midst of the civil rights battles of the sixties, both addresses this paradox and suggests a way out: "Now, it seems, we have to take the whole book again, since there is little relevant to our age that can be taken out of it. Today's Negroes, who reject martyrdom and intend to overcome, are ashamed of Bible-thumping Uncle Tom; George Harris, prophet of a vital Africa, has become a demagogue with two gold Cadillacs. If the book is to mean anything now, a good deal of the meaning must reside in the art."[5]

The "art" of *Uncle Tom's Cabin* is best understood in the largest possible terms. The writing itself is often lackluster, and the copious racial, social, and regional stereotyping is unarguable. But this novel explores the issues of freedom and bondage more memorably than any other American novel, and it does so in ways that have not been adequately recognized. Even to "liberate" *Uncle Tom's Cabin* from the demands of modernist aesthetics and to insert it into the mode of the jeremiad or the sentimental tradition does the novel a disservice as well as a service. Granted, Stowe is putting forth a revolutionary matriarchal scheme, and she is armed with sermons and tireless moral fervor; but her weapons and her tactics are *writerly* to the core. She is showing, sometimes in the oddest kinds of ways, the freedoms of speech that alone can offset the constraints of race and culture. Speech may free, not so much in terms of an Emancipation Proclamation but rather in terms of language itself overturning and undoing bondage, the language of the Bible which stakes out a spiritual realm behind the phenomenal one, and the language of this "God-authored" novel which was to change American history. Stowe's novel is more ludic, more interested in semiosis, in the production of meaning and the power of signs, than had been thought. In this study it deserves pairing with Twain's *Pudd'nhead Wilson*, for both texts share a fascination with disguise, and both texts are in search of a way out, a writerly way of breaking the prison.

That is not all. *Uncle Tom's Cabin* is the archetypal statement of our American commitment to remaking the world; with prophetic design it inaugurates the poetics of the dismembered family, and it seeks its restorative wholeness in the realm of art as well as belief. The self is under siege in this novel: treated as a thing, swapped and bartered, bought and sold, broken into and wasted. Stowe's project is to render this world of juggled and abused creatures, this malleability of the human thing, while seeking forms of redress. This redress is sometimes literally re-dress; at others it is to be found in the Bible, but the Bible as a place, a realm made enterable by language. At its most giddy, the search for freedom and self-determination becomes demiurgic, entails entering the spirit world by cunning and stealth, even to the point of ghosting. These ventures will be found again in every American text studied here: the project of self-making, on the one hand, and reconceiving the environment, on the other, is at the heart of our literature. Nowhere is the legacy of Stowe's novel more visible than in one of the contemporary texts to be discussed at the close of this book: Toni Morrison's *Beloved*, also a meditation on the forms of enslavement and the forms of redress, also vitally concerned with the dismembering and re-membering of the human family.

Much of the raw power of *Uncle Tom's Cabin* derives from its presentation of slavery as a system of human ownership. Blacks are shown to be objects of commerce, human merchandise, entirely subject to the laws of the marketplace. And private property is thereby exposed as the central religious doctrine of the United States. Hence, George Harris's owner says with genuine fervor and indignation: "It's a free country, sir; the man's *mine*, and I do what I please with him, — that's it!"[6] The Fugitive Slave Law (which was part of the Compromise of 1850), requiring northerners to return escaped slaves to their southern owners, is known to have been the great stimulus behind Stowe's decision to write this novel, and one feels that she was as incensed by the

hypocrisy of this legislation as by its evil; one of her targets, then, is the
self-deception of the North, its acquiescence in a pure property scheme dressed
up as patriotism. Thus, after presenting the unsavory trio of Haley, Loker,
and Marks outlining their plans for the recapture of Eliza and Harry, the
author heaves this broadside at her audience:

> If any of our refined and Christian readers object to the society into
> which this scene introduces them, let us beg them to begin and conquer their
> prejudices in time. The catching business, we beg to remind them, is rising to
> the dignity of a lawful and patriotic profession. If all the broad land between
> the Mississippi and the Pacific becomes one great market for bodies and
> souls, and human property retains the locomotive tendencies of this nine-
> teenth century, the trader and catcher may yet be among our aristocracy. (90)

Stowe's phrase "the catching business" itself catches some of the kinetic energy
of the scheme she wishes to present. Not only is a new breed, indeed a new
hierarchy, on the rise, but we are made to see that the view of America as
"one great market for bodies and souls" is a strikingly mobile proposition, a
formula for perpetual motion, for far-flung adventures of buying and selling,
escaping and retrieving. Her book is to do full justice to the "locomotive
tendencies" of her century and of her material, for the essential gravity of the
human being—a creature inscribed in a family, weighted with the density
of human connections—is disallowed for her blacks. Instead, we come to
understand that the universe looks entirely different, obedient to different
laws of motion, when people are literally, as we say in today's parlance, up
for grabs. With a kind of prescient prenuclear logic, Stowe has displayed
slavery as the moral splitting of the atom, the bursting of the family armature
and the "liberation" of the creatures positioned within it, an explosion of
forces and a repositioning of the human object according to the laws of supply
and demand. Here is the truly reified world view, and in it the human subject
is an assemblage of parts, but part of no assembly. In his negotiations with
Haley for purchasing Tom, St. Clare muses about how much he himself might
bring on the market, how much his "parts" are worth: "'I wonder, now, if I
was divided up and inventoried,' said the latter, as he ran over the paper, 'how
much I might bring. Say so much for the shape of my head, so much for a
high forehead, so much for arms, and hands, and legs, and then so much for
education, learning, talent, honesty, religion!'" (181). The dreadful human
cost of such inventory, the mutilated psychic state it produces, is more fully
explored in Morrison's *Beloved*, but already here we see human value as market value, as cipher. And we see in St. Clare's list the treatment given to the
nonmeasurables as well, the stuff one cannot put on a scale or palpate. What
happens to it?

The human-as-merchandise is most fully and institutionally on display in
the chapter "The Slave Warehouse." Stowe explains that we might expect such
a place to be a "foul, obscure den, some horrible *Tartarus 'informis, ingenus,
cui lumen ademptum,'*" but that in up-to-date New Orleans such places are

clean and well tended. At least they appear so to the naked eye, but she wants us to see a bit deeper into the matter:

> Then you shall be courteously entreated to call and examine, and shall find an abundance of husbands, wives, brothers, sisters, fathers, mothers, and young children, to be "sold separately, or in lots to suit the convenience of the purchaser;" and that soul immortal, once bought with blood and anguish by the Son of God, when the earth shook, and the rocks rent, and the graves were opened, can be sold, leased, mortgaged, exchanged for groceries or dry goods, to suit the phases of trade, or the fancy of the purchaser. (379)

It is in such passages that Stowe lifts the curtain from her realist depictions to show us the larger temporal and spatial backdrop, the fuller story of the human soul's origins and value, the searing drama of Christ's sacrifice which stands behind each one of these inventoried bodies. Jane Tompkins has written persuasively of the religious allegory that subtends the action in *Uncle Tom's Cabin*, and she has shown how persistently Stowe counterpoints her plot with biblical echo and citation.[7] But we are not meant to be transported into some "other" realm; instead we are supposed to understand that the selling, leasing, mortgaging, and exchanging of human beings is a virtually apocalyptic transgression, not merely because the "soul immortal" dare not be commodified but most especially because it must not be pieced apart, ripped and torn out of its larger home. Let us examine again the list of items in the warehouse: "husbands, wives, brothers, sisters, fathers, mothers, and young children." Stowe does not write "men and women, old and young"; she emphasizes the familial rather than the generic, and she does so with such vehemence that we may feel that "sold separately" is a heinous double crime, with the true horror falling on the second term. One wonders if *Uncle Tom's Cabin* would have been written had slave families remained intact and been protected by law *as families*. What is most cataclysmic in this book, tantamount to the shaking earth, the rent rocks, and the opened graves, is the sundering of the family. The family, more even than the human soul, is the center of gravity of life, the fundamental unit — emotional, moral, physical, spiritual — that is dismantled and mocked by the very machinery of the marketplace scheme, all those barbaric centrifugal energies let loose by the "locomotive tendencies" of the nineteenth century.

Critics have not failed to note the importance of Rachel Halliday's orderly, maternal Quaker kitchen as a kind of radiant domestic metaphor for the sound body politic.[8] And in a series of remarkable essays Elizabeth Ammons has spelled out the matrifocal ideology of *Uncle Tom's Cabin*, showing how both Eva and Tom are to be understood as figures of the female Christ, and how the institution of motherhood, far from being some kind of idealized retreat from worldly affairs, poses an authentic alternative to the systems of slavery and exchange which govern society.[9] But the family model needs to be assessed, above all, as an affective spiritual reality that is somehow *prior* to the "normal" scheme of individuated atomistic beings. We know that Stowe herself had six children, that she struggled hard to balance mothering and writing, that the material conditions (including poverty and poor health) in which she lived were often harsh; we know, too, that she lost one of the children, despite heroic efforts to save it, and that her own mother died when she was only five. These things we know. Harder to gauge is what these experiences actually meant for Stowe. But *Uncle Tom's Cabin* is an eloquent testimony to her profound sense of reality as umbilical, linked in the flesh. It is here that she differs radically from her male peers. One thinks of the proud, muscular individualism that breathes and speaks in Emerson, Thoreau, and Whitman, or the haunted sense of solipsism that shows in Poe, Hawthorne, and Melville. Not that these writers did not understand human relationships, but rather that they started with an imperious ego whose needs had to be assuaged, either in reality or in dream. Nowhere in their work does one encounter the view of self that bathes *Uncle Tom's Cabin*, a view of life as weave and connection, of home as mesh and fulfillment, of feeling itself as empathic and fluid. Stowe's novel is written under the sign of lost children and sundered kinships, of fleshly contracts that have been broken.[10] This will become a political matter, but it is first and foremost a visceral state of being, an experiential feeling of connectedness so strong that distance and death seem abstractions to it. Only when this primary sense of bonding and linkage is understood do the conventions and machinations of this novel become at last visible for the poetic devices they are.

Stowe's direct address to the conscience of mothers comes in a well-known passage at the end of the novel, and we see the unmistakable connection between the powerless slave mother and the author who cannot forget her dead baby: "I beseech you, pity the mother who has all your affections, and not one legal right to protect, guide or educate, the child of her bosom! By the sick hour of your child; by those dying eyes, which you can never forget; by those last cries, that wrung your heart when you could neither help nor save; by the desolation of that empty cradle, that silent nursery, — I beseech you, pity those mothers that are constantly made childless by the American slave-trade!" (514–15). This impassioned plea can be said to underwrite a great deal of *Uncle Tom's Cabin*, and we must come to terms with the urgency of this need, an urgency so authoritative that it authors, turns silence into cries, emptiness into fullness. The fundamental impetus of the novel is restorative, to make the family whole again; this healing project is no simple matter, given the damages done by slavery and death, and the greatness of the novel resides in its strategies for reassembling what has been sundered. Consider, for example, the episode of Senator and Mrs. Bird helping Eliza escape to the Quakers. Mrs. Bird's maternal passion quickly enough routs her husband's abstractions, and he, now prepared to help, suggests that they donate some of their own dead child's clothes for Eliza's son Harry:

> His wife opened the little bed-room door adjoining her room, and, taking the candle, set it down on the top of a bureau there; then from a small recess she took a key, and put it thoughtfully in the lock of a drawer, and made a sudden pause, while two boys, who, boy-like, had followed close on her

heels, stood looking, with silent, significant glances, at their mother. And oh! mother that reads this, has there never been in your house a drawer, or a closet, the opening of which has been to you like the opening again of a little grave? Ah! happy mother that you are, if it has not been so. (109)

We recognize the authorial voice again, but we see here just how inventive this voice is, how it structures its fiction according to the principles of loss and retrieval, how it goes about transforming, through plot and largeness of heart, fragments into wholes. Eliza's Harry will wear the clothes of Henry Bird, and this gesture of human patchwork, of family quilting, illuminates a great deal of Stowe's essential design. The novel is familial in a very special way (we will see that the project of remaking the family is also at the heart of Faulkner's *Light in August,* as well Morrison's *Beloved*) because it seeks, heroically and melodramatically, to put back together what was sundered, and to do so with borrowed clothes and palpable substitutes. Harry becomes Henry; the dead live; the family is doubly saved. And, as if the adventure in disguise were not enough to flaunt the new grouping, Stowe packs off the senator and Eliza and her child on a carriage ride that is as fascinating in its own homespun way as the famous ride in the carriage that Emma and Léon take together in *Madame Bovary*:

Know then, innocent eastern friend, that in benighted regions of the west, where the mud is of unfathomable and sublime depth, roads are made of round rough logs, arranged transversely side by side, and coated over in their pristine freshness with earth, turf, and whatsoever may come to hand, and then the rejoicing native calleth it a road, and straightway essayeth to ride thereupon. In process of time, the rains wash off all the turf and grass aforesaid, move the logs hither and thither, in picturesque positions, up, down and crosswise, with divers chasms and ruts of black mud intervening.

Over such a road as this our senator went stumbling along, making moral reflections as continuously as under the circumstances could be expected, — the carriage proceeding along much as follows, — bump! bump! bump! slush! down in the mud! — the senator, woman and child, reversing their positions so suddenly as to come, without any very accurate adjustment, against the windows of the down-hill side. Carriage sticks fast, while Cudjoe on the outside is heard making a great muster among the horses. After various ineffectual pullings and twitchings, just as the senator is losing all patience, the carriage suddenly rights itself with a bounce, — two front wheels go down into another abyss, and senator, woman, and child, all tumble promiscuously on to the front seat, — senator's hat is jammed over his eyes and nose quite unceremoniously, and he considers himself fairly extinguished; — child cries, and Cudjoe on the outside delivers animated addresses to the horses, who are kicking, and floundering, and straining, under repeated cracks of the whip. Carriage springs up, with another bounce, — down go the hind wheels, — senator, woman, and child, fly over on the back seat, his elbows encountering her bonnet, and both her feet being jammed into his hat, which flies off in the concussion. After a few moments the "slough" is passed, and the horses stop, panting; — the senator finds his hat, the woman straightens her bonnet and hushes her child, and they brace themselves firmly for what is yet to come. (111–12)

A bit of heavy-handed comic relief? Or a metaphoric rendering of the transformations and jolting changes that have just taken place? With a sure intu-
ition Stowe broaches the subject of the right road, the right way of life, much
as Faulkner will handle it in the Bundrens' effort to stay on the road while
crossing the swollen waters in *As I Lay Dying*; and, like Faulkner, she stresses
the violent and bruising confrontations that take place, so powerful that they
wreck private identities, recast the self, show it to be meshed with others in
vital and invasive ways. These tumbling bodies also point to the famous car
accident in Flannery O'Connor's story "A Good Man Is Hard to Find," in
which the nuclear family pitches headlong into a dark and savage realm, or
indeed Mrs. Shortley's vision of a "small room piled high with bodies of dead
naked people all in a heap, their arms and legs tangled together, a head thrust
in here, a head there, a foot, a knee, a part that should have been covered up
sticking out, a hand raised clutching nothing" from the newsreels about the
war in O'Connor's story "The Displaced Person."[11] These bodies of Stowe's
crash into one another, "tumble promiscuously," speak a language of human
connection that Stowe cannot articulate in any other fashion. In this type of
discourse we must understand that metamorphosis and disguise are going to
do heroic work, are going to be the central tropes for forging together what is
separate and separated.

The mutilations of the spirit depicted in *Uncle Tom's Cabin* are most
obviously and scandalously to be found in the routine ravaging of the black
family, but they cut, in some sense, deeper even than that, informing the very
scheme of selfhood in Stowe's mind, as if individuation were actually something of a mirage, a temporary islanded state that has never satisfied the spirit.
Self means orphan in Stowe; the family constitutes that prior integrity which
haunts the weaned individual. Her characters experience themselves preeminently in terms of lack, of yearning for reentry into the whole. The novel
familializes its readers, thrusts Tom by means of its title and story into the
reader's orbit as uncle, as figure of kinship. As we have seen, the figure of the
mourning mother is to be found behind much of the story's action, transfigur-
ing the exchanges into covenants, retrieving among the living the dead who
have been lost. The children return. St. Clare dies with the word "Mother" on
his lips, and we are to realize that this sophisticated, world-weary person has
completed his exile as self, has returned home. Every breakage is a fusion of
sorts: Eva will go "to our Savior's home," where it is "so sweet and peaceful,"
"so loving" (326); Tom undergoes his calvary at the hands of Legree, but his
death leads, through George Shelby's act of liberation, to the re-formed family, free at last from "the risk of being parted from home and friends, and
dying on a lonely plantation, as he died" (509). Perhaps the most spectacular
instance of bonding what has been separated is the case of Simon Legree,
reunited—at last, utterly against his will, by dint of human magic—with his
own mother, an unmistakable pendant to the deathbed reentry of St. Clare.

And it is in this light that we may interpret the flurry of embarrassing
reunions at the end of the novel: prodigal children returning, orphans finding
a home, a tempest of sibling and familial constellations ranging from Madame
de Thoux's "Mr. Shelby, George Harris is my brother!" (495) to Cassy's mis-

taken words to her new-found granddaughter, "Darling, I'm your mother!" (499). This profusion of families refound and reaffirmed may stick in the throats of today's hard-boiled readers, reminding us of the worst shortcomings of sentimental pulp fiction, but one can hardly quarrel with the logic or necessity of these final reconciliations. The major critical question here is: Are these coincidences somehow "earned," validated by the larger work? Long-lost cousins and nephews and siblings clutter up the ends of many books, even some great books—one thinks of Jane Eyre's most fortunate inheritance—but few works deal as richly with the poetics of orphanhood and family making as *Uncle Tom's Cabin*. The entire novel is about reunion, and one could even argue that, for Stowe, the very purpose of the novel, of art in general, is to make possible or visible this coming together of what has been sundered. Morrison's *Beloved* will take this theme of fissure and dismemberment as far as it can go, will question the very feasibility of healing and reunion, probing it for the psychotic and spectral possibilities it contains.

The ruptured family, from the *Odyssey* to *Beloved*, is in short a topos of all cultures, having to do with the alienations of war, economics, and race, as well as the social order. Harriet Beecher Stowe's moral outrage over this theme is well known. Less well understood is the role of human art in responding to this tragedy. Stowe writes at the close of her story that the reuniting of families is a perilous enterprise, and her terms are worth examining: "Deeds of heroism are wrought here more than those of romance, when, defying torture, and braving death itself, the fugitive voluntarily threads his way back to the terrors and perils of that dark land, that he may bring out his sister, or mother, or wife" (499–500). Stowe carefully juxtaposes the heroism of family making against the possible factitiousness of art, but her own language is large and prophetic: the lost family member is captive in a "dark land," and the way back to this figure is tortuous, a matter of "threading" one's way. We see here a version of the Orpheus-Eurydice myth (grafted onto a labyrinthine setting), and it serves as a capstone for the novel she has written, itself a mythical treatment of separation and reunion, the former caused by human abuse and desperation, the latter achievable by courage—and also by art.

Art would not seem to do very well in Stowe's book. On the face of it, the project of remaking the self, of alteration as redress, is predictably dismissed as both comic and spurious. St. Clare's servant Adolphe assiduously apes his white master, and he is presented to us as an affected fool. But is the matter so simple? Having himself called *Mr. St. Clare* "among the colored circles of New Orleans" (253), and making use of his master's fine clothes and even his way of speaking, Adolphe seems excessively histrionic, a figure out of place within the narrative economy of the book. St. Clare's own assessment of his servant has a distinct existential tinge: "As to Dolph, the case is this: that he has so long been engaged in imitating my graces and perfections, that he has, at last, really mistaken himself for his master" (208). Stowe is hardly Pirandello, but she is irresistibly drawn to the spectacle of disguise and impersonation. Once the St. Clare slaves are sold, poor Dolph gets his comeuppance at the hands of the crude Sambo: "'Lor, now, how touchy we is,—we white niggers! Look at us, now!' and Sambo gave a ludicrous imitation of Adolphe's

manner; 'here's de airs and graces. We's been in a good family, I specs'" (381).
There's a lot of acting (and considerable resentment as well) going on here, as
Sambo brings Dolph down. The matter becomes still more virulent in Marie
St. Clare's brutal punishment of Rosa: "I mean to shame her; that's just what
I want. She has all her life presumed on her delicacy, and her good looks, and
her lady-like airs, till she forgets who she is; — and I'll give her one lesson that
will bring her down, I fancy!" (374). It has been pointed out that mulattoes
occupy a very special position in Stowe's scheme. To be sure, they too are
slaves, and we can measure the anger which their posturing brings about,
among both blacks and whites. But it is also the case that they can get away
with the posturing because they are depicted as not only white-skinned but
also "white-mannered." Adolphe and Rosa mimic the whites out of vanity,
and they will be made to pay for it. But when we consider the actions of
George and Eliza Harris, it becomes clear that acting and disguise may be a
precious resource for achieving freedom and mobility. George, unlike Dolph
and Rosa, really can *pass*. Stowe is rather fulsome as to his particular trumps:

> We remark, *en passant*, that George was, by his father's side, of white
> descent. His mother was one of those unfortunates of her race, marked out
> by personal beauty to be the slave of the passions of her possessor, and the
> mother of children who may never know a father. From one of the proudest
> families in Kentucky he had inherited a set of fine European features, and a
> high, indomitable spirit. From his mother he had received only a slight mu-
> latto tinge, amply compensated by its accompanying rich, dark eye. A slight
> change in the tint of the skin and the color of his hair had metamorphosed
> him into the Spanish-looking fellow he then appeared; and as gracefulness of
> movement and gentlemanly manners had always been perfectly natural to
> him, he found no difficulty in playing the bold part he had adopted — that of
> a gentleman travelling with his domestic. (133)

Passages like this help us understand the controversy this book has generated among blacks ever since its publication. The Byronic, European-looking
George is granted an aristocratic bearing and a social seriousness that puts
him at sharp variance with the full-blooded blacks of the novel. Richard
Yarborough has shrewdly pointed out that George and Tom "inhabit different
worlds, parallel dimensions that never intersect. A full-blood Clark Kent and
a mulatto Superman, they are never on stage at the same time."[12] Yarborough's
pithy metaphor aptly translates the pecking order as well as the strategy to
which Stowe was committed, and it also points to the disguise motif itself
which is so rampant. Thus, it follows that Eliza will trim her hair to pass for a
male, and that little Harry will be altered into a girl; but is it necessary for
Eliza to blush and tell George, "There, an't I a pretty young fellow?" or for us
to learn "what a pretty girl" Harry-Harriet makes (448–49), so pretty even
that "the dark beauty of the supposed little girl drew many flattering remarks
from the passengers" on the boat (451)? There is an unmistakable element of
play, of maneuvering room, in these disguises, a sense in which the sheer
aesthetic pleasure of self-shaping, of refashioning color and identity, is registered and enjoyed. In a system where monolithic imprisoning labels abound,

it is hard not to savor these episodes as moments of mastery and ease, moments when the hounded subject begins to script the environment, starting with the contours of his or her own body. Stowe hardly goes as far as Twain does along this path, and we will not find in *Uncle Tom's Cabin* an obsession with masquerade and deception that matches the pyrotechnics of *Puddn'head Wilson*; but we do have a comparable meditation on freedom and ingenuity, on the political uses of art.

Adolphe and Rosa, George and Eliza, Harry/Henry/Harriet all evince a kind of morphological looseness, a slipperiness that makes it hard to pin them down, to "catch" them. Through them a certain slippage enters this text, and in that slippage we are entitled to discern a peculiar form of freedom: unsettling, sometimes generous and sublime, sometimes histrionic and vain, always multiple. This mobility can wreak havoc on orderly minds, and in one of the most remarkable chapters of the novel Stowe displays just how much epistemological violence may be generated by such creatures. On the one hand, we have the steadfast Vermonter of the text, the firm, unplayful, decent Ophelia, believing in order, set in her ways; and on the other, we have the astounding Topsy, Stowe's black alter ego to the angelic Eva. Their collision course is highly illuminating because it refuses to be limited or pinned down to the surface reading Stowe attaches to it.

On the face of it, Topsy presents no interpretive problems. Entering the St. Clare household on the terms "odd," "goblinlike" and "heathenish" (278), she is clearly enough defined as the ideal target of Ophelia's missionary efforts; she also appears initially to be no different from all those other "black heads" scattered about the household, "mopping and mowing and grinning between all the railings, and tumbling over the kitchen floor" (279). This presentation of the black ragamuffin as circus creature in need of Christian education must complicate our sense of Stowe's racial views, and the author makes doubly certain that we do not miss her point by pairing the black urchin with her white counterpart: "There stood the two children, representatives of the two extremes of society. The fair, high-bred child, with her golden head, her deep eyes, her spiritual, noble brow, and prince-like movements; and her black, keen, subtle, cringing, yet acute neighbor. They stood the representatives of their races. The Saxon, born of ages of cultivation, command, education, physical and moral eminence; the Afric, born of ages of oppression, submission, ignorance, toil and vice!" (287). Nothing enigmatic here: a straightforward, even allegorical portrait of the races. In the face of this luminous binary system Ophelia's mandate for education and conversion—conversion in more ways than one—is easily understood.

But it is not easily carried out. And that is not simply because Topsy is an ornery child. In Topsy, Stowe has expressed, to the dismay of many critics, her overt racial beliefs, but she has also expressed a good deal more than that, notably a kind of elemental freedom that is simply unchartable in her available conceptual scheme. It seems that nothing can be done to "change" Topsy, that she is impenetrable, utterly resistant to moral or physical suasion. Now, all readers know what Topsy's fate is: to be transformed by the instinctual love of Eva and the rather more contractual affections of Ophelia into an orderly little creature who can end up in Vermont. But Stowe's most fascinating pages have to do with the little heathen rather than the little Christian, and it is possible to see in this black child a kind of absolute integrity that no one else in the book enjoys. Her famous rejoinder to Ophelia's question "Do you know who made you?" is the most startling declaration of independence in the novel:

> "Nobody, as I knows on," said the child, with a short laugh.
> The idea appeared to amuse her considerably; for her eyes twinkled, and she added,
> "I spect I grow'd. Don't think nobody never made me." (282)

Eric Sundquist has remarked that these lines are an implicit critique of the family-as-property system itself, but one can go still further.[13] Topsy is repudiating the entire patriarchal principle, and her demiurgic response gives us pause, makes us rethink self-determination as a morphological notion, a matter of self-production. And the laughter and the twinkling eyes are not unrelated to this display of power, for Topsy's repertory is herself — her self — body, eyes, sounds, language. She is the novel's riddle of the Sphinx, its central heart of darkness, a purely alien code that is not amenable to the discourses of the regnant system. We have seen that black/white is Stowe's basic binary scheme; but truth/lie is no less crucial to the ordering of a manageable world, and Topsy's discourse obliterates that distinction:

> "Topsy," said Miss Ophelia, "don't you know it's wicked to tell lies?"
> "I never tells no lies, Miss Feely," said Topsy, with virtuous gravity; "it's jist the truth I've been a tellin now, and an't nothin else." (285)

Later, Topsy confesses to stealing and burning Rosa's earrings and Eva's ribbon, and her explanation is: "Cause I's wicked, — I is. I's mighty wicked, any how. I can't help it" (286). But there has been no theft or burning; the items are still there. Ophelia is bewildered:

> "What in the world did you tell me you took those things for, Topsy?"
> "Why, Missis said I must 'fess; and I couldn't think of nothin' else to 'fess," said Topsy, rubbing her eyes. (286)

This is no simple deceit. "Confession" means nothing here, since there is nothing prior to the words, nothing to refer to. Topsy's language is pure, unconstrained by referent, happily spewing out meanings. She reconceives words, flaunts their malleability. The "state" from which the "first parents" fell she labels, with twinkling eyes, "Kintuck" (293), not so terribly unlike Gatsby's claim, seventy-five years later, that San Francisco is in the Midwest. St. Clare acknowledges that Ophelia needs "to give her a meaning or she'll make one" (293), and this is because "one word is as good as another to her" (293). After her advent, we learn that Chloe confuses "poetry" and "poultry," that too an exercise in freedom and transformation. She is the play principle, the self as performance, the semiotic black hole at the core of Stowe's creation. With this in mind, we can reconsider her antics as a kind of freedom fighting, gestures of unfettered, even gratuitous expressiveness: "Topsy was soon a noted character in the establishment. Her talent for every species of drollery, grimace, and mimicry, — for dancing, tumbling, climbing, singing, whistling, imitating every sound that hit her fancy, — seemed inexhaustible" (289).

Moreover, Topsy, alone of the black characters, fights. True, the mulatto George wounds Tom Loker, but Topsy's martial exploits are, albeit devious, not to be dismissed. We learn that anyone in the household "cast[ing] an indignity on Topsy was sure to meet with some inconvenient accident shortly thereafter" (290), ranging from theft to destroyed clothing to "a libation of dirty slop" "unaccountably" deluging them. "Unaccountably," Stowe writes, for there was absolutely no way to prove Topsy the culprit; "not a scrap of direct evidence could be found" (290) to indict Topsy for these misdemeanors. In short, Topsy cannot be *tracked*; she does not have the luxury of looking like a Spaniard, but her actions are disguised nonetheless, resisting all efforts to pin down an origin, a source. That is no mean feat in this novel, when one thinks of the professional trackers, the blood on the ice that "marked every step" (79) taken by Eliza when crossing the ice-strewn river, pursued by creatures like the "mousing man" Marks. Markings are critical in *Uncle Tom's Cabin*, whether it be the "stripes" on one's back, the wounds on one's hands, or the darkness of one's skin. But Topsy is inscrutable. She is the anarchic principle incarnate:

> Topsy would hold a perfect carnival of confusion, for some one or two hours. Instead of making the bed, she would amuse herself with pulling off the pillow-cases, butting her woolly head among the pillows, till it would sometimes be grotesquely ornamented with feathers sticking out in various directions; she would climb the posts, and hang head downward from the tops; flourish the sheets and spreads all over the apartment; dress the bolster up in Miss Ophelia's night-clothes, and enact various scenic performances with that, — singing and whistling, and making grimaces at herself in the look-glass; in short, as Miss Ophelia phrased it, "raising Cain" generally. (291)

This "carnival of confusion" constitutes an ecstatic release of signifying and expressive energies. Topsy quite simply reshapes and re-forms her world, putting things to new uses, wearing feathers, reversing the direction of up and down, coopting sheets and spreads for her own apparel, boldly creating a "new" Miss Ophelia out of the bolster, commandeering the whole consort into a theatrical performance of her own making. All Miss Ophelia knows to say is "raising Cain," but we can say a bit more than that. Topsy is nothing less than Stowe's equivalent to Melville's white whale, and this chapter constitutes an eerie parallel to "The Whiteness of the Whale" because in both instances we have the encounter with a startling world that defies interpretation, a recognition that the ordering process itself, whether it be moral or conceptual, is a form of colonization, a kind of fiction that covers over the elemental energies that can be neither named nor corralled. Topsy is Stowe's rendition of the power of blackness — blackness seen as pure energy, unchanneled, unchained, unmappable. We are close to the very power of creation, a creatural vitality that precedes culture and epitomizes what we might mean by the word "freedom." Stowe is mesmerized by the semiotic and behavioral anarchy of Topsy, and it is to her credit as a writer that she, far more successfully than Hawthorne in his treatment of Pearl, could render this pulsing figure with all its mystery and integrity intact.

Topsy's fuller story cannot be told by Stowe.[14] The wild child's narrative will appear in Morrison, who turns her into a ghost haunting her origins and demanding her fill. Nor will Stowe pursue or develop those who could pass: Dolph will be reborn in Twain's *Puddn'head Wilson*; George Harris goes right off Stowe's map as he heads for Liberia; but Faulkner's Joe Christmas may be thought of as the psychotic portrait of such a figure, seen from the vantage point of intolerable racial and gender tensions, doomed to rage and mystery, headed for crucifixion. But could one imagine a synthesis of these forces, a character endowed with Topsy's indomitable spirit and dark power yet outfitted with the pigment and social graces to warrant narrative development? Needless to say, this rhetorical question leads us to the final figure of freedom to be discussed: Cassy. Stowe could tell Cassy's story, and in it she fused all the motifs that have interested us: the remaking of the family, disguise, the power of blackness, and the power of art.

Cassy is presented to us as the abused, damaged mother that Eliza could have become, that Stowe knows herself to be, by dint of the dead child. She has drained the entire cup of miseries. A beautiful quadroon, she has loved a white man with complete sexual passion and borne him children; she has been traded to be a partner to his cousin; she has seen her two children sold; she has tried to kill the cousin with a bowie knife; she has been bought by the kind Captain Stuart but has later deliberately put to death the child she bore him, out of memory of the other losses; and now she has become the crazed "mistress" of Simon Legree. There is an intensity of feeling and range of experience in Cassy that dwarfs that of Stowe's other characters. When we first meet her, she is half crazed with hurt and rage. But Uncle Tom's Christlike example reawakens her moral faculties, and she gradually moves, fully and confidently, into the key role she is to play: to free herself and Emmeline from the grasp of Simon Legree. That project of liberation, more even than the calvary and crucifixion of Tom, constitutes the novel's most significant and poetic display of human art and human freedom.

The symbolic disposition of Simon Legree's plantation has been much commented on; a place of rot and decay, near swamps and spongy ground, it is clearly enough meant to be a version of hell.[15] Its haunted house is Poe-like in its trappings, and Stowe is going to tell a ghost story to match those of Poe. But there are some significant differences. Cassy stresses to Tom how powerless they are in this place, how much it is a closed world unto itself, with absolute power resting in the hands of Legree:

> "You see," said the woman, "*you* don't know anything about it;—I do. I've been on this place five years, body and soul, under this man's foot; and I hate him as I do the devil! Here you are, on a lone plantation, ten miles from any other, in the swamps; not a white person here, who could testify, if you were burned alive,—if you were scalded, cut into inch-pieces, set up for the

dogs to tear, or hung up and whipped to death. There's no law here, of God or man, that can do you, or any one of us, the least good; and this man! there's no earthly thing that he's too good to do." (419–20)

This is more than bombast. We are to understand that Legree's plantation is a place where absolute power reigns, where no intervention is conceivable. We may even, with just a grain of poetic license, compare it to the ship world that Melville returns to in many of his narratives, also a universe unto itself, closed off from outside influences, subject to a law (and a tyranny) of its own. In particular the analogy of "Benito Cereno" comes to mind, because there we see the carnivalesque and histrionic possibilities of the ship world taken to their logical extreme. And most of all we can see in the person of Melville's black artist Babo the counterpart to Cassy. Babo is the mad artist of Melville's tale, the *metteur-en-scène* who scripts the roles for all the players, especially the two white officers, one of whom plays wittingly, one of whom plays unwittingly. The only realm open to Babo is art; the elaborate play on board the Spanish galleon testifies to a desire for revenge and a rage to hurt that cannot be assuaged by killing alone. And we must interpret the actions of Cassy in a similar way. She will oppose the absolute tyranny of Simon Legree with her own black magic, her fabricated ghost story. She will use artistic ingenuity to rival his despotism, and she will fashion a world of her own, replete with presences and voices; and Legree will be made to live inside it, just as he has coerced others into his own enclosure. This is not an act of madness; it is an act of art. In the words of Sandra Gilbert and Susan Gubar, for whom Cassy in the attic is as near perfect an emblem of the madwoman as one could find, "Cassy exploits impersonation of madness and confinement to escape maddening confinement."[16] They properly term her stratagem "a uniquely female plot," and it is that indeed: she is not just a female actor asserting her will in a male scheme, but is calling upon other female spirits, notably the ghost of Legree's dead mother. Legree will be forcibly connected to the mother he has betrayed, will suffer the classic Stowe connection of mother and child, and we are to understand that this forced reunion is, at least poetically, an atonement for the woman-artist who has killed her own child. Cassy's magic act is a culminating moment of the novel, and it warrants a closer look.

Magicians are not normally held in good odor, and it is all too easy to dismiss Cassy's prestidigitation as mere technique. It is true that she manages pretty much what the Delphic oracle managed, to become a vehicle for the voice of the gods, but she does so in a shockingly mechanical fashion: "In a knot-hole of the garret, that had opened, she had inserted the neck of an old bottle, in such a manner that when there was the least wind, most doleful and lugubrious wailing sounds proceeded from it, which, in a high wind, increased to a perfect shriek, such as to credulous and superstitious ears might easily seem to be that of horror and despair" (466). But we might also claim that the tempest on the heath in *King Lear* is strictly a meteorological affair. What strikes us in both cases is the way in which the elements are part of a larger sign system, and Stowe's character has taken the extra step of bottling the sound, channeling it for her listener, converting noise into language. Above all, we are obliged to hear the multiple voices in Stowe's orchestral arrangement, to grasp their composite sound. Hence, we note that Cassy's strategem is cut, almost filmically, against Tom's calvary, as if the Christian spectacle of submission and yearning for another life were to be juxtaposed against the secular scheme of fighting evil by *producing* the spirit world. It is not impossible to envision Cassy's "art" as a version of Tom's resurrection, since his bodily death and her conjured ghost are textual bedfellows. But Stowe wants us to understand that art itself is never merely technical or mechanical. Cassy has *earned* the role of pythia because she has suffered every evil imaginable. In the awful terms of the text, she has been repeatedly "broken" and "broken into." Legree's greatest pride consists in his prowess at "breaking people in," and Stowe is out to demonstrate not only that he will fail to break Tom but that he himself will be invaded by Cassy's art. Tom's sacrificial death seems an ingredient of that art, and Cassy herself must, in some important way, consent to die before she can become a potent and liberating spirit. When Tom urges her to escape, her response is significant: "I know no way but through the grave" (463). And when she and Emmeline lead Legree and his men on a wild goose chase, it is no accident that the two women must plunge "into a part of the labyrinth of swamp" (471), and that Cassy threatens Emmeline with death if she falters. According to Stowe, one remembers, rescuing one's family is an affair of threading one's "way back to the terrors and perils of that dark land" (499–500), and we cannot fail to see that this entire chapter of tricks and stratagems is ultimately a voyage into and beyond death, a way of keeping covenant with one's own dead, even those one has murdered. The ghostly emissary fashioned by Cassy will break into Legree, directly into that "dark, inner world" (466) that not even he can keep inviolate. Simon Legree, who has cast aside Mother and all softness, learns what Stephen Dedalus learns in the "Circe" chapter of *Ulysses*: the dead mother cannot be kept out; her embrace goes beyond the tomb; they will be brought face to face.

But there is little that need be thought of as supernatural in this outcome. Stowe has written her book from beginning to end with the certainty that mother and child remain an unfissured whole, despite the horrors of slavery and the appearances of flesh. Cassy has had to become a ghost to become a ghost; she has had to die to get to the dead; she has had to kill a child to save a child. There is nothing saccharine or facile in this chapter about human art, for it makes very clear that the prime ingredient of the artist's enterprise is his or her own flesh and blood. Only when we have accepted the severe logic of Cassy's geste can we come to terms with the sappy coincidences at the close of the book: "Darling, I'm your mother!" Somewhat like Bloom achieving an epiphanic encounter with his Eton-dressed dead son Rudy at the end of "Circe," so too do Cassy — and George and Eliza — earn their improbable co-incidences, merit their happy endings, suffer through to the high plateau of artful resolutions, so that the larger family may be at last brought together.

Uncle Tom's Cabin is not a metafiction. "Freedom of speech," when applied to Stowe's book, is not to be thought of as a modernist gambit that celebrates the spawning power of language to make a universe of its own. Yet

Stowe's novel occupies nonetheless a central place in this study because it documents, more forcefully than any other text under discussion, the palpable weight of oppression that may choke human life. Stowe wants to salvage the human family, and her closing formula for doing so, for ending slavery, is well known: "But, what can any individual do? Of that, every individual can judge. There is one thing that every individual can do, — they can see to it that *they feel right*" (515). What she has not said is that art can be a unique tool for achieving this effect.[17] Perhaps she has not needed to say it. Surely the function of literature is illustrated on virtually every page of her novel, especially as it is figured by the highest verbal exemplar she knew: the Bible. Tom's relation to the Book is total: he is actually defined as a living text, as "all the moral and Christian virtues bound in black morocco complete" (179), and we can hardly fail to see that his own life is an *imitatio Christi*. But we also see the book as a huge container, a kind of spatiotemporal human almanac and itinerary that keeps him in touch with the reality of his past, a living chronicle of his own life and of the people he has known and lost:

> As for Tom's Bible, though it had no annotations and helps in margin from learned commentators, still it had been embellished with certain way-marks and guide-boards of Tom's own invention, and which helped him more than the most learned expositions could have done. It had been his custom to get the Bible read to him by his master's children, in particular by young Master George; and, as they read, he would designate, by bold strong marks and dashes, with pen and ink, the passages which more particularly gratified his ear or affected his heart. His Bible was thus marked through, from one end to the other, with a variety of styles and designations; so he could in a moment seize upon his favorite passages, without the labor of spelling out what lay between them; — and while it lay there before him, every passage breathing of some old home scene, and recalling some past enjoyment, his Bible seemed to him all of this life that remained, as well as the promise of a future one. (174–75)

The "way-marks" and "guide-boards" of Tom's Bible image a form of tracking and recouping quite at variance with the likes of the slave chasers or the blood on the ice. In the Book one may find the fuller dimensions of one's life, including past and future. Eva, we may recall, put at the very top of her slave liberation program reading and writing: "I'd teach them to read their own Bible, and write their own letters, and read letters that are written to them" (310). St. Clare discovers, to his amazement and envy, that the words on the page of the Bible are *real* to Tom, and he wishes that he, too, had such eyes. Stowe even writes that those words have become for Tom "ingots of gold," and with this notation we may measure how far we have moved from the operative mercantile system of the novel. The word itself is precious, is the true agency of exchange, because it makes legible and visible all that our eyes do not see: the past, the future, the soul. Small wonder that Tom, so victimized and done to within the story, holds the Book dear: it makes him rich by giving him an estate that others cannot take away, no matter how hard they try to break into him.

By now it should be clear that Harriet Beecher Stowe has emulated the Bible in her own book. She has aimed for *Uncle Tom's Cabin* to have the kind of power and reach that the Bible itself has for Eva and Tom. And it seems fair to say that her book did have that kind of revolutionary power, that it did move from the realm of print into the realm of feelings and thence into the political arena as well. Only part of the full story achieved legendary status: Eliza crossing the ice, the Christlike travails of Uncle Tom, and the fate of the angelic Eva. Much of the rest is no longer part of public memory. And we know how the popularized versions of the text, winning public favor for half a century after the book was published, had less and less to do with the text that Stowe actually wrote, leaving us with a combination of minstrel show and hagiography.

But the whole of *Uncle Tom's Cabin* tells another story as well, a story of human cunning and human creativity, a story of art rivaling belief. The feats of Topsy and Cassy are remarkable instances of human passion as semiotic power, of the human creature as free spirit, with its freedom lodged in the capacity to alter the givens by dint of *language*. Topsy's language of body and visage is properly inscrutable, black, implosive, uncoercible; Cassy's language may seem to be an open bottle visited by the wind, but in fact it is a discourse that has been forged by a life of rage and abuse, and it reaches full articulation — making palpable the world of the spirit — only after a passage through death. In these strange triumphs of human will and human expression, Stowe is not betraying her biblical model. To move from the written character to the human character, to display textual freedom as a priceless index of human freedom: these gambits epitomize the astonishing play as well as the high seriousness of *Uncle Tom's Cabin*. She is showing us that the writer celebrates the freedom of the human spirit and bonds the human family together through words as writer, as someone who wants to alter the world and has only language to make us *feel right*.

4

Twain: The Twinning Principle in *Pudd'nhead Wilson*

A notoriously unsure judge of his own work, Mark Twain nonetheless recognized that the presence of the Italian twins, along with the embryonic romantic interest they kindle, constituted an undesirable tug of war in *Pudd'nhead Wilson*. Once he had discovered Sir Francis Galton's *Finger Prints*, Twain seems to have decided that his book should center on the plot of the exchanged infants and the fortunes of Wilson, and that it would not accommodate the more exotic material involving the freakish twins. As to the love angle, the infatuation that Rowena feels for the dashing aristocrats, Twain's reservations seem justified: love has no place in this fiction, and the passages devoted to its emergence are silly. Nonetheless, as every reader knows, Twain did not remove the twins. He merely "altered" them from the original Siamese version—a four-armed, two-headed creature on two legs—to the more usual variant: two separate young men who happen to be twins. And many readers have felt that Twain's famous "obstetrical" efforts in sorting out his two stores ("I pulled one of the stories out by the roots, and left the other one—a kind of literary Caesarian operation") made rather more of a mess than a success of these affairs, leaving odd reminders throughout the novel of the initial joint conception.[1] After all, the twins are still there, and they continue to disturb.

Why are they still there? Many years ago Leslie Fiedler remarked that Twain's instincts outran his judgment, that the twins were an integral feature of his book even though they violated conventional canons of propriety. Fiedler is worth quoting in detail, because he senses the audacity and elusive propriety of this strange book, even though he faults Twain with a failure of artistic nerve:

> All that the surrealists were later to yearn for and in their learned way simulate, Twain had stumbled on without quite knowing it. And as always (except in *Huckleberry Finn*) he paid the price for his lack of self-awareness; he fumbled the really great and monstrous poem on duplicity that was within his grasp. The principle of analogy which suggested to him linking the story of the Siamese Twins, one a teetotaler, the other a drunk, Jekyll and Hyde inside a single burlesque skin—to the tale of a Negro and white baby switched

in the cradle finally seemed to him insufficient. He began to worry about broken plot lines and abandoned characters, about the too steep contrast between farce and horror; and he lost his nerve — that colossal gall which was his essential strength as well as his curse. Down the well went the burlesque supernumeraries and finally out of the story; and the poor separated twins remain to haunt a novel which is no longer theirs.[2]

Fiedler reveals something of his own interest in freaks and gall, but, for the most part, these remarks constitute the most insightful commentary the novel has ever received. Yet it may be that Twain knew all along, obscurely perhaps, what he was doing. The twins are not cut out of the final version because they are nothing less than its metaphoric heart, however irrelevant or dangling they may appear in realist terms. It is time to see just what twinning entails, for Twain and for us.

Understood loosely, the twin phenomenon is found frequently in Twain's work. *The Prince and the Pauper* is an overt instance of its appeal, and we can see what Twain was drawn to in using it. To "swap" two physically identical but socially opposite youngsters is to open a number of narrative doors, leading at once to comedy, dramatic surprise, irony, and satire. As Marvin Fisher and Michael Elliot have noted, Twain displays "a long obsession with twins, intentional imposture, and accidentally confused identities."[3] *Pudd'n-head Wilson*, they argue, "is a partly intentional, partly intuitive analysis of what can happen when a supposedly organic community maintains a network of social fictions based on an inevitably deadly and socially divisive idea of human fractions."[4] Human fractions, as we know, abound in this novel, ranging from the $\frac{1}{32}$ black blood that brands a person to the canine version, half a dog. The fateful exchanging of Tom and Chambers, as alike at birth as prince and pauper, sets the course for a speculative fiction that is obsessed with *difference*; look-alikes with different careers point up the whole issue of definition, of how we see clear, of how we know who is who. How firm and how fixed a proposition, Twain seems to be asking, is a human subject? Selfhood, as he had already sovereignly displayed in *Huckleberry Finn*, comes from without as well as within, from environment as well as heredity, and it follows that any serious story of identity is at some level a story of mixed identities, of identity itself as a riddling mix of genes and society. Swapping the babies is Twain's entry into this material.

But why the Italian twins? Twain, ever interested in freaks and performers, was first drawn to the idea of the famous touring twins Chang and Eng, who came to this country in the 1820s; but the "real" origin of his story was presumably the spectacularly conjoined pair Giovanni and Giacomo Tocci, whom Twain learned about in the 1890s. These Siamese twins actually shared one body with separate arms and heads, and they clearly constitute the purest, most literal manifestation of the twinning principle, the creation of two who are bonded into one. In the original version of the novel they appear in their conjoined form, making it possible for the author to try out a wide number of Jekyll-and-Hyde scenarios. But Twain must have intuited that such a creature would do better in the circus than in the novel. *Pudd'nhead Wilson* comes of age as a novel precisely when the author severs and normalizes his Siamese twins, for—despite Fiedler's contention that Twain "fumbled" here—separated twins are infinitely more promising, tell us far more about doubling and duplicity, than conjoined ones. It is precisely when the physical bond, the actual flesh linkage, disappears that the great issues of this novel—identity and connection—come into focus. We then have the spectacle of linkage that is real but does not show, of individuality and autonomy that show but are not real. The "atomic" individual is in for trouble. No less so than the work of Conrad and Dostoyevski, *Pudd'nhead Wilson* is about secret sharing and unavowable doubles.

Twain's twins allow him to launch the fiercest attack yet on individual autonomy by painting, in the most graphic terms imaginable, the pluralist reality of self, the sort of dispersion and scattering that Rimbaud in his famous letter had prophetically announced: "JE est un autre." Twain and Rimbaud make strange bedfellows, but a glance at the American writer's work and life reveals not only that he was obsessed with alterity but that he knew firsthand what the slippage of self feels like. Figurative Siamese twin himself, he traveled throughout his life the umbilical cord connecting Samuel Langhorne Clemens and Mark Twain. Slightly further afield, Twain may have had his own fraternal dilemma, namely, in the grotesque career of his brother Orion (seen, in Justin Kaplan's words, as "his mirror image, his burden, his baseline for judging the distance he himself had come from Hannibal."[5] Here is already a version of the echo principle that may erode any belief in an integral self. The world sees our specificity, but we know our connectedness. *Pudd'nhead Wilson* is an affair of rebounds and reflections, an exercise in (invisible) comparatism. Luigi and Angelo are separated, but the twinning that counts is the figurative twinning, the existence of doubles and shadows and echoes in a world that claims to contain individuals, all black and all white, all master and all slave.

Twinning disturbs, and it is instructive to consider some of the folklore surrounding twins, for we shall better understand the malaise that exists between twins and Dawson's Landing. Twins introduce rivalry and ambiguity into areas that seem clear and unitary. The fable of Romulus and Remus deals as much with fratricide and instability as it does with founding. Or take the story of the Man in the Iron Mask, who was said to be the twin of the king and hence a threat to the monarchy. Fratricide, actual or virtual, hovers about the legends of twins, and there are many traditions in which one twin is put to death at birth just to avoid such ambiguities and such outcomes. There is an inherent scandal in twinning, for it undercuts the notion of legitimacy and primacy. Still more basic is the threat of replication itself. The single item proclaims its self-sufficiency, its definitional sharpness and integrity, but the replica erodes the very lines of identity and closure. It is hard to see clear in a world of twins, and it must follow that the forces of order will always want to suppress them in order to restore the reign of the "clear and distinct." In Twain's apparent tale of confusion, murder, and sleuthing, the real war may well be against replicas and doubles and the mysteries they announce. The social, political, and ethical ramifications of such a strategy must have been sensed by Twain. But could he have fully anticipated the writerly benefits he was to reap?

Few writers can fully gainsay twinning. Dawson's Landing may take refuge in single fixed identities, but Mark Twain is seduced by doubling. It opens the realms of virtuality and disguise to him, and it points to domains where multiplicity and shadow are the order of the day: those of language and the psyche. Those political and social forces that govern the community according to unitary values and strict binary oppositions — white versus black, rich versus poor, man versus woman — can be routed, as Twain was to discover, by means of the twinning principle. Twain knew all too well that his was a divided society, that the trauma of 1861–65 was still, some thirty years later, unhealed, that unity was a fiction. Hew knew also that the lawgivers believed in mono- lithic fixities — not just black/white, but lady/whore and gentleman/scoundrel and a host of others — which admitted of no admixtures, no nuances, no maneuvering room. *Pudd'nhead Wilson* is rife with verbal doublings, with carnivalesque and anarchic energies that wreak havoc on the fixed meanings of its good citizens. Such a strategy is particularly congenial to ex-citizen Mark Twain, who is playing with explosives (just as he did in *A Connecticut Yankee in King Arthur's Court*), taking measure of the determinisms that coerce hu- man life (color, birth, reputation) while fashioning a peculiar writerly counter- assault of his own. The twinning principle will be called on to open up a closed world, to create within the precincts of the text freedoms that are unallowable within the community. This process of opening and liberation makes it possible for us to see in *Pudd'nhead Wilson* an echo principle, a shadow play that recasts the figures and gestures that appear before us, pro- ducing something like a photographic negative of the events at hand, turning white into black, black into white, all the fixed principles into their opposites. But play is never simple, and, in ways that are as intriguing as the problematic close of *Huckleberry Finn*, so too does *Pudd'nhead Wilson* back off and close down shop, call a halt to the revolution, and put out the fires it has so assiduously been fanning.

Let us begin with the twins in Chapter 5, where Twain himself begins with them. Hints of doubling abound. Tom Driscoll has strutted about with his polished Yale manners, but his fancy clothing soon produces a dark replica: "And when Tom started out on his parade next morning he found the old deformed negro bell-ringer straddling along in his wake tricked out in a flam- boyant curtain-calico exaggeration of his finery, and imitating his fancy East- ern graces as well as he could."[6] Much is on show here, and we are not far from the clowning antics of Dolph in *Uncle Tom's Cabin*. But the whole proceeding here has a circuslike feel to it: Tom's walk is a "parade," a perfor- mance, and it is properly "deformed" in the servant aping his master, "tricked out," Twain says, and he hints at something of the energy and zest of such ventures. Here is the old high-low contrast that is dear to classical comedy, but we cannot fail to see that there really is something of a parade here, a positing of two where there was one, an echo principle that is verbal and morphological as much as it is satiric. One has a "wake" in Twain's book, as if we did not stop where we thought our contours ended, as if we were "leak-ing" or "extended" in some irrepressible but illuminating and confessional way.

Nothing in the book is more shrewd than Twain's actual introduction of the twins. We recall that Rowena's family is breathlessly awaiting their entry, and the author presents it with considerable flourish: "At last there was a knock at the door and the family jumped to open it. Two negro men entered, each carrying a trunk, and proceeded upstairs toward the guest-room. Then entered the twins — the handsomest, the best dressed, the most distinguished-looking pair of young fellows the West had ever seen. One was a little fairer than the other, but otherwise they were exact duplicates" (27). There is a great deal to admire here. The "two negro men" who enter through the opened door are a beautiful dramatic touch, and — at least for the reader — there has to be a momentary confusion with the twins themselves. The young aristocrats are, of course, white, but as we read that "one was a little fairer than the other, but otherwise they were exact duplicates," we are irresistibly reminded of the other pair of fair young fellows, also exact duplicates, enough so that they were exchanged in their cradles and nobody has noticed the difference. The Italians are doubles not only of each other but of Tom and Chambers. And Twain's discourse in presenting them speaks, eloquently if indirectly, of the major racial and economic issues of the novel. When the twins are initially mentioned, Rowena's ecstatic happiness is unmistakably that of an *owner*: "Just think, ma — there's never been one in this town, and everybody will be dying to see them, and they're all *ours*!" (26).[7] This emphasis on owning and being owned is sounded as well in the twins' own story: orphaned at an early age, obliged to be exhibited for nothing — a nightmarish version of Twain's own public career, the kind of thing he must have feared most — they repeat-edly refer to these years as "slavery." Twain has tapped the polysemous nature of poetry in this episode, and he is showing that prose, too, can have what Hemingway was later to call "fourth and fifth dimensions." Everything speaks in multiple tongues: the twins refer us to the swapped babies, and the whole consort is bristling with hints of slavery, of loss of freedom by dint of color or fortune. The whole sequence of their arrival comes to a brilliant and prophetic close in the twins' triumphal piano duet: "The young strangers were kept long at the piano. The villagers were astonished and enchanted with the magnifi-cence of their performance, and could not bear to have them stop. All the music that they had ever heard before seemed spiritless prentice-work and barren of grace or charm when compared with these intoxicating floods of melodious sound. They realized that for once in their lives they were hearing masters" (30). Leavis particularly admired this passage, and one can see how its fine closing term, "masters," completes the series of somersaults and rever-sals brought into the fiction by the twins. They are at once slaves and masters, circus freaks and noblemen, ridiculous and admirable. Strict definitions are to no avail here because the view of human nature that Twain is presenting is insistently multiple and elastic. There can be little doubt that they are most admirable in their guise as *performers*, for here is the mastery that Twain most takes to heart, the mastery that serves as a strange, aesthetic analogue and counterpart for the other mastery, that of white over black, which governs the social structure of his world.

All of Twain's cards are on the table in this scene: the twins bring excitement, art, multiplicity, and play to Dawson's Landing, and they are meant to give us pause. Their mobility is characterological and essential, not just writerly, but it is the writing itself, the author's writing, the deft shifting of registers, that makes us see it. The gambit consists in positing a rival structure of one's own devising, a verbal one that may alter and invert the givens through the agency of language. The introduction of the twins opens Twain's register, inserts the black-white issue into a larger, panoramic context of power and performance, and although it endows the writer with a demiurgic ability to reshape potent social forces that are movable in no other way, we are by no means certain that the twins themselves will benefit from such prowess. The ease with which the twins are moved from slave to master is the ease of metaphor, but metaphor itself is a liberating, explosive trope, inherently at war with fixed notions and codes. Even my own critical language—"are moved from slave to master"—indicates something of the passivity and marionettelike results of such authorial dexterity, showing us that verbal legerdemain is never entirely "for free," no matter how freewheeling it appears. *Pudd'nhead Wilson* is a nervous text throughout, imbued with an unsettling kind of fluidity, prone to slippage and reversal, as if all its issues were pirouetting on a tightrope and could show black or white, depending on the lighting or the angle.

This attitude toward one's materials is preeminently aesthetic; its sovereignty is the sovereignty of modern literature, the aristocratic ease with which a Joyce maneuvers his materials, making it possible for us to see many and contradictory things in them, to see the artwork itself as multiple and ambivalent rather than oriented or committed. Such play is never innocent, and in Twain's hands it offers the same heady liberation from bondage that it does in Joyce, the awakening from the nightmare of history which the writer negotiates in his own peculiar fashion. Such writing is especially desperate and arresting when the authorial gambits are demonstrably filling in for collapses within the text, when the only freedoms imaginable and realizable are the writerly ones. Twain will go this whole route.

The swapping of children may be a game, but it is a game at once scientific and fateful. Roxy exchanges the babies out of fear that her child may be sold down the river, but her deed wonderfully resembles that of the trained anthropologist or sociologist, for it is hard to imagine a better test case for the nature-nurture argument than the arrangements Roxy makes for the two children. Like mice in a Skinnerian maze, baby Tom and baby Chambers are to reveal the operative laws of the system; how each turns out will be a kind of racial proof of the pudding. The nineteenth century is thinking out loud in Twain's bizarre text, as the determinants for human behavior pass by us in review. At first all seems to be nurture, which, after all, is the enlightened view we would expect from a novelist we admire. As Pudd'nhead's Calendar puts it, "*Training is everything. The peach was once a bitter almond; cauliflower is nothing but cabbage with a college education*" (23). Habit works its own dreadful wonders, and by dint of treating Tom as master, Roxy soon begins to experience him that way: "The mock reverence became real reverence, the mock obsequiousness real obsequiousness, the mock homage real homage; the little counterfeit rift of separation between imitation-slave and imitation-master widened and widened, and became an abyss, and a very real one—and on one side of it stood Roxy, the dupe of her own deceptions, and on the other stood her child, no longer a usurper to her, but her accepted and recognized master" (19). We are a far cry here from the twin-*masters* displaying their authority by plying their art; instead, Twain is displaying something quite different for us, namely, accretive chains and links that bind us, by which we bind ourselves. Experience is the great deformer. It is questionable whether anything, even art, can counter it. The behavioralist model is taken to its grisliest extreme in the pathetic case of Chambers, whose fate, at the end of the novel, seems sealed, no matter how many rabbits Wilson and company may pull out of their collective hats:

> The real heir suddenly found himself rich and free, but in a most embarrassing situation. He could neither read nor write, and his speech was the basest dialect of the negro quarter. His gait, his attitudes, his bearing, his laugh—all were vulgar and uncouth; his manners were the manners of a slave. Money and fine clothes could not mend these defects or cover them up, they only made them the more glaring and the more pathetic. The poor fellow could not endure the terrors of the white man's parlor, and felt at home and at peace nowhere but in the kitchen. The family pew was a misery to him, yet he could nevermore enter into the solacing refuge of the "nigger gallery"— that was closed to him for good and all. But we cannot follow his fate further—that would be a long story. (114)

It is hard not to imagine that Faulkner had these lines in mind when he created Joe Christmas, the outcast between black and white communities who could "pass" everywhere but never be at home anywhere. Chambers is a true denizen of Dawson's Landing, blessed and cursed with an integral sense of selfhood; he is forever molded by his upbringing, and his very immobility figures forth the prisonhouse that Twain is seeking to explode. Although the hapless Chambers seems unitary enough and definable enough, hence remaining "black" no matter what the denouement brings, the epistemological going gets much rougher with the other characters in Twain's book.

Enlightened liberal thought may rest its case with environment as the explanatory factor in human behavior, but Twain had to contend with some powerful rival theories, notably the white-supremacy views held by the general populace and brought to their finest flower in the code of the F.F.V. To be sure, Twain treats the gentlemanly doctrine of the F.F.V. with considerable irony, but it is wishful thinking to imagine that he is free of its hold. One remembers the Sherburn episode in *Huckleberry Finn*, and we know something of the boundless cynicism apparent in the later Twain. In short, Twain cannot be absolved of his elitism; he reveres caste every bit as much as he despises it. When Tom behaves like the cad he (also) is, even the egalitarian Wilson chastises him for betraying the code: "You degenerate remnant of an honorable line! I'm thoroughly ashamed of you, Tom!" (63). But the most eloquent support of the F.F.V. line comes from the most unexpected quarter: Roxy herself. Chambers's life may be checked by his upbringing, but in Tom's case the arguments put forth most passionately are purely genetic. When Roxy learns that her son has refused to fight a duel in the proper F.F.V. fashion, she blasts him for his cowardice, and bases her argument on the most astounding genealogy in American literature:

> "What ever has come o' yo' Essex blood? Dat's what I can't understan'. En it ain't only jist Essex blood dat's in you, not by a long sight—'deed it ain't! My great-great-great-gran'father en yo' great-great-great-great-gran'father was ole Cap'n John Smith, de highes' blood dat Ole Virginny ever turned out; en *his* great-great-gran'mother or somers along back dah, was Pocahontas de Injun queen, en her husbun' was a nigger king outen Africa— en yit here you is, a slinkin' outen a duel en disgracin' our whole line like a ornery low-down hound! Yes, it's de nigger in you!" (70)

Put forth here is a not entirely comic version of the virulent blood argument that is to haunt American fiction, reaching its apotheosis in *Absalom, Absalom!* and *Go Down, Moses*, where the "family" is even more an amalgam of black and white and red, even more a shorthand history of colonization and racial mixing, even more pieced apart than it is here. There is a fine irony at work here because Roxy's genealogy is a specimen of *adulteration*, of the human being as mix and assemblage. Purity is a fiction. But the streams that flow in us are not of equal value, and Roxy plays Dawson's Landing's favorite game, that old game of human fractions, according to which Tom has got the wrong stuff in him: "Pah! it make me sick! It's de nigger in you, dat's what it is. Thirty-one parts o' you is white, en on'y one part nigger, en dat po' little one part is yo' *soul*" (70). The second shoe is dropping in these lines, because we can see that heredity is just as despotic and imprisoning as environment. Tom would be every bit as much a victim as Chambers. These can be distressing lines for the reader who wants the author to be more politically correct, beyond such a racist and genetic view of the subject.

Unless, of course, we decide that Twain is not speaking at all here but rather is exhibiting some of the strong medicine that he dished out in *Huckleberry Finn*, notably in that book's very finest moment, when Huck is ministering to an angry conscience that indicts him for wickedness in his protection of Jim. There is no more mature gesture in our literature than Huck's stating his willingness to go to hell in order to be true to his friend. Twain is probing very deep here, and he is demonstrating the terrible porousness of the human creature. In much the same way that Blake's exploited chimney sweeps dream their employers' dreams, so too does Twain illuminate the harrowing reaches of social indoctrination. It is nothing less than an ecological view of the subject (although Twain would be aghast at this terminology), in which the borders between "inside" and "outside" are eroded, so that the operative beliefs of the culture are to be found *inside*, not in edicts of law or newspaper editorials but rather in the thinking habits of human beings. One modern environmental term for such invasion is pollution, but even there we restrict its range of significance to the physical and the materialist; instead, as Louis Althusser and others have argued, we should rethink ideology itself as a form of pollution, as the very air that the subject breathes in and fashions his or her mental world out of. Hence, it follows that Huck demonstrates the stranglehold that culture has on us all, even though he takes the extraordinary heroic step beyond when he is prepared to go to hell if that is the price for keeping covenant with Jim. If Huck's conscience (consciousness) is false (that is, "constructed"), why shouldn't that be true for Roxy, too? And that is what is so harrowing about her indictment of her own flesh: "It's de nigger in you." She is displaying, with awesome purity, the workings of the system, and those old boys in the F.F.V. would be proud of her. What is on show here is less racism than brainwashing, or, in Stanley Brodwin's telling phrase, whitewashing.[8] Culture is insidiously active in Twain's work, harnessing consciences and whole vocabularies, speaking through people who think they are speaking for themselves.

Here, then, is the deep knowledge of bondage that accounts for the unusual amount of horsing around, tomfoolery, and play that one finds in Twain. It has often been remarked that there is an infantile dimension to his work, and it is a commonplace of American criticism that Tom Sawyer, Twain's consummate prankster and lifelong child, does everything he can to ruin *Huckleberry Finn* at its moment of high moral seriousness. Eliot, Trilling, Leo Marx, Forest Robinson, and a host of others have tried to account for the regressive high jinks that close Twain's masterpiece, but perhaps one needs to reconceive these matters, not so much on the level of a single text but rather in terms of a Twainian dialectic, a mix of determinism and freedom that cavalierly crosses the lines between politics and play, law and language. Robinson has argued in his impressive study of Twain's "bad faith" that Twainian casuistry and artful dodging are profoundly cultural maneuvers, allowing us (as well as his characters) to back off from intolerable racial and moral conflicts.[9] There is much truth in Robinson's argument, but must we be so damnably serious? Play and sidestepping constitute more than bad faith; they are ways to stay alive, to make space, to create breathing room, to avoid collisions. Ducking issues may be as mature as facing them, particularly if we cannot face them. And there is more: at its best — and Twain is not always at his best here — play may allow us to reconceive issues, to imagine resolution and transcendence rather than to confront impasse or failure. Every right-thinking Twain critic blasts the puerile antics of Tom Sawyer, but Twain needs Tom Sawyer, needs to thumb his nose at moral conversion as well as moral corruption, needs to have others whitewash his fences, for it is good to cover up dirt, and even better to trick others into doing it.

Again, in *Pudd'nhead Wilson* the twinning principle is a way of making elastic what would be rigid, of spoofing what would be solemn, of annexing more space and having more fun in quarters that are pretty cramped and dull. Twain has Roxy swap those babies, much as Pascal offers his famous wager, to introduce metaphysics and openness into the closed confines of the rationalist community, to give, as we might say, freedom a chance. And, on the face of it, the project is an abysmal failure: Chambers, as we saw, is the victim of nurture; although there is not one speck of black blood in him, he will always be the black slave he grew up as. And as for Tom, all of his environmental privileges go for naught, and neither Yale nor money nor white upbringing will offset the heredity poison he carries from birth, that drop of black blood that scripts his life. We lose, Twain seems to be saying, either way. Like Hawthorne before him and Faulkner after, Twain knows how *unfree* we are, and we cannot understand or enjoy his games until we see in them a ludic reprieve from necessity. Ludic reprieve has little to do with bad faith or wishful thinking; it has to do with the capacity of art to reshape events, to display something of the rich human potential that attends life even though it does not alter it, to make the forces of desire and yearning and fear visible even though they were not visible in recorded events. *Pudd'nhead Wilson*, far from being the flat, allegorical, strained narrative that most critics have seen in it, is Twain's most remarkable effort to tell it both ways, to treat the damning forces of his culture in such a fashion as to see past them without ignoring their authority.

The determinist prisons of heredity and environment do indeed bind, but freedom is like the cat with nine lives, and for the writer those eight figurative lives are as important as the one flesh-and-blood one. The Italian twins bring the circus to Dawson's Landing, even though they are no longer freaks. Just as the mirror projects a virtual space for those who look into it, twinning becomes a way in which the story of broken kinships, fissured identities, and racial divisions can be fully played out. That story is above all the story of Roxy and Tom, and we shall see that Twain's treatment of mother and son is charged with echoes and reverberations which enable us to discern an entire repertory of human possibilities. The story of bondage is to be doubled by a story of revenge, of the shackled and stuck characters coming unstuck by means of art, sometimes their own, as seen in the astounding array of masks and disguises, sometimes the art of the author, as seen in the metaphors and similes enlisted to render them, and in the peculiar turns of plot and intrigue that twist and refract the story.

"It's de nigger in you" advertises the essentialist doctrine that Twain could not quite disbelieve in, and *Pudd'nhead Wilson*'s most intriguing excesses, its array of doubles and shadows, are to be understood as the author's way of fighting back against such one-liners. A familiar critique of *Pudd'nhead Wilson* is that there are no fully realized characters in it.[10] Either they are stick figures, or else they are seen as overly schematic, overloaded to the point of being allegorized. But if we understand that Twain is doing battle with fixed labels and monolithic constructs, then characters such as Roxy and Tom take on more resonance because they make us reorder our sense of what "integrity" really means. Character begins to look like a capacious thing. Twain's depiction of Roxy has been seen as problematic ever since Fiedler waxed eloquent on her status as one of the few sexualized women in American literature (and the only one in the Twain corpus); the problem has to do with the peculiar mismatch between her bearing and her language. The author *describes* her, in her moments of passion, as a regal figure of unparalleled authority: "She raised her head slowly, till it was well up, and at the same time her great frame unconsciously assumed an erect and masterful [!] attitude, with all the majesty and grace of her vanished youth in it" (38). Yet when she *speaks*, her idiom is not just that of a black person but insistently servantlike and comic, as in the opening sally to Jasper (her stylized partner in Twain's minstrel show): "*You* is, you black mud-cat! Yah-yah-yah! I got sump'n better to do den 'sociat'n wid niggers as black as you is. Is ole Miss Cooper's Nancy done give you the mitten?" (8).

Like the Italian twins, she is both servant and master, but Twain is going to carry this oxymoron cleanly and defiantly into the realm of action. This journey from metaphoric license to actuality is spectacularly evident in the unforgettable sequence in which she forces Tom to get on his knees to beg, then rewards him in proper fashion: "Fine nice young white gen'lman kneeling' down to a nigger wench! I's wanted to see dat jes' once befo' I's called. Now, Gabrel, blow de hawn, I's ready. . . . Git up!" (39). It is a keen moment of mocking cruelty, and it causes us to realize that "minstrel show" language is not necessarily domesticated or comic at all, that this black speech has an edge and a wit all its own. Roxy is Twain's most fascinating female character because she cannot be contained by the prevailing paradigms offered by his culture; Roxy can be cruel and tender, submissive and haughty. The black idiom that Twain has always prided himself on knowing how to deliver is no longer predominantly the comic vehicle that it was even in *Huckleberry Finn*, and in Roxy's moments of passion it achieves an unsettling pathos. Just how far this was to go in Twain can be seen in the unfinished manuscript of 1902, "Which Was It?," in which the mulatto Jaspers uses that same idiom to launch a declaration of war: "You's a slave! . . . en I lay I'll learn you de paces! I been one . . . slave to de meanest white man dat ever walked—en he 'uz *my father* . . . en he sold my mother down de river, po' young thing, en she a cryin' en a beggin' him to let her hug me jist once mo' . . . en he hit her on the mouf, God damn his soul! — but it's my turn, now; dey's a long bill agin de lowdown ornery white race, en you's a gwyneter *settle* it."[11] It is hard not to see in this virulent indictment (and in the very details themselves: a mother sold down the river, a humiliated mulatto) the logical conclusion of a dialectic that is already unfurling in *Pudd'nhead Wilson*. "You's a gwyneter *settle* it" is nothing less than a verbal grenade; it elevates the previously docile idiom into something staggeringly potent. Roxy does not go quite as far as Jasper does, but she remains an imperious figure, filled with passions and resentments that will not be corralled forever. She is indeed the queen of the text, and although the white patriarchs take her to their beds, she enacts her revenge by plotting and interlacing the lives of the community. Unchecked by the constraints of race and sex, Roxy moves into the male domain as well, and little is more surprising than the scene in St. Louis when a man is seen stalking Tom, pursuing him into his lodging, and only later, after the door is closed, does this male announce "himself" to Tom as his mother. Twain-Hitchcock has quite simply altered Roxy by means of male disguise and has then gone on to fool his reader, as if to show how far this character might go—and how flexible the rules of fiction are. In all her guises, all her performances, Roxy is flaunting her access to power, her maneuvering room in a culture that says she has none at all.

But Roxy looks downright monotone in comparison to the meteoric, histrionic career of her son, Tom. He is the novel's greatest performer, and the text seems embarrassed by his successes. "Degenerate remnant of an honorable line," Wilson staunchly upbraids Tom; "it's de nigger in you," his mother informs him. And yet we cannot fail to see that the text lets him have his way, that he constitutes its vital center, perhaps its raison d'être. Tom Driscoll is arguably the most dislocated, displaced and disseminated character in nineteenth-century American fiction. Pious denunciations notwithstanding, Tom is doing something the text wants done, and he is doing it "under cover," because that is the way this text does things. Feminist criticism has helped us recognize rage and *ressentiment* in art by teaching us to look a bit more widely than we had before, and we need the same wide view here. Despite all disclaimers to the contrary, Tom's agenda is (imaginatively? morally?) sanctioned, just as Bertha Mason's is when she sets fire to the house and figuratively castrates Rochester as avenging angel, and we have learned to see Bertha's actions as the displaced rage that Jane Eyre has denied all her life. For Tom, it starts with the thieving: "He had been prowling about in disguise, stealing small valuables from private houses; in fact had made a good deal of a raid on his fellow villagers a fortnight before, when he was supposed to be in St. Louis" (42–43). Look at the language here: Tom Driscoll, under cover of being "one of us," is in reality a plague on their houses, a disease in the community that attacks "private houses" and "fellow villagers." This is not innocent. All the F.F.V. rhetoric in the world will not prevent us from seeing him as the avenging principle, the full-scale reversal of all the high-minded pieties that demand assent in Old Virginia.[12] Tom Driscoll is a gentleman's nightmare: not only is he arrogant, petulant, and cowardly, but he has this disturbing habit of disguising himself as black. But the fiction of the mulatto who can "pass" is a leisurely paced story, whereas Tom dizzily careens through his repertory, insolently flaunting the precarious and makeshift nature of racial and moral stereotyping. His entire life consists of crossing lines and breaking codes.

Why is he like this? It is worth attending to his words when he is initially confronted by his mother with the news that he is black: "Why were niggers *and* whites made? What crime did the uncreated first nigger commit that the curse of birth was decreed for him? And why is this awful difference made between white and black?" (44). With this grandiose claim, the entire patriarchy is on trial, and we soon see that justice is not long in coming. Tom cannot get at the God that created such an invidious state of affairs, but he can go after his representatives here in the community, those fathers who govern Dawson's Landings and a good bit else as well. Many critics have felt that Tom's eventual murder of his uncle is a thinly veiled version of parricide; Tom himself muses "that if his father were only alive and in reach of assassination his mother would soon find that he had a very clear notion of his indebtedness to that man and was willing to pay it up in full . . ." (70). Arlin Turner has shown that "Twain at one time planned a scene in which Tom confronts his father, hesitates, and then concludes he cannot kill him. But when his father pleads, 'O spare me! — I am your father!' Tom cries, 'Now for *that*, you shall die,' and kills him.'"[13] Oedipal energies are certainly in play here, but one feels that the institutional pieties, the fathers as a code of values and fixed entities, are even more stifling and intolerable, more in need of violation. In this light Tom's odd behavior is readable as a veiled societal allegory: the Black Man's Revenge. It is a noble concept, and it is all the more intriguing because the book never says this much, merely hints at it by dint of its bizarre plot. Here, then, would be the ideological fruits of the twinning process: the creation of characters who are apparently kept in line, but only apparently. This mother and her son are possessed of a kind of vital energy that eludes censorship and mocks propriety. Such a reading of *Pudd'nhead Wilson* highlights its subversive qualities, the ways that its figurative activity reverses or topples the priorities of the dominant order. But perhaps even this schema is too pat, too controlled. Twain's novel fascinates because one senses in it— Twain sensed in it—disequilibrium, a spawning principle that might not be controllable at all.

If Tom is a hero, he is a hero of multiplicity. Chameleonlike, he moves through a repertory of characters and disguises, making a mockery of any binding behavioral system. Brought up white and on top, he has plenty of arrogance; but it disappears whenever he is faced down by others. Sent to Yale, he easily adopts the eastern manner and polish. Short of cash, he does not hesitate to alter both his color and his sex, stealing in the disguise of a woman, sometimes white, sometimes black. He is, in all senses of the term, "on the make." Let us reconsider his climactic utterance about blacks and whites: "Why were niggers *and* whites made? What crime did the uncreated first nigger commit that the curse of birth was decreed for him? And why is this awful difference made between black and white?" Tom discovers *difference*. And the God that he faults is manifestly an artist-God, one (suspiciously like Mark TWain) who enjoys doubling and then seems to enjoy penalizing some of the creatures he has made. Once again one hears echoes of post–Civil War America, of a culture that has been cursed with difference although it dreams of unity. We can, of course, read these lines in biblical fashion, referring to the tribe of Ham and some anterior sin for which the black man is punished.[14] But we can also read the passage theatrically, taking terms such as "made" and "uncreated" as artistic terms, referring to a world in which "black" and "white" are something one makes or creates. It makes a difference which way we read the speech, and Tom himself will check out both versions. Convinced, initially, that "black" is his true essence (heretofore unknown), Tom "tries on" the "blood" psychology by responding to the "nigger" in himself: "He found the 'nigger' in him involuntarily giving the road, on the sidewalk, to the white rowdy and loafer. When Rowena, the dearest thing his heart knew, the idol of his secret worship, invited him in, the 'nigger' in him made an embarrassed excuse and was afraid to enter and sit with the dread white folks on equal terms. The 'nigger' in him went shrinking and skulking here and there and yonder, and fancying it saw suspicion and maybe detection in all faces, tones and gestures" (45). Yet—and this is crucial—the "nigger" phase does not last. It is another coat of clothing, another coat of skin. Yes, he is altered, but then that is what he does best: alterations. Twain hastens to assert that Tom "dropped gradually back into his old frivolous and easy-going ways and conditions of feeling and manner of speech" (45), but this claim, just like the earlier one that "the main structure of this character was not changed and could not be changed" (45), suggests a stable base, a solidity of character, which the performance of the novel radically denies. When Roxy tells him that she is his real mother, he enters into something like the Twain baptism, a maelstrom, "a whirlwind of disorganizing sensations and emotions" (41). The self can be "disorganized" in the same way it can be organized: as construct, assemblage, cultural package, fiction. There is a kind of extraordinary, random, "uncommitted" energy in such a view, as if the subject were structured much like the atom is said to be, and once we "unlock" it, once we get inside its armature, all hell can break loose. In this book of fractions and fissures, Tom alone seems to relish the giddy freedoms that are his for the taking. Twain never does get around to telling us *why* Tom dresses as a girl, just as, indeed, Huck dressed as a girl, or why Roxy dressed as a man when in St. Louis. To avoid detection is the pragmatist's view, but that view may be a cyclopic one. Defoe never explained either why Moll Flanders went into disguise in such a big way. We are obliged in these texts to recognize the precariousness and availability of the self that is on display, to see that masks and disguises are inebriating modes of expression as well as concealment, that they constitute, in the realm of action, that dream language that liberates in the realm of the psyche. Disguise is too central, too obsessive and authoritative, in these books to be just a tool, a device. Tom is fascinating as a character precisely because his repertory is so extensive and compulsive, however small his spirit may be. He is modern in the same way that Dostoyevski's Underground Man is modern: a man of roles and masks, a discovery that there are only roles and masks. The Russian author's urbane declaration, "Yes, an intelligent man in the nineteenth century must and morally ought to be preeminently a characterless creature," finds its homely counterpart in Roxy's suspicion about Tom that there "warn't nothing *to* him" (46) or Wilson's conviction that Tom "hadn't character enough" (98).[15] Nobody is here.

With this charge we come full circle from the view of Tom as black revenge, and we move closer to the modernist issues of doubling and twinning with which this chapter began. Tom's masquerade is not unlike that of Melville's Confidence Man, and it betokens the same slippage of identity and fascination with virtuality, but whereas Melville is in search of trust, Twain is in search of freedom. Even Dostoyevski's tale seems complacent when compared with *Pudd'nhead Wilson*, for Twain is not merely chronicling a cultural malaise; he desperately needs a character who can author himself, a figure who might get clear of the governing constraints of the community. But the program of subversion, of black assertion underneath black submission, turns out to be something of a launching pad, the threshold for flights and excursions that have no ideological agenda whatsoever. After all, open-ended research has no target in mind. Twain has put together a fiction with a surprising boosting power of its own, a genuinely "free enterprise" of extraordinary parity, with a decentered protagonist who could be anything at all, with equal rights for shadows and metaphors, with no discrimination between major and minor characters, major plots and subplots. Everything is going to be of a piece in this pluralist, collectivist fiction; everything will partake of everything else. The Italian twins, impudently useless along utilitarian narrative lines, have a place of honor in this consort because they are nothing less than reflective counters, walking mirrors, used to image other characters and events and issues. They are the novel's echo chamber, its stereophonic system, and they liberate the anarchic potential of Twain's fable. They are used to "speak" the other characters, to foretell and retell the central acts of the novel. Both their gestures and their speech attain, at critical moments, the density and allusiveness of poetry, obliging us to reconceive narrative coherence, to see that the peripheral and the gratuitous are homing in at every turn, are pointing to the secret heart of the novel.

The centerpiece for such a reading is to be found in the remarkable tale told by the twins concerning the knife and the murder. Angelo's minute description of the knife is larded with implications and unavowed twinships: "You notice what a curious handle the thing has. It is solid ivory, polished like a mirror, and is four or five inches long—round, and as thick as a large man's wrist, with the end squared off flat, for your thumb to rest on; for you grasp it, with your thumb resting on the blunt end—so—and lift it aloft and strike downwards" (52–53). Here is the murder weapon, Luigi's Indian knife, later to be brooded on by Wilson as the "text" he must decipher. Some deciphering is already possible: both phallic and reflective, it hints at libidinal and generative reaches, seems to tell us that it is more than just an ornament. Angelo's account of the murder itself is still more bristling:

> A native servant slipped into our room in the palace in the night, to kill us and steal the knife on account of the fortune incrusted on its sheath, without a doubt. Luigi had it under his pillow; we were in bed together. There was a dim night-light burning. I was asleep; but Luigi was awake, and he thought he detected a vague form nearing the bed. He slipped the knife out of the sheath and was ready, and unembarrassed by hampering bed-clothes, for the weather was hot and we hadn't any. Suddenly that native rose at the bedside, and bent over me with his right hand lifted and a dirk in it aimed at my throat; but Luigi grabbed his wrist, pulled him downward, and drove his own knife into the man's neck. (53)

The violence depicted and connoted in this passage is not easy to classify. Twain appears to be describing a murder, but the context (two [naked?] men in bed together truly twinned, perhaps a remnant of the original Siamese version) and the gesture (pulling the native downward, thrusting the [phallic?] knife into him) make it hard not to see something insistently sexual here, something resembling a homosexual rape. And although none of these details is "necessary" for the narrative business at hand, Twain must have obscurely sensed that he needed *these details* for the story he could not tell any other way. That story, we begin to see, is one of censorship and displacement, of moving laterally when one cannot move frontally. Here at last is violence in the bed, something the daytime Twain steers as clear of as possible. The fateful coupling that is at the origin of everything, the coupling of Roxy with Colonel Cecil Burleigh Essex (standing in, censorwise, for Judge York Leicester Driscoll), is unnarratable by Twain; but it will not disappear so easily, and we are invited to sense something of its murderous violence in this bizarre nocturnal episode. Only at the fringes of his narrative, in a seemingly unconnected anecdote, can Twain speak the sexual intimacy and violation that fuel his narrative. As it is in dreams and poetry, so is it true here: displacement is economy. How can we not see that this "dangling" tale of murder an-nounces — and deepens — the "real" murder of the novel: Tom Driscoll's mur-der of his sleeping uncle. And this native who seeks to murder Angelo is a dead ringer, or at least a ghostly double, for the young man who blackens his face with burnt cork before doing in his figurative father.

It is finally worth our consideration that this would-be murder is a graphic demonstration of one of the novel's most powerful impulses: the removal of doubling, the putting away of the half, the murder of the twin, all in the name of reestablishing unity and singleness. This murky episode spills the beans, images both the sexual and the epistemological scandal of the text. The waking mind is cunningly present as well, for it must be homicidal to twins, since it wants to see clear, to put dreams and doubles to rout; and this is what the dreamer knows. *Pudd'nhead Wilson* is oneiric rather than allegorical, a night-mare text with the kind of choreography and fluidity Joyce put into the "Circe" chapter of *Ulysses*.

The oneiric, as Freud has taught us, is a libidinal playground, a script in which the repressed returns, disguised or twinned so that we may finally attend to it. *Pudd'nhead Wilson* is Twain's dream text, the book where nighttime's metaphoric and associative logic advances into the light of day. Everything bristles here. The Italian twins cargo murder into the book well before Tom does his "uncle" in. In this light Roxy, too, rewards a second look, because she goes routinely beyond her prescribed narrative bounds, and she seems to carry a kind of libidinal energy and intensity that have escaped Twain's censor-ship, thereby retaining their originary darkness and vibrancy. Justin Kaplan has drawn attention to the analogy between the "one mature and explicitly sexual woman in all his fiction, Roxy the slave," and the remarkable dream Twain had a year or two later in London, a dream worth quoting in full:

I was suddenly in the presence of a negro wench who was sitting in grassy open country, her left arm resting on the arm of one of those long park-sofas that are made of broad slats with cracks between, and a curve-over back. She was very vivid to me — round black face, shiny black eyes, thick lips, very white regular teeth showing through her smile. She was about 22, and plump — not fleshy, not fat, merely rounded and plump; and good-natured and not at all bad-looking. She had but one garment on — a coarse tow-linen shirt that reached from her neck to her ankles without break. She sold me a pie; a mushy apple pie — hot. She was eating one herself with a tin teaspoon. She made a disgusting proposition to me. Although it was disgusting it did not surprise me — for I was young (I was never old in a dream yet) and it seemed quite natural that it should come from her. It was disgusting, but I did not say so; I merely made a chaffing remark, brushing aside the matter — a little jeeringly — and this embarrassed her and she made an awkward pretence that I had misunderstood her. I made a sarcastic remark about this pretence, and asked for a spoon to eat my pie with. She had but one, and she took it out of her mouth, in a quite matter-of-course way, and offered it to me. My stomach rose — there everything vanished. . . .[16]

There is doubtless much to be unpacked in this dream: the open hunger for food that covers the hunger for sex, the series of displacements and excuses, the increasing discrepancy between the verbal protests and the physical merging (as if the picture were coming ineluctably into focus at the close, with its unstoppable, unbearable intimacy as an expression of what Twain could never "say" in the daytime world). "Disgusting" claims the dreamer three separate times, as he moves closer and closer to sexual congress; "degenerate" is what the outraged Wilson brands Tom, but to no avail. Roxy's sexual vitality is the magnetic core of this novel, just as Tom's frenzied self-spawning charts its plot. Twain's dream is a telling dream, and it does beautiful justice to the facts and fictions of our lives, the unavowable hunger that moves us, and the screens we put up by way of defense and accommodation. Twain is dreaming for his culture here. We will see the same cluster of food, sex, and blackness in Faulkner's *Light in August*, but there is no rage at all in Twain's version, just an oneiric fable of mouth-to-mouth sharing, as elemental as it is in the episode on Howth Hill where Molly passes the seedcake from her mouth to that of Bloom, but adumbrating in this American text a moving, impossible-to-achieve, impossible-to-censor fable of connection between black and white, woman and man, that shimmers with its carnal beauty.[17] The antics of Roxy and Tom, the maneuvering of the twins, seem energized by this same dark libidinal energy, bent on transformation and murder rather than coupling, but no less unavowable (to Twain, to his culture, to traditional narrative) for all that.

Embodiments of Twain's dream logic, free to live, the twins, as Fiedler wrote, do actually haunt this text which they merely seem to visit. They may seem relics of an earlier design, awkwardly abandoned in the revised work, but we must not be fooled; they inhabit every nook and cranny of this book, twinning whatever they touch, thereby midwifing something quite miraculous: the expression of desire, the glimpse of another world. To put it in terms of purity, they *contaminate* and *adulterate* the novel by communalizing its elements, by showing, almost in incestuous fashion, how things do not (cannot?) stand alone but are paired and brothered and sistered. Theirs is the principle that accounts for the uncanny doubling of events, phrases, and images which permeates the novel. This is nothing less than an *ars poetica*, but it is an oddly familial one, a way of writing that flaunts connection rather than separation, that displays hidden kinships rather than private contours. And so it becomes possible to regard the writerly project of *Pudd'nhead Wilson* as a response to Tom's anguished discovery of "difference": Tom finds himself in a culture that marks and brands and ghettoizes, but the book he inhabits is one ongoing adventure in pairing and secret sharing.

At the very beginning of the narrative Twain offers a kind of traveling shot of Dawson's Landing, and gives us a close-up to remember: "Swinging

signs creaked in the wind, the street's whole length. The candy-striped pole
which indicates nobility proud and ancient along the palace-bordered canals
of Venice indicated merely the humble barber-shop along the main street of
Dawson's Landing" (3). On the face of it this is a characteristic Twain equation
of Old and New World in which the irony makes it hard to gauge what he
thinks of either one. But the face of things doesn't cover much in *Pudd'nhead
Wilson*. Much later, when Judge Driscoll is ridiculing the twins in his cam-
paign, again we see the Venetian-barber imagery, this time turned on its
head — "He said they were back-alley barbers disguised as nobilities" (83) —
and once dead, the Judge will be said to have been assassinated by "a profli-
gate Italian nobleman or barber" (95). It is truly a case, as the text says, of
"swinging signs," of metaphors and similes that can be actualized and inverted,
much as Tom Driscoll can become a black woman, and the dagger can become
a text unto itself. This is not merely a case of foreshadowing or loaded metaphors but rather the crafting of multidirectional narrative circuitry, a network
so energized and "egalitarian" that we can no longer distinguish between tenor
and vehicle, between center and periphery. Like the arterial flow of the human
organism, in which the ecosystem is such that blockage in the extremities is
tantamount to blockage in the heart, so too is Twain's novel astonishingly
democratic and decentered, and a chance simile here or a casual description
there or a seemingly innocuous anecdote on the side will turn out to be vital to
the book's design, will even turn out to be a major thoroughfare for the book's
figurative flow of life.

The economy of *Pudd'nhead Wilson* is truly remarkable, as if Twain allowed himself only a fixed number of episodes and then set out to see how
many times he could rework or reposition the givens he had selected. "In
der Beschränkung zeigt sich erst der Meister," Goethe wrote, and we are to
understand that restrictions in art are secret luxuries, that mastery consists
in pirouetting one's limited materials, liberating their multiple significances,
turning and returning them, as the polytropic text acquires its many shapes.
When we first meet Roxy, she is flirting with Jasper, and Twain refers to their
jousting as a "friendly duel" while they themselves are called "combatants"
(8). Innocent or no? In light of the twins' murder story there is at least a
figurative connection between loving and dueling. And doesn't this language
already signal the duel that is to come, the one between the Judge and Luigi?
Or, consider the seemingly innocuous instance of robbery that is recounted at
the beginning of the story. The Judge, as veteran Dawson's Landing denizen,
knows who done it: "Theft he could not abide, and plainly there was a thief in
his house. Necessarily the thief must be one of his negroes" (10). But "necessity" is no simple matter here; and although Roxy exchanges the infants in
response to this event, it continues to "play" in the text, so much so that we
cannot fail to hear its bizarre echo in Tom's later nocturnal activities: "He had
been prowling about in disguise, stealing small valuables from private houses"
(42). It does not seem fanciful to suggest that Twain planted the first instance
of theft so that we could savor the second, as if to show that the words of the
text have a life of their own, and we do savor such doubling, not merely
because Tom grows up to be the black thief of the beginning, but also because

it is pleasurable to see simple materials put to complex uses, to find segments of narrative that return sea-changed.

Twinning is scandalous because doubles could just as easily become triples, and after that, nobody knows. Twain is to discover that once we open a closed thing, be it a character or a culture, we may have a lot more than doubles on our hands. And how do we deal with that?[18] Not only do they call into question the supremacy of the one, but they also underscore the potency of spawning itself. We make, but do we know for sure what (or how many) we have made, especially if we have made it in the dark? In the culture of miscegenation the color of a baby brings, especially if it is dark, the shocking light of truth, and nothing better illustrates Twain's sense of these volatile matters than his peculiar sigh of relief when *Roughing It* was well reviewed by William Dean Howells in the *Atlantic Monthly*: "I am as uplifted and reassured by it as a mother who has given birth to a white baby when she was awfully afraid it was going to be a mulatto."[19] Just a metaphor? Each of us is moved differently, has a personal repertory of epithets denoting pleasure and danger, although it is tolerably obvious that our culture hands out verbal "ready-mades" in this arena. Birthing, for Twain, brings forth in the fullness of time a daytime denouement for nighttime intrigue; it constitutes something like a game of racial Russian roulette, and it ends not with a boom but in the advertising of a coupling that cannot be hidden. Birthing is a cliffhanger.

How could it not be? The birth of a child brings more than miscegenation to light; it crystallizes, as nothing else could, the warring issues that Twain was grappling with: the claims of racial and genetic determinism versus the capacity of humans to make something new. The male writer knows that, in the flesh, only women can do it, and from the evidence of *Pudd'nhead Wilson*, only black women do it well. But in the word it is a different story: there men may rival with women, spawning their own language creations, making something, at last, out of nothing. The twinning principle is testimony to male fertility, to the writer's capacity to generate new matter, to make his own version of genesis. Early in the novel Chambers rescues Tom from the river, much to the latter's humiliation, and as a result Chambers receives a new name, "'Tom Driscoll's Niggerpappy'—to signify that he had had a second birth into this life, and that Chambers was the author [!] of his new being" (21). As a character Chambers is utterly powerless, pure victim; but as a feature of this highly energized narrative he is also endowed with potency, with a signifying "room" all his own. "Niggerpappy" is a striking term for this writerly form of generation, and it unmistakably puts creativity on the dark, unavowable side of things, along with sexuality and deviance, a way of dishing up a world unlike that of the F.F.V. It is as "Niggerpappy" that Mark Twain wrote *Pudd'nhead Wilson*, for it is only as author that Twain could open up the closed scripts of his culture, shuffle the deck he had been given, redistribute not only the cards but the players as well.

Pudd'nhead Wilson treats birthing with all the complexity we should expect, given Twain's interest in freedom and constraint. It is thus fitting, as we approach the close of this chapter, to return to the story's origin. We shall discover, not surprisingly, that we are witness to twin births, each a face of the other, each a particular form of determinism, one of flesh, one of language. And we shall finally have to deal with the title figure of the novel, Pudd'nhead Wilson himself. What we see in Chapter 1 is a double birth sequence, a double genesis: that of the two children and that of David Wilson's fateful baptism into Pudd'nhead. We start with a panoramic description of Dawson's Landing, which then zeroes in on the chief inhabitants there, those who will play a role in the story. We move down the list of illustrious figures, from York Leicester Driscoll (the Judge) on to his sister, then Pembroke Howard, Cecil Burleigh Essex, and finally on to Percy Northumberland Driscoll, brother to the Judge. But observe how Twain fills us in on the family fortunes of Percy Driscoll:

> On the 1st of February, 1830, two boy babes were born in his house: one to him, the other one to one of his slave girls, Roxana by name. Roxana was twenty years old. She was up and around the same day, with her hands full, for she was tending both babies.
>
> Mrs. Percy Driscoll died within the week. Roxy remained in charge of the children. She had her own way, for Mr. Driscoll soon absorbed himself in his speculations and left her to her own devices.
>
> In that same month of February Dawson's Landing gained a new citizen. This was Mr. David Wilson, a young fellow of Scotch parentage. (5)

Into this chronicle of births Twain has inserted the birth of David Wilson; "gained a new citizen" certainly suggests as much. The novel bifurcates at this juncture, leaving the two babies in order to attend to David Wilson's transformation into Pudd'nhead. We now witness the creation, the genesis of his title, a title far more influential and despotic than any lordship brought over from England or Italy. It all starts with Wilson's hapless but characteristic response to the yelping and snarling of "an invisible dog":

> "I wish I owned half of that dog."
> "Why?" somebody asked.
> "Because I would kill my half." (5)

These remarks will be Wilson's undoing, and it is worthwhile speculating as to where the offense lies. The invisible dog calls forth a playful comment on "half" its self, and with that half the twins are into the novel. But the notion of something being adulterated, of being anything other than itself — $\frac{1}{32}$ black blood makes a person *all* black — is alien to Dawson's Landing. Later in the novel Twain tells us straight out that "irony was not for those people; their mental vision was not focussed for it" (25). Unable to grasp an imaginative structure, a fiction such as "half" a dog, the town begins forthwith to name and to nail Wilson. One sees the scaffolding going up, as their literalism brands Wilson over and over a fool: "What did he reckon would become of the other half if he killed his half? Do you reckon he thought it would live?" (5). "Killing a half" is a virtual leitmotif of this novel, expressing the fear and suspicion occasioned by twinning or doubling; but for the people of Dawson's

Landing it is merely a flagrant instance of nonsense. What kind of man would say the likes of that?

> "In my opinion the man ain't in his right mind."
> "In my opinion he hain't *got* any mind."
> No. 3 said: "Well, he's a lummox, any way."
> "That's what he is," said No. 4; "he's a labrick—just a Simon-pure labrick, if ever there was one."
> "Yes, sir, he's a dam fool, that's the way I put him up," said No. 5. "Anybody can think different that wants to, but those are my sentiments."
> "I'm with you, gentlemen," said No. 6. "Perfect jackass—yes, and it ain't gong too far to say he is a pudd'nhead. If he ain't a pudd'nhead, I ain't no judge, that's all." (6)

These solid Missouri citizens, for whom Twain has genuine affection and genuine contempt, go by the tangible and the measurable. Wilson offends. His "half" dog is a mental construct, a thing of words, and they will have none of it. They will truck only with the real.

But can the writer ever be in their party? The beauty of this passage lies in the way that Twain gently but firmly turns them on their heads. What we have witnessed is a naming ritual, a performance of "Niggerpappy" who is establishing the word as law: Wilson moves from having no mind to lummox, then labrick (Simon-pure at that), and thence to dam fool, penultimately resting with jackass and concluding with the term that will fit him so tightly that for "twenty long years" he will be unable to get out of it—Pudd'nhead. In this novel which tests one determinism against another, heredity against environment, black blood against white blood, nothing appears remotely as deterministic as the name given to David Wilson. Black and white, master and slave, may, at the hands of the artist, be juggled and interchanged; but the artist's weapon, his language, has a strange fixity of his own, and one's reputation, one's "name," may acquire the solidity of stone. Words are the truly potent force in Twain's contest. Not only do they mold people for good, limn them for life, but they can move cavalierly among the social and racial forces that appear so impregnable. The naming of Wilson as Pudd'nhead is hardly a celebration of freedom, but rather one step further along the determinist road, a recognition that our prisons are also verbal. Language may close as well as open.

Yet even here Twain has not been able to resist the twinning principle, and he does his own little writerly pirouette in the perfect final remark, "If he ain't a puddn'head, I ain't no *judge*, that's all" (emphasis added). Given the preceding list of worthies, presided over by the Judge himself, there is more than a little waggery in the metamorphosis of that sentence; we may even glimpse in it the seeds of the Judge's own death sentence. Such a glimpse reveals the new dispensation that is augured in this novel, for the writer's wordplay has a fabulous potential, and it may reap him imaginative victories over the F.F.V. every time he goes to the trouble to make his figurative l-e-a-p.

No writer, not even Joyce or Coover, can somersault his way throughout an entire narrative. *Pudd'nhead Wilson* has its share of traditional storytelling and unplayful language. And Twain does not regard the slavery issue merely as word play, whatever liberties he may take with it from time to time. But the carnival cannot go on forever. At the close of the novel, as we know, Pudd'nhead disappears, and only David Wilson is left: David Wilson, successful lawyer and mayor of Dawson's Landing. Pudd'nhead vanishes, and so too do the twins. Dawson's Landing is doubtless a more solid place than ever. But it is worth our while to take a good look at how it all happens, and nothing is more instructive in this light than the famous trial scene. We can hardly fail to observe that more than an isolated crime is on trial here. What is at stake is the twinning principle itself.

Wilson befriends the twins from the outset, and in some profound way they make common cause with one another. Pudd'nhead seems to intuit that his plight is bound up with "twinning," that if "half a dog" got him his dunce cap, the Angelo and Luigi will help him remove it. Wilson was branded a pudd'nhead because he had the bad judgment to consider words real, to trot out his putative half a dog as a thing among things. This is, of course, exactly the heresy that Twain is enjoying throughout the novel, but the citizens of Dawson's Landing won't stand for such nonsense. And Wilson knows it. His spectacular performance at the close of the novel clears the world of doubles (including his own sobriquet). Wilson's much-heralded solution of the novel's mysteries is a victory for single truths, for the entire fingerprint fantasia is little more than a cancellation of mystery, an erasure of the space and freedom between origin and end, a last-ditch effort to reduce the world to fixed labels.[20] In a regime of "natal signatures" and "physiological autographs," the twinning principle goes out of business. Wilson successfully identifies and nails "the one man in the whole earth whose hand can duplicate the crimson sign" (the assassin's prints on the knife), and we understand that the "signs" of Dawson's Landing are no longer "swinging." The deeper mysteries and doubling of psyche and character are essentially pushed off the stage as the virtuoso detective takes over. What is happening here?

Explanations have not been lacking concerning Wilson's performance. David Sewell has analyzed the trial scene in terms of speech act theory, and he has convincingly shown how Wilson "proves" nothing, but rather uses his sleuthing prowess to reinstate the social agenda of the community.[21] Wilson's assimilation into the dominant culture is of course signaled by his becoming mayor. Forest Robinson goes a step further, linking Twain's own reference to Wilson as "only a piece of machinery—a button or a crank or a lever, with a useful function to perform in a machine" to his critique of bad faith, leading to a view of Wilson as "utterly dispassionate isolato."[22] Apt as these strictures are, Wilson's fingerprinting solution requires interpretation also on its own grounds, as cancellation of mysteries and doubles, and once we enter that territory, we can see in the courtroom performance a rather fascinating "closing" gambit on Mark Twain's part. True, Wilson finally reenters the fold, but he does so most spectacularly as word tamer, as a man who can put the genie back into the bottle. There can be no mistake about it: the price he must pay for reentry is a double one, social and verbal. Tom Driscoll's magic must be undone, and we see him systematically "regressed"; his acting days all over, his bag of tricks open for public inspection and revealed to be paltry indeed, Tom goes from white to black to murderer to thing that will be sold down the river. The black threat to the community is at last disposed of. But, as we have had ample opportunity to observe, the more virulent threat to the community comes from the twinning principle, from the specter of an open-ended world where the lines do not hold between the sexes and the races, between figures of speech and creatures of flesh. Here is the real Terror that may come to Dawson's Landing, to those folks without irony, and although *Pudd'nhead Wilson* has been written along precisely those lines, its title character deals a death blow to such ludic freedoms by at last killing off "Puddn'head," getting rid of the doubles, and putting things in order.

We are forcibly reminded of Twain's equally desperate act of closure in *Huckleberry Finn*, and once again we may feel that the rich oneiric script of the dreamer—a script that makes a fluid ballet of black and white, man and woman, master and slave—has been regrettably cleaned up by the author in the light of day. Both books end by shutting down the revolution, and each time they do so by means of shenanigans and pyrotechnics that shore up the community. It may simply be that Twain cannot say no to spectacle and brio, even if he runs the risk of trivializing things a bit, of moving us from the dream to the kindergarten, thereby easing our exit from the text. But David Wilson carries the day less as future mayor than as consummate magician and emcee, a figure who recalls even more than any fictive creation Mark Twain the public orator and performer: "Wilson stopped and stood silent. Inattention dies a quick and sure death when a speaker does that. The stillness gives warning that something is coming. All palms and finger-balls went down, now, all slouching forms straightened, all heads came up, all eyes were fastened upon Wilson's face. He waited yet, one, two, three moments, to let his pause complete and perfect its spell upon the house; then . . ." (109). The relish that Twain must have experienced in these lines is almost palpable, and it is time to do a final tally of losses and gains. True, the univocal and the monolingual return. The mysteries of birth and characters are not mysteries for the man who can read natal autographs, and so things are nicely tidied up in Wilson's paroxysm of analytic prowess. Twain is, at least epistemologically, "cleaning up his act." And yet, this scene is not merely a sell-out, a cashiering of depth and opaqueness in favor of slick one-liners. Twain has never lost sight of the power issues at the core of his book, and David Wilson is finally enjoying in this courtroom scene a peculiar but very real form of power. Control of one's audience has a politics all its own, just as the twins became masters when performing their piano duet; such control may be the ultimate form of authority for the artist, the one form of leverage and clout that he is equipped for, whatever his social or economic station. Compromises may be necessary, but applause is real. Twain, veteran that he was, knew this better than most. So it would be churlish to be too critical of David Wilson's triumphal day in court.

But the question will not disappear, even if the mysteries do. How can we not posit a connection between Wilson's prowess and the departure of the twins, the solving of the mystery and the removal of the twinning principle? Pudd'nhead will be mayor, and the good citizens of Dawson's Landing will welcome him to their bosom, as Twain cunningly avoids the shoals and depths to which he has so brilliantly pointed. His book remains uncannily resonant, for its bizarre contours and its curious excesses point to dark reaches indeed, in to a realm where nothing is only "itself" but is also its opposite, where sexuality and violence and deviancy are all faces of one another. In such a realm the twinning principle leads inexorably to a version of self that is radically fissured and decentered. Conrad and Dostoyevski went that full route, and it is fair to say that Faulkner carried out the mission that Twain could only begin. His Club of Freethinkers was free only up to a point, and one can hardly start the revolution by signing on the judge and the mayor.

But faulting the book for what it does not do should not prevent us from praising it for what it does. *Pudd'nhead Wilson* remains an audacious modernist fiction, bolder in its structure than anything else Twain wrote. At its best it displays a playfulness and impudence that are at once social, philosophical, and verbal, thereby inverting most of the moral and conceptual pieties that his culture believed in. Finally, it picks up Schiller's dictum that play is the most mature human faculty, and its ludic energies are enlisted, at least for a good long while, in a peculiar colonizing effort, as if Twain dimly realized that "the Territory" of freedom that Huck was forever seeking may be on the far side of things altogether, a realm of doubles and echoes, a writerly West that is shockingly egalitarian in its dispensation of masks and words and deeds. For much of this we have the twins to thank.

III

THE VILLAGE MODERNISTS

5

Anderson: The Play of
Winesburg, Ohio

When Susan Sontag announced in 1964 that *Winesburg, Ohio* was "bad to the point of being laughable," she put something of a nail into the already formed coffin of Sherwood Anderson's falling reputation.[1] The put-downs had begun much earlier, right after the poor man's death, with Lionel Trilling's influential depiction of Anderson's work as arrested adolescence, and ever since then *Winesburg* has had the taint of damaged goods, even when dealt with sympathetically and generously.[2] The argument *for* Anderson has rarely been an exciting one: he is credited with (now dated) psychological discoveries, with sincerity, with love for his land, with a keen sense of the threats of modernism, with compassion. At the core of the disfavor is his provincialism, and Welford Taylor is right in pointing to the cosmopolitan bias that prompted such judgments. Benjamin Spencer, in his efforts to reclaim Anderson for the canon as a "mythopoeist," explains why it was that Sontag and that crowd could not abide Anderson: "Addicted to the New Wave of French fiction, with its commitment to sensory surfaces and psychic fragmentation as contrasted with Anderson's concern for inwardness and identity, her [Sontag's] verdict is inevitable."[3] We can begin to see why Sherwood Anderson is not at the center of things: considered "minor" (by himself as well as critics), unpossessed of continental sophistication, he has left us an uneven body of work that peaked with the publication of *Winesburg* in 1919 and has failed to spark much critical interest in the past several decades.

How viable is this? Have we really seen *Winesburg*? The artist of "Loneliness," Enoch Robinson, speaks for his creator when he addresses (in his fantasy) the critics: "'You don't get the point.' he wanted to explain; 'the picture you see doesn't consist of the things you see and say words about. There is something else, something you don't see at all, something you aren't intended to see.'"[4] Have we missed the point of *Winesburg*? It may well be a misread book, and perhaps it is not always best served by its most fervent admirers. Spencer's contrast of Anderson's "concern for inwardness and identity" with the French New Wave's interest in "sensory surface and psychic fragmentation" is ultimately wrong and must be rejected. Anderson was no small-town

Robbe-Grillet, but his best work thrusts sensory surfaces at us and challenges us to decipher them, to see how they come together and come apart in his tapestry of misfits and incongruity. There is psychic fragmentation aplenty here, along with a prose rendering that is much bolder than has been thought. Even Irving Howe, who could appreciate the importance of Gertrude Stein for Anderson, especially in connection with a compositional practice in which "words could have an independent value," failed to plumb that insight and labeled the language of *Winesburg* "translucent, leading quickly to the center of the book's action."[5] But Anderson's best stories are anarchic and polysemous, orchestrated in puzzling and daring ways, yielding a kind of narrative series of covers and screens that perfectly conveys his fables of dislocation and choked desire.

To look at *Winesburg* in terms of the freedom of speech, however, runs the risk of saying nothing new whatsoever. We have long known that Anderson's project was one of confession and exposure, of finding words for the pent-up secrets and yearnings that his small-town characters carried deep within themselves. As Edwin Fussell has indicated, his program is that of Pirandello: "For finally what the characters want of George Willard is to have their stories told (they are quite literally characters in search of an author)."[6] No one has better summarized the special "reality" of this undertaking than Alfred Kazin, "the reality beyond the visible surface world, the reality of all those lives that so many did lead in secret, that he had brought into American fiction[.] It was not his vision that was at fault, it was that human situation embodied in him, that story he told over and again because it was his only story—of the groping that broke forth out of the prison house of life and . . . went on groping; of the search for freedom that left all the supplicators brooding and overwhelmed."[7] Anderson's view of the human predicament was one of murk and repression, and the narrative strategy employed in *Winesburg* is perfectly attuned to this base-line picture of reality: George Willard, reporter extraordinaire, will listen to and draw out the closed denizens of Winesburg, thereby playing a cathartic role in the lives of these people and in the fictional project of the author. Yet readers have always sensed that the release occasioned by the young reporter is invariably brief and momentary, giving us an epiphanic glimpse of what lies hidden, but rarely leading to any kind of narrative development. Winesburg is a place where it is always too late, where the damage has already been done, where the best that can be hoped for is a stuttering moment of light and truth, to be followed either by a return to routine or by death. There is, as Howe long ago pointed out, "a deep malignancy" behind "seeming health," and the story of this bucolic village-before-industrialism is nonetheless "a fable of American estrangement."[8]

How significant, then, is George Willard's service to his fellow citizens? Consider the example of Elmer Cowley, exemplary choked member of the community, whose speech is ultimately freed to the point of his exclaiming: "I'll be washed and ironed. I'll be washed and ironed and starched" (200). This quaint cliché is then followed by a pummeling meted out to George as final expressive act before Elmer leaves Winesburg for good, issuing at the very last his epitaph: "I guess I showed him. I ain't so queer. I guess I showed him I ain't so queer" (201). With these kinds of victories to his credit, George makes it hard for us to gauge with certainty his therapeutic value to the community. At least Elmer gets out. Elizabeth Willard, George's frustrated mother, never gets quite so far. For her the only purgative release imaginable would be an exit of real magnitude: "I wanted to get out of town, out of my clothes, out of my marriage, out of my body, out of everything" (227); it does come, but only in death.

If there is no place to go, there still may be much to be said. But little else is more instructive in this light than the encounter between George and Helen in "Sophistication," a mute coming together in which they become "not man and woman, not boy and girl, but excited little animals" (242). This episode is genuinely touching, but it can be no more than that, and we are given to understand that contact between humans is, albeit urgent and necessary, beyond the ken of language: "For some reason they could not have explained they had both got from their silent evening together the thing needed. Man or boy, woman or girl, they had for a moment taken hold of the thing that makes the mature life of men and women in the modern world possible" (243). One thinks in this regard also of the fine story "The Untold Lie," singled out by Malcolm Cowley as epitomizing the Anderson epiphany and breakthrough, in which self-revelation and intimate sharing miraculously happen to happen. Yet, we also note that this story of a roughneck settling down, and of his companion's failure of nerve, is a haunting but sobering fable about the resources of language. Anderson manages to work inarticulateness and silence about as far as they can be worked, and he achieves, for his readers, a stuttering kind of eloquence, an eloquence that is all the more effective by being wholly absent within the story proper. Within those precincts nothing is sayable: "It's just as well. Whatever I told him would have been a lie" (209).

Nonetheless, seen globally, Anderson's tales are odd success stories, pairings in and through which release is effected. Purgative throughout, the fables in *Winesburg* tell us about letting off steam, about soothing encounters in the dark, exchanges that are all the more life-saving by being figurative, unspoken, sublimated. Marriages are entered, love is made, confessions are undertaken and very, very often to the wrong people, or to George Willard, who happens to be on hand. Alice Hindman, in "Adventure," begins by kneeling on the floor in her room and whispering in her prayers "things she wanted to say to her lover" (115). Given the sociostructural logic of *Winesburg*, she must be brought out into the open, allowed (perhaps even forced) to have her pitiable say to a half-deaf old man. We are not far removed from *Waiting for Godot*. At other times Anderson creates a carrefour narrative, a balletlike arrangement in which A speaks passion to B, who wants to hear it from C. In some writers this would be a formula for comedy, or indeed for tragedy (or both, as in *Cyrano de Bergerac*); but in Anderson C just happens to be walking down the road as A completes his or her utterance, thereby being magically present and able to get the coupling done that needs to be done. "An Awakening" follows exactly these therapeutic lines, and we see George's huffing and puffing for the vehicle that it is, a vehicle for bringing Belle Carpenter and the inarticulate Ed Handby together at last. Anderson is strangely optimistic in this regard, and even the emptiest lives in *Winesburg* have their actively displaced poetry. Much as Flaubert had shown in "Un Coeur simple" that even the poorest have their passions, Anderson has grasped the enabling powers of projection and sublimation, the countless ways by which feeling incessantly colonizes an alien world and translates it to size. This peculiar alchemy is everywhere operative, in nooks and crannies as well as on center stage. Consider young David Hardy's stay at the home of his semicrazed grandfather in "Godliness":

> Two of the old farmer's sisters were alive and still lived in the house. They were afraid of Jesse and rarely spoke when he was about. One of the women who had been noted for her flaming red hair when she was younger was a born mother and became the boy's caretaker. Every night when he had gone to bed she went into his room and sat on the floor until he fell asleep. When he became drowsy she became bold and whispered things that he later thought he must have dreamed. (79)

Here, in the details about marginal figures, is the characteristic Anderson weave, its view of the illicit always slipping in, its blurring of the line between dream and event, its utter commitment to expression. The discrete refuses to stay discrete in Anderson, and his strongest intuitions have to do with libidinal poaching, with strategies of displacement and fulfillment that will have their play in the starkest precincts. All too often Anderson is crude in his theatrical positioning, and Winesburg is of course wonderfully small, a place that is little enough for the "right" person to be credibly around the corner, heading our way. Ultimately there is a figural logic here that bids, in some of the most extreme stories, to blow mimesis sky high.

So, perhaps just stuttering or rubbing against one another is enough, is a step in the direction of sharing one's unsharable inner life. George Willard is, more often than not, simply in the right place at the right time, bumping into Winesburg types who are ready to explode. A little pressure is let off, a little light is achieved, and they can go back to their dark, stifling lives. These are momentary illuminations, and it has been said that Anderson did not have the equipment of a novelist, that he knew only how to package his vision in the short story form. As Joyce had shown in *Dubliners*, epiphany itself is a conservative, cool device, good for distilling the events of a lifetime, useless for changing them. We are treated in *Winesburg*, for the most part, to circumscribed units of narrative, to small, self-enclosed stories (of small, self-enclosed people) that have very little echo or resonance in the greater collection. It is the very ethos of a *local* vision, a single-minded scheme that may work wonders story by story, but is hard put to do much in the way of connecting stories, developing larger lines of contrast, expansion, or irony. One notable exception to this sealed-off feeling is the pair of stories, "The Strength of God" and "The Teacher," in which Anderson displays his bridge-making powers by moving from the fable of the troubled minister to that of the troubled woman whom he has been spying on (in her bed); here we see just how stereophonic Anderson might have become, how the private angles might have been corralled into a larger, more kaleidoscopic configuration. Yet, on balance, this odd diptych is too mechanical, too additive in its joint arrangements, and one feels that Anderson has done right to respect the closure of his single pieces, that little has been lost, for his real strength is precisely with the squeezed precincts of the single life.

Those single stories in *Winesburg* yield a cumulative portrait of a repressed village, a place where damaged people nurse their private injuries. Anderson has been credited with tapping into their inner lives, and his vision, especially sensitized to sexual denial, has often been allied with that of Freud, but always a primitive, "groping" Freud; he is seen as an intuitive writer who had no system at all, no program to speak of, just his instinctual sense of what made his people alternately function and malfunction. He is rarely thought of as sophisticated, and the old assessment of his technique offered in *Literary History of the United States* (1946) still rings true for most readers: "He often fumbled in his narrative, which is always honest but truly artless. The style, however, is effective, and deceptively ingenuous and impromptu."[9] What does it really mean to label a style "deceptively ingenuous" or to term a narrative "honest but truly artless"? Anderson may indeed be a "primitive" in some sense, but that sense is worth examining, just as it is worth examining in Faulkner and Picasso. Once we attend to the role of language in *Winesburg*, we realize that Anderson is talking about it all the time, that his "artless" book is larded with metacritical observations.

Kazin may have found the "groping" element of Anderson's writing to be his central weakness, but Elizabeth Willard is grateful that her son George "is groping about, trying to find himself. . . . He is not a dull clod, all words and smartness. Within him there is a secret something that is striving to grow. It is the thing I let be killed in myself" (43). The antithesis is an arresting one: all words and smartness make the dull clod, whereas groping is allied to depth, inner richness, and growth. Elizabeth obviously has her glib, fast-talking husband, Tom Willard, in mind, but the principled distrust of eloquence is found everywhere in *Winesburg*, and it is allied in Anderson's mind with the encroaching media invasion heralded by modern life in general. The urban industrial culture carries with it a kind of verbal pollution: "In our day a farmer standing by the stove in the store in his village has his mind filled to overflowing with the words of other men. The newspapers and the magazines have pumped him full. Much of the old brutal ignorance that had in it also a kind of beautiful childlike innocence is gone forever. The farmer by the stove is brother to the men of the cities, and if you listen you will find him talking as glibly and as senselessly as the best city man of us all" (71). But the issue is every bit as much artistic as it is cultural, for Anderson is, willy-nilly, telling us about the kind of language that is needed for his own art. One remembers, in this connection, Kate Swift's impassioned remarks to George about the nature of writing: "'If you are to become a writer you'll have to stop fooling with words,' she explained. 'It would be better to give up the notion of writing until you are better prepared. Now it's time to be living. I don't want to frighten you, but I would like to make you understand the import of what you think of attempting. You must not become a mere peddler of words. The

thing to learn is to know what people are thinking about, not what they say'"
(163). The "peddler of words" renders only the surface talk, whereas the
mature writer delivers what people are "thinking about." What are people
thinking about? What narrative shape does thinking have? Anderson at his
best gives us some unforgettable instances of what thinking looks like. But we
may have to redefine thinking as a sequence of mental and psychic operations
that have a special cogency and language of their own. The most memorable
scenes and stories in *Winesburg* are astounding in their figurative boldness, in
the shocking connections Anderson establishes between his materials, in the
flagrant disregard for "proper" storytelling, the kind of storytelling practiced,
no doubt, by the word peddlers.

At times this new language is in the service of character description. To
make us understand Elizabeth Willard's repressed inner life, Anderson is content to describe her from the outside, but he paints for us quite a picture: not
only had she been "stage struck," "much confused," fascinated with the theater, and seen in company with traveling men guests, but "once she startled
the town by putting on men's clothes and riding a bicycle down Main Street"
(45). It will not quite do to label Elizabeth merely another "grotesque," although Anderson himself indulges in such shorthand, for what he is really up
to is the articulation of Elizabeth's wildest and fiercest energies. Those energies
appear to us in their pure colors in the transvestite episode just mentioned,
and with that in mind, we can more fully savor the startling scene that Elizabeth imagines in the way of revenge on the man responsible for it all:

> The scene that was to take place in the office below began to grow in her
> mind. No ghostly worn-out figure should confront Tom Willard, but some-
> thing quite unexpected and startling. Tall and with dusky cheeks and hair
> that fell in a mass from her shoulders, a figure should come striding down
> the stairway before the startled loungers in the hotel office. The figure would
> be silent—it would be swift and terrible. As a tigress whose cub had been
> threatened would she appear, coming out of the shadows, stealing noiselessly
> along and holding the long wicked scissors in her hand. (47)

We begin to discern in this passage something of Anderson's reach, and as
readers of a later, more sensationalist age we are tempted to see in this episode
the kind of twisted sexual fury that Hitchcock depicted in *Psycho*, a film that
is astoundingly close to Anderson's vision in its mix of liberating disguise,
transgression, and sexual punishment.[10] One can even compare Hitchcock's
famous "holding-off" technique with the brilliant placement of those castrat-
ing scissors at the very end of the passage. Here, for a moment, as a pure
longing, Anderson has given us the plot that "fits" Elizabeth, and it threatens
to go off the Winesburg map.

But such fierce descriptions still play by the narrative rules we are accustomed to, and one has to look farther afield to find the kind of new figurative
language that Anderson sometimes fashions for his stories of release and
disguise. That language has a special thickness and propriety, as if Anderson
were intent on decentering and liberating his materials, strewing odd signifiers

and disconcerting parallels throughout his narrative, obliging his reader to reassemble the pieces in some new, quite unforeseen manner. It has been much noted that George plays psychoanalyst to the good people of Winesburg, that he allows them to express their neuroses and pent-up feelings. But it would seem that no one has applied the psychoanalytic model where it really belongs, to the text itself. George's purgative role in *Winesburg* is ultimately far less interesting than Anderson's creation of a new discourse, one that functions much like the dream discourse. In this discourse there are no details, and the polished surface is maddeningly significant. The modernist Anderson, the peer and friend of Gertrude Stein, is a maker of prose-poetry; as far back as "Hands" he defined his role (and his ambition) as "the poet who will tell the hidden wonder story of the influence for which the hands were but fluttering pennants of promise" (31). Let us take him seriously. Like a writer inventing a new script, like a deaf writer who needed to "sign" by use of his hands (and face and body), Anderson is strangely polytropic, using whatever means available to express what must out, fashioning a jerky, jarring prose that can be wonderfully nervous and unsettling. Anderson's best stories are fables of displacement and sublimation, texts that "speak" Anderson in ways that are freer and more disruptive than anything he can openly enunciate.

"Paper Pills," all of four pages long, is perhaps the most remarkable tale that Anderson ever wrote, and it deserves to be read as an American pendant to Kafka's "Country Doctor," for both explode the daytime logic of their ostensible subjects in order to testify to darker powers of sexual desire and violation. Although Kafka moves into the monstrous by erasing the line between event and metaphor, whereas Anderson respects the givens of his story and merely adorns it with metaphor, his way of adorning is no less estranging than Kafka's erasure. Doctor Reefy, the protagonist of the story, seems to offer a typical Anderson retrospective: "Winesburg had forgotten the old man, but in Doctor Reefy there were the seeds of something very fine" (35). It is worth attending to those "seeds," because they constitute the commanding figure of the story: the narrative will "hatch" these seeds, much the way the old writer gives birth to the youth and woman who "inhabit" him in "The Book of the Grotesque." Groping in Anderson is actually nothing more than the "birthing" necessary to bring to light and life the dark, concealed story of his characters. But in "Paper Pills" Anderson has fully developed the organic character of his seed metaphor, and thus we learn that the doctor married a girl who had been left "a large fertile farm," that the doctor's friend John Spaniard "owned a tree nursery"; and, most significant of all, the courtship of Doctor Reefy and the "tall dark girl" is presented to us in a strange parable that owes much to those seeds:

> The story of Doctor Reefy and his courtship of the tall dark girl who became his wife and left her money to him is a very curious story. It is delicious, like the twisted little apples that grow in the orchards of Winesburg. In the fall one walks in the orchards and the ground is hard with frost underfoot. The apples have been taken from the trees by the pickers. They have been put in barrels and shipped to the cities where they will be eaten in apartments that

> are filled with books, magazines, furniture and people. On the trees are only
> a few gnarled apples that the pickers have rejected. They look like the knuck-
> les of Doctor Reefy's hands. One nibbles at them and they are delicious. Into
> a little round place at the side of the apple has been gathered all of its
> sweetness. One runs from tree to tree over the frosted ground picking the
> gnarled, twisted apples and filling his pockets with them. Only the few know
> the sweetness of the twisted apples. (36)

Something strange is happening here. Nothing will stay put in Anderson's
narrative: the seeds and the fertile land and the nursery seem to have produced
the supreme metaphor of the twisted apples, but they too are on the move,
and one appreciates their sweetness only by biting into them, an act of getting
under the skin that is allied here to the doctor by dint of his knuckles, but
which will be extended even more crucially to the tall girl herself. Finally,
these twisted apples may originate in seeds, but they seem to eventuate in the
paper pills themselves, the little paper balls recording the doctor's wasted life,
balls of language which he throws at the nursery man and reads to his wife
during the brief season of her life.

   Is it possible to sketch the tree of life any more forcefully than this? "On
the papers were written thoughts, ends of thoughts, beginnings of thoughts"
(37), Anderson writes, and his story is a meditation on ends and beginnings.
We see the full spectrum of metamorphic operations, from seed to flower to
fruit to language, and Anderson insists on running it both ways, showing us
that language can be the first as well as the last term of the equation, the
origin as well as the end. Language here is properly generative. The young girl
had two suitors, and she discovered the shocking potency of words:

> For a time the tall dark girl thought she would marry the jeweler's son.
> For hours she sat in silence listening as he talked to her and then she began to
> be afraid of something. Beneath his talk of virginity she began to think there
> was a lust greater than in all the others. At times it seemed to her that as he
> talked he was holding her body in his hands. She imagined him turning it
> slowly about in the white hands and staring at it. At night she dreamed that
> he had bitten into her body and that his jaws were dripping. She had the
> dream three times, then she became in the family way to the one who said
> nothing at all but who in the moment of his passion actually did bite her
> shoulder so that for days the marks of his teeth showed. (37–38)

Once again we see the kaleidoscopic machine at work, transforming all givens
into other givens, rivaling words against flesh, disclosing the dream to be the
source of the event, so potent that it actually engenders. Granted, Anderson
squeamishly writes "she became in the family way," but he has more than
earned his euphemism by fleshing out, metaphorically, the actual erotic inter-
mingling that engenders life, an activity so threatening that it passes for vampirish and murderous, leaving not only a fructified seed but also marks in the
flesh. The seed analogy refers, then, to the girl in the family way, as indeed it
must, since we have known about biting into apples and the costs of sexual
knowledge ever since the Bible, and we realize that Anderson is giving us

nothing less than a creation myth here, a story about the seeds of life: from flesh to language and back.

The story is relentless: the tall dark girl has been bitten into, and in turn she has bitten into the doctor, for "she was like one who has discovered the sweetness of the twisted apples, she could not get her mind fixed again upon the round perfect fruit that is eaten in the city apartments" (38). She marries the doctor and dies. Why? Again, the story is rife with answers: tasting another's sweetness is deadly; more lethal still, perhaps, may be the ingesting of those round paper balls, the doctor's balls, the potent medicine, the paper pills that he gave her. And if we are not satisfied with those answers, the story dramatizes still a third one, more shocking and gruesome than the others:

> In the office of the doctor there is a woman, the wife of the man who kept the bookstore in Winesburg. Like all old-fashioned country practitioners, Doctor Reefy pulled teeth, and the woman who waited held a handkerchief to her teeth and groaned. Her husband was with her and when the tooth was taken out they both screamed and blood ran down on the woman's white dress. The tall dark girl did not pay any attention. When the woman and the man had gone the doctor smiled. "I will take you driving into the country with me," he said. (38)

Artless? Groping? It is as if Anderson were feverishly inventing languages for his story of sexual liaison. He whispers that this episode is unrelated ("The tall dark girl did not pay any attention"), but his text shrieks out the relatedness of it all: here is the friendly abortion performed by the doctor, happily displaced onto a dental scenario. More to the point, here is at last the body-to-body engagement that spawns life, taken beyond apples, moving past shoulders, spilling blood this time. The woman groans, and the drama of biting in and pulling out—no less effective in its way than Shakespeare's "making the beast with two blacks"—states the unspeakable, images the carnal fusion that fuels this tale. Anderson has found a language to express the world of motion and metamorphosis that is his true quarry: the cost of sexuality and pleasure, the making and ending of life, the ceaseless current of energy that moves from seed to flesh to paper to language to seed. On the surface it may be that this is just another sepia tale of a has-been, another grotesque, but if we attend to the figural dynamic that Anderson has put in place, we see one of the most striking stories of displacement in American literature.

"The Philosopher" is also a doctor story, and although it is far less urgent than "Paper Pills," it exhibits the same figurative high jinks, the same insolent play of metaphor beyond the needs of the ostensible story. Doctor Parcival is even more backgrounded by his narrative than was the case with Doctor Reefy. Shortly after introducing the doctor, Anderson abruptly shifts terrain and focuses—that is the term for it—on the events at Tom Willy's saloon, most particularly the spectacle of the saloon keeper's hands: "That flaming kind of birthmark that sometimes paints with red the faces of men and women had touched with red Tom Willy's fingers and the backs of his hands. As he stood by the bar talking to Will Henderson he rubbed the hands together. As he grew more and more excited the red in his fingers deepened. It was as though the hands had been dipped in blood that had dried and faded" (49–50). We are in classic Anderson territory. There is an unmistakable excess of meaning in those marked hands, and although we have no idea how they might be linked to the story of Doctor Parcival, the very insertion of this material announces that these exchanges must be, in some odd way, versions of each other, a signal that this story is about strange, "bristling" conversations. And it is obvious that these bizarre hands have a message of their own, a sign, a birthmark that we will need to decipher. Hands are frequently "independent" in *Winesburg*, as in the lead-off story of Wings Biddlebaum's uncontrollable, eloquent hands, those "fluttering pennants of promise." Speaking is centralized in each of these vignettes, but we are made to understand that speaking is a peculiarly somatic activity, a nonstop fleshly confession that broadcasts our inmost secrets without our permission, often without our knowledge. Let us look again at Anderson's signs. Henderson, the sensualist, enjoys talking about women to Tom Willy, whose blood-red hands move ever faster in his excitement. Much is on show: the dipped and dried blood hints at murder, and the violence has an undeniable sexual coloration, given what we know of these two men. Their "talk" is erotically and murderously charged, and we know it to be, in some undisclosed way, a prelude, a double for the other "talk" of the story, the enigmatic confession made by the doctor to George Willard.

Diffuse, discontinuous, "signing" all the while, the narrative drops the hands and returns to Parcival in order to emphasize the enigma of the doctor's identity. As Parcival explains that he has no obvious motive in talking to George, the reader knows just the opposite, that the motive is in the talking itself, that whatever is being said is somehow strategic, therapeutic. While Parcival focuses on his own mystery, Anderson focuses on Parcival's appearance: fat, unspeakably dirty. And we sense that speaking dirt may be purgative, a form of cleansing. This man is going to be "birthed" by Anderson, but hardly in a straightforward fashion; the more he reveals about himself, the more enigmatic, the more parceled out he becomes. Hence, he tells us of his background: a detailed account of a murder (of a doctor, no less) in which he had some strange unspecified involvement, and account of his mother who took in washing (remember his own filth), mention of his insane father, and, most spectacularly, a complicated narrative about his hated brother:

> "The Big Four paints its stations a nasty orange color. How I hated that color! My brother was always covered with it. On pay days he used to get drunk and come home wearing his paint-covered clothes and bringing his money with him. He did not give it to mother, but laid it in a pile on the kitchen table.
>
> "About the house he went in the clothes covered with the nasty orange colored paint. I can see the picture. My mother, who was small and had red, sad-looking eyes, would come into the house from a little shed at the back. That's where she spent her time over the washtub scrubbing people's dirty clothes. In she would come and stand by the table, rubbing her eyes with her apron that was covered with soap-suds." (52–53)

As Anderson's story gathers energy, it fairly pulsates with signifying power. The painted brother seems virtually spawned by the marked hands (or is it the other way around?), and the red eyes join in the color spree as well. Isn't this the outcome of a world in which "hands" might be "fluttering pennants," flags or signs that contain a "hidden wonder story," if only we knew how to tell it? No less than Blake's "London," Anderson's "Philosopher" is a story about "marks of weakness, marks of woe." Like Blake, Anderson knew that the world marks us and that we mark it in turn, and the resultant vision is one in which the public, shared, phenomenal world has become luminous with private meaning. For Blake the blood runs down palace walls, whereas for Anderson the blood is to flow in multiple deaths, in the hands of Tom Willy, and in the orange paint of Parcival's brother. The reason he calls himself a doctor but has no patients, Parcival says, "does not appear on the surface"; it lies, he says, in his character, "which has, if you think about it, many strange turns" (50). In Anderson's hands Parcival is literally polytropic, telling stories that "began nowhere and ended nowhere" (51), and he is ministering to the great disease of his life: his life as disease. There is logic here, in Anderson's arrangement, but it is not the directional one of conventional prose; rather, the story is relentlessly confessional and indicting, as if Anderson wanted to do a version of the talking cure, narrative with no discernible center, just a mix of voices and markers, spread out everywhere, all coming home.

The story moves towards its climax, but its materials stubbornly refuse to coalesce. Deaths begin to pile up. The insane father dies in a mysterious fashion, possibly involving criminal negligence, thereby recalling the (fictitious?) "murder" of Doctor Cronin; Parcival then recounts the death of his brother (run over by the car in which he lived: a familial death?). Then Anderson delivers the last death, that of child thrown from a buggy (also reminiscent of the brother run over by the train), and this one serves as a catalyst for the story's ostensible conclusion: Parcival, asked to attend the injured child, refuses to come to her aid and is subsequently overcome by fear that the townspeople will crucify him for this act of cruelty. It is then that he confides to George his culminating philosophical wisdom: "It is this—that everyone in the world is Christ and they are all crucified" (57).

"The Philosopher" is arguably Anderson's most decentered story, and yet its separate parts taunt the reader with an elusive sense of odd propriety and near coherence, a suspicion that the parts must be redistributed if the significance of the piece is to emerge. It is a question of opening that trunk of Parcival's that arrived with the doctor and occasioned a brawl, the (same?) trunk that contained the body of the murdered Doctor Cronin and was hauled across the city and thrown into the lake. To speak is to display one's wares, our hidden wares, the luggage we carry about, the corpses we maintain. Hence, the words are virtually painted red all over the town. Anderson is articulating a story of murderous self-knowledge here, but he has disseminated the "evidence" everywhere, much the way the daytime mind does, until the dream restores the pieces in some riddling form for us. We cannot hear the doctor's story until we see that everything in the piece "speaks" him. First, the doctor's initial mystery making about his professional identity is born out by the close of the story: he is shown to be a nondoctor and a co-murderer, betrayed not only by his refusal to aid the girl but by his self-indicting narrative as well. Second, the ongoing discourse of filth and cleanliness betokens the central torment of the story, the doctor's own dirt—that is, his hatred for his family and his own self-loathing—figured also in the series of murders, each a figurative version of what he wanted to do his "loved" ones, and of what that desire has done to him. Finally, the bold emphasis on markings—the moving hands and the painted body—signals Anderson's remarkable view that we ourselves are language rather than the "users" of it, that our faces and gestures and feelings constitute that fuller script—it writes us, we do not write it—which dwarfs any stuttering verbal utterances we might make.

Anderson has been wrestling, confusedly, with this theme throughout *Winesburg*: the need to make the material world luminous with spirit, to show that utterance is everywhere. In "Godliness" the crazed Jesse Bentley, obsessed with bringing "from God a word or a sign out of the sky," grips his grandson's shoulders and turns his face to the sky and shouts. Anderson writes: "The whole left side of his face twitched and his hand on the boy's shoulder twitched also. 'Make a sign to me, God,' he cried" (86). We cannot fail to see that the human creature has become language here, that the twitching face and hand have acquired a horrible eloquence beyond the ken of the character himself. "Godliness" incorporates Anderson's "signing" within a recognizable religious context, and the allegorical tends to be too shrill, too prepackaged. In "The Philosopher" we have a secular version of events, more decentered, more confessional, ultimately more grisly in its workings.

Anderson's story is properly hieroglyphic, and its emblems hint at a carnival world of the psyche that has no truck with realism. Perhaps the most arresting moment of the piece comes when Parcival goes to the asylum to bless his father's dead body. In telling us that "they treated me as though I were a king," he conjures up a world like that of *The King of Hearts*, a realm in which the labels by which we know ourselves have been definitively removed. Looking at the corpse of his father, Parcival says something that could stand over the gate to Winesburg, Ohio, as a cautionary note to the readers who come to visit: "Let peace brood over this carcass" (54). Much of *Winesburg* is packed into that phrase: the subject as flesh with its corollary of the wasted life as carcass, the peace that comes from accepting one's filth and frailty, the brooding that is needed before the script can be read and the vision of wholeness can be gained.

Most of the dark stories of *Winesburg* bear out Parcival's conviction that we are all Christ, all of us subject to crucifixion. Parcival's prophecy is meant as an indictment of the community, but its deeper logic is self-reflexive: we achieve our own homemade crucifixion by the simple procedure of living, for our memories are freighted with corpses and cadavers that refuse to die. The language of these fictions, as we have seen, is rarely straightforward or subservient to ostensible narrative ends; instead, there is a profusion of metaphoric activity, resulting in a decentered or multicentered fable in which the discrete elements often require regrouping if we are to perceive their overall coherence.

Sometimes, however, Anderson is manic in a light, whimsical way, unlike the grim performances I have analyzed. In the figure of Joe Welling, protagonist of "A Man of Ideas," Anderson has given us a strange self-portrait that differs radically from most of the tormented figures of Winesburg. Unlike the gropers and stutterers, the crucified ones who live mutely among ghosts and carcasses, Welling is a pathological talker, a human conduit for language, a vehicle of verbal messages from afar, a Delphic oracle in Ohio:

> He was like a tiny little volcano that lies silent for days and then suddenly spouts fire. No, he wasn't like that—he was like a man who is subject to fits, one who walks among his fellow men inspiring fear because a fit may come upon him suddenly and blow him away into a strange uncanny physical state in which his eyes roll and his legs and arms jerk. He was like that, only that the visitation that descended upon Joe Welling was a mental and not a physical thing. He was beset by ideas and in the throes of one of his ideas was uncontrollable. Words rolled and tumbled from his mouth. A peculiar smile came upon his lips. The edges of his teeth that were tipped with gold glistened in the light. Pouncing upon a bystander he began to talk. For the bystander there was no escape. The excited man breathed into his face, peered into his eyes, pounded upon his chest with a shaking forefinger, demanded, compelled attention. (103)

The metaphors tell us everything: Welling is a force of nature, and in him all is linked—seismic activity, precious stones (glistening gold-tipped teeth), untrammeled energy that manifests itself variously as fire, motion, ideas, words, and talk. With a touch of the poet, Anderson gives Joe his rightful position: Standard Oil agent in Winesburg. Welling is indistinguishable from the fuel and energy he dispenses. In the throes of an idea he is a little Niagara Falls: "Astride an idea, Joe was overmastering. His personality became gigantic. It overrode the man to whom he talked, swept him away, swept all away, all who stood within sound of his voice" (104). When Welling thinks (naturally enough) of the water up at Wine Creek, the thinking itself is liquid, kinetic energy: "Thoughts rushed through my head. I thought of subterranean passages and springs. Down under the ground went my mind, delving about" (105). For most of us activity has its counterpart: stillness. For Welling life knows only one state: ceaseless, raging energy. Decay, he explains to George Willard, is no idle matter:

> "Let's take decay. Now what is decay? It's fire. It burns up wood and other things. You never thought of that? Of course not. This sidewalk here and this feed store, the trees down the street there—they're all on fire. They're burning up. Decay you see is always going on. It don't stop. Water and paint can't stop it. If a thing is iron, then what? It rusts, you see. That's fire, too. The world is on fire. Start your pieces in the paper that way. Just say in big letters '*The World Is On Fire.*' That will make 'em look up." (106)

It is as if the spirit of Heraclitus were roaming Winesburg, revealing to all the locals his prodigious secret that the elements alone are real, that the originary fire burns through every gesture, every word. Make this man a coach for the baseball team and you have a natural disaster; he functions pretty much the way a magnet would if you snuck it into a room of iron filings:

> With runners of the Winesburg team on bases, Joe Welling became as one inspired. Before they knew what had come over them, the base runners were watching the man, edging off the bases, advancing, retreating, held as by an invisible cord. The players of the opposite team also watched Joe. They were fascinated. For a moment they watched and then, as though to break a spell that hung over them, they began hurling the ball wildly about, and amid a series of fierce animal-like cries from the coach, the runners of the Winesburg team scampered home. (107)

The wit of Anderson's story consists of positioning this peculiarly charged, virtually radioactive "natural" figure in a cultural bind: courtship and town politics. Welling talks love the way we might expect him to: "Under the trees they walked and Joe talked. His passionate eager protestations of love, heard coming out of the darkness by the cemetery wall, or from the deep shadows of the trees on the hill that ran up to the Fair Grounds from Waterworks Pond, were repeated in the stores" (108). To carry the day, however, he must work his "elemental" magic on both his lady, Sarah King, and her male protectors, "the two Kings, Edward the father, and Tom the son" (108). It is a classic "high noon" scenario, and there is a good deal at stake: we are to learn not only whether Joe can win the girl but, more significantly, whether the Welling power system is a match for the sinister Kings of Winesburg. Now, shoot-outs and collisions are sordid, dreary affairs, and they are figural expressions of closure and crisis, of that old determinist logic whereby horns are locked and only one comes out alive: the bigger, stronger, tougher, or richer. But Anderson gives us a preview here of what Fitzgerald is going to do in his "shoot-out" scene between Tom and Gatsby in the sweltering Plaza Hotel, and also what Coover will do in his ribald "Shootout at Gentry's Junction": he moves beyond the deadly binarisms into the liberating realm of play. Thus, little Joe Welling carries the two Kings "off their feet with a tidal wave of words" (110). He waxes lyrical to these two oafs and fashions for their slow but unresisting minds a creation myth of his own, a rival "King"dom: "Suppose this — suppose all of the wheat, the corn, the oats, the peas, the potatoes, were all by some miracle swept away. Now here we are, you see, in this county. There is a high fence built all around us. We'll suppose that. No one can get over the fence and all the fruits of the earth are destroyed, nothing left but these wild things, these grasses. Would we be done for? I ask you that. Would we be done for?" (110). In this world of nature, man plays second fiddle. The fruits can be destroyed, the land can go bad, the sky can fall in. How would the Kings manage in these straits? But Joe Welling is a prime mover in precisely this scheme. The fruits are destroyed? Well, that's not such a problem: "We'd begin, you see, to breed up new vegetables and fruits. Soon we'd regain all we had lost. Mind, I don't say the new things would be the same as the old. They wouldn't. Maybe they'd be better, maybe not so good. That's interesting, eh? You can think about that. It starts your mind working, now don't it?" (110).

Anderson's parable about power closes with little Joe taking on the Kings and sweeping them away by dint of mental and verbal energy. His only trump is Anderson's only trump: language, language as the conduit of thought, language as the currency of the world. The imperial word conquers all: "'Take milkweed now,' he cried. 'A lot might be done with milkweed, eh? It's almost unbelievable. I want you to think about it. I want you two to think about it. There would be a new vegetable kingdom you see. It's interesting, eh? It's an idea'" (111). The new vegetable kingdom which exists purely as a realm of thought and language is the place where Joe Welling can be King. Here is Anderson the mythopoeist, and here is a philosophical parable that testifes to the living life of the mind, not perhaps the way the continental philosophers would have done it, but done very smartly nonetheless. The little man who works for Standard Oil truly delivers energy to the community. As conduit for the elements and as pythia for the people, Welling plays out fully, even passionately, the double dream of Sherwood Anderson: the democratic scribe whose language liberates his fellows and becomes thereby a genuine "public utility," and the demiurgic wizard who overpowers the real world by the force of his words, thereby acquiring a kingdom of his own.

This assessment of Anderson's language in *Winesburg* is meant to rescue him from the charges of artlessness and naïveté that have been leveled at him over the years. He does not offer the pyrotechnics of Joyce or the programmatic innovations of Hemingway or Faulkner. But his most interesting stories pose an audacious challenge to the conventions of orthodox fiction. We encounter at every turn bristling metaphors, multiple centers of interest, a new kind of poetics in which disruption and displacement rule over a mixed field, linking figuratively what is unconnected on the surface, proposing a composite picture that regroups (and recoups) its discrete parts, fashioning a startling new script. Biting into apples, "painted" limbs, the mechanics of talking: these innocuous matters become poetry in the work of Anderson in that they catalyze entire units of narrative action, "bleeding" through into layer after layer of event and notation, proposing for us at the far side of the story an order of "definition" that we could never have suspected at the outset. Is this not how Gertrude Stein herself defined her friend?

> Dear Sherwood, as long as grape sugar is grape sugar and it always is, and oranges twenty-five for twenty-five cents are oranges, so long will Sherwood be Sherwood. And as grape sugar will always be, and oranges will be, so will he.
> One cannot cry when grape sugar is like that or twenty-five oranges for twenty-five cents are like that, and one cannot die when they are like that, so one does not cry for Sherwood nor does Sherwood die.
> No.
> Grape sugar and oranges twenty-five for twenty-five cents, they are Sherwood.[11]

Stein's wholly metaphoric vision of Anderson becomes the occasion for a small-town figural ballet that dances itself through time and mocks closure through its algebraic mix of numbers and fruit, its portrait beyond death. As readers of a time when oranges are no longer twenty-five for twenty-five cents, we may see in her equation both the moment of *Winesburg* and the timelessness of Anderson's achievement, those twisted apples and beautiful equivalences that constitute the best of his art.

In spewing out his odd mix of signs and markers, Anderson achieves a kind of prose-poetry that is the first of its kind in American fiction. But that is not all. We begin to detect in Anderson's strange verbal performances an insistent linkage between the binds, phantasms, and miseries of the near-autistic villagers on the one hand, and the fashioning of a bold, empowering language on the other. Anderson's gambit is tactical, strategic, throughout, and his success in having that larger "say" rivals with the countless, unrecountable failures experienced by his people. "Paper Pills" says something about the price of passion and the chain of being that not only fuses Wordsworth and Kafka, but allows us to see in the brief events of a small-town Ohio doctor's life a wondrous paradigm of human connection, profound enough and cosmic enough to be projected into a planetary myth. And he fashions, in "The Philosopher," a modern *conte philosophique* reminiscent not of Voltaire, whose elegance is alien to Anderson's garrulousness, but of Borges-cum-Faulkner: the metaphysical twists, detective fantasies, and forkingly assimilative strategy of the Argentine, along with the plaintive, musing introspection and the youth–old man encounter that we associate with the southerner who learned so much from him. "A Man of Ideas" has already been characterized as Heraclitean, and the connections it makes between the energies of nature and human discourse are remarkable indeed. No less remarkable is its home-town flavor, its utter prosaicness in the figure of Joe Welling: little man with a big voice, reminiscent of hawkers, drummers, con men, and snake charmers, small-town poet of the "Now that's interesting" variety, a recognizable crackpot we have seen and discounted for decades on end. Anderson's triumph is to re-present this fellow to us for inspection, to position him, oddly enough, at the heart of the community (delivering fuel and coaching baseball), to make us discern his magic, to overwhelm the reader — along with the other in-house Kings — with Welling's verbal and imaginative performance. We know that Welling's victory is suspiciously self-indulgent (on Anderson's part, that is, for Welling is unmistakably a self-portrait, a *porte-parole*), that Kings are not so easily swayed in the real world. Yet, this is a profoundly American fable about the freedom and the power of speech, a parable that does not, for once, pit man against the environment, but rather sets the little man against all the odds and then enlists the environment on his side. Walt Disney might have done something like it, but only Anderson could have shown that the power of language is of a piece with the flowing and pulsating energies of the elements themselves. "A Man of Ideas" is a bright chthonic parable, a poem of the earth: natural resources and verbal resources are alike in kind; the word is living.

Winesburg, Ohio has all too often been read as a small proposition, the tunnel vision of a provincial mind shedding light on ghosts of the past, a nightmarish but bucolic world irretrievably distant from contemporary concerns. But Anderson was, at his best, a mythic poet for whom the village anecdote was, if you knew how to look and "compose," cosmic event, for whom language, if you knew how to speak and write, was power. He could not do the long thing, and his writing, even in *Winesburg*, was often crude, sometimes vulgar, even silly. But what he did well has not been surpassed.

6

Flannery O'Connor and the
Art of Displacement

Flannery O'Connor's fiction poses almost as many challenges to modern readers as Kafka's stories do. Each moves through mimesis to get beyond it, to
show the workings of the soul in a materialist world. Yet Kafka's sibylline
parables and bureaucratic fables have imposed themselves as the illuminations
of a *Herabgesandter*, as the work of a spiritual geographer who wishes to
map the terrains of justice, guilt, purity, and authority but has at his disposal
only the drabbest, most concrete landscapes imaginable: boardinghouses,
muddy villages, alleyways, traveling circuses, shabby apartment buildings.
Flannery O'Connor has not met with Kafka's success, and many readers find
her work too regional in its purview, and too theological, indeed too doctrinal
in its assumptions. It is felt by some that her intense Catholic beliefs narrow
her work into allegory at every turn, that the fusion of the profane and the
divine is forced and overly rigid. Whereas Kafka's form of mystery seems
generic and nonsectarian, O'Connor's appears overdetermined, drenched in
local color, shaped by the stresses of dogma and established ritual. She insists
on writing about the Great Events — baptism, the Crucifixion, the workings of
grace — as if they were taking place today, every day, right there in that rural
Georgia that she has memorably labeled "Christ-haunted."

What is most intriguing and compelling about O'Connor's work is its relentlessly *pedestrian* concern with transcendence; she writes about, and from
the angle of, everyday life, but in her hands it begins to shimmer with "otherness." To locate the mystery right here among us, rather than in the beyond,
and to see the mystery as inseparable from the plain data of experience, is to
fashion a prose that is utterly mimetic and utterly revelatory at the same time.
The tribute O'Connor paid to Teilhard de Chardin is one that applies perfectly
to her own enterprise: "His is a scientific expression of what the poet attempts
to do: penetrate matter until spirit is revealed in it."[1] We can hardly fail to see
that the poetic and the spiritual are intricately linked in O'Connor's oeuvre, so
much so that we may want to see them as faces of each other, consubstantial
to each other. There is much violence in her work but, strangely enough, little
real dissension. As Peter Hawkins says, "The warfare she wages is not, in
fact, spirit against flesh, but, rather, spirit *in* flesh," and this omnipresence of

spirit leads to a very special view of language.[2] O'Connor's poetics derive from an astonishingly unified world view, and her verbal practice boldly parts ways with the entire modern, differential conception of language as closed, systemic, and conventional. Whereas the modern scheme harks back to Saussure's binary system of signifiers and signifieds, O'Connor's dark and beautiful fables are almost Edenic in their wholeness of expression, their linguistic integrity. She is out to show us, at every turn, that words speak and name beyond the reaches that we ascribe to them, that they possess a fullness of utterance that no one, including their speakers, initially sees. Her project is the direct opposite of the Derridean demonstration of incessant, "always already" difference and absence; she speaks oneness and presence, and the high drama of her stories consists in coming to terms with the devastations of oneness and presence, the incessant translation of misfit into fit, of fragment into whole, of dissonance into harmony, of misery into grace. Literature, she felt, was an incarnational art, and her work chronicles the adventures of signification, the increasing heft and weight of a language that is utterly inclusive, yoking the denotative and the connotative, the descriptive and the figurative, the factual and the spiritual, wherever it goes. And it goes further than we may think, further than the country folk of Georgia, and beyond the vagaries of the present moment. At her best she is properly and convincingly eschatological, fusing the particular with the universal, demonstrating that the Christ story is never played out but always playing.

O'Connor's view of art is extreme: not only is it epiphanic, but it is essentially ephiphanic at every moment, showing us that the common scene is always uncommon, if we know how to look. In this she is totalitarian; for her, spirit is everywhere, and there are no nooks and crannies where "ordinary" life can be indulged. Consider, by way of contrast and as a means of bringing O'Connor into focus, Auden's famous "Musée des Beaux Arts":

> About suffering they were never wrong,
> The Old Masters; how well they understood
> Its human position; how it takes place
> While someone else is eating or opening a window or just walking dully along;
> How, when the aged are reverently, passionately waiting
> For the miraculous birth, there must always be
> Children who did not specially want it to happen, skating
> On a pond at the edge of the wood:
> They never forgot
> That even the dreadful martyrdom must run its course
> Where the dogs go on with the doggy life and the torturer's horse
> Scratches its innocent behind on a tree.
> In Brueghel's *Icarus*, for instance: how everything turns away
> Quite leisurely from the disaster; the ploughman may
> Have heard the splash, the forsaken cry,
> But for him it was not an important failure; the sun shone
> As it had to on the white legs disappearing into the green
> Water; and the expensive delicate ship that must have seen
> Something amazing, a boy falling out of the sky,
> Had somewhere to get to and sailed calmly on.[3]

The view presented by Auden is urbane, and it is merciful: there are miracles and Great Events, yes, the stuff of myth and fable, but they are the poetic exceptions in a world of prose. The ordinary folk go about their ordinary lives, perhaps unaware of, certainly untouched by, such fireworks. Brueghel suits Auden's purposes beautifully because his paintings breathe a kind of ontological innocence, a naturalist world that just happens to contain miraculous events, but no one need worry about them. Such a view is merciful, for it posits a natural creatural life that manages without miracles, that is neither blessed nor cursed by the power of the spirit or the decrees of the Lord. In such a scheme art must be intrusive, the messenger from elsewhere who insists on news of the soul. Such art may be beautiful and meaningful, but it will always be profoundly unnatural, alien to the world it visits, at home only in museums, in some kind of *musée des beaux arts*.

If, however, we move from Brueghel to Bosch, we find a more apposite pictorial and moral counterpart to Flannery O'Connor. As Gilbert Muller has noted, both Bosch and O'Connor share a vision of life as hellish and filled with torment by devils and demons; their most striking parallel, however, is their joint predilection for the grotesque, "a violation of the limits which have been laid down by God for man."[4] Bosch is insistently allegorical, not to say visionary, and his canvases sovereignly mix levels of experience and orders of reality, fusing the "human" with the legendary and the bestial, thereby suggesting that they form one composite world. Perhaps "violation of limits" is best understood as a transgression of normative boundary lines. Yet for all their common interest in the grotesque, the parallel between Bosch and O'Connor is somewhat misleading in that the modern writer has no recourse to the supernatural, nor does she invent new amalgams of man-beast; her vision is no less eschatological than that of the fourteenth-century painter, but she finds all her materials right at home, for everybody to see. The devil may be afoot, but his foot itself is not cloven; he is likely to be a traveling Bible salesman or a drifter looking for wheels.[5]

If a third painterly parallel may be proposed, it is that of Rembrandt, especially the Rembrandt who illustrated the Old and New Testaments by using the common people of his acquaintance as models. Rembrandt finds in the most ordinary materials — faces lined by age and suffering, bodies worn down by time — what he needs to paint the philosophers, saints, and apostles. There need be no strict distinction between the folk of Leiden and those of Scripture or legend. And it is this capacity to discern and to render the spiritual aura of common things that makes his work so moving. O'Connor, it can be argued, works the same miracles with her ordinary materials, and she refuses to observe the boundary between prose and poetry, between the ploughman and the body falling out of the sky. Hence, her work is always threatening, oddly "nervous" in its unfurling, since the mysterious forces of grace and damnation may come into play at any moment; her world is one of incessant "translation," whereby the low-profiled denizens of her country tales suddenly take on their true proportions, give their fuller measure.

This kind of translation must needs be a kind of writing, a cunning verbal art that gives us surfaces so that it may burst through them. At a given point in most O'Connor stories, we can almost hear the machinery going into operation, and we can then begin to see into the distance and the depths. At these moments one realizes the odd and staggering propriety of her art, and one is then able to appreciate those strategies of displacement that have been at work all along, revealing in the transactions and encounters of her good country people the contours of that larger Passion play that is her true subject. In these moments our optic as readers is widened, and we take in that larger realm that she, again like Kafka, has been mapping all along; as she herself said, it is a question of distances: "The prophet is a realist of distances, and it is this kind of realism which goes into great novels. It is a realism which does not hesitate to distort appearances in order to show a hidden truth."[6] Great novelists, we are told, may well tamper with the given scene and do a little meddling (distorting), but they do so in order to be true to that more capacious realism of distances. For the reader it is a question of extending one's vision, both inwardly and outwardly, of being shocked into a recognition of the real reaches of ordinary things. And this effort, O'Connor always insisted, was essentially imaginative rather than moral.

For our purposes here the best of O'Connor is her short fiction, and the best pieces are the ones that work this theme of shock and discovery in double fashion; that is, they tell a story of trauma and revelation, and they occasion for the reader something of that same leap or fall. These fictions characteristically revolve around seemingly innocuous events — a family outing, a trip to the city, a risk-free flirtation, the signing on of a hired hand — and then they promptly take all parties (reader included) off the map. It may simply be, in Peter Hawkins's words, that her characters "walk out on ice, suddenly to fall into a depth they never knew was there," or it may be that these reaches go a good bit further than the bottom of the ice, all the way to the underworld self that must be explored, as Jefferson Humphries has argued in his provocative, gnostic reading of O'Connor.[7] But in all cases there is something of that "radiance of form" about which Jacques Maritain spoke, a kind of incandescence that illuminates the new circuits and lines of connection that we begin to sight as O'Connor's stories come to their odd conclusions.[8]

One of the most convenient places to begin an appreciation of O'Connor is her story "The River." Here the author is working with utterly predictable materials, and the reader *knows* that it will be a story of baptism. But the reader usually does not know just how much O'Connor has already taken into account such expectations and, most crucially of all, how wise O'Connor is about the reader's notion of baptism. As she said: "When I write a novel in which the central action is a baptism, I know that for the larger percentage of my readers, baptism is a meaningless rite; therefore I have to imbue this action with an awe and terror which will suggest its awful mystery."[9] Not only is baptism regarded as a "meaningless rite," but the word itself has been cheapened, shorn of its transcendental power, its authority as a vehicle for moving from one realm to another. Immersion in the water must, in "The River," somehow re-become for the reader the resonant act of spiritual cleansing and rebirth that O'Connor takes it to be; and words must be reinvested with their originary fullness, must be shown to leave their dictionary realms and to reassert their power over the earth and those who dwell on it. As the author tells us, "awe and terror" will be called in to do the job, and it is instructive to see just how this is done, to see that this empowering of language is in itself a fearsome and prophetic turn of events.

The first thing we notice is the victimization of the child, not only abandoned by his parents but somehow cheated in still larger ways, victimized by a setting that is implacably poor, morally poor: "The child stood glum and limp in the middle of the dark living room while his father pulled him into a plaid coat."[10] Everything conspires to produce soullessness here: "glum and limp" denote the undirected flesh, the aimless child who is "pulled" into his clothing. This "dark living room," suffused with the smell of "dead cigarette butts," is no place for living at all, and O'Connor paints an oppressive picture of familial impoverishment: hung-over mother, toneless voices, mutterings. When the child returns to this setting after his encounter with the river, he measures its insufficiency: a refrigerator with some shriveled vegetables, brown oranges, "something fishy in a paper bag," and a pork bone. His most gratifying home activity consists of emptying ashtrays onto the floor and carefully rubbing the ashes into the rug. In this wasteland setting life is a series of games, parties, meals eaten out. Words in particular have little weightiness: "They joked a lot where he lived. If he had thought about it before, he would have thought Jesus Christ was a word like 'oh' or 'damn' or 'God,' or maybe somebody who had cheated them out of something" (163). The child is to discover another realm, a place where there are no jokes, where words not only count but *name*, irrevocably. From Harry (or maybe Herbert) he will be translated into Bevul, a person who counts. To become Bevul, to receive his true name, the child must first leave the home of ashes and jokes; he must then, to achieve purity, cast the animal out from him, and O'Connor brilliantly locates this purgation in the barnyard, where the country children trick him into a face-off with the pig:

> "No you can lift up the board and put your face to the . . ." a quiet voice began.
> He had already done it and another face, gray, wet and sour, was pushing into his, knocking him down and back as it scraped out under the plank. Something snorted over him and charged back again, rolling him over and pushing him up from behind and then sending him forward, screaming through the yellow field, while it bounded behind. (162)

One sees here the economy of O'Connor's scheme. Perfectly naturalistic, a credible children's prank, the scene is nonetheless a spiritual manifesto, a form of double writing that brings into synchrony the material world and its other side. No less than that "other" face, gray, wet, and sour, that pushes into his, the unfurling events are coming from "within" as well as "without," and that collision course—wonderfully filmic, immediate, and relentless—is rife with violence, tantamount to rape. The animal is everywhere here, pressing hard, under the house, in the hogs, ultimately in the piglike face of Mr. Paradise, who flaunts his fleshly state in the cancerous purple bulge on his left cheek. In the illustrated book, we are told, Christ drove a crowd of pigs out of a man, just the sort of thing one might find in a Brueghel or a Bosch painting, and it is plain enough that the author intends to produce her own writerly version of illustrated proverbs. This consort of local event and scriptural parallel constitutes more than allegory; it is the author's way of making language more than a joke, of creating resonance, of imaging the very act of purification that we associate with baptism. Those fatigued words "baptism" and "purification" move from the linguistic to the phenomenal in this story, receive an astounding fullness of meaning. Every detail is shown to be echoing and double here: the "dark living room" of ashes must be left, and the animal must be exorcised (by means of a violent fleshly encounter) before the soul can enter the flow. The writer's task is to reveal the essences under the surfaces, to show how polysemous everything is: "Listen to what I got to say, you people! There ain't but one river and that's the River of Life, made out of Jesus' Blood. That's the river you have to lay your pain in, in the River of Faith, in the River of Life, in the River of Love, in the rich red river of Jesus' Blood, you people!" (165). Not unlike Edvard Munch, who in his painting *The Scream* wished to depict a sky that actually *was* coagulated blood, to go right through paint to become blood, O'Connor seeks to invest her words with immanence, to transform these brown waters into Faith, Life, Love, the rich, red river of Jesus' blood. By the end of this strange story Bevul has reentered these waters and has been accepted by them. We see the quintessential O'Connor here: in closing, the story comes into its full birthright, achieves that complete illumination of its materials, whereby river and name finally disclose their unsuspected power and reach. The reader who has attended the eerie synchronization at work here, the fashioning of a language and a story that function doubly, feels something of the mystery, awe, and terror that the author had in mind.

"The River" is among O'Connor's most conservative stories, for its plot is so visibly grafted onto an older sacramental story. In other fictions, however, she ranges more widely, achieves more dissonance between her secular anecdote and those spiritual paradigms that shimmer in the background. In "The Life You Save May Be Your Own," the one-armed carpenter, Tom T. Shiftlet, is endowed by the author with unmistakable, albeit grotesque, Christlike attributes: we read that his "face descended in forehead for more than half its length and ended suddenly with his features just balanced over a jutting steeltrap jaw" (146), but that "his figure formed a crooked cross" (146). A good deal of O'Connor is on show here: the grotesque, distorted figure is always defined in relation to the story of the cross, as if to measure just how far we have come from that originating event, as if to remind us that it is still the trope that ineluctably orders our secular lives. "A crooked cross" is the perfect emblem for many of her stories. Shiftlet has been seen by many as an Antichrist, but he surely speaks for the author when he expresses his belief in mystery and opaqueness:

"Lady," he said, and turned and gave her his full attention, "lemme tell you something. There's one of these doctors in Atlanta that's taken a knife and cut the human heart—the human heart," he repeated, leaning forward, "out of a man's chest and held it in his hand," and he held his hand out, palm up, as if it were slightly weighted with the human heart, "and studied it like it was a day-old chicken, and lady," he said, allowing a long significant pause in which his head slid forward and his clay-colored eyes brightened, "he don't know no more about it than you or me."

"That's right," the old woman said.

"Why, if he was to take that knife and cut into every corner of it, he still wouldn't know no more than you or me. What you want to bet?" (147)

Shiftlet, deceiving though he is, reliably displays the analogical principles at work in O'Connor's world. Mimicking with his own gestures the "analysis of the human heart," he makes it clear that his actions in the story are to be a gloss on the exploits of the Atlanta doctor: the heart on show, and yet the darkness still intact and nobody the wiser. How, the story seems to ask, do we know the truth of the heart, the genuine motives for behavior? Ordinary analysis may well "cut into every corner of it," but surgical probing is not knowledge. And the word seems to be no more reliable than the scalpel. After all, we live after Babel; and we can lie. What's in a name? "'Lady,' he said, 'nowadays, people'll do anything anyways. I can tell you my name is Tom T. Shiftlet and I come from Tarwater, Tennessee, but you never have seen me before: how you know I ain't lying? How you know my name ain't Aaron Sparks, lady, and I come from Singleberry, Georgia, or how you know it's not George Speeds and I come from Lucy, Alabama, or how you know I ain't Thompson Bright from Toolafalls, Mississippi?'" (147–48). How do you know? How do you go beyond the "joke" realm that Bevul lives in, those closed-off verbal precincts where "damn" and "Jesus" are just four- and five-letter words? How can the word become incandescent, so that Aaron Sparks and Thompson Bright would achieve the actual radiance promised by their names? Literature itself seems to be on the line here. What is there to believe in fiction? in human discourse? Words, used for day-to-day marketplace operations, are whimsical and fickle, amounting to little more than noise. The only question that matters is: When do they *count*? When does a name become one with its referent? In "The Life You Save May Be Your Own," the riddles remain unanswered, even though the heart is displayed on the page. We see nothing but displacements and reversals, the play of passion that has no fixed counters to side with. The automobile is invested with spiritual value, while the retarded Lucynell is treated like a thing. The final page of the story reads like bouts of disembodied rhetoric, warring verbal positions that have no people to fill them. Shiftlet has abandoned the sleeping Lucynell and has picked up a hitchhiker on whom he unloads his fulsome dithyramb about the beauty of mothers. Calling his mother an "angel of Gawd" (just the words earlier applied to Lucynell) and indicting himself for abandoning her (mother? Lucynell?), Shiftlet provokes from the hitchhiker a violent rejoinder: "'You go to the devil' he cried. 'My old woman is a flea bag and yours is a stinking pole cat!'" (156). The two registers fight it out, but the reader is in the dark about their spokespeople. O'Connor seems unable to mesh her words and her people, and she closes the story in a frenzy of atmospheric tumult: "The turnip [cloud] continued slowly to descend. After a few minutes there was a guffawing peal of thunder from behind and fantastic raindrops, like tin-can tops, crashed over the rear of Mr. Shiftlet's car. Very quickly he stepped on the gas and with his stump sticking out the window he raced the galloping shower into Mobile" (156). There is an unresolved violence in this story that ends up in the cosmos itself, as if O'Connor decided that all talk of spirit is twaddle in the degraded, paroxysmal world of turnips, tin-can tops, stumps, and galloping showers which reigns triumphant. Here is that "dead landscape" that John Hawkes appreciated in O'Connor, "quite ready for new humor, new vision, new and more meaningful comic treatments of violence."[11] But the spillover here never comes into focus; the mingling of realms achieves no clarity, and the furious words do not carry. The crookedness of the cross overshadows the cross itself.

O'Connor's best work is more laconic, less strained and emphatic than what we see in the final pages of "The Life You Save May Be Your Own." Her most remarkable stories maintain a perfect balance between mimetic reporting and spiritual event, and nowhere is this more in evidence than in "A Good Man Is Hard to Find." This little fable about a family outing that goes astray is arguably the most grisly and most perfect piece O'Connor ever wrote. It starts out in the purest secular tradition, with careful social notation and naturalist detail enlisted to render the operations and texture of this family in all their mediocrity and banality. If ever a group was designated as "this-worldly" and not-singled-out by fate, it would be this consort of grandmother and son and wife and children. Yet by the end of the story, not only has the family been shot dead, but we are made to feel that there is a disturbing propriety in their deaths. Here are the little people, much like Auden's ploughman; they find, however, that they are not witnesses to but actors in a drama they had never reckoned on. It is hard to imagine a more freakish story, and it is here, if ever, that O'Connor brings her two planes — the secular and the spiritual — onto a collision course that radically challenges the reader's sense of norms. The implicit burden of mimetic prose — to show things as they are, to give a slice of life — has been dealt a foul blow, and we are obliged to rethink how things are, how life is sliced.

As critical readers we have probably suspected some degree of trouble in this story from the outset. After all, the initial mention of the Misfit guarantees, according to the laws of literature (unlike, we hope, the laws of life), that he will show up in the course of events. He does. Likewise, we note the pretentiousness of the grandmother: her shrewd manipulation of the family, her vanity (she is dressed to the teeth, so that "in case of an accident, anyone seeing her dead on the highway would know at once that she was a lady" [118]), her romantic "Gone with the Wind" references to a privileged, decorous past, her relentless concern with social propriety. What reader does not suspect that she will meet with a comeuppance? But what reader suspects that it will be as lethal as it turns out to be?

There are no halfway measures in O'Connor. She *needs* all the brutality she can muster: "In my stories I have found that violence is strangely capable of returning my characters to reality and preparing them to accept their moment of grace. Their heads are so hard that almost nothing else will do the work."[12] The rhetorical and the essential are fused together here: violence must be done to the thick-skinned and hard-headed, and the reader inevitably shares in the trauma; but these bouts are to put folks back on track, to return them to reality. Finally, the seasoned O'Connor reader knows that this particular family setting is glaringly deficient in spirit, and that this deficiency is going to be their doom—if only we can read it. And so we look at the innocuous mimetic scene, the proasic country-folk version of Wallace Stevens's "Sunday Morning": the son, Bailey, "bent over the orange sports section of the *Journal*," the wife, "a young woman in slacks, whose face was as broad and innocent as a cabbage and was tied around with a green head-kerchief that had two points on the top like a rabbit's ears," the children "reading the funny papers on the floor" (117). Somewhat like the joke world of "The River," this setting is at once material and unreal, a mix of colors and vegetables and animals that is "innocent" of anything beyond the tangible and measurable. The "news" of this realm is to be found in the sports section and the funny papers, but other news, other tidings, are on the way.

Soon enough we realize that things are a bit unrulier and more dimensional than they seem: the animal metaphors become insistent, so that the "big black valise that looked like the head of a hippopotamus" sends us back to the wife's "head-kerchief" with its "two points on the top like a rabbit's ears." There is something of a hidden bestiary here, ranging from the figurative animals to the concealed cat, Pitty Sing, who is going to do so much damage, to the chained gray monkey at Red Sammy's. (And why is Sammy red?) This sense of lurking danger is also signaled by the mention of "patrolmen [who] hid themselves behind billboards and small clumps of trees and sped out after you" (119). This is a pulsating verbal world, one that is getting ready to jump out of its linguistic and conventional skin, so that metaphors will be actualized and the controlled landscape will explode, as if in frenzy or in seizure, with energy that is no longer containable, even though it has always been there.

Things are *bristling* in this story, and nothing is simply itself or quite what it seems. The children play a game of labeling the shapes assumed by the clouds, but how much of a game is it? Things have multiple shapes, and shapes have multiple meanings. Mr. Edgar Atkins Teagarden, genteel though he may be in one register, signals E.A.T. on another. Nothing can be trusted down here, for O'Connor, no less than Melville, sees a world of incompatible measures and time schemes. Thus, when Red Sammy's wife declares, "It isn't a soul in this green world of God's that you can trust," she adds significantly, "And I don't count nobody out of that, not nobody" (122), while looking directly at Red Sammy. The green world and the red Sammy are inscrutable, indecipherable, unpredictable, glowing signs in a language we suddenly realize we can't read. Things and people are not trustworthy because they are enigmas, not knowable because they do not know their own riddles. And thus it follows that a good man is hard to find because we have no registers or sensory apprehension of goodness; we see and we analyze and we assess, but we measure the wrong things, such as the precise time we leave Atlanta and the exact mileage on the car, but when it comes to "soul[s] in this green world of God's," our instruments have no purchase and our sights are off.

This family outing is headed into the immeasurable, and while the children exchange comic books, we note that the car passes "a large cotton field with five or six graves fenced in the middle of it" (119), that they have now moved "outside of Toombsboro" (124).[13] Thus, when Bailey takes the car off the highway and onto the dirt road, he may think he is headed for some plantation, but we know that another zone altogether is being entered. This entry entails leaving the known world of genteel romance and moving into explosive violence. And there won't be a tame word in the bunch:

> The thought [that the plantation was in Tennessee, not Georgia] was so embarrassing that she [the grandmother] turned red in the face and her eyes dilated and her feet jumped up, upsetting her valise in the corner. The instant the valise moved, the newspaper top she had over the basket under it rose with a snarl and Pitty Sing, the cat, sprang onto Bailey's shoulder.
> The children were thrown to the floor and their mother, clutching the baby, was thrown out the door onto the ground; the old lady was thrown into the front seat. The car turned over and landed right-side-up in a gulch off the side of the road. Bailey remained in the driver's seat with the cat—gray-striped with a broad white face and an orange nose—clinging to his neck like a caterpillar. (124–25)

It is a remarkable "passage" is more ways than one. The docile world of things is no longer "innocent"; the "newspaper top" no longer covers things. And the things themselves tumble. The animals have arrived fully on the scene at last, with a "snarl" that we are to hear again at the end of the story, and the humans find themselves in strange new alliances: Bailey is no longer paired with the woman "whose face was as broad and innocent as a cabbage" but rather with the "cat—gray-striped with a broad white face and an orange nose—clinging to his neck like a caterpillar." Although the prose indicates that he "remained in the driver's seat," we can easily enough see that he is no longer there, in the familiar sense of that metaphor: being in control. On the contrary, the normative world has loosened its grip and lost its control. The power of this passage derives from the astonishing transformations it ushers in. In the vein of Picasso's *Guernica*, O'Connor is painting a tableau of pure anarchy, a riotous unleashing of creatural (and other) energies gone amok: the dilating eyes and jumping feet of the grandmother, the springing cat, the children thrown to the floor, the mother and child out the door, the old lady into the front seat, the car over once lightly, the driver merged with the cat-caterpillar. This momentous regrouping announces the new dispensation at hand: the exodus from the familiar highway and the initiation into a new realm, that surreal O'Connor territory where spirit reigns and daytime logic is to no avail.

As we see a "big black battered hearselike automobile" (126) approach, we know that we are not "outside of Toombsboro" at all, but rather moving further and further into it, into the woods "tall and dark and deep" (125), woods that "gaped like a dark open mouth" (127), and into which, ultimately, each member of the family is to be led for shooting. We are not all that far from the mythic dark forest of Hawthorne's "Young Goodman Brown," a place that is rife with spirits and magic, a realm that inverts and recasts the kinships and structures we had thought operative in the world. The Misfit presides over this territory. Described by the author as "scholarly," the Misfit is a genuine intellectual, a man who is not content with appearances but must peer into what is behind them: "My daddy said I was a different breed of dog from my brothers and sisters. 'You know,' Daddy said, 'it's some that can live their whole life out without asking about it and it's others has to know why it is, and this boy is one of the latters. He's going to be into everything!'" (129). The showdown between the Misfit and the grandmother illuminates the utter frivolity of her genteel code. She insists that he's not common at all, that he's got good blood, whereas his view of life flaunts all the things she (and civilization) would hide, and hide from. Like the genius loci, he emerges from his realm, welcoming the grandmother to the new territory, intent on showing her the rules that apply here. Thomas Merton once compared O'Connor to Sophocles, and in the Misfit she has indeed given us a portrait of archetypal man as a parricide who has erased the memory of his act: "'It was a head-doctor at the penitentiary said what I had done was kill my daddy but I known that for a lie. My daddy died in nineteen ought nineteen of the epidemic flu and I never had a thing to do with it'" (130). This man who is "into everything," has been "buried alive," locked in a prison, walled off from right and left and up and down, cut off from his origins and his crime, is exemplary; he is Freud's modern man, and his life consists of trying to reclaim himself by retracing those instinctual paths of violence and murder that are the true bases of creatural life.

Theology has been much enlisted to define this strange character, but he needs to be seen as the avenger from afar, the one who brings news, opens up the scene, shows the grandmother and her family just how much there is between heaven and earth.[14] And he embodies the O'Connor enterprise in that he is in search of his own past, of the larger figure that he makes in the scheme of things. Punishment constitutes the facts of his life, but he is stymied by the failure to remember his transgressions, and he now *writes* everything he does to have a record of the "fit" between crime and punishment. We sense that this "fit" is no less than the calibration between deed and significance, word and meaning, matter and spirit, past and present, life and truth. John Desmond, in his excellent *Risen Sons*, has shown us a great deal about O'Connor's historical imperative, her concern to locate the present moment within its immense eschatological framework. Like so many O'Connor denizens, the Georgia family lives a shrunken, utterly materialist life, an unending series of daily escapes from the fullness of memory and history. Jesus looms large for the Misfit as the man who set the pattern, who yoked the contraries, who *may* have embodied the spirit and revealed the soul to be as real as the senses. Jesus is a maddening figure for the Misfit because he was pure illumination; in the benighted world after the Fall we can no longer see the connections between matter and spirit. If we could, what would things look like?

They would perhaps take on the strange new shapes that appear in this story. The grandmother has to be weaned from her reality of social pretension. She must come to see that her family is not merely Bailey and company—

nothing better marks this than her inability to recognize Bailey's shirt when the Misfit puts it on—but that she has other, perhaps deeper allegiances. The story tells us at the outset that "she wanted to visit some of her connections in east Tennessee," that "Bailey was the son she lived with" (117), and we are meant to ponder these statements, perhaps to return to them as the story reaches its climax. Certainly the moral high point of the grandmother's life, her one true spiritual discovery, comes when she finally goes beyond "the peculiar feeling that the bespectacled man was someone she knew" (126) and recognizes him as her own flesh: "'Why you're one of my babies. You're one of my own children!' She reached out and touched him on the shoulder" (132).

This epiphanic moment cannot be sustained or even borne. The Misfit "sprang back as if a snake had bitten him and shot her three times through the chest" (132), reminding us, analogically, of Jesus himself, who "thrown everything off balance" (131). The animals remain in charge here. There is no way out of the woods, indeed "nothing . . . but woods" (131). But there is not only darkness; the spiritual contours in these woods are momentarily glimpsed, even though such discovery means leaving both one's road and one's life: "'She would of been a good woman,' The Misfit said, 'if it had been somebody there to shoot her every minute of her life'" (133). This cryptic utterance has been interpreted in countless ways, but we can hardly miss its relevance to the title of the story; a good person is hard to find because only death and trauma, only murder every minute of our life, is likely to effect the necessary transformation, the kind of violent metamorphosis, that would reveal the spiritual contours of our own fleshly exile. Kafka did something like this when he depicted the fate of Gregor Samsa. But whereas Kafka alters his protagonist in the flesh, O'Connor alters the scene, makes it erupt with violence and cataclysm, actualizes her metaphors, takes her people into the woods, and operates her magic on them there, in order to reconceive the human family and to display our terrible fit within it.

The basic structure of O'Connor's fiction seems inevitably binary, since her abiding theme is the fit between the secular and the spiritual. But the fuller picture she bequeaths us is one of unity, of terrifying mesh. In the stories I have examined no mediating figure is necessary to bring the "collision" into focus; we simply follow the child's adventures in "The River" and the family's fate in "A Good Man Is Hard to Find." The perspective flits back and forth a bit in "The Life You Save May Be Your Own," but there is no Jamesian center of consciousness reflecting on these matters. In some of her most complex work, however, O'Connor entrusts the narration to a commonsensical figure who is demonstrably unequal to the events; the result is a sumptuous interplay of voices and visions, somewhat like that achieved by Melville in "Benito Cereno," in which each perspective makes visible its limits as well as its' authority.

"Good Country People" displays the beginnings of this technique. O'Connor initially complicates her account of Hulga and the Bible salesman by introducing the imperturbable Mrs. Freeman, whose tics and accounts of her daughters Glynese and Carramae add an extraordinary "country" flavor of "white trash" philistinism, pungent observation, and folk humor. Mrs. Free-

man offers a lovely backdrop for the spiritual issues at hand; consider her
report of her daughter's marriage:

> "Carramae said when her and Lyman was married Lyman said it sure felt
> sacred to him. She said he said he wouldn't take five hundred dollars for
> being married by a preacher."
> "How much would he take?" the girl asked from the stove.
> "He said he wouldn't take five hundred dollars," Mrs. Freeman repeated.
> "Well we all have work to do," Mrs. Hopewell said.
> "Lyman said it just felt more sacred to him," Mrs. Freeman said. "The
> doctor wants Carramae to eat prunes. Says instead of medicine. Says them
> cramps is coming from pressure. You know where I think it is."
> "She'll be better in a few weeks," Mrs. Hopewell said.
> "In the tube," Mrs. Freeman said. "Else she wouldn't be as sick as she is."
> (281–82)

There is no other writer who can rival O'Connor for getting across the tone
and vision of this kind of character, and we see the inextricable mix of marriage, ecstasy, money, intestines, and the tube which passes for a certain
country wisdom. Mrs. Freeman is utterly unequipped to perceive a spiritual
happening, and if she did, she would probably consign it to the lower intestine.
But O'Connor is not able at this point to bring this perspective fully to bear
on the story she wants to tell.

That story is about revelation, and it focuses on the one-legged Joy/Hulga,
thirty-two-year-old daughter of Mrs. Hopewell, replete with Ph.D. (in philosophy) and boundless contempt for country people. Hulga, like the Misfit, is
an intellectual, but she is a credentialed intellectual, and, rather than trying to
corner God, she prides herself on being unillusioned and radically self-
sufficient. We recall that Harry/Herbert became Bevul through baptism, and
that transformation entailed bursting through the factitious joke world of
empty words. Joy has done it all on her own, the other way, baptized herself
anew, exerted the power of the Creator by reconceiving herself, flaunting her
control over language and destiny.

> She considered the name her personal affair. She had arrived at it first purely
> on the basis of its ugly sound and then the full genius of its fitness had struck
> her. She had a vision of the name working like the ugly sweating Vulcan who
> stayed in the furnace and to whom, presumably, the goddess had to come
> when called. She saw it as the name of her highest creative act. One of her
> major triumphs was that her mother had not been able to turn her dust into
> Joy, but the greater one was that she had been able to turn it herself into
> Hulga. (275)

Intellectual pride of considerable magnitude is expressed in this yearning for
autogenesis and utter independence. Her university training has taught her
that we live in a perceptual and moral world of our own devising, that we are
free agents equipped with language, able to analyze, able to name. Needless
to say, Hulga's self-confidence is supreme when she elects to toy with the
Bible salesman; she intends to use him as an experiment in sensations. "I don't

even believe in God," she informs him, and she adds, when he urges her to say that she loves him: "In a sense, if you use the word loosely, you might say that. But it's not a word I use. I don't have illusions. I'm one of those people who see *through* to nothing" (287). Just words. Educated people are careful about their terminology, don't use "God" or "love," for they cannot be handled with the scientific precision proper to philosophical reasoning.

But O'Connor has a surprise reserved for Hulga, namely, that she will travel her name in reverse, rebecome Joy for a moment, before being even more thoroughly maimed than before. This story is about control—of the name, the body, and the heart—and O'Connor wants to show how limited and illusory our "ownership" is. It comes about when the salesman, Manley Pointer, asks to see where her wooden leg joins on. The kissing and the sexual excitement have up to now been easily controllable, and her lucidity has never faltered. Now it all changes, and the cerebral "nothing" is blown away, yielding to rapture and fullness:

> The girl uttered a sharp little cry and her face instantly drained of color. The obscenity of the suggestion was not what shocked her. As a child she had sometimes been subject to feelings of shame but education had removed the last traces of that as a good surgeon scrapes for cancer; she would no more have felt it over what he was asking than she would have believed in his Bible. But she was as sensitive about the artificial leg as a peacock about his tail. No one ever touched it but her. She took care of it as someone else would his soul, in private and almost with her own eyes turned away. "No," she said.
>
> "I known it," he muttered, sitting up. "You're just playing me for a sucker."
>
> "Oh no no!" she cried. "It joins on at the knee. Only at the knee. Why do you want to see it?"
>
> The boy gave her a long penetrating look. "Because," he said, "it's what makes you different. You ain't like anybody else."
>
> She sat staring at him. There was nothing about her face or her round freezing-blue eyes to indicate that this had moved her; but she felt as if her heart had stopped and left her mind to pump her blood. She decided that for the first time in her life she was face to face with real innocence. This boy, with an instinct that came from beyond wisdom, had touched the truth about her. When after a minute, she said in a hoarse high voice, "All right," it was like surrendering to him completely. It was like losing her own life and finding it again, miraculously, in his. (288–89)

There is probably no more passionate moment in all of O'Connor's work. The girl is indeed face to face with real innocence, but it is her own innocence, not his. All of her self-sufficiency is gone, and she experiences the mystery of being opened and entered. Like Christ, like Mrs. Shortly in "The Displaced Person," Hulga is to be dismembered before she can be whole. Her helplessness is rendered all the more poignant, of course, because the body is taken literally apart, and the story closes with utmost brutality as the girl's discovery of ecstasy is followed by the boy's cynical act of pillaging. "To take someone's innocence" is an old truism about the loss of virginity, but surely nobody with a Ph.D. believes such clichés anymore. In this freakish story of a country boy stealing an educated woman's leg, O'Connor has fleshed out a parable with the same brilliance that we see in Brueghel's illustration of proverbs. Here, at the close, the world of banal transactions, of intestines and hustlers, turns shimmering with light, yields up its figural meanings, points to events of extraordinary moment. Mrs. Freeman is brought in to close the story, but she never begins to take the measure of what has transpired, although she does achieve, for the reader, a colloquial exit from these garish events. Only in O'Connor's richest and most complex story of all, "The Displaced Person," will the different perspectives finally be orchestrated together into a fully stereophonic fiction.

One of the more striking features of "The Displaced Person" is the poise with which O'Connor interweaves the various stories she has to tell. Mrs. Freeman who is not "quite" white trash reappears here as Mrs. Shortley, and in her interactions with Mrs. McIntyre, the widow who owns the farm, we enjoy once again the rich ore of southern class relations which O'Connor mines with such skill and humor. But Mrs. Shortley is a thoroughly strategic creation, as well as an inherently interesting one in her own right, and she is the person through whom the story comes, from the beginning as she witnesses the arrival of the Guizacs, on to later bouts of downright sleuthing ("She stationed herself at a crack between two boards where she could look out and see him and Mrs. McIntyre strolling toward the turkey brooder . . . " [211]), and continuing right on to her death and beyond, through to the grisly end, in the person of her husband, who has replaced her and picked up a fallen banner. In short, there is a Shortley world established here, replete with values, language, and interests, and O'Connor is at pains to bring it into collision with the strange events that befall the McIntyre farm.

Whereas Mrs. Freeman epitomizes the day-to-day mind and speech habits of "good country people," Mrs. Shortley is a far more formidable creation, a figure of outsized physical and mental proportions, one who has the requisite stature to measure and wage war with the arrivals from across the water. She is a philistine, contemptuous of the softer virtues, devoid of charity, conniving, out for herself and her own; but she is a visionary philistine, and her passionate rendition of events gives this story a rare kind of moral power. O'Connor has drawn her with consummate skill, sketching her as an enormous, prophetlike woman-mountain, yet not forgetting her sexual tastes and her tenderness for her husband. When this woman's large stomach trembles, "it was as if there had been a slight quake in the heart of the mountain" (196), but when her husband does his cigarette-butt-in-the-mouth number, "it nearly drove her wild and every time he did it, she wanted to pull his hat down over his head and hug him to death" (200). Mrs. Shortley has heft, and she also has inner visions, featuring herself as "a giant angel with wings as wide as a house, telling the Negroes they would have to find another place" (200).

Place counts for a great deal here, and the story sets out to measure just how much it does count, just what our connections are with the place we live in. Everyone, it will be seen, yearns for fixity and views his or her bond with the land as natural, but everyone can be, and will be, moved. Guizac comes from Poland to this place, the priest visits it, the Shortleys are trying to stay in it, the blacks may have to leave it, Mrs. McIntyre married into it. This dance of people and place, the dance of displacement, is utterly intolerable and quite deniable because our connection with place seems so established, so constitutive of what we are. "The Displaced Person" is Flannery O'Connor's most profound meditation on regionalism, on what it means to inhabit a particular place, to be part of a particular culture; as such it is also a meditation on history, on what binds people and what separates them, on how they define their identity.

The perspectival strategy of the story is designed to express conflict, the encounter with alterity, and that encounter does all the defining that is necessary. Mrs. Shortley, "the giant wife of the countryside" (194), inaugurates the story by examining the black car driving onto the farm, and then scrutinizing its occupants, "a long-legged black-suited old man with a white hat on and a collar that he wore backwards" (195), followed by the Displaced Person and his family, giving to their onlooker the image "of the three bears, walking single file, with wooden shoes on like Dutchmen and sailor hats and bright coats with a lot of buttons" (195). For Mrs. Shortley their name is Gobblehook. Since the adults don't speak English, Mrs. Shortley wonders if "they'll know what colors even is" (195). These Gobblehooks have escaped from "over there," and we are given a vivid picture of what that escape and what "over there" mean to Mrs. Shortley:

> Mrs. Shortley recalled a newsreel she had seen once of a small room piled high with bodies of dead naked people all in a heap, their arms and legs tangled together, a head thrust in here, a head there, a foot, a knee, a part that should have been covered up sticking out, a hand raised clutching nothing. Before you could realize that it was real and take it into your head, the picture changed and a hollow-sounding voice was saying, "Time marches on!" This was the kind of thing that was happening every day in Europe where they had not advanced as in this country, and watching from her vantage point, Mrs. Shortley had the sudden intuition that the Gobblehooks, like rats with typhoid fleas, could have carried all those murderous ways over the water with them directly to this place. If they had come from where that kind of thing was done to them, who was to say they were not the kind that would also do it to others? (196)

America the Beautiful is on show in this extraordinary passage: the butchery of the camps is registered as something indecorous and obscene, what you might expect "over there," "where they had not advanced as in this country," and the proper response is to view these escapees as diseased, as carriers of a pestilence they might infect us with.

It has been thought that O'Connor's sense of history is strictly eschatological, that the fullness of time and space she ushers into the lives of her people is fundamentally biblical; and, given what we know of her southerners astray in the North, there seems to be an undeniable regional *parti pris* in her work, a suspicion of the world beyond Milledgeville. But genocide comes to Georgia in these lines depicting Mrs. Shortley's vision, and the reader is stunned, both by the haunting picture of body parts crammed into a room and by the xenophobic reaction to it. Those who consider Flannery O'Connor a local colorist would do well to reread "The Displaced Person," because it ranks, once again, with Melville's "Benito Cereno" as a definitive portrait of Americans caught in a world they do not understand, of how we must suffer through to knowledge. Captain Delano never does grasp the full meaning of the conflict between the blacks and the Spaniards on board that ship, but the Shortleys are destined to drain the full cup of "displacement" as the common fate. World War II and Catholicism seem equally exotic and abhorrent to Mrs. Shortley, unrelated to the everyday issues of life, just as the mention of Christ in conversation embarrasses Mrs. McIntyre "the way sex had her mother" (225). But the bigger world cannot be kept out, and the familiar "country" pragmatism, the no-nonsense perspective that regards the peacock with its wondrous tail where "tiers of small pregnant suns floated in a green-gold haze" (226) as just "another mouth to feed" (198), is to be found wanting, for it misses the fuller scene, not only as it is imaged in creatures but also as it is enacted in front of one's eyes. Here, as O'Connor does in everything she writes, she displays the larger stage on which events transpire, and she teaches us to hear the full resonance and see the extended reach of her regional materials.

To acquire that fuller view can be, as the grandmother learns, lethal. We fight to maintain the same way of looking, the same way of talking. Wars have never been fought about anything else. Thus, it is entirely apt that Mrs. Shortley envisions her conflict with the Guizacs as a battle over language:

> She began to imagine a war of words, to see the Polish words and the English words coming at each other, stalking forward, not sentences, just words, gabble gabble gabble, flung out high and shrill and stalking forward and then grappling with each other. She saw the Polish words, dirty and all-knowing and unreformed, flinging mud on the clean English words until everything was equally dirty. She saw them all piled up in a room, all the dirty words, theirs and hers too, piled up like the naked bodies in the newsreel. God save me, she cried silently, from the stinking power of Satan! And she started from that day to read her Bible with a new attention. She poured over the Apocalypse and began to quote from the Prophets and before long she had come to a deeper understanding of her existence. (209)

The spectacle of the words stalking forward, gabbling, grappling with one another, beautifully images the conflict of cultures (filth, purity, truth) as a linguistic transaction. The beliefs for which we live and die turn out to be verbal, and Mrs. Shortley takes refuge in narrative, in the Bible, in Apocalypse for appropriate fables that would give shape to her dilemma and her special role within it. The Book may teach us something about the shape of our lives, but it must be in our own language if we are to take heed. The Polish Bible wars with the English one. Language emerges as the bedrock of cultural identity here, and it clearly cuts deeper than color. According to Mr. Shortley, China and Africa are all right to visit, because we know immediately about the differences; but in other places, where we've let "all them people onto English" (233), there is nothing but trouble. Guizac is aligned with the German enemy, the monolithic lingual alien from "over there," and Mr. Shortley is finding that the war still isn't over: "Gone over there and fought and bled and died and come back on over here and find out who's got my job—just exactly who I been fighting. It was a hand-grenade come that near to killing me and I seen who throwed it—little man with eye-glasses just like his. Might have bought them at the same store. Small world . . . " (232).

Opposed to this lingual and cultural impasse is the common ground on which stand the Georgians, both black and white. And that ground is astonishingly verbal as well. Nothing is more indicative of the verbal fabric of commonality than the way in which the Shortleys and the blacks carefully dish up to Mrs. McIntyre the words and phrases that are her legacy and identity. These utterances are, of course, not hers at all, since most of them come from the Judge, and they are shown in the story to be lingua franca, the currency and cement of cultural cohesiveness. "Judge say the devil he know is better than the devil he don't" is more than a comment about the Other as devil; it is also a bond with Mrs. McIntyre's past, just as "We seen them come and we seen them go" asserts Astor's tenure at the farm and his unstatable but genuine legitimacy there, in contrast to the Guizacs. The most explicit instancing of community through language is doubtless offered by Astor's policy of sporadic soliloquies under Mrs. McIntyre's window, consisting of countdowns on her peacocks and her husbands: "I remember when it was twenty of you walking about this place and now it's only you and two hens. Crooms it was twelve. McIntyre it was five. You and two hens now" (217). We see here a confederacy that Guizac and the priest can never vanquish or penetrate, but we also note, as the passage itself flaunts, the diminished and diminishing character of the bond. The peacocks are disappearing, and the husbands are gone. The story reveals the passing of an order, and there is a distinct elegiac underlay to its gruesome events. Things and people become obsolescent, are undone by the passage of time. The tractor has replaced the mule. The Guizacs bid to replace the blacks. There is something almost Darwinian in this picture of a lazy rural way of life having to shape up, having to put up or shut up when it finally meets efficiency and cost-effectiveness in the person of Guizac, having to take in the horrors of war-torn Europe and the "overflow" of displaced persons that reaches even Georgia. O'Connor has taken a wide-angled look at that so-called larger world, and she has given us a memorable tableau of its many points of intersection with the people and the paradigms among which she lives.

These people are encountering displacement. Guizac-Gobblehook, willing to work and to marry his cousin to a black, is estrangement in person for this community: he has been uprooted from whatever life he knew, and his arrival causes more of the same. What is a displaced person? "It means," Mrs. Shortley explains to Astor, "they ain't where they were born at and there's nowhere for them to go—like if you were run out of here and wouldn't nobody have you" (198). At the very end of the story Mr. Shortley "left without notice to look for a new position and the Negro, Sulk, was taken with a sudden desire to see more of the world and set off for the southern part of the state" (235). But the other departures are less voluntary. Upon overhearing that she and her husband are to be given notice, Mrs. Shortley, her face "an almost volcanic red," elects to clear out. Her exodus from the farm is an unmistakable replay of the Guizacs' expulsion from Poland, and she finally experiences, from the inside this time (something that has been rigorously avoided throughout the story), what it feels like to be torn apart:

> Fierce heat seemed to be swelling slowly and fully into her face as if it were welling up now for a final assault. She was sitting in an erect way in spite of the fact that one leg was twisted under her and one knee was almost into her neck, but there was a peculiar lack of light in her icy blue eyes. All the vision in them might have been turned around, looking inside her. She suddenly grabbed Mr. Shortley's elbow and Sarah Mae's foot at the same time and began to tug and pull on them as if she were trying to fit the two extra limbs onto herself.
>
> Mr. Shortley began to curse and quickly stopped the car and Sarah Mae yelled to quit but Mrs. Shortley apparently intended to rearrange the whole car at once. She thrashed forward and backward, clutching at everything she could get her hands on and hugging it to herself, Mr. Shortley's head, Sarah Mae's leg, the cat, a wad of white bedding, her own big moon-like knee; then all at once her fierce expression faded into a look of astonishment and her grip on what she had loosened. One of her eyes drew near to the other and seemed to collapse quietly and she was still. (213–14)

The volcanic explosion, that "overflow," has finally come, and it is in the nature of an intense, killing inner vision. Mrs. Shortley — one leg twisted under her, a knee into her neck, tugging and pulling on Mr. Shortley's elbow and Sarah Mae's foot — is Guizac; she has finally understood alterity in the only way that it is understood: she has become the Other, to the extent of entering the camps, moving into the newsreel so as to be finally inside that "small room piled high with bodies of dead naked people all in a heap, their arms and legs tangled together, a head thrust in here, a head there, a foot, a knee, a part that should have been covered up sticking out, a hand raised clutching nothing." The story of displacement, she now knows, is a story of dismemberment; like Christ and other sacrificial figures who have been taken apart, Mrs. Shortley must be fissured before she can be whole, must be pieced apart before she can make her journey, a voyage even greater than that of Guizac from Poland to Georgia: "Her huge body rolled back still against the seat and her eyes like blue-painted glass, seemed to contemplate for the first time the tremendous frontiers of her true country" (214).

This "true country" suggests a homeland and a birthright beyond Georgia. Guizac will also be torn into pieces, but we have no indication that he moves into a promised land. Christ, we are told, "was just another D.P." (229), and he, too, informed people that the turf they were walking on was neither stable nor their own; he, too, was in some sense an alien bringing tidings of dispossession, making it hard for people to be at home in the places where they had ruled, bringing displacement. Eliot's Magi sound the same plaint: "We returned to our places, these Kingdoms, / But no longer at ease here, in the old dispensation, / With an alien people clutching their gods. / I should be glad of another death."[15] The final displacement is, of course, that of Mrs. McIntyre, the veteran survivor who has participated in a drama more far-reaching than any of her dealings with husbands, blacks, and hired hands; her "removal" follows hard on the death of Guizac, as she uncomprehendingly watches him receiving the final sacraments and then begins to exit her own, hitherto familiar life: "She felt she was in some foreign country where the people bent over the body were natives, and she watched like a stranger while the dead man was carried away in the ambulance" (235). O'Connor relentlessly removes her "belongings": her cows, use of her limbs, eyesight, voice. She too becomes the displaced, bereft of Guizac, stripped to nothing, abandoned by all except the priest, who visits weekly and sits by the side of her bed and explains the doctrines of the church.[16]

It is a fierce and uncompromising story, as ferocious a critique of self-sufficiency and hardness of heart in its own way as *King Lear*. It seems to be saying that the body must be both uprooted and dismembered before the spirit can be made whole. The lesson is a severe one. But it also expresses a yearning for wholeness in the flesh, as Mrs. Shortley fathoms in her vision: "She stood there, tottering slightly but still upright, her eyes shut tight and her fists clenched and her straw sun hat low on her forehead. 'The children of wicked nations will be butchered,' she said in a loud voice. 'Legs where arms should be, foot to face, ear in the palm of hand. Who will remain whole? Who will remain whole? Who?'" (210). The answer is: those who suffer to the point of transfiguration. Can it be incidental that Guizac's "whole face looked as if it might have been patched together out of several others" (222) or that Mrs. Shortley's final gestures, in the throes of death, are profoundly "connective"? "She suddenly grabbed Mr. Shortley's elbow and Sarah Mae's foot at the same time and began to tug and pull on them as if she were trying to fit the two extra limbs onto herself." The response to being dismembered is to create a whole body out of separate parts. That is also the only conceivable act that is commensurate with displacement. "To fit the two extra limbs onto" oneself is to redefine the human self and the human family. That act of assimilation stems from a sense of connectedness that is so visceral as to be organic. The overlapping ventures of separateness and turf protection which are the base of this story can be transcended only through a generosity of spirit that can see sameness beyond difference, family beyond self, community beyond the individual. And, ultimately, "beyond" is the wrong word; "in" is what is needed: to see like *in* unlike, to see spirit *in* matter, to see Great Events *in* local anecdotes.

Such double vision can be brought about only by the canniest use of language, the fashioning of a verbal strategy that respects discrete particulars while never losing sight of universals. Such an art form will yoke together the apparently dissimilar and will thereby produce dissonance and the grotesque on the surface while achieving a larger harmony and consonance in the depths, attaining that realism in the distance which is O'Connor's stated goal. The anarchic self-sufficiency of words and their limited reference must be overcome, liberated into a fuller marriage of meanings. Mrs. Shortley's vision exposes the problem: "She began to imagine a war of words, to see the Polish words and the English words coming at each other, stalking forward, not sentences, just words, gabble gabble gabble, flung out high and shrill and stalking forward and then grappling with each other" (209). This privatist, regionalist linguistics must be overcome because it expresses the place-bound, ego-centered "I" that shuns connection and fears alterity. Death is, of course, one solution to the problem: death yields a vision of solidarity in this story. But language and art may provide another way of expanding vistas, of creating vistas. The larger verbal home can be fashioned by means of a text that brings the camps into Georgia, brings galaxies into the tail of the peacock, brings the dismemberment and fate of Christ into the affairs of Gobblehook on the farm. Displacement is traditionally thought to be the strategy of the psyche that works under cover, that censors its desires, that disguises its agenda in a culturally acceptable form. Here, on the contrary, all is revealed, all becomes revelation. Flannery O'Connor's is an art of displacement, for it fuses the story of the ploughman with that of the boy falling from the sky, thereby showing that the story of the soul is as much "at home" in rural Georgia as it might be in some *musée des beaux arts*.

IV

THE AMERICAN
MODERNISTS AND
FREEDOM OF SPEECH

7

Fitzgerald's *Great Gatsby*: Fiction as Greatness

In a study of self-making and freedom of speech in American fiction, *The Great Gatsby* stands inevitably as a sort of flagship in the armada, and if it sinks, the whole fleet deserves to go down. Fitzgerald's text picks up all the strands of this study: the crafting of identity as demiurgic activity, the American scheme of self-worth in terms of documentation and material possessions, the play of desire as maneuvering room for the American subject, the pivotal role of language as instrument of assertion, and, most crucially and most underrecognized, the mysterious nature of *belief*—the sustaining and actualizing forces that make us real to one another, that marshal our energies and affections, that fuel the very system of free enterprise, that underlie the transformation from Nobody to somebody, that keep the fleet afloat. Credit itself, the sort of thing that sustains Donald Trumps and Jay Gatsbys, means belief.

More than half a century after its publication, *The Great Gatsby* is still a vexed case, seen variously as a portrait of the twenties, a picture of the American Dream that is at once lyrical and critical, and an example of point-of-view narrative that draws shrewdly on James and Conrad.[1] All these things Fitzgerald does, no one would deny; what is vexing is what to make of them. Is the novel ultimately a critique of either Gatsby or his dream? What, ultimately, does Nick Carraway or the reader learn? Finally, what does the greatness of Gatsby and of Fitzgerald's novel consist of? It may well be that such ultimacies are themselves readerly myths, in that art rarely treats us to these bottom-line handouts of knowledge and truth. Yet, readers have always felt that Fitzgerald's book is telling us something vital about American culture, and that we must somehow plumb his vision, transform his fable into some kind of workable assessments and critical notions that might help us to see—both our society and ourselves—better.

In looking at Fitzgerald criticism, one frequently discerns a certain petulance: Gatsby's dream itself is thought, especially in an age of ideological awareness and political conscientiousness, to be so meretricious and vulgar, why all the ado? Nick himself, our arbiter in this matter, often seems too smug on the one hand ("I am one of the few honest people that I have ever known") and too conniving on the other (Jordan Baker's not-so-broad hint at the book's close). Or else, in the more sweeping variety of "correct" readings, Fitzgerald the author comes up short, unable to see through his tinsel materials, unable to sort out his ironies, unable to curb his rhetoric. With hindsight the book seems to be imbued with excess: the tawdry materialism of the Flapper Age, the wild parties, the flashy and not-so-flashy possessions of Gatsby, the excesses of capitalism, the sentimental and blinding excesses of the rags-to-riches story itself, the American Dream. It is in this light that *Gatsby* criticism often seems to dig its heels in, roll up its sleeves, and do what it loves best: to perform *analysis*, that is, to reveal, for the eye-opening benefit of those readers who may have been taken in, these puffed-up appearances and myths for what they truly are — spurious, specious and inflated. The critical act itself, practiced in all our disciplines, seems imaged here: to see through, to become undeceived, to deflate, to deconstruct. Fitzgerald criticism, even more than most, is marked by the moral fervor of exposure and judgment.[2]

On the face of it, indeed, *The Great Gatsby* falls into the nineteenth-century tradition of "great expectations" and "lost illusions," as two of its greatest exemplars termed it. Such a fiction chronicles the lure of worldly success and the gradual education of the hero as he comes to measure the moral cost involved in secular achievement. The focus of such texts is quintessentially critical, as Pip, Lucien and Rastignac, and their followers encounter and expose the rottenness of social systems, and hence the *illusory* nature of any triumph within that context. Nick Carraway begins the narration of *Gatsby* in a posture much like that of Pip as he finishes his narrative: he has seen — and seen through — the parade and pretensions of high society, and he returns to the Midwest, where principles might still be found. "Conduct may be founded on the hard rock or the wet marshes, but after a certain point I don't care what it's founded on. When I came back from the East last autumn I felt that I wanted the world to be in uniform and at a sort of moral attention forever."[3] The figurative gesture of peering behind or beneath appearances, zeroing in on the "foundation," can in fact be recognized as the fundamental realist act.

It is worth passing a minute with this critical metaphor of examining foundations. One thinks of Mrs. Eberhardt whom Myrtle Wilson mentions at her party, Mrs. Eberhardt who "goes around looking at people's feet in their own homes" (31). The "base" for Gatsby's show, we already suspect, is not going to bear much looking into. Thus, Nick Carraway is at the outset appropriately *dis*enchanted, *dis*illusioned, for the grand pageantry has been exposed for a very small and mean operation. Seeing clear is crucially linked, in this critical tradition, to deflation, to trimming down to size. Dickens calls Pip's expectations "great," just as Renoir titles the illusion of his film "grande"; we see a recurring feature of realism in this movement from large appearances to *small* explanations. As I have suggested, a good deal of *Gatsby* criticism works along these lines: the critic begins work, if you will, on July fifth, just as Nick listed the names of those who came to Gatsby's parties on an old timetable of July 5, 1922, and metaphorically sizes up the damage done the night before. Things always look smaller, less glamorous, on July fifth because the magic, the *Rausch,* is over, the grand and ecstatic moments of the party are now, in the harsh light of day, lesser propositions, not to say embarrassments. Criticism deflates, exposes, shows the ugly underpinnings that support the show. Nick expresses the sobering effect of such an education in graphic terms: his stint with Gatsby and Co. is akin to his carefree twenties, indeed the entire nation's twenties; but now he is thirty, and one can hardly avoid thinking of the Great Depression waiting in the wings, the American thirties, here: "Thirty—the promise of a decade of loneliness, a thinning list of single men to know, a thinning briefcase of enthusiasm, thinning hair" (136). "Thinning" betokens the same shrinkage that July fifth brings, and the question that must be posed here is: Is Gatsby still great once the novel is over? What, if anything, remains of the party once it is over? How thin does it get?[4]

There can be little doubt that Gatsby appears dreadfully exposed in his own underpinnings. Surely the thinnest, barest document in the novel is the pathetic SCHEDULE on the flyleaf of *Hopalong Cassidy* which graphically spells out the young Gatz's program for success, including exhortations such as "Practice elocution, poise and how to attain it" and "Read one improving book or magazine per week" (174). Here is the meanest prop of all, a July fifth document if ever one existed, the vulgar, irreducible blueprint underlying Gatsby's fabulous career, a humble and humbling Fitzgeraldian *Ding an sich* which emerges at the novel's close. In its factual, evidential status, as ultimate as an X ray, this SCHEDULE wrings the neck of fiction and glamour, showing it all to be no more than a con game. One imagines Tom Buchanan's glee in the face of such a document, the final demystification of Gatsby, brought back at last to his lowly origins. Let Gatsby be pegged as no more than the outgrowth of his SCHEDULE, and immediately an edifying congruence is revealed between first stages and last stages, origins and destiny, illuminating the kind of causality achieved by centripetal thinking, homing in on the hidden source, moving mercilessly from the grand circumference back to the pitiful center: Jay Gatsby and his mansion exposed as Jimmy Gatz and his SCHEDULE.

But of course, that is not *The Great Gatsby,* or more precisely, it is *Gatsby* in reverse. The living truth of the novel is centrifugal rather than centripetal, projected outward rather than homing in, generating reality rather than proving it, invested in a "fattening" rather than a "thinning" enterprise, dedicated to the heroic cause of making July fifth rival with July fourth, the chronicle of the dream thereby capturing its enduring beauty and magic, its "elusive rhythm," as well as displaying the "foul dust [that] floated in the wake" (2). I share Hugh Kenner's conviction that Nick Carraway's role is not so much to critique Gatsby as to preserve him, that, in Kenner's words, "a man hard to convince shall have been convinced of his worth," because, as Kenner concludes, "it is important, in short, that Gatsby shall be Great. It is important because the central myth of the Book has to do with Appearance made Real by sheer will: the oldest American theme of all."[5]

It is doubtful whether Americans have a monopoly on that particular theme, but Fitzgerald's book is peculiarly modern in its focus on belief rather than truth. Ford Madox Ford, in a different book entirely devoted to the dismantling of illusions, expressed the nostalgic hope that beauty is not destructible, even though destruction is real, that the dream continues strangely to live even if it has been wholly discredited: "You can't kill a minuet de la coeur. You may shut up the music-book, close the harpsichord; in the cupboard and presses the rats may destroy the white satin favors. The mob may sack Versailles; the Trianon may fall, but surely the minuet—the minuet itself is dancing itself away into the furthest stars. . . ."[6] Fitzgerald's interest, I think, is in that minuet that can't be killed. His book stands, then, on the far side of the divide marked by Balzac and Dickens; exposure and education are their central purposes, whereas *Gatsby* is about the power of belief. In that light the death of Goriot is radically different from that of Gatsby: Balzac's figure dies so that all can witness the collapse of an ethos, but Gatsby's death is, in words he himself applied to Daisy's love for her husband, "just personal," in no way affecting his potency as a figure, a legend, an image.

Images, more than minuets, may be said to have a life of their own. They certainly appear to do so in *The Great Gatsby*. It is no accident that Henry Gatz so treasures the *photograph* of his son's house that it seems "more real to him now than the house itself" (173). The so-called "real thing" can hardly compete with its representations, the constructs of desire; hence, a green light on a dock can embody and figure forth all of Gatsby's longing, but such magic, as Gatsby is tragically to learn, can have no truck with real people. Reunited with Daisy, Gatsby realizes that "it was again a green light on a dock. His count of enchanted objects had diminished by one" (94). Gatsby himself senses that the flesh-and-blood Daisy cannot measure up to the image he has made of her: "There must have been moments even that afternoon when Daisy tumbled short of his dream—not through her own fault, but because of the colossal vitality of his illusion. It had gone beyond her, beyond everything. He had thrown himself into it with a creative passion, adding to it all the time, decking it out with every bright feather that drifted his way. No amount of fire or freshness can challenge what a man can store up in his ghostly heart" (97). In responding to such a passage we are at a very real critical crossroads. To be sure, Fitzgerald is not shying away from the theme of disappointment, but his ultimate game, I think, is the bigger game of belief and fantasy. Gatsby, even knowing that Daisy is incommensurate with the dream, goes on, and much of the novel's pathos hinges on his efforts to remake the world, the past, to fashion a reality of his own that would correspond to the dream. Whereas a writer such as Flaubert is corrosive when it comes to dreams and hyperbole, Fitzgerald's subject is more truly that of creation rather than deflation. Note the sense of magnitude expressed in that passage: "colossal," "beyond her, beyond everything," and finally, we are told that the "ghostly heart" outrivals matter, that it generates and stores up visions to which flesh and blood and things cannot measure up.

The mean, phenomenal world of flesh, blood, and things is ultimately of interest to the writer only to the extent that it can be transformed into "enchanted objects." Even the most debunking literature gets an unavowable mileage out of enchantment. The scalpel-like probing and lucidity of Flaubert and Joyce depend, parasitically, on the prior energies of belief: Emma and

Frédéric and Félicité, Stephen in *Portrait of the Artist* and all the huffers and puffers of *Ulysses* are so many entryways through which the indispensable stuff of dreams can be freighted into the work. Indispensable because the "after" critique feeds on a "before" illusion, just as getting thin hardly makes sense if you haven't been fat; but indispensable also because literature has always known itself to have common cause with illusion, has always taken con men like Gatsby to its bosom because they have been the truest apostles. Whereas the realist mission is "to show things as they are," Fitzgerald seems altogether more committed to the project of making things from nothing. Daisy does not measure up because Gatsby's dream cannot be outfitted with checks and balances, or any kind of external referent; it is instead supremely autonomous, autogenerative, fed from within.

The larger thesis I want to develop is that the notion of making something from nothing, or in Kenner's words "appearance made real," is not only an American theme but also a paradigmatic formula for literature itself. *The Great Gatsby* depicts things being made from nothing, and objects becoming enchanted objects. Both these operations depend, quite simply, on belief. Nothing in the novel is more endowed with this magic power than Daisy's voice. Everyone remembers Gatsby's own definition of that voice: "Her voice is full of money" (120), and money has long been seen as the central magic in Fitzgerald's scheme. We know as well the famous exchange between Fitzgerald and Hemingway: "The rich are not as we are"; "No, they have more money."[7] The Hemingway rejoinder has always been seen as the realist deflation of Fitzgerald's infatuation, but once we think about it, money itself is the archetypal semiotic launch pad, uninteresting in its material thingness but endlessly potent as the source of dreams. A voice full of money tells us that speech is also the currency of desire. In Daisy's voice Fitzgerald finds a miraculous equivalent to the dream, something beyond disenchantment: "I think that voice held him most, with its fluctuating, feverish warmth, because it couldn't be overdreamed—that voice was a deathless song" (97). Daisy's voice is a veritable siren song, enchanting all men who come her way, Tom and Nick as well as Gatsby, and we would do well to attend to it, indeed, as voice, as language: "Daisy began to sing with the music in a husky, rhythmic whisper, bringing out a meaning in each word that it had never had before and would never have again. When the melody rose her voice broke up sweetly, following it, in a way contralto voices have, and each change tipped out a little of her warm human magic upon the air" (109). This voice, which "men who had cared for her found difficult to forget" (9), transforms the world in a remarkable way: its magic is equated with new meanings, meanings never before seen and never to be seen again. Daisy's voice has the promise of genesis, of making things anew. Daisy's voice points us to a world of dazzling freshness and mobility, a world responsive to our will, unbound by old definitions and dispensations. Daisy's voice announces a narrative program of remarkable dimensions, outfitted with a language of full potency, capable of metamorphosing the objects it names. This is to be Fitzgerald's New World, and it is also his book.

Thus, the characters and setting in *The Great Gatsby* are oddly maneuverable, alterable. In this realm the World Series is quite naturally "fixable" and alterable rather than given. The dog bought by Tom for Myrtle Wilson is significantly both a boy and a bitch, and at Myrtle's party everything seems to be strangely fluid: people's names seem especially up for grabs, as Nick tries to read a chapter of *Simon Called Peter*. Myrtle's sister Catherine is "said to be very beautiful by people who ought to know" (28), much as they "say [Gatsby is] a nephew or a cousin of Kaiser Wilhelm's" (33). Note that "saying" is enough here, is a sufficient warrant for truth. The entire party has a theatrical, improvisational dimension; characters seem to be posing, as if Mr. McKee, who is in the "artistic game," were going to photograph them. Things are strangely malleable here, so that the tapestried furniture, with its "scenes of ladies swinging in the gardens of Versailles," seems to spawn a new Myrtle Wilson, one whose "personality had also undergone a change," and whose vitality "was converted into impressive *hauteur*" (30–31). Anything can happen in these precincts, just as Nick claimed of Fifth Avenue that he "wouldn't have been surprised to see a great flock of white sheep turn the corner" (28). There is a "musical chairs" element to *The Great Gatsby*, and at critical junctures Myrtle Wilson will mistake Jordan for Daisy, and Gatsby will be fatally mistaken for the driver of the car, just as the party will predictably go to and from New York in swapped automobiles.

One might argue, feebly I think, that the plot requires some of these confusions, but we will be on firmer ground if we acknowledge that *The Great Gatsby* has a bizarre ludic quality, that its materials refuse to stay put, that Fitzgerald, in pirouetting his materials, is doing pretty much the same kind of thing that he ascribed to Daisy's voice: "bringing out a meaning in each word that it had never had before and would never have again." The mean phenomenal world can be altered. As the song intones "I'm the sheik of Araby," we sense a yearning for metamorphosis as well as romance, an opening onto nominal adventures and purchases that dizzily extend the singer/signer. Innocent prose reveals odd linkages and twinning: "We backed up to a grey old man who bore an absurd resemblance to John D. Rockefeller" (27).[8] Just as some chemicals, when brought to a certain temperature, decompose and change form, so does Daisy become catalyzed by the New York heat: "We'll meet you on some corner. I'll be the man smoking two cigarettes" (126). None of these passages has any literal truth, nor do they further the plot; but they are indexes of the novel's figurative activity, of the play of metaphor and masquerade, of self-projection and self-creation, which are at the heart of the book. To be free from the constraints of proof or evidence, to alter one's identity, to be multiple rather than single, to overcome the laws of time and space and background: such are, Fitzgerald wants to tell us, precisely the virtues of fiction. How can we not see, at the same time, that they are the central articles of the American Dream, and that they make possible Jay Gatsby?

All the items just named involve the creation of belief, the making of something from nothing, the sovereign power of language and imagination over against the paltriness and inertness of evidence. Gatsby is the consummate hero of belief: his belief in Daisy, in the green light, is of such a magnitude as to make and to move worlds; no less important is others' belief in him. It is possible to regard Fitzgerald's novel as a willed experiment in semiosis, the ways in which meaning is produced and belief established. This text is especially illuminating from this point of view because it spews forth signifiers, sometimes as metaphors, sometimes as lies, sometimes just as an exercise in dissemination; but its secret truth is that there is no truth, no reliable referent, no fixed center to which the signifiers point, no foundation ultimately worth checking out. Fitzgerald has discovered that the secret of the self-made man is hardly a secret for the novelist, for such a man is preeminently made of words rather than flesh and thus heir to a peculiar freedom which flouts all constraints.

And what is the American Dream if not a limitless freedom of the sign?[9] The American Dream, like Daisy's voice, may be confused with money, but it is ultimately an exhilarating kind of liberty which deifies the individual will and either transcends or erases all its obstacles. The American, more than most, dreams of being freed from his or her origin, so as to make his or her self and world in an endless process of generative activity. Thus, that "green breast of the new world" which the Dutch sailors saw, like the "pap of life" and the "incomparable milk of wonder" which Gatsby sucked and gulped, are Edenic in their promise that desire and reality shall be one, that "fiction" and "fact" shall be coerced into a new etymological unity as *made* things, subservient to human will. In this dream, as perhaps in all dreams, the word produces the deed, the desire forges the object, the imagination makes the world. Desire and will are entirely potent here, capable of producing their own artifacts and setting up their own regime. Not only is the traditional bugbear of social origin transcended, but, in the process, all impediments to self-enactment are removed. This New World is a Sorcerer's Apprentice world in which naming something brings it into existence, in which the signifier is endlessly potent. Granting some exaggerations, such is the ontology of the American Dream; it is also the modus operandi of the con man and the writer, specialists as well in passing off the word for the thing itself, dependent on belief for whatever success they are to enjoy.

We have come at last, although obliquely, to Gatsby, and this is as it should be, since no single path leads to him, no single past has produced him. Like the ancient gods for whose birth multiple legends can be found, so Gatsby is at once "a nephew or a cousin to Kaiser Wilhelm's," "a German spy during the war," "an Oxford man," "a bootlegger," "a person who killed a man." Mysterious, elusive, multiple, "Mr. Nobody from Nowhere," Gatsby has no single referent. He is not there when you look for him, and mysteriously present when least expected, such as in Nick's first encounter, or when Nick arranges his meeting with Daisy. He seems endlessly replicated and mirrored in the text, and there is something apt in Daisy's admiring claim: "'You resemble the advertisement of the man,' she went on innocently. 'You know the advertisement of the man—'" (119). Likewise, when Tom Buchanan announces that he has "made a small investigation of this fellow," Jordan's humorous reaction seems closer to the poetic truth: "Do you mean you've been to a medium?" (122). Jordan, as we shall see, is close to the mark in pointing us to the spirit world if we want to find Gatsby's origins.[10]

It is in this light that the delayed disclosure of Jimmy Gatz and his SCHEDULE must be seen as essentially a foil, the mockery of an origin. To be sure, the "young roughneck" that Nick sees derives biologically from Mr. and Mrs. Henry Gatz, just as James Gatz was "really, or at least legally, his name" (98). The search for origins, which is a hallmark of realist fiction (and the grounded self, and traditional societies, and much else), is not absent from this novel, but it is rendered quaint and peripheral; it is quite simply upstaged by the dazzling appearances, the performance of Gatsby as persona, and the impact he has on others. The book itself is a testimonial to his enduring reality, and Nick invariably identifies Gatsby with the future: his "heightened sensitivity to the promises of life," his "extraordinary gift for hope," his "romantic readiness." Even in the most literal sense Gatsby cannot be pinned down: "He was never quite still; there was always a tapping foot somewhere or the impatient opening and closing of a hand" (64).

And there is the matter of his smile. Like Daisy's voice, Gatsby's smile is infinitely seductive, for it projects the archetypal magic fable to which we never fail to respond: it serves us up our own "rounded" life, confirmed. Here, too, Gatsby's business is with the future, a future for us, one that we like. Gatsby's smile is truly generative, "constituting" not so much himself as "you": "It was one of those rare smiles with a quality of eternal reassurance in it, that you may come across four or five times in life. . . . It understood you just so far as you wanted to be understood, believed in you as you would like to believe in yourself, and assured you that it had precisely the impression of you that, at your best, you hoped to convey" (48). This smile is a triumph of *making*, a mutual confirmation that our daily acts of personal genesis have succeeded, have carried the day. It is also a social contract, not so terribly different (despite appearances) from the larger one articulated by Rousseau; both have to do with responsibilities, and both issue from writers with a profound sense of anxiety and precariousness, a deep knowledge of how much balm recognition confers. It is easy to lower the critical boom here, to highlight such a passage in terms of bad faith and complicity, but we would do well to ponder the enabling generosity at work here, the well-nigh ontological energies in play. Gatsby embodies the power of belief. He extends it to others, and he exists only insofar as they extend it to him. Belief, as I have repeatedly said, does not require evidence or proof or referent or origin. The believer makes his own world, and that is what Gatsby has done: "His parents were shiftless and unsuccessful farm people—his imagination had never really accepted them as his parents at all. The truth was that Jay Gatsby of West Egg, Long Island, sprang from his Platonic conception of himself" (99). There is doubtless no more perfect piece of Americana in all of literature. Horatio Alger, rags-to-riches, the American Dream, upward mobility: it is all there. Fitzgerald has grasped the immensity of the American cliché the self-made man, and he has properly understood it to be a spiritual, even an artisanal phenomenon, every bit as much as an economic statement. Yet we who are positioned outside this text know that self-made men are cluttering the offices of analysts and doctors all over the United States, looking backward, often painfully, to determine where in fact they came from. Gatsby, as we also know, finished up supine as well, lying afloat in a pool, abandoned by all except Nick Carraway. We know, finally, that Gatsby's exploits are even a bit darker than those of con men, that his shady dealings and obsession with power mirror some of the most diseased aspects of the American psyche and culture. Ultimately, one must also ask just how far fiction can take us, at what point the world of fact and referent finally catches up to the high-flying gold-hatted imagination that longs to make its own world.

The Great Gatsby is great, I think, because it is willing to hint, more than once, that fiction just might take us all the way. This book is, from beginning to end, despite its revelations and wary narrator, committed to the power of the dream, or more precisely and more to the point, to the power of fiction. It is now time to substantiate this claim by looking at some central passages that depict the complex war between fact and fiction. Let us begin with Gatsby's own impassioned statement or origin to Nick: "'I'll tell you God's truth.' His right hand suddenly ordered divine retribution to stand by. 'I am the son of some wealthy people in the Middle West—all dead now. I was brought up in America but educated at Oxford, because all my ancestors have been educated there for many years. It is a family tradition'" (65). This sequence begins right at the top, as God, the final guarantor of all utterances, the one who separates the true from the false, is invoked as authority. God's truth would be pure referent, and Gatsby's speech act would be totally at one with its meaning, so much so that divine retribution is standing by to punish any and all discrepancies between language and truth. This assurance of verbal legitimacy has, as its social cohorts, "all my ancestors," "family tradition," and Oxford itself, all venerable displays of origin, all respected emissaries of the Old World. Now, my argument all along has been that Fitzgerald is depicting a New World, one that dispenses with those fixed entities and either invents or projects its own data. Nick indeed suspects that Gatsby's claim is spurious:

> "What part of the Middle West?" I enquired casually.
> "San Francisco."
> "I see."
> "My family all died and I came into a good deal of money."
> His voice was solemn, as if the memory of that sudden extinction of a clan still haunted him. (65–66)

One hardly knows what to admire most here: Gatsby's answer of San Francisco or Nick's assent, " I see." Where is God's truth here? For there is a choice. Either this is outright balderdash, part of Gatsby's flimflam, the sort of thing we would expect from a bootlegger; or this just may be, on some level, real if not true. Or true if not real. Nick's "I see" functions a bit like Gatsby's smile, and it opens just the tiniest bit of space for squeezing San Francisco into the Midwest, but a very special map will be needed for this, a new dispensation altogether. The more Gatsby talks—and he talks very little in this book—the more extravagant and overtly fictive he becomes: "After that I lived like a young rajah in all the capitals of Europe—Paris, Venice, Rome—collecting jewels, chiefly rubies, hunting big game, painting a little, things for myself only, and trying to forget something very sad that had happened to me long ago" (66). The hackneyed character of these clichés is so pronounced, the phrases themselves, as Nick realizes, are "so threadbare," that the whole performance seems patently theatrical, literary, evoking "no image except that of a turbaned 'character' leaking sawdust at every pore as he pursued a tiger through the Bois de Boulogne" (66). But now the fun begins, for in this novel fraud can be the beginning rather than the end of things. Gatsby quite simply (and hugely) authenticates his performance; he produces signs of legitimacy, such as the military decoration from Montenegro and the Oxford photograph, and in the face of such evidence Nick is (willing to be)"converted": "Then it was all true. I saw the skins of tigers flaming in his palace on the Grand Canal; I saw him opening a chest of rubies to ease, with their crimson-lighted depths, the gnawings of his broken heart" (67). Nick's musings are deliciously tongue-in-cheek, but they are hardly an indictment; on the contrary, they are an homage to Gatsby's version of things, and they express Nick's willingness to play Gatsby's game, to add furnishings of his own to Gatsby's place. If charades is what we do, then by all means let us play charades. We see Nick moving into Gatsby's sphere in this passage, and it is worth noting that the whole transition from hoax to belief has a distinct *literary*, even factitious coloration. And yet, this house of cards has a peculiar dimensionality. Once we give them a try, we find that the romantic clichés are found to have some life left in them, so that even the jaded and condescending Nick Carraway can come under their spell.

Breathing life back into melodrama is just one of Fitzgerald's tricks. At privileged moments in this narrative we may see objects become enchanted and characters spawn new identities, as Fitzgerald gently reminds us that literature has a pulse and a heartbeat of its own. Consider, for example, the fine passage when Nick and Gatsby cross the Queensboro Bridge and encounter the city. Fitzgerald ushers in this scene with language that pointedly foreshadows his famous concluding image of Dutch sailors and the New World: "The city seen from the Queensboro Bridge is always the city seen for the first time, in its first wild promise of all the mystery and the beauty in the world" (69). As we shall see, this New World is very much, to use Tony Tanner's significant phrase, a "city of words," a place whose verbal freedom turns it into a "lexical playfield."[11] Here is what Nick sees:

A dead man passed us in a hearse heaped with blooms, followed by two carriages with drawn blinds, and by more cheerful carriages for friends. The friends looked out at us with the tragic eyes and short upper lips of southeastern Europe, and I was glad that the sight of Gatsby's splendid car was included in their somber holiday. As we crossed Blackwell's Island, a limousine passed us, driven by a white chauffeur, in which sat three modish negroes, two bucks and a girl. I laughed aloud as the yolks of their eyeballs rolled toward us in haughty rivalry. (69)

On the face of it we have here an innocent slice of American life; if pushed, one might claim that this scene has a mildly symbolic dimension, a discreet evocation of the American Dream *in petto*.[12] In this light we see America the melting pot, with its southeastern Europeans and its Negroes and the possibility of limousines and wealth for all; looking still more closely, we note the death or decline of the Europeans and the rise or dawning of the blacks, this too an apt figure for American freedom and mobility. But the more one scrutinizes this passage, the more playful and sibylline it becomes. There is an uncanny fixation with eyes, as each segment concludes with an ocular close-up, and one begins to wonder if there is not something pathological in this book about perception, perspective, Owl-Eyes, T. J. Eckleburg, and the like.[13] One is also entitled to question whether southeastern Europe is as fixed a proposition as is the location of San Francisco in the Midwest. Certainly the Negroes appear to have come verbally from "Blackwell's Island," indeed to have emerged from the "sombre holiday," every bit as much as to make a social statement. The passage starts to appear far more pictorial than social, with its arrangement of black and white, its flower-heaped hearse and splendid cars. It is a pageant of life and gaiety, and the lead-off item that begins the process, the man with the four-letter adjective "dead," is no more without life than "black" and "white" are sociological. "A dead man passed us . . . ," and he is merely, grandly, part of the parade, filled with verbal life, here in Fitzgerald's New World where language actualizes "the wild promise of all the mystery and the beauty in the world." And tucked in the middle of this mystery and beauty is one of the most shimmering sights of all, that of Gatsby's car, which can demonstrably bring to life as well as put to death. Nick himself sums it up: "'Anything can happen now that we've slid over this bridge,' I thought; 'anything at all . . . '" (69). To "slide" over that magic bridge is seductively easy in Fitzgerald, for the glamour of that other world, its "haughty rivalry," beckons to us at every turn. That bridge turns out to span realms more distant than Queensboro and the city, and the final scene I want to analyze illustrates the freedom Fitzgerald found on its far side.

On that far side we encounter what is arguably the most fascinating sequence in *The Great Gatsby*, and the most ignored: namely, the saga of "Blocks" Biloxi. This is the centerpiece of my interpretation, and therefore I quote it in full:

> "Imagine marrying anybody in this heat!" cried Jordan dismally.
> "Still—I was married in the middle of June," Daisy remembered, "Louisville in June! Somebody fainted. Who was it fainted, Tom?"
> "Biloxi," he answered shortly.
> "A man from Biloxi. 'Blocks' Biloxi, and he made boxes—that's a fact—and he was from Biloxi, Tennessee."
> "They carried him into my house," appended Jordan, "because we lived just two doors from the church. And he stayed three weeks, until Daddy told him he had to get out. The day after he left Daddy died." After a moment she added, "There wasn't any connection."
> "I used to know a Bill Biloxi from Memphis," I remarked.

"That was his cousin. I knew his whole family history before he left. He gave me an aluminum putter that I use to-day." The music had died down as the ceremony began and now a long cheer floated in at the window, followed by intermittent cries of "Yea-ea-ea!" and finally by a burst of jazz as the dancing began.

"We're getting old," said Daisy. "If we were young we'd rise and dance."

"Remember Biloxi," Jordan warned her. "Where'd you know him, Tom?"

"Biloxi?" He concentrated with an effort. "I didn't know him. He was a friend of Daisy's."

"He was not," she denied. "I'd never seen him before. He came down in the private car."

"Well, he said he knew you. He said he was raised in Louisville. Asa Bird brought him around at the last minute and asked if we had room for him."

Jordan smiled.

"He was probably bumming his way home. He told me he was president of your class at Yale."

Tom and I looked at each other blankly.

"Biloxi?"

"First place, we didn't have any president — "

Gatsby's foot beat a short, restless tattoo and Tom eyed him suddenly.

"By the way, Mr. Gatsby, I understand you're an Oxford man."

"Not exactly."

"Oh, yes, I understand you went to Oxford."

"Yes — I went there."

A pause, then Tom's voice, incredulous and insulting: "You must have gone there about the time Biloxi went to New Haven." (128–29)

Perhaps it is best to start with the truism that *The Great Gatsby* is never regarded as an experimental novel, nor is Fitzgerald generally appreciated as the creator of narrative high jinks, say, in the manner of Joyce or Faulkner. We have never been instructed to look out for tricks in the Fitzgerald delivery. Moreover, these are not laughing matters, and we seem a long way from Joyce's brothel setting or Darl Bundren emptying himself for sleep. Finally, this particular scene is positively crucial, from a realist point of view: it is, in effect, Fitzgerald's showdown scene, his "high noon" moment of truth in a sweltering New York hotel room where the two males finally fight it out for the golden girl. Tom has done his sleuthing, and Gatsby has finished his courting. Who will carry the day? Here, if ever, Fitzgerald needs tame, reliable, univalent prose, needs to etch this battle with clarity and force.

But what do we have? Coming out of nowhere — and this from any perspective in which we care to examine it — is "Blocks" Biloxi. He enters this story very like an unbidden but irrepressible ghost, like tidings that must be proclaimed. As if he were virtually distilled by the book's textual chemistry, catalyzed by its weird enzymes and juices, spawned by this seminal flow, "Blocks" Biloxi emerges. Almost like an epiphany, he is a radiant image of what Gatsby has only been striving to be: the complete self-made man.

More even than other fictional characters Biloxi is a construct of words: "A man named Biloxi. 'Blocks' Biloxi, and he made boxes — that's a fact — and he was from Biloxi, Tennessee." Like a child's game, "Blocks" are put together to make Biloxi; he is a fabrication, an assemblage, and he makes such objects for others: "he made boxes," boxes which contain whatever fictive meaning we insert in them. To emphasize the pure artifice of this gambit, Fitzgerald makes name and place exactly the same, much like a child who has only one kind of block for two separate purposes: "and he was from Biloxi, Tennessee." We are indeed in a New World, a writerly wonderland, where the artist's blocks and letters and boxes can deliver up a geography and a history all of their own making, claiming as truth—"that's a fact"—all his magic, including the location of Biloxi in Tennessee, which can only have "left" Mississippi in the same way San Francisco "moved" to the Midwest: by verbal fiat.[14]

Outfitted with a dazzling specious origin, the Biloxi character can now begin to perform within the fiction. Jordan first contributes to his career by appending the story of Biloxi's momentous stay at her house. He enters the house supine (from drink, supposedly), and his exit three weeks later triggers the supine departure of Daddy (from death this time). Jordan hastens to explain, "There wasn't any connection," but the reader who has any experience with blocks is bound to suspect a pattern here, at least a metaphorical linking, a Wolfsheim-type "gonnegtion" forged by the text's generative activity. Coming into Jordan's house "just two doors from the church," Biloxi is perhaps even more a ghost than we thought, a somehow holy figure whose presence is life and whose leaving is death.

Nick joins in the collective fabulation and spreads Biloxi a little further, adding a block: "I used to know a Bill Biloxi from Memphis" Jordan provides the missing referent ("cousin"), and returns to the mystery of origin: "I knew his whole family history before he left." This is, of course, oral history, "Blocks's" own tale of his past, forcing any "constructive" reader to think of that other inventor of his past, Jay Gatsby. The "gonnegtion" between Biloxi and Gatsby is just beginning.

As the noises of the marriage ceremony and the subsequent jazz music filter into the hotel room, Daisy muses, "We're getting old. . . . If we were young we'd rise and dance." She is cautioned by Jordan, "Remember Biloxi," causing the reader once again to ponder the connections here. Daisy is obviously recalling her own marriage to Tom, but beyond that she is encountering time itself. "We're getting old" is a recognition that one's romance and youth are going (if not gone), and her wistful statement, "If we were young we'd rise and dance," connotes a "rising and dancing" of special poignancy, a retrieval of youth, a hint even of resurrection. Jordan warns her by referring to Biloxi, yet Biloxi's presence maintains life; only when he leaves do we die. How can we not recall Gatsby's own imperious desire to stop time, his spirited answer to Nick's earlier warning:

> "I wouldn't ask too much of her," I ventured. "You can't repeat the past."
> "Can't repeat the past?" he cried incredulously. "Why of course you can!" (111)

I do not for a moment suggest that the ghost imagery I have used—Biloxi as holy spirit—has any orthodox religious significance. But it is clear that the issue of lost youth and irretrievable past is at the heart of the book, as it is at the heart of the dream. And the radiant answer, the splendidly American response, is to recreate what has been lost, to invent one's past and to harness desire as the very reality principle itself. The generative power of the dream is so strong in *Gatsby* that it not only incorporates the open future but also annexes the past as its truest field of operation. Gatsby, unlike so many heroes of desire, reverses the romance trajectory by attempting to remake what he has already had, to repossess what was already once consummated. In this sense his entire project is akin to the yearnings of the Dutch sailors who sensed in the open continent something not only commensurate with their capacity for desire but something already crucially behind them. It is here that the Fitzgeraldian trajectory announces the scheme of energy and desire that animates the world of Faulkner; and although the Faulknerian mode seems altogether darker and more brooding, moving toward the closure of curse and doom, the southern writer nonetheless presents a comparable picture of desire harnessed by the past, of all living projects scripted by the hunger for impossible repossession. Quentin Compson's longing for the (fictive) purity of childhood innocence and virginity has its parallels with the voracious appetite that Gatsby expresses in his certainty that the past can be repeated. Nothing need be over for the self-made man. The "gift of hope" may be illusory, but it is life-sustaining, and once it is gone, once "Blocks" Biloxi leaves the house, life is not worth living.[15] The "realist" exposure of illusion, the sleuthwork of Tom Buchanan and his ilk, is not so much an education as a loss of something magic and indispensable. This Fitzgerald took to be the burden of his novel: "the loss of those illusions that give such color to the world so that you don't care whether things are true or false so long as they partake of the magical glory."[16]

But the dreamer has to awake, and no fiction can permanently ignore the inescapable constraints of reality. Moreover, the object of the dream cannot be protected against time, nor can *its* beauty ever match that of the dream. Finally, the achievements furthered by the dream may be tawdry and corrupt, although the dream never can be. Fitzgerald had no choice but to expose his quester for a fraud, the quester's materials as vulgar and meretricious. But the deeper challenge he faced, and the one he met so perfectly that *The Great Gatsby* continues to perplex its readers today, is the dilemma of conveying the beauty and power of the dream while discrediting its object, its "occupant," and its effects. The power of belief is Fitzgerald's true subject, and he brilliantly saw that it is allied to semiosis, to the production of meaning. He intuitively grasped that the virtues of the dream are synonymous with the virtues of language. Time cannot kill it, nor can origin or fixed referent determine or immobilize it. Language "rises and dances" in *The Great Gatsby*, and it offers its most perfect performance in the figure of "Blocks" Biloxi. Biloxi, the put-together amalgam of person and place, spewing cousins, putters, and death in his wake, commences to look more and more like Gatsby. No one knew him, but he was allegedly "a friend of Daisy's." She claims that he was not, that he had come down in "the private car," which points at both Gatsby and the railway coach. Biloxi made his own story, claiming that he knew Daisy, was raised in Louisville, had done more yet. His most extraordinary achievement, the novel's very finest transposition of fiction to fact, dream to reality, and language to deed, is the rank he acquired: "He told me he was president of your class at Yale." No longer "out there" in Tennessee or even Louisville, Biloxi has finally come home, home to the Fitzgerald citadel where he takes his rightful place on the throne. Here is the "high noon" showdown at last, in a different key, reminiscent more of Quixote's encounters than those of gunfighters. If "Blocks" Biloxi can be president of your class at Yale, then not only is America a genuine "rags-to-riches" virgin land, but literature has finally out-trumped life by getting its own man elected.[17]

The forces of order man their defenses at once:

> Tom and I looked at each other blankly.
> "Biloxi?"
> "First place, we didn't have a president — "

But it is manifestly too late in the game for such reneging, and Tom Buchanan rises oddly to the occasion, dropping Biloxi and moving on to Gatsby, with a sure sense that the story of one is the life of the other and vice versa. Closing in on Gatsby's Oxford stint, approaching ever more closely the so-called boundary between fact and fiction, Tom finally makes the ultimate connection and delivers one of the most perfect lines of the book: "You [Gatsby] must have gone there [Oxford] about the time Biloxi went to New Haven." At this point Gatsby produces a compromise answer, and the interlude with Biloxi comes to a close. In a sense the remainder of the book is something of a comedown, a return to reality and its unavoidable assortment of evidence and corpses and cold fried chicken.

But the issues raised in the Biloxi episode and the ringing identification of Biloxi and Gatsby as one, their careers as intertwined — these concerns illuminate the larger purposes of the novel, and to shed light on them has been the object of this study. "Blocks" Biloxi is not only a "made" person, a construct; he is also positioned in a homemade world of the group's devising, the kind of place where Biloxi can be in Tennessee and San Francisco in the Midwest. This flimflam man who manufactures his past, crashes the wedding, does in Jordan's father, and is president of the class at Yale is a potent figure, free of all prior conditioning and constraints (since he is shaped and constructed in front of our eyes) and strangely memorable (he is "there" in the narrative only because he is memorable). Pure artifice, yet he intrudes into the real world, leaving Jordan a putter and leaving her father to die. His meteoric career is a bold parable of Jay Gatsby's life, a shorthand version of the same magic and creation of belief that constitute Gatsby's particular greatness. "Blocks" Biloxi is the liberated signifier, the unit or "block" of language that can be molded and connected in countless ways, to yield countless boxes, each with countless possible contents or signifieds. His adventures are a crucial piece of American life. His shadow looms large in American fiction, hinted at already in Wakefield and Bartleby, related to Twain's twins, nightmarishly in the wings in the tortured antics of Joe Christmas, still to be graphed in the dance of clowns staged by Coover and DeLillo.

The novel does not close with Biloxi, nor shall I. Jay Gatsby is also a hero of self-creation, but unlike the enigmatic Biloxi, he is a passionate, tragic character, one who brought to the potential of signs the energy of his life. His smile, his parties, his love are profoundly creative, constitutive gestures, enabling others to take form and life. He is the prime mover in Fitzgerald's scheme, the "Son of God" who is a consummate fiction maker, acting through the shape he gave to himself and to others. There is a remarkable kind of freedom in this act of shaping, and I have argued that it can be understood as a peculiarly American freedom, an imperious desire to make reality rather than to undergo it. But this freedom can be exercised only by dint of energy and will. The con man, like the artist, replaces the given world with a construct of his own, but it can rival reality only if he invests it with life, with his life. Those splendid parties of Gatsby's and the aura that surrounds the scattered details of his life, these are the properties of legend, and they bear witness to a strange kind of public belief, a kind of reciprocity whereby Gatsby is himself brought to life by those who surround him. What are legends if not stories that retain an echoing truth over time, stories that subsequent generations keep alive? The "scattered" and disseminated Gatsby is public domain, and even though his funeral is so scandalously underattended, he is nonetheless "out there" for good, located doubtless "somewhere back in that vast obscurity beyond the city, where the dark fields of the republic rolled on under the night" (182).

Such reciprocity also defines the basic aesthetic miracle that brings art to life, that makes the page seem real, that makes it endure. Why else do we read? Fitzgerald has undertaken in *Gatsby* to deliver the belief system of an era, and he has shown us how much reciprocity, how much give-and-take, how much public "financing" goes into the fixing of legends. This compact little novel distills the very poetry of capitalist America, and it offers us a classic treatise on the nature of fiction. Above all, it speaks to us of the pact between the artist and the rest of us. Hero of dreams, Gatsby is dreamed by others. Only in such a way can the artist then act on his public, appeal to or coerce their belief, and ultimately withdraw from the scene, confident that his creation is alive, kept alive by the belief of his public.

Fitzgerald achieved that final transfer (perhaps only) in *The Great Gatsby*, and the book is endowed with an indigenous energy and power that mock both closure and exposure. This brings me back, even if circuitously, to the question with which I began: What is Gatsby's greatness? My answer is in my chapter title: fiction is greatness. There can be no fixed, measurable index of greatness, no specifiable number of dollars or military victories or literary prizes which must be earned before greatness is bestowed. I am not suggesting that it therefore does not exist. Greatness has common cause with fiction because it hinges on belief, because it can be achieved only if it is conferred. To be great requires a crucial measure of *public* endorsement; indeed, it requires being "ratified," much as one must be "elected" president of your class at Yale.

Three quarters of a century have passed since *Gatsby* was published, along with a couple of wars, and it is fair to say that "greatness" is not in especially good odor these days; it smacks of fascism, of surrender and hero worship. We have only to think of the films of Bertolucci, or to see how DeLillo treats this theme, to understand how much the world has changed since Fitzgerald chronicled the twenties, how suspicious we have become of individual aura and magnetism. Legends today will be dismantled tomorrow. What is not exposed in the newspapers will be deconstructed in the academy. In our desire to see clear, to recognize the stranglehold that culture has on us, "belief" shades into benightedness. And yet nothing in our more critical era quite matches the zest and splendor of Fitzgerald's book. It may well be that the power of belief, like that of the dream, has an integrity that no amount of muckraking or exposé can finally discredit. There is something dazzling and forever young about the high-flying Gatsby and his fictive surrogate, Biloxi.

Yet they are not alike. One could say that the career of "Blocks" Biloxi testifies to the success of the simulacra in American culture that Jean Baudrillard has been talking about, or, more in keeping with my theme, that it flaunts, with rare chutzpah, the insolent sovereignty of language itself, the triumph of the word in replacing the deed. Well before "The Electric Company" appeared, Fitzgerald showed us that Letter Man might be elected. Biloxi, as we know, achieved his ghostly triumph in these precincts, yet his more flesh-and-blood cousin Gatsby remains ultimately the more compelling candidate for greatness. The fiction making for which he stands is a passionate act of transformation not unlike Rimbaud's *alchimie du verbe*, but it can make its magic and enchanted objects only through the gift of self and the response of others. Gatsby gives his life to the dream, and although we may be inclined today to interpret these events as a cautionary fable, it is also good to see it the other way: desire invests the world with magic, and belief is the name we give to our contract with others and with art. To phrase it that way is to run the risk of Gatsby's own "appalling sentimentality," but it is also to underscore the humane value of belief, even fictional belief, as the goal of language and literature.

8

Faulkner's *As I Lay Dying*:
The Voice from the Coffin

At an early moment in William Faulkner's novel about dying, Doctor Peabody treats us to a view of death that is worth pondering: "I can remember how when I was young I believed death to be a phenomenon of the body; now I know it to be merely a function of the mind — and that of the minds of the ones who suffer the bereavement. The nihilists say it is the end; the fundamentalists, the beginning; when in reality it is no more than a single tenant or family moving out of a tenement or a town."[1] Faulkner's interest, in this book as in all his books, lies with the communal as much as with the individual, and we can expect him to pay as much attention to the tenement as to the tenant. In fact, we will come to see that death is only to be understood as a kind of "moving" venture. The more one considers this notion, the more we have to credit Peabody with a theory of fiction: death as the fiction of cessation and finality in a world of pure process. Death, understood as "end stage," is close to the very bedrock of our Western metaphysics; it authorizes our belief in time and meaningful sequence, and it is never distant, ontologically, from our notions of presence and absence, here and there, now and then, or, as Faulkner likes to say, *is* and *was*. *As I Lay Dying* stands as Faulkner's most remarkable text about death, a stark mediation and gloss on the medieval memento mori, on the scandal of matter and decomposing flesh, on the rituals of burial and bereavement that bear witness to every culture's deepest beliefs.[2]

What is most arresting about this novel, however, is that nothing is arrested or over, that there is only flux and motion, an endless shuttling from one tenement to another. In this new dispensation the old pacts and dichotomies are dissolved, and all those founding distinctions of sanity and order — presence versus absence, now versus then, animate versus inanimate — are scandalously blurred, are ultimately washed away. Everything is in the present; everything is joined and fused. The title says it all: "as I lay dying," an ongoing activity, a present participle, a process that is without end, a moving out and a moving in. *Saying it* is, of course, the writer's great trump card in his dealings with death. Present participles, outfitted with their imperial "-ing" endings, flaunt the presence, the presentness, of language. The wedding of living language to living matter is what *As I Lay Dying* celebrates, page after page. Nothing ever being really over, how can it surprise us that Addie Bundren *speaks* long after she has been put in her coffin? Her central, highly explanatory chapter comes well after she has supposedly left the living, and she thereby illustrates one of the book's central laws: the mother lives. But her famous monologue is only one of the occasions when she speaks. At other moments the tenement she has moved to, the coffin itself, achieves voice and utterance, renders the speech of its tenant. Here is how it sounds to Darl: "The breeze was setting up from the barn, so we put her under the apple tree, where the moonlight can dapple the apple tree upon the long slumbering flanks within which now and then she talks in little trickling bursts of secret and murmurous bubbling. I took Vardaman to listen. When we came up the cat leaped down from it and flicked away with silver claw and silver eye into the shadow" (143). If we read this passage as an index of Faulkner's world — what he sees and what he hears — rather than as a picture of Darl's peculiar psyche, then we can better grasp the strange poetry of *As I Lay Dying*. Almost monosyllabic, blatantly alliterative, the language here figures forth a metamorphosed scene where the elements are at once ludic and triumphant.[3] The breeze and the moonlight are the shapers, the form givers, in this drama of shapes and shaping, and the personified coffin ("long slumbering flanks") houses the still-speaking Addie, whose words are fluid and liquid, like the voice of the river, "little trickling bursts of secret and murmurous bubbling."[4] It would be a mistake, I think, to refer this evocation altogether to some decomposition scenario; instead, Faulkner is positing a world of ceaseless energy and ceaseless expression, a scheme that is profoundly lingual in nature, in that its most characteristic manifestations appear as *voice*. "Voice" becomes "voices" quickly enough, as the speaking elements shift and recompose, yielding a medley of sounds. The coffin, we note, is at once the source and the container for these voices, and it appears to us as a thing of mystery and magic as well as speech, even a source of riches, as we see the "silver" eye and claw of the cat performing their antics (much as the Bundrens are doing) around the dark shadow. A great deal of *As I Lay Dying* is on show in this passage: the metamorphic scheme that foregrounds the coursing elements, the vocal imperative that governs Faulkner's view of nature and art, casting the writer (like Vardaman) into the role of *listener* as well as speaker.

The supreme emblem of the Faulknerian flow is, of course, the river. In *Absalom, Absalom!* he will call it the "geographic umbilical" that serves as a blood conduit for the divided land, and that view of the river as vital channel of communication is nowhere more in evidence than in *As I Lay Dying*. Here, however, the umbilical river actually speaks: "it talks up to us in a murmur become ceaseless and myriad," and "it clucks and murmurs among the spokes and about the mules' knees," making a "plaintive sound, a musing sound" (93). All is animate in this novel, seething with motion and speech, radically overturning our complacent and anthropocentric view of nature as background, of humans as the moving figures on a stage that is supposed to be docile. Here the stage moves and talks, and the people are seen precisely as elements, unprivileged parts of the scene.

One suffers the world, for it comes at us and takes us incessantly, sweeps us up in its design, uses us as its commodity. Hence, the "red road lies like a spoke of which Addie Bundren is the rim" (69), and this family will—why not?—be visited by flood and fire in the pilgrimage. Faulkner takes great pains to render this energized setting in such a way as to stress its anarchic and ubiquitous power. The river takes imperial honors, but the so-called still places are not still either: "I enter the hall, hearing the voices before I reach the door. Tilting a little down the hill, as our house does, a breeze draws through the hall all the time, upslanting. A feather dropped near the front door will rise and brush along the ceiling, slanting backward, until it reaches the down-turning current at the back door: so with voices. As you enter the hall, they sound as though they were speaking out of the air about your head" (14). Everything is upended and unmoored here: the house tilts, the breeze moves up, the feather rises, all partakes of the strangely coursing energy, the "down-turning current" which is pure flow, the dance of the molecules that consorts throughout the novel and sets everything to its tune. *So with voices*: human voice is sound, air, and breeze, a "speaking" that comes from nowhere and everywhere, "about your head," at once sourceless and demiurgic. We enter this book as we enter this hall, this tenement that overflows with voices. One listens, astonished and penetrated, and one sees that language is being systematically decentered, severed—just as the river appears to sever the body from its base—from its human sources; instead, speech emerges from things usually thought voiceless: water, air, dead flesh.

The self is immersed in this flux, deprived of its autonomy, everywhere porous and partnered in the dance. In this new poetics and new physics there is an exquisite awareness of the body's fit among the elements. Thus, Darl's memory of adolescent masturbation is a memory of air and flow, of a passive body submitting to nature's caresses: ". . . so I could lie with my shirt-tail up, hearing them asleep, feeling myself without touching myself, feeling the cool silence blowing upon my parts . . . " (8). Dewey Dell, bearing a "living seed" within her, finds her place in an arrangement that is virtually symphonic: "The cow breathes upon my hips and back, her breath warm, sweet, stertorous, moaning. The sky lies flat down the slope, upon the secret clumps. Beyond the hill sheet-lightning stains upward and fades. The dead air shapes the dead earth in the dead darkness, further away than seeing shapes the dead earth. It lies dead and warm upon me, touching me naked through my clothes. . . . I feel like a wet seed wild in the hot blind earth" (42). Again we notice, through Faulkner's cunning language, the displacement of life and energy into and onto new areas. A new dispensation appears here, entirely sexualized, an affair of breathing, touching, and moaning. Nothing can resist; even the secret clumps receive the sky that lies on them. The word "dead" is repeated five times, but its conventional meaning is undone, reversed, transformed into sultry warmth and downright sexual aggression. The cow's breathing envelops Dewey Dell, the sky lies down with the other animals, and the scene is typically atilt as the lightning stains upward and fades, leaving us with the all-pervasive medium of the air, air which we normally never perceive but which is thickly present here as the source of life and even of perception, shaping what can be seen, lying "warm" upon Dewey Dell and touching her naked, as if the touching, the central activity here, were peculiarly transitive, made naked. Faulkner's work has been thought to be obsessed with purity and virginity, and it is, perhaps nowhere more so than here and in the sister text, *The Sound and the Fury*. But we cannot fail to see that virginity is an impossible proposition in this scheme, that touching and penetration and fusing are conditions of life, preceding and mocking all acts of violation and moral codes, no more to be accepted or refused than air is accepted or refused.

The air shapes and touches, makes visible and naked, is seen to be the medium of both life and art; sulphuric, heavy, warm, the air itself breathes in this text, takes on the role of source, much the way the sun or the fire does in primitive mythologies. *As I Lay Dying* is arguably Faulkner's most pagan novel, for in it the physical world reigns with such utter and devastating authority that the schemes of men and morality are inevitably seen as fragile constructs, and the antics of humans are no more than "furious attitudes, dead gestures of dolls" (139). Not that it is all sound and fury; the book is shot through with a kind of country wisdom, a knowledge of the earth and the elements, which can be as serene as the taste of water that has "set a while in a cedar bucket. Warmish-cool, with a faint taste like the hot July wind in cedar trees smells" (8). Drinking it at night, Darl sees the water's dark surface as "a round orifice in nothingness, where before I stirred it awake with the dipper I could see maybe a star or two in the bucket, and maybe in the dipper a star or two before I drank" (8). There is almost a throwaway lyricism here, a primeval sense of magic and deity, of the dipper being in our hand as well as in the heavens, of the stars being present in our drink of water; and underlying this poetic fullness is its heady complement of nothingness, of the abyss we drink into, of the something out there or in there that we may be stirring awake.[5] In this novel very often "it" is stirred awake, for not only do the elements rule, but they rule despotically, and they are, as it were, liberated by, through, and throughout the text, brought to the attention of the Bundrens and the reader in ways that are unforgettable. Life here is terribly coerced, as Doctor Peabody has understood, "like our rivers, our land: opaque, slow, violent: shaping and creating the life of man in its implacable and brooding image" (30). Tull puts the matter in terms of sorrow and affliction, but imagery of the elements broadcasts clearly enough the subject's role as victim: "Now and then a fellow gets to thinking. About all the sorrow and afflictions in this world; how it's liable to strike anywhere, like lightning" (46). Once again, with the economy of the poet, Faulkner announces loudly the power of nature while whispering softly that "brooding" and "thinking" are the terrible conductors that hook us up to the system, that make us receptacles of lightning. There is precious little safety or stability in this scheme, but there is much spectacle.

Nowhere is the spectacle grander than when the Bundrens seek to cross the swollen river. Here is the primal Faulkner scene, with the elements roused up to a furious pitch, displaying their awesome power against human puniness. The water speaks its own language, as I have already indicated, but it is not like the water we are used to. Darl, drinking, saw the stars, and Tull—

commonsensical, barometric outsider—sees the river as matrix, as living, killing container: "The water was cold. It was thick, like slush ice. Only it kind of lived. One part of you knowed it was just water, the same thing that had been running under this same bridge for a long time, yet when them logs would come spewing up outen it, you were not surprised, like they was a part of the water, of the waiting and the threat" (90). One is tempted to say that the Bundrens have finally come home, come to that realm of pure flux and violence that has been lying in wait up to now. As Darl faces the "thick dark current," he feels "as though just beneath the surface something huge and alive waked for a moment of lazy alertness out of and into light slumber again" (93). In this apocalyptic setting nothing holds, and uprights are overturned, "uprooted" from any ground whatsoever: "Above the ceaseless surface they stand—trees, canes, vines—rootless, severed from the earth, spectral above a scene of immense yet circumscribed desolation filled with the voice of waste and mournful water" (93). Darl knows that they have "reached the place where the motion of the wasted world accelerates just before the final precipice" (96), and in this supreme moment of immersion the fictive world of order is abolished. The surging log that both looks like Christ and has foam "like the beard of an old man or a goat" (98) strikes the fragile Bundren wagon with its precious human cargo, and the Faulknerian baptism takes place.

Faulkner may be a pagan, but he is also a modernist, and the cataclysmic encounter between the Bundrens and the swollen waters is emblematic of something more personal and psychological in nature: the (potentially lethal) contact between self and Other which is at the heart of the book. To plunge into the maelstrom of the river and to penetrate the nakedness of the Other are twin faces of the same awful collision. Darl and Cash experience it: "He and I look at one another with long probing looks, looks that plunge unimpeded through one another's eyes and into the ultimate secret place where for an instant Cash and Darl crouch flagrant and unabashed in all the old terror and the old foreboding, alert and secret and without shame" (93). The purity of this encounter is immediate and immaculate, achieved by a stupendous peeling away of veneers, not only of custom and decorum but also, one is tempted to say, of time and evolutionary history. Crouching "flagrant and unabashed," entering each other with "long probing looks," Cash and Darl reach back to prehistoric cavemen, to the "old terror and the old foreboding," a time prior to language itself, a time when there was neither cover nor mediation. There is something properly terrifying at work here, for terror sets in when we realize that no defenses are going to hold, that the body and the mind come to us here as naked, as targeted for unstoppable penetration.

From Hawthorne's prying narrators and Melville's Drummond light to James's center of consciousness and Faulkner's interior monologues, narrative literature hinges crucially on the dynamics of vision, of seeing "inside" the characters. *As I Lay Dying* is especially poignant in this regard because it posits a view of the human subject as guarded, fearful of violation, closed in. "The Lord can see into the heart" (6), Cora Tull solemnly assures us at the outset of the novel, and it would seem that such exposure may be all right if it comes from the Lord, but there's trouble if it comes from anywhere else. That is what Peabody terms Addie Bundren's "pride": "that pride, that furious desire to hide that abject nakedness which we bring here with us, carry with us into operating rooms, carry stubbornly and furiously with us into the earth again" (31). Even the fish that Vardaman catches is described by Tull as being "ashamed of being dead, like it was in a hurry to get back hid again" (21). In a very influential essay Calvin Bedient has argued that pride is the conceptual center of the text, and he has focused especially on the success of Addie and the failure of Darl to cover nakedness.[6] There can be little doubt that Darl fails at concealment, that he cannot manage to build an "I"-tenement to house his consciousness, and that special dysfunction warrants a full discussion. No less striking, however, is Darl's key role as invading angel, as penetrating gaze that no one can resist. He is the seer who enters whatever he sees, who narrates from afar (since he need not be present in body if he is ubiquitous in spirit), who thus constitutes an unbearable threat to those who have something to conceal: Dewey Dell and her pregnancy, Jewel and his illegitimacy, even Addie Bundren in her status as carrion. It comes as no surprise that he is viciously attacked by his siblings at journey's end.

Yet the general view of Darl as the text's Hamlet, its suffering intellectual who is, much like Quentin Compson, paralyzed by consciousness, is seriously flawed. There is nothing cerebral in these matters. Eye contact is physically traumatizing: it is a current that connects two holes. When Dewey Dell looks at Peabody ("he could do so much for me if he just would"), the doctor says it's "like the stream of a hose touches you, the stream at the instant of impact as dissociated from the nozzle as though it had never been there" (30). Darl's vision is alien not only to those it visits; it is also alien to Darl. Faulkner repeatedly describes Darl's eyes as nonhuman, as part of the *land*: Dewey Dell thinks of him at the supper table "with his eyes gone further than the food and the lamp, full of the land dug out of his skull and the holes filled with distance beyond the land" (18). Anse mentions his eyes, "full of the land all the time" (25). Later, again, Dewey Dell says: "The land runs out of Darl's eyes; they swim to pinpoints. They begin at my feet and rise along my body to my face, and then my dress is gone; I sit naked . . . " (78).[7] Faulkner is graphically conflating vision and earth, as if we were *of* the land as much as *on* or (crucially here) *in* the land. From dust to dust, the old text says, but the newer one posits earth and water as the elements of the human body, constituting it in life as well as in death. To make water and to make wind are time-honored descriptions of bodily functions, but Faulkner must surely be among the first to plumb narratively this metaphysics of elements, and he bypasses altogether the small game of peeing and farting in order to go after the larger prey: living and breathing, looking and dying. Darl's vision rises along and into his sister's body like the flood; nothing mental here at all.

Darl's eyes invade, but he touches no one. In the figure of Addie Bundren, however, Faulkner has dramatized a far more visceral form of encounter. Her mode of dealing with others has exactly the kind of elemental, stupefying brutality that we see in the river scene. Addie's monologue is one of the most virtuoso sequences Faulkner ever wrote, and it illuminates all the issues at hand: the elements, human connection, language. Addie wastes no time in telling us what kind of a schoolteacher she was: "I would look forward to the times when they faulted, so I could whip them. When the switch fell I could feel it upon my flesh; when it welted and ridged it was my blood that ran, and I would think with each blow of the switch: now you are aware of me! Now I am something in your secret and selfish life, who have marked your blood with my own for ever and ever" (114). Here is perhaps the most haunting image of human contact in the whole of Faulkner, and it reminds us that touch is more likely to be murderous than tender, such as Wash Jones's ominous "I'm going to tech you, Kernel," which is uttered just before he cuts Sutpen's head off, and where "tech" functions beautifully as both "teach" and "touch," each signifying a fatal lesson. The isolation of the subject, the distance between people (where Cash and Darl crouched "flagrant and unabashed in all the old terror and the old foreboding") can be bridged, if at all, only by the most violent embrace. We see, too, just how resonant the "flowing blood" can be in Faulkner, for it images not only kinship and continuity but also a kind of violent, even homicidal fusion, a means of entry into the secret places of the other. Blood constitutes the purest and ultimate flow in Faulkner; as elemental as water and air and fire, it is virtually palpable in his books, imaging the reaches of family and history as well as the waterway of the body and the land. Thus, when Anse repeatedly says that the dead Addie must be taken to Jefferson because of the family burying ground and "them of her blood waiting for her there," we may glimpse something eerily literal in the phrase, an embodied community of spirits that cannot be gainsaid, blood figures waiting for Addie to join them.

And join them she will. There is no better way to expose death as a fiction than to carry out one's will *d'outre tombe*. Her famous monologue confirms what we already know: she lives on in the minds of her family, in the burial project they jointly undertake. What most strikes us about this fearless and deathless woman, however, is her rage for authenticity. To achieve this she was and is ruthless: beating her students, flaunting her pride, and above all coercing her family, first in life and then in death. Readable as the governing and repressive desire of the text, the tyrannical force of closure that seeks to sculpt all Bundren life into her funeral project, Addie's imperious *design* already forecasts Sutpen's monomaniacal scheme.[8] But above all, Addie quests to be herself, to be authentic rather than counterfeit, to be gesture rather than word: "I would be I; I would let him be the shape and echo of his word" (117). Language, she discovers (about the same time Saussure did), is a cheat, in that language, being a system based on difference, can never *be* the things it names. The scandal of life is that the word is substituted for the deed: "We had to use one another by words like spiders dangling by their mouths from a beam, swinging and twisting and never touching, and that only through the blows of the switch could my blood and their blood flow as one stream" (115–16). In a vision of surreal power, Faulkner expresses the built-in deceit of language, the play of substitution and difference that keeps us apart, at word's length, twisting and spinning. We are not far from the world of myth here, a legendary fable of blood and spiders that finds pictures for our disinherited state, our nostalgia for immediacy and connection. Again and again Addie imagines authenticity in terms of the flowing blood: "I believed that the reason was the duty to the alive, to the terrible blood, the red bitter blood boiling through the land" (117), and "My children were of me alone, of the wild blood boiling along the earth, of me and of all that lived; of none and of all" (118). One cannot fail to recognize the river in these lines, to see that the coursing blood and the swollen waters are the very conduits of life, and that all else is sham.

Addie Bundren's cult of the flowing blood likens her to the imperious river, but even she cannot maintain her form forever, and now she lies dying. That is the meaning of the flow, the cost of authenticity: it dismantles us. "I" is a provisional structure, not a home. We are a tenement house for the elements, and the elements can regroup. Addie fights these consequences with all that she has, and in her battle with entropy Faulkner is returning to the doomed battle he staged between Quentin and his father in *The Sound and the Fury*, the battle about "temporary" and its annihilating effect on all that is human. *As I Lay Dying* focuses on the same unwinnable war, but it does so without pathos or sentimentality. Addie wants to make her mark; she wants her life to be, in the language of *Absalom*, "nothing fault nor false." As Richard Godden has pointed out, she refuses to be a copy: "Addie has a conviction, beyond personal arrogance, about the representative originality of everything in her life. Her virginity, to her, was the first that was ever lost; her adultery occurs in the eye of God; her children might well be divided tribes; her refusal of Anse is murder and her words are as new as Adam's— none of them is expendable since each word must contain what it names, in a word so ideally natural that it need not be said and can be left silent."[9] But it is more than language that plays Addie false. She inhabits Faulkner's world of flux, and, like the log that is to strike her coffin, she too is carried by the flow. Her resistance to the flow goes by the name of pride: pride that her body would not soil itself, pride that her feelings can be kept in, pride that her will can be carried out. But her body will rot, her feelings are broadcast everywhere, and her will is carried out in such a monstrous way that we are on the border of pure travesty. The war against mobility and metamorphosis cannot be won. Anse is dead right when he consistently refers to his dead wife as a "particular" woman, a woman who would not want her corpse to travel in somebody else's wagon but rather in "ourn" ("*We'll wait for ourn, he said. She'll want it so. She was ever a particular woman*" [59]). But "particular" is the language of "I," of Somebody; it connotes a regime of propriety and proprietorship that is utterly untenable. Anse is also right when he wages war against the road, for he understands it, too, to be the agent of flux, and he wants none of it:

A-lying there, right up to my door, where every bad luck that comes and goes is bound to find it. I told Addie it want any luck living on a road when it come by here, and she said, for the world like a woman, "Get up and move, then." But I told her it want no luck in it, because the Lord put roads for travelling: why he laid them down flat on the earth. When He aims for something to be always a-moving, He makes it longways, like a road or a horse or a wagon, but when He aims for something to stay put, He makes it up-and-down ways, like a tree or a man. And so he never aimed for folks to live on a road. . . . Because if He'd a aimed for a man to be always a-moving and going somewheres else, wouldn't He a put him longways on his belly, like a snake? It stands to reason He would. (24)

There is arguably no other Western writer who can match Faulkner's ability to do metaphysics in such a homespun way. Anse is very much Addie's mate in his tribute to stability, to the dignity of verticals in a world of threatening and moving horizontals. But the novel will undercut Anse, and the road turns out to be in cahoots with the river, both of them imperious channels of flux and motion that govern all human comings and goings, convert all human behavior into comings and goings. And one feels that this is every bit as much a "road novel" as a "river novel," that the entire Bundren pilgrimage is little more than a roadlike calvary, a blood-red road lying "like a spoke of which Addie Bundren is the rim." On the move, the Bundrens are to discover that motion is all, that within and without them is ceaseless traffic, as impersonal as the play of atoms. Addie Bundren is moving into a new tenement, a new material form, and the question is: Is that still Addie Bundren? Among the uprights that are swept away is the fixity of self, the fiction of identity. And Addie is hardly alone in being undone. All the Bundrens are moving, on parade, and we are witness to a genuine family "outing."

Ever since Olga Vickery charted the binary systems and polarities and dialectical axes of *As I Lay Dying* back in the early 1950s, it has been customary to read the book in terms of counterpoint: Darl versus Jewel, talking versus doing, consciousness versus being, life versus death.[10] In this light Dewey Dell's experience of pregnancy is enlisted as an opposite number to Addie's dying. But the novel is less schematic, more organic, more of a piece than such interpretation allows. Dewey Dell is being initiated into the same processes that her mother is encountering; she travels, in every sense, that same red road of which Addie is a spoke and Anse a victim. As Daniel Ferrer has eloquently shown, there is a systematic and ongoing equation between death and birth, the coffin and the fetus: "The equivalence of the body in the coffin and the foetus in the womb is carried on throughout the book: the journey is a shortened pregnancy (the burial takes place *nine* days after Addie's death) or a prolonged delivery (the ambiguity of the word travail, a doublet of travel, designating too the labour of childbirth, is more than once exploited) . . . ; the coffin's shipwreck corresponds to the breaking of the waters; the rope joining the waggon to Jewel's horse represents the umbilical cord. . . ."[11] Yet even this sustained analogy is too formal, too structural. The book's integrity lies in the sameness of the traumas it depicts. The pregnant daughter and the dying mother are both coming apart. Says Dewey Dell: "I feel my body, my bones and flesh beginning to part and open upon the alone, and the process of coming unalone is terrible" (59). As Eric Sundquist has argued, the entire novel hinges on the realization that the subject is always "coming un-alone," that familial and sexual consciousness always entail fusions of self and not-self, experienced as incursions and invasions, requiring a redefinition of ego along new, "corporate" lines.[12] Perhaps even this is too abstract, too much an affair of consciousness. Faulkner is out to chart the generic adventure of the self as "a tub of guts," a body-tenement on the move, immersed in the flow of elements. The nightmare of such a scheme is that "self" is annihilated; that is Dewey Dell's nightmare:

> *When I used to sleep with Vardaman I had a nightmare once I thought I was awake but I couldn't see and couldn't feel I couldn't feel the bed under me and I couldn't think what I was I couldn't think of my name I couldn't even think I am a girl I couldn't even think I nor even think I want to wake up nor remember what was opposite to awake so I could do that I knew that something was passing but I couldn't even think of time then all of a sudden I knew that something was it was wind blowing over me it was like the wind came and blew me back from where it was I was not blowing the room and Vardaman asleep and all of them back under me again and going on like a piece of cool silk dragging across my naked legs* (78–79)

This passage is a roll call of fictions that can be disassembled, of binarisms and constructs that collapse: name, gender, time, the line between sleeping and waking. Only the wind is real; it is "passing" and "blowing," and we realize that everything is both made and unmade by it, that the wind blows the house up as well as down, that it posits Vardaman asleep, that it keeps, if we are lucky, the whole consort in place, "all of them back under me again," but that it can just as easily redistribute the parts and the players, the people and the things, the time and the place, the selves and the settings.

A tub of guts is a weighty matter. For all its airiness and wateriness, *As I Lay Dying* gives its due to the density of flesh: skin, bone, organ, and blood have a specific gravity which Faulkner never forgets. Peabody's 250-pound body has to be hauled up the hill, and Addie's corpse is heavier in the coffin than anyone expected. In some ways the novel is an extended conceit about *gravity*, about the weight and fate of flesh which has only one direction to go: down. Anse may think that trees and men are equipped for being upright, but supine is the nightly posture of flesh while it lives, and the permanent condition of it dead. One lies dying; one does not stand dying. No accident that Cash first broke his leg falling off a church roof, and Tull sees this as an omen for what is to come: *"If it takes wet boards for folks to fall, it's fixing to be lots of falling before this spell is done"* (58). No less than in the Joycean *danse macabre* of "32 ft. per sec.^{2}," which spells out one of the authority schemes in *Ulysses*, falling bodies are at the core of Faulkner's novel, and he goes out of his way to pay homage to the texture, smell, and weight of matter, both carnate and incarnate. This is why Darl is a figure of such pathos: the land may run out of his eyes, but he himself is adrift, unmoored, atilt, weightless. The wind blows like cool silk dragging across Dewey Dell's naked legs, and we can feel her heavy sentience, her stint as pièce de résistance in the nightmare of passing and blowing. Darl, however, leaks land through his eyes and has no ground of his own. In one of the most remarkable passages in modern fiction, Faulkner graphs for us what living in the body-tenement can feel like from the inside, when the building is threatened:

> In a strange room you must empty yourself for sleep. And before you are emptied for sleep, what are you. And when you are emptied for sleep, you are not. And when you are filled with sleep, you never were. I dont know what I am. I dont know if I am or not. Jewel knows he is, because he does not know that he does not know whether he is or not. He cannot empty himself for sleep because he is not what he is and he is what he is not. Beyond the unlamped wall I can hear the rain shaping the wagon that is ours, the load that is no longer theirs that felled and sawed it nor yet theirs that bought it and which is not ours either, lie on our wagon though it does, since only the wind and rain shape it only to Jewel and me, that are not asleep. And since sleep is is-not, and rain and wind are *was*, it is not. Yet the wagon *is*, because when the wagon is *was*, Addie Bundren will not be. And Jewel *is*, so Addie Bundren must be. And then I must be, or I could not empty myself for sleep in a strange room. And so if I am not emptied yet, I am *is*.
>
> How often have I lain beneath rain on a strange roof, thinking of home. (52)

Not unlike his brother Cash the carpenter, Darl is studding up his house in this passage, working to create those uprights that will keep the edifice intact, make it endure. The painful elaboration of *is* and *was* has a building-block character to it, like a primitive game that is played to shore the self up, to tide it over during its daily bouts of vacancy and absenteeism. In sleep, the tub of guts shakes off consciousness entirely, exists fully as thing; to do that, a prodigious emptying is necessary, a careful removal of "I" from the tub, on the order of a scientific experiment in which oxygen is removed in order to create a vacuum. Like a Mississippi Descartes, scrupulously working out his cogito, Darl Bundren is inventorying his estate; Descartes did as much, we recall, and he found the truth criteria put forth by the medieval authorities wanting, whereas Darl tragically reverses the procedure, finding the world to be real and the "I" to be a construct. Where does "I" live? Is it a flicker in the tub? A neural synapse in the tenement? We are to understand that full versus empty is not some static, polarized schema (like present/absent) but rather a kind of ebb and flow, the ceaseless rhythm of life that knows neither beginning nor ending, that orders all we do, from sleep to food to sex to death, with the animallike regularity of the lungs and the heart, the systolic and the diastolic. "I" is lying dying in this passage, casting about for parameters to frame it and pin itself down, running through its repertory of proprietary strategies, finding that the world is unownable and free, that the self is no more than a fictive point on a graph where the flowing line alone is real. Darl is performing the dance of Nobody's Home. There can be no greater fiction than the shape and career of the ego, the claims of continuity and coherence put forth as "I"; the fraudulent self dissolves, and in its place there is only a nameless flux, as anonymous and elusive as "the load that is no longer theirs that felled it and sawed it nor yet theirs that bought it and which is not ours either, lie on our wagon though it does."

Addie Bundren lies metamorphosing in her coffin, and in this shape she continues to script and to shape the lives of her family. Her unwanted son Darl comes apart. More even than it could be said of Benjy, Darl Bundren is the "natural," the creature without an "I": "As though the clotting which is you had dissolved into the myriad original motion . . . " (110). The struggle to uphold identity is both futile and exhausting; Darl wants to let go and to play out: "If you could just ravel out into time. That would be nice. It would be nice if you could just ravel out into time" (140). The tone here is one of wisdom as much as fatigue, a seemly exit out of an unseemly mess, a country boy's genteel version of "la commedia è finita." At the end Darl literally ruptures and fissures. He has known all along of his intermittency and his multiplicity ("That's why I am not *is. Are* is too many for one woman to foal" [65]), and, at the end, he splits, like a chemical compound when exposed to the right temperature and pressure. The pluralized Darl is taken away to Jackson, laughing, affirming, querying, musing over separations and fusions, speaking the flow, becoming all the voices "about your head":

> Darl is our brother, our brother Darl. Our brother Darl in a cage in Jackson where, his grimed hands lying light in the quiet interstices, looking out he foams.
> "Yes yes yes yes yes yes yes yes." (172–73)

"I" dies in this sequence, as the tenement is finally imploded into a welter of voices and visions.[13] The horror of this book derives from the fear that containers will not hold. One's first sense of these matters is that of overflow. Like the swollen waters, so too the rotting, flowing body threatens to "out" from the coffin. Cash's injury triggers the same perception: "Cash broke his leg and now the sawdust is running out. He is bleeding to death is Cash" (139). And here we see the Darl(s) running out. But this essentialist view is only one view. Even more terrible is the spreading of *nothingness,* the heinous view that the container—skin, coffin, name, what-you-will—is only a shape around a *hole,* and that hole may grow, like cancer. As Daniel Ferrer has commented, "There is the risk that the hole will spread out, that the text will run, stitch by stitch."[14] When the "I" dies, fiction is turned inside out, self-cannibalized. Without the governance of the ego (as fictive container if nothing else), discourse is scandalously free, goes on a "wilding." This "outing" of the self is brought to its spectacular conclusion in Vardaman's succinct account of Darl's journey: "*He went to Jackson. He went crazy and went to Jackson both*" (171). How can you write past this?

Those who have found it odd that Darl Bundren, Mississippi farmer, sounds at times like Descartes or Hamlet must find it odder still that Addie Bundren, also of Mississippi, sounds at times like Lacan and Derrida and Irigaray. When she gets on the subject of language, her monologue seems for all the world like a Yoknapatawpha *Séminaire* (with worms as auditors), and in her pithy utterances Faulkner displays a savvy about the nature of his medium that remains unmatched in pathos and sheer intellectual brilliance. Her discourse on theory moves us, unlike most discourses on theory, because it is utterly experiential, grounded in the facts of her life. And it is for this reason that *As I Lay Dying* occupies a central place in the West's "Unbehagen der Sprache," that anguish about utterance that subtends all the activities of the speaking species and haunts, in a very special way, the professional writer. Addie has never recovered from the shock of falseness that all words occasion, and her trauma enables us to measure, with rare perspicuity, the endless sham that speaking entails. It started with the birth of Cash: "That was when I learned that words are no good; that words dont ever fit even what they are trying to say at. When he was born I knew that motherhood was invented by someone who had to have a word for it because the ones who had the children didn't care whether there was a word for it or not. I knew that fear was invented by someone that never had the fear; pride, who never had the pride" (115). The linguist tells us that words are systemic and differential, but the novelist puts some bile into it, produces a motive for the gap between sign and referent: deceit, abuse, invention. Faulkner is positing here an ethics of language and silence whereby those who *do* do not speak, while those who speak are choosing the verbal substitute, have no interest in the "real thing." Language becomes the plaything of cowards and dodgers, a rival never-never land of pure conventions, a specious tenement that contains nothing.

Thus we have the indictment of names as empty shells. Anse, the professional nondoer of the novel, epitomizes the hollow word: "Why Anse. Why are you Anse. I would think about his name until after a while I could see the word as a shape, a vessel, and I would watch him liquefy and flow into it like cold molasses flowing out of the darkness into the vessel, until the jar stood full and motionless: a significant shape profoundly without life like an empty door frame; and then I would find that I had forgotten the name of the jar" (116–17). This passage points already to the notions and imagery that Sartre will employ to articulate the viscosity of being—although "cold molasses" is unsurpassable—and the drama of consciousness as a hopeless yearning of the *pour soi* for the *en soi*.[15] Note that the jar is real enough though its name is forgotten, just as the thick nameless flow is genuine albeit expressible. Beckett's entire project in the trilogy is foreshadowed in these lines as well, especially his desperate gambit in the final volume, *L'Innommable*; one critic has even evoked the famous jar in Tennessee that Wallace Stevens wrote of, suggesting that Addie's jar takes dominion everywhere in the novel, and that it symbolizes the "tension between the perfection of the artist's dream and the failure of his art, between the plenum of silence and the poverty of vocabulary."[16]

The "plenum of silence" has often been thought to be at the center of Faulkner's poetics, a plentitude unmarred by language's tricks, a fullness essentially undeliverable but there nonetheless, beyond the words, seemingly daring the writer to come at it, to yoke it into his operation, actually damning him to failure. Yet this plenum emerges ineluctably as a vacuum when it is textualized. Addie completes her molasses rendition of Anse by turning the camera selfward and measuring her own inner space: "I would think: The shape of my body where I used to be a virgin is in the shape of a   and I couldn't think *Anse*, couldn't remember *Anse*" (117).[17] One remembers Quentin Compson's obsession with virginity, his hopeless and fatal yearning for the presexual and the prelingual, for the nonbeing that comes with his entry into the Charles River. Purity, silence, virginity: these are refusals that life cannot abide. Nor, Faulkner seems to be saying, can art. The hole in the body becomes the hole in the text, and it is insidious, corrosive, undoing. The blank page had an evocative beauty and perfection for Mallarmé, but Faulkner is drawn to our struggle with blankness, our negotiations with purity, silence, virginity, and words. He is interested in dying, not in death. Even Darl is a man emptying himself for sleep, not an empty man. And so words, sham that they are, are all the writer has. Deeds, Addie tells us, go terribly along the earth, clinging to it, while "words go straight up in a thin line, quick and harmless" (117). If that is so, as readers our job is to turn our sights upward, to watch that spectacular thin line, to see where it goes and what it does. But it may be as well that Faulkner makes a liar out of Addie, that he secretly feels that words also go terribly along the earth, that he can feel it in the very writing of the phrase itself. And it may also be that Addie champions words every bit as much as she indicts them, that her very mode of contact with others stands as a paradigm for language, the language of fiction that Faulkner is crafting: "When the switch fell I could feel it upon my flesh; when it welted and ridged it was my blood that ran, and I would think with each blow of the switch: Now you are aware of me! Now I am something in your secret and selfish life, who have marked your blood with my own for ever and ever" (114). Addie's own language has a kind of heft and density reminiscent of folklore; as Richard Godden says: "Words come to her mind much as domestic utensils might come to her hand—pots, doorframes, spiders, molasses, clothes, and blood."[18] But look at the passage: her communication with her students is a language, and it is scandalously active and immediate, imaged as marking and gouging and inscribing, as entry into the Other. *As I Lay Dying* may be understood as a sister text to Kafka's "In der Strafkolonie," for each of them seeks a visceral language of flesh and blood; each dramatizes the writer's mad desire to devise a writing that rips open the skin of the Other, that projects the author into the reader's "secret and selfish life" by marking his blood for ever and ever.

Addie has discovered that words are only signs, that they can never fuse with their referents. For her, language is a sham. But Faulkner has discovered that the gap between words and things is the very space of fiction. As a writer he is always in the black, even if his story is nothing but deficits. Darl empties himself for sleep, and Addie keens about the failure of words, but Faulkner is engaged in *filling* (the gap, the page, the reader), in making words do things they never did before, much as the Reverend Shegog performs his virtuoso oratory in *The Sound and the Fury*'s Easter sermon.[19]

Only signs, laments Addie: doorframes, jars, vessels. Only signs, exults Faulkner: the shape of a where Addie used to be a virgin, the   that Addie is lying in, the 3 mi, 2 mi to Jefferson, the 13 reasons for doing the coffin on a bevel, the semiotic spectacle of life itself: the gathering clouds that betoken the rain, Dewey Dell's conviction that "God gave women a sign when something has happened bad" (39), the world of myriad and changing shapes that we interpret throughout our lives; both figurable and nonfigurable, some legible to humans, some legible only to animals: "Looking back once, their [the mules'] gaze sweeps across us with in their eyes a wild, sad, profound and despairing quality as though they had already seen in the thick water the shape of the disaster which they could not speak and we could not see" (97).

Layers of unspeakability are peeled off in this novel, as Faulkner works to find a language for the unsayable and the invisible, to work the entire spectrum of speech acts, ranging from geometric figures, numbers, and blanks in the text, on the one hand, to luminous metaphors and similes on the other, devices for capturing the flow of life and energy in which the Bundrens are awash, always with the intent of surrounding us with voices, "as though they were speaking out of the air about your head." "La vraie éloquence se moque de l'éloquence," Pascal said, and Faulkner understands something similar about the laws of rhetoric; sinking your enterprise keeps your enterprise afloat, and flaunting the artifice of your medium gives it a peculiar authenticity. Perhaps it is a question of *qui perd gagne*, a way of losing battles so as to win wars. This is how Addie Bundren goes about discrediting the carrying power of language:

> And then he died. He did not know he was dead. I would lie by him in the dark, hearing the dark land talking of God's love and His beauty and His sin; hearing the dark voicelessness in which the words are the deeds, and the other words that are not deeds, that are just the gaps in people's lacks, coming down like the cries of the geese out of the wild darkness in the old terrible nights, fumbling at the deeds like orphans to whom are pointed out in a crowd two faces and told, That is your father, your mother. (117)

It is a curious passage. Anse's unreality is real enough to us at this point for us to extend it to his sexual connection with Addie. But when Whitfield seems to enter the scene (one has trouble imaging Anse speaking of God's beauty and his sin), and we feel heat and passion in this rhetoric. Here would be the words that are deeds, that express the "dark voicelessness" much the way the land runs out of Darl's eyes, and they are contrasted with other words, factitious words that are empty and stem from lack rather than plenitude. And then the sequence simply lifts off the ground — maybe this is what it means for words to "go up in a thin straight line" — as the cries of the geese come down, and we feel that language and lovemaking (never far apart in Faulkner) are both figured here in the "fumbling," and then are both transcended in the dazzling familial metaphor of orphans in a crowd seeing their father and mother. I have already suggested that the river serves, imagistically, as a blood conduit, a kind of umbilical cord that binds humans; here we have the umbilical cord once again, the tenuous link of genetic and blood lines that relates child and parent, conferring identity on each, and Faulkner asks us to imagine the link between word and meaning (even between sexual congress and human connection) in those terms. Yes indeed, we remind ourselves, this passage is a broadside against language; but no reader of the novel will ever see it that way because of its spellbinding eloquence, because of the mind-wrenching aptness of its figurative logic. Faulkner fully understands, just as Beckett would in the decade that followed, that the crisis of failed language is a passionate, fiery, and wonderfully verbal crisis.

Unlike Beckett (or Saussure or Derrida), however, Addie's monologue on metafiction lasts all of eight (8) pages. There is really very little *about* language in the fifty-odd other sections of the novel. Yet Faulkner is nonetheless taking up Addie's gauntlet, page after page, showing us that it is indeed possible to create a language that holds on to "doing," that fully delivers the strange and powerful transformations and upheavals that are his topic. In the Vardaman sections Faulkner achieves his most perfect expression of liberated, pulsating things, creating a panorama of flow and process. The vision is decentered:

> Then I can breathe again, in the warm smelling. I enter the stall, trying to touch him, and then I can cry then I vomit the crying. As soon as he gets through kicking I can and then I can cry, the crying can.
> "He kilt her. He kilt her."
> The life in him runs under the skin, under my hand, running through the splotches, smelling up into my nose where the sickness is beginning to cry, vomiting the crying, and then I can breathe, vomiting it. It makes a lot of noise. I can smell the life running from under my hands, up my arms, and then I can leave the stall. (36)

"Smelling" and "crying" and "vomiting" are nouns as much as verbs here, independent forces, and they have no need for human agency, since they come first, imperially, and the so-called subject follows in their wake. "He kilt her. He kilt her" is usually given honors in this cluster, thought to be the psychological ground on which the jumbled perceptions rest. But we are equally entitled to see the sandwiched motive as merely a part of the anarchic scene, and it makes good sense to read the passage as an affective workout, a tracking of "life" in all its neurological and bodily guises, a picture of the human subject as a welter of ungovernable sensations, much like the horse that Vardaman is touching. Precarious like Darl, Vardaman spends a lot of his time pinning himself and others down; in several notorious instances, however, he goes "off" ("My mother is a fish" being the briefest and most radical chapter in the novel), displaying a kind of malleability and propensity for fusion that would be comic if it were not also true, and a family trait:

> "Jewel's mother is a horse," Darl said.
> "Then mine can be a fish, cant it, Darl?" I said.
> Jewel is my brother.
> "Then mine will have to be a horse, too," I said.
> "Why?" Darl said. "If pa is your pa, why does your ma have to be a horse just because Jewel's is?"
> "Why does it?" I said. "Why does it, Darl?"
> Darl is my brother. (65)

Much ink has been spilled to account for Faulkner's bestiary. André Bleikasten has spoken of primitive totemism and made pertinent analogies to Picasso's treatment of animals in *Guernica*. Eric Sundquist has suggestively referred the entire analogical mania of the text to the workings of grief, "the possibility of relocating the lost integrity of one object in another as a way of expressing the maintenance of emotional connections that are threatening to disappear."[20] Nonetheless, the origins of such behavior, the rationale for the animal displacements, are what is behind the scenes, and it is the scene itself, the moving scene, that commands our attention. What is most striking is the slippage of identity and the crossing of species, the sheer kinetic energy that courses through the picture and rewrites the familial nexus, makes us see that this business of moving into and out of tenements is going on all the time. The river and the road house us, and they are moving. One thinks of that electric train that Vardaman so covets, as it sovereignly seems to run in and out of his mind on unchartable tracks. A new mix is in the offing here, a cinematic kind of writing that cuts time and place in its own imperious way, that reconceives the family to be a potpourri of humans and fish and horses and rabbits, all thrown together. Here is Dewey Dell sitting on the wagon watching Darl, desiring Darl to turn the mules toward New Hope for an abortion:

> *Suppose I tell him to turn. He will do what I say. Dont you know he will do what I say?* Once I waked with a black void rushing under me. I could not see. I saw Vardaman rise and go to the window and strike the knife into the fish, the blood gushing, hissing like steam but I could not see. *He'll do as I say. He always does. I can persuade him to anything. You know I can. Suppose I say Turn here.* That was when I died that time. *Suppose I do. We'll go to New Hope. We wont have to go to town.*   I rose and took the knife from the streaming fish still hissing and I killed Darl. (78)

Everything moves: not only the rushing void, gushing blood, hissing steam, and streaming fish, but the players themselves, as we fade from Darl sitting on a wagon to Lafe in the field, and we hear the echo of Dewey Dell's powerlessness (*"Dont you know he will do what I say?"*), all constituting a replay of her dying "that time," reaching its libidinal crescendo in the fantasized murder of Darl. This is how things are: swept by currents, we darkly strike.

In *As I Lay Dying* Faulkner's prose is never still nor —*pace* Addie Bundren — hollow. It keeps pace with the turmoil of the elements, and it renders the pulsing scene. Even when the language is clichéd and frozen, as in the barrage of biblical quotation and homily issuing from Cora Tull, Faulkner is more cunning and strategic than meets the eye. "Brother Whitfield wrestled with [Addie's] spirit," intones Cora, and the reader relishes this promiscuous language, this speech that has the spawning energy of malapropisms, always saying more and other than the speaker knows. Addie also uses fixed language: "He [Jewel] is my cross and he will be my salvation. he will save me from the water and from the fire. Even though I have laid down my life, he will save me" (113); but then the author rather hugely makes good on her prophecy, goes about actualizing the scriptural figures, shows that language has its own staggering indwelling power.

We know that Faulkner altered a good bit of the prose in his revisions of this novel, and that he invariably introduced complexity and ambiguity into notations that may have seemed too straightforward in the first drafts.[21] The evocations of Jewel's horse are among the most dazzling instances of revised prose that explodes on the page, and in them, once again, we can gauge the writerly project at hand: to fashion a language that makes visible and palpable the flowing life that our habituated vision fails to see. Here is how the horse moves: "Moving that quick his coat, bunching, tongues swirling like so many flames" (9); and a moment later we are treated to this hieratic frieze. "When Jewel can almost touch him, the horse stands on his hind legs and slashes down at Jewel. Then Jewel is enclosed by a glittering maze of hooves as by an illusion of wings; among them, beneath the upreared chest, he moves with the flashing limberness of a snake" (9). It hardly needs to be said that this is the potent, thickened language of a poet. In the first phrase one does not know whether "coat" is the subject or object of "moving," whether "tongues" is a noun or verb (an especially apt slippage for this text). The second passage is metamorphic in its range and thrust, as birds and snakes come onto the scene. And in both cases there is a fine sense of hot energy, and "flames" and "flashing" are literally dazzling, too bright and too quick for static notation. This kind of prose causes us to realize how frozen and paralyzed the natural scene appears under the gaze of most writers. Faulkner restores motion to things, invests them with the dizzying energy found in the river and the wind. So conceived, the things become kaleidoscopic and prancing: "He galloped up and stopped, his heels in the horse's ribs and it dancing and swirling like the shape of its mane and tail and the splotches of its coat had nothing whatsoever to do with the flesh-and-bone horse inside them . . ." (87). The continuous explosion on the page is one more tenement, this one occupied by a flesh-and-bone horse.

The "liberated" horse takes its place in a vision that is at war with unity, at war with the stable, complacent, reified world view that passes for normal, dictating that A is A and B is B. Little remains discrete and "itself" in this novel; instead, things transmute and fuse, move out of themselves and into odd mergers, come to be seen as elements of a despotic recombinant force, bent on *shaping* and coupling without end. This is the book for telling us that a nickel has a woman on one side and a buffalo on the other, that a French spyglass features a woman and a pig with two backs and no face. Indigenous color and shape may undergo sudden alteration: "Your foot looks like a nigger's foot, Cash," Vardaman tells him, as it turns black; likewise, Jewel's back "looks like a nigger's" (151–52). Faces and organs are reconfigured, redistributed: "From behind pa's leg Vardaman peers, his mouth full open and all color draining from his face into his mouth, as though he has by some means fleshed his own teeth in himself, sucking" (33). Cash, shielding the coffin from the rain is *inverted* by the light of the lantern and the wet shirt, "as though he had been abruptly turned wrong-side out, shirt and all" (50).

We watch Cash acquire a cement leg and then lose it at the cost of "sixty-odd square inches of skin," and we understand that the human figure, like the flesh-and-bone horse, has acquired a morphological repertory, is subject to endless permutations. But the most spectacular new amalgam, issuing forth with a power and authority that partake of the legendary, is to be found in the sublime scene when Jewel rides the coffin of his mother out of the burning barn:

> We see his shoulders strain as he upends the coffin and slides it single-handed from the sawhorses. It looms unbelievably tall, hiding him. I would not have believed that Addie Bundren would have needed that much room to lie comfortable in; for another instant it stands upright while the sparks rain on it scattering bursts as though they engendered other sparks from the contact. Then it topples forward, gaining momentum, revealing Jewel and the spark-ings raining on him too in engendering gusts, so that he appears to be enclosed in a thin nimbus of fire. Without stopping it overends and rears again, pauses, then crashes slowly forward and through the curtain. This time Jewel is rid-ing upon it, clinging to it, until it crashes down and flings him forward and clear and Mack leaps forward into a thin smell of scorching meat and slaps at the widening crimson-edged holes that bloom like flowers in his undershirt. (149–50)

The unavowable sexual link between Jewel the illegitimate son and Addie Bundren, pointedly echoing in the refrain "your mother is a horse," achieves finite shape in this passage as Jewel mounts his mother and rides the coffin out. More than human, Jewel is a primitive deity, part centaur, part fire god, crashing through the "curtain" of human limitation in a dazzling feat of autogenesis ("engender" twice repeats the message).[22] The storm has come: the thundering Jewel and his mount "crash," the sparks "rain," and the fire "gusts" as the humans enter the play of elements; in this realm there is only energy, and the scorching meat is one and the same as the blooming flowers, as Faulkner once again makes the ("widening crimson-edged") holes of his text incandescent.

As everyone knows, neither nature nor fiction is all crescendo. *As I Lay Dying* has its eddies and quiet spells as well as its moments of flood and apotheosis, and the prose is understandably tamer and less self-flaunting in those passages. The spectrum of tones and "idiolects" in the novel as a whole has been frequently remarked, and there is little doubt that Faulkner revels as much in the laconic, the garrulous, and the fundamentalist as he does in the surrealistic and the metaphoric. Yet one feels that crisis and trauma are the bedrock of his world, that, once one thinks about it (as Tull does), "it's liable to strike anywhere, like lightning" (46). So, the conversational coexists with the apocalyptic because it helps to make the apocalyptic bearable. We see it when the men, standing awkwardly around Addie's coffin, reminisce about the washed-out bridge, remembering Peabody's crossing it to deliver a baby ("'If I'd a crossed it every time your wife littered since, it'd a been wore out long before this, Billy,' Peabody says" [57]). The same crucial dialectic appears in the river scene. Staring into the raging waters, and simultaneously exchanging plunging looks into each other's secret places, Cash and Darl proceed to make the smallest possible talk. Punctuated by the faintly meta-phoric "I reckon we're still in the road," their leisurely words meander about the old days when Tull cut the two big white oaks which used to mark the ford. And as Jewel rides his horse into the depths, Darl remembers the circum-stances of his birth, and Cash recalls that the pillow was longer than the child, to which Darl responds, "Neither his feet nor his head would reach the end of it" (95). Measures are being taken here. Faulkner himself labels this exchange "talking quietly of old security and old trivial things" (94), and one glimpses a theme that is to become increasingly important in the later work, namely, the significance of civil talk, the redemptive capacity to humanize by reminiscing and storytelling. In *The Hamlet* we encounter the true hero of such delicate articulations, Ratliff, but in this novel talk emerges as a fragile counterpoise to the fury of the natural world. In a book where language is branded as counterfeit, whatever credible poise or balance there is must be located in the realm of "doing." And that is precisely what is achieved in the Bundrens' ordeal with the river.

"It aint on a balance," Cash repeatedly warns, and he thereby articulates the central human issue of the novel: not only how to maintain the coffin and the wagon afloat and secure—which cannot be done—but how to find any equilibrium at all in the maelstrom one inhabits. Ultimately, Faulkner knows, one unravels. No one resists the "myriad original motion." But there is more to life than "ultimately"; before that final dissolution there is the business of living and even the business of dying. Faulkner subjects the Bundrens to everything he can throw at them, but they emerge as more than victims. Initially the Bundrens are simply overwhelmed, hurled into that thick water that "clucks and murmurs"; but as they *reenter* the river, voluntarily, to re-trieve Cash's tools, they go the elements one better. One would be hard put to find in all of modern literature a scene that better images the fragile human community pitted against the forces of nature. They go back into the water, and they go together:

> We submerge in turn, holding to the rope, being clutched by one another while the cold wall of water sucks the slanting mud backward and upstream from beneath our feet and we are suspended so, groping along the cold bottom. Even the mud there is not still. It has a chill, scouring quality, as though the earth under us were in motion too. We touch and fumble at one another's extended arms, letting ourselves go cautiously against the rope; or, erect in turn, watch the water suck and boil where one of the other two gropes beneath the surface. (106-7)

The elements are on parade; everything moves, sucks, and boils. This is the Faulknerian scheme. And the humans enter it. Forming a veritable human chain, the Bundrens bring back from the depths of the swollen waters the delicate, precise instruments of human measure and balance: the rule, the square, the hammer, the saw, the chalk line. Although narrated with great simplicity, this scene has considerable pathos, for these are the tools of human "doing," the means by which human beings make whatever inroads they are to make against natural anarchy. Some twenty years before the (for some, bloated) rhetoric of the Nobel Prize speech, Faulkner is able to show, cleanly and starkly, that humanity will both endure and prevail.

Darl the dreamer unravels, but Cash the carpenter makes. Faulkner's gambit consists in utilizing all the writerly tools he can find in order to take the measure of the anarchic scene. He wants to build something that will both reflect and withstand the elements. It can therefore be no wonder that this novel opens with a man building something that will "hold," and it never stops asking the twin questions: Will it hold? What does it hold? *As I Lay Dying* is about the fictions of containment, imaged in the body holding its fluids and guts, the word "talking at" its meaning, the subject emptying himself for sleep, the human harboring a soul, the womb harboring a seed, the space where Addie used to be a virgin, the coffin-tenement with its final cargo. At a crucial moment the coffin-container is immersed in the flow, enters the raging waters. Can the container hold against the twin stresses of inside and outside?

Addie Bundren watches with approval as her son makes her final dwelling place, her last tenement, because making something well is a supreme achievement. Cash the craftsman builds the archetypal container of the novel, and he waxes eloquent on its construction, listing all his reasons for making it on a bevel. Still empty, the finished coffin is already a reverent thing, imbued with great powers; the men carry it in knowledge of its worth: "It is light, yet they move slowly; empty, yet they carry it carefully; lifeless, yet they move with hushed precautionary words to one another, speaking of it as though, complete, it now slumbered lightly alive, waiting to come awake" (52). Once again: we know that nothing can withstand the flow. The self unravels, the coffin is a scandal, and the words cheat. We cannot rival with the elements. Yet the human geste has meaning, and against the imperious flow of nature (that of the world and that within) humans can assert the balance of form. It is "as though, complete," man-made forms have a magic of their own. What do they contain? Dewey Dell feels that Cash has sawed "the long hot sad yellow days up into planks" (18); Cash speaks almost religiously of "form and content" when he claims that nothing justifies the deliberate destruction of "what a man has built with his own sweat and stored the fruit of his sweat into" (161).

Addie Bundren's monologue is a dirge about lost origins, lost essence, severance from being. But her radical critique of language and/as containers is contained within Faulkner's novel. Not only does the novel counter her charge; the novel *is* the countercharge. The coffin crafted in love, "now slumber[ing] lightly alive, waiting to come awake" (52), is a potent alternative to the "empty door frame." Much, very much of the novel's criticism deals with the *content* of that coffin: Is it Addie Bundren? Is it still Addie Bundren? Should it be rushed into the earth or escorted to Jefferson? Is it Mother or carrion or a rabbit or a fish? These are, indeed, the right questions to ask, and one is inescapably led to do so. But the *fact* of the novel, the made thing of the novel, is the coffin itself, not the endless speculations to which it gives rise. We make forms: that is the difficult and gallant task. We make do with the tools we have—our bodies and our words—because our making and our doing invest them with a peculiar magic of their own.

It is hard not to see the coffin as a figure for Faulkner's art. Words are all he has, with which to grasp the dance of the elements. They are, as Calvin Bedient says, his "pride": "Faulkner's metaphorical prose is, at its densest, not so much a mimetic instrument as the preening expression of the pride of the imagination in itself. This is to say that Faulkner's very language is proud, and proud precisely as a defiantly 'free' response to the threat always present in the perilous nakedness of the self and the world."[23] With words he must be true to what he sees, and also make something that endures. Anarchy and dissolution are everywhere, the raging blood within and the raging water without; the lightning, as Tull said, is liable to strike anywhere. So he finds words for the many voices—of the dead mother and the pilgrim family, of the river and of the air, of the beleaguered psyche and the doing body—and he orchestrates them, puts them together. He is a maker of coffins.

Thus, one admires in both Cash Bundren and William Faulkner more the coffin maker than the moralist, because the made thing is what endures. *As I Lay Dying* revolves around a voice coming from a coffin, but for the artist the speaking voices he makes and writes are the imperishable coffin. In the climactic river scene the Bundrens and the coffin enter the water, and that is lightning striking; the Bundrens then retrieve that coffin and the measuring tools that built it, and that is humanism. At the beginning of the novel the boards of the coffin are "yellow as gold, like soft gold" (3); after its rescue from the waters the wet coffin rests "in the wagon bed," and Faulkner tells us that the planks are "hushed a little with wetting yet still yellow," then adding, casually, perfectly, "like gold seen through water" (105). In that coffin made of gold we see a figure of Faulkner's art and his belief.

9

Faulkner: Fusion and Confusion
in *Light in August*

There is an unforgettable moment in *Light in August* when Lena's newborn infant is "fused" and "confused" with the infant Joe Christmas. In calling the child "Joey," Christmas's grandmother, Mrs. Hines, greatly bewilders Lena herself, who is afraid that "she might get me mixed up, like they say how you might cross your eyes and then you cant uncross. . . . "[1] This mixing up, as Alfred Kazin has suggested in his well-known essay on the novel, confuses the reader as well, who comes to it "with a shock," encountering "Faulkner's desperate eagerness to wrest all the possible implications from his material . . . his attempt to will his painful material into a kind of harmony that it does not really possess."[2]

When one thinks about it, it is evident that Kazin's critique is hardly limited to this scene; it has been leveled at the entire novel and indeed, at one time or another, at most of Faulkner's novels. Faulkner's work, more than most, flaunts its piecemeal quality, its fragmentation: whether it be the separate narrative voices in *The Sound and the Fury*, *As I Lay Dying*, *Absalom, Absalom!* and the like, or the separate short stories posing as a novel in *The Hamlet* and *Go Down, Moses*, or the tit-for-tat interweaving of *The Wild Palms*, Faulkner makes it devilishly hard for us to see his works as unified wholes. Where order and integrity are achieved in some kind of overview, the result is either frenetic and inflated, as with Gavin Stevens, or teasingly enigmatic, as with Dilsey's famous "I seed de beginnin, en now I sees de endin." Most Faulkner readers never quite see so much, caught as they are in the author's furiously juxtaposed voices, times, and stories.[3] It may be "fusion" seen from the proper Olympian perspective, but down at the narrative level, in the arena, it looks a great deal like that primal "confusion" imaged in *Absalom, Absalom!* by Judith Sutpen's figure of the loom:

> You get born and you try this and you dont know why only you keep on trying it and you are born at the same time with a lot of other people, all mixed up with them, like trying to, having to, move your arms and legs with strings only the same strings are hitched to all the other arms and legs and the others all trying and they dont know why either except that the strings are all

in one another's way like five or six people all trying to make a rug on the same loom only each one wants to weave his own pattern into the rug. . . .[4]

Pattern certainly exists, but we are the ingredients rather than the makers of it. And the makers themselves seem petulant and willful, as if life were not so much a loom as a puppet show in the hands of angry children. We see, too, the crowdedness of an ecosystem that is not likely to respect privacy, that may indeed specialize in incursion, disruption, and trauma. Finally, this passage tells us, as a narrational formula, how the Jamesian novel, with its single figure in the carpet, is given a special, rather manic, even cubist turn of the screw by Faulkner's flirtation with incoherence as he strives for multiplicity. Faulkner experiments incessantly with the forms of fractured consciousness, isolated voice, jagged point of view, and bewildering connection because that is the experience for which he must find a shape. Fragmentation and confusion are his themes, and competing patterns on the loom must be his form. But the final stature and maturity of his work lie in his capacity ultimately to assess and to frame these shards, these pieces, to "fuse" them — somewhat analogously to Eliot's and Joyce's earlier "fusings" — into a very special composite, a harmony of his own. To understand the nature of that harmony is the task of this study, and we can do so only when we have fully faced the confusion. So let us return to the beginning and consider again Lena's distress:

> She looks at Hightower; her eyes are questioning, intent. "She keeps on calling him Joey. When his name aint Joey. And she keeps on. . . ." She watches Hightower. Her eyes are puzzled now, questioning, doubtful. "She keeps on talking about — She is mixed up someway. And sometimes I get mixed up too, listening, having to . . . . . ." Her eyes, her words, grope, fumble.
> "Mixed up?"
> "She keeps on talking about him like his pa was that — the one in jail, that Mr Christmas. She keeps on, and then I get mixed up and it's like sometimes I cant — like I am mixed up too and I think that his pa is that Mr — Mr Christmas too — " She watches him; it is as though she makes a tremendous effort of some kind. "But I know that aint so. I know that's foolish. It's because she keeps on saying it and saying it, and maybe I aint strong good yet, and I get mixed up too. But I am afraid. . . ." (701)

Let us understand what kinds of certainties and stabilities are undermined here. The making of a child by a woman and a man would appear to be the quintessence of cause-and-effect logic, of reliable sequence, of the tangible, measurable, provable positivist world view. Lena is hardly a philosopher, but she recognizes the inherent scandal — and, indeed, the threat — of Mrs. Hines's assertion. It is as if she were being indoctrinated into the loom world, and she is now to experience — firsthand, in her own skin — the odd coupling that seems to govern the text she inhabits. What is real if one's child, one's flesh, is not one's own? And how can the begetting of a child be anything other than direct, immediate, knowable to both parties involved? Or, at the very least, to the mother? There is yet another dislocation at work here, one that looms astonishingly large in Faulkner's work, and it is the rupture between name and person: "Keeps on calling him Joey. When his name aint Joey."

Things are coming unglued in this passage, but they are then reconnected in some strange fashion, issuing in new alliances, "wedding" Lena to Joe Christmas, a man she has never seen before, christening her child "Joey" although she insists "I aint named him yet" (702). Confusion or fusion? What is unmistakably clear is that we have an encounter here—and does it truly matter whether we term it figurative or not?—between the integral Lena Grove and the man who personifies fragmentation, Joe Christmas. Why the wedding?

Faulkner was drawn, from the very outset of his career, to shell-shocked heroes, those walking wounded—like Donald Mahon or Bayard Sartoris—who had been so undone by their experiences as to be permanently disabled, and mute in the bargain.[5] We soon see, however, a new language of astonishment and outrage which will accommodate the damaged psyche: hence Benjy and Darl and Vardaman exhibit a kind of generic amazement and precariousness, a kind of ontological instability which, because it can take nothing for granted, ceases to distinguish between self and world. Thus, the cows can run up and down the hill, the bowl can go away and come back, the chopped-up fish is lying in the "bleeding pan"; severed from the scene and unaware of its own mediation, such a consciousness is easily jumbled, and it speaks its own poetry in phrases such as "my mother is a fish" or "Caddie smelled like trees." Most poignant of all is the homelessness of such a psyche, locked in its own machinations, even, in the case of Darl, aware of its solipsism. Emptying himself for sleep, desperately sorting out "ours" and "theirs," negotiating and renegotiating the ontological distance between *is* and *was*, Darl Bundren epitomizes the type of psychic exile that haunted the early Faulkner. Such a character knows itself to be Nobody, a fiction, a construct, an assemblage; it will, under stress, "unravel," "as though the clotting which is you had dissolved into the myriad original motion. . . ."[6]

Within *Light in August* Joe Christmas's ancestry may be enigmatic, but with the Faulknerian oeuvre his forebears are present and accounted for. What is new about Christmas is the remarkable social and sexual coloration which Faulkner has grafted onto this familiar psychic profile. The neurological antics of alienation and solipsism could now, as the novelist must have seen, serve as a wedge into a new range of cultural and behavioral issues. Even more deprived of origin than Darl, Joe Christmas has no givens, no purchase in the world. Black in the white world and white among blacks, he is a living "negative," in the photographic as well as the moral sense, existing only insofar as others define him, taking shape through outside illumination, whether it be the determining gaze of others or even the headlights of a car.[7] As a child at the orphanage he learns his fate from a black yardman whom he has asked, "How come you are a nigger?" The answer resonates throughout the novel: "And the nigger said, 'Who told you I am a nigger, you little white trash bastard?' and he says 'I aint a nigger' and the nigger says, 'You worse than that. You dont know what you are. And more than that, you wont never know. You'll live and you'll die and you wont never know . . .'" (683). Joe

Christmas receives his initiation here, is prophetically baptized as Nobody, understands his life to be an unanswerable riddle.

Nobody is by no means an empty or ideal proposition, however. Whereas Fitzgerald made his Mr. Nobody from Nowhere a hero of desire and dreams, Faulkner is intent on tapping the epistemological rage generated by these conditions. His rendition of Christmas is, as most critics have recognized, a bristling portrait of a man in search of wholeness, of integrity in the literal, formal sense of the word. And Faulkner's narrative gambit consists of denying him that integrity over and over again, and in ways that are worth focusing on. Especially effective are the metaphors he introduces to render Christmas's distance from others, from himself. When he storms into Bobbie's room, following the disastrous encounter with McEachern, he sees Max and a stranger there as well. The scene is narrated in a remarkable fashion, as if Christmas were on an operating table, going into or coming out of anesthesia, seeing and hearing but failing to comprehend:

> He [the stranger] and Max might have been brothers in the sense that any two white men strayed suddenly into an African village might look like brothers to them who live there. His face, his chin where the light fell upon it, was still. Whether or not the stranger was looking at him, Joe did not know. And that Max was standing just behind him Joe did not know either. And he heard their actual voices without knowing what they said, without even listening: *Ask him*
>
> *How would he know* Perhaps he heard the words. But likely not. Likely they were as yet no more significant than the rasping of insects beyond the closedrawn window, or the packed bags which he had looked at and not yet seen. (557)

The reference to the African village conveys the quasi-anthropological character of Joe's estrangement from his fellows, the perceptual blockages that can jam all communication. Faulkner is the master of static and noise, and much of his work is, in that sense, the polar opposite of the exquisite verbal duets of Henry James, those fine scenes of nuanced repartee; instead, the pronouncements of others are at a terrible distance from us, at our periphery, muffled, getting "in," if at all, only syllablewise. Everything so sharply etched and present in this scene — whether the stranger was looking, where Max was standing, what they were saying — is peculiarly islanded, out of Joe's cognitive reach, presented as undecipherable code.

But the distance of Others is only part of the problem. Joe Christmas is equally cut off from his own internal workings. In him the rift between mind and body is virtually absolute: his consciousness invariably lags after or precedes events, so as to produce dislocations of this sort: "'Get on back to town,' he said. 'I'll be there soon as I . . . .' Apparently he was not aware of what he was saying nor of what was happening; when the woman turned suddenly in the door of the car and began to beat him in the face he did not move, his voice did not change: 'Yes. That's right. I'll be there as soon as I—' Then he turned and ran, while she was still striking at him" (551). Few writers can match Faulkner in mapping those moments when the body mutinies, becomes the locus of ungovernable stresses akin to the electrical overload that produces epileptic seizure. In his work we come to appreciate how miraculous human balance is, how the human creature is an intricate assemblage of firing neurons that just may go haywire; and we attain a deepened sense of "fit," of how fine it is when cerebral command and bodily response are in sync with each other. Often enough things go the other way: the body takes the lead, pursues its mad dark logic, and informs — later — the brain of its activities. These neural and affective "wildings," unsponsored and ungovernable, not only unownable but heinously independent, write large for us the very somatic language of Nobody.

We are not far, in Faulkner's world, from those badly dubbed films in which the sounds uttered and the lip movements uttering them are out of phase, and it is painful to watch such films, doubtless because they reveal the talking self to be a machine that can malfunction, a human phonograph that depends on relays and speakers, on fine-tuning, if speech is to occur. Perhaps the silent films, with their jolting rhythms, their plenitude of gesture and thinness of word, their systematic disjunction between motion and imprinted language, convey even more forcefully the halting, checked, out-of-sync nature of the Faulkner subject. In his work the time lag separating language and flesh can reach monstrous proportions, and — unlike in film, where the disjunction is mechanical and uncommented — Faulkner has taken this *décalage*, this rift between the neural and the somatic and the verbal to be part of his theme.

Hence, in *Light in August* there are sequences in which Christmas is strangely present and absent at the same time, and it is altogether characteristic that we see him *discover* that he is brandishing a revolver in front of frightened teenagers, or a razor in front of a group of blacks. To deliver the "feel" of Christmas's severed condition, Faulkner has brilliantly chosen to narrate from the inside, to convey to us the precariousness of a subject constantly on the verge of "losing it," a subject never at one with its "own" data. This form of disconnectedness finds perhaps its most extreme image in the scene I have already commented on, when Christmas has been beaten up by Max and the stranger: "He did not know how long he lay there. He was not thinking at all, not suffering. Perhaps he was conscious of somewhere within him the two severed wireends of volition and sentience lying, not touching now, waiting to touch, to knit anew so that he could move" (561). The electrical imagery of broken circuitry and severed wire ends constitutes a graphic, neurological figure for Joe's condition, and it illuminates in a peculiarly high-tech fashion the force field that images life in this novel, retaining the intricacy of interlocking parts suggested by the loom figure, but now energized in terms of checked and flowing current. Except that the subject/Nobody is on the receiving end: Christmas is shown throughout as discontinuous, moving between "plugged" and "unplugged," a bewildered spectator of his own life. How many times do we hear him say, "I am going to do something," or in its more appropriate passive formulation, "Something is going to happen to me"?

So out of sync is Christmas with himself and his world, it actually comes as no surprise that he balks at "natural" animal functions, especially in the realms of food and sex. He violently rejects food that is offered him, calling it "woman's muck," and his sexual malaise extends from nausea and disgust at menstruation to pathological violence bordering on rape, imaged literally in the women he brutalizes, imaged figuratively in the metal tins of liquor he pierces, the buttons that he obsessively cuts off, the cracked urns that he imagines from which "there issued something liquid, deathcolored, and foul" (538). Christmas's woman trouble—his horror of smoothness and softness, of flow and connection—is the obverse side of his evident preference for man-to-man binary arrangements, oppositional affairs ranging from the beatings by McEachern (mirrored in the wrestling match with Joanna) to the oddly physical coexistence with Brown, the "other wife."[8]

Nowhere is Joe's fragmented self more in evidence than in the famous toothpaste scene. After the child ingests the phallic sweet paste while overhearing the sexual intercourse between the dietician and her friend, he again discovers and displays the radical disjunction of his nature: "In the rife, pink-womansmelling obscurity behind the curtain he squatted, pinkfoamed, listening to his insides, waiting with astonished fatalism for what was about to happen to him. Then it happened. He said to himself with complete and passive surrender: 'Well, here I am'" (489). Again one cannot fail to see the prophetic import of these lines, and the suggestion of victimization, even by one's body, is reinforced into something larger still, more akin to a scapegoat, a ritual sacrifice. "Well, here I am" is the Faulknerian "Ecce homo," and this man who is profoundly estranged and fragmented, broken into wire ends and component parts, will in effect play out the fuller sacrifice that is contained in his name: disconnected in his life, he will be dismembered at his death.

I have sketched out the dimensions of Joe Christmas's disconnectedness in order to show just what it is that Lena Grove encounters in that strange scene of confusion with which this chapter began. Still stranger is the fact that they never do literally meet, that they never have met, strange because the whole novel is preparing us for that meeting. Not only do the conventions of fiction usually require that main characters come into contact with one another, but *Light in August* in particular seems little more than a stage on which the Lena Grove phenomenon is meant to confront the Joe Christmas phenomenon. In view of his modality, condition, and emblematic name, Joe Christmas may be thought to represent the fall from nature and loss of integrity inherent in modern life itself, and indeed he has been widely interpreted along these lines. In search of his identity, the tool of culture and the victim of society, Joe Christmas literally embodies neurosis, displays Faulkner's acute sense of anarchy and psychic ungluing. He makes us understand the grisly truth of our homely phrase for malaise: being at loose ends.

Regardless of whether they meet in the flesh, Lena Grove is Christmas's opposite number on virtually every count. Her perspective is ceaselessly natural rather than cultural: she moves into that Mississippi community and into Faulkner's novel on a kind of timeless treadmill, like a denizen from another world, bringing pastoral news of urns and nature's cycles. Ready to have her child, confident that the Lord will see to it that the husband comes forth and the family is reunited, she exposes the nullity of all social codes and moral structures. Each successive farmer and his wife do Lena's bidding, no matter how reluctantly; their moral disapproval is utterly weightless and irrelevant. Lena is an embodiment of natural grace: in marked contrast to Christmas, she reveres the physical world and is both at home in and at one with it. She eats her "sourdines" decorously, and she conducts the birth of her child with equal decorum. Her pledge to nature is both total and totally unconscious, leaving her with no awareness, no inner life whatsoever to speak of. Earth mother, pagan goddess, carrying in her body the most elemental plot known to the human species, Lena Grove is integral and vital; hers is the orbit, the natural rhythm, the very life principle by which and against which the community and its scapegoat, Christmas, must be measured.

That Faulkner has intentionally chosen to juxtapose these two stories is evident even in the novel's packaging. Lena's comments on her coming "clean from Alabama" and her closing refrain, "My, my. A body does get around," effectively frame the Joe Christmas material, leaving unanswered only the larger, more crucial questions: Can Lena Grove really contain, "get around," Joe Christmas? Can the life story encircle the death story, other than by authorial fiat? If the characters meet only figuratively, how can we speak of interaction? This last query leads us back to the scene of fusion and confusion, in which Lena the harmonious and unconscious seems to experience something akin to thought, the notion of an encounter that would be somehow figurative and still true. Can Lena's child be Joey? Even stranger, can Christmas be its father?

This baby, whose lurking, pressing whereabouts are signaled from the very outset of the novel, is a kind of human time bomb, a relentless reminder that what looks closed is not, that what looks fixed is not. That unborn child who thrusts every so often makes it abundantly clear that he intends out, and that he will alter the scene. The familiar prisonhouses of morality, language, and the body will be to no avail: the nameless child will emerge from the apparently closed body of its mother, in accord with principles that have little to do with Mississippi. Not only does his entry into the ranks celebrate the life principle, but it does so in a spectacularly verbal way. Lena's child is a peculiarly "communal" infant; just as Lena's own vital presence yokes others into life, turns Byron from a machine into a person, makes a doctor out of Hightower and brings him briefly into the community, so too does the baby "touch" just about all the characters in the novel. The birth of the infant is a relational mesh, a kind of magic web in which all are caught, mirrored, and linked. Part of the magic involved here is verbal. When we read, for instance, of "Byron Bunch borning a baby" (689), we must pause and try to gauge the strange truth of Faulkner's phrase. With similar figurative logic, Hightower hopes that the baby will be named for him, thinks of precedents for such namings. Somewhat more distantly, but no less vitally in terms of the novel's design, the child stands for the infant Joanna Burden wanted but never had, or indeed the grim "reward" that Lucas Burch had but never wanted. Most pointedly and most confusingly, the baby is Joey, the child of Mrs. Hines's Milly.

The birth of this child is the long-awaited center of the novel, as Lena climactically becomes "light in August." The way in which Faulkner has "shared" the child "out" through linkage and metaphor makes us realize that "origin" is never so discernible as we might think. Lena's child is not pinned down, and although that might confuse us, it also obliges us to see in this birth the very play of a freedom that is at once writerly, biological, and social. Radically different in tone and manner from the Fitzgeraldian gambit visible in the playful making of "Blocks" Biloxi, Faulkner's project is nonetheless a highly self-conscious meditation on freedom and writing. With this infant Faulkner moves into the theme of Nobody's Home, treats us to a vision of liberated language, of a free, undetermined entity, unbound by referent, by cause and effect, having multiple origins. Lena insists that she "aint named him yet," and he is therefore available for all names—unlike Joe Christmas— but victim of none. Christmas suffers the tyranny of name unto death, not just his own name but those monolithic imprisoning codes of black and white, codes that Faulkner powerfully depicts as *nominal*, although no less despotic for being only words; whereas Lena's baby is splendidly "unfixed," an elo- quent testimony to the very principle of generativeness and freedom. In Lena's confusion over the child's multiplicity, Faulkner speaks to our own disarray at the spectacle of the open-ended sign, the freedom that must be unnamed if it is to be. Homespun, country to the core, devoid of the magnificent metalan- guage of Addie Bundren's monologue, this scene about Lena's child, about the claims on Nobody, is as beautiful and profound as anything Faulkner ever wrote about the relation between words and flesh.

The birth of Lena's child gives rise to questions and to freedoms that are ultimately more than verbal. One of the oldest stories of our culture involves the birth of a child whose father cannot, in any ordinary sense, be named. It was, for all those who used human logic, a confusing story. What is more unfathomable than a fatherless infant or a virgin birth? What sense of identity would that child have? How would one trace those origins? The Christ story is the death of realism, for its coherence transcends the dictates of both reason and flesh, the twin deities of realism. This is not a matter of doctrine or received religious views, and Faulkner always referred to the Christian ele- ments of his work as familiar, usable paradigms rather than articles of belief. But Faulkner was forced to devise a narrative strategy that would be true to the world as he saw it and felt it, a world animated by forces that are meta- physical as well as physical. He wrote out of the conviction that spirit and imagination and love have the capacity to project their own rival world, one linked and connected in ways that defy ordinary logic, one whose fusion can only seem to be, at least initially, confusion.

Hence, in this version of the Story, Lena Grove gives life to that child in the manger where Christmas and Brown have lived. And she is told that her child is more than her own flesh and blood, has another name; and she is afraid, as if dimly aware that she has been acting a larger role in a stranger play than she realized. The play is literally a creation play, centered on the making of life, of new life, ultimately of eternal life. The severed connections and wire ends of Joe Christmas's life have yielded to a vision of mysterious connection, of unwitting alliances, of triumphant linkages. The birth of a child is the flesh-and-blood evidence of the spirit, the creation of two where there was one, the making of something from nothing. It is Genesis, as Byron senses: "Then he heard the child cry. Then he knew. Dawn was making fast" (695). To connect dawn and birth is to hint that each is a face of the other, to see the life principle in its many guises. No thing is a single thing in the visionary model, especially not birth. Speaking of the same fabled birth in a manger that is mirrored in Faulkner's novel, T. S. Eliot's wise man expresses confusion comparable to that of Lena Grove:

> All this was a long time ago, I remember,
> And I would do it again, but set down
> This set down
> This: were we led all that way for
> Birth or Death? There was a Birth, certainly,
> We had evidence and no doubt. I had seen birth and death,
> But had thought they were different; this Birth was
> Hard and bitter agony for us, like Death, our Death.
> We returned to our places, these Kingdoms,
> But no longer at ease here, in the old dispensation,
> With an alien people clutching their gods.
> I should be glad of another death.[9]

Eliot's poem, with its modulated irony and its grumbling, British, sharply focused list of particulars, begins, we recall, with a highly descriptive, evocative picture of the Magi's journey: camels, melting snow, silken girls, sherbet, night fires, running stream, water mill, old white horse. Things and places and smells and sights can be recounted in that vein. This is knowable material: surfaces and sequences behave. But when he comes to the event itself, the wise man falters, is confused. The birth of Christ signals more than a new religion: it is the death of the Magi's modus operandi, and even his language opens onto a void. The "old dispensation" is the familiar "positivist" one maintained precisely by means of "evidence" and "no doubt"; but the scene he has witnessed proclaims an authority beyond logic and realism, and it testifies to fusions and linkages, traffic between spirit and flesh for which he has no precedent or paradigm. Neither mimesis nor irony will convey what he has to say, but he has no tools other than mimesis and irony. Faulkner was drawn to the challenge of this theme perhaps even more forcefully than Eliot, for his need to discover or invent an alternative to determinism, an overpass beyond realism, a new dispensation, was particularly urgent. The traditional novel form itself, with its conventions of plot and character, as he well knew, has common cause with directionality and death, with closure and evidence. In asking how fiction could embody the coursing life that he believed in, the lines of force that mesh together spirit and flesh, that are capable of wedding strangers, he saw that his language would have to undermine single meanings and fixed essences, that strange affinities would have to be made visible by the text, affinities between seemingly distinct characters, between concepts as opposed as birth and death.

There is also a death in *Light in August*. When Joe Christmas completes his sacrificial career and is both shot and castrated by Percy Grimm, Faulkner insists on describing this garish and violent ending as a lyrical and pastoral beginning:

> Then Grimm too sprang back, flinging behind him the bloody butcher knife. "Now you'll let white women alone, even in hell," he said. But the man on the floor had not moved. He just lay there, with his eyes open and empty of everything save consciousness, and with something, a shadow, about his mouth. For a long moment he looked up at them with peaceful and unfathomable and unbearable eyes. Then his face, body, all seemed to collapse, to fall in upon itself, and from out the slashed garments about his hips and loins the pent black blood seemed to rush like a released breath. It seemed to rush out of his pale body like the rush of sparks from a rising rocket; upon that black blast the man seemed to rise soaring into their memories forever and ever. They are not to lose it, in whatever peaceful valleys, beside whatever placid and reassuring streams of old age, in the mirroring faces of whatever children they will contemplate old disasters and newer hopes. It will be there, musing, quiet, steadfast, not fading and not particularly threatful, but of itself alone serene, of itself alone triumphant. (742–43)

This scene attempts no less than the depiction of life after death, and it simply runs off the realist map. Christmas is at first seen in his characteristic passive position, a thing, mishandled by others and disconnected from itself. It is the determinist story of Nobody reaching its unpreventable, inalterable climax. But the climax is not what we expect. A great release comes into being, and it powerfully fuses motifs of sexual orgasm, of the holy spirit, of ascension and final peace and serenity. Christmas's death has a potency that not only projects him permanently, now as a dominant insider, into the psychic landscapes of the community, but figuratively enacts the release of seed and semen that could father Lena's child. Things are coming together here, and this new dispensation makes visible a kind of propriety, a kind of fit that we could not have suspected. At last "steadfast," "serene" and "triumphant," dwelling in "peaceful valleys, beside . . . placid and reassuring streams," Joe Christmas appears to take on Lena's very character, to embrace her in some ghostly fusion.

Certain chemicals when heated to the proper temperature alter their state, recompose. In Faulkner's best novels his materials are worked in a comparable way, brought to that pitch which will catalyze them. "Someone has to rake up the leaves before you can have a bonfire," as we learn in *Absalom, Absalom!*, and the heat of the bonfire is a liberating heat, an explosive force which spawns new forms, new alignments. What produces the heat? I think we have to ascribe this radiant energy to the brooding mind, the mind—of Faulkner, of his reader—that returns over and over to the bare data of experience and dwells on them, works them up, ponders their prismatic form, their multiple significances, their striking and unpredictable parallels and patterns. To think is to rake up the leaves; to think hard enough is to make a bonfire. We are forced to think about the data of *Light in August*, to ponder the fit of its materials. The birth of Lena's child precedes Christmas's death; knowing the linear scheme that largely governs our bodies and our plots, we are likely to think in terms of *chronos*, to cast the unnamed child onto the treadmill that leads to crucifixion, to see Christmas's black shadow fall on the baby. Such is precisely Joanna Burden's mixed perspective on black and white:

> But after that I seemed to see them for the first time not as people, but as a thing, a shadow in which I lived, we lived, all white people, all other people. I thought of all the children coming forever and ever into the world, white, with the black shadow already falling upon them before they drew breath. And I seemed to see the black shadow in the shape of a cross. And it seemed like the white babies were struggling, even before they drew breath, to escape from the shadow that was not only upon them but beneath them too, flung out like their arms were flung out, as if they were nailed to the cross. (585)

This view of echo and double accounts for much of Faulkner's art, both his treatment of blacks and whites and also his notion of language itself. To see in each white birth a black crucifixion is to translate the birth-death sequence into a familiar kind of Faulknerian doom, a punishment of cultural and racial crimes, and that forbidding assessment of the novel remains open. But, just as Eliot's wise man is obliged to rethink the connection between birth and death, so too is Faulkner's reader invited to consider another reading, one that reverses the direction, moves from death to birth, from determinism to freedom, from violence to peace, from crucifixion to resurrection. To be sure, the journey through contingency beyond death flouts both flesh and reason, but it can be *imagined*. Mrs. Hines imagines it:

> "I never saw him when he could walk and talk. Not for thirty years I never saw him. I am not saying he never did what they say he did. Ought not to suffer for it like he made them that loved and lost suffer. But if folks could maybe just let him for one day. Like it hadn't happened yet. Then it could be like he had just went on a trip and grew mangrown and come back. If it could be like that for just one day. After that I would not interfere. If he done it, I would not be the one to come between him and what he must suffer. Just for one day, you see. Like he had been on a trip and come back, telling me about the trip, without any living earth against him yet." (686)

This "one day" reprieve sought by Mrs. Hines, this miracle which could momentarily undo or transcend the world of fact, is, of course, what she experiences when she sees Lena's child, sees him as Milly's baby Joey. The onslaught of experience is so brutal and ungovernable in Faulkner's world that we frequently encounter his dream of innocence, of a kind of virginal prior state, a precious alternative and second chance; Quentin Compson's entire life is cued to this premise, and he dies for it. With Mrs. Hines, however, we understand the desire to erase the slate to be a matter of imagination and vision, unavailable in the realm of facts but achievable, perhaps, as a fiction. But the heart of the matter lies with us, not with Mrs. Hines. We must be the ones to fathom Faulkner's language, to piece together his disparate images and faces and colors, to fuse the birth and the death, to see the cross and to see in it both crucifixion and rebirth. The fragmented and dismembered Joe Christmas can be fully understood only when "we" make him whole, only when his transgressions and his suffering are encompassed within a larger Passion story, just as the fragmented Compson story must be placed against the backdrop of the Easter sermon and the black congregation if its pattern is to emerge. Vision, Faulkner is saying, is aggressively shaping, not passively retinal. It does not depict the world; it constitutes the world. To go beyond the separate, given pieces, to reassemble and connect, is to transform the old world of fact and death into a new world of spirit and life. Like dawn and the infant, it is a new beginning, a new slate, "like the world never had anything against him yet." Faulkner's best fiction is devoted to the making of new constellations, of supreme fictions, of might-have-beens that are truer than truth.

It must be emphasized that we are dealing here with no escape into symbol, no "desperate eagerness to wrest all the possible implications from his material." The journey to these new vistas requires overpassing, much as the birth follows long labor, and we must rake up the leaves before we can have the bonfire. The visionary mode is "earned" in Faulkner; on the far side of things, it is reached only after the things have been measured, "suffered," and transcended. For the most part this new world is an expanded picture of what we knew, but the "new dispensation" stresses linkage rather than separation, and it binds over space and time rather than stopping with them. One discovers connection, in the blood and in the flesh as well as in the imagination, so that the individuals find themselves enmeshed in a new family. The two boys at Harvard become the two southern youths in *Absalom*, and they mount, all four of them, the same horses; likewise in that novel Quentin goes beyond Judith's loom view of entanglement as he realizes the folly of individuation, the absurdity of thinking that anything has a beginning or an end: "Maybe we are both Father. Maybe nothing ever happens once and is finished. Maybe happen is never once but like ripples maybe on water after the pebble sinks, the ripples moving on, spreading, the pool attached by a narrow umbilical water-cord to the next pool which the first pool feeds, has fed, did feed . . ." (261).

There is only connection. Incest and miscegenation are the magnetic poles of much of Faulkner's fiction, precisely because they stand for fusion where there "should" be distance. The past *is* rather than *was*, because the mind works through fusion and metaphor, rather than tedious sequence and logic. The magnetic force field imperiously links and bonds the creatures within it. The separate pieces can cohere dreadfully, in schemes of incest and parricide, as Sophocles demonstrated long ago in his Oedipus story, as Faulkner was to demonstrate in *Absalom* and *Go Down, Moses*. But in Faulkner's culture (like that of Dickens and Balzac, who are equally drawn to the emergence of denied and occulted linkages) which specializes in segregation—blacks versus whites, North versus South, men versus women—the connective vision is both scandalous and necessary. And the process can be redemptive when it allows us to move beyond the *huis clos* of single bodies, the prison of the here and now. Joe Christmas is a terrifying creation because he is Nobody, irremediably alone, cut off from everything. The pattern and art of *Light in August* are in the service of connection, of unsuspected umbilical cords and metaphoric fusions. Even Lena Grove, paragon of wholeness that she is, comes into the novel alone, looking for a husband; her isolation is the social fact of her life, yet she knows she is in the Lord's hands, and the Lord connects: "Her voice is quiet, tranquil, stubborn. 'I reckon a family ought to be together when a chap comes. Specially the first one. I reckon the Lord will see to that'" (414). The Mississippians scoff at such naïveté, but the author structures his story to bear her out. Her "realist" family may be long gone, and Lucas Burch will renege on his role, but there is something undeniably familial in the sight the doctor takes in when he visits the mother and child: "He entered the room, where a young woman whom he had never seen before lay wan and spent on a narrow army cot, and an old woman in a purple dress whom he had also never seen before, held the child upon her lap. There was an old man asleep on a second cot in the shadow. . . . He went to the old woman who held the child. 'Well, well,' he said, 'Byron must have been excited. He never told me the whole family would be on hand, grandpa and grandma too'" (692). There is nothing "reckless" or "desperate" here. On the face of it just realistic notation: a young woman, an old woman, a child, an old man. And we note the stress of foreignness: the doctor has never seen any of these people before; we are not too far from the anthropological perspective chosen to render Joe's fading in and out of consciousness. But then things come together. Faulkner is once again heating up his materials, hinting at a figurative propriety, a level of connectedness that we had not seen. There is something profoundly modernist in Faulkner's gambit, a recognition that the family we were born into is either dead or damaged, whereas the family we need has to be built. And it can be built. Kinship may be literal and genetic, but it may also be figurative and of the spirit. Even the most biological of bonds, such as the "blood"—the sort of link we inherit rather than elect—can be liberated into metaphor, into an *imagined* sense of continuum which is chosen rather than suffered. Again the four boys on the two horses in *Absalom* come to mind, fused into a new family: "not two of them there and then either but four of them riding the two horses through the iron darkness, and that not mattering either: what faces and what names they called themselves and were called by so long as the blood coursed—the blood, the immortal brief recent intransient blood which could hold honor above slothy unregret and love above fat and easy shame" (295).

The family that is *made* rather than *given* can also stand for the central paradigm of Joyce's *Ulysses*. Robert Scholes has written of the "structuralist imagination" as it functions in Joyce, and one of its results is the creation of "open," unbounded characters, characters "sharing" in their environment.[10] Joyce is everywhere seeking to juxtapose consented spiritual kinships against suffered biological ones, to portray the work of art and language as a special progeny which is contrasted to the flesh-and-blood child. The fundamental dynamic of Bloom and Stephen as variously complementary figures bears witness to the same need to create symbolic networks that might replace one's biological and social matrices. Such activity is not only an exercise of authorial freedom (whereby the artist enjoys a sovereignty peculiar to art alone), but also a provocative challenge to the traditional limits and hegemony of "self" as a rigid, closed figure of individuation. In such art we begin to see what an ecological fiction might look like, and we are helped to a view of interconnection and interdependence, of the potential "traffic" that takes place between discrete selves, one that the classical novelist, respectful of distances and individual contours, cannot easily render.

In *Light in August*, no less than in *Absalom, Absalom!*, Faulkner attempts to move beyond "the central I-am's private own." The flowing blood of *Absalom* and the metempsychosis of *Ulysses* are both figures of plurality and connection, and the work of each author tests the powers of the self in a scheme that both surpasses and informs it. Continuum is all. Lena's baby demonstrates the cyclical pattern in action, and Hightower imagines more children coming from her: *"More of them. Many more. That will be her life, her destiny. The good stock peopling in tranquil obedience to it the good earth; from these hearty loins without hurry or haste descending mother and daughter"* (699). The round of life, like the blood, is anonymous, knows no names, moves "without hurry or haste." Here is the continuum and vitality from which Joe Christmas has been severed, the "tranquil obedience to the good earth" which is pure process, pure harmony. Many are the ways of dealing with this central, irresistible force, and Faulkner would seem to have dramatized all of them. Christmas fights it, Joanna Burden has a first and final ecstatic fling with it, Hightower is magnetically drawn to it, Byron is wholly altered by it.

To make a family is the artist's way of rendering homage to this force. All parties must be born again, reshaped, and reconstituted. Hence, as we have seen, the baby unites the various actors of the novel, yokes them—figuratively if not literally—into a paradigm of family or fatherhood. The beauty and pathos of the novel lie in the fact that this sea change, this transformation, is not achieved simply by authorial sleight of hand. Just as Quentin and Shreve must experience love and generosity before they can "become" Charles Bon and Henry Sutpen, so must Hightower be *knowingly* forced into life and birth, just as Joanna must "die" after menopause, after her connection with fertility is severed. Christmas, as we've seen, is altered only through death and dying, but he seems then to attain the peace and plenitude denied him in life. Perhaps the most fascinating transformation is that of Byron, who must make the tiny but miraculous journey from *Bunch* to *Burch*.

It is worth pausing a moment to consider the nature of this name change because it says a good deal about Faulkner's writing practice. Verbally Bunch and Burch are so alike as to be taken for each other, and indeed Lena Grove is at the outset misled by this similarity, coming to Byron Bunch thinking he is Lucas Burch. Yet the poetic logic of this novel is such that this initial confusion will become a fusion, in that Byron Bunch will, in a crucial sense, become Lucas Burch, become the missing husband and father—or at least try to. What we have, in narrative terms, is a remarkable case of verbal similarity

leading to substantive similarity, external sign likeness leading to internal referent likeness. But the narrative terms are soon exhausted and left behind as
Faulkner takes his experiment right off the ground, shows us that word games
can evolve and move toward issues of life and death, that the altering of
language points mysteriously to the transformation of self.

If we compare the Bunch-to-Burch phenomenon to its Joycean counterpart
of Blephen-and-Stoom, then we see even more clearly what it is that Faulkner
and Joyce are and are not doing. Blephen-and-Stoom is slapstick and authorial: slapstick because it appears as one of the circuslike transformations that
Stephen and Bloom undergo, along with other equally improbable constructs
based on age, background, and the like; and authorial because Joyce is ex-
ploiting both ways, insisting on difference every bit as much as likeness, hinting that the young man looking for a father and the older man looking for a
son can come no closer than a modest name change, a kind of verbal plastic
surgery, hinting also, a bit more broadly, that the young man and the older
man are no more than words in the artist's hands, that they can be altered and
merged into each other at will (that is, at the author's will), since they are
totally malleable verbal materials before being anything else. The *convention*
of character is underscored by Joyce, and as we look on at the wiring and the
props, we see the puppeteer's strings, much as Judith Sutpen saw them in her
loom image.

Once these conventions are foregrounded, all forms begin to look like
constructs, and the old essentialist world view is in for a bad time. Husband,
it comes as no surprise, is every bit as artificial an arrangement as father and
son, and therefore Bloom need harbor no individualist illusions as he enters
the bed on which Molly lies: "If he had smiled why would he have smiled? To
reflect that each one who enters imagines himself to be the first to enter
whereas he is always the last term of a succeeding one, each imagining himself
to be first, last, only and alone, whereas he is neither first nor last nor alone
in a series originating in and repeated to infinity."[11] This view of life as endless,
indiscriminate serial chain has some similarity to Hightower's view of Lena:
"from these hearty loins without hurry or haste descending mother and daughter." Both authors recognize the power and authority of the generic, along
with the corresponding puniness of the individual; but, whereas Joyce exploits
the comedy inherent in this discrepancy, Faulkner achieves a strange blend of
the heroic, the tragic, and the futile. He knows that the self is a construct,
that it can "unravel." But he knows, too, that it is the fictive home for our
experiences. Thus, Byron Bunch, who knows that he *weeded another man's
laidby crop* (706), must go the whole route and become that other man.
One actually feels that character is coming to life here, declaring its strange
autonomy, showing us that the authorial game is now over and that the existential one has begun. It is here that we move into the heart of things. At
some critical moment in Faulkner's novels words must be overpassed, so that
the frontiers imposed by names can at last be crossed. Names either bind or
confuse. *The Sound and the Fury* has too many Jasons and Quentins, but at a
certain point the confusion stops, and the dead brother can never be con-

founded with the rebellious niece. In *Absalom*, when enough heat has been generated and leaves raked up, the two roommates begin to understand each other *à demi mot*, no longer stymied by the "he's" and "she's" of their furious dialogue. Now, Byron must also go beyond the words' contours to see what they conceal and contain:

> *And this too is reserved for me, as Reverend Hightower says. I'll have to tell him now. I'll have to tell Lucas Burch* It was not unsurprise now. It was something like the terrible and irremediable despair of adolescence. *Why, I didn't even believe until now that he was so. It was like me, and her, and all the other folks that I had to get mixed up in it, were just a lot of words that never even stood for anything, were not even us, while all the time what was us was going on and going on without even missing the lack of words. Yes. It aint until now that I ever believed that he is Lucas Burch. That there ever was a Lucas Burch.* (695–96)

Something roughly akin to fission is taking place in these lines, as we see Byron burst through the word fence that everywhere encloses and imprisons meaning. To crash this barrier is, as Faulkner would say, to "abrupt" onto a new realm, to encounter Difference, Difference understood as alterity itself rather than some interstitial nothingness or mental category. There is a creatural trauma here of extraordinary proportions, and it seems fair to say that Byron Bunch is experiencing a rupture of self that must be close to the elemental "opening out" which characterizes the birth of a child. Byron must go beyond the enclosed linguistic system, break free into a kind of no-man's land where all is immediate, and we have no defenses. Names fall away. The subject can now author its own change. Such is the metamorphosis of Byron Bunch: for Bunch to become Burch, he must confront, replace, and assume the man who has sired Lena's child.

> The hill rises, cresting. He has never seen the sea, and so he thinks, "It is like the edge of nothing. Like once I passed it I would just ride right off into nothing. Where trees would look like and be called by something else except trees, and men would look like and be called by something else except folks. And Byron Bunch he wouldn't even have to be or not be Byron Bunch. Byron Bunch and his mule not anything with falling fast, until they would take fire like the Reverend Hightower says about them rocks running so fast in space that they take fire and burn up and there aint even a cinder to have to hit the ground." (712)

Yes, this is the edge of the world, and, in its modernist fashion it is bristling with the territorializing and baptismal energies that we find in Renaissance texts of exploration. To career past the borders of self is tantamount to falling out of language, and one senses a kind of primeval awe at work here, akin to the discovery of new elements, a new planet. This is a moment that many writers doubtless strive for, when the words become so incandescent with meaning that they volatilize, go up in smoke, shed their tired name skins and reveal their true mysteries. Faulkner images this "overpass" in terms of weightlessness, estrangement, and cosmic energy, an event in outer space where the meteoric return and disintegration hauntingly point to and complete the "black blast," "the rush of sparks from a rising rocket" of Joe Christmas's death. In this moment of self-eclipse, the prison of individuation is broken and the elements, freed from their old labels, may now regroup and find new ones. Here, as we saw, Christmas fuses with Lena. Here, Bunch may become Burch. That act of metamorphosis, radically different from the game of Blephen-and-Stoom, mirrors a new world, a spiritual configuration toward which the novelist's language must point.

The novelist's words are always poor and borrowed, every bit as generic and nonindividuated as the birth and death processes of his fable. How, then, can the creation story be told? How can the miracle of life be narrated by language, and how can the language of narration be kept alive? Faulkner's answer in *Light in August* is to narrate poetically, to compose characters who initially seem realistic and "closed" but gradually come to fuse with or be confused with others, to yoke seemingly discrete stories into a strange composite, to suggest that visible actions have less visible echoes and resonances, that unfurling gestures neither begin nor end where they appear to, that birth and death may be faces of each other, that names deploy as well as denote. Thus, we are warned to pay heed, to look beyond the words when we first hear of Joe Christmas: "And that was the first time Byron remembered that he had ever thought how a man's name which is supposed to be just the sound for who he is, can be somehow an augur of what he will do, if other men can only read the meaning in time" (422). Faulkner's language is charged in this novel, and by "language" I mean all the devices of structure and symbol as well as vocabulary and syntax. He wants to energize this fiction, to go beyond the apparent meanings and thereby liberate the stranger correspondences and potencies that are his ultimate quarry. Hence, everything can be resonant; all things speak, and all connections may be symbolic. Early on Byron begins to suspect that his world is teeming with signs. Thus, the burning house has a message, if we know how to read: "It seemed to him that fate, circumstance, had set a warning in the sky all day long in that pillar of yellow smoke, and he too stupid to read it" (459). This new language of signs and strange fusions is, in the "time-release" format that Faulkner cunningly gives to it, endlessly generative and potent; it is meant to perform the great miracle of art: to do what Lena Grove does, to create life.

Faulkner always acknowledged that he sought in his work to arrest time, to make life on the page. He put it to Jean Stein in these terms: "The aim of every artist is to arrest motion, which is life, by artificial means and hold it fixed so that a hundred years later when a stranger looks at it, it moves again since it is life."[12] It is not hard to grasp why Keats's "Ode on a Grecian Urn" so fascinated him that it echoes in countless of his novels; Lena Grove is fittingly described in terms of this same urnlike imagery, and Faulkner had reason to believe that in *Light in August* he had performed such a feat. In speaking of his remarkable period of masterpieces, Faulkner expressed this view in a most interesting fashion:

I think there's a period in a writer's life when he, well, simply for lack of any other word, is fertile and he just produces. Later on, his blood slows, his bones get a little more brittle, his muscles get a little stiff, he gets perhaps other interests, but I think there's one time in his life when he writes at the top of his talent plus his speed, too. Later, the speed slows, the talent doesn't necessarily have to fade at the same time. But there's a time in his life, one matchless time, when they are matched completely. The speed, and the power, and the talent, they're all there and then he is "hot."[13]

Much is on show here: the flesh-and-blood writer caught in an entropic scheme that no one escapes, and then Writing itself, the deathless verbal medium that one taps into when one is writing "at the top of [one's] talent." We write as we live: in time, against time. One cannot fail to be struck by the parallels between the statements regarding the writer's aims and the imagery and themes of *Light in August*. From *The Sound and the Fury* to the Stockholm address, Faulkner is looking for what will *endure*. The full force of this concern is best felt when we apply it to the writing itself, as well as his major theme. *Light in August* plays out this drama in every conceivable hue. The title itself, signifying both the birth of a child and the quality of light, is part of Faulkner's new language. August, not April, would be the cruelest month, for it flaunts the discrepancy between human cycles and natural cycles, exposing our heat and passion to be one time only, end-oriented, doomed to death rather than regeneration. What is needed, as Mrs. Hines laments, is a reprieve, a language and a fable that would be so constituted as to defy closure, to give us a second chance. Hence, this is a novel of Indian summer, of Joanna Burden's Indian summer of feverish passion: "It was summer becoming fall, with already, like shadows before the westering sun, the chill and implacable import of autumn cast ahead upon summer; something of dying summer spurting again like a dying coal, in the fall" (591), or "It was as if she knew somehow that time was short, that autumn was almost upon her, without knowing yet the exact significance of autumn" (592). Thus, Joanna's move through her time into menopause, into the impossibility of creating new life, is perfectly rendered as "that final upflare of stubborn and dying summer upon which autumn, the dawning of half-death, had come unawares" (595). There is a rich seasonal language in Faulkner, a cogent imagery which leads Rosa Coldfield, in her desire to mate with Sutpen, to claim repeatedly that she "might be sun for him," the same imagery which finds the writing, when it is good, "hot." In Lena and her child Faulkner has succeeded in meeting the seasonal challenge, for she is the life principle triumphant. The birth of her nameless child is an act of moral and writerly freedom, a celebration of the "round of life" which transcends individual contours and duration.[14] Faulkner paid his homage to this force as an artist, and he fashioned and pieced together his verbal materials in such a way as to keep them resonant, endlessly signifying, flowing. How else can a story of carnage become a story of love? In the birth of that child there is a figurative redemption for the death-dealing Calvinism of the community and the alienated, sterile consciousness of Joe Christmas. Ultimately, *Light in August* is a peculiarly seasonal Passion play, a spectacular meditation on what lives and what dies, what is separate and what is connected. The "language" of the novel is no less than its vexed linkages, the complex emerging story of kinship — biological and spiritual — which severely tests our notions of reality and order. Faulkner is obliging us here, as indeed he has always done in his best novels, to move beyond the apparent confusion so as to grasp the bold metaphoric fusions at work. If we do this, we grant his language that extra dimension it seeks, and we thereby make his art endure.

10

Hemingway's *Garden of Eden*: The Final Combat Zone

The Garden of Eden, written "on" between 1946 and 1958, finally published in 1986, is incomplete, perhaps incompletable, but even in its partial state it is something of a Hemingway summa, a replay of grand old themes—the traumas of love and/as war, the hunt as quest, the transformation of experience into art—but on a new turf, in a new key, in a new manner. Its status in the Hemingway canon is sure to be disputed for some time, and most of the serious attention it has received distinguishes sharply, and properly, between the 1,500-page manuscript in the Kennedy Library and the sleek 247-page *récit* edited by Tom Jenks at Scribner's. Jenks has cut out the subplots, removed a number of central characters, reduced Hemingway's rather baroque multicouple mirror grouping to a cleaner triangulated fable, and served up a far more digestible fiction than the intransigent piece that Hemingway himself never got around to taming. Where appropriate, in this chapter I will refer to distinctions between the genuine manuscript and the edited novel, but the governing premise of my study, taking into account the American literary canon's debt to figures such as Max Perkins, is that time and oblivion will have their way, that *The Garden of Eden* will come to have canonical status, to be regarded as *echt* Hemingway, long after the editorial brouhaha has subsided and been lost from sight. And then the question that will be asked is: What does this posthumous work add to the Hemingway corpus? How does it change our vision?

To be sure, the Old Master's touch is recognizably the same, and once again the sensuous immediacy of life is delivered up to us on our plates, replete, in John Updike's words, with "that liturgical gravity which Hemingway invented."[1] Eden may come in many guises, but surely these culinary delights deserve to be part of it:

> On this morning there was brioche and red raspberry preserve and the eggs were boiled and there was a pat of butter that melted as they stirred them and salted them lightly and ground pepper over them in the cups. They were big eggs and fresh and the girl's were not cooked quite as long as the young man's. He remembered that easily and he was happy with his which he

diced up with the spoon and ate with only the flow of butter to moisten them and the fresh early morning texture and the bite of the coarsely ground pepper grains and the hot coffee and the chicory-fragrant bowl of café au lait.[2]

There is something miraculous, almost sacramental, in this ongoing, "and"-punctuated prose, this reverent, close-grained notation of the pungent visual and olfactory and tactile pleasures to be had in Hemingway's garden of earthly delights, a sumptuous yet simple feast located here in the Grau du Roi, but "moveable" to Cannes, Hendaye, Madrid, even Africa. Such zoom-shot prose can cause salivation and hunger pangs, and although literature may have nobler subjects than gastronomy, *The Garden of Eden* is winning indeed in its fresh and vivid appeal to the palate.[3] For this, much thanks.

The famous clean style is still much in evidence, suggesting by its very presence that the best things in life and art are keen, immediate, and to be savored. Here is the first Eden: a realm of touch and taste, where things have their plenitude and where writing effortlessly serves them up, owing to that magical style that is, to cite Updike again, "Edenic, an early-morning style wherein things still have the dew of their naming on them."[4] But often enough one has the feeling that the clean style seems somehow to have grown up, to have become conscious of itself, of its beauties and of its risks. When David tells Catherine, "The sea was very good," she snaps back: "You use such interesting adjectives. They make everything so vivid" (134). This stinging rejoinder has itself "the bite of coarsely ground pepper grains," and we see in it the reflexivity of *The Garden*, a charged reflexivity, one that amounts to a series of writerly checks and balances, lending the text a downright pugilistic tone when the going gets rough:

When they came back from the beach they found Catherine in the garden.
"So you got back," she said.
"Yes," David said. "We had a good swim. I wish you'd been there."
"Well, I wasn't," she said. "If it's of any interest to you."
"Where did you go?" David asked.
"I was in Cannes on my own business," she said. "You're both late for lunch."
"I'm sorry," David said. "Do you want to have anything before lunch?"
"Please excuse me, Catherine," Marita said. "I'll be back in a moment."
"You're still drinking before lunch?" Catherine asked David.
"Yes," he said. "I don't think it matters if you're getting a lot of exercise."
"There was an empty whiskey glass on the bar when I came in."
"Yes," said David. "I had two whiskeys actually."
"Actually," she mimicked him. "You're very British today."
"Really?" he said. "I didn't feel very British. I felt sort of half-assed Tahitian."
"It's just your way of speaking that irritates me," she said. "Your choice of words."
"I see," he said. "Did you want a shot before they bring the chow?"
"You don't have to be a clown."
"The best clowns don't talk," he said.

"Nobody accused you of being the best of clowns," she said. "Yes. I'd like a drink if it isn't too much work for you to make it."

He made three martinis, measuring them each out separately and pouring them into the pitcher where there was a big chunk of ice and then stirring.

"Who is the third drink for?"

"Marita."

"Your paramour?"

"My what?"

"Your paramour."

"You really said it," David told her. "I'd never heard that word pronounced and I had absolutely no hope of ever hearing it in this life. You're really wonderful."

"It's a perfectly common word."

"It is at that," David said. "But to have the sheer, naked courage to use it in conversation. Devil, be good now. Couldn't you say 'your dusky paramour'?" (154–55)

Quoted in its entirety, this segment displays a kind of verbal sparring that perfectly conveys the deeper tensions of the text. David has just finished getting some particular "exercise" with Marita, and Catherine's testiness is doubtless spurred by jealousy. But his real fitness is verbal: words are his "discipline" in the most literal sense, and it is on that plane that Catherine sets out to challenge and mock him. Nothing better images David's efforts to establish control than the meticulous martini-measuring sequence, done in the slow-motion, monosyllabic, limpid prose that has always nailed things down in the past. Early on, David asks himself: "Do you suppose the Grau du Roi time was all simple because you could write a little of it simply?" (37); and now, as the words begin to pirouette in and out of brackets and quotation marks, the Hemingway terrain begins to shake, and the surface begins to open up. In David's early writing "the sinister part only showed as the light feathering of a smooth swell on a calm day marking the reef beneath" (42). That reef beneath, and the depths beneath the reef, constitute the true territory that *The Garden of Eden* aims to chart.

One's apprehension of that reef is delayed and put off, largely because the sensual beauty of *The Garden of Eden* is so overwhelming, so seductive. But Hemingway's text has the cautionary power of *The Scarlet Letter*, and it deserves, like its nineteenth-century counterpart, to be seen as an American fable about freedoms and limits: sexual, moral, and writerly. Closer to home, we see Hemingway moving clearly into Fitzgerald territory here, and the *Garden* explores the darker and tragic reaches of hedonism in much the same way *Tender Is the Night* does. Here, too, we see the erotic antics of handsome, monied Americans on the Côte d'Azur, and we end up with a fight to the death that is every bit as "sinister" as the doomed relationship of Dick Diver and Nicole Warren. Indeed, the Fitzgeralds themselves seem silhouetted in this book, as Hemingway plays out, once again, the story he knew all too well: that of the writer married to a woman who undermines his power, who bankrolls him and demands her share. We know that Zelda Fitzgerald was such a woman in Hemingway's eyes, and we get a memorable taste of such a creature's venom in the remarkable tongue-lashing that Frances metes out to Robert Cohn in *The Sun Also Rises*. But there is no Robert Cohn to take the heat in *The Garden*, and so David Bourne must encounter female aggressivity head-on. Catherine is quite capable, in a few well-chosen words, of leveling the entire edifice of machismo that has seemed the be-all and end-all of Hemingway males throughout the years: "'O I know he's a satisfactory lover,' Catherine said. 'He's always that. That's just like his martinis or how he swims or skis or flew probably. I never saw him with a plane. Everyone says he was marvelous. It's like acrobats really I suppose and just as dull'" (156). And Catherine is mistress of the proprietary tone (that unctuous tone so calculated to drive the Hemingway male mad): "You know, I've never read a story of David's. I never interfere. I've only tried to make it economically possible for him to do the best work of which he is capable" (156). Hemingway, as we know, was especially sensitive to the charge of being a "kept" writer, since he had a knack for marrying women with money, at least with more money than he had. And in Catherine Bourne's final act of war — burning David's *cahiers* — we see an unmistakable replay of the lost *cahier* incident of 1922 (in which Hadley lost the greater part of Ernest's manuscripts at the Gare de Lyon), a writerly trauma so deep-seated, so rife with betrayal innuendo, that we cannot help seeing Hadley here, a Hadley now transformed into warrior. A good bit of Hemingway marital and erotic arrangements are on show in this novel, especially the period of the ménage à trois when Ernest was "shifting" from Hadley to Pauline, a time — in Paris and in Hemingway's private life — of sexual experiment and gender crossing.

If Hadley is visible in the destroyed manuscript episode, it is nonetheless Zelda Fitzgerald who seems targeted in the portrait of Catherine Bourne: a woman locked in a Darwinian struggle with her writer-husband, enlisting all manner of erotic tactics in her battle for power, using womanly wiles to encroach on the male preserve of art. Fitzgeraldian echoes abound: David regards Catherine as sick, urges her to seek medical (read: psychiatric) attention in Switzerland, thereby repeating Nicole's career in *Tender Is the Night*. And Catherine's final phase is likened to dementia, expressed in terms that are again recognizable: "I broke myself in pieces . . . all it did was break me in pieces" (192). Crack-up would be the ultimate Fitzgeraldian metaphor, applicable both to the oeuvre and to Scott and Zelda, and critics who read *The Garden of Eden* as a pendant to *A Moveable Feast* — that is, as a kind of (barely) literary chronicle of Hemingway and his acquaintances — will find much to work with.[5]

All the same, the Fitzgeraldian echoes are only echoes, and the novel has an intrinsic life of its own. What Hemingway may have seen in Scott and Zelda, what kinds of resentment he may have experienced vis-à-vis his enabling and competing wives, is to be found less in biographical anecdote than in the very texture and plot of *The Garden of Eden*. This novel is mercifully posthumous, for it spares no one, least of all its author. In contrast to *A Moveable Feast*, which is demonstrably a settling of scores, this final text boldly and relentlessly goes "in," actualizes much that was previously implicit in the Hemingway corpus. It does not remain at the surface, even though its surface is brilliant, but rather moves vertically, offers a powerful oneiric formulation of what was always there but never quite sayable. Despite its sensuous account of the Mediterranean good life, there is a rigor and austerity here of no mean proportions, a willingness, finally, to go all the way, to give definitive form to the ghosts and stresses and doubts that make a battle zone of the artist's life. In the temperament and ominous trajectory of Catherine Bourne, Hemingway has at last created a magisterial rival for his male artist, and her enormous project of transformation and transcendence endows this seemingly privatist novel with genuine metaphysical reach, placing Hemingway in a large and rich tradition of spiritual and erotic quests ranging from Hawthorne and Melville to Proust, Joyce, and Faulkner.

Catherine Bourne does not come from nowhere, and once we get a fix on her antecedents, we can better grasp her significance for Hemingway, her final "coming out," after the long line of women who indirectly announce her. The first unmistakable sign that trouble is brewing between the Bournes comes when Catherine has her hair cut as short as a boy's. This is not new in Hemingway. As far back as "Cat in the Rain" (in *In Our Time*) we find a wife with hair "clipped close like a boy's" complaining about this hair, while George, the husband, is quick to tell her he likes it that way. It may be that he likes it far more than the story indicates. In *The Sun Also Rises* Brett, of course, is notoriously short-haired, and it seems a sign of her stylishness and sexual freedom. We recall that Romero significantly wants her to let her hair grow out, to conform to his idea of a wife, and at this (as much as at anything else) she bolts; but, within the confines of the text, she is a distinctly short-haired Circe, and no male (including Romero) fails to respond. Consider, finally, Maria in *For Whom the Bell Tolls*—Maria whose head was shaven by the Fascists and who is loudly judged by all parties (including herself) to be quasi-deformed by the loss of her hair. Yet who can fail to observe that her crew-cut hair constitutes a powerful aphrodisiac for Robert Jordan, a source of sexual excitement (rather than moral sympathy), and countless are the moments when he rubs his hands over her cropped head. These are the most erotic moments of the novel, and Hemingway coyly tells us that Jordan's throat "thickens" each time he caresses her head. There is a typology at work here, a coming into focus of the woman as most erotic when most boylike. And the Hemingway male's ongoing albeit sublimated interest in these matters constitutes an envy of female breasts and genitalia, even to the point, as Robert Gajdusek has shown, of "feminizing" the male body, of metaphorically assuming its attributes.[6] There is, then, a genuine line of forebears for Catherine Bourne, a "sisterhood" of sorts, but only in Catherine is the androgynous behavior and the boy's haircut brought center stage, *willed*, insolently bereft of any "cover story," outfitted with a veritable program, chosen at last for the sense of pleasure, liberation, and self-mastery it affords, has perhaps always afforded.

In his important 1986 biography of Hemingway, Kenneth Lynn has taught us a great deal about the author's anxieties regarding his masculinity, and he has placed particular emphasis on the Ernest-Marcelline connection, the "look-alike" older sister/double whose imprint is discernible in much of the psychic behavior displayed in the novels.[7] The great frustration with biographical criticism, however, lies in its deference to the recorded life as ultimate authority. Granted, Ernest was dressed as a girl for a longer time than most young children at the turn of the century, but this small piece of juvenile evidence is simply incommensurate with the real issues at hand: the guises of erotic behavior, the radical project of self-sculpting, the varieties of fusion and self-transcendence made possible by love and desire. Fixation with Marcelline or fear and/or longing for the mother have their place in any account of Hemingway psychology, but they will not carry us far enough when it comes to interpreting the work, for the work is precisely the arena where such initial proclivities are finally played out, actualized, given their due. And the unfurling and unleashing of psychic energy, albeit distantly referrable to sibling relations and the like, has a directionality and dimensionality of its own, yielding, in *The Garden of Eden* (and perhaps only there), a large and rich weave, larger and richer than the secrets of Oak Park.

Let us return, then, to the close-cropped Catherine and give her haircut its full valuation. Catherine courts change. In her insistent, almost pathological behavior in the novel we see a major theme: the human body as artistic material. Catherine is going to alter herself, to craft herself. Whereas Maria's head was shaved by the Fascists, Catherine takes hers to artist figures, such as Jean, coiffeur-sculptor par excellence, who tells David that haircutting "is as important to me as your métier is to you" (80). A strange note, this, in the Hemingway scheme. If we have learned anything from his novels over the years, it is that the human body takes a beating. The male body is menaced by bullets, grenades, the horns of bulls, the fists of other males, the "inside" ravages of syphilis, gangrene, dysentery, impotence, and the like. As for the female body, it is customarily reified, an object of desire (Brett eyed by the Basques, Maria ravaged by the Fascists); and it receives its dosage of trauma from nature itself, most notably and tragically in the birthing process, shown as grisly and potentially unsurvivable (by the male) from "Indian Camp" on to the intolerable ending of Catherine Barkley in Switzerland, caught and then smashed in the biological trap: "I'm almost done, darling. I'm going all to pieces. . . . I'm all broken. They've broken me. I know it now."[8] Here is the generic and sisterly context for assessing the huge project of self-shaping that Catherine Bourne undertakes. The object at last becomes the subject. The changes are self-wrought, not suffered or inflicted. Self-shaping is not a matter of vanity and coiffures; it is mastery.

The novelty and stature of Catherine Bourne impressed reviewers from the very outset. In her, Updike feels that the author has finally been able "to touch upon the feminine within himself, the seducibility from which only his writing (for a time) was safe, and to conjure up, if only to exorcise, the independent will within women, of which he doubtless had more experience that his typical heroes let him express."[9] In much the same vein, E. L. Doctorow ascribes to Catherine "the stature of a self-tortured Faustian," and goes on to characterize her as "a brilliant woman trapped into a vicarious participation in someone else's creativity," terming her "the most informed and delicate reading Hemingway has given to any woman."[10] But, whereas Doctorow critiques as naive the premise of sexual fantasizing as madness, we would do well to attend very carefully to Catherine's "shaping" ventures. Hemingway is telling a wildly energized and inverted Pygmalion story, and through his rendition of desire as demiurgic, transformational, he is doing the last thing on earth many of us would expect from the alleged macho writer of the century: he is deconstructing gender, showing it to be a construct, a structure one can alter.[11] Catherine begins her metamorphic odyssey by having her hair cut close, like a boy's, and we are hard put to sort out her various motives. She clearly seeks to "look like" David, and we understand "look like" to be a kind of entry, a form of fusion. Looking like David is tantamount to becoming David. This desire for a more perfect union would seem a sublimely personal quest: Catherine becoming David. But is it so simple? Catherine's project of alteration is utterly *generic*, a re-forming of the gender she was outfitted with at birth. To "look like" a boy is the first step toward "being" a boy, and here is an epic journey that has little to do with catherines and davids. And there is still another unmistakable component to Catherine's enterprise: in her feverish efforts to recompose herself, we may discern the makings of an odd "homing" venture, an undoing of all that culture and race and gender have "imposed," a voyage to some anterior state before gender, some essentially dark, originary self. We are now squarely in the Garden, and we can begin to see that Catherine Bourne is Hemingway's Edenic figure—at once and interchangeably Adam, Eve, and the snake—seeking a knowledge that might, miraculously, be a higher innocence, striving for a form of self-liberation that is strangely, undeniably, also a search for love and a more perfect fusion.

Liberation and union are inextricably connected in *The Garden of Eden*. Not that Hemingway hasn't always seen them as faces of each other. Embrace and union with the loved one must always entail, in some sense, the transcendence of self. One remembers Catherine Barkley's self-effacing love: "There isn't any me. I'm you. Don't make up a separate me" (115). Or Maria's yearning, in *For Whom the Bell Tolls*, for a fusion with Robert so total that it would collapse their separate identities and make them into a new single figure:

"Afterwards we will be as one animal of the forest and be so close that neither one can tell that one of us is one and not the other. Can you not feel my heart be your heart?"

"Yes. There is no difference."

"And feel now. Thou has no heart but mine."

"Nor any other legs, nor feet, nor of the body."

"But we are different," she said. "I would have us exactly the same."

"You do not mean that."

"Yes I do. I do. That is a thing I had to tell thee."

"You do not mean that."

"Perhaps I do not," she said speaking softly with her lips against his shoulder. "But I wished to say it. Since we are different I am glad that thou are Roberto and I Maria. But if thou should ever wish to change I would be glad to change. I would be thee because I love thee so."

"I do not wish to change. It is better to be one and each one to be the one he is."

"But we will be one now and there will never be a separate one." Then she
said, "I will be thee when thou art not here. Oh, I love thee so and I must
care well for thee."[12]

The radical idealism of the ending of *For Whom the Bell Tolls* is poignantly
foreshadowed here, as Maria makes her brave pledge against death, asserting
that the couple still lives through the love of each partner. There is a tragic
generosity at work here, a desperate search for something beyond self that
would outlive destruction and transcend individuation, a view of coupling that
moves so powerfully from flesh to spirit that something new and composite is
brought into a being, an ecstatic hybrid creature that is free at last of contingency. The selflessness and idealism of these earlier texts are equally present
in *The Garden of Eden*, but the meditation on fusion itself has evolved considerably. The female desire for loosening the grids of sexual identity can no
longer be checked. Catherine Barkley tells Frederick at night, "I want us to be
all mixed up," and Maria has confessed to Robert Jordan that she wants to go
beyond all differentiation, that the two of them might "change" still further,
in ways not available to conventional lovemaking. But Frederick Henry and
Robert Jordan will not go this far; they want to retain the old demarcations,
the differences that bound identity.

With Catherine Bourne the genie can no longer be kept in the bottle. The
old view of female self-effacement ("I want what you want. There isn't any
me any more. Just what you want" [*A Farewell to Arms*, 106]) is perhaps at
last understood by Hemingway to be a male fantasy that screens out the real
issue at hand: female desire. Catherine Bourne prophetically takes the lead,
asserts her sexual desire as the modus operandi of the couple, assures David
that he too will like it, that she will initiate him into the mysteries, that the
passage he is to make is something to be proud of. And so the woman woos
the man here. And she is after large game. The close-cropped hair is a first
step only: "'You see,' she said. 'That's the surprise. I'm a girl. But now I'm a
boy too and I can do anything and anything and anything'" (15). There is a
madness for assertion here, a flaunting of *doing* in the sexual sphere, a magical
overcoming of gender and limit. And how does David respond to his altered
woman? "'Sit here by me,' he said. 'What do you want, brother?'" (15).
The vocabulary counts. Catherine is becoming his companion, his sibling, his
incestuous, same-sexed mate—that is, so long as he remains a boy. But the
alterations need not be one-sided; David can play, too. His male equipment,
like Catherine's breasts, can become merely his "dowry," what the accidents
of biology have endowed him with; the whole body can become erogenous, all
zones play zones and combat zones, the seesaw of penetration and reception
as "democratic" and shifting as polymorphous desire could desire.[13] It is at
last dark, and we can now see what getting "mixed up" entails:

He had shut his eyes and he could feel the long light weight of her on him
and her breasts pressing against him and her lips on his. He lay there and felt
something and then her hand holding him and searching lower and he helped
with his hands and then lay back in the dark and did not think at all and only

felt the weight and the strangeness inside and she said, "Now you can't tell who is who can you?"

"No."

"You are changing," she said. "Oh you are. You are. Yes you are and you're my girl Catherine. Will you change and be my girl and let me take you?"

"You're Catherine."

"No I'm Peter. You're my wonderful Catherine. You're my beautiful lovely Catherine. You were so good to change. Oh thank you, Catherine, so much. Please understand. Please know and understand. I'm going to make love to you forever." (18)

It is an extraordinary sequence, and it immediately puts Hemingway in the company of his international peers, of Proust and his complex scenarios of sexual transformation and disguise, of Joyce who wrote "Circe" and altered the name and sexual equipment of his creature Bloom in order to achieve the polymorphous ideal he had in mind. The passage displays Hemingway's characteristic blend of concision and ellipsis, saying cleanly what it has to say, suggesting volumes in the interstices of its utterance. He cunningly avoids any real specifications in describing the sexual activity at hand, limiting himself to issues of weight, holding, and searching, and strangeness on the inside. We are free to imagine Catherine's "taking" of David however we see fit, with her hand, with special aids, with whatever our imagination supplies. As Mark Spilka has said, "For them as for us, it is the edenic invitation to forbidden mysteries and disturbing sexual ambiguities that matters."[14] It is Hemingway conversation at its best, studded with lacunae that the reader negotiates, but now carried out in a new medium, in a wholly sexual key.

And the verbal shifts are as interesting as the erotic ones. The name changing is endlessly signifying: it is the ultimate fusion of lovers, this time each as the other; it is the great high of sexual invention, a particular way of "making it new" (experiencing pleasure from the "other" side); and, who knows, it may also be the ultimate narcissist dream, Catherine making love to David *as Catherine*, Catherine finally consummating the sex act with herself, an act achievable only through the agency of David as "go-between." We have come a long way from Jake Barnes's pimping efforts to bring Brett and Romero together. Hemingway seems to have discovered that lovemaking is the ideal cubist arena, the place where bodies and names metamorphose, offer recombinant possibilities only hinted at in the earlier texts. The bedroom is the new atelier for the artist, and this is because sexual desire is now seen to be the great dismantling, demiurgic force, equipped with a creative and associative-dissociative power akin to nuclear fission.

"I'm going to make love to you forever," Catherine informs David. The woman's bid for power is spectacularly multileveled: she takes the lead, she initiates the male, she inaugurates the morphological play and role swapping; finally, she boasts of an endless potency (could David do as much?) and makes us see that her form of erotic activity makes of intercourse a kind of pleasure that could go on forever. Hence, her litany to David—"please be slow, please be slow"—underscores the advantage she has over him when she makes up the rules and transforms their lovemaking into something radically different, beyond his male scripts. David knows this. He accepts her lead, but he knows there will be a price to pay. Catherine may pledge to make love to him forever, but he feels, on the contrary, that something is over forever: "The young man put his arms around the girl and held her very tight to him and felt her lovely breasts against his chest and kissed her on her dear mouth. He held her close and hard and inside himself he said goodbye and then goodbye and goodbye" (18). These words are unmistakably elegiac, a charting of distances traversed and a kind of helpless leave-taking. Hold her though he does, "close and hard," David can no longer immobilize the liberated body, and all the gender-specific, proprietary help in the world (the young man, his arms, the girl, her lovely breasts, her dear mouth) will not do the trick. The box is opened, and fixed identities, stable sex roles, are out for good.

The metamorphoses of Catherine Bourne open up *The Garden of Eden*, much the way a false bottom is removed from a suitcase, allowing us to see that there is more underneath, concealed because it needs to escape censorship and the light of day. More, too, in the sense of volume, resonance, and echo. Catherine's quest is dark in ways that are cultural and racial, reminiscent of the blonde and the brunette in Cooper, Hawthorne, and Melville, Jim's role in *Huckleberry Finn*, Charles Bon's role in *Absalom, Absalom!*, hinting at unavowed kinships that are going to be acknowledged and made good on. Catherine, changing, stands for a crumbling white world, a gender-specific daytime effigy that will become polymorphous and Other at night: "During the night he had felt her hands touching him. And when he woke it was in the moonlight and she had made the dark magic of the change again and he did not say no when she spoke to him and asked the questions and he felt the change so that it hurt him all through and when it was finished after they were both exhausted she was shaking and she whispered to him, 'Now we have done it. Now we really have done it'" (20). If we didn't know, we might think we were watching a scene from some female version of *Dracula*: transformation under the light of the moon, dark magic. More than sex, more even than the body is being altered here. Note the pain, the exhaustion, the shaking, the sense of finality. These are forbidden rituals, taking Catherine and David figuratively far beyond Cannes, toward another world. Catherine cannot get black enough:

> "I want to get behind my ears and neck tanned and over my cheekbones. All the new places."
> "You're awfully dark, brother," he said. "You don't know how dark."
> "I like it," the girl said. "But I want to be darker." (22)

When instructing the coiffeur how to cut, Catherine tells him to do it like Eton, but then to keep cutting, to go past Eton: "It feels like an animal," she tells David. "You're my good lovely husband and my brother too," she reassures him, and then comes the clincher: "I love you and when we go to Africa I'll be your African girl too" (29). David patiently explains that the season is wrong for Africa—he cannot tell her, perhaps he does not even know, that

Africa is *his* place, not hers—but her quest for a more primitive state is not so easily checked:

> "Did you think I could ever be this dark?"
>
> "No, because you're blond."
>
> "I can because I'm lion color and they can go dark. But I want every part of me dark and it's getting that way and you'll be darker than an Indian and that takes us further away from other people. You see why it's important." . . .
>
> "How dark are you going to get?"
>
> "As dark as I can. We'll have to see. I wish I had some Indian blood. I'm going to be so dark you won't be able to stand it. . . ." (31)

Later, after making love, David wonders, "how dark can she become . . . how dark will she ever really be?" (31). It is entirely apt that David's friend the Colonel sees Catherine at the Prado and thinks *African*, "the young chief of a warrior tribe who has gotten loose from his councillors and was looking at that marble of Leda and the Swan" (62). Beneath the simple hedonism of Hemingway's story is to be found an exploratory critique of civilized roles and boundaries, a yearning for the primitive reaches of the psyche—including dark lions, Indians, and Africans—where a freer play of desire might be possible. Catherine is no practicing artist; she pointedly tells David as much ("The whole way here I saw wonderful things to paint and I can't paint at all and never could. But I know wonderful things to write and I can't even write a letter that isn't stupid" [53]). But she is very much a rival creator bent on self-expression at all costs, seeking hungrily a new multiplex, rainbow, plural identity.

Catherine's material, as we have seen, is her (and David's, and then Marita's) body, and the possible forms of sexual and imaginative intercourse available to these bodies are much more diverse than anything previously shown in Hemingway's work. In the past the night was always a time of unease and precariousness: Jake Barnes cried then, Frederick Henry was *croyant* when the dark came, and Robert Jordan had oneiric sex with Garbo and Harlow. In *The Garden* as well Catherine initially promises David, "We won't let the night things come in the day" (22), but it is a pledge that cannot be kept, and by the time they reach Madrid, Catherine has started to "show the dark things in the light and there would, it seemed to him, be no end to the change" (67). In short, the anarchic power of desire, kept at bay in so much of Hemingway, kept under wraps and acknowledged only at night, is both ferocious and authoritative in *The Garden*, and it bursts onto the daytime agenda.

The old discipline and the old *pudeur* are gone. If we recall Catherine Barkley's shame when her image is displayed in the three mirrors of the hotel room where Frederick takes her ("I never felt like a whore before"), we can better measure the distance Hemingway has traveled. The mirror, one is tempted to say, is the chief furnishing of *The Garden of Eden*, the vehicle of self-dissemination and self-replication: not only do Catherine and David arouse each other by mirror gazing, but they actually have their landlord buy a big mirror for the bar; and, finally, it is not very hard to see Marita herself,

the "swing" figure who loves both Catherine and David, whom both love, as
the ultimate mirror of the text, the body that serves as "common ground" for
the husband and wife. Hence, a line such as "Go and talk with her David.
And if you want to fuck her then fuck her good for me" (149–50) is to be
understood in almost direct, nonmetaphoric fashion, as if you could fuck
someone for somebody else, as if that were what you were probably doing
anyway. Here is the peculiar dimensionality and cubism of Hemingway's
book. Mark Spilka has rightly charged Tom Jenks with rather ruthlessly cutting Marita's role from David's complex "caretaker" and wise alter ego to "the
'good wife' who ministers to the creative mystery but has no creative life of
her own"; but for mirroring and reflecting purposes, for exercises in virtuality
and vicariousness, the Marita of the published version adequately performs
her structural task.[15] We all know the famous definition of the kind of prose
Hemingway was attempting to writer, what he called a "fourth and fifth
dimension that can be gotten," and one is struck by the consonance of that
narrative ideal with the erotic situation in *The Garden of Eden*. Lovemaking,
we now see, is — forgive the pun — an affair of "layering," of substitutions and
displacements, of effigies and mirrors. It is strictly within the logic of Catherine's project to alter herself and others, to push David toward three-way sex
and round-robin performances. Ultimately, the writerly project and the erotic
project both aim at a kind of endless play, a prose that is more difficult than
poetry, a lovemaking of "infinite variety" that might go on forever.

Catherine Bourne is nothing less than the female Rimbaud. She wants to
passer outre. She is the one who could say:

> "Je ne comprends pas les lois; je n'ai pas le sens moral, je suis une brute:
> vous vous trompez."
> Oui, j'ai les yeux fermés à votre lumière. Je suis une bête, un nègre. Mais
> je puis être sauvé. . . .[16]

The erotic pas de deux of Catherine and David Bourne recalls the ecstatic and
wrenching experiments of Rimbaud and Verlaine, the *vierge folle* and the
époux infernal, for she too proclaims, "L'amour est à réinventer" (224), and
not only does she believe that "à chaque être plusieurs *autres* vies me sem-
blaient dues" (233), but she is determined to live out these *other* lives that are
her due: lion/*bête*, African/*nègre*, girl/boy. Above all, she plays out the cardinal Rimbaud belief, "JE est un autre" (345), and her obsession with alterity
lends *The Garden of Eden* a remarkable surrealist power unlike anything seen
in Hemingway before.

Once we see Catherine Bourne for the demiurgic, form-giving, form-
altering, protean figure that she is, a figure who, in Spilka's words, "manipu-
lates their [David's and Marita's] lives . . . like a maternal novelist arranging
close relations," we have a text that leaves the real-life figures of Hadley and
Zelda and Grace far behind, and we are then able to grasp the nature of the
quest that informs the novel's erotic activity.[17] In the original manuscript we
understand that Catherine's verbal wit and repartee constitute a significant
part of her artistic weaponry and credentials — Marita pointedly compares her

to David in this respect—but the published novel rightly locates her rival powers in the area of self-making and remaking. Catherine's metamorphoses constitute the figural drama of David's life, and that drama is an old familiar story in the Hemingway oeuvre. Her transformations are a version of the elemental fluidity that threatens the male prerogatives of fixity and pattern. In *In Our Time* we encounter its basic anarchic power: "*Water buffalo and cattle were hauling carts through the mud. No end and no beginning. . . . Women and kids were in the carts crouched with mattresses, mirrors, sewing machines, bundles. There was a woman having a kid with a young girl holding a blanket over her and crying. Scared sick looking at it. It rained all through the evacuation.*"[18] Pulsating life, animal and procreative, without end or beginning: here is the violent world that cannot be ordered. We see here the primal ooze that is regnant on the quai at Smyrna, in the "blue bunch" of entrails and pumping blood of the gored horse, in the hemorrhaging death of Catherine Barkley, in the retreat from Caporetto in the rain. Sometimes this natural force takes on more finite shape, as in the rushing bull or bullets that come at us. Sexual intercourse comes increasingly to partake of this uncontrollable, unmanageable energy. When Robert Jordan and Maria experience lovemaking as the earth moving, it all seems romantic initially; but the earth does move in *For Whom the Bell Tolls*, and its seismic activity may well obliterate human life:

> Then, through the hammering of the gun, there was the whistle of the air splitting apart and then in the red black roar the earth rolled under his knees and then waved up to hit him in the face and then dirt and bits of rock were falling all over and Ignacio was lying on him and the gun was lying on him. But he was not dead because the whistle came again and the earth rolled under him with the roar. Then it came again and the earth lurched under his belly and one side of the hilltop rose into the air and then fell slowly over them where they lay. (321)

We are meant to remember the lovemaking in the sleepingbag, and to see in this description of the bombs landing a grotesque replay of sexual intercourse: the moving earth, Ignacio lying on him, the gun lying on him, the earth obscenely rolling and lurching "under his belly," the entire hilltop rising and falling "over them where they lay." Nothing stays still here, nothing even stays itself, and it is intolerable, just as Picasso's *Guernica* is intolerable in its monstrous rupture of form and identity. These are the cataclysmic upheavals that chart the Hemingway landscape, and their virulence and violence are what is lurking, "sinister," under the surface of *The Garden of Eden*. Catherine Bourne completes a grand procession, and it is less a procession of women than of elemental threats, of violent natural forces that place the Hemingway male in his inevitable situational drama: under siege. But at last the rules of the game have changed; the very field on which it is played has changed. Catherine is the avenging angel, assertive and insatiable, and her powers in this story are unmistakably artistic as well as erotic, making her the most formidable rival to the male in the entire Hemingway corpus.

It is possible to feel that *The Garden of Eden* has had too much editing plastic surgery to be credible. The very substantial Sheldon subplot has been excised, and with it a significant dimension of the original project has been jettisoned: the fuller, more nuanced spectrum of artistic, sexual, and cultural crises that Hemingway had wanted to pack into this ambitious novel.[19] The version assembled by Jenks has a formal elegance and a propriety of the editor's making, and they hinge, first and foremost, on the remarkable counterpointing that the published text exhibits between the hunting story and the David-Catherine-Marita love triangle. We will never know how Hemingway might have sorted out his materials, nor if he would have juxtaposed these two narrative strands and ventures in such a fascinating way. At first glance it may seem that several different projects are being carried out at once, resulting in a jarring conflation of an African short story (what Spilka has termed "the Kipling impulse") and a Mediterranean novel.[20] The relationship between these two ventures is not simply a matter for the critics; it is of vital importance within the novel proper. Moreover, the bold figurative logic that it displays points to a reflexivity and sense of poetic form that Jenks may have "midwifed," but which emerge unmistakably from the deepest experiences and principles of the Hemingway career and oeuvre. As the sexual intrigue becomes more and more frenetic, more stereophonic, and equipped with doubles and mirrors, David Bourne turns increasingly to the African stories he is writing. Until then, we recall, he has been writing about the events of the present, an account of his experience with Catherine. When he persists in this new writerly direction, Catherine is sharply resentful: "Can't you see? Jumping back and forth trying to write stories when all you had to do was keep on with the narrative that meant so much to all of us. It was going so well too and we were just coming to the most exciting parts. Someone has got to show you that the stories are just your way of escaping your duty" (190). As both David and Catherine argue that they don't want to get the work "mixed up," we realize that the writerly issues are inseparable from the erotic tensions, that writing itself is a terrain for mixing and doubling. Above all, Catherine wants to control the textual field, to shackle David's writing to their joint experiences so that there would be no private realm for him alone, no arena for him that was inaccessible to her. This is penetration of a sort, and it accounts for the extraordinary hostility she feels for David as *independent writer*: she loathes the clippings he receives about the reception of his earlier work, she flaunts her own financial support of and control over his writing, and, at the end, she goes the full route and destroys his work.

It is quite possible to view these matters in terms of Hemingway's personal biases, a kind of writerly misogyny that converts women into jealous shrews when it comes to their men's writing. But that is only part of the picture. A number of critics have pointed out that the Hemingway male *needs* this kind of challenge and "input," that all the novels involve a male's coming to terms with his womanly side.[21] Spilka sees Hemingway's entire career in seesaw terms, as an "oscillation between novels of failed sexual relations (*The Sun Also Rises*, *A Farewell to Arms*) and tales of stoic male endurance," and he speaks persuasively of the author's "reactive strength," his "self-defining resistance to his own androgynous propensities," his "dependency and openness to the manipulations of many wives and mistresses whom he desperately needs, and with whom he secretly identifies."[22]

But how much "accommodation" is achieved? Catherine wages war against the African stories because she knows that David is taking refuge in them, that he is building, through them, a space of his own. And that writerly reprieve, as private as the tomb, constitutes the "separate peace" that Hemingway has been seeking all his life. Early on in their *éducation sexuelle*, David wakes up and realizes that writing is to be his salvation: "The sun was bright now in the room and it was a new day. You better get to work, he told himself. You can't change any of it back. Only one person can change it back and she can't know how she will wake nor if she'll be there when she wakes. It doesn't matter how you feel. You better get to work. You have to make sense there. You don't make any in this other. Nothing will help you. Nor would have ever since it started" (146). It couldn't be put more clearly. Writing is (to be) David's fiefdom, his turf; it is the arena he can control. Catherine prodigiously changes herself (and even him) at will sexually, but David can change nothing on that front. It is a risky, possibly fatal game that she is playing — "she can't know how she will wake nor if she'll be there when she wakes" — but David is going to hold onto himself, to keep his ego intact in his writing, "there," since he doesn't make any sense "in this other." Here, then, is the challenge to David Bourne, and it accounts for the novels' odd binary struggle: writing is called upon to create a space for the beleaguered male, a preserve that will offer sanctuary from the erotic play of the coupling lovers. Writing has always been given a place of prominence in Hemingway's books, whether it be the satirical view of Robert Cohn or the admiration Robert Jordan feels for Pilar's pithy prose, but never before has it been shown to be the life-and-death affair that we know it really was for Hemingway. Writing itself is under siege here: it is not by accident that Catherine wants to put Marita in David's study, to put eros between the author and his work. But the most remarkable instances of this dialectic are precisely those moments when the text "changes direction," gets "mixed up," moves from *her* sexual agenda to *his* hunting story. In short, all of the apparent indecisiveness of this text, its apparent uncertainty as to its subject, its weaving from one plot line to another — these are the features of the book that make it so dazzlingly modern. Like Proust's *Recherche* or Faulkner's *Absalom, Absalom!*, Hemingway's book enlists writing and storytelling as a form of action, a way of staying alive, a way of coping with the murderous events that one cannot otherwise cope with: "You have to make sense there. You don't make any in this other." Much the way Faulkner's two Harvard roommates travel back through time to a war fifty years earlier, David Bourne learns not only that writing has a time and space of its own but that one can live there: "It was the third day of the wind but it was not as heavy now and he sat at the table and read the story over from the start to where he had left off, correcting as he read. He went on with the story, living in it and nowhere else, and when he heard the voices of the two girls outside he did not listen" (107).

We are so accustomed to viewing the Hemingway writer as a spartan, austere figure seeking one true sentence, doing battle with the gods in front of his typewriter, that we may fail to give writing itself its astounding life-saving due in *The Garden of Eden*. Catherine Bourne is indeed the demiurgic, meta-morphosing life force in this book, and we have seen that her project is ultimately metaphysical, that her Rimbaldian quest for total freedom is dark and primitive and African. Now we see that David Bourne, helpless and mal-leable in the face of her desire, is going to propose his own African venture, a writerly land where Catherine is denied access, a preserve that will shore up David's identity and guarantee his integrity. Hemingway shows us, in countless beautiful passages, the *passage* itself, the exit from one realm and the entry into another, the trip to Africa:

> When he sat down the sun was not yet up and he felt that he had made up some of the time that was lost in the story. But as he reread his careful legible hand and the words took him away and into the other country, he lost that advantage and was faced with the same problem and when the sun rose out of the sea it had, for him, risen long before and he was well into the crossing of the gray, dried, bitter lakes his boots now white with crusted alkalis. He felt the weight of the sun on his head and his neck and his back. His shirt was wet and he felt the sweat go down his back and between his thighs. When he stood straight up and rested, breathing slowly, and his shirt hung away from his shoulders, he could feel it dry in the sun and see the white patches that the salts of his body made in the drying. He could feel and see himself standing there and knew there was nothing to do except go on.
>
> At half past ten he had crossed the lakes and was well beyond them. By then he had reached the river and the great grove of fig trees where they would make their camp. The bark of the trunks was green and yellow and the branches were heavy. Baboons had been eating the wild figs and there were baboon droppings and broken figs on the ground. The smell was foul.
>
> But the half past ten was on the watch on his wrist as he looked at it in the room where he sat at a table feeling the breeze from the sea now and the real time was evening and he was sitting against the yellow gray base of a tree with a glass of whiskey and water in his hand and the rolled figs swept away watching the porters butchering out the Kongoni he had shot in the first grassy swale they passed before they came to the river. (138–39)

Writing is "the other country," and there is little in Hemingway to match this African genesis, this race against the sun, this brutal but redemptive "over-pass" from the Mediterranean hotel to the gray, dried, bitter lakes and the boots white with crusted alkalis. The clean plain style is paying its way now, and the sheer palpable weight and presence of Africa—the hot sun, the wet shirt, the sweat between the thighs, the salts of the body, the wild figs, the baboon droppings, the foul smell—is going to provide the desperately needed counterweight, the heft, necessary to David Bourne's survival. Africa will be the real place and the real time, and "there," at least, David will make sense.

Catherine began her African quest at Grau du Roi. David's Africa goes further back: it was where he grew up; it was the subject of his first novel.

Thus, the reminiscences that fuel his writing are nothing less than a *return*, a recapturing of the past; but here too the project is one of transformation, of becoming once again the child he was. That child was part of a family, a complex human and racial network every bit as problematic as the ménage à trois of himself, Catherine, and Marita; this African family consists not only of his father but also of "his Kamba servant and brother" (129), another "dark brother" in the procession of doubles. To come to terms with this first family, these origins, is the burden of David's writing, and this artistic quest constitutes a brilliant doubling of the novel's surface story of love and marriage. Much the way Lily Briscoe's painterly project both rivals with and recasts the relational themes of *To the Lighthouse*, so too does David's African story vie with the erotic project of his wife; and both Virginia Woolf and Hemingway achieve thereby the density and resonance that are proper to poetry, the kind of metaphoric economy in which everything speaks for everything else. Woolf has long been credited with such narrative breakthroughs, but *The Garden of Eden* appears to be the only real metafiction that Hemingway wrote, the only text that fully gauges and dramatizes the role of art itself as a way of staying alive.

What about the thing itself, the actual piece that David writes when he puts pencil to paper? This African story is, in all respects, astonishing. The actual narrative, which David dismisses as a young child's story, is one of the most luminous fables that Hemingway wrote. In this account of an elephant hunt, or more specifically the pursuit of a wounded elephant, Hemingway delivers a quest narrative of epic stature, not only recalling his own *Old Man and the Sea* but calling to mind some of the greatest hunt stories in American literature, Melville's chase for the white whale and Faulkner's story of the bear. Even these echoes do not take us far enough, and one is reminded as well of Proust's epic quest, this time conceived as a feat of memory and resurrection and time travel. Like Proust's Marcel, David is searching in his past for the key to his present; and even though Hemingway's narrative leaves its segments unlinked, we are invited to ponder the larger, enduring ramifications of the elephant hunt, to see in it a story of innocence and knowledge, a story about the human heart and the betrayals it causes and courts. Ultimately the elephant hunt succeeds miraculously as an embedded narrative of limpid, childlike clarity on the one hand and as a provocative coda for the adult love story on the other, a metaphoric assessment of its risks, transgressions, and meaning.[23]

The ten-year-old David Bourne will be initiated into the values and priorities of the adult world much the same way that Isaac McCaslin is initiated into the wilderness and the twin curses of ownership and racism. If Hemingway does not strive for quite the "lateral" cultural reach that Faulkner does, he moves "vertically" instead with great deftness, showing us that "rites of passage" is a staggeringly kinetic proposition, that the "passage" in question is at once temporal, moral, and perceptual. Following the wounded, great elephant with the legendary tusks, David comes to understand a good deal about himself (why did he alert his father to the beast's whereabouts?) and the adult community he is in the process of entering (a community of trackers, followers of blood, willing to use all means, including gut-shooting and cunning manip-ulation of the elephant's noblest virtues). Unlike the big fish that Santiago pursues, David's elephant is a spiritual creature animated by love and fidelity; he is trackable precisely because his final trek is a homage to his dead friend, his *askari*, and the human hunters, those who killed his *askari*, know this "dirty secret." With very pure metaphoric logic the hunt reveals its essential doubleness: the blood that gushes from the elephant's wounds becomes lumi-nous as a sign of spirit, as a physical language of fidelity written onto the landscape. Thus, the hunters are following a double script, rich with signifi-cance and dark in its portents. David encounters many truths here, although he is not to understand them with finality until he recaptures this childhood experience through his writing. He learns that the heart will betray us, that love for others is a death pact, that the lives of true friends and lovers are transparent in their markings, culminating in a return to a skeleton, heinously on show to hunters and trackers.

Already, as a child, David grasps the deadly law of cause and effect at work here. "Never tell anyone anything ever. Never tell anyone anything again" (181), the boy grimly warns himself, realizing that he is to blame for this dreadful slaughter, for it was he who alerted his father and Juma to the elephant's presence. But the scene has a radiance and a figurative power that give special resonance to the boy's words. The heart can kill us if it speaks, and the bleeding, homeward-bound elephant is living language to his pursuers, a language of blood that simultaneously expresses and betrays. "Never tell anyone anything ever" is a desperate strategy for self-protection, for immu-nity. But that is not all. David is, even then, speaking as a writer, and he is expressing with great clarity Hemingway's fear of confession and exposure. "Friend or enema" Frederick teases Catherine Barkley, and we see that the great enemy of the Hemingway hero is enema, the expulsion of what wants out but must be kept in. The heroic code is tight-lipped, and the writer's task is to convey inner turmoil without "telling" it, the way it is done, say, in "Big, Two-Hearted River." Hemingway is very close to the Faulkner of "The Bear" in this hunting story, but whereas "tracking" is aligned with reading in Faulkner's text (reading of the wilderness and reading of the ledgers), Heming-way's focus is more on language as bleeding, as palpable sign of the suffering heart.

Ultimately, more even than this is at stake in David's recollection of the elephant hunt. His African past, like Catherine's African project, is essentially a meditation on Eden, and together they fuse the central issues of the novel: innocence, knowledge, and art. One is free to read *The Garden of Eden* as multidirectional, to see its two ventures in terms that are absolutely double: expulsion from the Garden and return to the Garden, loss of innocence and recovery of innocence. Catherine's art, as we have seen, is that of the human body and the metamorphoses that sexual desire may occasion for it; David's art is, of course, writing, and his reflections on the elephant hunt of his past constitute the most luminous *ars poetica* in the whole of Hemingway:

That was where he stopped in the hunt that morning. He knew he did not have it right yet. He had not gotten the enormity of the skull as they had come onto it in the forest nor the tunnels underneath it in the earth that the beetles had made and that had been revealed like deserted galleries or catacombs when the elephant had moved the skull. He had not made the great length of the whitened bones nor how the elephant's tracks had moved around the scene of the killing and how following them he had been able to see the elephant as he had moved and then had been able to see what the elephant had seen. He had not gotten the great width of the one elephant trail that was a perfect road through the forest nor the worn smooth rubbing trees nor the way other trails intersected so that they were like the map of the Métro in Paris. He had not made the light in the forest where the trees came together at their tops and he had not clarified certain things that he must make as they were then, not as he recalled them now. The distances did not matter since all distances changed and how you remembered them was how they were. But his change of feeling toward Juma and toward his father and toward the elephant was complicated by the exhaustion that had bred it. Tiredness brought the beginning of understanding. The understanding was beginning and he was realizing it as he wrote. But the dreadful true understanding was all to come and he must not show it by arbitrary statements of rhetoric but by remembering the actual things that had brought it. Tomorrow he would get the things right and go on. (182)

Much is familiar here to the Hemingway reader. The code of authenticity, the heroic efforts to get it right, not to cheat, to be true to experience: all this we have seen before. But never has it been quite so bathed in the light of poetry. The "journalistic" Hemingway was always something of a misnomer anyway, but here we learn, with utmost clarity, that writing is a visionary activity, that it operates a magic return to the past, that it recovers innocence and, in doing so, loses the innocence it recovers. David's beautiful list of the particulars he has "left out" of his narrative, far from nailing down the scene, lifts it up onto a new plateau, invests it with the enchantment of an archaeological discovery, the sighting of a new planet. Note the insistent expansion that is taking place. He had not gotten the great length of the whitened bones nor the great width of the elephant trail. The skull is more enormous than he had said; it lies not on the ground but rather over an entire network of circuits and channels. Note also the telling metaphors at work: those "deserted galleries or catacombs" hint of lost civilizations, of huge expanses of bodies and skeletons sacrificed by the hunters. The ancient cities and ruins of Europe shimmer through this prose, and Hemingway's comparison of the intersecting trails to the Métro in Paris is an appropriate modern conclusion to his epic similes. Yet the expansion is finally more than historical and cultural; ultimately it is perceptual. Seeing the elephant is where we start; seeing what the elephant sees is where we end. Here, too, Hemingway is true to the mythic aims of the hunt, namely, the ecstatic fusion of hunter and hunted, but David Bourne's version of it is insistently perceptual, imaginative, empathetic. This is a *rite de passage* in more ways than one, because David actually transcends his own limits and bearings, learns, by dint of great effort, to become what he pursues. Likewise, he tells us that tiredness brought the beginning of understanding, which means that his own fatigue carries him into the fatigue of his father, merges him with a point of view that is not his own, makes him Other. Such is the passage from innocence to knowledge, for knowledge means knowledge of the Other, the dark Other whom one may become through love. David's project, we now realize, is every bit as much about alteration and transcendence as is that of his wife. But in his case writing is to be the agency of such metamorphosis and generosity.

Earlier on, David had thought about the prodigious transformations that writing and reading entail: "It was not him, but as he wrote it was and when someone read it, finally, it would be whoever read it and what they found when they should reach the escarpment, if they reached it, and he would make them reach its base by noon of that day; then whoever read it would find what there was there and have it always" (129). It is not so much a question of writing *about* the adventure of the hunt; writing itself is such an adventure, and reading is its magic counterpart, a kind of special treasure hunt where the quarry you see is another life, and if you find it, you have it always.

Writing is the encounter with alterity. Entering the perceptual field of another may be as intimate as sexual intercourse, and it brings its own special knowledge. David's story resembles Proust's great novel in that it effects a return to one's past and to those who are ghosts, including the ghost of oneself. The father does not come off as a hero in David's tale, and yet the entire piece is infused with understanding, even with forgiveness. Something resembling a separate peace seems to have made.[24] Why, then, is the writing of the story construed by Catherine as an act of war? The jealous-wife syndrome will take us only so far. More to the point is the rivalry that emerges between David and Catherine. David writes, as I have noted, to assert control, to save his life; but his African project and her African project are competing paths to Eden, radically incompatible strategies for metamorphosis, transcendence, and innocence. The rifts and divisions of the novel are seen to be strategic and tactical in nature, the necessarily opposed ventures of the two major figures. Brilliant editing at Scribner's may be responsible for this binary structure, but even if that is the case, we are entitled to feel that the spectacular conflicts of this novel have been in the making for the whole of Hemingway's life.

As we know, the book is outfitted with an ending that sticks a little in the throat. Catherine has burned the *cahiers* and has conveniently disappeared; David is left with Marita, who is able (incredibly) to share his writerly world, and at the end we have a scene reminiscent of the close of *Hedda Gabler*, in which David magically retrieves his work from oblivion. It is very saccharine, and its inadequacies have not gone unnoticed.[25] Rather than closing this chapter on that note of specious closure, I would prefer to return to the question of warfare in order to consider one final time why Catherine burns David's African stories. We recall that Catherine has proposed to market David's work, to line up some artists (Marie Laurencin, Derain, Dufy, and Picasso) and make the necessary arrangements. David predictably balks. Then Catherine closes in for the kill, and she berates David once again for abandoning the story of their relationship (a story she controls) in favor of Africa: "It's [*their* story] certainly much more interesting and instructive than a lot of natives in a kraal or whatever you call it covered with flies and scabs in Central Africa with your drunken father staggering around smelling of sour beer and not knowing which ones of the little horrors he had fathered" (189).

What is one to make of this? The reader certainly hasn't seen any African story of this stripe. Here is a dark Africa for David that has little to do with elephants. We remember the line about David's "Kamba servant and brother," and one wonders. "It's bestial" was Catherine's earlier violent reaction to David's African material. Hemingway, once again, but ever so discreetly, is in Faulkner country here, hinting at incest and miscegenation, giving David a dark brother just as Charles Bon darkly twins Henry Sutpen, hinting at a monstrous father, on the order of Carothers McCaslin, one whose transgressions are on the far side of any act of forgiveness. Those transgressions are not recounted in *The Garden of Eden*. But the genuine fury they arouse in Catherine—and, indeed, David's equally angry reply, "There goes the ball game"—gives pause. For there is transgression in this book. The entire sexual fantasia has only appeared to get off scot-free. Perhaps Hemingway is expressing, in Catherine's violent repudiation of the African stories, something of his own unresolvable moral ambivalence regarding the events that are front and center in his novel. The hedonism and sexual license of his beautiful young people may be too good to be true, too audacious to go unpunished, and so the censor makes his ineluctable appearance, but he does so, muffled, by means of displacement. There is, finally, judgment being pronounced here, and one feels that it may cover more than any single item in David's past. In this light the war that finally breaks out confers on this sunny text a foretaste of apocalypse. The *cahiers* were destroyed, and who believes they can be made good? Ernest Hemingway could not pull it off himself, in 1922. And Catherine Bourne is broken by her experiments. "Now all I am is through. You're a girl and a boy both and you really are. You don't have to change and it doesn't kill you and I'm not. And now I'm nothing" (192). Back as early as *The Sun Also Rises*, Brett told us the truth about sexual desire: "It's tearing me all up inside" (183). So, perhaps, crack-up really is Hemingway's theme, even though he has trumped it up in strange new colors in *The Garden of Eden*. Rimbaud did not finish well either. Self-invention can be a formula for disaster.

To regard Catherine's violent destruction of the story as a displaced version of judgment, even final judgment, even final judgment meted out by the author to himself as author, is to pay tribute to the dazzling artistry of Hemingway's last book. There is a generosity of vision here that is new. Seeing the elephant can lead to seeing what the elephant saw. The woman-as-(desiring)-subject stands (at last) at the tragic center of this fable, and Hemingway has been able to see it her way, even as he measures her intolerable threat to his male surrogate, even as he punishes her act of hubris. In this book, as many critics have noted, Hemingway was "braver than we thought" because he had the courage to "remake" himself and his art by displaying in a new key the guerrilla warfare at the core of his life. Above all, he has fashioned (with the help of Tom Jenks) an astonishingly resonant and poetic narrative, a meditation about the freedom and limits of "shaping" that will take its place in American fiction. To see one thing in another, to be tight-lipped while having one's say, to reach Africa and Eden through sex and writing is possible only in a capacious, virtually cubistic narrative that consists, like the Parisian Métro, of endless passages and intersections, luminous moments where people fuse and alter, come together and come apart, turn and return. This is the prose that is harder to write than poetry because in it we actually imagine those fourth and fifth dimensions that Hemingway sought to render.

V

THE AMERICAN
POSTMODERNISTS AND
FREEDOM OF SPEECH

11

John Hawkes, Skin Trader

We encounter, as entry to John Hawkes's *Blood Oranges*, lines cited from one of the master tales of foiled desire in modern fiction, Ford Madox Ford's *Good Soldier*: "Is there then any terrestrial paradise where, amidst the whispering of the olive-leaves, people can be with whom they like and have what they like and take their ease in shadows and in coolness?" It will be recalled that Dowell, Ford's broken narrator, closes his vision of desired harmony by contrasting it to the cacophony he had experienced: "Or are all men's lives like the lives of us good people—like the lives of the Ashburnhams, of the Dowells, of the Ruffords—broken, tumultuous, agonized, and unromantic lives, periods punctuated by screams, by imbecilities, by deaths, by agonies? Who the devil knows?"[1] This plaint could effectively stand over a great many of Hawkes's novels, for it signals, in its duet of mellifluous nostalgic tones and bitter reprisals, the double bind that marks Hawkes's world: the curse visited on desire and the writerly project of fashioning a realm where it may be—somehow—gratified. Life, in Ford's text, emerges as an affective syntax, an utterance that is structured, parsed, and punctuated by pain and madness, a rhythmic punishment and denial of pleasure. Hawkes, too, understands the dialectic of pleasure and pain to be rich in syntactic and narrative possibilities, and we see in his novels an effort to move past the multiple constraints that Ford displays: not just the throttling of desire but also the linearity of its representation, the chain of sequence itself that must proceed from hunger to hurt. Could one, Hawkes seems to be asking, do it somehow all at once, create a script of many tongues, speaking pleasure and pain, ease and dis-ease, music and cacophony, simultaneously?

Desire itself, in the Hawkesian scheme, is predictably no cheerful matter, for it seems to include the full spectrum of Ford's affective possibilities: a vision of ease that is never far from agony. Although his work has tended to move from the anarchic and bestial to the more refined and patterned, the originary darkness remains intact. The Hawkesian narrative is both sumptuous and shrewd, and it cargoes an enormous amount of affective material into its decorous forms. Underneath Hawkes's modulated song is a primitive and uncensored imagination, endlessly serving up its findings and carving them in front of our eyes. His people are moved by lust, savagery, and murder, and they routinely court mutilation and torture. But there is, especially after *The Blood Oranges* (1970), a recognizably French stamp on much of the writing: a delight in the palate and the flesh, a feel for texture and sensuous immediacy, a fascination with the Old World's forms, its overt monuments, and its darker folklore.

Yet, despite his kinship with figures such as Baudelaire and Lautréamont, the writer whom Hawkes perhaps most closely resembles is his compatriot Hawthorne. Even the names hint at likeness, and although Hawkes would doubtless reject the comparison, Hawthorne is his model in a number of crucial ways: the drive to romance and allegory, the punitive streak and the fascination with the illicit, the obsession with evil, and, finally, the dialectic of repression and displacement that configures the entire writerly project. But in Hawkes the sternness and rigor of Hawthorne are given an overlay of sensuality and dream, yielding a kind of fiction that is as exacting and vengeful as *The Scarlet Letter*, but as dreamlike and sumptuous as anything in Rimbaud or Huysmans. The fit between these two strains is uneasy, and that uneasiness accounts for the astounding density and cunning of Hawkes's prose, a kind of baroque fashioning that rivals Cellini in its sinuous movement and lush artifice, yet remaining taut, muscular, even severe in its moves, achieving a remarkable economy of utterance.[2] Hawkes's thickened language proves that words and phrases can be endowed with a radiance and materiality that give the reader the kind of hedonistic pleasure one might experience in touching a richly textured fabric or desired human flesh. This prose, however, is rarely ornamental as such, and it is mistakenly classified all too often as decadent or self-contained; rather, Hawkes is using language in a colonizing project, using it to render a landscape that, in becoming representable, is richly mediated in character, shown to be always already inflected by human desire. The great challenge consists in landing this quarry, in delivering the scene with all its shimmering undercurrents and overlays, and at his best, when he captures the beast still living, John Hawkes manages a richer, fuller, more complete say than virtually any other American writer of this century.

That "say" is in the service of character and event, as one would expect, but it is also enlisted in the making of an environment, not so much a physical space as a perceptual realm, a cognitive and sensual domain where person and place are no longer truly separable. Hence, recognizable sites in Hawkes's books can be shorn of their ordinary markings as they are subjected to the crucible of the writer's alchemical power, and they are thus transfigured into psychic landscapes, places that live with unusual intensity. Poe famously claimed that the horror he wrote of was not that of Germany but of the soul, and it could be said likewise that the war-torn Germany of *The Cannibal* is a landscape to be found on no map, that the British and American settings in *The Lime Twig* and *Second Skin*, rendered with such fine and precise notations, are destined, at crucial moments in the fiction, to disappear, like a suddenly drawn curtain when the central business of the play is to occur. The unspecified pastoral setting of *The Blood Oranges* and the unreal marshland and prison of *The Passion Artist* again testify to Hawkes's high mission: to invent a place with such cunning that we recognize it, that we know we have lived there, even if only for the time-space of the fiction.

It is in this light that *Adventures in the Alaskan Skin Trade* is such a notable achievement, for in it Hawkes appears to be seeking new company, to be rivaling both Michener and *National Geographic*, as he gives his readers a heady but informative grand tour of the North; and, for once, he finds an existing landscape utterly commensurate with his capacity to create. This book acquires thereby a kind of epic dimensionality; not only does it offer, at long last, an accessible entry into the Hawkes universe, but it places Hawkes in the grand tradition of exploration narrative, enabling him to locate, finally, his dreamscape on terra firma.

Adventures in the Alaskan Skin Trade sheds a salutary light on the entire Hawkes corpus because its manifest surface realism, its declared project of Alaskan portraiture, make us rethink the earlier books and help us to perceive their (now visible) sociohistorical dimensions. For too long John Hawkes has been regarded exclusively as the artificer of hermetic, self-indulgent, forbiddingly private dreamscapes; he is indeed that, but it is time to recognize that these "internal," often infernal books are no less a map of culture and history for all their inwardness and word magic. This is an ear attuned to frequencies we have blotted out; Hawkes depicts a cancerously active world, makes visible and audible for us the seismic energy of the earth, the tug of gravity, the sounds behind the sounds, behind the silence. He forges unforgettable images of violation and destruction, and although these affective vistas, largely bereft of recognizable data or dates, are not being passed off as history, they nonetheless restore to us and for us something of the horror that can attend our lived histories, both on the grand and on the intimate scale. The dark bloodletting in *The Cannibal*, the bomber that enters the flat in Dreary Lane in *The Lime Twig*, the "kissing bandits" who go AWOL in *Second Skin*, the women who break out of La Violaine in *The Passion Artist* are potent images of derailment and misadventure, of programs gone foul, of high-sounding directives travestied and gone amok, of the visceral flesh-and-blood base that subtends our fine abstractions. The characteristic Hawkesian response to such fiascoes is to keep plunging, all the way to the bottom. Sometimes the plunge is into further violence, as in the murderous finale of *The Lime Twig*; at others it entails exit and the making of a place of one's own, as in *Second Skin*; in *The Passion Artist*, Konrad Vost finishes, fatally, his education in the very prison he shunned at the outset, but willingly now, even gratefully.

Hawkes's last great explorer, John Burne Deauville, known as Uncle Jake, completes the line of surveying, colonizing heroes, but his Alaskan exploits are different from anything that has gone before. Uncle Jake is Hawkes's version of Kafka's K, the *Landvermesser*, the man who charts and chronicles the New World, the man whose secret longing is to sound its depths, illuminate and thereby possess its mystery. Whereas Kafka's world of castle and village is to be found on no known map, Uncle Jake is our tour guide to a real-life Alaska, bursting with flora and fauna, waiting for its story to be told. This exploratory fable is rich in echoes, and one thinks back to Columbus and

Cortés, men who encountered, charted (and violated and misread), entire continents. But Jake is no mere colonizer, and he does not seek actual gain of any sort; instead his aims are grander still, because he knows himself to be a latecomer on the scene, to a country no longer virgin (Has there ever been a virgin land? Whose fantasy is this?) and he regards his mission as a dual one: to inventory and also to redeem. Jake is out to save Alaska, to purify it, and in this sense his exploits have in them something of an *imitatio Christi*, but with secular, folkloric, and cartoon elements more proper to Superman and Captain Marvel and other one-dimensional heroes of yore. This oddly swollen, oddly vacuous figure is the final one in Hawkes's parade of questers, and his mystery—still haunting, long after his death, his narrating daughter Sunny— and aura constitute both the dark center of this novel and also a measuring standard for assessing, retrospectively, other Hawkes pilgrims: William Banks, Skipper, Cyril, Konrad Vost. And thus we can see in *Adventures in the Alaskan Skin Trade* a meditation on the Hawkes oeuvre, but rendered in surprisingly American hues and marching to a familiar American beat: the libidinal fable and family romance acquire now the echoes of cultural myth, and the familiar plunge into the interior is now embodied in a pioneering saga of the New Frontier. Our country, 'tis of thee.

But we will not fully savor the Alaska fiction unless we are willing to double back, to retrace something of the route Hawkes has taken in his homing journey to the North. And that itinerary can be fully illuminated by an examination of the Alaska text's most conspicuous forebear, *Second Skin* (1963), Hawkes's best-known novel and one of the great fictions of our century. Separated by more than twenty years' interval, the early text narrated by an older man, the latter book told by a young woman, these two novels constitute the central diptych in Hawkes's fiction: they signal each other in countless ways, and each shadows the other, echoes the other, fills in the other's silences, and resonates the other's phrases. The central axis on which each book turns is the father-daughter relationship, seen from the father's angle in the early novel, refracted from the daughter's perspective in the Alaska saga. Moreover, each text graphs the comedy and poetics of heroism, the moves and doges by which a man may conquer the forces of adversity and environment, the cost he pays for doing so. Finally, each of these novels is an endgame narrative, an ongoing skirmish with death; and the game—and it is a game—remains largely the same even though the optic changes. How does the imagination go about transmuting disaster into song? How can writing convey the comedy, pathos, and magic of human gesture and desire?

Skipper, protagonist of *Second Skin*, has the most remarkable voice in Hawkes's fiction, and he deserves to be placed alongside Joyce's Bloom in terms of street aphorisms and minute epiphanies for the short haul, and a mix of creatural cunning and self-dramatization for the longer haul. Zanier than Bloom, endowed with a comparably low center of gravity but tilted a bit more toward the grotesque, Skipper is the person who, bombarded by snowballs in the dark, thinks: "Escaped homing pigeons? A covey of tiny ducks driven berserk in the cold? Eaglets?"[3] Small-time metaphysician, he is the fellow who muses, "Anyone who has gotten down on his knees to vomit has discovered,

if only by accident, the position of prayer" (127). Hawkes has made it clear
that he intended Skipper to be recognizable as a survivor, yet it is not by way
of plot but through the peculiar heroics of vision and voice that he endures.
We would expect such a figure to reward us in moments of crisis, but he is no
less gratifying when it comes to minutiae and daily chores; this is how he
shaves: "Laughing while I was making irritable impatient faces in the bathroom mirror. Giving myself a close shave for the high school dance. Trying to
preserve my exhilaration against hers. And it was pleasurable. After a particularly good stroke I would set aside the razor and fling the water about as
wildly as I could and snort, grind my eyes on the end of the towel. Then step
to the window for a long look at the black night and the falling snow" (73).
How does one go about assessing this kind of episode? Plotwise there is really
nothing to report; morally as well this sequence is small potatoes. But that is
merely to say that this kind of perception makes a mockery of plot and morals
because it operates such a close-grained zoom look at the human creature that
those unwieldy constructs become hopelessly inoperative. Joyce, we know,
displayed the antics of his trio in *Ulysses* in comparable fashion, exposing the
artifice of our received views concerning the shape of person and event. But
there is more zest in Hawkes than in Joyce, and a good deal needs to be said
about the particular adrenaline released in the episode at hand, and in the
writing that delivers it. Plot and morals do not simply collapse or disappear;
instead, we may say that they are reconceived, even rediscovered, in the creatural gambits of the living, gambits consisting of dodges, feints, and minute
roller-coaster rides such as the shaving-snorting-grinding sequence just depicted. These are the units of measure that life has, once our picture acquires
sufficiently high definition to make them visible. The tiny lifts and peaks at
hand here, the little affective workout, the closing dash of poetry that brings
the black night and the falling snow into the bathroom, these exercises flaunt
a kind of irrepressible hedonism, got on the cheap, capable of flourishing in
the barest, most impoverished places, constituting with their mix of lather,
spray, and sound a very special little *son et lumière* spectacle by and for a
party of one. And with that, morality is back in the game — morality redefined
as the life-affirming gestures that keep us going, that instill zest and pizzazz
into the banal and homely routines performed by the living.

Skipper baffles criticism. Child of a suicidal undertaker, surrounded by
death and destruction, he counters with song. The narrative voice we hear
throughout the novel is a kind of singing; to live, to keep living, to keep others
living. The deaths mount up anyway: his father's, his mother's, Fernandez's,
Cassandra's. Still he sings, and of course he does not "know" his songs; filled
with incestuous longings, he cares only for the pleasure they offer, not their
moral coefficient. He lovingly explores his daughter's black bag as if it were
her coveted body; he relishes the sexual pleasure Fernandez will give her; he
throbs as she is "kissed" by the Kissing Bandits; he dedicates his life to shep-
herding hers. The temptation to label or tag such behavior is real (and most
Hawkes critics have succumbed to it), but we blur and erase what is most
marvelous in this text when we engage in such assessments. Hawkes's first-
person creation is endowed with a kind of narrative independence and maneu-

vering room that both invite our censure and defy us to pin it on the author; as moralist, the critic is in grave danger of going out of business here. We simply do not possess a scale for measuring these acts and urges of Skipper's, and their vitality and energy constitute something sui generis that no ethical code can capture within its nets. Hawkes seems to be reminding us that life is incomparably richer than the measures we foist on it, and he is out to show us that literature, done finely enough, is capable of rendering this human dance.

Huge man, king of the belly-bumpers, Skipper is a fully rounded character in more ways than one, and we could say that he effectually "rounds" others by dint of his solicitude and desire: he turns the cold Cassandra into his warm nugget; he is alive to the bravura of Fernandez, the loyalty of Sonny, the threatening sexual storm of Miranda, the animal warmth of Catalina Kate. What does Skipper achieve? Perhaps nothing. Perhaps his very modus operandi makes "achieve" into something quaint or irrelevant. Hero of alterations, he alter's life's stimuli—harsh or sweet—into the tones of his song, into the stitches of his embroidery; in this he differs radically from Uncle Jake, "doer" par excellence but man without a song. *Second Skin* becomes thereby a bottomless fiction, an unplumbable narrative with no reliable truth coefficient. Although it may appear to us that Skipper's ordeals on the cold, dark island are followed (?) by his paradisal stint as Artificial Inseminator on the tropical isle, this "sequence" (and the empirical bases it connotes) is by no means assured, and Tony Tanner has persuasively argued that the two islands are to be seen as imaginative grids, as interpretive frames for Skipper's experiences.[4] But this is no argument for mirage or chimera. We do not wake up from disaster and find that it was just a nasty dream. The sexual humiliation suffered at Tremlow's hands, the failure to shield Cassandra, the imposing stack of corpses that litter Skipper's trail—these facts are not to be undone.[5] But Hawkes is out to show us that they can be rivaled by the siring performances of life and art, through love and through pipette. Artificial insemination means, among other things, that artifice is seminal, that the artist makes life, no matter how much life unmakes him.

Hawkes's writing is in the service of Skipper's libidinal fullness, and it gets its man across in all his astounding innocence, that uncensored and unlabeled flow of desire (and fear) that carries the thing called Skipper.[6] Cassandra has him lovingly punctured; he is attracted to Jomo's artificial hand; Miranda's brassiere lashes its tail and her enormous chest roars of beehives; and these remain the figures of Hawkes's story, violent and pure, liberated metaphors on parade. There is a logic here, a tale of violation, a primitive arrangement of bare, forked creatures, but it is for us to piece it together. The puncture of Skipper's tattoo causes a scream that is "a strenuous black bat struggling, wrestling in my bloated mouth" (19), and that insistent image of invasion is just waiting to be sexualized and pinned down to Tremlow ("the sudden recall of what Tremlow had done to me that night" [19]); 128 pages later (!), Skipper finally finishes recounting the Tremlow saga, and the pattern becomes still darker, yet surfacing to the light: "Oh, I grunted at them, gagging in blood, grinding the top of my bald head into the invisible deck, and I flexed every possible muscle and bucked, did my best to buck, thrashed around good and plenty in the darkness with someone breathing his hot breath into my ear and the cloth ripping away from my flesh as if they were running the tip of a hot wire down the length of my thigh" (147). This scene, filled with grunting, gagging, grinding, flexing, bucking, thrashing, breathing, but nary a spoken word of the King's English, richly displays Hawkes's freedom of speech. We see here the language of the victimized subject, doing his best to buck, fighting carnal oppression carnally, losing the struggle against penetration, winning the struggle to keep it mum, displacing Tremlow (and his member?) into a black bat and a hot wire (the better to repress it? to convey it? to repress and convey it?).[7] The body has so few resources; it never can do much more than thrash and buck, with a little grinding on the side, and it is destined to lose all its fights, to be punctured and penetrated all the days of its life. But there is a peculiar form of dignity expressed here, the dignity of huffing and puffing, the dignity of a cover-up, the dignity of returning the repressed to a kind of vibrant elemental language that would do it justice. (One remembers Bloom's exquisite response to the Honourable Mrs. Mervyn Talboys's order that he take down his pants: "[*Trembling, beginning to obey.*] The weather has been so warm." Joyce, like Hawkes, understands the language of cover-up, understands that cover-up is in fact the essential language of culture.)[8]

The world of *Second Skin* is animate and legendary: iguanas and birds and snakes and lizards and bees and fish predominate.[9] The AWOL soldiers are first seen "traveling on their bellies," and they arrive "all little tight tendons and daggers and hand grenades and flashing bright points and lizard eyes" (40), ready to "drop their eggs," ready to give Cassandra "foamy" kisses (?) while Skipper "stood there trembling, smiling, sweating, squeezing her hand, squeezing Cassandra's hand for dear life and in all my protective reassurance and slack alarm" (42). There is no simple way to make this passage "behave"; we are at a loss to know what is cover for what, and every single word that Hawkes uses is both literal and figurative, announcing and concealing, standing for and standing in for. The soldiers who strip off their uniforms and weapons are depicted as desert lizards, are said to be dropping their eggs, and this vista recolors our view of the war itself in shocking hues: reptilian, erotic, violent. And for Skipper's performance, there is simply no bottom at all: What is he squeezing? What is he feeling? What is he doing? What is happening? This is not merely riddling prose. If there is word magic here it is to be understood as a language for the complex, tortured, yet preening psyche, the mind-body that negotiates with and in the bestiary, the animal kingdom that undergirds *Second Skin.*

The primeval life of Hawkes's creatures is rendered seismically, in flashes of metaphor, and the result is a brilliant and sonorous textual world, unified by bold correspondences — the bite of the tattoo, Tremlow's sodomy, the iguana mounted on Catalina Kate, the dead fetus in the jar and the inseminated cow, the seeds of death and the seeds of love, and finally all the radiant images of "second skin": penetrated flesh, lizard's cover, the oil skin, condom, the fabric of art, the clothing of life. Second skin means living twice, moving through death to life, through suicide to celebration, from the dark island to the sunny isle. To render this double vision a special palimpsest language must be devised, a language skin that displays both its own shimmering surface and the flesh and bones beneath: "Because I know and have stated here, that behind every frozen episode of that other island—and I am convinced that in its way it too was enchanted, no matter the rocks and salt and fixed position in the cold black waters of the Atlantic—there lies the golden wheel of my hot sun; behind every black rock a tropical rose and behind every cruel wind-driven snowstorm a filmy sheet, a transparency of golden fleas" (48).

Hawkes's language has the waywardness and seductive power of Joseph's robe of many colors, and his wildest, most manic scenes, such as the splendid belly-bumping sequence, are strange hieroglyphs, efforts to write with the body itself, to "sign" with it, to tattoo the skin and to make the skin a tattoo. If such writing sometimes appears extravagant or hermetic, we would be well advised to take a better look, to try harder to grasp the expressive outreach of his prose. Our life itself, Hawkes is showing us in his epic of closed and punctured bodies, is hermetic; all of us are hermetically sealed in and off, entombed, buried alive, much the way the dead fetus is still kept in the jar. Hawkes's art calls to mind the Book of Revelations, for his mission consists in opening the seals, bringing to language the closed off and twisted frequencies of fear and desire, transmuting them into song. Let there be no mistake: contact is not thereby achieved. Others can be neither reached nor saved; we never do more than "thrash around good and plenty in the darkness"; but they can be loved, bathed in the light of an imagining, desiring mind that "keeps" them—not out of harm's way, that is impossible—living for us.

Second skin. It is said that our cells change entirely over the course of seven years, and skin doubtless participates in the round. But we are unlike snakes and cannot shed our skin. And we allow or suffer it to be opened at our peril. Fleshly skin is all too penetrable, woundable; human skin is a one-time affair, and the horrible relics of the camps—lampshades made of human skin—have the disturbing power of a taboo, of an obscene after-life, of living beings drastically reified and commodified. And this is why the power of art and the freedom of speech are precious. Fiction, especially the fiction of John Hawkes, has its endemic cunning, its special secrets of disclosure and utterance, making it possible to do in writing what we cannot do in the flesh: to reverse time, to double back, to hold off, to *tell* in such a way that fullness is achieved. Great fiction, like pregnancy, delivers events "in the fullness of time," but it also reclothes them, re-skins them, shimmers forth their prismatic reality, reverses their linear fate, illuminates them, like cubism, forward and backward, inside and outside, all at once.

Consider, in this light, Hawkes's rendition of Fernandez's death. We follow Skipper on shore patrol into the flophouse right up the stairs and into the "hideaway." We note the butchery, the naked body: "Stabbed, beaten, poked and prodded, but he was finally choked to death with the guitar string" (156). Only then do we learn about the fingers:

> And the fingers. Yes, all five fingers of the left hand. All five. The clasp knife, the wine-dark pool, the fingers themselves, it was clear, too clear, what they'd done and that the severed fingers were responsible for the spidery

red lines scattered over everything. The wild tracings, the scene of blood — I touched him on the shoulder once and then I managed to reach the corridor and, while the blonde held me under the arm and cupped her wet hand on my forehead, I doubled over and let everything in my hot stomach boil up and out. (156)

Hermetic? *Au contraire*, the body is opened, displayed for viewing, aspiring to the level of art, on the way to becoming script. Fernandez's pierced body is a writing instrument in the hands of his killers. Nothing is "hidden away" any longer, and Skipper's insides are no exception. Skin is the medium and the message.

The blonde explains to Skipper that a big guy, still bleeding from a fight, had come in, forced himself on her, and when it was over — "and it wasn't bad, all things considered" — while she was doing her hair, he told her about the killing, how "he and a couple of others had killed a little fairy spic upstairs, that it was a game they had to let some fairy pick them up and then, when they were in the flophouse room to pull out their knives . . . " (157). Artifice inseminates. Language makes real, writes on us like a tattoo. First the picture, then the words: "He waited, you see? Waited until he was done to tell me. So now for ten bucks the blood's on my hands too, and all over I'm dying, I can feel it" (157). There is a time for telling, for making the saying of something so intolerably full and rich and poisonous that it can kill. The fractured narrative structure of *Second Skin* is devised for such time-release utterances, for inserting the pieces together in such a way that the shards retain their cutting edge even as the mosaic takes on form, so that seeing and being cut are inseparable, facets of each other. Such narrative skill endows speech with a kind of luminous purity and striking potency, as if it were issued from the pythia or the oracle not as prediction but as enactment, erasing the gap between word and deed, achieving the immediacy of fate.

Second Skin closes with the utterances of a Skipper become Prospero:

Now I sit at my long table in the middle of my loud wandering night and by the light of a candle — one half-burned candle saved from last night's spectacle — I watch this final flourishing of my own hand and muse and blow away the ashes and listen to the breathing among the rubbery leaves and the insects sweating out the night. Because now I am fifty-nine years old and I knew I would be, and now there is the sun in the evening, the moon at dawn, the still voice. That's it. The sun in the evening. The moon at dawn. The still voice. (210)

The magician's flourishing hand transforms the orders of man and nature, makes all things into its expressive signs. And hence the sun appears in the evening, not at dawn, and the moon is to be seen at dawn, not in the evening. By these things you shall know Prospero. And it is done by the voice, the still voice, the voice still.

It may be that *Second Skin* was an impossible act to follow, and one may feel that nothing Hawkes has written since has quite the same poise. Both Frederick Karl and Marc Chénetier have charted the Hawkes career as a downturn, as a costly move away from darkness and opacity toward sun, heat, and consciousness.[10] This, however, is why *Adventures in the Alaskan Skin Trade* (1985) satisfies. On the one hand, it plumbs the old terrain of darkness and death, and, on the other hand, it constitutes a truly new departure, an epic fiction that merges comic travelogue and American quest. It is well to acknowledge, straight out, that the Alaska book has no voice in it comparable to Skipper's, and that its prose is, in long stretches, far more workmanlike, the kind of thing necessary to make us see the Great North in all its details and wonder. In the realm of popular fiction Hawkes is in league with Michener, but we also hear older American echoes, going back to Parkman and Fennimore Cooper, trailblazers, guides to the new land. In Hawkes, however, the territorial quest is at once geographic and psychic; the voyage out is also a voyage in, a search for the father:

> Dad?
> Where are you, Dad?
> To the north. To the west. To the far north and the receding west. Where the seas are black and the fish dead. Where the rivers flow and the mountains rise. Where the fog drifts and the rain falls. Where the birds fly off course and the caribou limps and the wolverine hunts itself along the water's edge. Where the wind sings and the log rots and moss grows on glaciers. Where the sun is cold and the white bear grins on his bed of ice that turns and floats on the salty currents through the night. To the north that is mine. To the west that is mine. To the bones and teeth and pinnacles and silence of the north and the west that are mine, Sunny, still mine.
> Westward ho![11]

Hawkes has brilliantly rolled all his quests into one here: the return to the father, the return to origins, is seen to be a cultural and continental affair, a return to the originary American hunger, the imperious desire to explore and to exploit ("mine, Sunny, still mine"), to perceive and to possess ("mine, Sunny, still mine"). The vigor of this prose supports a project that is virtually cosmological in scope: to extend the continent, to encounter a heightened and special world where the elements appear to behave—the rivers flow, the fog drifts, the rain falls, the wind sings—but where something is askew and amok: the birds fly off course, the caribou limps, the wolverine hunts itself. Why is the bear grinning? There is both grandeur and darkness in the sweep of this scene: not only is the sun cold but death is everywhere visible, in the black seas and the dead fish and the rotting log, in the disoriented animals. Hawkes's Alaska book, unlike the apparently sensual and erotic projects charted in his Mediterranean texts, is unmistakably a death book: filled with lusty characters and quixotic dreamers, faithful to the topography of the great land it explores, it is nonetheless a haunted text, touched everywhere by blackness and emptiness. Hawkes's gambit is to trumpet the grandeur, to paint the epic fresco in bold strokes, but to do so with a strange chiaroscuro, to interweave the discursive and the subversive, the mimetic and the metaphorical, to devise hollowing and muffling strategies, to *tell* in such a way that we both see Alaska and see through it death, posited everywhere as the complement of desire, the fellow traveler in all territorialist ventures. In this, Hawkes calls to mind the central American dream text, Fitzgerald's *Great Gatsby*, and he seems to be picking up the gauntlet flung down by the famous last page, the lyrical depiction of the great deadly hunger that is America:

> And as the moon rose higher the inessential houses began to melt away until gradually I became aware of the old island here that flowered once for Dutch sailors' eyes—a fresh, green breast of the new world. Its vanished trees, the trees that had made way for Gatsby's house, had once pandered in whispers to the last and greatest of all human dreams; for a transitory enchanted moment man must have held his breath in the presence of this continent, compelled into an aesthetic contemplation he neither understood nor desired, face to face for the last time in history with something commensurate with his capacity for wonder.[12]

Jay Gatsby's project, we know, flaunts the splendor that can be built on nothing, and Fitzgerald's version of the dream—half enamored, half critical—stands as a resonant model for Hawkes's Alaska tale. For Sunny, as for Gatsby and the Dutch sailors, the future is "already behind them," and her obsession with the dreamer is both more libidinal and more desperate than Nick Carraway's fascination with Gatsby. In search of her father, trying to render him with finality so that she might finally be free of him, Sunny the daughter still suffers the coercive presence of her father; yet her tracking and storytelling are rivaled by those of her subject, for Jake too is a tracker and teller. They symmetry is sharp and cruel, for Sunny is enthralled, still held captive, by her father, while Jake is in love with Alaska, the great object of his desire, the North that is mine, the West that is mine. Hawkes's pieces are in place: the girl who desires her father, the father who lusts for the land, the land that turns either to rot or to ice in its pledge to death.

We are now in a position to see that *Adventures in the Alaskan Skin Trade* is of a piece with *Second Skin*. Each book hinges on the father-daughter relationship, but they are inverted images of each other. The libidinous, bumbling Skipper has become the heroic but cold Uncle Jake. The cold, desirable, but rebuffing Cassandra has become the sensuous but spurned Sunny. The most crucial (and costly) shift is that of narrative voice: whereas Skipper's inimitable voice creates the very medium of *Second Skin*, the much "tamer" Sunny narrates much of the Alaskan story, and when Jake does speak, he comes forth as Boy Scout, mindful of merit badges and honor code, possessor of a voice equipped for describing glaciers and bears and seaplanes but utterly bereft of the sexual timbre that marks Skipper. The father moves full circle, from desiring subject to sought-after object, and the daughter makes the same moves in reverse. Calling to mind Hemingway's change of direction in *The Garden of Eden*, the Alaska books posits its female protagonist as subject in her own right, but this particular sex change creates as many problems as it solves.[13] A price is paid for Hawkes's 180-degree rotation: Skipper's inimitable wit and song are lost; Jake's circumstantial reports on his outings can be painfully informational and devoid of psychic or sensual overtones; and Sunny's voice is sometimes uneven and unconvincing. Her motto, "heed hedonism," and her exploits as proprietor of the brothel Gamelands seem occasionally contrived and forced, and her cheerful sexuality sounds a strident note in the Hawkes music, too innocent and weightless to be believed.

One feels that Sunny's generalized hedonism covers for her real but repressed feelings for Jake, but the lid is on surprisingly tight in this sprawling novel. Jake, prig that he is, cannot hear the words "suck" and "sex," and although his daughter describes and details her womanly breasts and hips often enough, she does it breezily, like a tour guide herself, yet without personal orientation, as if for generic consumption. Sex would appear to be confined to Gamelands, because there seems to be no time for it in the scheme of the novel. Jake is too busy being Superman and Eagle Scout, making Alaska safe for democracy and chasing every varmint in the North, usually in the most dangerous fashion possible, with drunken pilots and leaky vessels. Not that these yarns are not handsomely executed: Jake's exploits with the bear (Old Unholiness), with the marital and dental needs of Swedes and Scoots, with the search for copper peaks and old totem poles, have a dewy-eyed freshness and excitement that are new in Hawkes's work. From our point of view it is hard not to think of poor Skipper when one encounters these exploits — Skipper the buffoon who is always *de trop*, the man who snorts and thrusts and grinds and achieves nothing whatsoever. Not so with Jake: he is a doer, a man of action with notches on his barrel, a striking-looking, elegant man, a man who awes all who see him — Sissie, Sunny, Frank Morley, Hilda Laubenstein, even the dental assistant Nancy. We sense, in every one of these instances, a fascination with Jake that is appetitive as well as admiring; men and women alike are drawn to this handsome hero, can't get close enough to him, can't get enough of him at all. Each one of them goes hungry, is thwarted, is cast aside by Jake, who is maniacally centered on one thing only: Alaskan heroics.

There is humor in the Alaska book, but John Burne Deauville is utterly humorless, almost a stuffed shirt. Knowing how much Hawkes values the adjective "comic" — he has repeatedly labeled some of the darkest happenings of his books "comic," much to the bewilderment of critics — we must wonder what kind of valuation Jake is to receive. He comes across, undeniably, as larger than life, but that is a heavy cross to bear. The writing that renders him has, regrettably, little of the rich, opaque music that was Skipper's. Uncle Jake is a bona fide hero, and heroes are, in the final analysis, a sad lot, risky business for all parties: authors, family, and friends.

And therein lies the challenge Hawkes has set himself in *Adventures in the Alaskan Skin Trade*: to take the hero's measure, to balance his heroics against his emptiness, to savor his exploits but to see and to render the cost they entail — Sissy's misery and death, Sunny's nightmares, Jake's own expropriation of the land. Hawkes is fascinated by Uncle Jake, not merely as a meditation on his own father but much the way Faulkner is fascinated by Thomas Sutpen, and he is out to position this mythic figure in a textual world that both celebrates and critiques him, shows his doings and makes us see his lacks. Given that Sissie and Sunny and Jake himself are conspiratorially bound and under oath to applaud his exploits and to censor any doubts, the damning evidence has to be cargoed in sideways, on the sly. In Sunny's dreams. In innuendoes expressed by Hilda and Nancy. In grotesque alter egos, such as Doc Haines the satyr-dentist. And, most wonderfully, in the very texture and replay of Jake's own heroics. Let the family cheerlead and whitewash as much as they want; Hawkes's gift for dislocation and displacement will freight the missing carnality and violence into every nook and cranny of the text. Jake himself may take his cues from the *Scout's Handbook*, but Hawkes's novel is a capacious thing, and both Jake and his doings find themselves matched and paired in the most embarrassing ways. It is the mix of flat heroics and psychosexual insinuation that confers a special seesaw feeling to this novel, and in it Hawkes displays both his signature and his special mastery in sounding, simultaneously, a spectrum of notes: the epic, the bawdy, the macabre, the surreal. It is time to ride the seesaw.

Like everything else Hawkes has written, the Alaska book is wise about its own delivery, keenly attuned to the communicative possibilities life offers, ready to pounce on those occasions when "speech" occurs, among people and among things, those privileged moments when the dead becomes the quick, when the still moves into the vocal. Bellies collide with one another in *Second Skin* as a furious statement of human contact; in this northern fable Hawkes changes venue but his "speech-conversion" practices are equally flagrant, and he actually brings in deaf-mute characters, the McGinnises, not only to depict their expressive powers but also to make his larger truth visible: "signing" is the very life of fiction. Like the blood that must find new pathways, open new veins when the old ones are removed, so too is the flow of speech imperious and undeniable, an affair of continually opening conduits and circuits, located in the strangest places, not unlike the flow of dark water once the ice has cracked. McGinnis speech, digital and facial rather than aural, mesmerizes Sunny: "How swiftly and mysteriously their fingers moved! How eloquent the speech no one else could hear or read!" (173). But, in this novel of sublimated energies and deep-flowing currents, all bent on reaching the surface, on finding expression, the straining McGinnises are the rule rather than the exception, and they constitute a living allegory of Hawkes's semiotic imperative: to convert all dumb things into speech, to make them alive, even incandescent with signification. The scene where Jake is trying to carve the stubborn Christmas ham in the presence of old friends and new McGinnises is exemplary of Hawkes's art, luminous and many-tongued:

> The Uncle Jake put down his fork, surveyed the table—with disdain? chagrin? bemusement? anger? — and slowly reached out his hand and, looking not at his hand but at Robert McGinnis, seized the unruly ham in a firm grip. Frank Morley groaned. Faster went Robert McGinnis's fingers, voluble became his grunting. Sissy gasped and Hilda, our brazen unjudgmental Hilda, leaned slowly and sedately forward toward the captive ham. And slowly all eyes on hand and ham, Uncle Jake tightened his grip, the juices of the red meat and the crusty glaze of brown sugar oozing up between his fingers—his wedding band, his Deauville signet ring—and in long deft revengeful strokes began to carve. And carve he did, never relinquishing his hold on the now

hapless ham, and suddenly, squirming as I was beside Uncle Jake, hardly able to contain my child's pleasure at this new sign of the unexpected, suddenly I wanted Uncle Jake to lick his fingers and to allow me to put my own small hand where his had been. I wriggled, I laughed, I watched as Uncle Jake held Hilda hypnotized while he stared straight at Robert McGinnis as if there were no other way to carve a ham. Uncle Jake could do whatever he wanted to do—so said the dripping knife, the ruthless greasy hand which he himself ignored. (173–74)

Not a word is spoken here, yet there is a tumult of voices, and the scene is indelibly rendered as mute but eloquent contact: eye to eye, face to face, flesh with flesh. Fastidious Uncle Jake has a rendezvous with flesh here, real "red meat," and he is obliged to grip it with all his forces, to get his hand on and in it with such vehemence that all social niceties disappear, just as the rings of marriage and family go under the ooze. Jake, saying nothing, vanquishes with his blade the squirming ham, but the "dripping knife" speaks, does him homage—he "could do whatever he wanted to do"—as does his own butchering body, "the ruthless greasy hand which he himself ignored." Jake's hand is "signing" with the same energy that is gathered in Robert McGinnis's face, and we cannot fail to see that this visceral plunge of hand and knife into flesh constitutes a strange congress for these two men: it is their potent speech. But the rending of flesh speaks to and for *all* of them: Frank groans, Robert grunts, Sissy gasps, and Hilda hypnotically gazes. Last but not least, the scene speaks deeply, even searingly, to and into its narrator, Sunny. She too watches, aroused, her elegant father assault and conquer resisting flesh, and her "squirming" and "wriggling" echo both the movements of the ham and a good bit more as well; finally, "suddenly" and ineluctably, Sunny desires entry into the initiation scene she has witnessed—"I wanted Uncle Jake to lick his fingers and to allow me to put my own small hand where his had been"—a scene of resonant carnal encounter that is close to being "primal" in this repressive text.

It might help, in order to measure what Hawkes is doing here, to refer to the famous Christmas dinner in Joyce's *Portrait of the Artist*; both writers have a way with the creatural, and the body makes its presence felt in the spitting and digesting at the Irish table, especially in the consonance of the ingested meal and the narrated story of politics and religion. Hawkes does not capture anything like the bitter Irish history that Joyce packs into his episode, but he is unmatchable in his way of bringing the "things" to life, displacing the "story" he wants to tell onto the very bodies and gestures of the participants, and he thereby makes us rediscover in the carving of meat and the hunger of guests something of the ancient primitive power that attended the sacrificing of animals and the sharing of food.

Jake, I have noted, is as mute as Robert McGinnis when it comes to the mention of sex, and in Hawkes's hands he is something of a figure in charade, showing but not telling the muffled erotic violence that is deep (and hidden) within him. But, as if he had absorbed a single but large dose of Freud, enough to posit sexuality itself as the displacement of the death instinct, he can indeed hold forth on death; and so the piercing of the ham evolves, issues out into the larger Alaskan current of death that subtends all language and gesture in this book:

> "I'm talking about Alaskan death, Robert, death as big and important as this Territory itself. Why, up here a fellow's winding sheet is a whole winter of icy snow. The howl of a wolf dog is the howl of death. Hardship. Privation. Misfortune. Up here a fellow dies in a gulch filled with skunk cabbage or on some bare and lonely mountain. Up here, Robert, we respect the death that awaits us on the heart-breaking way to failure or in a nameless game. Up here a man embraces death. He walks along, he mushes along, he crawls along until he stops. Then someone else, years later, gaunt and near death himself, finds the first man's note tacked to a tree: 'Hell can't be any worse than this trail,' says the dead man's note. 'I'll try it.'" (175)

Here is the book's high road of discourse. Jake, deaf and blind to so much, has a grasp on death that parallels his grip on the ham. Once again we see the impulse toward speech, the decoding of signs. And death is the ubiquitous code: the winter of snow signifies winding sheet; the dog's howl is death; and even the nameless grave advertises itself through notes tacked on trees. All activity is death-oriented: embracing, walking, mushing, crawling, writing. The Alaskan community is a Morse Code of death, a parade of diers over time who record epitaphs. Is that not Sunny's job in this book: to read her father's unwritten testament?

Now comes the low road. Jake's passionate diatribe on death works its way into Robert McGinnis's brain, goes right through his deafness, touches him to the quick. "Wrinkles of delight" "disfigure" his face, and in his excitement "Robert McGinnis shoved aside his plate and, with a sound as of bubbles hotly bursting, eagerly agreed, it seemed, with all that Uncle Jake was saying" (175). And this vital, almost spastic connection between people — unwilled, animal, irrepressible — figures what is *living* in Hawkes's scheme, what redeems the death program. Struggling, stuttering, McGinnis wants somehow to *say*, to find some expression for his entente with Jake. And, oddly reminiscent of some of Kafka's locked-in characters whom music alone might deliver, he fashions a language of his own:

> It was embrace, the tenderest embrace that Robert McGinnis had in mind because helpless in the very tangle of himself, and too overwhelmed, too overwrought, too frustrated to pursue any longer his attempts to express himself directly to his rigid host, now Robert McGinnis turned away from host and table and lumbered in a few steps to Sissy's piano. And still swaying and lumbering, Robert McGinnis sat down at Sissy's piano, exposed the keys, and grandly, liltingly, lovingly, played the golden Steinway for Uncle Jake. (177)

It does not seem fanciful to say that this moment is both more tender and more erotic than any so-called sexual union depicted in the book. It is in these passages that the very pulse of Hawkes's enterprise is felt, the uncanny sense he has of our stuttering and stumbling efforts to speak and touch. "Helpless in the very tangle of himself" describes not only the muteness of Robert McGinnis but the generic muteness of human beings, and this sequence is wise about the spectrum of communicative possibilities, the languages at our disposal, the rich network of frequencies and sign systems by which we word-lessly communicate. Practiced in mummery, Hawkes has magisterially painted and outfitted his figures. He may deny them outright speech by biology and *pudeur*, but we see and hear them speak *quand-même*, as the seesaw moves from carving a ham to Alaskan death to the golden Steinway, always meaning more than it says, radiant with body heat and animal need, covering the gamut of utterances and gestures from knife wielding to Schumann.

Adventures in the Alaskan Skin Trade is written, melodically, in these multiple registers, and we soon enough come to understand its multilingualism and musical score. Not unlike Wagnerian leitmotifs, the same themes are likely to appear and reappear, but different the second time around, as if Hawkes had decided to limit his number of signifiers or instruments while expanding the range of meanings and produced sounds. There is a peculiar economy at work here, a kind of calculated risk or *gageure* that is out to explore how much mileage can be gotten out of the same one or two vehicles. Or, to use a metaphor closer to Hawkes's heart, the same bodies come back, but they seem to have traded skins, and these second skins make for a special narrative song and dance. Let us consider, as a specimen of this recombinant art, the episode of Sissie's dental initiation.

Whereas pulling teeth would seem like straightforward material for most writers, the stuff of trauma but not of shifting registers, Hawkes chooses to invest it with sexual innuendo, and he thus depicts Sissie's stint with Doc Haines, the book's wisest sensualist, as a scene of musical seduction and intercourse. Waiting in the other room, during the middle-of-the-night emergency visit, while Sissie is inhaling the laughing gas, Jake and Sunny find themselves tuned in to a concert they had not anticipated: "The three machines began to pulse and probe while Sissie's laughter rose to gay heights, changed to a sweet pattern of giggling, and then soared on uncontrollably" (182). Jake becomes increasingly frantic as the sexual aura of the business in the other room becomes heavier and more insistent, and we gauge just how desperate he is to keep clear of such areas, to remain undefiled. Sunny, meanwhile, is blissfully picturing the erotic play at hand (and mouth), and she intuitively knows that Doc Haines "should be wearing a white coat but was instead leaning over Sissy in a crimson bathrobe" (183); she is, above all, attentive to the larger erotic ramifications, the potential "spill-over" that would engulf Jake as well, thanks to the input of Haines's "assistant," the loose Nancy, there in the waiting room eyeing Jake, ready to make a foursome of it. As Sissie's cries come into the waiting room, mingled with laughter, termed "the lively sounds of a young woman being pushed high in a swing in summer or rippling with unexpected pleasure behind a tree" (183), Jake can take it no more and bolts. Shaken by the penetration drama on the other side of the wall, speaking darkly of the scoundrel dentist who "jammed a gleaming blade into my poor cousin's rotten tooth" (184) and killed him, Jake wants his wife out of there; but Nancy has been waiting for just such a move, and Hawkes moves in for the choreographic kill:

> And now the crimson-clad Nancy blocked the closed door and held firm before Uncle Jake, who in his momentum had stopped just short of her. They were together, touching and not touching, the towering man elegant, disheveled, dressed for the street in his beige and crisply tailored overcoat, the robed and slippered woman dressed for warm darkness and quilts and pillows. She took the half-step necessary to push herself against him. She seized his soft lapels. She made certain that the tall man was breathing in the very breath that she exhaled.
>
> ". . . breathe deeply," came the young and confident voice behind the door, "a few more deep breaths, Cecily." (184)

It is obvious to the reader, albeit not to Jake, what is happening in this scene of elaborate coupling and intermingled bodies and breaths. In Hawkes the very air one breathes is charged, invested with narcotic or erotic power, and sooner or later all breathing parties must partake of it, willingly or no.

What is considerably less obvious, less predictable, is the bizarre rewrite that Hawkes will offer of this dental escapade, and it is here that we get the second-skin effect, the chutzpah of a writer who seems to be saying: not only can dental work carry libidinal cargo, but it can then be replayed, turned into pure expressive sign, mystifying us by its odd reach. This time Jake is to play the dentist, and he gets his chance with the old Indian Olo; this scene, too, has its muffled eroticism ("that old fellow had the most beautiful eyes I'd ever seen" [224]), and it is "capped" by an excruciating amount of pushing and pulling, all of which culminates in the ingenious solution of *unscrewing* the recalcitrant tooth. We are in no-man's land here—and this is the writerly Alaska that Hawkes has been constructing for some time now—since no narrative exigency could ever require such a scene, but Hawkes is following a very pure metaphoric logic, unpacking his materials, reveling in the affective density they can be shown to have, repackaging them in strange new narrative twists. This episode closes in the realm of myth, as Jake (about whom there seems to be a touch of the artist) outdoes nature by making a set of teeth for the old Indian chief, a set of deer teeth embedded in a wooden plate. Deep-seated Hawkesian obsessions come to mind here—Jomo's steel hand in *Second Skin*, the gruesome chastity belt discovered in *The Blood Oranges*, Vost's silver hand in *The Passion Artist*—and we sense an elusive propriety in effect, a fascination with the human body, especially its appendages and orifices, that is coupled with monstrous human craftwork, human engineering feats to replace or shut off the equipment, to abet or repress natural function. These artifacts have a kind of beauty and obscenity about them, as if they were themselves eroticized, transformed into sexual tools of entry and violation, the tools of art, the outreach and ingress of the artist. Deer teeth in human mouths epitomize second skin because they figure forth a world become malleable, "plastic," reshapable, and disturbingly expressive, displaying a kind of wild liberty akin to the cubist painter's dismantling and redistributing human parts in order to make a face of his own devising. The episode of the "un-screwed" tooth comes to a close, and in its light, in the air it makes, we may perceive the breathing space of Hawkes's art, a space for having a second look, for gauging the now palpable affective, erotic energies at work under the surface. What "happened" in the dental office or the teepee has become mysterious, underlaid and overscored, endowed with suggestive life, converted into sign, into speech.

Such pirouetting language was also used to convey the bumbling, untram-meled Skipper, but one is tempted to say it was wasted on him, that he reveled in his hues and colors, whereas it is absolutely required as a vehicle for getting Uncle Jake into the book, and then getting around him the way Hawkes is bent on doing. John Burne Deauville is the little boy who never grew up. His pieties and gestures have a certain narrow grandeur to them, but their sources remain veiled. Ever on the lookout for wrongdoing in Alaska, ready to eradicate evil, seeker of ever greater challenges to his courage and stamina, shunner of ever greater demands on his intimacy and feeling, champion of justice, denier of women, Uncle Jake is a very curious Hawkes phenomenon, a man unattuned to just those frequencies Hawkes hears so finely and renders so insistently. Jake, then, not Robert McGinnis, is the deaf-mute figure of the novel, and in him Hawkes has given us an unforgettable picture of *Vir americanus*, or perhaps *Puer americanus*.

Coming from Hawkes, Jake's gallant descriptions of combat and trial ring false, and one is never without the feeling that Jake is in deeper than he knows, that he is whistling in the dark. The man needs a second skin, and he will get it. Jake, the single-minded and fanatically true, is to be shown multiple and contaminated, and this by the ludic play of language and event that presents and contains him. It is here that Cooper and Parkman and Michener are inverted, or better, set into motion, for the great epic of Alaska is to be revealed as a kaleidoscopic affair. We have already seen how Hawkes plays his dental card twice. Let us now consider his handling of the classic wilderness contest, the contest that no trailblazing author with self-respect (and a knowledge of Faulkner) could afford to omit: the bear hunt.

The killing of His Unholiness is, we recall, Jake's maiden venture into heroics. Jake will have himself airlifted into the wilds, rescue the wounded Johnson, the infamous Harrison, and he will have his bear. The business of heroics, after all, has its rules: "It was understood that Rex and Johnson would remain just behind the screen of dripping boughs and up to their knees in skunk cabbage while I alone entered the clearing. They'd have a perfect view but the stage would be mine—as it had to be" (85). The potent smell of the bear, "hotter, spicier, more foul than Johnson had thought it was" (85), is shown to be rich in significance, betokening "an actual history of regal savagery, the meat and teeth of his combats, the grass and ferns and baby deer he had devoured and then excreted in all the steaming piles I'd seen" (85). It is a striking notation. We see how capacious smell can be, as if Proust had come along on the trip to Alaska, to show that sensations are to be understood as universes, as multidimensional, bringing with them past time, encapsulating history. Once again—as with the resonant tracks left by the elephant in Hemingway's version of rites of passage—we see the Hawkes script as richly textured, a *trace* that rewards our scouting efforts, invites us to perform the exploratory work that doubles the trek through the wilderness. But Jake himself has no stomach for such musings, and it is highly fitting that the climax of the bear slaying comes to us in Kiplingesque tones: perfect specimen, noble, impressive, good fortune.

At least it seems to. True to form, Hawkes will replay the bear hunt, and on the second go-around, when it gets its second skin, he will bring out into the open its extraordinary ferocity. We will finally get our fill of the bear smell, "hotter, spicier, more foul that Johnson had thought it was." The sibling story is told by the quasi-mythic Martha Washington as she flaunts her amazon naked scarred body before the eyes of Sunny and Hank Laramie. Martha's tale rotates, completes Jake's, bathes it in the aura of sadism, sexuality, and brutality that Hawkes has never lost sight of. The grueling account of Martha's torture by the she-bear and her cubs—her being raked by the unsheathed claws, her shoulder chewed, her scalp opened—closes doubly with a crushing embrace ("I had met my match") and, the next day, when she is conscious again, a lethal vendetta: first the she-bear between the eyes, then the cubs, replete with exploded skull, as if tit were being rendered for tat. Once again we see the structural wizardry of Hawkes's novel: provocatively exposing her wounded and healed voluptuous body, Martha Washington speaks, passionately and arousingly, of carnage, and she thereby sounds the registers of Hawkesian speech, a discourse that sees murder and lust, copulation and maiming, as inseparable, as the now exposed libidinal underpinnings of bear hunting.

No Kipling in sight here. Instead the naked body, larger than life, scarred by seventy-six puncture wounds, posited as irresistible. Hawkes's art of inscription, already familiar to us as the central trope of *Second Skin*, makes a spectacular return here, and we see that the inscribed body is the eroticized body. Hank Laramie abandons Sunny on the spot, and she herself realizes that this woman is a version of her father "reincarnated." A few skins need to be traded, but once that is achieved, we begin to experience some of the sexual chemistry at work here, and we sense that this brazen woman is the *embodiment* of the Other Jake, the one kept at bay and under cover by all parties except the author, the penetrated and lusting figure whom Sunny desires, who "haunts" this text and its hero like a bad dream, like a bad smell. The scarred Martha Washington is no less than the tattooed Jake, and she brings to the surface, makes legible for us, what he has spent his life concealing: lust, carnage, and death.

But Hawkes is out to write Jake in other ways still. Nowhere is the Other Jake more visible than in the indicting dreams Sunny has of him. In one he appears a murderer, a child killer to be exact, clubbing baby seals to death, in cahoots with professional sealers, party to the soundless slaughter: "The ice is running red with crimson rivulets that cross and recross the ice as far as I can see. Ice, dead seals, seals attempting to escape, the sealers themselves—everything is turning that color of red that is like no other, the wet red color of blood when it is first exposed to the air, the shining red color of blood before it blackens" (113). The Alaskan sea, so prominent in this book, is finally shown in its original color, and it is used virtually as a pigment — both paint and ink — with which the writer expresses his vision.

In another dream Jake is accused of "unlawful cohabitation," and the list is presented: Three Way Mary, Moose Neck Betty, Skagway Lil, The Chinless Filly. Sunny then makes her plea to the chief magistrate: "Hang him! I cry. He's innocent!" (250). His innocence, like that of Faulkner's Sutpen, is indeed a crime of the heart, a deficiency of feeling, and in Hawkes's scheme it is more unforgivable even than the alleged acts of bestiality. In still another vision Jake is trapped in a wrecked airplane, and in a dazzling purgatorial scene worthy of Dante, Hawkes pronounces judgment on the guilty aviator:

> And now I [Sunny] realize at last what is so peculiarly frightening about his wrecked plane. It is this: that soon, in another few minutes, the old salt-encrusted plane that looms before me will be entirely submerged. At every high tide the metal wreckage sinks from view, goes under. That which is meant to fly is beneath the sea. Then as the tide goes out the tip of the rudder appears, the tip of a wing, the tip of the wooden propeller, and slowly the wrecked plane emerges, dripping and covered with fresh barnacles. Day in, day out, with every rising and falling tide the plane must undergo its drowning. (309)

It is in majestic images of this sort that Hawkes frames and points his Alaskan fable.[14] Jake's ceaseless forays into the wilderness, his furious need to vanquish the elements, are definitively exposed as vain and derelict, instances of overweening pride which recall the doomed flight of Icarus, that fully warrant punishment by the gods, meted out on a cyclical basis, much as it was for Sisyphus and Prometheus. In still another, Jake is only a voice, and in the desolate log cabin there is a lone sled dog of great size and ferocity, surrounded by bones and tufts of fur; Jake's Boy Scout voice cries, "Sunny, that darn dog," and we grasp the cannibalism of the scene, the revenge of the animals and the elements.

All of these dreams record Jake's enduring hold on Sunny — she can no longer heed hedonism, she will never leave Alaska, never get to France — as well as a full-scale, virtually surrealist depiction of his sins: failure to love, failure of flesh, rape of the land, hubris. Perhaps the most emblematic dream has Jake frozen solid, lying on his side "like a toppled statue," larger than life, with a fur cap that "looks like a bishop's mitre" (253). Coldness of heart is the crime. It is what we have seen but not fully understood ever since the first dream, at the beginning of the novel, showing us Jake "inside the glacier, the King of the North in his tomb" (16). Hawkes's novel comes to resemble the desolate wintry landscape of Ibsen's plays, a northern myth of arrogance and frigidity, an anti-Pygmalion fable of humans being revealed as statues.

The Great Alaskan Death that Jake describes to Robert McGinnis is something that he knows all too well. Uncle Jake stands convicted in all his roles: adventurer, colonist, father. And with his fall, down go Superman and Captain Marvel as well. A large enterprise is coming unraveled here. Hawkes elects to crown his portrayal of the derelict father by reciting one final misadventure: the quest for the totem pole, the supposed masterpiece of Indian art that figures America's father, Abraham Lincoln. We sense that the entire novel is gathering up its energy in this escapade, preparing to make its fullest utterance on the status of heroism and the functioning of fathers, ready now to indict an entire nation for its deathly ways. The Indians have a saying, "May your totem pole stand long in the land" (343), but there is no erect pole to be found here, only a "toppled statue," a rotting facsimile. As Jake's party of questers approaches the site of the totem pole, Hawkes invests the scene with overtones of birth: Jake brings a "long wooden cradle," and he is hell-bent to deliver Lincoln. In pursuit of the Great Father, on the trail at last of his own totemic Other, Jake pronounces his eulogy in the purest Boy Scout warble: "And to think that it took these strange birds, the Suslotas, to comprehend the freedom that had been granted to them and to all their kind in Alaska, and then to acknowledge their indebtedness to Mr. Lincoln and honor him the way they did. I tell you, Frank, it seizes the imagination like nothing else I've heard of, that's for sure" (367). With this starry vision of the White Man's Burden to fuel his efforts, Jake makes his way through sacred ground, through a wasteland of black stumps. Blood, we recall, is bright red before the air blackens it, and we have seen Hawkes paint the sea with it; he can also paint with it once it turns black, and he does so now, blackening his people, blackening the skins of his American pioneers, using the very stumps as writerly implements, devices for making second skins, tools for signing. The reckoning is nigh. Black Jake and his black crew come upon Mr. Lincoln in Alaska; he too is black. The guide disappears into thin air, the lemmings cease to move, the yellow owl is gone. The quest has been completed: we have moved back through time, to the origin, to the Father. Jake, at long last, encounters his effigy, face to face. Here is the long-awaited scene of self-knowledge, a moment of tattoo and signature, a moment of revelation. All that remains is to possess the icon, to partake of the godhead, to remove the treasure. The men make their preparations. But Lincoln is not to be moved. Yet the questers are determined, will not be gainsaid. With the sure logic of ancient myth and modern surgery, Hawkes boldly and exquisitely resolves the dilemma. The white men bring out their knives, section Lincoln in pieces, roll him onto his face, and then discover the Alaskan truth: the Father is not hard but soft, delicate, crumbling, "punk," a Lincoln "diseased through and through with rottenness" (378).

We are not far from a Götterdämmerung here. The saga of Uncle Jake has been an American story all along, a chapter of American history that is coming to a close. The settling of Alaska is the last great gasp of American pioneering, the last frontier, and Hawkes has succeeded in conveying both the glamour and the excitement, as well as the rapacity and hubris, that attend our drive to the north, to the west. Sunny's search for her father is an elegiac plaint, a song that measures both the scope of Jake's achievements and the crimes of which he is guilty. A portrait of American hunger and innocence emerges here, and in it we can see portentous connections between exploration and colonialism, between the heroics of doing and the failure of feeling. As we finish this sprawling novel, we realize that Hawkes has graphed a very special American trajectory, a coming of age that moves from exuberance to loss. In the end we may feel that the writer has followed his subject into the very grave, has delivered an autopsy of the American Dream.

But such a grim reading goes counter to the vibrancy of Hawkes's vision, the spawning and saying power of his language. Even death, in this scheme, is an opening rather than a closure, an affair of appetite and energy, a source of power as elemental as that of the sun. The boat carries in its hold a cargo of rotting fish, and the stench they give off, like the hot, spicy stench of the bear, is the pungent smell of life. It cannot be evaded, just as "suck" and "sex" cannot be evaded. Rot is nothing more than metamorphosis, a trading of skin. Sitka Charlie tells the story of a doctor's wife and a young Chilkat woman who "fished through the same hole where they defecated and dumped the slops" (264), and although that is a strange view of sanitation, it tells us a great deal about the wellsprings of life and art. In the final analysis, the Great Alaskan Death constitutes a morphological principle of great beauty, and in Hawkes's art it becomes a new way of seeing and saying. Let us remember Sunny's handling of the old skull found in the Indian burial ground: "Suddenly I ran the middle three fingers of my left hand lightly around the surface of one of the skull's eye sockets and, raising my eyes to Robert McGinnis's, stuffed my fingers into my mouth and licked them clean of the soot which was all that remained of the smoke that once had been the dead man's flesh" (214). It is all on show here: the cannibalistic transformation of death into life, decay into nourishment; the silent, pungent, potent communication between people face to face, finger to eye socket; the magic, unflinching stubbornness and beauty of Hawkes's vision, which seizes on life and chokes its secrets into utterance, reveals every surface to be a sign, a *trace*, a rich script that moves over time from flesh to smoke to soot to us.

12

Robert Coover: Fiction as Fission

Robert Coover's work occupies a place of honor in what can now be seen as the American tradition of freedom of speech. His novels exhibit a dazzling, sometimes frantic experimentalism, and they offer, above all, a testament to language as imperialist design, language as not only protean but downright parasitic, not only capable of changing forms but intent on taking over, rivaling all forms of experience and cancerously invading them, adapting them to its own frequencies and modalities. It used to be that one believed in certain fences, certain limits and proprieties, so that the verbal—grand and aggrandizing though it might be—was nonetheless stationed in its own precincts, neither constituted nor equipped to "do" the things done in other fields: film and music and dance, but also, in some crucial sense, experiential realms such as sex and memory; that is, the novelist could *write about* these things, but one always knew the things themselves had their own different savor and integrity. That is how it used to be. Coover has changed a lot of that, and he comes across as the PacMan of American fiction, the writer who chases his prey, crosses all manner of conceptual boundaries, poaches like crazy in these territories, and gets it all back home into language, makes us see it *as language*. Coover's fictions, then, corral a large territory: myth and politics, song and dance, sports and film, sex and religion, and he disports himself with truly evangelical zeal, out to prove that language is the great converter, the alchemist that transmutes all it encounters into its verbal performance.

Doubtless the modern writer whom Coover most calls to mind is Joyce, especially the Joyce of *Ulysses*, who wrote: "Aeolus," "Cyclops," and "Circe," with their mix of word play, satire, and metamorphosis. But ultimately one must go further back, not only to the father of fictions, Cervantes, whom Coover salutes in *Pricksongs and Descants*, but perhaps more strikingly to the arch-fabulator of the Renaissance, Rabelais, whose bawdiness, barnyard humor, ribald creatural fantasy, and stupendous verbal inventiveness seem to be an uncanny model for the Coover undertaking. The fit may be an apt one in other ways as well, for Rabelais's work, filled with giants and assorted sexual-cum-political extravaganzas, expresses through its voracious appetite the vigor of an epoch, the bristling energies of an era of exploration, discovery, and rediscovery. This same youthfulness, this ferocious desire to go all the way, typifies Coover's oeuvre at its best and marks it as the cultural document of a restless, inventive age, an age obsessed with power of all stripes, a time of perceptual and cognitive breakthrough: relativity, fission, media, computers, cinema. His zany novels yield a map of our time.

Coover's early work is poised and mature. *The Origin of the Brunists* (1966) displays his capacity for shrewd cultural and social denotation, as well as his already mythic sense of the religious impulse in American affairs. More Joycean and self-reflexive is *The Universal Baseball Association, J. Henry Waugh Prop.* (1968), a prodigious effort to get *Homo ludens americanus* into the proper artistic and metaphysical framework, showing something of the narrative mileage that Coover can get out of American fun and games. These large-souled fictions were followed (in print if not in conception) by the elegant and influential volume of short pieces, *Pricksongs and Descants* (1969), in which we see the makings of a bolder, more whimsically playful kind of metafiction, a sign of what was to come. A number of these vignettes are classically postmodern in their impulse to reconceive and parody older materials. Thus, Coover gives us a version of Noah's ark as told by "The Brother" in a rural, good-old-boy twang that puts a shocking spin on the biblical parable. Coover has a number of tongues at his disposal, but his most powerful and biting work frequently employs country-boy lingo, a kind of sprawling, gutsy redneck flow of speech that is remarkably resilient and muscular, able to get into intellectual corners one wouldn't think it capable of, a language performance that gives pleasure and seems to take pleasure as well, strutting its stuff. Coover's prose smacks. You can feel it.

That is why the central parable of *Pricksongs*, "The Magic Poker," disappoints as much as it delights. This Prospero-like fable of the colonizing imagination, with its emphatically phallic poker at the heart of things, establishes once and for all the centrality of eros in all things magic, according to Coover. Yet, the mix of fairy-tale frame, romantic reverie, and realist notation seems at times overly cute, cloying, and self-indulgent in ways that Coover avoids in his more explosive later work. The two stories in the collection that stand out are "The Elevator" and "The Babysitter," and each of them is something of a cubist experiment, a bid for a special fourth-dimensional prose.[1] We recall that Hemingway sought prose's "fourth and fifth dimensions" by dint of ellipsis and repression so as to yield a muffled echo effect in which the reader conspires to fill in the blanks, invent the missing material. Coover's project goes the other way, sets out to unpack and play out every possible avatar of his original donnée. He understands all narrative elements to be ripe and rife with alternative permutations, and he understands the human mind to be the theater where these permutations are played out, under the guise of paranoia, desire, or memory. But that is where the fun starts, where the real work begins. The job consists in finding the proper architecture for these teeming virtualities, the proper composite form that at once liberates its discrete parts and coordinates them, achieving the strangest imaginable music along the way. The geometricians have an astonishingly precise analogue for the Coover layout: it is called the hypercube, and it displays three-dimensionally the spatial form of a cube that has been rotated on its axes, turned fourth-dimensional; it looks like a cube with excrescences and outgrowths, a cube whose walls grew cancerous and launched new extensions, a liberated and unrepressed cube that has finally become all it could be.[2]

"The Elevator" is the story of the little man, Martin, in cubist form, involving fifteen versions of Martin-in-the-elevator going to or from work. Distinctions between real and imaginary lose all value here as Coover orchestrates within a tiny urban cubicle a version of civilization and its discontents *in petto*. Predictably enough, the body is a key player once the constraints of realism are overthrown, and Martin runs the whole gamut of libidinal trials, from the humiliation of false farting charges to fantasized *Liebestod* with the female operator on to gargantuan (Rabelaisian) phallic power, culminating in Martin's ultimate ascendancy as the elevator hurtles down to destruction. Walter Mitty and Charlot are not far from this rhapsody, and we can begin to get a fix on Coover territory: the trials and exploits of the little guy, the spectacular outbreak of libido into *carnaval*, the making of the hypercube fiction.

"The Babysitter" is comparably dazzling. Here, Coover unpacks the entire repertory of possibilities—encompassing romantic desire and nightmarish fear—attendant on the homely American ritual of babysitting. Mr. and Mrs. Tucker go to a party, leaving their children Jimmy and Bitsy and the baby with the babysitter, who is being "courted" by her boyfriend Jack (and his friend Mark). This kernel supplies Coover with 107 (one hundred and seven) vignettes that map the Tuckers' night out sub specie aeternitatis, plotting every conceivable twist of the story, plugged into six different subjectivities, having a big time. As we have come to expect by now, a good number of these venues are going to be shocking (isn't that what fear and desire traffic in?): the baby drowns in the tub; the baby is stabbed by a pin; the babysitter is raped by (a) Jack, (b) Mark, and (c) the horny Mr. Tucker; Mrs. Tucker is buttered (buttered) by all the guests to fit back into her girdle while nursing her fears of being sent to a nursing home. Coover skates in and out of these garish corners with consummate ease, flaunting the textual reality as his sole authority, defying us to close up shop. That old baseline of reality/illusion has gone up in smoke quite a while back, which means that there is no place to come home to. The story has to end, nonetheless, and it points, in good old American fashion, to the Last Frontier: "'What can I say, Dolly?' the host says with a sigh, twisting the hot buttered strands of her ripped girdle between his fingers. 'Your children are murdered, your husband gone, a corpse in your bathtub, and your house is wrecked. I'm sorry. But what can I say?' On the TV, the news is over, and they're selling aspirin. 'Hell, *I* don't know,' she says, 'Let's see what's on the late late movie.'"[3] There we have it: those two familiar American rituals—the party and the movies—are vehicular channels of fantasy and desire, moving us both into and out of murder and mayhem, beckoning the writer to make use of them as artistic conduits. With hindsight we can see here the genesis of Coover's two most extremist fictions, *Gerald's Party* (1985) and *A Night at the Movies* (1987). But in the time between, or better (for Coover), in the space between, he published what still looks to be his magnum opus, *The Public Burning* (1978), a rich cornucopia of all his styles and manias, a book of imperial proportions chronicling a crucial chapter of paranoia in American history—the trial and execution of the Rosenbergs in 1953—but ultimately crafting a surreal operatic fantasia commensurate with the mythic dimensions of the American way of life.

The third and final intermezzo of *The Public Burning*, a "Last-Act Sing Sing Opera," stages the last-ditch maneuvers of the government to wring a confession from the Rosenbergs and closes with the couple's stubborn assertion of innocence and love, their disbelief that such "political prosecution" could take place in America, and their final effort to embrace before dying. They are separated by prison officials, and Julius proclaims to the audience: "WHAT WILL BE THE ANSWER OF AMERICA TO ALL THIS?"[4] All parties exit the stage, and a lone spotlight lingers on a sign that reads "SILENCE."

It is tempting to see Coover's book as a response to this silence, this shameful oblivion into which the Rosenbergs disappeared. Hence, his text is to be a "public burning," a bringing out into the open, twenty-five years later, of these events; and the burning is to be not merely that of the convicted Rosenbergs but the incandescence of Coover's writerly assault. The electric chair is now placed front and center, in Times Square, and Coover is out to rival with it in "high-noon" fashion, to concoct his writerly showdown with these events so as to release their power, to *write* them somehow into the skins of his readers, to fashion a script that marks and burns—much the way Ethel Rosenberg is said to have done to the strikebreakers ("I am a scab," she painted on their behinds; "I am a scamp," she is to paint on Richard Nixon's behind), much the way Kafka's formidable penal-colony machine writes into the flesh of its prisoners the name of their crimes. Coover's penitential carnival of the 1950s is more raucous and loony than Kafka's severe fable of the island prison, but they are both dead serious about the meaning and composition of death sentences, about the textual machinery needed for such a script.

At the heart of the drama and the book is Coover's Richard Nixon. He understands that the Rosenberg trial has mythic resonances, is "like a little morality play for our generation" (147), and he is utterly cognizant of his own role as *metteur-en-scène*:

> I was more like a stage manager, an assistant director or producer, a presence more felt than seen. This was true even of the trial itself: I felt somehow the author of it—not of the words so much, for they were, in a sense, improvisations, but rather of the *style* of the performances, as though I had through my own public appearances created the audience expectations, set the standards, keyed the rhetoric, crystallized the roles, in order that my generation might witness in dramatic form the fundamental controversy of our time! (148)

We can see in these lines the complexity and strategic importance of Coover's Nixon. Not only is he an artist figure of sorts, but his is also the major (albeit partial) consciousness of the text, a mind that creates and responds to events, both overdetermined by its own political indoctrination and yet surprisingly open, curious, restless, wanting to go further than the script or clichés of the era allow. Shaper and shaped, he partakes of a figural drama in which the

artistic and the political are inseparable, as if power itself had a form imperative, and the mark of a leader was to leave a mark, to make visible and legible
the dark forces of the times. Nixon comes across as a peculiarly intriguing
comic creation, a man more sinned against than sinning, a manipulative polit-
ico and also a schlemiel, a canny interpreter of events and also a brazen
demagogue.[5]

With Nixon at the hub, Coover does indeed fashion his modern morality
play, placing in the key roles of God and the devil their secular counterparts,
Uncle Sam and his archenemy, the Phantom. And with this we enter immediately into strange precincts, the land of cartoon figures and jingoist rhetoric,
a place that would seem shrill and one-dimensional, about as far from the
hypercube as we could get. In some sense *The Public Burning* stands or falls,
depending on how we cotton to Uncle Sam, because this ranting and raving
stick figure, this shape shifter extraordinaire, occupies a good bit of the text,
and one needs to accept Coover's premise that such tutelary divinities do
indeed occupy our American scene and need to be heard. It is a bold premise,
and Coover makes astonishingly good on it. First of all, he pulls off a mixed-
media fiction, a stage that has on it both humans and cartoons, somewhat
like the film *Who Framed Roger Rabbit?* Given Coover's zest for textual
experiment, the very gambit itself of putting the Superheroes out there with
ordinary folks has to have been irresistible. But that is just the beginning.
This mixed-media approach is an uncanny rendition of the way power and
ideology play in our day-to-day lives. Slogans, icons, mottoes, bumper stick-
ers: these do's and don't's, kill-for's or die-for's, have finally found a narrative
expression, and old Uncle Sam has finally been liberated from his posters in
post offices and draft boards and given a chance to walk the streets and do his
thing in good old democratic fashion. A venerable tradition of American folk
laughter is reinvoked here, and it is not hard to see a good bit of Mark Twain's
frontier humor in Coover's cavorting narrative.[6] It is utterly right that the
American creed should be spoken by a cartoon figure, because only such a
figure could have the unswerving *clarity* of our famous first principles. The
rest of us are rather murkier, distracted by the facts of our lives, intent on
just getting by, dimly aware that life cannot be packaged in one-liners; the
Superheroes work around the clock, don't need more than one dimension, are
ever true to their ideological mission.

This theoretical defense of Uncle Sam makes his presence in the novel
plausible enough, but it begs the real question: Does Uncle Sam "work"? And,
if so, why? And the answer is: yes. And the reason is: Sam's language. What
Coover has done is to focus so intently and passionately on the slogans of
American jingoism that he has found their poetry. And in finding their poetry,
he has produced some of the most rollicking and vibrant prose of the century.
It is quite a feat: to take clichés of the coarsest and plumpest sort and to make a
rich rhetoric of them by "entering" them and showing what a carny scene the
world becomes once we are located on that *galère*. So it is that Sam Slick,
the novel's "prairie, boondock Zeus," has the juiciest language in the novel,
the raunchiest and often the most brilliant running commentary on the American *res publica* ever to have been penned.[7] When this man opens his mouth,

just sit back and enjoy the ride. In his homespun malapropisms Coover's malice and wit have a field day. Here is his version of the founding:

> "Now is the seed time of Continental union, faith and the clash of resounding arms, the Original Merrycunt Revilusion. I know not what chorus others may take, but as for me, stick a feather in your girl and call her Maggie Rooney! Whee-oo! I must fight somethin' or I'll ketch the dry rot — burnt brandy won't save me! C'mon you varmints, the harder the conflict, the more glorious the massacree! Laxation without intoxification is tyranny, so give me Milly Stark or liberty sleeps a widder!" (523–24)

Sam Slick is one mean customer, and his vigilance for the American cause is unrelenting. Thus he mouths the purest form of American Manichaeanism, and we know who the Bad Guys (in 1953) are:

> "I wish to remark," remarks Uncle Sam, setting his plug hat firmly back on his hoary brow, "and my langwidge is plain, that for ways that are dark and for tricks that are vain, the foe's most abominable lop-eared lantern-jawed half-breed whiskey-soaked and generally onscropulous and haughty host do take the cake, if you don't watch 'em! They are disgraceful, depraved and putrescent, endowed by their Creator with certain gangrene hearts and rottin' brains and similar unalienated blights, and given to sech public frothin' and fumin' as to wound and disease the body politic like thorns in the flesh and other eeroginous zones. But hey! if the Red slayer thinks he slays, boys, he knows not the sub-tile ways I keeps whippin' the she-double-I-it outen any slantindicular sidewinder what trifles with freedom, swells the caress of disunion, incites domestical inch-erections amongst us, eats out our substance, or notherwise bites the hand what lays the golden egg of peace, property, and the bottomless pork barrel! (613–14)

Sam, for the most part, has the legendary arena to himself, and his overheated tirades are a kind of jingoist solo performance. The awesome Phantom, much maligned, is thought to be everywhere behind the scenes, but we don't really get a look at him, except for one memorable occasion when Nixon is escaping from protesters and discovers, to his amazement, that his cabbie is none other than the Evil One. Their exchange is fascinating and telling: the Phantom makes himself known by the utter salaciousness of his views, by his phenomenal repertory of dirty jokes about American power. After assessing U.S. presidents along the lines of their fornication record, he then moves into the matter at hand, the nature of the Rosenbergs, and he delivers a blistering portrait of Ethel as queen of burlesque turned atom-spy:

> ". . . twirlin' her tits, suckin' up quarters with her cunt, things like that. We didn't realize she was suckin' up a lot more than quarters, and then flushin' it all straight to Russia! You read about it, Nick: she had A-bombs up there, Jell-O boxes, Red herrings, passport photos, Klaus Fucks, the Fifth Amendment — shit, she could probably get a whole P-38 up her snatch and have room for Yucca Flat and the Sixth Fleet to boot! They say there was a ray gun in her navel, a walkie-talkie hid in her G-string, and a camera stuffed up her ass. . . ." (337)

Phantom though he is, this guy has an extraordinarily carnal imagination, and the picture he offers of Ethel systematically transmutes sex into spying, makes the woman's body over into the site of espionage and warfare, operates the classic translation of this novel: politics reconceived as sex. And this is indeed a translation, a speech act, a raunchy new code for telling a story of political intrigue. Like the burlesque show itself, such a telling is meant to inflame and arouse, to burn. It is hot rhetoric, and it wreaks havoc with the "facts" that it translates. Then, in a moment of remarkable reflexivity, the Phantom calls for time-out, exposes the very wiring he (and the novel) are made of: "'Look,' he said, his voice mellowing, losing its hard twang, 'can't we get past all these worn-out rituals, these stupid fuckin' reflexes? . . . They got nothin' to do with life, you know that, life's always new and changin', so why fuck it up with all this shit about scapegoats, sacrifices, initiations, saturnalias—?'" (338–39). Coover's book is taking its own pulse here, creating a brief intermission where we might get a glimpse of life and politics without carnival and drumbeating; one is reminded here, mutatis mutandis, of the special quiet moment in *Ulysses* when Bloom stands up to the Citizen—that episode, too, an affair of martial rhetoric and roller-coaster murder and mayhem—with his simple apology of love as the only sanity. And of course Nixon goes right past it, never even registers this possibility of encounter without histrionics. Coover is being true to the paranoid logic of political rivalries—the "Evil Empire" sort of thing—but one is obliged to say that he is also opting in favor of his own rhetorical proclivities, his own writerly commitment to a grotesque and sensationalist view of power and politics. The question remains: Can the translation of history into comic book and burlesque yield a vision of moral seriousness?

The question itself is a rhetorical one—this is intermission time—for it would hardly be asked if there were no affirmative response waiting in the wings. Yes, there is ethical power and nuance in *The Public Burning*, and we will get to it. But it seems essential to give this book its due as pure spectacle, to take its fun more seriously, to take, if possible, the actual measure of its vaudevillian excesses, to study and to appreciate its frenetic new code of ENTERTAINMENT as the central idiom and script of American life, and only then to "translate back," only then to reverse the Coover procedure by putting the morality back into the comedy. There is only one way to gauge Coover's antics: not to back off from them (into political analysis, sermon, and homily) but to go right into and through them; if he wants to give us a 3-D film, we must needs put the glasses on and *see* the spectacle in all its hoary dimensions. So we go to Times Square, "this place of feasts, spectacle, and magic . . . the ritual center of the Western World" (205). It is here that the public burning will take place, and Coover brings in the whole gang to witness the ritual execution:

> . . . everybody jamming up together, old and young, great and small, of all creeds, colors, and sexes, shoulder to shoulder and butt to butt, missionaries squeezed up with mafiosos, hepcats with hottentots, pollyannas with press agents and plumbers and panty raiders . . . workers in dungarees, million-

aires in tuxedos . . . all the top box-office draws and Oscar winners, all the Most Valuable Players . . . Heisman Trophy and Pulitzer Prize winners, blue ribbon and gold medal takers, Purple Hearts and Silver Stars, Imperial High Wizards, Hit Paraders, Hall of Famers, Homecoming Queens and Honor Listees . . . The Sweetheart of Sigma Chi, Yehudi Menuhin, Punjab, Dick Button . . . José Iturbi and Consuelo Vanderbilt, John L. Lewis and Georg Mikan. Esther Williams turns up in her tanksuit, hand-in-hand with the Oscar-winning cat-and-mouse team, Tom and Jerry—and old Mickey Mouse himself is there, too, celebrating his twenty-fifth birthday and elbowing his way through the crowd with Minnie, Goofy, Horace, and the rest of the aging Rat Pack. (439–40)

This list does for America pretty much what Joyce's swollen lists in "Cyclops" (to which it is indebted) does for Ireland: it mythicizes the culture, links together celebrities of show business, cartoons, sports, the academy, even the fraternities, and displays—again following Joyce—their commonality as witnesses to the execution. Such heightening and leveling underscores the business of America as show business, and it flaunts the truly democratic operation of our cultural machinery: whatever you are good at, whatever eminence you've achieved, puts you into a special fraternity of winners, puts you on parade as America's entertainment Légion d'Honneur. A system of salutes and recognitions is on show here, the apparatus of a society that measured the best minds by $64,000 questions, the best bodies by Heisman trophies and homecoming queenships, and decked out its finest in purple hearts, silver stars, gold medals, and blue ribbons.

And it gave us front-row seats at the burning. Zapping the atom spies is shown to be the greatest show on earth in 1953. In one of the most burlesque but spellbinding episodes of the novel, Coover plays out the execution drama in the medium of the American sitcoms of the fifties. Out come Jack Benny and Rochester, Edgar Bergen and Charlie McCarthy, capped by a finale from the Marx brothers. Coover lovingly fashions out of execution materials the skits and dialogues for these groups, breathtakingly true to their individual styles and tics, showing us that the medieval "gallows humor" is still alive, has merely undergone an electronic paradigm shift. It's the wonderful world of comedy. You'll just die laughing:

Boris Karloff and Elsa Lanchester work a Frankenstein act with all the electrical paraphernalia, then Dean (Ethel) Martin drags Jerry (Julie) Lewis around the Death House set by his lower jaw while singing "One Fine Day" from *Madame Butterfly* in a drunken falsetto. Amos 'n Andy turn it all into a blackface minstrel show, with Kingfish doing the lawyer's part, very wily, but bungling things up as usual, and then Jimmy Durante and Garry Moore come out and play it for pathos, using the letters to the children. Out front the people glance up at the Paramount clock, their eyes filling with tears of laughter and unabashed sentiment, as Jimmy and Garry climax their skit with Jimmy sitting in the electric chair in a curly wig, playing the piano, and singing: "Oh, *who* will be wit' chew when h'I'm: *far* h'way, when h'I'm *far* h'way from H—YOU?" (530)

What better way to speak American hysteria than to make it hysterical, hysterically funny, hysterically sick. No excess or liberty that Coover can take could possibly exaggerate the madness of the historical event itself. There is a lithe political intelligence at work in these buffooneries, and it is abetted by an even savvier literary intelligence that knows it can mine this ore, that it can break genuinely new ground by heeding Marx's well-known dictum that history is repeated as farce. As word man extraordinaire, Coover knows that we get from "farce" to "force" in no time flat: "As when Buster Keaton, sitting deadpan in the electric chair, calmly turns and throws a custard pie at the Executioner just as he's about to throw the switch: SPLAT! Some have contended that it was America's love of pie-throwing that led the nation to develop the atomic bomb" (559). There is genuine ludic wisdom in these lines. Coover utilizes the shock value of monstrous associations with the same zest that Lautréamont and the surrealists did, with the difference that he is writing cultural history and anatomizing the American psyche at the same time, taking American "innocence" dreadfully seriously, exposing our politics as the games of children who saw too many circuses, lit too many firecrackers. There is also a peculiar kind of joy in these manic creations, a *Heiterkeit* (didn't Schiller say that the play instinct is humanity's most mature attribute?) that is at once Olympian and egalitarian: Olympian in its panoptic vision of politics and bloodletting as play, egalitarian in its radical leveling of all discourses to the banter of show biz. Rather than diminishing the stature of his subject and materials, Coover strangely exalts them by displaying their obsessive presence everywhere we turn, onstage and offstage, in the papers and in drag, the only show in town. Although it has been claimed that *The Public Burning* is wanting in political analysis, it could be argued that no other novel in history has ever made ideology more visible—*pace* Althusser—and audible than Coover has. The familiar criticism leveled against postmodernism—that its commitment to metacommentary is evasive, self-referential, and judgment-shy—has been angrily applied to Coover's book ever since it appeared.[8] And it is doubtless true that *The Public Burning* will neither be read as historical record nor be enlisted for getting people to the barricades. But, as we have seen throughout this study, the relations between art and ideology are not so simple, and the ludic text may sometimes be understood as both a last-ditch utterance of moral outrage and the experimental arena of a rival moral vision. At bottom this is a prodigious translation performance, a replaying and recoding of history, a sovereign exercise in the freedom of speech which finds maniacal and explosive new voices for the silent dark past that must be made to burn.

What is especially striking about Coover's achievement, given the garish nature of his materials and the covenant with frenzy that is part of his plan, is the remarkable balance he nevertheless manages to maintain between the sensationalism on the one hand (cartoon figures, rabid jingoism, carnival extravaganza) and a compelling, thoughtful meditation on the Rosenberg affair on the other. *The Public Burning* is the product of a very considerable amount of archival research and historical empathy, and it is crammed full of the facts and figures surrounding those events of 1953: informed portraits of not only Ethel and Julius Rosenberg, their co-defendants, and the informants who named them, but lawyers and judges, senators and congressmen, with special cameo appearances by Dwight Eisenhower and a full-bodied evocation of Richard Nixon. The central figures are presented vertically (from childhood up, by means of flashbacks) as well as dramatically, shown to be the products of their complex pasts as well as players in an unfurling drama. Actual correspondence, legal testimony, public speeches, FBI memoranda, newspaper and magazine articles are scrupulously brought into play (I choose my words with care) and cohabit the pages of the novel along with fictional improvisation and invention, yielding a rich composite textual weave. In his excellent 1986 essay on *The Public Burning*, Jackson Cope persuasively reads Mikhail Bakhtin's dialogic theory into Coover's project, showing how Coover is reaching for a culturally stereophonic model.[9] To a large extent Cope takes his cues from Coover's own pronouncements regarding the circus dimension of the Rosenberg novel;[10] in this light we can better understand not only the clown role of Nixon but even more crucially the frenzied carnivalization at the heart of the novel. But the Coover pyrotechnics are also part of a shrewd narrative economy. Not entirely unlike the strategic ballast that cetology gives to *Moby-Dick*, the richly detailed sociopolitical fresco painted by Coover serves as a legitimizing base for his crucial spurts of fantasy, for the massive liberties he is going to take with the known record.

A number of those liberties have been witnessed already in the actualized Uncle Sam and the brilliant song-and-dance routines that are to herald the Rosenberg's public burning in Times Square. But the more crucial liberties that Coover takes (invents) are located in the realm of motivation rather than spectacle, and they are centralized in the complex figure of Richard Nixon. How free, we may ask, is Coover free to be here? Do no rules apply? Can the historical record be simply a happy hunting ground for the postmodernist writer? In some crucial sense our American creed of liberty at all costs, of "free enterprise" in the writerly as well as the political and the commercial arenas, of "mobility" as the American way of life, justifies Coover's inventings — or at least rationalizes them. But it may well be that our "can-do-ism" constitutes the essence of American hubris. Americans may *think* themselves free agents from cradle to grave, but the historical record writes large the actual forces and vectors that inform(ed) our maneuverings. Coover's novel is about exactly these matters, this classic tug-of-war that permeates and "tenses" American life. And no one understands this better than Coover's Nixon. Acutely aware of external geopolitical forces, Coover's Veep has a virtually Hegelian sense of the significance and necessity of the Rosenberg execution:

There's the mounting world pressure, of course, the military build-up on both sides, the threat of an all-out nuclear exchange, but it's more than that — it's almost as though there is something critical about the electrocutions themselves, something down deep inside, a form, it's as though there's an inner momentum now that can no longer be tampered with, the nation is too deeply committed to this ceremony, barriers have already come down, the ghosts have been sprung and there's a terror loose in the world, an excitement: if the spies don't die, and die now, something awful might happen, the world's course might get bent. (262)

What freedom here? What maneuvering room?

Hence, the Richard Nixon of *The Public Burning* is to play out an American destiny. Life-size rather than Superhero, man-in-the-gap trying to fathom his role in these great events, questioning and probing where Uncle Sam had ranted and raved, Richard Nixon will undergo the paradigmatic struggle reflected and refracted in every American literary text under inclusion in this study: the struggle to be free and to make a self. On the one hand, Nixon — like Gatsby and so many others — shares the dream:

> I'm like Teddy Roosevelt, I like to be down in the arena. They used to say of Roosevelt that "when Theodore attends a wedding he wants to be a bride; when he attends a funeral he wants to be the corpse." I'm like that. And what's most important, I have the faith: I believe in the American dream. I believe in it because I have seen it come true in my own life. TIME has said that I've had "a Horatio Alger-like career," but not even Horatio Alger could have dreamed up a life so American — in the best sense — as mine. (366)

Nixon, then, would be the American protagonist, the Gatsby of the 1950s, but unlike Fitzgerald, Coover has chosen to plunge us deeply into the mind and feelings of this emblematic figure, and what we find there — contrary to the assured, centered person we might expect — is a strangely vacant, almost ghostly figure, someone who knows himself to be only a *figure*, an "ontologically insecure character," a "cash-and-carry" personality that is pure expediency, ready to move, poised to embody the American will — remember this line — a channel waiting for the current to fill it.[11] Here is No-Man. From Hawthorne's Wakefield to DeLillo's Oswald, this specter haunts the American imagination, and whenever he is on the scene, we can expect to see a flurry of strategic activity:

> You're not born with "character." You create this as you go along, and acting parts in plays helps you recognize some of the alternative options — most people don't realize this, and that's why they end up such shabby characters. . . . The extempore contests taught me agility, coolness in crisis situations, and how to manipulate ambiguities when you don't have the facts and aren't even sure what the subject matter is. I learned in debates that the topic didn't count for shit, the important thing was strategy. . . . (365)

Unburdened by fixities or even by pieties — his pieties are essentially provisional, functional — Coover's Nixon is, in the purest sense of the term, an *opportunist*, a man waiting for the right events, not so much to shape them as to be shaped by them, to be instanced and made whole by them. In his active performances he is an impressive version of *Homo americanus*, a man on the move, "genuinely" theatrical, a man for all seasons.

But, as we have occasion to see over and over, ghostliness and insubstantiality mark his inner life. For such a person others, too, are figural, annexes or appendixes to the action at hand. Nixon's reflections about his wife, Pat, could have been written by Hawthorne or James (or Borges):

> It occurred to me that I had been living with Pat for nearly thirteen years, thirteen years this Sunday, and yet in a real sense she was a complete stranger to me. Only when she was chewing me out did she become somehow real, but the rest of the time . . . Well, it was almost as if I'd married some part of myself, and Pat was only the accidental incarnation of that part. Do we all do this? Is this what marriage is all about, finding fleshly embodiments of our ghostly selves, making ourselves whole? (251)

Thinking, kinetic, speculating, this Nixon is filled with constant chatter, a busybrain that flurries a great deal, seems to revel in the workings of its own circuitry. And that circuitry extends into corners and realms that transcend time and space, making its "owner" something of a fellow traveler *malgré lui*. Fatigued, going endlessly over the Rosenberg data looking for a breakthrough, Coover's Nixon takes some strange trips:

> I'd thought, stretching out: I must do what I always do, I must consider all the worst alternatives as cold-bloodedly as I can, and reach an analytical conclusion. But instead I'd dozed off and found myself in bed with the guy I slept with at Duke. He had been studying so hard he'd set his ass on fire, and he was trying to show me the burns. Curiously, he had a thin black moustache and wire-rimmed glasses, was wearing a double-breasted suit jacket, white shirt, and tie. "Don't be embarrassed," I said, as I pried the cheeks of his butt apart to see what was the matter. We didn't have any electricity in that place and it was dark, but by peering closely I could tell that the whole area was festering and badly inflamed. It was almost like somebody had taken a meat cleaver to it. I felt nauseous and sorry for what I'd done. I wanted to comfort her but I was worried what the lasting impression would be. Dad came in and suggested a poultice of hot mustard. He didn't seem to understand the problem. I shouted: "Summer solstice, not poultice!" He seemed utterly abashed and ashamed of himself. I was ashamed too, because I knew he'd never finished school. Pat lay naked on the bed, her eyes closed, moaning softly, literally shedding light. I was at the sink. Perhaps I'd been washing the dishes, or else I'd been vomiting. "She's the Sweetheart of Sigma Chi," Dad said solemnly. He was dressed up for church and his ears stuck out. I went outside, thinking: Didn't they know *I* could die, too? (222–23)

We are indisputably in the province of fiction here, beneficiaries of a rather enormous liberty Coover has taken, made privy to a rich and bristling dreamscript, written in the languages of displacement and condensation, energized by libidinal fear and desire, recasting the discrete elements of the Nixon biography — wife Pat, unschooled Dad, Duke Law School — into a shocking but fluid narrative line, one that moves briskly through cover stories and wordplay and stand-ins in order to present the Nixonian psychic apparatus. A number of bogeys come out into the open: homoeroticism (wanted? feared?), fixation with the anus and/as genitalia, varieties of guilt (over sex [practices?], over his parents, over Pat), fear of exposure, fear of death. We note that the lead-off article in this oneiric script is a burned butt that is insistently looked into. Some thirty pages later Nixon looks into it again as he ponders the connections between fire hazards and recent legislation:

> Lot of goddamn fire in this case. Everything from the Greenglass kitchen stove to talk of an atomic holocaust. Holocaust: burnt whole. Just what the Rosenbergs had to look forward to. "Flaming Reds," the papers called them. "This infernal conspiracy." The day's hot news story. "Gonna put their feet to the fire," Uncle Sam had told me out at Burning Tree: "They've inflamed a lotta passions out in the world, let 'em get their own frizzed a little!" Maybe that was what my dream last night about Pat's burning bush was all about. . . . (253)

The bold poetic logic on show in this passage is unmistakable, and it sends us both into the interior of the Nixon subconscious but also outward toward seemingly independent strata of the story: stoves, Holocaust, epithets for communists, headlines, punishment, passion, genitalia. Nixon "reads" these private fires into a public burning, corrals the discrete particulars of the case into a unified code, into a coherent language, and he startles us into rethinking the rationale of these events, for we are invited to trace everything back to a potent, governing structure, a form of *correspondences* that we discern often enough in the arrangements of art and psyche but never in life. Coover's reach is more audacious still: we recall the first momentous meeting between Nixon and Uncle Sam at the Burning Tree golf course, and we note now that last night's dream of an "ass on fire" undergoes a prudent sex change to become "Pat's burning bush." Once we factor the proper mythic echo of Moses and the Burning Bush into this heady equation, we are in a position to measure the "infernal" intensity of Coover's recombinant strategy. Using a visionary paradigm from the Old Testament to configure Nixon's encounter with the American God is witty enough, but this pairing is exponentially heightened and complicated when it is made to signify—at the same time—a burning male anus and/or female vagina. In this dazzling equation we have the makings of a psychosexual rendition of Manifest Destiny, a version of the Burning Bush epic that conflates divine revelation with genital conflagration and sexual taboo.[12] To regard the dictates of ideology as (also) an erotic code is to effect a scandalous fusion of realms, to invert public and private, to suggest that the august politics of the nation flow from (toward?) our sexual fantasies, to give uncommon density and clout to our term "body politic."

Coover has chosen, ultimately, not to travel very far down this route, not to delve into Nixon's "Nighttown" material, no doubt thinking that the book is pyrotechnic and zany enough not to need Nixon on a couch. He must also have decided that Nixon's psychic malleability, his elasticity, his associative forays could be shown in still other ways, more frontally, even more explosively. Vice President Nixon, the man with a (well-warranted) fear "of getting lost in some maze of emotions, of surrendering my self-control, afraid of . . . afraid of exile. From myself" (368), is to be sent by Coover into parts unknown. His involvement with the Rosenbergs and the public burning will be many things: an exile, a pilgrimage, a metamorphosis, a bid for freedom, a fable about the power of fiction to depict/defeat the facts of history.

The more research Nixon does into the Rosenberg case, the more astonished he is by the resemblances and parallels that come to light, twinning him with the atom spies. The Rosenbergs, like himself, were "carried along by a desire . . . to reach the heart of things" (150); young Julius had "been elected vice president of the Young Men's Synagogue Organization. Like me, at Christian Endeavor. He had had lessons and had even considered becoming a rabbi, just as my mother had always thought I might become a Quaker missionary" (159–60). Even differences and dissimilarities hint at a pattern: "We were more like mirror images of each other, familiar opposites. Left-right, believer-non-believer, city-country, accused-accuser, maker-unmaker" (169). Nixon even wonders "what would happen if Tricia and Julie grew up and fell in love with the Rosenberg boys" (252), and we cannot fail to see that a new expanded family identity is emerging. We also see the liberty Coover is taking, the brooding liberty of hindsight that works on the poor isolated facts of the case, shines and polishes them into multifaceted surfaces, puts them into a new mosaic, converts research into art. Nixon's growing obsession with the Rosenbergs encroaches on his own (never firm) identity, leads to extraordinary and unintended feats of empathy, to an interweaving of his past and theirs, so that the recall of his California childhood is overlaid with other, unbidden memories:

> I seemed to remember things that had never happened to me, places I'd never been, friends and relatives I'd never met who spoke a language I didn't know. I recalled narrow streets filled with trucks, lined with crude stalls, stacks of trousers and shirts and underwear, chicken feathers in the gutter. I distinctly remembered a kind of tacked-up wooden cross with work gloves hanging from it, ties draped over it, sweaters and slips heaped and tumbled below, short fat men with glasses and flat-billed caps haggling with women dressed in long shiny black dresses and bell-like bonnets down around their ears. . . . (179)

"Hey—where did I get these memories?" the Vice President then asks, as he unwittingly takes his place in a long and distinguished literary parade of empathizing poachers, of bridge-making narrators: Melville's lawyer and scrivener, Baudelaire and his *petites vieilles*, Carraway and Gatsby, Zeitblom and Leverkühn, Quentin and Shreve and the Sutpen saga, Roquentin and Rollebon. But Nixon's vicarious experience of the Rosenbergs is special, because they are the Enemy. They are the Other who is branded, by the country at large, as subversive, noxious, invasive. Nixon himself makes the connection: "All those disturbing apparitions, those images out of a life not my own. . . . It was as though something had got into me last night, like an alien gene, and I'd lacked the strength to fend it off—all my Early Warning rhetoric about 'boring from within': I'd suddenly begun to understand it for the first time" (216). Once again we experience, as readers, the jolt of synchronization, the pleasure that attends coming into focus, and Coover's textual weave now looms large, insistently tying together the warp of public rhetoric and the woof of private experience, reconceiving politics along lines of creatural panic, bonds of empathy, and bacterial invasion. With these lines in place, we begin to understand the Red Scare as a 1950s version of the plague that visited Thebes in the time of Sophocles and struck Europe in the mid-fourteenth century, and thus the boundless paranoia of American isolationism is revealed as a desperate yearning for intactness, for impenetrability, for a true blue country that cannot be invaded because its people are steadfastly themselves, integral and impenetrable, immovable.

Nixon fascinates because he lives out the myth and its undoing. Part of him craves fixity, but the major adventure Coover has provided for him is an exercise in motion and slippage. His growing identification with the Rosenbergs does not stop with Julius; it extends even more powerfully to Ethel:

> We were both second children in our families, we both had an older brother, younger brothers, both had old-fashioned, kitchen-bound mothers and hard-working failure fathers, were both shy and often poor in health, I admit it, both preferred to be by ourselves except when we were showing off publicly on a stage, both were honor students, activists and organizers, loved rhetoric and drama, worked hard for our parents, had few friends, never dated much and mated late, had dreams. (388–89)

The astute reader, especially if he or she has read any Coover before, senses what kind of mileage the author is planning to get out of these parallels and kinships. The noxious pestilential Other who threatens the body politic with plague and invasion is a figure of fascination, an Other who seduces. Richard Nixon is embarked on an exploration of the Rosenbergs, and from that point on they have *entered* both him and the novel, have gotten on the inside and are busily working their magic there. Seduction means "to lead astray," but Nixon's seduction is a richer affair: he is led Other-wards, and this also means that he is making the voyage *in*, into the dark heart. Even that formulation does not go far enough. Nixon begins to grasp that his growing engagement with the Rosenbergs is an American quest, that he is moving ever deeper into the true American ethos of freedom. His connection with the spies is an opportunity for unprecedented liberties. Wanting to be a player, to go to the heart of things, to be the man of destiny, Nixon becomes a Freedom Fighter. And he lurches into a great American discovery: reality is not a given; it is something you *make*: "There were no scripts, no necessary patterns, no final scenes, there was just *action*, and then *more action*! Maybe in Russia History had a plot because one was being laid on, but not here—*that was what freedom was all about!*" (449). It is worth pausing over these lines. Coover's book has been, all along, a meditation on freedom and determinism, and it "writes" that meditation in as many tongues as it can: philosophical, political, historical, artistic. Perhaps only Thomas Mann's *Doktor Faustus* offers a comparably rich playing-out of this dialectical struggle, and Mann's bold fusion of themes—the Faustian pact, the *Durchbruch* of the German state, the parallel stories of Nietzsche and Schönberg as refracted through

Leverkühn, the belatedness of modern art — stands as a suggestive earlier model for the epic scope of Coover's enterprise. We have never had any troubling granting philosophical status to Mann's very (very) serious book; but Coover's traveling circus has seemed too formalist, too excessive, too raucous, too impolite to warrant such consideration.

Yet there is an audacious synthesis building in this sprawling novel. We should remember that Nixon's theatrical and writerly version of American freedom versus Russian determinism (with its scripts, scenes, plots) has been sounded earlier by the oracular Sam Slick, and it is worth quoting this Wild West panegyric at length, since it both displays Coover's stylistic exuberance and highlights the philosophical agon of the novel:

> "Dead before they're born! . . . If those lizards ever get their world revolution, it'll be all over for 'em. . . . This excitement out on the perimeter is all they've got. Inside, son, there's nothing but old mold and fungus. They're learnin' the hard way what our Old West was all about, all that tumult and butchery and wild unsartinty. Two pollrumptious screamers shoot it out on a dusty Main Street over a saddlepack fulla gold: now them two fellers is about alive as anybody's ever *gonna* be! Socialists are skeered of this, they want everything buttoned down fair and logical and all screwin' up antedeluvian *quiet*, which is to say, they don't want nothin' to *happen*! What's there to live for in a world like that, I ask you — all them sissies runnin' your life for you. No, the earth belongs to the livin', boy, not to cold pickles! You can't tame what don't stand still and nothin' in this universe does! Einstein put his finger on it a long time ago — oh, he's gone off the deep end lately, I know, but listen, he knew what America was all about: don't let the grass grow under your feet! Saddle up, keep movin', anything can happen! . . . Bodies in motion just don't age as fast, that's what it boils down to. America, by staying off its ass, was stayin' young! . . . This here's a country of beginnin's, of projects, of vast designs and expectations! It's got no past; all has an onward and prospective look! The fountain of youth! (254–55)

There is both poetry and truth in these overheated but oracular lines, and Coover emerges here as both the lyricist and the mythographer of American culture. His predilection for frontier humor has a surprisingly philosophical base, and the references to Einstein's views on time, space, and motion may seem casual, but they are offered with deadly seriousness, and they will be integrated into the very structure and theme of his novel, as we shall see. The cult of youth, the religion of mobility, and the suspicion of government stand for the America of the 1990s as much as that of 1953 or 1978; but, just as Einstein said, nothing stands still, and the satire of socialism has a very strange and prophetic ring to it, now that the Berlin Wall is down, eastern Europe is reshaping itself, and the Soviet Union is a historical memory.

Coover's Nixon has fire in his belly, and — unlike his "real" counterpart, who made a career out of closure, paranoia, and fear — he will make good on American freedom and mobility; he will write his own role, throw off ideological blinders altogether, because he knows that no prior script is binding: "There was no author, no director, and the audience had no memories — they got reinvented every day! I'd thought: perhaps there is not even a War between the Sons of Light and the Sons of Darkness!" (448). Inebriated by the vistas of freedom and self-invention, Nixon feels catapulted beyond the constraints of consistency and cogency. What, he understands, are "character" and "identity" and "self" if not conventions? Sounding as though he lived in one of Borges's stories, he expresses his belief "that men contain all views, right and left, theistic and atheistic, legalistic and anarchical, monadic and pluralistic; and only an artificial—call it political—commitment to consistency makes them hold steadfast to singular positions" (449). Liberated from prior binds and bonds, aware now of "the real meaning of the struggle against the Phantom: *it was a war against the lie of purpose*" (449), free agent at last and fast becoming Superhero, Richard Nixon wants to bring his new tidings to his people, to "provoke a truth for the world at large to gape at: namely, that nothing is predictable, anything can happen" (452).

Thus the stage is set for the showstopping central event of the novel, the dramatic climax that threatens to upstage even the public burning at Times Square. Nixon's exercise in freedom merges into his fascination with the Rosenbergs: defying prior scripts, he will go to Sing Sing, encounter Ethel Rosenberg in person, and make history.[13] What happens is more than anyone (except Coover fans) bargained for: Nixon experiences wild sexual desire for Ethel Rosenberg, and Coover stages a full-scale, deeply burlesque and deeply serious rendition of their encounter. He kisses her, and in that probing, questing, many-paged kiss we see the continued journey of Nixon into the Rosenbergs, the final entry into the Other. As their tongues explore each other's mouths and their hands move into each other's furrows and extensions, Coover operates something of a miracle of geography and history, of the past recaptured, of Einsteinian mobility and American freedom. It goes on and on, too long for full quotation, but as it crescendoes, it looks like this:

I closed my eyes: my mind seemed to expand, it was as though her hand were kneading it, stretching it, her tongue lapping its edges, her other hand digging in for its root far below. Oh what a mind! I hardly recognized it! It was full of hidden memories, astonishing thoughts, I'd never seen it like this before, a vast moving darkness and brilliant flickering pictures, new and strange, called forth by the charged explorations of our mouths and hands. Some were frightening: girls knocked down by fire hoses, men gassed in trenches and run down by police on galloping horses, villagers buried in bomb-rubble, lives blighted by disease and poverty, children monstrously deformed by radiation or eaten up by vermin—yet it was all somehow exciting, I reveled in all this experience and knew it to be good. I grasped Ethel's bottom and saw the face of a child. He seemed to live in a great city. I couldn't tell if he was black or white, Mexican, Italian, or Polish, but it didn't matter. I shared his dreams: he was a poet, a scientist, a great teacher, a proud craftsman. He was America itself, everything we've ever hoped to be, everything we've dared to dream to be. But he awoke—we both awoke—to the nightmare of poverty, neglect, and despair. He failed in school. He ended up on welfare. He was drafted and died in Korea. I saw all this as my tongue roamed behind Ethel's incisors. I was weeping, but it was as if with joy, because I also saw Grandma Milhous and she was smiling. Why are you nervous? she seemed to be saying. Ethel was clawing through the hair on my chest. The child was reborn. There was peace. My peace and Grandma's. I was trying to get both of Ethel's breasts into one hand. I saw the villages rebuilt and the demeaned lives uplifted. I smelled Mom's hot pies, felt my fingers moving brilliantly on the organ keys, playing "My Rosary," heard the magical call of faraway train whistles in the night, and it was the sweetest music I'd ever heard. I saw the shackles of work gangs fall away, walls between peoples come tumbling down (I had them both in my hand for a moment, soft and firm and full—One if by land, I thought, two if by sea—then let them slip away, reaching up for her face), slum tenements emptying their multitudes into sunny green meadows. I licked feverishly at Ethel's bruised lips and tasted fresh hot bread, stroked her throat and smelled the fragrance of roses, explored the cleft between her buttocks and felt a peace and warmth and brotherhood I had not known since those mornings we all huddled around the kitchen stove in Yorba Linda and we were all still alive. (542–43)

There will be readers who have no stomach for this passage, who find it tasteless, obscene, farcical, bloated, sentimental, or all of the above. But it is arguably the most splendid piece of writing in Coover's entire oeuvre. With its dazzling, filmic cutting of erotic close-up with recovery of the past, it looks unmistakably ahead to later, still more polished and audacious renderings of this slippage and fusion in *Gerald's Party* and *A Night at the Movies*. In its handling of Americana—the ethnic youngster with dreams, Mom's hot pies, faraway train whistles in the night—it keeps covenant with the original folk-loric strain in Coover's fictions. And in its presentation of ecstatic power, of liberation from ideological blinders, it sovereignly completes Nixon's transformation into American hero of freedom. His final embrace with Ethel causes him to feel "an incredible new power, a new freedom. Where did it come from? Uncle Sam? The Phantom? Both at once? From neither, I supposed. There was nothing overhead any more, I had escaped them both! I was outside guarded time! I was my own man at last!" (547). We are confronting here a very pure version of the freedom of speech, the creative shaping power of language and imagination, as the enabling principle of American fiction. The projects of autogenesis that make up American fiction—Wakefield's, Gatsby's, Catherine Bourne's, Beloved's, Lee Harvey Oswald's—give resonance to the Nixon venture here; and the breaking free from societal markings has the kind of birthlike purity, the yearned-for second chance, that shimmers under the narrative surface of our fictions: discernible in the swapped babies in *Puddn'head Wilson*, in the vortex of forces stirred up by the nameless infant that Lena Grove delivers when her time is come. All of these texts bear witness to the coercions and determinants of culture, and in each one of them we see the makings of a writerly freedom, a writerly reprieve.[14]

But if we are to take the full measure of Coover's reach here, we must turn to Faulkner's *Absalom, Absalom!*, where imagination and love and language are called on, years and years later, to make amends for brutality and death and war, to fashion an alternative to fratricide by means of a "marriage of speaking of hearing" effected, briefly, in a Harvard dormitory. The Faulkner-ian "overpass to love" is created by a cunning narrative strategy of ellipsis, dislocation, and empathy, and tonally it bears little resemblance to the winking and burlesque that are still present in Coover's scene of exalted coupling. Nevertheless, what they share is the same temporal fullness and emotional generosity, the magic view of love as "boosting power," love as the fueling energy that propels us out of our closed skins and into the bodies, minds, and pasts of Others.

Let there be no mistake here: this is not a sentimental but a political proposition. Nixon uses his new freedom to discover and recover a crucial working past — his own lost childhood from an earlier America, and also that of Ethel, with its European and Jewish components — and these perceptions grow wider still, go beyond the private altogether into a vision of girls knocked down by fire hoses, men gassed in trenches, villagers buried in bomb rubble, youths on welfare, boys dying in Korea. Whereas Faulkner's Mississippian at Harvard or indeed Joyce's young Irish artist regard history as a nightmare from which they are trying to awaken, Coover the postmodernist presents it as an inrushing film, "a vast moving darkness and brilliant flickering pictures," that floods us with responsibilities, exposes — by its sweeping environmental logic and flow — the utter idiocy of all "isolationisms," be they of America the beautiful or of the imperial self. Only here does Coover deal frontally with the brutality and blindness of all warmongering "-isms," those potent forces that are clothed in jingoist, Manichaean prose and are responsible for the economic and physical misery of the human race. The fusion of Richard Nixon and Ethel Rosenberg is a freedom of speech, and it proposes a fictive alternative to the historical extermination, a joyous, incandescent, writerly burning instead of the silent butchery and electrocution of the "record." The Rosenbergs are finally granted, through the offices of fiction, the reprieve they desperately sought from the courts of the land; not that Nixon and Ethel are to be imagined riding off together into the sunset, but that Nixon has finally grasped the human reality of the Other, has finally understood the human density of history. That understanding of the Other — visceral, empathetic, from the "inside" — is the only thing that will prevent atrocities such as the Rosenberg execution and the national paranoia whose child it was.

Fiction does not alter history. It may be, as in *Absalom, Absalom!*, a creative elegy, an effort to imagine an alternative to the record. At its most exalted, fiction brings its readers into its tapestry and helps them to experience, vicariously of course, the turmoil of events at which they were not present. Faulkner did that: he was able to render, as a writer, the fratricidal holocaust experienced by America in the Civil War. And his overpass to love is offered as the only way to understand, and thereby avoid, such carnage. But one can hardly claim that *The Public Burning* has the emotional density or seriousness of *Absalom*. The encounter between Nixon and Ethel does not bear fruit: the spies will be burned. Their embrace is, indeed, properly ecstatic, offers a genuine epiphany, a radiant image for understanding and peace; but it does not stamp the novel. We do not finish Coover's novel thinking it to be a tragic love story. At most their embrace instances the freedom of what Coover has called "dream time":

> In effect, dream time is an act of artistic creation, and I realize now that's
> what I'm doing. Most of the society's effort goes into forging the construct,
> the creative form in which everybody can live—a social contract of sorts. It is
> the job of the politicians—chiefs or whatever—to organize it. Whatever form
> they set up is necessarily entropic: eventually it runs down and is unable to
> propel itself past a certain point. When it does that, it becomes necessary to
> do everything that has been taboo: wear women's clothes, kill the sacred
> animal and eat it, screw your mother, etc.[15]

Nixon has become a hero of liberty by entering dream time. But his geste is
more than anarchic. What is it? The coercive, entropic order has been transcended. What is coming? What has the author wanted to leave us with?

We can perhaps begin to answer this question by returning to the Rosenbergs' alleged crime. Their trespass, Coover wants us to understand, is a
mythic transgression, akin to Prometheus's theft of fire, it too a desperate
assertion of individual freedom against the order of the gods:

> In the middle of the Western World stands this empty chair: and only the
> Rosenbergs can fill this emptiness. Not the Nazi war criminals, not the dis-
> loyal union agitators or the Reader's Digest Murderers, not even the grisly
> necrophile John Reginald Halliday Christie can sit that seat tonight. For the
> Rosenbergs have done what none, not even these, may dream to do. They
> have denied Uncle Sam, defied the entire Legion of Superheroes, embraced
> the Phantom, cast his nefarious spell upon the innocent, and for him have
> wrested from the Sons of Light their most sacred secret: the transmutation of
> the elements. (435)

We are dead center. Coover's enabling conception, his own secret, is spelled
out here. *The Public Burning* aims a spotlight on the famous execution of the
atom spies in 1953, but its larger ambition is to explore the deeper significance
of their crime itself. The rhetorical and political drumbeating may stem from
the paranoid Manichaeanism of the fifties, but that does not go far enough; a
longer view establishes a different, more profound, more sinister causal chain,
and we may view all the political and journalistic hullaballoo as symptoms, as
radii issuing from a center. That center is not the theft of the sacred secret; it
is the secret itself, the transmutation of the elements. Coover's novel takes the
measure of our modern era that is inaugurated by one fateful historic event,
the quintessential triumph of American can-do-ism: the discovery of atomic
energy, the nature of atomic fission.

Like the Joyce of *Ulysses*, the Mann of *Doktor Faustus*, and the Faulkner
of *Absalom*, Coover has taken the measure of his cultural crisis by *giving its
measure*, by translating its revolutionary new view of power into the very
structure, language, and dynamic of his epic novel. He has understood that
the "transmutation of the elements" heralds a new, utterly mobile order of
things. Uncle Sam laid claim to Einsteinian relativity as the key to American
restlessness and energy; we now see that "energy" is a polysemous term, that it
signifies atomic energy as much as get-up-and-go. Relativity ushers us into a
world shorn of the grids and directional signals and solid bases we take for

granted in our perceptual scheme: up/down, here/there, now/then, you/me. To "wrest from the Sons of Light their most sacred secret" virtually images the (illicit?) discovery of nuclear fission: to break through the armature of the atom in order to liberate its prodigious indwelling energy. Finally, as each of the foregoing remarks implies, "the transmutation of the elements" is a writerly formula, for it challenges the writer to "transmute" physics into language, and it should be readily apparent by now that *The Public Burning* is to be a transmutation of atomic energy into narrative.[16] The fabled American freedom that Nixon is questing for, the freedom from prior scripts that he finds, the liberating mobility that takes him to Sing Sing, the brilliant radiance and 'boosting power" of his epiphanic trip through time and space as he embraces Ethel Rosenberg and experiences history: all this is the writerly version of nuclear fission.

Not just the major themes of the novel reflect the dynamic of nuclear energy; the very way the text is written and composed flaunts a *Kuntswille* that is true to Einsteinian relativity. How would you write a "free," a "freed" book? Well, you'd try, for starters, to liberate your words, to exalt their signifying energies without tying them down to specific referents. One way to get protons and neutrons on the move, verbally, is to rhyme and pun madly, accentuating to the point of idiocy and anarchy the verbal and phonic counters of your espionage materials:

> Knock knock! Who's dere? Police? Police who? Uh, Police tuh meet yuh, lady. Thistle be quick. Chester routine inquiry. Hassan body here seen a spy ring? We all aspiring, Mister, it's a Mary kin way! Clem the ladder of success, you know? Gopher broke. Hokay? Well, yeah, but . . . C'mon, Thomas money, copper, and Eisenhower late as it is! Yes'm, Czar Rhee tuh bother yuh. Dewey have your pardon? Sure, son, Hiss all right, to err is Truman. Better luck on the—knock, knock!—Nixon. . . . (21)

Or you might go on a numbers spree, just to democratize your text a bit, to give numerals their day on the page, to let them fight it out with the words, so that the representational conventions and rival orders of your medium were good and illuminated: "Eighth Race: Perón arrests 7 Radicals, a 4-nation chase nets 6 thieves, The French crisis enters its 5th week, Nick Condos was Martha Raye's 4th husband, and Willi Goettling, leaving 3 dependents, is shot between his 2 eyes by the Russians, losing his 1 life. 37 Down: *zero.* NIL" (244). Or you might trot out a whole paragraph of familiar song titles and refrains, coerce them firmly into narrative service, make 'em into one long sentence, and create thereby a panoramic "united states" of throbbing lyrics, a new national anthem of heartfelt clichés, tapping into the humming static just below the threshold of speech that pollutes the American mind and constitutes a bona fide *lieu commun* for all our citizenry:

> So hand me down my walkin' cane and let us go then, you and I, beyond the sunset, the river, and the blue, down to that crowded hole above Cayuga's waters, travelin' on down the line from on the wide Pacific to the broad

Atlantic shore, over hill, over dale, up a lazy river and down the road feelin'
bad dashing through the snow on a bicycle built for two to catch the night
train to Memphis, comin' round the mountain on a wing and a prayer and
tramp! tramp! tramp! leaving the Red River Valley white with foam to walk
in the King's Highway down Moonlight Bay, prospecting and digging for
gold. . . . (494–95)

You would find writerly ways to be a fellow traveler in Nixon's "war against
the lie of purpose," and target number one would be the purposive tyranny of
narrative itself, the coercive pressures of your plot line. You might thumb
your nose at these hierarchical proprieties by promoting other verbal arrangements, such as the mosaics of newsprint, the egalitarian mix of articles, types,
stories, and subjects that cohabit the journalist's page. *The Public Burning* is
such a text, replete with headlines, subheads, and different-pointed characters.
And its canny interlacing of carnivalesque theater and Nixonian consciousness, of historical record and manic fantasy, of metaphysical conundrums and
wacky one-liners, of political tragedy and raunchy comedy does indeed have
the intended Brechtian effect, makes it possible for us to laugh at the serious
and to cry at the comic, forces us to see our reality in terms of rollicking,
frolicking discourses.

In a moment of insight Nixon realizes that the *Times* crossword puzzle
epitomizes the field picture that configures our lives, "a kind of matrix, a field
of play which mirrored the structure of the newspaper and thus of history
itself, the paradigmatic range of 'news' and possibility, crossed with real 'time-
arrow chain-of-events'" (256). With customary brilliance Coover "transmutes"
our weekly rituals into resonant fables, and he exposes another of his sacred
secrets: namely, that the dismantling of narrative and the war against the lie
of purpose are themselves ur-narratives, dramatic renditions of the human
subject's (shrinking) place in a wildly energized force field delineated by the
text. The crossword puzzle is radically decentered, starts and stops all over the
place, has strange neighbors and bedfellows, is fueled by multidirectional
signifying power. Einstein and atomic fission again come to mind, but this
time with a twist: How does one negotiate this scheme? How do we make our
way? As Robert Morace has written: "Even as Coover becomes more and
more wildly inventive, his characters steadily lose ground in their struggle
for autonomous existence and imaginative freedom on the one hand, and
community on the other."[17] This is not a coincidence; it is a dialectic. Coover's
writerly freedom and Nixon's "liberation" take, like all explosions of energy,
the ground out from under us. *The Public Burning*—in its systematic assault
on linear narrative, its proliferation of discourses, its prodigious display of
power in all modalities, its associative logic and multiple circuitry—is Coover's
bomb-text.

Readers of postmodern fiction in general—one thinks of the work of figures such as Robbe-Grillet or John Barth or Italo Calvino or Julio Cortázar—
must learn to orient themselves to these energized textual precincts, where
nothing remains either still or itself, where the freedom of speech is being
exercised page after page. Thus it is that Coover has placed in the middle of

his book, as a kind of bonus for his dazed readers, their own garish self-portraits in the figure of the man who has seen the 3-D film *The House of Wax* and has kept his 3-D glasses on while walking the streets of New York.[18] Giving us a preview of coming attractions (*A Night at the Movies*), this man's perceptual and cognitive dilemma both mirrors our own disarray and bears witness to the quality of vision that a bomb-text produces and inflicts:

> He's about to exit by way of a plate-glass window when the fruiterer collars him and pushes him brusquely out what is probably the door, plunging him reeling back into the heart of the maelstrom, past a newsstand where, grasping for support, he acquires some newspapers and magazines, and then, though this is not exactly his intention, on into a subway entrance. He fumbles, clutching newspapers and grapefruit, down the stairs, one lens showing him an advertisement of *Dangerous When Wet* with Esther Williams in a swimsuit, a moustache under her nose and a Ulysses S. Grant beard between her legs, the other a time-lapse overview of traffic patterns on the subway platform. At the bottom, pausing to wonder if "the Balance of Terror" is a communicable disease which he's somehow caught, he tries to locate himself—without success—in a gum-machine mirror. All he sees there is Abraham Lincoln with his beard on fire. A train pulls in, arriving from separate directions in the two lenses, and he allows himself to be swept aboard by the crowd. Or perhaps he wishes to take the train, he isn't sure. He finds an empty seat, but when he sits down it isn't there. (353)

It used to be reported—anecdotally and, doubtless, apocryphally—that Thomas Mann, during his stay at Princeton, gave Albert Einstein a copy of Kafka's "Metamorphosis," and that Einstein, after reading it, is said to have commented: "The human mind is not that complex." One wonders what he might have said if he had been offered the passage just cited; one wonders especially if he might not have recognized in Coover's funhouse a fictional replica of what life could look like if the relativity theory governed our perceptions. The train comes from several directions at once, one enters places one had not intended, the mirror does not reflect one's image, one sits down and it isn't there. To be sure, Coover is packing a little Freud in here too, and the Freudian view of repression has its own paradigm of armature breaking when it comes to jokes, slips of the tongue, dreams, and the work of neurosis itself. But what we see, above all, is that the "balance of terror" really means *imbalance as terror*, as the text becomes a mine field for its human occupants. But the man in 3-D glasses is there to prime us for worse still, for one final transmutation of the elements.

Richard Nixon's giddy moment of "incredible new power," of "a new freedom," comes to naught. The scripts cannot be broken; the covenants cannot be remanded. The spies convicted of stealing the atomic secret will be put to death by the gods, killed by powers like those they stole. The show must go on, and Coover's prose delivers at last the public burning. Moving beyond the optical fun-and-games of 3-D glasses, Coover shows us with unbearable precision just what it looks like when the human body—Ethel's body which Nixon has held—enters the force field of the bomb-text:

> Ethel Rosenberg's body, held only at head, groin, and one leg, is whipped
> like a sail in a high wind, flapping out at people like one of those trick images
> in a 3-D movie, making them scream and duck and pray for deliverance. Her
> body, sizzling and popping like firecrackers, lights up with the force of the
> current, casting a flickering radiance on all those around her, and so she
> burns — and burns — and burns — as though held aloft by her own incandescent
> will and haloed about by all the gleaming great of the nation. (640–41)

This scene remains horribly true to the entertainment code of the novel, but
that code has now become surpassingly eloquent, capable of expressing the
kind of American crucifixion that we see in the deaths of Stowe's Uncle Tom,
Faulkner's Joe Christmas, O'Connor's Displaced Person, DeLillo's Lee Harvey Oswald.

One expects *The Public Burning* to end with this haunting, almost intolerable event. But Coover has added an epilogue. As if to mitigate the effects of
this American nightmare, and to make us, once again, capable of laughing at
the tragic, he returns to the novel's penultimate movement of high farce when
Nixon — on public display with "I am a scamp" painted on his rear, with
his pants tangled around his ankles — seizes the moment and challenges the
American people to drop their pants for America. This call for patriotic display and self-baring, based on the famous "Checkers" speech, touches the
hearts and genitals of the thronging masses, with one exception: Uncle Sam.
In classic debater fashion Nixon then pressures Sam Slick himself to lower his
pants, creating thereby a major blackout (and, in its way, a version of the
bomb itself). This moment of Nixonian hubris is not to be forgotten or par-
doned, and in the final pages of the novel Sam performs on the body of
Richard Nixon his own act of freedom: he sodomizes him.

This scene, gruesome though it is, and distasteful though some may find
it, displays the final transmutation of the elements, the final alchemical trick
that Coover has in store for his readers. Nixon resists heroically, but he yields
at last when Sam threatens to open him with a hatchet: "'*No!*' I shrieked,
giving way. And in he came, filling me with a ripping, all-rupturing force so
fierce I thought I'd die! This . . . this is not happening to me alone, I thought
desperately, or tried to think, as he pounded deeper and deeper, destroying
everything, even my senses, my consciousness — but to the nation as well!"
(659). It is a sublime line, a final audacious transformation of hackneyed
political cliché into American myth, worthy of the classical writers' depictions
of Jove's sexual exploits, conceiving power once again as sexual, showing that
the pastime of the gods is to put it to the nation: Uncle Sam is fucking
America. And with this realization Nixon finally understands the American
presidency: "I recalled Hoover's dazed stare, Roosevelt's anguished tics, Ike's
silly smile: I should have guessed . . . " (660). Here, then, is the final grotesque "incarnation" of power, the final "embodiment of the American will"
that Nixon has been seeking. In proper Rabelaisian spirit Coover closes his
book in explosively corporeal fashion, but, more even than his Renaissance
precursor manages to do, the American novelist displays by his brilliant

"transmutation of the elements" just how open-ended the story of the body politic can be.

Where does a writer go after *The Public Burning*? Fascinating as some of them are, none of the five books Coover published after 1978 has the scope or heft of this American epic. *Spanking the Maid* (1983) is a fastidious postmodern performance, reminiscent of Robbe-Grillet's stylized work, consisting of variations on a motif with a persistent erotic substratum that is never fully brought into play. We encounter again the Coover of "The Magic Poker," and although some critics have seen in this fable the vintage Coover theme of wrestling with the constraints of style and genre—defined now in terms of domestic and erotic routine—the author seems, nonetheless, a thinner, less compelling presence than fans of *The Public Burning* would wish.[19] In 1985 *Gerald's Party* appeared, and with it the master of orgiastic ceremonies reappeared, giving us a party to end all parties. Murder story and metaphysical tale, *Gerald's Party* strives, even more systematically than the book on the Rosenbergs, to achieve simultaneity in fiction. In some ways we are now able to see what "The Babysitter" and "The Elevator" were pointing toward. But no hypercube or numbered sequences are going to be necessary. Sovereignly interweaving the voices of memory, consciousness, and a sprawling array of drunken guests, Coover creates a mix of saturnalia and *Gesamtkunstwerk*; this powerfully erotic book is not for the timid, and it orchestrates sexual intrigue, quick-witted repartee, and bracing vulgarity with a kind of impish zest that has become Coover's trademark. Reminiscent of some of Buñuel's film satires of the bourgeoisie's eating and fornicating rituals, Coover's book has the unremitting close-ups, warts and all, of *Homo americanus ludens*, but larded with lyrical and philosophical gleamings, and, most astoundingly, packaged with a kind of juxtapositional frenzy that fractures all narrative happenings in order to restructure them into a higher syntax of its own. This passage comes at the close, when (1) Gerald and his wife are making love, (2) Gerald's mother-in-law is telling a story to Gerald's son, and (3) Gerald is (also? associatively? "enablingly"?) recalling a past conversation with Alison, after whom he has unsuccessfully lusted during the entire party:

> I gripped her buttocks now, one taut flexing cheek in each hand ("Did she look like you, Gramma?"), feeling the first distant tremors deep in the black hole of my bowels ("A bit . . .") and remembering one night at the theater when, the stage littered with fornicating couples meant to represent the Forms of Rhetoric (the sketch was called "A Meeting of the Minds"), she'd leaned toward me and whispered, "I know they want us to feel time differently here, Gerald, more like an eternal present than the usual past, present, and future, but the only moment that ever works for me is at the end when the lights go down ("No, Peedie doesn't die," her mother was saying, "not yet . . .") and the curtains close. And I'm"—her feet kicked up over my back, crowding her own hands away, so she reached up to clutch my neck and hair—"not sure I like it." "*Great!*" she moaned now, her head tipping back off the edge of the sofa, her back arching, her hips convulsing, and mine too were hammering away, completely ("Don't worry . . .") out of control—it was a kind of pelvic

hilarity, a muscular hiccup (had Pardew compared this to murder?), our
pubes crashing together like remote underwater collisions, as ineluctible as
punchlines. (314)

The gambit here is unmistakably Proustian in its delight in aesthetic query
and composite arrangement, especially in its prodigious efforts to suspend the
moment, to unpack it mentally and verbally and viscerally, and then to fashion
a writerly scaffolding (itself deliciously self-reflexive, as in "ineluctible as
punchlines") that bodies forth this affective cluster with all its teeming life.
We see here a new confidence and poise in using the very typographical conventions of writing itself, a capacity to use quotation marks and parentheses
the way a carpenter uses nails and planks, to craft a narrative utterance that
extends, vertiginously, our reach in time and space. The Coover speech imperative is visible in the fornicating couples who represent the Forms of Rhetoric,
and, indeed, *Gerald's Party* is essentially an effort to create a new, all-
encompassing grammar, a computerlike project of display and retrieval that
maps the semiotic power and the affective density of the body. And yet, for
all its brilliance, Coover's party book does not have the intensity or mythic
resonance of *The Public Burning*. Although both books are meant to be
extravaganzas, the story of the atom spies satisfies us more deeply by the
remarkable congruence of its parts, the uncanny "fit" that it proffers between
cultural history and narrative machinery.

Coover has since published three books: a further installment of Nixoni-
ana, *Whatever Happened to Gloomy Gus of the Chicago Bears?* (1988), which
is presided over by a Saul Bellow–type narrator and displays a serious concern
with the social issues of the 1930s, but nonetheless lacks for the most part the
exuberance and sparkle of his greatest work; *Pinocchio* (1991), a sprawling
mix of fantasy and sacrilege that dishes up the old puppet story in Fellini-like
hues and colors; and, in 1987, *A Night at the Movies*, which I take to be his
most unmoored, brilliant, and inventive book to date, the text that will bring
my discussion of Coover to a close. Building on the 3-D sequence from *The
Public Burning*, Coover proposes here nothing less than a tribute to the most
popular art of our time — film — and he then goes on to abscond with the
jewels, to poach shamelessly in the great filmic preserve, to show that the
fabulous technical possibilities of film (dissolve, panning, cutting, montage)
have, must have, for the writer obsessed with the Forms of Rhetoric, their
verbal counterparts. Knowing Coover's appetite for experiment and his imperialist view of language as expressive medium, we might have expected him
sooner or later to "do" a "film book." But who would have thought that his
takeover from film to language could have the sheer brilliance and exploratory
reach that it does? Not only has he explored the exotic, escapist, and "bovaris-
tic" dimensions of film — the sort of thing Woody Allen has done within the
genre with *The Purple Rose of Cairo* — but he has made film *speak*, shown it
to be an expressive medium beyond our wildest dreams. Hence, *Top Hat* is
stupefyingly translated into a sociopolitical meditation on the individual versus the group, and those scenes of Fred Astaire soloing "against" the troupe
of dancers and "gunning them down" with his cane will never look the same

to anyone who has read Coover. His rare gift for discerning rhetorical power, for seeing gestural eloquence where the rest of us see mere motion, becomes, in fact, a rare gift for his readers because it expands their perceptual scheme, endows *seeing* with the kind of wit and intelligibility that most of us find only in language. This is doubtless a generational argument, and the people who "grew up" on the movies have a visual literacy and sense of discrimination that remains, for older folks, language-bound. Be that as it may, *seeing* is so automatic, so taken for granted and "given," that there is something uncommonly handsome and enriching in this book, as if we were being helped, through Coover's language vision, to special lenses, to a picture of higher definition, to a more articulated and refined awareness of what our eyes process.

But Coover has, characteristically, other, more unsettling, gifts in mind for us. "Charlie in the House of Rue" begins by presenting Chaplin's inimitable maneuvers and sight gags, and Coover is miraculously able to deliver Chaplin's dance verbally, to make us see—because we are reading it—just how intricate and exquisitely modulated these comic routines are. Charlie blows his nose on tapestry, doffs his derby to a suit of armor, takes a cigar, offers one to the armor, peers in the visor, drops it, finds the edge of his cigar chopped off, reopens the visor, tosses a lighted cigar into it. Quickly enough, however, the game gets more complicated, as Charlie finds, much the way the man with the 3-D glasses found, that the setting is both bizarre—a maid who twinkles her behind at him, an old man pouring an eternal drink, a beautiful lady hanging, a policeman striking at ducks in a bathtub—and, worse still, mobile and metamorphosing. Out of his normal orbit, like Nixon at Sing Sing, Charlie too experiences a prodigious freedom, but it is invested entirely in the environment, as though he had strayed into the precincts of the atom, with the energy understood to be libidinal as well as physical. The episode with the maid perfectly illustrates the Coover procedure: "Charlie pulls himself painfully to his feet and, in a rage, hurls himself at her, but even as he plunges it is into darkness as again the lights go out. . . . She pops out, legs spread, and whipping her bodice open, flashes her breasts at him. They glow in the gathering dimness as though lit from within, pimpled by dark little nipples like pupils of frightened cartoon eyes" (105). As Charlie seeks ever more frantically to get out of this erotic trap, all the devices of Coover's style trip him up: he flees, but into a mirror; he threatens her with the cane, and she invites it with her backside; the room darkens and brightens, "her eyes sparkling, her flesh glowing, the black patch of pubic hair winking at him from behind the fluttering white apron like the negative of a sputtering lightbulb" (105). He finally exits, but into a closet, thumps against the wall, and

falls back in a thick bind of knotted gowns and petticoats, straddled by the grinning maid. He clambers to his feet, losing his derby between her squeezing thighs, and tries to escape, but she backs him up against the wall and, standing on his trousers, rips his shorts away. He opens his mouth to cry out: she stuffs it full with one of her plump breasts, then pushing his derby down around his ears, her knee jammed between his legs, commences to trim away his little moustache with the scissors. He closes his eyes, shudders: the maid slips and the scissors jabs his nostrils. He gasps in pain and seems to get the maid's breast caught in his throat. He staggers about, gagging and snorting, crashing into things, taking pratfalls, dragging the startled maid with him. Tears are streaming down his puffed-out cheeks. The maid is pushing on his face, hanging on to his ears, prying at his jaws, her own mouth agape with torment and effort. At last the breast pops free and they fall apart, somersaulting away from one another as though spring-loaded. The maid, clutching her breast, crawls over by the dressing table, tears clouding her darkly lined eyes. Her belly has gone soft, the soles of her feet are dirty, her hair is snarled. (105–6)

Seen against the earlier "straight" passages of Chaplinesque, this episode explodes with surprises and broken promises, new vistas, and uncharted realms. We recall that Artaud discerned revolutionary anarchy in the Marx brothers, and we can assume that Coover "reads" Chaplin in a comparably violent fashion. But there is more to it than that: Charlie is in the House of Rue, and Coover intends to cut Poe in with the American comic, to work the 3-D scheme again, not with separate lenses but with separate fables, importing a bit of Sade as well into the act, cunningly using and undermining the conventions of each set, brilliantly exposing what they "conceal" by dint of his crossings. Hence, the assured comic routine of the little man takes him into deep waters, and we see a parable of American innocence in trouble, as the erotic energies of this coupling drama sweep its players all about the stage in a virtual mimicry of the earlier pratfalls and comic routines. It is vintage Coover, too, in its vision of sexual assault, of potential castration and powerlessness (think of how many Coover protagonists are trapped with their pants down or, worse still, literally caught in the act, as Gerald is, when he is unable to withdraw his penis from Sally Ann, who has "seized" on him), of the hilarious and figural antics performed by little players caught up in elemental forces.[20] Ultimately this episode closes as a parable about desire, about the spending of one's energies, about the fuel that makes Chaplin go, that brings us to the cinema. Coover's improbable conflations and syntheses — Chaplin and Poe as a pair? — seem to be the whimsical antics of a comparatist flexing his muscles (turning literary history into vaudeville), a writer for whom nothing remains single or discrete, for whom all events, all acts (cultural, political, sexual) can, if handled right, disclose their indwelling grammar.

No account of Coover is complete without some mention of his "supreme fiction" to date, "You Must Remember This," the astounding remake of *Casablanca* which completes *A Night at the Movies*. Coover's gambit is quite simple here: he focuses on the scene in which Rick (Bogart) returns to his room to find Ilsa (Bergman) waiting for him. In the film this is their great romantic reunion, their "recovery" of Paris, and it makes possible the gallant ending of noble resignation and high idealism. Coover has elected to "unpack" this scene and to fill in a crucial narrative ellipsis by offering his readers what the film has genteelly omitted: the mix of dialogue, memory, and sexual acrobatics enacted by Rick and Ilsa. Capitalizing on Bogart's tough-guy sentimentalism and Bergman's Scandinavian accent, Coover fashions a farcical yet intensely moving and provocative story about freedom of speech. What is most captivating about this piece is its wise knowledge of its own textual status, its prior scripts, displayed through continuous ironic references to the tower light, the "Marseillaise," the underground (consider "She slides her thighs between his and squeezes his penis between them, as though to conceal it there, an underground member on the run, wounded but unbowed" [163]). The players' awareness of their "roles," of the always/already written drama of which they are a part, makes this story a sustained, often lyrical meditation about freedom, about breaking through time and space.

Lovemaking, as we've come to expect in Coover, emerges as the quest par excellence, the ur-exploration that works through sensorial and cerebral associations to discover and to recover the past. Thus, Coover will have Ilsa reexperience her Nordic childhood and Rick his Parisian idyll through the good offices of their spectacular coupling bouts, and, to top it off, he will "write" this episode filmically as well, as an affair of getting between the frames. In so doing, Coover produces some of the most adventurous writing of our century, writing that is so ambitious, so "cocky," so committed to taking on all endeavors and making them into speech that he now rivals with sex itself, finding, no doubt, in the machinery of ecstasy, in the dynamics of desire and pleasure and orgasm, a more humane and life-sustaining analogue for atomic fission:

> He douses his cigarette in the wet towel, tosses it aside, wraps his arms around her thighs and pulls her buttocks (he is still thinking about time as a pulsing sequence of film frames, and not so much about the frames, their useless dated content, as the gaps between: infinitesimally small when looked at two-dimensionally, yet in their third dimension as deep and mysterious as the cosmos) toward his face, pressing against them like a child trying to see through a foggy window. He kisses and nibbles at each fresh-washed cheek (and what if one were to slip *between* two of those frames? he wonders—), runs his tongue into (—where would he be then?) her anus, kneading the flesh on her pubic knoll between his fingers all the while like little lumps of still taffy. She raises one knee up onto the cushions, then the other, lowering her elbows to the floor (oh! she thinks as the blood rushes in two directions at once, spreading into her head and sex as though filling empty frames, her heart the gap between: what a strange dizzying dream time is!), thus lifting to his contemplative scrutiny what looks like a clinging sea anemone between her thighs, a thick woolly pod, a cloven chinchilla, open purse, split fruit. But it is not the appearance of it that moves him (except to the invention of these fanciful catalogues), it is the smell. It is this which catapults him suddenly and wholly back to Paris, a Paris he'd lost until this moment (she is not in Paris, she is in some vast dimensionless region she associates with childhood, a nighttime glow in her midsummer room, featherbedding between her legs) but now has back again. (173–74)

Saluting and parodying Proust, Coover presents ecstasy as a breaking out of the here and now, with the risk of self-annihilation as well. Ilsa, "unsure of who or what she is," wonders, "Is she one person, several—or no one at all?," wonders, "hugging Richard's hairy cheeks (are they Richard's? are they

cheeks?)" (179). We are not so far from the bomb-world of *The Public Burning*, and once again we see that the exercise of human freedom can be a
vertiginous affair, that it can blast you free—for a moment—from prior
scripts, including the armature that makes you "you." We may feel the shadow
of Borges here, the supreme metaphysician of the self in the labyrinth, but the
drama/challenge of metamorphosis is as old as Ovid, and Coover himself has
signaled his debt to the Roman writer.[21] Yes, it is all protean, within and
without, but the Forms are prior: shifting, tumbling, fictive, but prior. Whereas the historical record proved immovable, unalterable in the Rosenberg story,
Coover the modern Quixote is tilting against the actual film script this time,
the fixed parameters and frames that originally gave life to Rick and Ilsa.
And we understand that their spontaneous lovemaking tripped the circuits,
pulled them out of the loop, and now they need to return. All the other
characters are waiting for them. But everything is, as always, in motion; the
doorway has been moved, and that's not all: "Who the hell rearranged the—
ungh!—goddamn geography?" (187).

Both free and bound, like so many American figures studied in this book,
they have to make their peculiar covenant with determinism and come to
terms with history, time, and space. Creatures of culture, textualized, they
have slipped out of their moorings for a brief ecstatic time, but now their
reentry is awaited so that The End can take place. They—even they—cannot
fornicate forever, but they still have language at their disposal, allowing them
their special say, their own utterance within the web that enmeshes them. So
they return, rivaling through their "private" story the story that frames them.
Ilsa makes her special bid for fixity:

> "Richard, it's a crazy world . . . "
> . . . .
> "But wherever you are . . . "
> . . . .
> " . . . Whatever happens . . . "
> . . . .
> " . . . I want you to know . . . "
> . . . .
> " . . . I luff you . . . " (187)

And each of these utterances is coupled by Rick's efforts to keep it moving, to
make more story: "*And then*—?"

And that is how it closes: " . . . And then . . . Ilsa . . . ? And *then* . . . "
(187).

"I luff you" and "And then?" are the two basic forms of human continuity
and human transcendence. Love, we have always known, can be ecstatic and
liberating, allowing us to come into our estate and to enter that of others.
Storytelling—"And *then*?"—is also, we now see, in its way, ecstatic, because
it too takes us out of the phenomenal world and creates its own order, its own
special triumph over endings, its freedom of speech.

13

Dis-Membering and Re-Membering in Toni Morrison's *Beloved*

Toni Morrison's novel *Beloved* serves as a virtual culmination to this study of freedom of speech in American literature. Her book on the trauma of slavery, endowed with the kind of searing power that we find in narratives that have come from survivors of the camps in our own age, rewrites a large chunk of our literary history, and she provides thereby a strange second look at much that we think we have seen.

Beloved has unmistakable echoes of Stowe's great book on slavery, and it is possible to read the modern text as a continued meditation on Stowe's two major themes: the mother-child connection that cannot be broken, and the piecing apart of the human family. But whereas Stowe packages her vision in the conventions of sentimental fiction and stereotypical characters, Morrison's text radically subverts traditional narrative form and even more radically calls into question our notion of character and the project of self-representation. Thus, if we reconsider Melville's spectral portrait of Bartleby, especially his maddening "emptiness" and vacancy, we see what a leisurely, almost free-floating creation Melville has given us, particularly when juxtaposed against the "tactical" emptiness of Morrison's people, a kind of willed amnesia that alone enables them to survive the trauma of their slave past. Going still further back, back to the beginning of this book, we note that Hawthorne's parable of self-making, as figured in the bizarre career of Wakefield, has elements of volition and control, even an aura of whimsical *experiment*, that are unthinkable in the hounded lives of Morrison's figures. Twain's *Puddn'head Wilson*, likewise, looks a bit different when seen from the *éclairage* of *Beloved*: his individualist fantasia of swapped (male) babies and remade identities and his meditation on power as performance show for the masculine enterprises they are. The libidinal reservoirs of energy that the white male Twain can only disguise and sublimate are, however, the very nexus of *Beloved*, and nothing better illustrates their respective terrains than the famous Twain dream already cited:

In my dream last night I was suddenly in the presence of a negro wench who was sitting in grassy open country, with her left arm resting on the arm of one of those long park-sofas that are made of broad slats with cracks between, & a curve-over back. She was very vivid to me—round black face, shiny black eyes, thick lips, very white regular teeth showing through her smile. She was about 22, & plump—not fleshy, not fat, merely rounded & plump; & good-natured & not at all bad-looking. She had but one garment on—a coarse tow-linen shirt that reached from her neck to her ankles without a break. She sold me a pie; a mushy apple pie—hot. She was eating one herself with a tin teaspoon. She made a disgusting proposition to me. Although it was disgusting it did not surprise me—for I was young (I was never old in a dream yet) & it seemed quite natural that it should come from her. It was disgusting, but I did not say so; I merely made a chaffing remark, brushing aside the matter— a little jeeringly—& this embarrassed her & she made an awkward pretence that I had misunderstood her. I made a sarcastic remark about this pretence, & asked for a spoon to eat my pie with. She had but the one, & she took it out of her mouth, in a quite matter-of-course way, & offered it to me. My stomach rose—there everything vanished.[1]

Here is Twain's repressed dream material: the commonality of food and sex, the repressed and twisted oedipal fixation with the nurturing black mother, the white (southern) male association of such sexual and maternal plenitude with blacks, the censoring and sublimating devices needed if such material is to be cargoed at all ("disgusting," and so on). One could argue that a great deal of *Beloved* is discernible in this libidinal cluster: nurturance is to be its great theme, and the mouth-to-mouth intimacy that Twain cannot stomach is unforgettably rendered in Morrison's story of female bonding.

But the American writer whose work is reconceived in *Beloved* has got to be William Faulkner. All of Faulkner's major novels take a curtain call: from the dying mother of *As I Lay Dying* to the birthing baby of *Light in August*, from the claustrophobic family tragedy of *The Sound and the Fury* to the Civil War epic of *Absalom, Absalom!*, Morrison works and reworks the Faulknerian material, and in so doing she makes us see ever more clearly the whiteness and the maleness of the Faulkner oeuvre. Whereas Lena Grove's baby is the freedom principle incarnate, Morrison shows us that birthing is hard, that babies can be maimed and murdered, that they can become ghosts every bit as imperious as the old ancestors who usurp the minds of Faulkner's people. Even where Faulkner is at his greatest, in the capsizing of a mind such as Quentin's or Darl's, in the "overpass to love" that recaptures the lost past in *Absalom*, Morrison is pressing him hard, adding urgency and cultural density to his themes by presenting the retrieval of the slave past as something so unbearable, so annihilating, that transgressions uncovered in the House of Sutpen seem almost benign in comparison with the barbarisms suffered by nineteenth-century blacks.

And the list could go on: the capitalist fantasy of self-creation in *Gatsby* shines with privilege—both white and male—when measured against the despotic social and psychic schemes of *Beloved*; the entrapment of Winesburg is leisurely when juxtaposed against the various *huis clos* of Morrison's text; even the polymorphous perversity that Hemingway unleashes in *The Garden of Eden* pales beside the ferocity of the mother-daughter bind in *Beloved*.

Finally, Morrison's novel belongs in the company of the other contemporary texts under discussion because, appearances notwithstanding, they have common cause: the dark libidinal energies of the father-daughter relation in Hawkes are recast and regendered here; the sanctity of the family against the stresses of a world that is wildly energized links her to DeLillo; the effort to work language into the kind of play that could offset the tragedy of history has common ground with Coover's *Public Burning*. In every one of these cases language is called on to perform heroics: not merely to depict the events at hand but to fashion a verbal power over them or an exit from them or an alternative to them. We shall see that *Beloved*, too, looks to language as a genuine way out of the labyrinth, but it is to be a special language, an *écriture féminine* that reassembles the broken pieces of the human enterprise — broken bodies, broken families, broken selves — in its bid for integrity.[2]

Beloved is Toni Morrison's effort to remember and to retrieve the forgotten ones, *los olvidados*. Beloved's was "not a story to pass on," we read as a triple refrain in the book's final pages, and Morrison herself has described her task as "assuming responsibility for people no one's ever assumed responsibility for. They are those that died en route. Nobody knows their names, and nobody thinks about them. In addition to that, they never survived in the lore. . . . I suspect the reason is that it was not possible to survive on certain levels and dwell on it. People who did dwell on it, it probably killed them. . . ."[3] But this view of the lost ones as simply vanished and unstoried is misleading in one key respect, for Morrison's ghosts refuse to turn over and die. *Beloved* is filled with unquiet graves, and her revisionist history of nineteenth-century America is downright choral in its orchestration of angry voices from the past. Paul D gets a job in a Cincinnati slaughterhouse, but the terrain he traverses is measured vertically, temporally, so that we hear the old story of usurpation:

> A route that took him smack dab through the middle of a cemetery as old as sky, rife with the agitation of dead Miami no longer content to rest in the mounds that covered them. Over their heads walked a strange people; through their earth pillows roads were cut; wells and houses nudged them out of eternal rest. Outraged more by their folly in believing land was holy than by the disturbances of their peace, they growled on the banks of Licking River, sighed in the trees on Catherine Street and rode the wind above the pig yards.[4]

Here is the Morrison cosmos. Everything in it is living and vocal, and the people under the earth are ceaselessly active — perhaps ceaselessly passive would say it better — because their abuse knows no end; but they have acquired voice, and the elements speak their violation, make their sorrow and anger known to those who walk over them.

We know that Morrison grew up in a family that believed in multiple registers and channels of expression; according to Nellie McKay, her "grandfather played the violin, her mother sang in the choir and decoded dream symbols, and there were signs, visitations, and ways of knowing that transcended concrete reality. Storytelling, especially of ghost stories, was shared activity for the men and women in her family."⁵ The logic of ghosts is wonderfully pure. It announces that spirit is real, outlives flesh, and refuses to be silenced. It is the very voice of history, the stubborn vocal evidence that others preceded us, that we despoiled them, that we too were Other and have despoiled ourselves. Ghosts announce that nothing is ever over. They are a strident language of permanency that punctures the here and now, keeps the wounds bleeding, shows what awful material "progress" is made of, brings unwelcome tidings. For white readers this novel can be hard going. The history that Morrison wants to tell in *Beloved* is so strewn with corpses and atrocities that we can hardly be surprised by the phantom afterlife. Paul D reflects on the damages he has seen:

> During, before and after the War he had seen Negroes so stunned, or hungry, or tired or bereft it was a wonder they recalled or said anything. Who, like him, had hidden in caves and fought owls for food; who, like him, stole from pigs; who, like him, slept in trees in the day and walked by night; who, like him, had buried themselves in slop and jumped in wells to avoid regulators, raiders, paterollers, veterans, hill men, posses and merrymakers. Once he met a Negro about fourteen years old who lived in the woods and said he couldn't remember living anywhere else. He saw a witless colored woman jailed and hanged for stealing ducks she believed were her own babies. (66)

Note how it all converges: the physical deprivation, the ubiquitous threat, the becoming invisible, and finally the "*dérèglement de tous les sens*": vacated memory, ducks for children. We hear of Aunt Phyllis, who sleeps with her eyes open, and Jackson Till, who sleeps under the bed (97). Stamp Paid gives us perhaps the crowning panoramic description of the ravages of war, the injuries suffered by blacks:

> Eighteen seventy-four and whitefolks were still on the loose. Whole towns wiped clean of Negroes; eighty-seven lynchings one year alone in Kentucky; four colored schools burned to the ground; grown men whipped like children; children whipped like adults; black women raped by the crew; property taken, necks broken, he smelled skin, skin and hot blood. The skin was one thing, but human blood cooked in a lynch fire was a whole other thing. . . . But none of that had worn out his marrow. None of that. It was the ribbon. Tying his flatbed up on the bank of the Licking River, securing it the best he could, he caught sight of something red on its bottom. Reaching for it, he thought it was a cardinal feather stuck to his boat. He tugged and what came loose in his hand was a red ribbon knotted around a curl of wet woolly hair, clinging still to its bit of scalp. (180)

This, for Stamp Paid, is close to the breaking point. But we are to understand that this extraordinary history of abuse and genocide will not be silent or acquiescent. When Stamp feels strangely rebuffed each time he tries to enter Sethe's house, he finally understands what is in there: "The people of broken necks, of fire-cooked blood and black girls who had lost their ribbons" (181). And they speak: "What a roaring" (181). The events at 124 are both luminous and resonant, and in them Morrison has told a story that voices the pain of thousands. That is why the first line of the novel (and Morrison packs a lot into her first lines)—"124 was spiteful. Full of a baby's venom"—only looks particularized.[6] By the time we have finished this novel, we feel what Baby Suggs meant when she admonished Sethe: "Not a house in the country ain't packed to its rafters with some dead Negro's grief. We lucky this ghost is a baby" (5). This venomous baby ghost is a dreadful inversion of the child Lena Grove delivers in *Light in August*; Faulkner's infant—nameless, freed from origin—brings life and freedom into the death-haunted community, makes possible the fashioning of a new family. But this baby is drenched with history and spilled blood, and Morrison's novel is about the enduring spell it casts on the living.

The book opens with a spiteful baby ghost, and it closes with the exit of Beloved, full-grown and ready to deliver, disappearing into the stream behind 124. The life cycle is displayed here in all its plenitude, from the spirit of the dead child to its fleshly embodiment all the way into motherhood itself, with its promise of birth and starting anew. But we know as well that this entry into the phenomenal world of flesh is shadowed by unreality and mystery, that this is the story of a "haint," one of those "unknown ones" whose life must be the subject of fiction rather than history; and thus Beloved's fate, like that of the unquiet Miami who groan under the earth that white men trod on and build up, leaves the memory of men and enters the elements: "The rest is weather. Not the breath of the disremembered and unaccounted for, but wind in the eaves, or spring ice thawing too quickly. Just weather" (275). The serenity of these final lines beautifully seals Morrison's novel, but that is possible only because the ghost has been delivered, the roar of all that collective misery and suffering has finally been heard. That baby's venom is narrative itself: the stories, the unspeakable past, must be told, exorcised, if there is to be peace; until then the unquiet dead will growl and sigh, and the denied ghosts will tear the place up, much the way 124 is terrorized by the virulence of its dictatorial haint.

Thus we hear, in spurts and unwillingly, sometimes as release, sometimes as hemorrhage, of the old wounds, of the scar tissue that is not quite dead. Morrison displays, in freighting this repressed material to us, a narrative brilliance that nothing in her earlier work quite points to.[7] Paul D arrives at 124 with shared memories of Sweet Home, with unforgotten desire for Sethe, and it takes his embrace, his "cradling" of Sethe's breasts, his caress of the branches in her back become a chokecherry tree, for the story to begin to emerge. Sethe recounts the saga of leaving Sweet Home six months pregnant, of sending the two boys and the baby girl on ahead, of having her milk taken by Schoolteacher's two boys, of having her back turned into a tree because she told Mrs. Garner what the boys had done. But, even in their horror, these events initially come across as flat, as over and done; only later will we understand the fullness of these acts, a fullness consisting of the meaning of milk, the premature birth of the infant, Denver, the whereabouts of Halle during the boys' violation of Sethe, and the final crowning events on the "other side" with Baby Suggs and the murder of Sethe's child. Much the way

Faulkner does in *Absalom*, Morrison cunningly withholds information, lets the reader absorb bits and pieces before realizing their larger pattern or significance; but unlike in Faulkner, the logic for withholding is not aesthetic but self-preservative, as if too much disclosure, too much density, would be lethal to the teller. Paul D keeps the story of Halle and butter to himself, for a while at least, just as he only later tells Sethe about his prison ordeal in Alfred, Georgia. Denver, alone of the characters, dwells lovingly on the past, but it is a highly selective rememoration, involving the events of her own birth; she never tires of rehearsing Sethe's account of the white girl, Amy Denver, and her miraculous intervention in the birth of herself, the "little antelope" that wants out from the mother's bloody, swollen body.

These stories, these highly edited stories, are sharable, and the telling of them is intimate and bonding. But they are the tip of the iceberg, and the mission of *Beloved*/Beloved is to move into the deeper and darker reaches, to reclaim large areas that have been placed off-limits, to restore full circulation to a system that has been grievously blocked and clogged. Perhaps this arterial image best conveys the systemic and somatic nature of Morrison's enterprise, and nothing better exemplifies this drama of infusion and flow than Amy's massaging of Sethe's monstrously swollen feet, an act of tenderness and vitality that is almost unbearably painful, making Sethe cry "salt tears" (35). "It's gonna hurt, now," Amy tells Sethe, because "anything dead coming back to life hurts" (35). The whole book is imaged in these lines—the project of rememoration, the mutation of dead tissue into living flesh, the pain, the rhythmic coupling of bodies in an act of love—and we begin to see just what kind of a new narrative discourse Morrison has created. Love alone sanctions and makes possible disclosure, and even then it might kill. Consider this exchange between Sethe and Paul D:

> "Maybe I should leave things the way they are," she said.
> "How are they?"
> "We get along."
> "What about inside?"
> "I don't go inside."
> "Sethe, if I'm here with you, with Denver, you can go anywhere you want. Jump, if you want to, 'cause I'll catch you, girl. I'll catch you 'fore you fall. Go as far inside as you need to, I'll hold your ankles. . . . " (46)

"Going inside" is tantamount to speleology or tightrope walking: you could fall, you might never come back, you don't go unless somebody is holding on to you.

Paul D enters the novel as a man who "had shut down a generous portion of his head" (41), and his response to trauma—to close up shop—is well-nigh generic in this text. His experiences are stored not in his mind or heart but in "the tobacco tin lodged in his chest" (113), and "by the time he got to 124 nothing in this world could pry it open" (113). The case of Denver is even more acute: she simply went deaf when a schoolmate asked her whether her mother had, what?—been in jail? murdered the baby girl?—and we sense that her body turned off, blew a fuse, because this question contains the greatest threat of all: maybe Sethe will murder her too, something that her brothers also feared and finally could not live with. This episode from the past and this possible threat in the future cannot be faced; a sizable chunk of Denver's life is "un-ownable." The normal state of life for these people, we begin to see, is akin to autism. To live at all, they have had to sign off from their past, from themselves.

We are made to realize that this state of permanent severance is instanced, above all, in the plight of the family. Baby Suggs had eight children, and every one of them was taken away: "Four taken, four chased, and all, I expect, worrying somebody's house into evil" (5). She claims she cannot remember: "My first-born. All I can remember of her is how she loved the burned bottom of bread. Can you beat that? Eight children and that's all I remember" (5). Sethe answers her, "That's all you let yourself remember" (5), but we can see that the loss of memory is the birth of ghosts, that the absent children are operative as spirits. Like the amputated limb that still throbs, the ghosts assert the continuum of what has been severed. Paul D thinks he rids 124 of its spiteful ghost, but Beloved materializes in response.

With utterly graphic logic Morrison gives us a world that is defined entirely in terms of human dismemberment: the body is pieced apart, the family is divided, the subject is cut off from its past. Baby Suggs preaches the plaint of dismemberment:

> "Here," she said, "in this here place, we flesh; flesh that weeps, laughs; flesh that dances on bare feet in grass. Love it. Love it hard. Yonder they do not love your flesh. They despise it. They don't love your eyes; they'd just as soon pick em out. No more do they love the skin on your back. Yonder they flay it. And O my people they do not love your hands. Those they only use, tie, bind, chop off and leave empty. Love your hands! Love them. Raise them up and kiss them. Touch others with them, pat them together, stroke them on your face, 'cause they don't love that either. *You* got to love it, *you*! And no, they ain't in love with your mouth. Yonder, out there, they will see it broken and break it again. What you say out of it they will not heed. What you scream from it they do not hear. What you put into it to nourish your body they will snatch away and give you leavins instead. No, they don't love your mouth. *You* got to love it. This is flesh I'm talking about here. Flesh that needs to be loved. Feet that need to rest and to dance; backs that need support; shoulders that need arms, strong arms I'm telling you. And O my people, out yonder, hear me, they do not love your neck unnoosed and straight. So love your neck; put a hand on it, grace it, stroke it and hold it up. And all your inside parts that they'd just as soon slop for hogs, you got to love them. The dark, dark liver — love it, love it, and the beat and beating heart, love that too. More than eyes or feet. More than lungs that have yet to draw free air. More than your life-holding womb and your life-giving private parts, hear me now, love your heart. For this is the prize." (88–89)

Affirming the body amounts to re-membering it, putting its pieces back together in spite of the system that fragments and abuses it, and only love can accomplish such wholeness. We see at once that this act of re-membering, of "ownership," is mental and temporal as well, signifies the possession of one's disparate parts by means of memory, and this too is possible only through love, because only love makes such possession bearable in the face of the mutilations the body has endured. "Over yonder" in the world the black person is dismembered, in body and in psyche. Over there "definitions belonged to the definers" (190), and this familiar dictum of ideological criticism—the control of discourse is effectively the exercise of power—is given a shockingly carnal expression, brought home to us (as readers) in the flesh. Thus the pieces of the black body can be redefined, remade: collars can redesign your posture; bits can be put into your mouth to give you a permanent smile; the body can be redistributed so that what is hanging in the trees has "Paul A's shirt on but not his feet or his head" (198). Beloved's recurrent nightmare is that she will fall apart: "Pieces of her would drop maybe one at a time, maybe all at once" (133). She has two dreams: "exploding and being swallowed" (133). This world of fragmentation and anarchy reifies and atomizes the black subject, turns him or her into merchandise. Paul D is forced to discover the "dollar value of his weight, his strength, his heart, his brain, his penis and his future" (226).

Morrison, like Stowe, has seen slavery to be a denial of the human family, but she has, as it were, "gone inside" as well, and given us a close-up view of the psyche every bit as sundered and plundered as the body. The freedom that ultimately counts, in Morrison's scheme, is in the aftermath, on the far side of escape; it is a matter of putting together, Humpty Dumpty–like, what has been taken apart, an arduous, almost Frankensteinian process of self-assemblage, a coming into one's own true estate as owner rather than slave. That is what Baby Suggs discovers when she finally gets to the "other side" and sets foot on free ground: "Something's the matter. What's the matter? What's the matter? she asked herself. She didn't know what she looked like and was not curious. But suddenly she saw her hands and thought with a clarity as simple as it was dazzling, 'These hands belong to me. These *my* hands.' Next she felt a knocking in her chest and discovered something else new: her own heartbeat. Had it been there all along? This pounding thing?" (141). This itinerary of proprietorship culminates in language: Baby Suggs tells Garner, for the first time, that she is not Jenny, that she is Baby Suggs, that she has a name independent of the slave commerce. In slavery definitions belong to the definers; in freedom the subject defines himself or herself. Baby's experience of self-ownership is close to genesis: in the dazzling light of autofecundation she becomes a person, assumes her appendages and organs as her own, announces her name, achieves, lame though she is, wholeness. Slavery not only reifies and atomizes the subject; it eradicates all notions of possession and integrity and turns the black person into a list of parts, all belonging to someone else, outfitted with a label that is also provided by someone else. "My niggers is men," Garner brags, but we see their victimization in the very tags they go under—Paul A, Paul D, Paul F—and we are not surprised when Paul D agonizes about his manhood, experiences his drastic lack of autonomy and integrity as a series of parts, is sexually humbled by the rooster of Sweet Home, appropriately named Mister. Morrison is illuminating the reaches of alienation and dispossession brought on by slavery, the extent to which the subject can be despoiled and invaded, can lose all sense of dignity.

That is why the moments of self-possession are so moving in this text. Baby's creed of loving and re-membering is one such instance. Even more luminous is the coupling of Paul D and Beloved, because this blatantly "inappropriate" lovemaking—in any conventional sense it would be betrayal—is presented as a dark, elemental current that cannot be resisted, a force that *moves* Paul D and betokens union in more ways than one: union of the sundered self, of name and body, of blocked past and present state. "I want you to touch me on the inside part and call me my name" (116), Beloved orders Paul D, and when he does, it is his own choked and dead life that comes back to life: "'Beloved.' He said it, but she did not go. She moved closer with a footfall he didn't hear and he didn't hear the whisper that the flakes of rust made either as they fell away from the seams of his tobacco tin. So when the lid gave he didn't know it. What he knew was that when he reached the inside part he was saying, 'Red heart, Red heart,' over and over again. Softly and then so loud it woke Denver, then Paul D himself. 'Red heart. Red heart. Red heart'" (117). With this passage we are at the center of the novel's mystery. Here we see the miraculous view of love that Morrison has presented, a love that at once unites and restores lovers to themselves by means of a generosity and a need so great that the dead limbs come to life, the blood flows again, the "beat and beating" heart is rediscovered and reexperienced, and the name and the body are united. Sexual fusion acquires here the power of a blood transfusion, of opening clogged arteries, of lifesaving. "Red heart" moves out of sentimental and psychological discourse to become a cardiac term, used to denote the creatural pulse and flow of the living body. Finally, it is of crucial importance that Beloved herself makes possible this opening of circuits, for that is precisely the pivotal structural role that she is to play throughout the novel: to *move* others, to be the fluid principle of linkage and connection, to bond.

Beloved is the red heart of the novel, the "returnee" from "over there" who re-fuses what violence and death have sundered. One remembers the ecstatic moment of bonding enacted by Quentin and Shreve in *Absalom*, the moment when four boys ride two horses into the war of another century, and they do so by shedding their names and faces and navigating the great Faulknerian waterway, "the blood, the immortal brief recent intransient blood." It is as if Morrison had set out to literalize Faulkner's metaphors, to drench her story of "flesh upon flesh" with real blood, to endow the ghost of the past with ravenous hunger, to bypass the theme of empathy and move directly into that of fusion. Beloved's return reestablishes the broken circuits, makes us see by her very presence the central act of violence at the core of things (again as in *Absalom*) and the incredible overpass that is at hand. Beloved's entry onto the scene is narrative magic because it brings out into the open the great hidden trauma that has been repressed: Sethe's murder of her baby girl. Whereas Faulkner works his way finally into the fateful disclosure of Thomas Sutpen to Henry that Charles Bon, his brother, is black, Morrison moves magisterially into the scene of the murder, starting with the arrival of the four horsemen and narrating it from their perspective: Stamp as a "crazy old nigger . . . in the woodpile with an ax . . . grunting—making low, cat noises like," and inside the shed

> two boys bled in the sawdust and dirt at the feet of a nigger woman holding a blood-soaked child to her chest with one hand and an infant by the heels in the other. She did not look at them; she simply swung the baby toward the wall planks, missed and tried to connect a second time, when out of nowhere—in the ticking time the men spent staring at what there was to stare at—the old nigger boy, still mewing, ran through the door behind them and snatched the baby from the arch of its mother's swing. (149)

Here is the novel's secret, the hitherto unseen curse of the past that has accounted for everything we have encountered: the haunted house, the venomous baby ghost, Baby Suggs's decline, Sethe's status as pariah, Denver's autism. For the whites the scene is unreadable: schoolteacher, pragmatist that he is, recognizes, quickly enough, that "there was nothing here to claim," that the "pickaninnies they had hoped were alive and well enough to take back to Kentucky, take back and raise properly to do the work Sweet Home desperately needed, were not" (149). The nephew stares in disbelief, shakes uncontrollably, asks over and over: "What she want to go and do that for?" (150). At last out in the open, this scene is delivered blatantly as scene, as spectacle defying interpretation. Thus, Morrison stresses eyes:

> They [schoolteacher, nephew, and slave catcher] didn't look at the woman in the pepper plants with the flower in her hat. And they didn't look at the seven or so faces that had edged closer in spite of the catcher's rifle warning. Enough nigger eyes for now. Little nigger-boy eyes open in sawdust; little nigger-girl eyes staring between the wet fingers that held her face so her head wouldn't fall off; little nigger-baby eyes crinkling up to cry in the arms of the old nigger whose own eyes were nothing but slivers looking down at his feet. But the worst ones were those of the nigger woman who looked like she didn't have any. Since the whites in them had disappeared and since they were as black as her skin, she looked blind. (150)

Sethe's murder of her child is the primal scene in *Beloved*, the originary event that has maimed or arrested every life connected with it. It is what is waiting "inside," and we now see why Sethe prefers not to go in. It cannot be looked upon: Buglar and Howard will never get over it; Stamp's eyes turn into slivers; Sethe's disappear altogether, making her look blind, making her blind. Now, eighteen years later, the scene must be seen again. The reader confronts it for the first time. Paul D looks at the photo of Sethe/murderess. Stamp's own memory of the event now comes to us, a memory of how Sethe "flew, snatching up her children like a hawk on the wing; how her face beaked, how her hands worked like claws" (157). First depicted as blind, now transformed into wild bird of prey, Sethe is moving out of the precincts of realist fiction, taking on the attributes of legend. Our final angle on the infanticide comes from Sethe herself, as Paul D questions the circling, spinning woman, and we hear of a truth so simple and elemental that it is at one with the growling Miami, the sighing wind, and the spring ice thawing:

> Simple: she was squatting in the garden and when she saw them coming and recognized schoolteacher's hat, she heard wings. Little hummingbirds stuck their needle beaks right through her headcloth into her hair and beat their wings. And if she thought anything, it was No. Nono. Nonono. Simple. She just flew. Collected every bit of life she had made, all the parts of her that were precious and fine and beautiful, and carried, pushed, dragged them through the veil, out, away, over there where no one could hurt them. Over there. Outside this place, where they would be safe. And the hummingbird wings beat on. (163)

Here is Morrison's parable of motherhood: Sethe does not destroy her children, she saves them. Refusing to be separated from her own flesh and blood, she gathers them/herself up, "all the parts of her that were precious and fine and beautiful," responds to the warnings of the wings and beaks, and makes her great final pilgrimage, a second crossing of the river that takes her "through the veil" altogether, finally arriving at an "over there" that would be permanently safe.

Only when we have read this full sequence devoted to the murder do we begin to grasp the fuller significance of Beloved's "return." Her entry into 124 is living proof that the family is still intact, that the child was indeed safe "over there" and has now come home again, "through the veil" once again. Beloved reunites the divided family. She is the sister Denver has lost; she turns Paul D's tobacco tin into a red heart; she is, above all, the living child, and she displays for us the indestructible mother-daughter bond at the core of Morrison's vision. The world of slavery is one of atomized parts, and schoolteacher is its metaphysician of abstract measurements and labels. But the other view, the view from "over there," is one of pure continuum, of endless connectedness, of the integral and holy body, of fusion rather than separation. That other view is the one preached by Baby Suggs, and in the ghostly figure of Beloved, Morrison gives that ethos its fullest, most haunting embodiment.

We often think of ghost stories as shadowy affairs. Countless films have treated us to creaking doors and the moon breaking through the clouds. Poe has given us exquisitely spectral versions of the intercourse between the living and the dead, and James, in stories such as "The Turn of the Screw" and "The Jolly Corner," has shown how much psychological sublimation and displacement the ghost narrative affords. *Beloved* rings a drastic change on the genre because it dispenses entirely with veils and lighting and twilight zone in order to present its wandering spirits. Instead, these denizens from "the other side" are utterly incarnate, flesh-and-blood creatures that walk, eat, sleep, and have sex. There is nothing esoteric or even "psychological" about Morrison's enterprise; the ghost has the same dense corporeal reality, the same carnal authority, that all her other folks have.

This is a world of bodies, first and foremost, and perhaps Morrison's greatest achievement lies in the sensuous depiction of animate life that she has offered us here. (Her other novels seem cerebral by comparison.) *Beloved* makes us see that a literature of the senses is possible, that most of what we read is ideational and schematic, unrelated to the career of the body. Nothing is strident or trumpeted here: no discourse on theory or critique of patriarchy or apology for some kind of "women's writing." Just the thing itself, the miraculous speech of flesh. The body has its own language: it expresses itself in fluids such as urine, milk, and blood. What other book has ever put onto the page in quite this way the primacy of the body's fluids? Sethe sees, on the way home from the carnival, that strange figure in a black dress with two unlaced shoes beneath it, and her bladder speaks with imperious urgency. Morrison's language is worth attending to, because it is all about body speech:

> Not since she was a baby girl, being cared for by the eight-year-old girl who pointed out her mother to her, had she had an emergency that unmanageable. She never made the outhouse. Right in front of its door she had to lift her skirts, and the water she voided was endless. Like a horse, she thought, but as it went on and on she thought, No, more like flooding the boat when Denver was born. So much water Amy said, "Hold on, Lu. You going to sink us you keep that up." But there was no stopping water breaking from a breaking womb and there was no stopping now. (51)

The body is making itself known here, articulating the cogency of its existence, displaying a logic that may appear animal (full bladder, like a horse) but is actually deeply human; it is talking about mothering, about birth, and the breaking womb is the body's way of accommodating the flow of life, the movement of the fetus from inside to outside, a primal event of bonding— mother and child and friend, Sethe and Denver and Amy—which broadcasts the connectedness of creatures. That connectedness is exactly what is at stake: the uncanny remembrance of Sethe as baby girl, attended by the eight-year-old, looking at the mother, and now the mother, attended by her youngest child, looking at the dead baby come home. That flowing water that seems "endless," that is "flooding" and unstoppable, has the biblical resonance of God's Flood as well as the human resonance of the woman's flow; it is given to us as prior, as preceding shape and form and name and identity, prior in the same way we know the human body itself to be over 65 percent water.

Most of the literature we know presents the story of humans in a more structured, contoured fashion: it respects the shapes and paradigms of charac- ter and plot, it believes in social and financial and ethical labels, it measures life by individual event and episode, it distinguishes between people, between living and dead, between reality and dream. At its most reductive, most litera- ture is the work of schoolteacher, a literature of measurement and categoriza- tion, a literature of lists and appendages, a grid for parceling out experience and life into coherent boxes, a logic that is binary and differential at every turn. We have learned in recent years to label such a view of life "phallogocen- tric" (although to give such a label to anything is to be guilty of it). Morrison's *Beloved* is, without any fanfare whatsoever, an example of what *écriture féminine* might mean.[8] Morrison is telling a story of the body (is making the body speak), and we realize just how gendered such knowledge is, how alienated masculine writing and thinking often are from the life of the body. Could a man have written these lines about the brief reprieve that Sethe experienced on "the other side," the brief month of freedom before the murder:

> Sethe had had twenty-eight days—the travel of one whole moon—of unslaved life. From the pure clear stream of spit that the little girl dribbled into her face to her oily blood was twenty-eight days. Days of healing, ease and real-talk. Days of company: knowing the names of forty, fifty other Negroes, their views, habits; where they had been and what done; of feeling their fun and sorrow along with her own, which made it better. One taught her the alphabet; another a stitch. All taught her how it felt to wake up at dawn and *decide* what to do with the day. That's how she got through the waiting for Halle. Bit by bit, at 124 and in the Clearing, along with the others, she had claimed herself. Freeing yourself was one thing; claiming ownership of that freed self was another. (95)

Morrison's entire agenda is on show here. The passage ends with an evocation of community, of people learning from one another to be free. We cannot fail to see that freedom here is imagined in terms of ownership and proprietorship, but that it is crucially made possible by our intercourse with others. The communal life is profoundly domestic: one can be a self only when one is part of a family, a family that teaches domestic arts such as making language and clothing. But the domestic perspective itself is made possible by a female logic that is as old as the species, a logic that counts out events by monthly cycles in connection with the moon and the womb, a logic that finds its purest expression in the creatural flow of mothers and children: "oily blood" and "the pure clear stream of spit."

In keeping with Baby Suggs's injunctions, the body—beaten though it is by whites—is revered in this book. Amy Denver lovingly massages Sethe's grotesquely swollen feet, helps her deliver her baby. Baby Suggs kisses Sethe on the mouth when she arrives, all bloody with her baby, gives the newborn to a "young woman in a bonnet, telling her not to clean the eyes till she got the mother's urine" (92). An old world of folk medicine and women's remedies comes into view in these scenes of nurturance and caring. There is poetry in Baby's discovery of Sethe's mutilated back:

> As she turned to go, Baby Suggs caught a glimpse of something dark on the bed sheet. She frowned and looked at her daughter-in-law bending toward the baby. Roses of blood blossomed in the blanket covering Sethe's shoulders. Baby Suggs hid her mouth with her hand. When the nursing was over and the newborn was asleep—its eyes half open, its tongue dream-sucking—wordlessly the older woman greased the flowering back and pinned a double thickness of cloth to the inside of the newly stitched dress. (93)

The sanctity of the human body, the ethos of *physical* kindness, the wisdom of a nurturing corporeal culture merge here to yield a shocking (and utterly unsentimental) poetry. The whipped body creates flowers, roses of blood that blossom, and this beauty in flesh is inseparable from the compassion and tenderness shown by the older woman. It is not a question of metaphor; it is the body that speaks—speaks through its closed, hidden mouth, speaks wordlessly in the language of flowers, the alphabet of stitches, the caring of women, the dream-sucking of infants.

The body comes first. It will deafen and go out of business when intolerable messages come. It will tremble, uncontrollably, when too much abuse has been suffered. It will shine when it experiences desire and is ready to mate. These are languages. Slavery appropriates the body of the Other and monstrously deforms its speech: the bit makes the face smile when it isn't smiling; the mouth sucks iron instead of breasts; the white "mossy-toothed" nephew usurps the milk; the husband, amok, rubs his face with clabber and butter, milk gone sour, congealed. Milk is the flow of life, the fluid umbilical cord that connects mother and child, the supreme proof of connectedness as the primal state. Three times at the beginning Sethe explains to Paul D that the boys took her milk, and he, like the reader, both understands and does not understand.[9] The burden of the book is to translate the crimes of slavery back into natural organic language, to locate the monstrous social scheme against the somatic one of nurturance and creatural survival. Only later do we grasp the enormity of Morrison's corporeal logic, the sacramental importance of mothering. Sethe returns to these matters when Paul D finally asks her about the murder, and she describes the fullness she had achieved, a fullness of cosmic proportions:

> We was here. Each and every one of my babies and me too. I birthed them and I got em out and it wasn't no accident. I did that. I had help, of course, lots of that, but still it was me doing it; me saying, *Go on*, and *Now*. Me having to look out. Me using my own head. But it was more than that. It was a kind of selfishness I never knew nothing about before. It felt good. Good and right. I was big, Paul D, and deep and wide and when I stretched my arms all my children could get in between. I was *that* wide. (162)

The nurturing mother is the fully extended and fully assembled self: big, deep, and wide. This capacious body is nothing less than a world, a "Sweet Home" unlike the other one that has been left, and we come to see that Morrison's book retells, in inverted form, the story of Genesis, the exodus from the slave Garden, the coming into personhood. Here is the authentic "over yonder" that Morrison wants to chart, a fluid place at once coterminous with the female body and constituting its own topography, a place freer than Cincinnati, a place we get to only by crossing mighty rivers, including the Styx as well as the Ohio. It is only when Paul D finally grasps the territorial reach of Sethe's scheme that he backs off: "This here new Sethe didn't know where the world stopped and she began" (164). This is a map he cannot deal with, and in rejecting her, he goes unerringly to the fluid, demiurgic principle that is in play: "Your love is too thick" (164).

Thick love is once again almost cardiac: blood that flows but is also viscous and dense, possessed of a materiality that binds flesh and creates substance.

Sethe's thick love annihilates the boundaries that govern ordinary life: life versus death, there versus here, you versus me. Morrison is showing here that the origin of ghosts, their etiology, has nothing to do with the gothic genre at all: it is a matter of thick love. The very title *Beloved* is something of an ontological experiment, the creation of a noun-thing out of the verb "love," as if love could be intense and fertile enough to go beyond mere nurturance, milk, and actually create matter. And what would happen if it did? When does love get so thick that the flow stops and the creature dies?

The entire plot of *Beloved* revolves around the beauty and terror of thick love. The venomous baby ghost, initially routed by Paul D, returns in the shape of the flesh-and-blood young girl, and Sethe's bladder tells her immediately what she only later comes to believe rationally: this is her dead child returned. Beloved's return seems, on the one hand, as we have seen, to open up the closed circuits, to reconfigure the family by giving Denver a sister, Sethe a child and even Paul D a siring role. But Morrison will not leave things so pat, and she goes the full route in imagining the significance of thick love, of the dead child made whole again. Thus, soon enough Paul D is expelled out of 124. On the face of it his departure stems from his inability to live with Sethe's murder, but we sense a deeper logic and economy at work here, a restoration of the mother world: 124 begins to look very like a house turned womb as the three women — Sethe, Denver, and Beloved — compose their gynecocracy of three. One feels that the life in 124, now fatefully sealed off from the external world, has become the "other world," that safe zone "over there" where Sethe was prepared to consign her children through murder. Here is where the experiment in thick love and female bonding will be taken to its logical extreme, the mother and her daughters welded and fused together into a new body, an airtight realm of its own. As Sethe puts it: "Whatever is going on outside my door ain't for me. The world is in this room. This here's all there is and all there needs to be" (185).

Beauty and terror. At last the separations and amnesia of the black family are overcome. The mutilations meted out by the whites, the even worse mutilations self-inflicted by the blacks, are miraculously healed and made whole. Death does not exist for thick love. Even Sethe's ultimate act of violence — cutting her own child's throat — is at last seen for what it always was: a maternal act of love, an act of protection. The baby, put safely away "over there," has come back full-grown. The baby was indeed saved, not lost; 124 is the triumphant family, the proof that dismembering is only temporary, that nothing on earth can permanently separate mother and child. "Obviously the hand-holding shadows she had seen on the road were not Paul D, Denver and herself, but "us three." The three holding on to each other skating the night before; the three sipping flavored milk. And since that was so — if her daughter could come back home from the timeless place — certainly her sons could, and would, come back from wherever they had gone to" (182). And thus we see in the return of Beloved that the basic reality principle of this novel is the indestructible mother-child continuum, that it cannot be ruptured because thick love holds, binds together, more than slavery or even handsaws can separate.

But there is nothing very cheerful about it. In stark contrast to the fairy-tale assembly that completes a book such as *The Color Purple*, the reunion of the family in *Beloved* is, if anything, almost more agonizing than its dismemberment. The returned child is insatiable. The mother's remorse is inconsolable. Thick love preserves life but it tortures. The ghost remembers abandonment, is obsessed with greed for the nurturance it lost. The mother explains: why she killed, how it was for safety's sake, how it was an act of love. Beloved and Sethe cannot be appeased, for each speaks out of the ineradicable loss she has sustained. Desire is an unfillable lack. Denver, recluse and womb inmate though she is, recognizes that 124 is becoming a torture chamber, that the fateful trip "in" may not be survivable. The ghost returns with unstillable appetite, with confused but unbearable memories; the mother receives the child, but she can never erase her geste, never eradicate its violence, no matter how redemptive and loving it was. Above all, thick love is tyrannical, will stop at nothing. It led to murder once, and it is leading to it again—but in reverse. Sethe pleads for forgiveness, but Beloved thinks only abandonment. Sethe gives, Beloved takes. Finally, Sethe shrinks and Beloved grows, and the metamorphosis actually takes place: mother into child, child into mother:

> Then it seemed to Denver the thing was done: Beloved bending over Sethe looked the mother, Sethe the teething child, for other than those times when Beloved needed her, Sethe confined herself to a corner chair. The bigger Beloved got, the smaller Sethe became; the brighter Beloved's eyes, the more those eyes that used never to look away became slits of sleeplessness. Sethe no longer combed her hair or splashed her face with water. She sat in the chair licking her lips like a chastised child while Beloved ate up her life, took it, swelled up with it, grew taller on it. (250)

There is a fierce somatic logic at work here, a terrifying picture of infant cannibalism, of a parturition that cannot ever take place, of the fetus gone wild and eating up the mother. This is what "nurturance" looks like, seen up close: a murderous devouring, a vampirish undoing of the mother. Sethe is performing her maternal role to the bloody end, is being "weaned" from external life, is becoming autistic as she nurses the succubus-child that takes her blood. As enlightened readers we "know" that Beloved is pregnant (doubtless with Paul D's seed), but what we actually see is the mother-daughter continuum in its purest form: the transformation of daughter into mother, the mother into child, indeed into child/corpse. Needless to say, this nightmarish portrayal of maternity is not easy medicine for many readers, especially for feminists. Judith Thurman has argued that Sethe is a figure of drastic confusion, mistaking her pride and her selfhood for maternity, thereby becoming, "in every sense, a slave/mother."[10] Here, on the mother-daughter terrain, according to such a view, is the true locus of the novel's view of slavery:

> It is important to the story that one of Paul D's first acts when he moves in with Sethe is to break her house up—smash her furniture and dishes—as a way of ridding her of the ghost. But he can't destroy her perverse attachment to the memory, to the idea of Sweet Home—in part because the roles of

master and slave, mother and child, have been fused within her. This fusion is, I think, what we experience as most sinister, claustrophobic, and uncanny in the novel, and it's what drives home the meaning of slavery.[11]

Sinister, claustrophobic, and uncanny, yes, but also the living truth of the novel. Sethe murdered her baby out of love, and her baby is now doing it to her. This is the reward that thick love has brought to Sethe, and there is no normative code on earth to measure it with. The giving of life is inseparable from the taking of life, and in Morrison's portrait of the birthing/dying process we see the same kind of creatural horror, beauty, and economy that we note in the reproductive practices of insects, animals and other living organisms. In rendering the theme of thick love and motherhood with such brute power, Morrison has moved beyond any conceivable "agenda" or programmatic goal. Nothing is going to be easily built on any foundation here. But there is indeed a foundation that is emerging into view.

Up to now this discussion has treated Beloved as if she were Sethe's actual dead baby come back to life. Sethe surely believes that to be the case. And, in the fullest poetic sense of the term, it is indeed true. But the careful reader senses that things are not quite this clear, not quite this simple. Reading more closely we see unmistakable evidence that Beloved has her own (multiple) origins, "independent" (as if such a notion were possible in this text) of Sethe altogether. The drama of irreconciliation at 124, the unsatisfiable hunger that both Sethe and Beloved experience with each other, has a prosaic as well as a poetic origin: they are (also) *not* mother and daughter. Consider their actual exchanges:

> She [Beloved] took the best of everything—first. The best chair, the biggest piece, the prettiest plate, the brightest ribbon for her hair, and the more she took, the more Sethe began to talk, explain, describe how much she had suffered, been through, for her children, waving away flies in grape arbors, crawling on her knees to a lean-to. None of which made the impression it was supposed to. Beloved accused her of leaving her behind. Of not being nice to her, not smiling at her. She said they were the same, had the same face, how could she have left her? And Sethe cried, saying she never did, or meant to—that she had to get them out, away, that she had the milk all the time and had the money too for the stone but not enough. That her plan was always that they would all be together on the other side, forever. Beloved wasn't interested. She said when she cried there was no one. That dead men lay on top of her. That she had nothing to eat. Ghosts without skin stuck their fingers in her and said beloved in the dark and bitch in the light. (241)

Beloved is referring to a real past, rich with horrors of its own: slave ship, abandonment, sexual abuse. We see how the pieces begin to fit: the story of the dead white man who had kept a black girl locked up with him for years, the extraordinary evidence provided by Beloved herself in the lyrical passages of the novel where she remembers her origins. Deborah Horvitz has suggested that Beloved has a double identity: she is the specific murdered child and "at the same time she represents the spirit of all the women dragged onto slave ships in Africa and also all Black women in America trying to trace their ancestry back to the mother on the ship attached to them. Beloved is the haunting presence who becomes the spirit of the women from 'the other side.'"[12] From the Olympian perspective of the reader/critic, all these "identities" enrich the novel; but within the framework of the text, within the confines of 124, we have a murderously foiled quest, a hunger that cannot be gratified. Why has Morrison given us a "misfit," a misalliance?

The most immediate answer would be that she has not wanted to give us a ghost story, pure and simple. Hence Beloved, with her own "actual" history, would anchor the story, give it a realist ballast. Quickly enough we see through such an explanation. After all, the house shook before Beloved came. Nothing will explain away the ghosts. More satisfying is the notion that the reunion of Sethe and Beloved is, if anything, more poignant, more tragic, even more significant if we postulate that Beloved is not the dead baby. Then we perceive the fuller story of loss that is being depicted: a woman seeking her dead child and a child seeking her dead mother, united, seeing the other as what she has lost, hopelessly trying to make good on the spilled blood and lost love. This view of the novel endows those final episodes at 124 with overtones that are both exquisite and absurdist, a kind of ballet or pas de deux being played out where the two can never mesh, never fulfill each other. Ultimately, however, even this reading will not quite wash, because the drama at 124 is a drama of connection, not misconnection. True enough, Beloved *is not* the dead baby, and Sethe *is not* the dead mother, but what we see, what the entire thrust of the novel makes visible to us, is that Beloved *becomes* the child and Sethe *becomes* the mother. The mother-daughter bond is actualized in front of our eyes, and it seems not to matter a great deal that the actual players are miscast. How can this be?

The only answer that makes sense is that the real mission in *Beloved* is to present the mother-daughter continuum with such transcendent power that we see in it the shape of reality itself. Much the way that Faulkner *made* a figurative family in *Light in August*, put together his story of Joseph and Mary and the child in such a way as to offset the murderous violence of his materials, so Morrison has written her facts of dis-memberment into a fiction of re-membering. And what we can perhaps now begin to see is the writerly dimension of her achievement. Her task was to depict the conditions of severance and blockage, but to reconfigure them, by dint of the very language by which they were conveyed, into a fable of connection. For such a project fluidity rather than line was necessary; for such a novel the body must receive its due and find its long-muted voice. Finally, in such a venture we must see connectedness as the very shape of experience rather than the isolated, contoured world of individual careers and discrete objects. Thus, Sethe and Beloved both are and are not who they think they are. Biologically and historically they are discrete figures, thwarted questers; but spiritually they are bound to each other, are part of each other, own each other.[13]

> When I tell you you mine, I also mean I'm yours. I wouldn't draw breath without my children. I told Baby Suggs that and she got down on her knees

to beg God's pardon for me. Still, it's so. My plan was to take us all to the other side where my own ma'am is. They stopped me from getting us there, but they didn't stop you from getting here. Ha ha. You came right on back like a good girl, like a daughter which is what I wanted to be and would have been if my ma'am had been able to get out of the rice long enough before they hanged her and let me be one. (203)

"The other side" where Beloved comes from is the same place where Sethe's ma'am is waiting, and we see that there can be no islanded figures in this text, that Sethe herself is daughter as well as mother, that there is only a long chain of mothers and daughters.[14] This chain may appear in the eyes of some to be a chain of bondage, but it may also be thought to be a sign of linkage, an indication of the human family that survives the mutilations of history. The purpose of writing is to make that continuum visible. Here is the secret knowledge shared between mothers and daughters: the story of fusion and origins, the mystery of sameness-in-difference. True, Denver loves the story of her own birth, for the first stories we learn are creation stories, accounts of our own coming. But this particular story reaches beyond Sethe and Amy Denver all the way back to the first mother, and it is shrouded in mystery and strangeness, as if it were an opaque language, a script of some unknown history written in prelingual signs:

Of that place where she [Sethe] was born (Carolina maybe? or was it Louisiana?) she remembered only song and dance. Not even her own mother, who was pointed out to her by the eight-year-old child who watched over the young ones — pointed out as the one among many backs turned away from her, stooping in a watery field. Patiently Sethe waited for this particular back to gain the row's end and stand. What she saw was a cloth hat as opposed to a straw one, singularity enough in that world of cooing women each of whom was called Ma'am.
  "Seth — thuh."
  "Ma'am."
  "Hold on to the baby."
  "Yes, Ma'am."
  "Seth — thuh."
  "Ma'am."
  "Get som kindlin in here."
  "Yes, Ma'am."
Oh but when they sang. And oh but when they danced and sometimes they danced the antelope. The men as well as the ma'ams, one of whom was certainly her own. They shifted shapes and became something other. Some unchained, demanding other whose feet knew her pulse better than she did. Just like this one in her stomach. (30–31)

A great deal is on show in this sustained memory: Sethe's mother as cloth rather than straw hat, the dancing adults, the metamorphoses. It is a primitive language of sexuality and joy, as well as anonymity and work, and Sethe has called her baby an "antelope" to hark back to this spectacle of shifting forms that contains, somehow, Mother. Everytime Sethe's mother enters the text, she enters as foreign language, exotic code, as strange speech that, if only understood, would signify connection. Denver ushers in the first such memory (thereby illustrating the chain), and Beloved does it the second time, asking Sethe whether "her woman" ever fixed up her hair, and again we get the odd story of distance and markings, of a lingual code that wants deciphering.[15]

> "So to answer you, no. I reckon not. She never fixed my hair nor nothing. She didn't even sleep in the same cabin most nights I remember. Too far from the line-up, I guess. One thing she did do. She picked me up and carried me behind the smokehouse. Back there she opened up her dress front and lifted her breast and pointed under it. Right on her rib was a circle and a cross burnt right in the skin. She said, 'this is your ma'am. This,' and she pointed. 'I am the only one got this mark now. The rest dead. If something happens to me and you can't tell me by my face, you can know me by this mark.' Scared me so. All I could think of was how important this was and how I needed to have something important to say back, but I couldn't think of anything so I just said what I thought. 'Yes, Ma'am,' I said. 'But how will you know me? How will you know me? Mark me, too,' I said. 'Mark the mark on me too.'"
> (60–61)

Here are Sethe's earliest memories, more primal than the events at Sweet Home, the ur-narrative that fuels all the others. We see it to be a story about markings, about the fashioning of a "kinship language" that would traverse the monstrous gaps that slavery has imposed, a physical language of breasts and skin symbols that would signify the unbroken family even in the midst of dismemberment. Even as Sethe explains these matters to Beloved and Denver, she triggers still further memories, loosens material that had been utterly forgotten or repressed up until now. The forgotten story of Sethe's origins surfaces at last, focusing on the woman, Nan, who yanked her back from the hanged body of her mother just as she was looking for the mark:

> Nan was the one she knew best, who was around all day, who nursed babies, cooked, had one good arm and half of another. And who used different words. Words Sethe understood then but could neither recall nor repeat now. She believed that must be why she remembered so little before Sweet Home except singing and dancing and how crowded it was. What Nan had told her she had forgotten, along with the language she told it in. The same language her ma'am spoke, and which would never come back. But the message — that was and had been there all along. Holding the damp white sheets against her chest, she was picking meaning out of a code she no longer understood. Nighttime. Nan holding her with her good arm, waving the stump of the other in the air. "Telling you. I am telling you, small girl Sethe," and she did that. She told Sethe that her mother and Nan were together from the sea. Both were taken up many times by the crew. "She threw them all away but you. The one from the crew she threw away on the island. The others from more whites she also threw away. Without names, she threw them. You she gave the name of the black man. She put her arms around him. The others she did not put her arms around. Never. Never. Telling you. I am telling you, small girl Sethe." (62)

Coming a quarter of the way through the novel, this passage appears to be what we reductively call background, but we gradually understand that the quest in *Beloved* is precisely for background: the characters' tortured and blocked sense of their own origins, Toni Morrison's effort to remember the forgotten ones, the ones who had forgotten themselves. And by the time we finish this novel, we can see in this story of Sethe's "ma'am" the central enabling paradigm of the entire fiction: to make and/or recover the forgotten mother language. The philosopher Johann Georg Hamann once wrote, "Die Poesie ist die Muttersprache der Menschheit," and Morrison's novel may be understood as poetic in just that sense: a mother language long lost but now refashioned, an *écriture maternelle* that reestablishes the mother-daughter chain and thereby grounds the human subject. Sethe remembers this "code" although she no longer understands it; but what she does understand is the human love that — miraculously — existed at the source of her life: in the midst of the abusive and anonymous sex, amid the nameless babies thrown away, Sethe sprang from a chosen union, a full embrace. This recovery of the mother eloquently offsets the disabling countertruth of slave culture: the absent mother, the abandoned child, the ungrounded self.

Morrison has insistently presented Sethe's origins in terms of a forgotten language because that remote, shadowy story is to be part of her own writerly strategy. The mother at sea haunts this narrative, a kind of ghost script that is everywhere operative, governing Sethe's giving birth to Denver in the boat by the Ohio, hinted at by the flooding waters that Sethe releases when she sees Beloved, most powerfully and movingly instanced in the lyrical medita-tions of Beloved herself about her own origins, in the extraordinary suite of "remembrances" that constitutes the novel's tribute to desire and con-nection. Here at last is the ultimate female discourse, the voice of linked women, the gynecocracy that no man can enter. Stamp Paid tried to get in, but couldn't:

> When Sethe locked the door, the women inside were free at last to be what they liked, see whatever they saw and say whatever was on their minds.
>
> Almost. Mixed in with the voices surrounding the house, recognizable but undecipherable to Stamp Paid, were the thoughts of the women of 124, unspeakable thoughts, unspoken. (199)

Thus, Morrison dives into the wreck, makes language for what was never said. She moves first into Sethe's (incurably proprietary) thoughts — "Beloved, she my daughter. She mine" (200) — and after chronicling Sethe's calvary at Sweet Home and her rapturous experience of recovery and reunion, she en-ters Denver — "Beloved is my sister. I swallowed her blood right along with my mother's milk" (205) — thinking and feeling it her way, finding words for the child's stunted growth and autism and final precious gift of a sis-ter. These untrammeled meditations, yielding a narrative flow that bears the entire family history felt from the inside, are completed by the richest, most opaque utterances of all, the ones that begin: "I AM BELOVED and she is mine" (210).

There is something futile and faintly obscene in the critical project of "pinning down" what Morrison "says" in the four pages allotted to *Beloved's* own remembering, exploratory voice. Not only do we encounter here a poetic voice that has the density and splendor that Faulkner achieves in the Rosa Coldfield fifth chapter of *Absalom*, but also we see that the gathered, imperious metaphors coursing in her mind constitute the book's deepest meaning, reconceive its narrative logic in pure, luminous images, the picture book of her life. Binding these pictures is the speech of utter longing, an almost prenatal speech of connectedness threatened over and over by severance. There are no boundaries in Beloved's somatic life: "I am not separate from her   there is no place where I stop   her face is my own and I want to be there in the place where her face is and to be looking at it too" (210). The fusion of bodies is prior, and the plight of mind is to recapture this wholeness, to expand subjectivity beyond self, by actually moving into the Other, to "be" her face and to "be looking at it too." This dirge is punctuated by images that signal faraway places: perhaps Africa (a place of flowers, round baskets, leaves, and grass), most certainly the memory of living packed together in the hold of a slave ship ("there will never be a time when I am not crouching and watching others who are crouching too") and experiencing great thirst ("the men without skin [white men] bring us their morning water to drink   we have none"), the horrid conditions ("I am not big   small rats do not wait for us to sleep"), the confused memory of both mass dying and single deaths, blending the dying slaves on board with the white man who "kept" her and died. We see the expulsion of dead black bodies into the sea ("the men without skin push them through with poles"), and we see, above all, the enigmatic mother figure whose face is Beloved's, who abandons the/her child by going into the sea, going into the sea over and over, yielding a choral refrain of loss:

> the woman is there with the face I want   the face that is mine   they fall into the sea which is the color of bread. . . . the woman with my face is in the sea. . . . I am sure she saw me   I am looking at her see me   she empties out her eyes. . . . I cannot lose her again. . . . she is going to smile at me   she is going to. . . . they push my own man through   they do not push the woman with my face through   she goes in   they do not push her   she goes in   the little hill is gone   she was going to smile at me. . . . I see the dark face that is going to smile at me   it is my dark face that is going to smile at me. . . . she goes in the water   with my face. . . . she took my face away   there is no one to want me   to say me my name. . . . I see her face which is mine   it is the face that was going to smile at me in the place where we crouched   now she is going to   her face comes through the water. . . . her face is mine   she is not smiling   she is chewing and swallowing   I have to have my face   I go in. . . . my face is coming   I have to have it   I am looking for the join   I am loving my face so much   my dark face is close to me   I want to join   she whispers to me   she whispers   I reach for her chewing and swallowing   she touches me   she knows I want to join   she chews and swallows me   I am gone   now I am her face   my own face has left me   I see me swim away   a hot thing   I see the bottoms of my feet   I am alone   I want to be the two of us   I want the join. . . . (210–13)

Here is the story of dis-membering and re-membering writ large. In Beloved's memories Morrison has found a language for the elemental processes of being, the infant's fusion with the mother, the intolerable experience of separation, the primal hunger and greed that fuels this fable of stolen faces, of stolen selfness, the mother-child bond as a lethal quest for wholeness (entailing cannibalism and mutilation), all issuing into a Narcissuslike tale of plunging into one's image/mother right on through to death and then beyond: one Beloved remaining on the bottom of the water and watching the other one rise up to the surface to find Sethe: "Sethe's is the face that left me. . . . she is my face smiling at me   doing it at last   a hot thing   now we can join   a hot thing" (213).

Beloved's story is the quintessence of the novel. Its message of loss and join is properly stereophonic, with echoes of Sethe's own mother and the slave ship, strong women who cannot be broken, even picking up tones of Paul D's prison-gang ordeal in Georgia, pointing toward a flesh-and-blood, abandoned, abused child while at the same time singing the chant of ghosts, completing the novel's melodic tale of loss and dismemberment. In Marianne Hirsch's words: "Beloved's is a composite personal and cultural memory that boldly equates the womb with the tomb with the slaveship, the crouching in the middle passage with the fetal position, the sea with uterine fluid, milk with blood."[16] We may read Beloved's threnody as the dirge of an unhinged mind, but we are also entitled to see in its flowing discourse a new language altogether, a communal script, a woman's way of reconceiving *les mots de la tribu*.[17] By writing it the way she has, as the generic and multivalent speech of mothers and daughters, Morrison has underscored its status as language, as the binding speech of "join," of speech itself as the vehicle and fabric of "join," yoking together by its very plaint and polysemousness the fissured lives and bodies it commemorates. It is in this light that *Beloved* hauntingly recasts my theme, the freedom of speech in American fiction, for Morrison has actually devised a fluid language of continuity and kinship, a verbal art that conveys the beauty and the terror of wholeness, of re-membering, even as it tells its slave narrative of dismemberment. A radical alternative to schoolteacher's measuring and defining prose, Morrison's script confers a kind of perceptual power to those people who had no power, and it defines for us a world—staggeringly rich, essentially black and maternal—far beyond the precincts mapped out by the definers.

14

Don DeLillo: Rendering the Words of the Tribe

The work of Don DeLillo is not easy to size up. Like a latter-day Balzac or Zola, he seems to have some giant composite plan in mind, an all-encompassing scheme that, when completed, will bear witness to how we lived, worked, played, and sounded in the second half of the twentieth century. DeLillo's zest for rivaling with the *état civil* has led him to some exotic subjects and oddball places: football, professional mathematics, Wall Street, rock music, pornography, terrorism, espionage, the college campus, the nuclear threat, and, more recently, America's founding trauma: the Kennedy assassination.

One finds amid this teeming variety of DeLillo subjects a number of constants that make his work both recognizable and developmental, as if a large argument were gathering force over the course of some nine novels. There is, first of all, the remarkable DeLillo style: cool to the point of being hip, close to the vest, drawn to the jargons and tics of coteries and the argots of professions, informed by the concepts of the media, wry, distant, exquisitely focused on the inane, the bizarre, the surreal, and yet capable of pathos and power.

And then there seems to be a fixed number of DeLillo themes: fascism, espionage, communication, power in all its guises, and finally the antics of the individual subject in his encounter with a systemic world.[1] Whereas artists such as Coover or Bertolucci conceive of fascism in terms of spectacle, mass movements, and paranoia, DeLillo is more theoretical and cerebral, at once more oblique and more various. *Great Jones Street* chronicles, for example, the career and retreat of an idolized rock star; DeLillo is drawn to the big-business sleaze around the performer as well as the visionary desperation of the lyrics themselves. The figure of Hitler runs in filigree in DeLillo's texts. The much-coveted, sought-after film footage in *Running Dog* is thought to be a pornographic rendition of final events in the bunker, and the novel cunningly interweaves, on the one hand, the obsession with the sexual antics of the doomed Führer, and, on the other, a grainy story of intelligence and counterintelligence, of hired killers and coerced sex.

Hitler reappears as the academic specialty of Jack Gladney in DeLillo's comic masterpiece, *White Noise*, and once again we perceive the reaches of DeLillo's theme by dint of the way he pairs and replicates it, this time in the guise of "twin" academic departments: Gladney's program of Hitler Studies may receive an American complement through the proposal for an Elvis Studies program. Comic fiction though it is, *White Noise* explores to great effect the cult of power and death that fascism entails, and in that light it is surprisingly more informative than the book on Lee Harvey Oswald, *Libra*, in which one expects a full-fledged rendition of Kennedy fascination to complete the series of portraits in power. Instead, *Libra* has a rather different orientation, and it chronicles the special "world within a world" of the CIA and international intelligence communities, thereby adding to the already masterly depiction of such circles and antics in *Great Jones Street, Running Dog*, and the extraordinary account of middle-management Americans caught up in Middle Eastern terrorism and cults in *The Names*, a novel of 1982 that is certain to gain in stature as DeLillo's novelistic status becomes clearer to us in the coming years.

But the cornerstone of DeLillo's work, the reason why he deserves inclusion in a study of "freedom of speech" in American fiction, is his peculiar, always fascinating, sometimes visionary concern with language. I have already mentioned his ear for the private jargons and codes of today's technocratic society (he is like Balzac here); at other moments he actually fashions a new discourse (here he is breaking new ground), as in the language of rock music or the project of the eerie questers in *The Names*. At all times DeLillo is concerned to render for us either sounds that we have heard without knowing it—the "white noise" of our Muzak age—or to usher us verbally into those other, unsuspected worlds behind the scenes of business and diplomacy, the academy and the cocktail party. In the tradition of Fenimore Cooper and Balzac, DeLillo is out to guide his readers into verbal precincts they have never entered before, but in his hands that guided tour becomes an explosive and dangerous affair, an encounter with sounds that can kill. Consider, in this light, the view of music-language as pure kinetic energy, as articulated by Bucky Wunderlich, the rock star of *Great Jones Street*:

> The true artist makes people move. When people read a book or look at a painting, they just sit there or stand there. A long time ago that was okay, that was hip, that was art. Now it's different. I make people move. My sound lifts them right off their ass. I make it happen. Understand, I make it happen. What I'd like to do really is I'd like to injure people with my sound. Maybe actually kill some of them. They'd come there knowing that full well. Then we'd play and sing and people in the audience would be frozen in pain and some of them would actually die from the effects of our words and music. . . . People dying from the effects of all this beauty and power. That's art, sweetheart. I make it happen.[2]

A vertiginous linguistic and cultural meditation is under way here; the manifestations of power and of art are collapsed together, are understood as speech phenomena. Life and death are graphed as language.[3] DeLillo occupies a very special place in my argument about freedom of speech, for his books always circle around the issue of utterance, and they make us understand that language is the *Urgrund*, the ultimate stage on which a society or a culture lives and goes through its antics and its rituals. "Le monde est fait pour aboutir à un livre," Mallarmé wrote, and in DeLillo's work of lingual crises and unheard-of frequencies we may glimpse the *aboutissement* of the reality-as-language equation, but trumped up now in the tribal and technocratic jargons of our media age.

DeLillo's cumulative project resembles at times that of Roland Barthes, especially the Barthes of *Mythologies*, for he is scrupulously attentive to the ways in which belief and passion are displaced, renamed, formated, and commodified in a materialist age. And he succeeds in these ventures largely because he has the eyes of the anthropologist as well as the ears of the linguist, perceiving the peculiar poetry of everyday rituals and services, chronicling the muffled spiritual impulses concealed within our mundane comings and goings. DeLillo's modernity lies in his sense that our myths are on the surface rather than in the depths, recorded in the print of our newspapers rather than in dark, oneiric scripts. Hence, in *Libra*, the CIA agent's wife, Beryl, no longer writes letters to her friends; she merely cuts clippings out of the papers and sends them instead: "She believed these were personal forms of expression. She believed no message she could send a friend was more intimate and telling than a story in the paper about a violent act, a crazed man, a bombed Negro home, a Buddhist monk who sets himself on fire. Because these are the things that tell us how we live."[4] Our myths are broadcast in the news, on the front pages, but we do not come easily to the realization that these acts of violence and melodrama somehow *speak us*, are devious utterances of our own private wishes and fears. That seems to be DeLillo's major accomplishment, book after book: to enter, as roving eye and roving ear, into and behind the worlds of finance, diplomacy, and violence, and to make us aware that these realms, apparently "argotized" and other, are actually "ghostlier demarcations" of ourselves.

DeLillo first gained a wide audience with *White Noise*, winner of the American Book Award in 1986, chronicle of the terrors lurking in the environment and the family, infused with a deadpan survivalist humor that marks it as one of the landmark fictions of our time. But *The Names*, published in 1982, leaner and more metaphysical than *White Noise*, constitutes the proper entry into DeLillo's world, for it sounds his major themes; an analysis of its exploratory ventures will make it possible for us, then, to hear the fuller resonances and to savor the unusual warmth and pathos of the later text. My consideration of DeLillo will be capped by some remarks on his most controversial work, *Libra* (1988), which both extends his exploration of high-level espionage and leads, in the eyes of some, out of the world of fiction altogether, although we may come to believe that the distinctions between history and fiction have now lost all meaning entirely.

The Names looks, initially, to be in the tradition of American expatriate novels. James, the narrator, is an "international risk analyst" stationed in Athens, and he measures, early on, the gap that separates him and his fellows from the experience of the Lost Generation of the twenties: "The deep terraces spill over with lantana and jasmine, the views are panoramic, the cafés full of talk and smoke into the early hours. Americans used to come to places like this to write and paint and study, to find deeper textures. Now we do business."[5] This declaration gently but firmly marks the distance between modernism and postmodernism, not in terms of writerly codes and imperatives but in the sense of a changed globe, a changed definition of what it means to be "American." Much of DeLillo's interest is devoted to defining the "new" American abroad; no longer the bumbling innocent of Melville or Twain or the Jamesian seeker of refinement or the Hemingway seeker of authenticity or the Fitzgerald seeker of pleasure, DeLillo's people are middle-management types, representing huge multinational conglomerates, trying to cope with a world of precarious allegiances and the ubiquitous threat of terrorism. Jake Barnes knew which Parisian restaurants to eat in, what hotel to stay at in Pamplona; this group has different expertises:

> We were versed in percentages, safety records, in the humor of flaming death. We knew which airline's food would double you up, which routes connected well. . . . We knew which airports were efficient, which were experiments in timelessness or mob rule; which had radar, which didn't; which might be filled with pilgrims making the *hadj*. . . . We advised each other on which remote cities were well maintained, which were notable for wild dogs running in packs at night, snipers in the business district at high noon. We told each other where you had to sign a legal document to get a drink, where you couldn't eat meat on Wednesdays and Thursdays, where you had to sidestep a man with a cobra when you left your hotel. We knew where martial law was in force, where body searches were made, where they engaged in systematic torture, or fired assault weapons into the air at weddings, or abducted and ransomed executives. (6–7)

The clipped, air-conditioned DeLillo style, larded with savvy particulars, nicely conveys the ironies and absurdities of this new dispensation: on the one hand, "we," the corporate Americans, "were versed," "knew," "advised," and "told each other"; on the other hand, this terrain defies charting and mapping, and from the doubled-up stomach to the running dogs and the man with the cobra, we learn that the natives and their exotica are no longer so manageable. This passage announces a change in America's place in the world, and the earlier pilgrim seeking knowledge is out of place in these precincts. The world — that extended version of the virgin West — is no longer open to explorers and tourists in the same way, and we see that the American bildungsroman has been turned on its head, that the educational scheme has become one of survival. The imperialist self is also in trouble here: DeLillo's people take up little space, have small appetites, are good at standing sideways, and are happy to come out with their skin. The contrast with Hemingway's Paris or even Hawkes's Alaska is striking and revelatory. American hegemony is a thing of the past.

And yet, *The Names* is still in the great quest tradition of Westerners seeking the wisdom and secrets of Europe and the East. Ever since Marco Polo we have known that a little business can also be done on the side, but there is an undeniable spiritual hunger in this text, reminiscent of figures such as Forster and Hesse, and DeLillo's triumph is to encode his quest parable in a mimetic narrative of capitalist maneuvers in the Middle East.

Needless to say, Americans are not the only ones who have to be careful in this territory. The Turkish businessman Vedat Nesim explains to James that his own sphere of operations is a veritable mine field:

> "You are a target only outside your country. I am a target outside and inside. I am in the government. This makes me a marked man. Armenians outside, Turks inside. I go to Japan next week. This is a relatively safe place for a Turk. Very bad is Paris. Even worse is Beirut. The Secret Army is very active there. Every secret army in the world keeps a post office box in Beirut. I will eat this shrimp in garlic and butter. Later I will eat profiteroles in thick chocolate sauce. After Japan I go to Australia. This is a place that should be safe for a Turk. It is not." (195)

We shall see, in *Libra*, that Americans are not advantaged over Turks at all, that they too are targets both outside and inside. But the real power of the passage resides in its uncertainty, its staccato list of places and particulars that do not cohere. This is vintage DeLillo style, and the lovely insertion of shrimp and profiteroles perfectly finishes off the old tourist paradigm, a sequence of colorful, discrete items for visiting and ingesting, with a twist: they could kill you.

Rich in exotica, this setting is also rich in secrets and indecipherable codes, in surprises and reversals. But how do we get there from here? Interpretation requires a stable base to which mysteries and enigmas are referred. But DeLillo's people are decentered: "The sense of things was different in such a way that we could only register the edges of some elaborate secret. It seemed we'd lost our capacity to select, to ferret out particularity and trace it to some center which our minds could relocate in knowable surroundings. There was no equivalent core" (94). Such an environment resists all interpretive grids except one: conspiracy. And this is because conspiracies are nothing but purposeful, interconnecting, secret relations that we do not comprehend, and secrets themselves are a nostalgic term for cogency, the cogency that eludes us, from which we as outsiders are excluded. This epistemological imperative has as its flip side paranoia, the certainty that the world is packaged in plots devised by others, in which we ourselves play unwitting roles as targets.

The central (impossible) activity within such a scheme is that of decoding, of getting a grasp on the grammar and the system at hand, so that one's own place in the composite can be understood. In *The Names* DeLillo has presented that paradigm in the purest possible form: the deciphering of languages, the understanding of the Names. And even though DeLillo is not a formally playful writer, has no verbal tricks or pyrotechnics to display, it is hard to think of any Western narrative that matches *The Names* in its exploration of language as high adventure. At the center of this exploration is the novel's chief quester, Owen Brademas, farm boy from the prairies turned archaeologist and éminence grise, in search of ancient inscriptions and the secrets they harbor. This insistent metaphysical tug is convincingly linked to the novel's commercial foreground by the involvement of other, less "pure" characters in Owen's (more or less conscious) mesh: Kathryn (James's wife), who works under his leadership at the dig on the Greek island; Tap (James's son), who is writing a quasi-novel about Owen; and most especially two males who track the tracker into the Greek hinterland: Frank Volterra, who wants to film Owen's involvement with a putative secret cult, and James himself, who becomes Owen's younger alter ego, who helps him complete the pattern. The secret cult at the heart of the matter is, not surprisingly, a language cult.

All of Owen's historical and archaeological pursuits are now transfigured into a project that is profoundly linguistic: erasing the gap between words and things. As if he had absorbed large doses of Saussure and Derrida, DeLillo has imagined a quest for the *natural language*, a language that would eclipse difference, dissolve the space between sign and referent, and install a regime of pure presence. DeLillo's materials become incandescent at this juncture, as if they were acquiring a signifying potency beyond the bounds of ordinary narrative. For instance, Owen explains to Tap the etymology of "character" (the ironies abound here, given that Owen is "also" a "character" in Tap's novel): "Owen says 'character' comes from a Greek word. It means 'to brand or to sharpen.' Or 'pointed stake' if it's a noun" (10). "Character" is on the move here, exiting the realm of the literary or even the print convention and moving in the direction of pure action or pure object. The cult that Owen has come upon exercises the central fascination of the novel because it is devoted to the power of letters, of the alphabet itself. The search for ancient inscriptions reveals itself to be a quest for originary language, language that is immediate and immanent. Such a quest can never be distant from the professional writer's generic interests — one thinks of Emerson's essay on language, or, in a much more sinister vein, of Kafka's story of the penal colony and its fable of body inscription — but DeLillo takes pains to show that even the business interests of the novel are part of a linguistic tradition. After all, as Owen explains, the old inscriptions were nothing but inventories, records of commodities, evidence of the view that "the first writing was motivated by the desire to keep accounts" (35), and with that theory in place James and his middle-management buddies acquire a strange linguistic aura of their own, appear to us as the keepers of a scribal tradition so all-encompassing that all labor ultimately reverts to it.

But the most vexing and arresting link between the secret language cult and the international business community is the common terror that informs both: terrorism as the new global fact of political and economic life, and violent death as the uncanny signature of the cult itself — "terrorists of textuality, agents of literacy's mastery and alienation infiltrating oral cultures," is how Thomas LeClair terms the cult — a signature that betokens nothing less than the fusion of person and place, sign and referent.[6] Here is the terrible synchrony that would erase difference: the cult brutally murders its victims in places where the initials of the place and the person coincide. All the players of the novel are obsessed with these ritual killings because they all know obscurely that their own lives are written out of this archaic grammar, that these ritual murderers are composing a new map and a new human language, by collapsing agent into setting, and by energizing the word so utterly that "character" once again becomes "pointed stake." Finally, one is tempted to posit terror itself as the ground for the psyche in DeLillo, an indwelling creatural horror that underlies all the codes and systems, that endows these books with a muted affective plaint beyond the cool surface ironies. We shall see more of this in *White Noise*.

The beauty of the novel lies in the radiance of its theory, its elegant fusion of esoterica and realpolitik. Yet even to consider *The Names* as a dualistic text is too fixed and schematic, for DeLillo's real game is to transmute all his materials, to achieve that fourth and fifth dimension in narrative that Hemingway was aiming for, in which the newspaper clippings of today not only speak our private myths but keep covenant with the primitive rites of the past. In such a text foreground and background are no longer separable, just as center and circumference become interchangeable. DeLillo's grasp of history confirms his belief in fluidity and plasticity. He is interested in etymology, the flow of names over time, and he is also drawn to the man-made changes, the fate of names such as Persia and Rhodesia, the alphabetical merry-go-round of modern Asia and Africa. Gatsby, we recall, placed San Francisco in the Midwest, but the mobility of the Fitzgerald text never gets much beyond "Biloxi, Tennessee"; DeLillo is bent on staking out a territory that mixes up characters, turns all stakes into pointed stakes, and works according to a directional code and gearshift that wreak havoc. James's friend David is struck that cars come at him in reverse:

> He was always finding himself driving down a narrow street with a car coming toward him backwards. The driver expected him to move, or ascend, or vanish. Eventually he saw what was so fearful about this, a thing so simple he hadn't been able to isolate it from the larger marvel of a city full of cars going backwards. *They did not reduce speed when driving in reverse.* To David Keller, between wives, this seemed an interesting thing. There was a cosmology here, a rich structure of some kind, a theorem in particle physics. Reverse and forward were interchangeable. (65)

Once again we are in classic DeLillo territory, a place for measuring the weather of the mind, a setting of velocities, sensory impressions, and careening lives atilt and akimbo. "To David Keller, between wives, this seemed . . . interesting" acquires the mathematical precision of a graph, with its double axes and mysteriously moving lines of force. We are not far from the trope of palm reading, but the face of fortune is no longer static and inscribed once and for all on the hand; instead, all of the elements are lurching in their own ways, propelled in their different channels and circuits, the erotic career and the moving cars melding a textual weave, a vehicular map of lines and intensities that recalls the Fates with their famous scissors.

This new cosmology brings with it a new poetics, a writerly physics in which statements signify doubly, move in forward and reverse. The language of the text becomes especially heated and active as DeLillo closes in (and opens up) on the language quest. Consider, for example, Owen's tale-within-a-tale of the Englishman Rawlinson, who wanted to copy the inscriptions (in Old Persian, Elamite, and Babylonian) on the Behistun rock. The rock being dangerously inaccessible, the Englishman makes use of a Kurdish boy to achieve his ends: "The boy inched across a rock mass that had only the faintest indentations he might use for finger-grips. Fingers and toes. Maybe he used the letters themselves. I'd like to believe so. This is how he proceeded, clinging to the rock, passing below the great bas-relief of Darius facing a group of rebels in chains. A sheer drop. But he made it, miraculously according to Rawlinson, and was eventually able to do a paper cast of the text, swinging from a sort of bosun's chair" (80). This fine passage epitomizes the richness, economy, and multidirectionality of DeLillo's project. We see the language quest in full swing, and we are struck by the physicality of the signs: the boy finding footholds and toeholds in the very lettering itself. The "characters" in play here are close to the "pointed stake," for the writing itself "brands" and "sharpens" not merely the rocky script "in" the passage but especially the colonialist narrative that delivers it, the brutal "inscription" of the Kurdish boy into the Englishman's design, the kind of invisible, systematic exploitation that has conditioned the stage now occupied by James and his cohorts.[7]

Taking still another step away, we see what may be the central paradigm of DeLillo's book: the arduous recovery of a secret script and the complex mediations required to make it happen. In that light this casual scene comes close to being the absent center of the novel. Some two hundred pages later Owen himself will arrive at his final destination, Rajsamand, to read the great stone inscriptions of the seventeenth-century Sanskrit poem, and he will make use of a young Indian boy to speak what he sees: "Together they read aloud, slowing, the man deferring to the music of the boy, pitching his voice below the other's. It was in the sound, how old this was, strange, distant, other, but also almost known, almost striking through to him from some uncycled memory where the nightmares lay, the ones in which he could not speak as others did, could not understand what they were saying" (284). Lines, many lines, are being blurred and erased in these sequences. Owen merges with the boy, with the Indian past, with his own traumatic childhood encounter with speaking in tongues, even his own preverbal fears from infancy, as the text ceases to distinguish between forward and reverse. Nothing remains discrete. The Kurdish boy becomes the Indian boy, who may be thought to fan out into the stalking, listening figures of Frank Volterra and James—Frank with his feverish desire to film the cult murders, James as the indispensable scribe-mediator for Owen, the one who finds Owen dying and takes down his story so it can be passed on.

We cannot fail to see that the getting of the script and the meaning of the script are akin, and that they have a common base in some elemental violence. This unspecified, unlocalizable violence is at the core of the novel, just as it seems to be at the origin of language itself. The ritual murders performed by the cult are nothing less than acts of exorcism and control, for they derive from a belief system strangely parallel to that described by René Girard in *La Violence et le sacré*, a world view that supposes originary violence, a flowing violence that precedes culture and language, that must be decorously chan-neled through the institutions of sacrifice and effigy if civilization is to be. DeLillo has given a linguistic turn of the screw to this theory of sacrifice, so that the indwelling violence of life is released by acts of verbal synchrony, by moments when the Names assert their all-encompassing authority, erasing distinctions of person and place. Hence, these dazzling murders establish the primacy of the letter above all else, and they remind us that the writer's narrative project is always, at least in some sense, a lethal quest for a magic script, an alchemical script that would liberate the original power of the word by dint of annihilation.

Such moments have an epiphanic, almost nuclear clarity in *The Names*, for they make visible a kind of blinding truth that has almost entirely disap-peared from the day-to-day lives of these characters. The major fact of these lives is that they are in the dark and are interchangeable. They are living the reality of forward slipping into reverse. Owen thinks himself a scribe, but the cultists insist he is a member of their group. People cross lines. James infuri-ates Kathryn by listing his version of her view of his flaws. The Kurdish boy shades into the Indian boy. Andreas confuses James the risk analyst with David the banker.

Yet the benightedness of such a perceptual and conceptual murk is argua-bly preferable to the fatal light of identity, the moment when the letter speaks. One thinks particularly of Borges in this regard, the Borges of "Death and the Compass," who works with the topos of fatal illumination, of the unity be-tween naming and killing. Here is the sinister side of DeLillo's Pauline medita-tion about seeing through the glass darkly, about knowing and being known, and in that sense he tells us something about the status of knowledge and information in a computerized, terrorist age. Michaelis Kalliambetsos is mur-dered at Mikro Kamini. Will the same thing happen to James Axton at Jebel Amman? It very nearly does. James is possibly shot at while jogging in Ath-ens, and David is hit. Mistake? The deadly revelation of the Names is not an archaeological dig, not a whimsical scholarly interlude. To be named, to be revealed in full light, to have total consonance between sound and substance, letter and person, is risky business for risk analysts. James learns, belatedly, from others, that the company he works for, Northeast Group, is a CIA cover, and we see once again DeLillo's brilliance in weaving his strands together. To learn that one's corporate identity is CIA is to learn a new grammar; in many parts of the world it is a death sentence. Remember Vedat Nesim's words: "I am in the government. This makes me a marked man." Branded. Marked by a pointed stake. Like the characters in Beckett's work, especially those of *L'Innommable*, the people of *The Names* are awaiting deliverance, to be spo-ken at last; but they may not outlive the utterance.

Writing is thus a form of Russian roulette, for letters can be loaded, and when the inscription is right, when the conditions are right, the violence of naming occurs. Melville's Bartleby, we are told after his death, may have been the disabused handler of dead letters. For DeLillo the letter is potent, deadly rather than dead, and his book closes with the final avatar of Owen Brademas, his letter-alike Orville Benton, protagonist of the fiction authored by the boy

Tap, last in the series of youths who mediate the script. Orville Benton, through the agency of Tap, lives out Owen's confused stirrings of the encounter with tongues, the preverbal past, "some uncycled memory where the nightmares lay, the ones in which he could not speak as others did, could not understand what they were saying" (284). Savvy postmodernist that he is, DeLillo knows that language precedes its speakers, that it got there first. So Tap uses what he has, does not even attempt to invent some new language. Early on he had, like so many youngsters, his version of pig latin, his "Ob" code.[8] But in the novel he writes, he rearranges (by ignorance?) the letters themselves, breaks (and breaks into) the fixed orthographic armature of the old words to liberate their indwelling violence and energy: "Seal the old language and loose the new!" Orville hears the preacher say, just as Owen remembered it. And it is done: "He was in the middle of a crowd, tongue-tied! There was a daise like a drunkerds skuffling lurch, realing in a corner" (335). Is this not the nightmarish but vitalizing encounter between self and sign? Using the child's memory of the revival meeting, DeLillo has found words here for the bondage from which we all come, the autism with which we all begin life, the universal crisis of being "in the middle of a crowd, tongue-tied," or, as the theorists remind us today, *infans*, "speechless."[9] The precariousness and the dazzling vistas of this scene are the conditions for one another: the flower and animal worlds press in with "daise" and "drunkerds," and "realing in a corner" perfectly delivers the DeLillo breakthrough, the regrouping of the Letter that removes our conceptual floor, throws us into a "skuffling lurch," while making possible a brave new "real" of its own. Orville is struck by the "glossylalya" he encounters, the way "people burst out in sudden streams," and the initiatory baptism he records is a would-be entry into the flux of the Names, the epic journey into the community of words. This *passage* rivals the Lacanian schemes for depicting our traumatizing and fissuring entry into language, for the journey into words is a (tragic?) exit from things: "He looked in vane for familiar signs and safe places. No where did he see what he expected. Why couldn't he understand and speak? There was no answer that the living could give. Tongue tied. His fait was signed. He ran into the rainy distance smaller and smaller. This was worse than a retched nightmare. It was the nightmare of real things, the fallen wonder of the world" (339).

DeLillo closes his novel on a pre-Babel note, leaving us to ponder the circularity of his materials (Owen the quester is now launched), the beauty of his fashionings: "looked in vane," "his fait was signed" (entailing a French, even a semiotic view of destiny itself), "a retched nightmare" that thrusts, convulsively, the body back into language where it was at the beginning. Tap's narrative is all of five pages long; DeLillo is not redoing *Finnegans Wake*, and he is content, here at the end of his story of death (of Owen, of James's marriage with Kathryn), to close with the voice of the child, to insist on continuum. Orville Benton, exiled into language, finds himself nonetheless entering the "nightmare of real things, the fallen wonder of the world," but his account is shot through with radiance. His journey is to be filled with surprises, a quest rather than a trip, one that lies at the core of this travelogue-fiction and shapes the lives of its "characters," all of them, in the final analysis, risk analysts, lurching into identity and synchrony, stumbling into "a self exposure we are never prepared for no matter how often we take this journey, the buried journey through categories and definitions and foreign languages, not the other, the sunlit trip to the east we thought we'd decided to make" (255). In taking the measure of its political and commercial schemas by reaching to the archaic poetry beneath them, *The Names* testifies to a noble and spirited view of utterance, an art form that is half palimpsest, half travelogue, outfitted with large vistas and dealing in high (pointed) stakes.

If *The Names* recalls, in its exoticism, the great travel and quest narratives of the past, *White Noise* displays DeLillo's no less prodigious gift for focusing his anthropological gaze homeward in order to deliver an anatomy of America the Beautiful in such a way that we discover a world we live in but have never seen, shimmering in its defamiliarized rendition of how the natives work and play. There is no undercover activity, no reportage on slums or cults or youth groups or hired killers or political campaigns. On the contrary, DeLillo sets his sights on the humdrum routines of middle America: the "new" family with its children of previous marriages, the presence of the media, the life of the campus, the threats to the environment, the adventures of consumerism, the management of dread. DeLillo is, of course, not Updike, and *White Noise* is not of the "around-the-house-and-in-the-yard" school of American fiction, nor is its reportage focused on "marriages and separations and trips to Tangle-wood."[10] Savvy mix of the planetary and the minute, it is a Drummond-light fiction, out to reveal to us our placedness and our surroundings.

As Murray, the resident guru of the novel, explains to his students, we "have to learn to look as children again."[11] We have to *see*; and DeLillo emerges as a writer of extraordinary perceptions, the Jamesian figure for whom nothing is lost, but a chronicler in a world unlike any James would have selected for notation. A visit to the supermarket (how many novelists take us to supermarkets?) yields this: "A woman fell into a rack of paperback books at the front of the store. A heavyset man emerged from the raised cubicle in the far corner and moved warily toward her, head tilted to get a clearer sightline. A checkout girl said, 'Leon, parsley,' and he answered as he approached the fallen woman, 'Seventy-nine.' His breast pocket was crammed with felt-tip pens" (19). *White Noise* is larded with such moments of zany mishap, given in deadpan style, without exclamation points, and invariably sandwiched into other "bytes" of cultural routine. The episode is finely seen; from the adverb "warily" to the felt-tip pens, it depicts a jungle, a precarious place pinned down with numbers, data, and codes. It is vintage DeLillo in its refusal of pathos, its leveling, egalitarian inclusiveness that calls to mind Whitman's democratic project a century earlier, stripped of all affect but no less canny in its sense of "fit" and "grouping." DeLillo the systems thinker is visible in these evocations, and he shows himself to be a savvy observer of environmental forces, wise about the clutter that surrounds and informs us.

The capacity to be insider and outsider, "to look as children again," enables the author to depict the known world with the eye-opening vision of a Martian visitor, an anthropologist seeking religious patterns in the daily routines of Americans.[12] Let us return to the supermarket:

Steffie took my hand and we walked past the fruit bins, an area that extended about forty-five yards along one wall. The bins were arranged diagonally and backed by mirrors that people accidentally punched when reaching for fruit in the upper rows. A voice on the loudspeaker said: "Kleenex Softique, your truck's blocking the entrance." Apples and lemons tumbled in twos and threes to the floor when someone took a fruit from certain places in the stacked array. There were six kinds of apples, there were exotic melons in several pastels. Everything seemed to be in season, sprayed, burnished, bright. People tore filmy bags off racks and tried to figure out which end opened. I realized the place was awash in noise. The toneless systems, the jangle and skid of carts, the loud-speaker and coffee-making machines, the cries of children. And over it all, or under it all, a dull and unlocatable roar, as of some form of swarming life just outside the range of human apprehension. (36)

Here is where we have lived, walked with our children, frolicked in the garden where all things are in season, partaken of the artfully arranged, bountiful harvest, wrestled with the filmy bags, arranged children and produce in the carts, taken in the noise, taken out the goods, paid our dues, exited, returned. There is "swarming life" here, and Murray, the expert on cultural studies, thinks it rigorously comparable to the spiritual transactions of Tibetan theology, thinks that is why we make these weekly pilgrimages:

This place recharges us spiritually, it prepares us, it's a gateway or pathway. Look how bright. It's full of psychic data. . . . Everything is concealed in symbolism, hidden by veils of mystery and layers of cultural material. But it is psychic data, absolutely. The large doors slide open, they close unbidden. Energy waves, incident radiation. All the letters and numbers are here, all the colors of the spectrum, all the voices and sounds, all the code words and ceremonial phrases. It is just a question of deciphering, peeling off the layers of unspeakability. (37–38)

Let there be no mistake: "peeling off layers of unspeakability" stands for the major activity of this novel, and it is a full-time job, unlike peeling fruit or unwrapping groceries. To see like a child again is to see dimensions, to perceive auras, to grasp the connectedness of what is discrete, the particulars of what seems joined, the odd magic of the material world we have made. DeLillo is the metaphysician of the kitchen and breakfast room, the poet of fast food; he actually *looks* at our gadgets: "I watched the coffee bubble up through the center tube and perforated basket into the small pale globe. A marvelous and sad invention, so roundabout, ingenious, human. It was like a philosophical argument rendered in terms of the world—water, metal, brown beans. I had never looked at coffee before" (103). There is something literally wonderful about this kind of writing, a kind of conceptual generosity that restores our doings to light and language, brings awe back to the world.

As one might expect, however, it can be a double-edged vision. The routines and trivia acquire radiance, but the "heavy" traditional icons are seen with a more jaundiced eye. This eye is alert to posturing, and it delights in exposing the song and dance of American packaging, the assiduous cultivation and merchandising of Americana. Hence, we have "the tourist attraction known as the most photographed barn in America," about which Murray wisely states, after seeing the array of slides, cards, and camera wielders, "Once you've seen signs about the barn, it becomes impossible to see the barn" (12). DeLillo's project of "innocenting" vision is rigorously counterpointed by the awareness of vision as construct, the awareness of the media's enormous shaping (and occulting) role in the way we see. Part of *White Noise* consists in seeing, like a child, the cultural machinery; the other part consists in examining, like an adult, the "unreal" vistas manufactured by that machinery — "unreal" in the sense that they are mythic constructs, making it "impossible to see the barn." We are dealing with more than the machinations of advertising; DeLillo wants to highlight the inevitable disjunction, *décalage*, between the concepts handed to us by the social order and the retinal evidence our eyes take in. Jack Gladney muses over the American nostalgia for yesteryear when he goes for a check-up at the medical laboratory with state-of-the-art facilities named Autumn Harvest Farms: "Was this an attempt to balance the heartlessness of their gleaming precision equipment? Would a quaint name fool us into thinking we live in pre-cancerous times? What kind of condition might we expect to have diagnosed in a facility called Autumn Harvest Farms? Whooping cough, croup? A touch of the grippe? Familiar old farmhouse miseries calling for bed rest, a deep chest massage with soothing Vicks Vapo-Rub. Would someone read to us from *David Copperfield*?" (275–76). DeLillo is touching here on the conceptual and rhetorical lag that informs all our lives, the ways in which we live in the past, still using Newtonian physics or medieval theology to explain events in our consciousness, busily applying to the present scene a host of models that have been defunct for centuries.

The story in *White Noise* takes place in a lazy college town called Blacksmith, and although DeLillo exploits the ironies made possible by his bucolic setting, he is not about to give us a cultural narrative in the manner of George Eliot. He has put his cultural experts in the book itself, and these folks are abrasively modern, on the lookout for today's icons; their view of rites of passage and cultural self-definition revolves around key queries such as "Did you piss in sinks?" "Where were you when James Dean died?" These folks, some of whom "read nothing but cereal boxes," are the connoisseurs of "American environments," and DeLillo is out to map that environment with the thoroughness of a cartographer-journalist who sees everything twice: both straight and at a tilt. Blacksmith is a town where Old Man Treadwell and his sister are lost for several days at a giant mall, where the technocratic order has made inroads everywhere, not merely in supermarkets and hospitals but in homes and people's minds. The human scale and unit of measure that governs *David Copperfield* (and most modern fiction as well) is eclipsed here, and we are witness to an array of compromises and uneasy truces, of skirmishes and negotiations between humans and their gadgets, humans and their environment. Sometimes it is delicious: "The smoke alarm went off in the hallway upstairs, either to let us know the battery had just died or because the house was on fire. We finished our lunch in silence" (8). This is what Hemingway's separate peace looks like sixty years after World War I. Make no mistake about it: American environments can kill you:

> They had to evacuate the grade school on Tuesday. Kids were getting headaches and eye irritations, tasting metal in their mouths. A teacher rolled on the floor and spoke foreign languages. No one knew what was wrong. Investigators said it could be the ventilating system, the paint or varnish, the foam insulation, the electrical insulation, the cafeteria food, the rays emitted by micro-computers, the asbestos fireproofing, the adhesive on shipping containers, the fumes from the chlorinated pool, or perhaps something deeper, finer-grained, more closely woven into the basic state of things. (35)

One senses that such deadpan writing stems, nonetheless, from an imagination of apocalypse, and DeLillo succeeds in bringing to the surface our repressed fears about cataclysm and nature's revenge, about the hubris of our technological feats and the day of reckoning that is on the way. He is the modern Kafka, the man who is at home in bureaucracy and who sees the lunacy of our engines of civilization and progress; like Kafka, DeLillo is the bookkeeper who starts in the red and goes downhill from there, wise about the myriad ways we are cornered and dispossessed, but at peace with his dark vision, palpably happy to inventory the mess we find ourselves in.

DeLillo also emerges as the poet laureate of the media age, for he understands the crucial role that television plays in the American environment, making it possible for us to savor erupting disasters, to watch, with relative impunity and vicarious thrills, the endless parade of world-class miseries visited on others and visiting us in our living rooms:

> That night, a Friday, we gathered in front of the set, as was the custom and the rule, with take-out Chinese. There were floods, earthquakes, mud slides, erupting volcanoes. We'd never before been so attentive to our duty, our Friday assembly. Heinrich was not sullen, I was not bored. Steffie, brought close to tears by a sitcom husband arguing with his wife, appeared totally absorbed in these documentary clips of calamity and death. Babette tried to switch to a comedy series about a group of racially mixed kids who build their own communication satellite. She was startled by the force of our objection. We were otherwise silent, watching houses slide into the ocean, whole villages crackle and ignite in a mass of advancing lava. Every disaster made us wish for more, for something bigger, grander, more sweeping. (64)

Needless to say, the pleasures of such spectating depend on the feeling of being untouchable. When it begins to look as if Blacksmith is having its own catastrophe, Jack is convinced there must be a mistake: "Society is set up in such a way that it's the poor and the uneducated who suffer the main impact of natural and man-made disasters. . . . Did you ever see a college professor rowing a boat down his own street in one of those TV floods?" (114). The media play a pivotal role in *White Noise* because they perform the double function of actualizing and derealizing, as if one's experience itself were not real until packaged and narrated and, ideally, served up on the evening news. Thus the folks in Blacksmith will feel a collective resentment when the catastrophe that has their name on it comes, goes, and never makes the news.[13] But it makes the novel.

Eerily paralleling Bhopal in a gentler key, DeLillo has arranged for his bucolic college town a small environmental disaster, to be coolly named the airborne toxic event. A tank car loaded with toxic gases is punctured, and the Gladney family's yearning for a disaster "bigger, grander, more sweeping" is fully satisfied. Here we have the novel's pièce de résistance, and DeLillo's evocation of the event, the evacuation, and the ensuing circus is both hysterical and bone chilling because no reader can escape the feeling that "it could happen here."

The description of the toxic cloud itself, seen in the mad exodus from the town, has the resonance and reach of myth:

> The enormous black mass moved like some death ship in Norse legend, escorted across the night by armored creatures with spiral wings. We weren't sure how to react. It was a terrible thing to see, so close, so low, packed with chlorides, benzines, phenols, hydrocarbons, or whatever precise toxic content. But it was also spectacular, part of the grandness of a sweeping event, like the vivid scene in the switching yard or the people trudging across the snowy overpass with children, food, belongings, a tragic army of the dispossessed. Our fear was accompanied by a sense of awe that bordered on the religious. It is surely possible to be awed by the thing that threatens your life, to see it as a cosmic force, so much larger than yourself, more powerful, created by elemental and willful rhythms. This was a death made in the laboratory, defined and measurable, but we thought of it at the time in a simple and primitive way, as some seasonal perversity of the earth like a flood or tornado, something not subject to control. (127)

LeClair has shrewdly observed that the nuclear cloud—"packed with chlorides, benzines, phenols, hydrocarbons"—is presented in consumerist terms, like a new item on the supermarket shelf.[14] Hence, to be understood, internalized as real experience, this event has to be not only packaged and presented but made over into narrative and thereby rendered consumable; in the "refugee camp" for the evacuees, Jack's son Heinrich provides for his fellows precisely this special human mediation, and in so doing he becomes a boy for his time, peculiarly altered by the disaster, both fulfilled and fulfilling:

> What a surprise it was to ease my way between people at the outer edges of one of the largest clusters and discover that my own son was at the center of things, speaking in his new-found voice, his tone of enthusiasm for runaway calamity. He was talking about the airborne toxic event in a technical way, although his voice all but sang with prophetic disclosure. He pronounced the name itself, Nyodene Derivative, with an unseemly relish, taking morbid delight in the very sound. People listened attentively to this adolescent boy in a field jacket and cap, with binoculars strapped around his neck and an Instamatic fastened to his belt. No doubt his listeners were influenced by his age. He would be truthful and earnest, serving no special interest; he would

have an awareness of the environment; his knowledge of chemistry would be fresh and up-to-date. (130)

With a brilliant sense of economy, DeLillo uses the catastrophe to cash in his chips. Jack's wife, Babette, has been reading tabloid articles to Old Man Treadwell, and here at the camp, under the shadow of the great cloud, these mawkish stories of Marilyn Monroe and John Wayne and Howard Hughes returning from the dead, often in UFOs, to consult with privileged viewers or to advise the president, seem no more implausible, no less credible than the actual events taking place. Murray was doubtless right: we are trafficking with the spirits wherever we go, into supermarkets or out of nuclear disasters. The tabloids are paying their way.

A lesser novelist would have dealt with the airborne toxic event in terms of tragedy and heroism: the individual pitted against the elements. DeLillo exploits this episode for the light it sheds on our deep-seated need to believe in the supernatural. In so doing he gives the disaster the kind of authority it rightfully deserves in *White Noise*, the authority of subject not object, of agent not setting. Here is the American environment at its most potent and demonic. And we realize we've been hearing it all along. "White noise" means, for scientists, "aperiodical sound with frequencies of random amplitude and random interval," whereas in music it signifies "sound produced by all audible sound-wave frequencies sounding together."[15] "Panasonic" was an earlier working title for this novel, and DeLillo has actually embodied this sense of an all-pervasive sound scheme, strangely analogous to what Melville was after visually in his meditation on the whiteness of the whale: a scaled picture of tiny space occupied by humans in the larger spectrum of noise and image made audible or visible or imaginable by the text's semiotic strategy.

The people of Blacksmith are only now comprehending the extent of their powerlessness, but DeLillo has been presenting all along a world view that divides up the power, puts humans in their proper, puny place. He has done this in a writerly fashion by divvying up narrational power, by writing a choral narrative in which the environment — now understood as a cultural rather than a physical force — speaks as much as the protagonists do. The novel is literally stereophonic:

> Upstairs a British voice said: "There are forms of vertigo that do not include spinning." (56)
>
> The TV said: "Now we will put little feelers on the butterfly." (96)
>
> The radio said: "It's the rainbow hologram that gives this credit card a marketing intrigue." (122)
>
> The voice upstairs said: "Now watch this. Joannie is trying to snap Ralph's patella with a *bushido* stun kick. She makes contact, he crumples, she runs." (257)

Sometimes this voice is not even discursive, just a list, a sequence of terms coming from out there: "MasterCard; Visa; American Express" (100). And it can be used to extraordinary point, as in the melodramatic episode in which Jack has learned from Babette of her Dylar venture and fear of death:

> We held each other tightly for a long time, our bodies clenched in an embrace that included elements of love, grief, tenderness, sex and struggle. How subtly we shifted emotions, found shadings, using the scantest movement of our arms, our loins, the slightest intake of breath, to reach agreement on our fear, to advance our competition, to assert our root desires against the chaos in our souls.
>   Leaded, unleaded, super unleaded. (199)

In striking Joycean fashion DeLillo achieves a tonal and philosophical counterpoint here that conveys the full force of the agon he is truly drawn to: the human story of love and passion, rendered with delicacy and power, juxtaposed against (undone by?) the technological indices of power and fuel, the marketing slogans that move our vehicles as well as our bodies.

At the end of the novel, when Jack is embarked on his fateful venture of revenge, the list achieves its darkest eloquence, as if to show that human madness is matched (abetted? produced?) by social and technological chaos of even greater import: "Random Access Memory, Acquired Immune Deficiency Syndrome, Mutual Assured Destruction" (303).

It is hard to imagine individual autonomy or dignity in this view of things, for the echoing, growling world out there continually noises its presence and power. And corresponding to this verbal, tonal bullying is an entire philosophy of the human being as automaton, as complex biotechnical entity ruled by forces unknown and ungovernable. Jack's son Heinrich is the youthful but formidable exponent of this weltanschauung, and his debates with his father on the nullity of human will, direction, and knowledge provide some of the keenest exchanges of the novel. When asked, innocently, by his father whether he wants to visit his mother for the summer at an ashram in Montana, Heinrich answers with the suavity that Voltaire displayed in *Candide*:

> "Who knows what I want to do? Who knows what anyone wants to do? How can you be sure about something like that? Isn't it all a question of brain chemistry, signals going back and forth, electrical energy in the cortex? How do you know whether something is really what you want to do or just some kind of nerve impulse in the brain? Some minor little activity takes place somewhere in this unimportant place in one of the brain hemispheres and suddenly I want to go to Montana or I don't want to go to Montana. How do I know I really want to go and it isn't just some neurons firing or something? Maybe it's just an accidental flash in the medulla and suddenly there I am in Montana and I find out I really didn't want to go there in the first place. I can't control what happens in my brain, so how can I be sure what I want to do ten seconds from now, much less Montana next summer? It's all this activity in the brain and you don't know what's you as a person and what's some neuron that just happens to fire or just happens to misfire. Isn't that why Tommy Roy [the convicted killer with whom he plays correspondence chess] killed those people?" (45–46)

Heinrich's biochemical, mechanized, will-less view of the human subject is perfectly calibrated to fit in the electronic world where the phone rings and "a woman's voice delivered a high-performance hello. It said it was computer-generated, part of a marketing survey aimed at determining current levels of consumer desire. It said it would ask a series of questions, pausing after each to give me a chance to reply" (48). *White Noise* is ultimately akin to the world of the body snatchers because it registers with great wit and accuracy the shrinking space we occupy, the limited autonomy we enjoy, the technological encroachments we endure, the peculiar hybrids we have become.[16]

Thus we are far indeed from *David Copperfield*, far from the reassuring schemes of psychological fiction that do honor to the human subject even when the going is rough. "La littérature de l'âme," in Barthes's phrase, is in trouble here, and DeLillo is offering to American letters an especially genial version of nonanthropocentric fiction, somewhat the way Robbe-Grillet did in his geometric fashion for the French some thirty years ago. The famed *inner life* of traditional fiction, the commodity that has sustained centuries of humanism, is not doing very well in *White Noise*. If the subject's consciousness is revealed to be a program of firing and misfiring neurons, what is to be said for its body, that place that harbors items such as heart, feelings, desire, and so forth? What is life really like on the "inside"? Jack, on the way to Autumn Harvest Farms, is bringing his most intimate disclosures with him: "I carried with me several specimen bottles, each containing some melancholy waste or secretion. Alone in the glove compartment rode an ominous plastic locket, which I'd reverently enclosed in three interlocking Baggies, successively twist-tied. Here was a daub of the most solemn waste of all, certain to be looked upon by the technicians on duty with the mingled deference, awe and dread we have come to associate with exotic religions of the world" (275). It is the supermarket vision gone "inside" for a stint, replete with filmy plastic bags and shiny, "burnished" specimens on parade. DeLillo is quite the master of the wide-angled shot in these precincts as well, as if Jack's privatist intestinal purview required enlarging, opening up to the roomier expanses of the whole family's waste system, yielding—in good supermarket logic—a more generic view of the inner life; and so Jack, looking for the fabulous Dylar medication that Babette has been secretly taking, inspects the compacted garbage of the week and runs headlong into a familial intimacy and exhibition of artifacts he had never suspected:

> I unfolded the bag cuffs, released the latch and lifted out the bag. The full stench hit me with shocking force. Was this ours? Did it belong to us? Had we created it? I took the bag out to the garage and emptied it. The compressed bulk sat there like an ironic modern sculpture, massive, squat, mocking. I jabbed at it with the butt end of a rake and then spread the material over the concrete floor. I picked through it item by item, mass by shapeless mass, wondering why I felt guilty, a violator of privacy, uncovering intimate and perhaps shameful secrets. It was hard not to be distracted by some of the things they'd chosen to submit to the Juggernaut appliance. But why did I feel like a household spy? Is garbage so private? Does it glow at the core with personal heat, with signs of one's deepest nature, clues to secret

yearnings, humiliating flaws? What habits, fetishes, addictions, inclinations? What solitary acts, behavioral ruts? I found crayon drawings of a figure with full breasts and male genitals. There was a long piece of twine that contained a series of knots and loops. . . . Some kind of occult geometry or symbolic festoon of obsessions. I found a banana skin with a tampon inside. Was this the dark underside of consumer consciousness? (258–59)

Once again, DeLillo's linguistic obsessions are on show. Perhaps this is the "natural language" of the species today. Organspeak. In a culture increasingly worried about industrial and nuclear waste, *White Noise* impudently suggests that we are to be known by our detritus, that our private waste is literally a form of ex-pression, of utterance.

And what do these secrets look like? Drawn, in all of his novels, to the dynamics of espionage and discovery, DeLillo is toiling in the same fields here, even though the terrain is now the family. Jack Gladney is a man who finds calm and peace in watching his children sleep. As he sits gazing at his daughter Steffie, he hears words she is murmuring:

Two clearly audible words, familiar and elusive at the same time, words that seemed to have a ritual meaning, part of a verbal spell or ecstatic chant.
Toyota Celica.
A long moment passed before I realized this was the name of an automobile. The truth only amazed me more. The utterance was beautiful and mysterious, gold-shot with looming wonder. It was like the name of an ancient power in the sky, tablet-carved in cuneiform. It made me feel that something hovered. But how could this be? . . . She was only repeating some TV voice. Toyota Corolla, Toyota Celica, Toyota Cressida. Supranational names, computer-generated, more or less universally pronounceable. Part of every child's brain noise, the substatic regions too deep to probe. (155)

One hardly knows what to make of these renderings, these epiphanic moments when DeLillo transmutes dross into gold, makes out of the pollution of advertising a beautiful postmodern lyricism and tenderness.[17] But we can hardly fail to see that, once again, "outside" has gotten "inside," that the TV is no longer "out there" at all; it is PacMan writ large: we are the machines gobbled up by other machines. Not that DeLillo's people have no "insides" or secrets: Wilder's marathon crying jag points to a dark core of pure affect, perhaps of terror, underneath it all, and DeLillo reveres that ultimate opaque language that is prior to all codes and grammars.

But the famous "inside story" which has been the burden of art and literature for centuries is passing "un mauvais quart d'heure" in this novel, is in fact being mauled into something quite unrecognizable, a series of weights and measures that graphs life and death, sickness and health, in utterly material fashion. Proust once assessed the magnificent absurdity of the thermometer that has a knowledge of our body that we, however self-aware we may be, can never possess. Overexposed to the toxic cloud, Jack Gladney seeks today's soothsayer with his computerized crystal ball. No secrets here:

"You're generating big numbers," he said, peering at the screen.

"I was out there only two and a half minutes. That's how many seconds?"

"It's not just you were out there so many seconds. It's your whole data profile. I tapped into your history. I'm getting bracketed numbers with pulsing stars."

"What does that mean?"

"You'd rather not know."

He made a silencing gesture as if something of particular morbid interest was appearing on the screen. I wondered what he meant when he said he'd tapped into my history. Where was it located exactly? Some state or federal agency, some insurance company or credit firm or medical clearinghouse? What history was he referring to? I'd told him some basic things. Height, weight, childhood diseases. What else did he know? Did he know about my wives, my involvement with Hitler, my dreams and fears? (140)

This passage is an uncanny and prophetic version of "freed" speech, empowered speech. Language is displaced but overflowing here because the machines and disks and data now speak us, frame us within their printouts, pronounce on our likely and unlikely futures, chart the curves and graph the risks. The subject is having his fortune told. Biology, chemistry, and mathematics have become myth. And business. And available. Our history is something somebody else taps into.

Once we grasp the disproportionate strengths and forces in the conflict DeLillo has staged, the profound imbalance between the human and the technological order, then we are in a position to measure the heroic role allotted to the family. Distinct from every other book DeLillo has written—each one cool and spare in its focus on cultural dynamics— *White Noise* is a singularly warm and effusive novel, filled with the poetry (and cacophony) of human relationships, tinged with melancholy at the fragility of the human, rich with laughter at the comedy of connection. The family is to be understood as a last gasp for consoling order, for human assertion. At least, that is Murray's theory:

Murray says we are fragile creatures surrounded by a world of hostile facts. Facts threaten our happiness and security. The deeper we delve into the nature of things, the looser our structure may seem to become. The family process works toward sealing off the world. Small errors grow heads, fictions proliferate. I tell Murray that ignorance and confusion can't possibly be the driving forces behind family solidarity. What an idea, what a subversion. He asks me why the strongest family units exist ꞌ. the least developed societies. (81–82)

DeLillo indulges fully in the farce of misinformation, and many of the Gladney family conversations seem to be a surrealist version of TV quiz shows, larded with garbled data, built on nonsequiturs, overflowing with runaway, homeless facts. But the truth coefficient of family discourse is ultimately irrelevant to the novel's deeper purposes, and the textural reality of human relationships has a richness and density all its own, utterly independent of the whims of true versus false:

> Babette came in from running, her outfit soaked through. Murray walked
> across the kitchen to shake her hand. She fell into a chair, scanned the room
> for Wilder. I watched Denise make a mental comparison between her mother's
> running clothes and the wet bag she'd dumped into the compactor. I could
> see it in her eyes, a sardonic connection. It was these secondary levels of life,
> these extrasensory flashes and floating nuances of being, these pockets of
> rapport forming unexpectedly, that made me believe we were a magic act,
> adults and children together, sharing unaccountable things. (34)

Even in the midst of catastrophe this tapestry of woven relationships displays
itself, shows the warp and woof of our lives, the threadwork and needlepoint
that are the homely but profound art of people living together over time: "It
was a period of looks and glances, teeming interactions, part of the sensory
array I ordinarily cherish. Heat, noise, lights, looks, words, gestures, person-
alities, appliances. A colloquial density that makes family life the one medium
of sense knowledge in which an astonishment of heart is routinely contained"
(117). Thus, many scenes in *White Noise* take place in the kitchen, "where the
levels of data are numerous and deep, as Murray might say" (48), or in the
bedroom or TV room, all turned into social rooms, places of multileveled
exchanges and transactions, material for endless study, response, and delight.
DeLillo has gotten a bum rap for coldness and abstraction, for failing to
produce rounded, believable characters. The children in the Gladney household have a rare fictional presence, and DeLillo shows himself to be a truly
democratic writer, widening our environment in more ways than one, letting
the TV and the toxic cloud speak, but also broadening the community of
human players, expanding our sense of communal enterprise, making us see
just how varied and surprising our actual natural resources are. There is nothing maudlin about this, nothing even programmatic in the family-versus-
destiny vein. Just a deepened sensitivity to sight and sound, an uncanny appreciation for the odd integrity of little folks and big folks. And this is a
modern family: children from prior marriages, former spouses dropping in,
youngsters flying out, Chinese takeout on Fridays, joint sprees at the supermarket and the department store.

Once again, DeLillo succeeds in avoiding the sentimental, in acknowledg-
ing the stress and paranoia of family while nonetheless depicting its richness,
its gratifying reality as environment, human this time instead or chemical or
media based. Jack Gladney is an astonishing character in the way Leopold
Bloom is, by dint of his capacity to imagine the other fellow, to take the
world as real rather than as screen for his own fantasies. But unlike Joyce's
protagonist, he is animated by fiercer loyalties and he is rewarded by familial
pleasures that Bloom has lost: the sight of children sleeping, the routine skirmishes with them, the endless tugs that give heft and rhythm to one's place on
the planet. Listening to Heinrich hold forth about the toxic environment, the
father in Jack wants to counter: "I wanted to tell him that statistical evidence
of the kind he was quoting from was by nature inconclusive and misleading. I
wanted to say that he would learn to regard all such catastrophic findings
with equanimity as he matured, grew out of his confining literalism, developed
a spirit of informed and skeptical inquiry, advanced in wisdom and rounded

judgment, got old, declined, died" (175). There is an exquisite balance in these lines between love, admiration, and irony, including self-irony. Such passages are no less eye-opening, no less exploratory than the anthropological trips to the supermarket, and they go a long way toward positing a center of gravity for *White Noise.*

Much of the novel's power derives from the elemental conflict it stages between the family unit, on the one hand, source of poetry and frail structure against chaos, and the omnipresence of death on the other, death depicted magisterially by DeLillo in an astounding array of colors and hues. The airborne toxic event merely makes public and communal and visible an ongoing presence of destruction that has been making private visits for some time now. Known variously as the reverse Darwinism that punishes survivors, or the brutal myoclonic jerk that wracks the body out of sleep, as the secret goal of all plots, or the terror just beneath the surface in all plane flights, as the secret origin of our sense of déjà vu, or the staple material of the media which fascinates the living, or indeed as the beyond depicted earlier in the *Egyptian Book of the Dead* and felt to be gathering apocalyptic force in the "floods, tornadoes, epidemics of strange new diseases" (136) seen in the hilarious Beckett-like countdown that Vernon pronounces over the entropic decay of his body, Death is of course the major white noise of DeLillo's scheme, the ubiquitous, lurking, palpable dread that is anatomized in this novel. Society's greatest weapon for warding off death is technology, but we have here a vision of technology gone amok: computers that replace our history with pulsing stars and bracketed numbers, toxins that escape to form a great Norse death ship and threaten entire communities, medications such as Dylar that are intended to eradicate the fear of death but instead give rise to death plots of their own.

If technology represents the West's failure to conquer death, fascism represents its supreme effort to serve it. The concern with fascism runs throughout DeLillo's work, but only in *White Noise* does it achieve its true proportions. Not only do the surging crowds that massed around the speeches of Hitler and Goebbels make an eerie return in the evacuation and cosmic threat of the airborne toxic event (with Heinrich playing the role of a child-führer in the improvised camp/*Führerbunker*), but Hitler is finally understood to be a magic talisman against death itself, the kind of epic figure to whom "helpless and fearful people are drawn," not so much larger than life as "larger than death" (287). Fascism is ultimately the conversion experience for Jack Gladney, his transformation from "dier" into "killer."

DeLillo brilliantly plays his German card to the full in *White Noise,* moving from the innocuous metamorphosis of Jack into a more menacing, dark-glassed J.A.K., then accelerating into the fuller homicidal reaches of the Hitler persona. Jack's transformation is insistently coded in linguistic terms, ranging from the rudimentary German lessons to the final descent into Germantown and murder.[18] Recalling, strangely yet precisely, Roman Polanski's gradual and meticulous enmeshing of his people at last in Chinatown (in the film of that name), a place where we do not know who is who, DeLillo propels his lovable protagonist into a crazed search for revenge that takes him to the

Dylar czar in Germantown, one Willie Mink, who has had sex with Babette as the condition for giving her the notorious pill for removing fear of death. Germantown, like Chinatown, is the metaphoric heart of the text, the center of the labyrinth, where Jack Gladney finally goes "inside." In this book, with its view of the subject under siege both inwardly (misfiring neurons, decaying organs, death sentence) and outwardly (the environmental invasions, cultural, climactic, media, electronic, nuclear), with Babette's prohibition of the very term "entering" ("We're not lobbies or elevators," she says [29]), it is disturbingly appropriate that Willie Mink define his nefarious enterprise as an inside room: "The point of rooms is that they're inside. No one should go into a room unless he understands this" (306). If there is anything *White Noise* teaches its readers, it is a respect for the dignity of surfaces, and we sense something outright invasive in the strange poetry of DeLillo's end gambit. The author persistently images Jack's "entry" in liminal and nuclear terms: "I was moving closer to things in their actual state as I approached a violence, a smashing intensity" (305); "I continued to advance in consciousness. Things glowed, a secret life rising out of them" (310). Willie Mink is the living embodiment of white noise, the originary generator of waves and rays, the source itself of the static and babble of technology that has punctuated this text in its choral refrains. Here there is light, and at last the murk of the human lifts, dissolves: "Water struck the roof in elongated orbs, splashing drams. I knew for the first time what rain really was. I knew what wet was. I understood the neurochemistry of my brain, the meaning of dreams (the waste material of premonitions). Great stuff everywhere, racing through the room, racing slowly. A richness, a density. I believed everything. I was a Buddhist, a Jain, a Duck River Baptist" (310). But this entry into truth, this blinding light, dismantles all human constructs, those of being and those of doing. Willie Mink is, in his very syntax and utterances, the death of narrative:

> "She wore a ski mask so as not to kiss my face, which she said was un-American. I told her a room is inside. Do not enter a room not agreeing to this. This is the point, as opposed to emerging coastlines, continental plates. Or you can eat natural grains, vegetables, eggs, no fish, no fruit. Or fruit, vegetables, animal proteins, no grains, no milk. Or lots of soybean milk for B-12 and lots of vegetables to regulate insulin release but no meat, no fish, no fruit. Or white meat but no red meat. Or B-12 but no eggs. Or eggs but no grains. There are endless workable combinations." (310-11)

We wind up inside the machine. This realm of interchangeable mechanical systems, the very speech of computer-generated discourse, spews forth a kind of biotalk of "endless workable combinations," but it is alien to human connection, to the human and syntactical linkages that alone figure life in this death-obsessed book. Jack Gladney submits to the fascist lure, becomes a killing machine deep in Germantown.

And, in a turn of pure genius, DeLillo chooses this moment to illustrate the virtues of Dylar, a drug that cannot ward off death but can, instead, produce magic language, turn words into deeds. The text at last speaks German. Jack merely *says* "Hail of bullets," and Mink ducks; says "Fusillade," and Mink takes cover behind the toilet. We are close, here (albeit in Marx brothers fashion), to the quest for potent language that is at the center of *The Names*, finally and fatefully moving past the mediations of signs into the very pith of violence and terror. It is here that we appreciate the mellowness of *White Noise*. DeLillo indeed underscores in this later text the lethal character of "natural" language, but he goes on to display his abiding commitment to the network of human players, the clowns who use and misuse the verbal codes. The verbal and metaphysical fantasia is cut short here, as Jack wounds Mink, takes him to the hospital, returns the stolen car, and reenters the bosom of his family. The life-affirming rhythm of comedy prevails, and the book closes with an image of immersion into the flow, this time entailing the child Wilder's entry onto the freeway, into the traffic, as if to show that life moves everything and everyone into its gravitational pull, that the child—so long viewed adoringly by his parents as magically suspended in time—is no more a talisman against death than Dylar or technology or fascism. And life continues its round. Even the products on the supermarket's shelves are rearranged.

Lacking the philosophical and linguistic boldness of *The Names*, lacking even more sorely the affective density, surreal humor, and cultural satire of *White Noise, Libra*, the fictional 1988 account of the making and unmaking of Lee Harvey Oswald, is nonetheless a story that DeLillo seems almost destined to have written. Building on the essay "American Blood: A Journey Through the Labyrinth of Dallas and JFK," published in *Rolling Stone* in 1983, *Libra* is, in some strange way, DeLillo's version of elegy, conceived almost entirely in terms of media and technology, in honor of America as Humpty-Dumpty, irremediably fissured on November 22, 1963, blinded by "six point nine seconds of heat and light" no less devastatingly than Oedipus was, with the searing intensity of a nuclear explosion.

Reminiscent of Dowell, the narrator of Ford's *Good Soldier*, who sees his work as the labor of a scribe following the sacking of a city, DeLillo's "book-man" Nicholas Branch, retired senior analyst at the CIA, is in the fifteenth year of his assignment to write the secret history of the Kennedy assassination, a task he will never complete, given the endless and increasing flow of computerized data that surrounds and threatens to bury him: the facts, the theories, the biographies, the histories, the countless trails and crossings, a retrospective weave that makes Oedipus's fateful encounter at his crossroads look achingly clean and clear in its spelling of origins and ends. Here, then, is DeLillo's model of the aftermath, the deluge: slain president, lost innocence, and a special purgatory of epistemological murk, of never again seeing clear, of permanent exile in the realm of information glut and data overload. From this morass there can be no credible deliverance, no redeeming truth. Only fiction remains, and that is the project he undertakes here: to understand Lee Harvey Oswald as a fiction, as a theory, in his own eyes, in the eyes of those who used him, in the eyes of history. Ultimately DeLillo has written a Sophoclean parable about the shaping of a life and the limits of knowledge, and this parable is luminous as a fable about the resources of fiction after the fall, the freedom of speech when vision is gone.

Libra is bound to disappoint readers looking for the portrait of an era. It pays attention to the pro- and anti-Castro elements, the ripple effect of the Bay of Pigs, the intricate shadow worlds of the CIA, the plotting and counter-plotting within its many factions, but everything is muffled and under cover, far from the strident realities of news media, national opinion, the fresco of a nation in trauma. Unlike Coover's *Public Burning*, DeLillo's book is not seri-ously concerned with the themes of American politics, not even with the paranoia and lunacy that he has chronicled so magisterially in earlier books. He is not even interested in Kennedy—and this amazes, given his persistent zeroing in on figures of power. He is only mildly interested in Jack Ruby—and this amazes, too, given his brilliance in rendering ethnic types like Ruby (in fact, the few pages devoted to Ruby in *Libra* have a gratifying heft and flavor unlike anything else in the book).

DeLillo's prey is the elusive Oswald, the Libra figure who could go either way, who is seeking to find his form, to leave his imprint, the man who defined happiness in a letter to his brother as "taking part in the struggle, where there is no borderline between one's personal world and the world in general" (1). Like a (thwarted) latter-day Hegelian, Oswald is trying to develop his world consciousness, to merge his destiny with the forces of history. As Nicholas Branch pores over Oswald's dealings with the CIA and the KGB, his education in New York and New Orleans, Minsk and Moscow, his lifelong efforts to be mover rather than pawn, surveyor of systems rather than cipher or dupe, the rich parallels and concatenations of American fiction begin to come into focus. Lee Harvey Oswald, putative candidate for regicide, is actu-ally *Homo americanus*, a man trying to forge his identity, utterly at home in our line of figures that starts with Wakefield and passes through Gatsby and Joe Christmas en route to beleaguered types such as Coover's version of Rich-ard Nixon and Rick Blaine. Such a figure haunts, seems (both to himself and others) fictive and even ghostly, engages the narrative imagination: behind the pallid Oswald we can discern the enigmatic Bartleby, the unmoored Darl Bundren, the riddling Misfit, the disembodied Beloved. The world of *Libra* is the labyrinth where Nobody lives, and like so many American texts it displays the desperate countermeasures of art to encroach on the real, to offer rhyme as a bid for reason. As readers, therefore, we are in strangely familiar terri-tory: once again, our desire to see clear is thwarted by the novelist's insistence on doubles and shadows, ranging from the twinning high jinks of *Puddn'head Wilson* to the transformational antics of Anderson, Faulkner, and Heming-way, right up to Hawkes's twin islands and the house of games negotiated by Coover's 3-D man and his fictive Chaplin. In these gambits we see the irresist-ible double game of the American writer, the craft and craftiness of the writer as rendition of, and alternative to, coercion. These are the generic features of self-making and freedom of speech in the American novel.

Libra plays by these rules but operates, nonetheless, a small but crucial paradigm shift. The shapers are now in the text and in the world. The writer's power has passed into the creation. *Libra* completes DeLillo's series of con-spiracy texts, of subjects encountering systems and environments beyond their control. The fate of Oswald is emblematic of the enmeshed, fettered self, trapped in others' designs, Libralike in its own uncertain allegiances, in search of its fit. *Libra* is the deadpan tragicomedy of information gathering, whether it be Branch's investigation, Guy Bannister's detective agency, Oswald's cross-cultural education, or the surveillance performance of the top secret U-2 aircraft. And the results are always the same: much data, little truth.

But the data itself we now understand to be made rather than given; planted, posited, put there to be "discovered." Thus *Libra* offers a prophetic vision of theory empowered, turned demiurgic, of models leaving the lab, of the Frankenstein scenario becoming routine business within the intelligence community, and beyond it. The shapers are in the system, and the central conceit of DeLillo's book is the *making of a man*, not by self-determination but by paste and glue. An entire American tradition of self-making (vitally embodied in most of the works studied here) is now biting the dust. Win Everett (rebuffed CIA veteran of the Bay of Pigs) has a grand design, and it consists of fabricating a life, doing "the whole thing with paper" (28), planting a paper trail, enlisting his disaffected cohorts in the project of selecting from the ranks of the living "a name, a face, a bodily frame they might use to extend their fiction into the world" (150). Life will yield to design:

> He would put someone together, build an identity, a skein of persuasion and habit, ever so subtle. He wanted a man with believable quirks. He would create a shadowed room, the gunman's room, which investigators would eventually find, exposing each fact to relentless scrutiny, following each friend, relative, casual acquaintance into his roomful of shadows. We lead more interesting lives than we think. We are characters in plots, without the compression and numinous sheen. Our lives, examined carefully in all their affinities and links, abound with suggestive meaning, with themes and involute turnings we have not allowed ourselves to see completely. He would show the secret symmetries in a nondescript life. (78)

One can almost taste the pleasures produced by plotting, the great opportunity to make good on design and intelligence, to bring the world to order by imposing one's fiction. But this subtle Jamesian view of complexity and pattern is quickly escalated into a Grand Guignol frenzy of uncontrolled intrigues, of cancerous and anarchic schemes instigated by competing factions and individuals, each intent on imposing its own design, making reality its own way. The result is a world of pure carnival, abounding in doubles and replicas: multiple Kennedys and Oswalds, clones, plants, lookalikes, masks. This histrionic, baroque profusion of images and effigies has its dark side. Here is how agent David Ferrie, former Eastern Airlines pilot, fully hairless, interested in young boys, defines himself: "Forty-five. Perfect astronaut age. I'm the dark scary side of John Glenn. Great health except for the cancer eating at my brain" (65). And DeLillo's project has the same lurking "who is who?" terror that doubles have implied ever since Jekyll and Hyde. Suzanne, the child of one of the agents, is never clear of "the dark scary side," and she goes to sleep with her special Little Figures of a clay man and a clay woman: "The Little Figures were not toys. She never played with them. The whole reason for the Figures was to hide them until the time when she might need them. She had to keep them near and safe in case the people who called themselves her mother and father were really somebody else" (366).

Role playing, double roles, effigies, double selves, no selves: this is the utterly unplayful world of espionage. The Little Figures with multiple identities. Stalin's name was Dzhugashvili; Trotsky's name was Bronstein. Lee Harvey Oswald will take on pseudonyms—Alek, Leon, O. H. Lee, and Osborne—but he is most fully revealed by the name Hidell:

> Take the double-*e* from Lee.
> Hide the double-*l* in Hidell.
> Hidell means hide the *L*.
> Don't tell. (90)

The vision of *Libra* and the DeLillo metaphysics are best summed up by the Dallas disc jockey Weird Beard:

> "I know what you think. You think I'm making it up. I'm not making it up. If it gets from me to you, it's true. We are for real, kids. And this is the question I want to leave with you tonight. Who is for real and who is sent to take notes? You're out there in the depths of the night, listening in secret, and the reason you're listening in secret is because you don't know who to trust except me. We're the only ones who aren't them. This narrow little radio band is a route to the troot. I'm not making it up. There are only two things in the world. Things that are true. And things that are truer." (266)

If *Libra* comes across as a frustrating book, oddly weightless even in its density, it is because the theatrical world of doubles and covers has finally become spectral and triumphant (true and truer), an affair of voices in the night, clones in the day, aliases and acronyms. Oswald's concept of happiness as the erasing of the "borderline between one's own personal world, and the world in general" turns out to be simply the erasing of one's personal world, the disappearance of self altogether into the world's designs.

Six point nine seconds of light and heat, of unbearable clarity, when all the phantoms traveling their separate routes converge and collide, from which new, unsuspected amalgams emerge. Ruby finds himself wedded to Oswald. The indistinct Oswald merges in death with his spy-double Powers, the downed U-2 pilot: "It is the white nightmare of noon, high in the sky over Russia. Me-too and you-too. He is a stranger, in a mask, falling" (440).

These epiphanic lines epitomize DeLillo's achievement. The nightmare is our daytime reality. The stranger, in a mask, is falling, but his estrangement is inseparable from ours, "Me-too and you-too." That is why DeLillo takes the risk of closing his novel with Christlike accents: three times Oswald asks Marina to live with him in Dallas, and three times he is denied; Marguerite Oswald refers pointedly to biblical precedent—"If you research the life of Jesus, you see that Mary mother of Jesus disappears from the record once he is crucified and risen" (453)—as she makes her final utterances. Buried in the ground in a final alias, as William Bobo, Lee Harvey Oswald is the exemplary victim of our culture, the No Man whose story is one long anti-bildungsroman, a "how-not-to" book on social purposiveness, an ongoing disappearing act that registers, in full, the forces that cause us to disappear. Here is the definitive portrait of the American Nobody, the man seeking to construct himself while being constructed by forces beyond his ken. With this text we come to the last of our self-made-men, but — in true DeLillo fashion — forward and reverse have become interchangeable: everything is going the other way now, and this man is made by others, converted neatly from life into fiction. Only he never knew.

The agent Parmenter's wife, Beryl, watches, along with much of the nation, Oswald's televised death, and she feels the terrible pull of this man's fate: "He is commenting on the documentary footage even as it is being shot. Then he himself is shot, and shot, and shot, and the look becomes another kind of knowledge. But he has made us part of his dying" (447). Shot by revolver and by camera, Hidell is exposed and undone, is witness to his own execution, shares in the packaging and distribution of his own death, leaves us his dying as a legacy for the living. Like Bartleby dying in the Tombs, or Joe Christmas dismembered, the final mystery of No Man does not die with the victim but passes on, living, into our lives and dreams.

Conclusion

A colleague once confided that the central myth shared by all his students is their conviction that they are somebody, possessing a unique identity: *a self*. Whereas, he added, if there is anything we have learned in the past century, it is the extent to which we are *products*: of our culture, our genes, our family, our environment, our media, our signs.

And who can deny it? Even to use the possessive pronoun "our" is highly misleading, since the salient fact common to culture, genes, family, environment, media, and signs is that they *precede* us, that they are the potent shaping forces, the veritable force field in which "we" are positioned, of which "we" are made. Let us add the monoliths of class, race, and gender to this mix, and it becomes still clearer that ideology informs and shapes identity, that much of any individual repertory is preformed, choosing us rather than being chosen by us, displaying in the antics of self a whole host of deep structures and impersonal forces whose creature self is.

It is no exaggeration to say that education and maturity jointly teach us this lesson throughout our lives. The more we know about history, social forces, biology, genetic coding, economics, psychology, psychoanalysis, language, semiotics, anthropology, myth, the more we understand the organic, integral, and unique self to be a fantasy. The older we get, the more we recognize in our gestures the sounds and motions of our parents, the more we hear in our speech the tones and slogans that have formed us, the more we see in our very bodies the genetic continuum that we instance, the more we comprehend our most profound ideas and feelings to be prepackaged and overdetermined, the harder it is to sustain the view of self as original or atomic.

Why, then, do our students persist in this myth? The view from the academy would doubtless be that we possess knowledge they do not have. But could one not consider the alternative: that they possess a kind of instinctual certainty, a quasi-religious belief in self that education and time gradually but relentlessly erode? This American agon, many-colored — comic, tragic, fantastic, evasive, determinist, ecstatic — has been front and center in our literature: selfhood as American bedrock, as inalienable right, as political and economic myth driving our culture and fueling our lives; and selfhood as

American fantasy, as illusory construct, as mirage that the impersonal forces of language, politics, and the environment obliterate, do in. This book has attempted to capture the high drama of that agon, to show that the gut conviction of the (especially American) young that they are Somebody has a history and repertory in the literature of this country, that it taps into the vitalizing energies of personal and national life in remarkable ways. Here is a war of independence that most of us fight every day of our lives.

One thing remains certain: whatever its status as fact, self can never be discredited as fiction. It stands as the supreme fiction of our books and our lives. It constitutes the ongoing work of art—the shaping enterprise of a lifetime—that consumes all our days as we traffic in résumés, stories, reminiscences, all the narrative bric-à-brac of self-positing. There is more than nostalgia or blind illusion at work here. A very primitive but very powerful energy fuels the work of self-making, of self-assertion, and the spectrum of literary texts from "Wakefield" to *Libra* displays some of the vitality and tenacity of this primal American activity. Perhaps it is time to move past the true-false concept of self, even to jettison the given-made dichotomy, in order to recognize that all notions of identity contain these dialectical elements, that the *process* of every life, wittingly or not, is a dynamic interaction of these strains and stresses. As long as we live, we are staking our claim, making our mark, "signing" all the while.

One thing we can gain from this American parade of self-making and freedom of speech is a better understanding of the plight and making of Nobody. To be a ghost to oneself or to be a thing for others is intolerable. Both of these conditions are profoundly social because connection with others actualizes us, either by touching our humanity or by recognizing it. This is every bit as much the work of culture as of individual initiative. Sexism and racism, reification and commodification are practices that produce Nobody. Let us return to the image of the student who thinks he or she has an identity, a self, and let us juxtapose that student with the (black) Memphis garbage collectors in 1968 whose signs read "I am a man." They wanted recognition; they knew, from the inside, what it meant to be Nobody. And therein lies the connection between the theme of Nobody's Home and the tribal culture that dominates our society today. Never has there been a time of comparable awareness and anger about the way society treats persons it regards as marginal, Other. Although disenfranchised groups may have much in common— namely, the refusal of human dignity to their members—the upshot has been a medley of competing voices and groups, a fragmented culture of causes and cases, each asserting its bid for recognition. And the vitality of American life owes much to this stridency, a stridency wholly in accord with the powerful desire for selfhood displayed throughout the pages of this book. To see how far back this theme goes, how much unity it confers on very different kinds of American texts and times, is perhaps to gain a fuller sense of common ground, of real bridges between apparently separate causes and concerns. If so, it might point beyond the obsession with Difference that seems to stamp so much of today's thinking.

Another thing we might learn from this parade of self-making figures is the sheer vitality and variety of these ventures, the manifold ways by which self is fashioned, the surprising role that language and its realm of virtuality may play in our drama of self-enactment. It is tempting to envision these performances as variegated portraits of the artist, as illustrations and case studies of the maneuvering room made available by and in literature. But this self-enclosed view will not take the measure of what we have seen. The writerly game of self-making is a serious one, and its stakes can be surprisingly secular. Our verbal extensions and projects, the sentences we write, have a way of becoming life and death sentences in the material world. When Lincoln greeted Mrs. Stowe as the little woman who started the big war, he was saying something about the power of the word, its capacity to go well beyond the precincts of the page and to play its part in the arena of history. In our day the notorious case of Salman Rushdie is an equivalent (and forbidding) example of the virulence of art. To render, in a book, either the slave or the god as human is to exercise a potent and dangerous freedom. In ways both wonderful and terrible, life does follow art.

Finally, I would hope that this book contributes in some way to a richer and more generous understanding of self-making and freedom of speech as bona fide American ventures. It has been fashionable for some time now to critique American individualism for its imperialist and colonialist appetites, and we all know something about the excesses and horror stories connected with U.S. greed and power, with the overreaching and arrogance that often typifies the self-made person. We know that the empowered self is frequently a blind and dangerous figure, closed off to the needs and even to the existence of others or of the environment. But the powers of belief, creation, and purpose which go into self-making have something magic and fine about them. They testify to a "can-do-ism" that is the very gauge of freedom, and they ceaselessly transform the world of closure—body, name, race, gender, class, even death—into something open, possible, imaginable.

When I studied at Princeton in the early 1960s, we all knew the anecdote of the "fabricated student applicant": a paper construct whose SATs had been forged, whose application had been filled out and submitted, for whom letters had been written, and whose career enchanted us, for he was said to have gone right on through, earning his degree, unimpeded (helped?) by his status as unreal. I later found this fellow in *Gatsby*, under the name of Blocks Biloxi, but even then, as students ourselves, we found something marvelous in this Odyssean story of cunning and pluck and forgery, this parable about beating the system through the agency of language. In their distinct ways every book under consideration in this study—even those such as *Uncle Tom's Cabin, Light in August, Beloved*, and *Libra* which are chronicles of entrapment and coercion—goes through the same prancing motions as our "fabricated student." They map for us the large terrain of self and setting, and in the intricate picture they offer of that crucial interplay between subjectivity and environment, they illuminate a spectrum of strategies and fates that may be ours. Ultimately these are colonialist narratives, not because they succeed in controlling the world but because they reflect our belief that being a person matters. Reading them, we may be strengthened to a richer view of our own resources, especially the resource of language, so highlighted in their very matter and manner, thereby making us freer, more empowered in our projects of utterance and self-fashioning.

Those projects, unlike the books we write or the classes we teach, are long-term projects, indeed lifelong projects, since the shaping at hand begins with our birth and ceases only with our death. It is doubtless the longest and most incessant artistic activity that we know, and the widespread view that art and aesthetics are elitist frills is sadly out of touch with the human crafting that living entails. In a 1990 essay the neurologist Oliver Sacks approaches this issue from a radically different direction, but his conclusion buttresses the fiction argument made throughout this book. Sacks claims that our bodies, even though systemic and generic, are personalized by living: "The nervous system adapts, is tailored, evolves, so that experience, will, sensibility, moral sense, and all that one would call personality or soul becomes engraved in the nervous system. The result is that one's brain is one's own. One is not an immaterial soul, floating around in a machine. I do not feel alive, psychologically alive, except insofar as a stream of feeling—perceiving, imagining, remembering, reflecting, revising, recategorizing runs through me. I am that stream—that stream is me."[1] Sacks goes on to critique Hume's denial of identity by asserting, "We are not incoherent, a bundle of sensations, but a *self*, rising from experience, continually growing and revised."[2] It is worth emphasizing the terms used by the neurologist: imagining, remembering, reflecting, revising. These are the resources and activities of a creature bent on individuation as much as on survival. And these processes are common to art as much as they are to memory, dream, and consciousness; indeed, the very control and discipline that stamp them, the "working" of our facts into forms and fictions, into patterns of wholeness, makes it unmistakable that we are close to the world of art here, that the human subject is an inveterate artist, transforming the data of experience into the attributes of self. American fiction, more than most, is hospitable to these homing ventures, and the light that it sheds on these dark matters testifies to a wonderfully irreducible human energy, a kind of man-made sun that creates, for its readers, blazoned days.

Notes

Introduction

1. Cited by Tony Tanner, "Frames and Sentences," in *Representation and Performance in Postmodern Fiction*, ed. Maurice Couturier (Montpellier: Delta, 1983), p. 22.

2. Wallace Stevens, "Notes Towards a Supreme Fiction," in *The Palm at the End of the Mind*, ed. Holly Stevens (New York: Vintage, 1972), pp. 207–34.

Chapter 1

1. Hawthorne's tale of the "crafty nincompoop" has drawn a certain amount of critical attention, mostly in journals. It has never been thought of as part of the Hawthorne heavy artillery: the famous novels, the major stories. The generalists who have assayed Hawthorne — Trilling, Kermode — have not touched it, and the specialists — Feidelson, Male, Fogel, Waggoner, Crews, et al. — touch it only in passing. Hyatt Waggoner's judgment — "a failure of development, a failure of creative energy" (*Hawthorne: A Critical Study* [Cambridge, Mass.: Harvard UP, 1955], p. 63) — is typical enough of the put-downs the text has received. The current "new historical" work on Hawthorne is understandably not drawn to this London-based text.

2. Nathaniel Hawthorne, *Tales and Sketches* (New York: Library of America, 1982), p. 295. Subsequent references to "Wakefield" and other Hawthorne tales are to this edition and are cited in the text.

3. John Wright, "Borges and Hawthorne," *TriQuarterly*, 25 (Fall 1972), 338.

4. See George Monteiro's fine article entitled "Hawthorne, James, and the Destructive Self," *Texas Studies in Literature and Language*, 4, no. 1 (Spring 1962), 58–71, for a cogent view of Wakefield as egocentric and destructive.

5. Martin Green's caustic but illuminating essay "The Hawthorne Myth: A Protest" in *Essays and Studies*, ed. S. Gorley Putt (London: John Murray, 1963), pp. 17–36, makes the fullest case against Hawthorne in terms of coldness and "unreality."

6. Robert Chibka's "Hawthorne's Tale Told Twice: A Reading of 'Wakefield,'" *ESQ*, 28, no. 4 (1982), 220–32, makes the argument for narrational authority very effectively.

7. Frederick Crews, *The Sins of the Fathers* (New York: Oxford UP, 1966).

8. Deborah West and Michael West, "The Psychological Dynamics of Hawthorne's 'Wakefield,'" *Archiv für das Studium der neueren Sprachen und Literaturen*, no. 220 (1983), 70.

9. Herbert Perluck, "The Artist as 'Crafty Nincompoop': Hawthorne's 'Indescribable Obliquity of Gait' in 'Wakefield,'" in *The Nathaniel Hawthorne Journal*, ed. C. E. Frazer Clark, Jr. (Detroit: Gale Research, 1978), pp. 181–94.

10. Roberta F. Weldon, "Wakefield's Second Journey," *Studies in Short Fiction*, 14 (Winter 1977), 69–74, has offered a very persuasive reading of the story as the account of a midlife crisis told mythically.

11. *The Portable Hawthorne*, ed. Malcolm Cowley (New York: Penguin Books, 1977), p. 617. Subsequent references are to this edition and are cited in the text.

12. Nathaniel Hawthorne, *The Scarlet Letter*, in *Nathaniel Hawthorne: Novels* (New York: Library of America, 1983), p. 243. Subsequent references are to this edition and are cited in the text.

13. Crews, *Sins*, p. 126.

14. Barton St. Armand, "Hawthorne's 'Haunted Mind': A Subterranean Drama of the Self," *Criticism*, 13 (Winter 1971), 1–25, examines a very different kind of Hawthorne text in terms of Jungian self-exploration, and one would have to agree that the head-on encounter with the dark Other, even in dreams, is generally sabotaged or begged; all the more reason, therefore, to conceive of this journey of self-knowledge in more figural terms, bypassing consciousness altogether.

15. Quoted by Harold Beaver, "Introduction," in *Herman Melville: Billy Budd, Sailor & Other Stories* (Harmondsworth, Eng.: Penguin, 1967), p. 15.

16. Quoted in *Studies in Classic American Literature*, ed. D. H. Lawrence (New York: Viking, 1964), p. 83.

Chapter 2

1. Herman Melville, "Bartleby the Scrivener: A Tale of Wall Street," in *Herman Melville: "Pierre," "Israel Potter," "The Piazza Tales," "The Confidence Man," Uncollected Prose, "Billy Budd," "Sailor,"* ed. Hayford & Harrison (New York: Library of America, 1984). Subsequent references are to this edition and are cited in the text.

2. The Christlike dimension of Bartleby has been very prominent in a good deal of the secondary literature. The most influential reading along these lines is that of Bruce Franklin in his *Wake of the Gods: Melville's Mythology* (Stanford: Stanford UP, 1963), pp. 126–36. See also Donald Fiene, "Bartleby the Christ," in *Studies in the Minor and Later Works of Melville*, ed. Raymona Hull (Hartford, Conn.: Transcendental Books, 1970), and William Bysshe Stein, "Bartleby: The Christian Conscience," in *A Symposium: "Bartleby the Scrivener,"* ed. Howard P. Vincent (Kent, Ohio: Kent State UP, 1966).

3. Dan McCall, *The Silence of Bartleby* (Ithaca: Cornell UP, 1989). McCall gives a very thorough and judicious account of the "candidates" and "origins" that have been proposed for Bartleby; he devotes a whole chapter to "A Passive Resistance" (for Thoreau), still another to "Hawthorne: A Problem," and yet another to "A Little Luny" in order to list the range of psychological disorders that have been suggested. Bartleby as "stranger in the city" was proposed by Leo Marx in his influential essay "Melville's Parable of the Walls," *Sewanee Review*, 61 (1953), 602–27. The view of Bartleby as expression of psychic automatisms is to be found in Robert E. Abrams's fascinating essay "'Bartleby' and the Fragile Pageantry of the Ego," *ELH*, 45, no. 3 (Fall 1978), 488–500; one of the best general Marxist studies is Louise K. Barnett, "Bartleby as Alienated Worker," *Studies in Short Fiction*, 11, no. 4 (Fall 1974), 379–85; and see Patricia Barber, "What If Bartleby Were a Woman?" in *The Authority of*

Experience: Essays in Feminist Criticism, ed. Arlyn Diamond and Lee R. Edwards (Amherst: U of Massachusetts P, 1977), pp. 212–23, for an eye-opening discussion that is revisionist in the best sense.

4. See Otto Reinert, "Bartleby the Inscrutable: Notes on a Melville Motif," in *Americana Norvegica: Norwegian Contributions to American Studies*, ed. Sigmund Skard and Henry H. Wasser (Philadelphia: U of Pennsylvania P, 1966), pp. 180–205, for a view of the scrivener as utterly asocial; Milton Kornfeld, "Bartleby and the Presentation of Self in Everyday Life," *Arizona Quarterly*, 31 (1975), 51–56, makes valuable use of Erving Goffman's views; Nancy Blake offers, in "Mourning and Melancholia in 'Bartleby,'" in *Delta: Revue du Centre d'Études et de Recherches sur les Écrivains du Sud aux États-Unis*, no. 7 (Montpellier, France, 1978), a very thoughtful psychoanalytic reading.

5. See Stanley Brodwin, "To the Frontiers of Eternity: Melville's Crossing in 'Bartleby the Scrivener,'" in *Bartleby the Inscrutable*, ed. M. Thomas Inge (Hamden, Conn.: Archon Books, 1979), p. 176; and Abrams's fine study of psychic mobility, "Fragile Pageantry of the Ego."

6. Francine S. Puk, "'Bartleby the Scrivener': A Study in Self-Reliance," in *Delta*, no. 7, p. 7.

7. Thomas Joswick, "The 'Incurable Disorder' in 'Bartleby the Scrivener,'" in *Delta*, no. 6, p. 91.

8. Herman Melville, *Moby-Dick*, in *Herman Melville: Redburn, White-Jacket, Moby-Dick* (New York: Library of America, 1983), p. 996. Subsequent references are to this edition and are cited in the text.

9. Blake, "Mourning and Melancholia," p. 164. Franz Kafka, "Ein Hungerkünstler," *Sämtliche Erzählungen*, ed. Paul Raabe (Frankfurt: Fischer, 1969), p. 171.

10. Herman Melville, *The Confidence Man* (New York: New American Library, 1984), p. 913. Subsequent references are to this edition and are cited in the text.

11. See R. W. B. Lewis, *Trials of the Word* (New Haven: Yale UP, 1965), and Paul Brodtkorb, Jr., "*The Confidence Man*: The Con-Man as Hero," *Studies in the Novel*, 1, no. 4 (Winter 1969), 421–35, for the argument that *The Confidence Man* is Melville's most prescient text, in view of the direction that modern fiction was going to take. For a book-length study of the "confidence" motif in American letters, see Warwick Wadlington, *The Confidence Game in American Literature* (Princeton: Princeton UP, 1975).

12. McCall, *Silence*, p. 93.

13. Lewis H. Miller, Jr., "'Bartleby' and the Dead Letter," *Studies in American Fiction*, 8, no. 1 (Spring 1980), 5.

14. Régis Durand, "Le Cadre de la fiction," in *Delta*, no. 1, 105.

15. Herman Melville, "Benito Cereno," in *Herman Melville: "Pierre"* . . . (New York: New American Library, 1984), p. 755.

16. See Barnett, "Bartleby," and Barber, "What If?" and see Allan Silver, "The Lawyer and the Scrivener," *Partisan Review*, 48, no. 3 (1981), 409–24.

17. Barber, "What If?" p. 223.

Chapter 3

1. Jane Tompkins, "Sentimental Power: *Uncle Tom's Cabin* and the Politics of Literary History," in *The New Feminist Criticism*, ed. Elaine Showalter (New York: Pantheon, 1985), p. 91.

2. See Sacvan Bercovitch, *The American Jeremiad* (Madison: U of Wisconsin P, 1978), for the treatment of this literary concept. For discussion of the larger aesthetic issues involved in modernist criticism's blindness to Stowe, see Philip Fisher, *Hard Facts: Setting and Form in the American Novel* (New York: Oxford UP, 1985).

3. The major responses of black writers and critics to *Uncle Tom's Cabin* are anthologized in *Critical Essays on Harriet Beecher Stowe*, ed. Elizabeth Ammons (Boston: G. K. Hall, 1980). These matters are also dealt with by Eric Sundquist in his "Introduction" to *New Essays on Uncle Tom's Cabin*, ed. Eric Sundquist (Cambridge: Cambridge UP, 1986).

4. The commentary by James is cited by Edmund Wilson in his discussion of Stowe in *Patriotic Gore: Studies in the Literature of the American Civil War* (1962); the Wilson essay is reprinted in Ammons, *Critical Essays*, pp. 117–21.

5. Burgess's article "Making de White Boss Frown," from *Encounter*, 27 (July 1966), is reprinted in Ammons, *Critical Essays*, pp. 122–27.

6. Harriet Beecher Stowe, *Uncle Tom's Cabin*, in *Harriet Beecher Stowe: Three Novels* (New York: Literary Classics of the U.S., 1982), p. 524. Subsequent references are to this edition and are cited in the text.

7. See Tompkins, "Sentimental Power," for the most illuminating discussion of Stowe's biblical echoes and insertions.

8. Eric Sundquist does a good job of assessing the central importance of Rachel Halliday and her Quaker kitchen in his "Introduction" to *New Essays*; and most of the feminist criticism of Stowe's book pays considerable attention to the Halliday episode as well.

9. See Elizabeth Ammons, "Heroines in *Uncle Tom's Cabin*," in her *Critical Essays*, pp. 152–65, and her equally fascinating essay "Stowe's Dream of the Mother-Savior: *Uncle Tom's Cabin* and American Women Writers Before the 1920s," in Sundquist, *New Essays*, pp. 155–95.

10. Philip Fisher's excellent discussion of Stowe (*Hard Facts*, pp. 88–127) also highlights the emphasis placed on separation, although his perspective is rather different from mine.

11. Flannery O'Connor, "The Displaced Person," in *The Collected Stories* (New York: Farrar, Straus and Giroux, 1983), p. 196.

12. See Richard Yarborough, "Strategies of Black Characterization in *Uncle Tom's Cabin* and the Early Afro-American Novel," in Sundquist, *New Essays*, pp. 45–84, 53.

13. Sundquist, "Introduction," p. 26.

14. A possible literary forebear for Topsy would seem to be Goethe's Mignon in *Wilhelm Meisters Lehrjahre*. Goethe's wild child has a number of protoromantic trappings, but she too is an intriguing instance of amorality and enigmatic behavior, and her origins also are shrouded in mystery.

15. I would like to express a general debt to Karen Halttunen's fine essay "Gothic Imagination and Social Reform: The Haunted Houses of Lyman Beecher, Henry Ward Beecher, and Harriet Beecher Stowe," in Sundquist, *New Essays*, pp. 107–34.

16. See, of course, the classic text on the subject, Sandra Gilbert and Susan Gubar, *Madwoman in the Attic* (New Haven: Yale UP, 1979), p. 534.

17. Fisher links this issue of "feeling right" to the powerlessness inherent in Stowe's formula, and he positions the novel's entire discourse within the topos of *ruins* — involving witnesses who see the work of destruction and cannot reach in to alter things — arguing that such stories "because they are deep in the past invite no compensation and provide no hope of redress, [but] offer, instead, training in pure feeling and response" (*Hard Facts*, p. 121).

Chapter 4

1. Samuel Langhorne Clemens, *Those Extraordinary Twins* (New York: Norton, 1980), p. 119. The fragment of the twins' story excised by Twain as he worked on *Pudd'nhead Wilson* in the early 1890s was, in fact, published along with *Pudd'nhead* in the American Publishing Company edition of 1894, with its own title. Criticism of *Pudd'nhead Wilson* has been dogged by questions of structure and overall "fit," especially in connection with the "residual" twins. Leavis considered the twins to be a "large" fault, but, he added indulgently, "not, after all, a very serious one" ("Introduction," in Clemens, *Pudd'nhead Wilson* [New York: Grove Press, 1955], p. 27). Most Twain criticism regards the structure of the book to be flawed.

2. Leslie Fiedler, "As Free as Any Cretur . . . , " (1955); reprinted in Samuel Langhorne Clemens, *Pudd'nhead Wilson* (New York: Norton, 1980), pp. 220–21.

3. Marvin Fisher and Michael Elliot, "*Pudd'nhead Wilson*: Half a Dog Is Worse Than None," (1972); reprinted in Clemens, *Pudd'nhead Wilson* (Norton), p. 305. Susan Gilman's *Dark Twins: Imposture and Identity in Mark Twain's America* (Chicago: U of Chicago P, 1989) appeared after this chapter on Twain was completed, but it is obvious that she takes the 'twinning principle" in a distinctly different direction, seeing in it the culture's hold on Twain rather than the artist's revenge. What I read as maneuvering room she reads as evasion.

4. Fisher and Elliot, "*Pudd'nhead Wilson*," p. 305.

5. Justin Kaplan, *Mr. Clemens and Mark Twain* (New York: Pocket Books, 1968), p. 269.

6. Clemens, *Pudd'nhead Wilson* (Norton), p. 24. Subsequent references are to this edition and are cited in the text.

7. See George M. Spangler, "*Pudd'nhead Wilson*: A Parable of Property," (1970); reprinted in Clemens, *Pudd'nhead Wilson* (Norton), pp. 295–303, for further discussion of these matters.

8. Stanley Brodwin, "Blackness and the Adamic Myth in Mark Twain's *Pudd'nhead Wilson*," (1973–74); reprinted in Clemens, *Pudd'nhead Wilson* (Norton), p. 339.

9. See Forest G. Robinson, *In Bad Faith: The Dynamics of Deception in Mark Twain's America* (Cambridge, Mass.: Harvard UP, 1986).

10. For an early and influential put-down of the novel, see Richard Chase's chapter on *Pudd'nhead* in his *American Novel and Its Tradition* (New York: Anchor, 1957), pp. 149–56.

11. This is quoted in Arthur G. Pettit, *Mark Twain and the South* (Lexington: U of Kentucky P, 1974), p. 171.

12. The best argument for Tom as avenger is made by James Cox in his magisterial study *Mark Twain: The Fate of Humor* (Princeton: Princeton UP, 1966), pp. 222–46.

13. This is quoted in Arlin Turner, "Mark Twain and the South: An Affair of Love and Anger," (1968); reprinted in Clemens, *Pudd'nhead Wilson* (Norton), p. 276.

14. See Brodwin, "Blackness," pp. 339–40.

15. Fyodor Dostoevsky, *Notes from Underground* (New York: Dutton, 1960), p. 5.

16. Kaplan, *Mr. Clemens*, p. 404.

17. Kaplan goes on to add, "And it is, in fact, precisely his casualness about symbolic content that permitted him to write down his dreams without being afraid of violating any taboos" (ibid., p. 405). For such "casualness," many thanks.

18. I cannot resist including here a personal anecdote that bears on this issue. I am a twin, and I still remember vividly how my mother described the reactions to my

birth. No one knew that she was going to have *two* babies, and therefore there was both shock and some consternation as well when I (as baby number two) arrived on the scene ten minutes after the entry of my brother. Most of all my mother remembers my father's startled exuberance, as he kept shouting into her ear: "There are *two* of them, *two* of them!" At the same time, however, there was the frightened, faintly horrified look of my grandfather, who obviously saw in this double birth something potentially akin to the making of a litter, with no guarantees that it would stop with "two." He must have felt there might be still more waiting in there. My mother kept reassuring both men: "It's OK, it's OK."

19. Quoted in Kaplan, *Mr. Clemens*, p. 168.

20. Leslie Fiedler, in his fine piece "As Free as Any Cretur," has some pertinent remarks on the detective's peculiar appeal for Twain (p. 228).

21. David Sewell, *Mark Twain's Languages* (Berkeley: U of California P, 1987), pp. 110–25.

22. Robinson, *In Bad Faith*, p. 127. The Twain quote appears in Robert Rowlette, *Twain's "Pudd'nhead Wilson": The Development and the Design* (Bowling Green, Ohio: Bowling Green U Popular P, 1971), p. 109.

Chapter 5

1. Susan Sontag, *Against Interpretation* (New York: Dell, 1969), p. 286.

2. Lionel Trilling, "Sherwood Anderson," in *The Liberal Imagination* (New York: Viking, 1950), pp. 22–33. Irving Howe's fine study *Sherwood Anderson* (New York: Sloane, 1951) also stands as a major statement on Anderson's limits and achievements as seen through the eyes of the New York critical establishment of the time.

3. See Welford Dunaway Taylor, "Anderson and the Problem of Belonging," in *Sherwood Anderson: Dimensions of His Literary Art*, ed. David Anderson (East Lansing: Michigan State UP, 1976), pp. 61–74, and Benjamin T. Spencer, "Sherwood Anderson, American Mythopoeist," reprinted in *Sherwood Anderson: A Collection of Critical Essays*, ed. Walter Rideout (Englewood Cliffs, N.J.: Prentice-Hall, 1974), p. 150.

4. Sherwood Anderson, *Winesburg, Ohio* (New York: Penguin, 1960), p. 169. Subsequent references are to this edition and are cited in the text.

5. Irving Howe, "The Book of the Grotesque," in *Sherwood Anderson*; reprinted in *"Winesburg, Ohio": Text and Criticism*, ed. John Ferres (New York: Viking, 1966), p. 409. This early edition of this text contains some essential Anderson criticism, including the makings of an argument for the "poetic" Anderson which I have in mind. See, especially, Sister M. Jocelyn, O.S.B., "Sherwood Anderson and the Lyric Story," pp. 444–54, and Epifanio San Juan, Jr., "Vision and Reality: A Reconsideration of Sherwood Anderson's *Winesburg, Ohio*," pp. 468–81.

6. Edwin Fussell, "Art and Isolation," in *"Winesburg, Ohio": Text and Criticism*, p. 380.

7. Alfred Kazin, *On Native Grounds* (New York: Doubleday, 1956), pp. 172–73.

8. Howe, "The Book of the Grotesque," p. 413.

9. R. E. Spiller et al., eds., *Literary History of the United States* (London: Macmillan, reprinted 1969).

10. "Mother" is, if anything, even closer to the *Psycho* scenario that I have indicated. Tom Willard, as much as his wife, is the victim of a ghost-filled, haunted hotel: "The hotel in which he had begun life so hopefully was now a mere ghost of what a hotel should be. As he went spruce and business-like through the streets of Winesburg, he sometimes stopped and turned quickly about as though fearing that the spirit of the

hotel and of the woman would follow him even into the streets" (39). At one point he says to his son George: "You're not a fool and you're not a woman. You're Tom Willard's son and you'll wake up" (44), and we realize just how much pirouetting and inversion is taking place, given the interest in transvestite escapades and states of mind between waking and dreaming.

11. As quoted by Linda Wagner, "Sherwood, Stein, the Sentence, and Grape Sugar and Oranges," in Anderson, *Sherwood Anderson*, p. 88.

Chapter 6

1. Cited by John H. Desmond, *Risen Sons: Flannery O'Connor's Vision of History* (Athens: U of Georgia P, 1987), p. 23.

2. Peter S. Hawkins, *The Language of Grace: Flannery O'Connor, Walker Percy, and Iris Murdoch* (Cambridge, Mass.: Cowley, 1983), p. 24.

3. W. H. Auden, "Musée des Beaux Arts," in *A Little Treasury of Modern Poetry*, ed. Oscar Williams (New York: Scribners, 1952), pp. 454–55.

4. Gilbert H. Muller, *Nightmares and Visions: Flannery O'Connor and the Catholic Grotesque* (Athens: U of Georgia P, 1983), pp. 3–4.

5. See John Hawkes, "Flannery O'Connor's Devil," reprinted in Melvin Friedman and Beverly Lynn Clark, eds., *Critical Essays on Flannery O'Connor* (Boston: G. K. Hall, 1985), p. 92.

6. Flannery O'Connor, *Mystery and Manners*, ed. Sally Fitzgerald and Robert Fitzgerald (New York: Farrar, Straus and Giroux, 1969), p. 179.

7. Hawkins, *Language of Grace*, p. 24, and Jefferson Humphries, *The Otherness Within: Gnostic Readings in Marcel Proust, Flannery O'Connor, and François Villon* (Baton Rouge: Louisiana State UP, 1983), pp. 95–112.

8. Jacques Maritain, *Art and Scholasticism and the Frontiers of Poetry*, quoted in Desmond, *Risen Sons*, p. 104.

9. Flannery O'Connor, "The Role of the Catholic Novelist," *Greyfriar* (Siena College, Loudonville, N.Y.), 7 (1962), 11.

10. Flannery O'Connor, *The Complete Stories* (New York: Farrar, Straus and Giroux, 1983), p. 157. Subsequent references to O'Connor's stories are to this edition and are cited in the text.

11. Hawkes, "Flannery O'Connor's Devil," p. 92.

12. O'Connor, *Mystery and Manners*, p. 112. See Claire Kahane's essay, "Flannery O'Connor's Rage of Vision," in Friedman and Clark, eds., *Critical Essays*, pp. 119–30, for a strong critique of violence in O'Connor.

13. O'Connor aficionados are familiar with the amazing photograph taken by the author of a man standing on the side of the road with his hand on a sign reading "Toomsboro: City Limit," reprinted in James A. Grimshaw, Jr., *The Flannery O'Connor Companion* (Westport, Conn.: Greenwood Press, 1981), p. 41.

14. O'Connor herself referred to the Misfit as the devil when she discussed this story with Andrew Lytle; see Sally Fitzgerald, ed., *Flannery O'Connor: The Habit of Being* (New York: Farrar, Straus and Giroux, 1979), p. 373. Is it that simple?

15. T. S. Eliot, "Journey of the Magi," in T. S. Eliot, *The Complete Poems and Plays* (New York: Harcourt, Brace and World, 1962), p. 69.

16. Oddly enough, we know that O'Connor herself regarded the end of the story as a failure because she did not feel that she had conveyed the "purgatorial" dimension of Mrs. McIntyre's suffering over her role in the murder of Guizac. Yet the displacement theme itself is carried out with grisly perfection in those final paragraphs, and one could not wish them to be more "articulated" than they are.

Chapter 7

1. Fitzgerald's debt to Conrad is a commonplace in the secondary literature. The Jamesian influence (center of consciousness, *ficelle*, and so on) is equally pervasive but more diffuse. James E. Miller, Jr., offers a fine discussion of Fitzgerald's borrowings, and he also highlights the possible connection with Willa Cather in his *F. Scott Fitzgerald: His Art and His Technique* (New York: New York UP, 1964), pp. 87–92; Lawrence Thornton has made the case for Ford's influence in *Fitzgerald/Hemingway Annual* (1975), 57–74.

2. This posture in Fitzgerald criticism seems to set in right at the outset, with H. L. Mencken's review of *Gatsby* in the *Baltimore Evening Sun* (May 2, 1925), reprinted in *Fitzgerald's "The Great Gatsby": The Novel, The Critics, The Background*, ed. Henry D. Piper (New York: Scribner's, 1970), pp. 121–23. A later variant can be seen in the jaundiced but brilliant Fitzgerald commentary offered by Hugh Kenner in *A Homemade World: The American Modernist Writer* (New York: Morrow, 1975), pp. 20–49.

3. F. Scott Fitzgerald, *The Great Gatsby* (New York: Scribners, 1925), p. 2. Subsequent references are to this edition and are cited in the text.

4. The cultural slogan of the 1980s – "you can't be rich enough or thin enough" – reminds us how the wheel turns. Making money and dieting are (were?) seen as Olympian exercises of will, and the beauty of the "proverb" lies in its inherent frustration and failure, its view that there can be no limit or reachable destination in either of these ventures. Of course, this is what finances them. Kafka's Hunger Artist seems nearby here, and perhaps the most sensual and gratifying binges imaginable are those of denial. Yet one misses the fulsome richness of the Gatsby scheme, the confident certainty of bygone days that more was better than less.

5. Kenner, *Homemade World*, pp. 37–38. I acknowledge my general indebtedness to Kenner's reading of Fitzgerald in particular, and of American literature in general. His notion of the "homemade world" and his frequently zany illustrations of such American tinkering strike me as a useful framework for considering *Gatsby*. In particular, Kenner adds a ludic and wacky note to the more sober ideological studies of individualism in American fiction, and although I do not share his disdain for the American primitive who invents both the game and the rules in his garage, I think he is absolutely on target in his view of American "can-do-ism," of the American writer as amateur *bricoleur*.

6. Ford Madox Ford, *The Good Soldier: A Tale of Passion* (New York: Knopf, 1927), p. 6.

7. This exchange is a commonplace of both Fitzgerald and Hemingway criticism. See Alfred Kazin's classic *On Native Grounds* (New York: Anchor, 1956), p. 245.

8. It turns out that most of these delightful, surrealist touches were added when Fitzgerald was revising *Gatsby*; see Kenneth Eble, "The Craft of Revision: *The Great Gatsby*," reprinted in Piper, *Fitzgerald's "The Great Gatsby,"* pp. 110–17.

9. I realize that a semiotic interpretation of the American Dream will seem harebrained to those who regard this topic as a strictly "substantive" history-of-ideas proposition, dating at least from the legacy of Benjamin Franklin. Yet the dynamic of the dream is what fascinates Fitzgerald, and it clearly fuels his narrative; there is a crucial volitional element in both language and desire, and I think there is considerable evidence (see the Blocks Biloxi section later in this chapter) that Fitzgerald was aware of their common virtues.

10. One wishes that more Fitzgerald critics had heeded Jordan's warning. All too numerous are the claims made for "discovering" who Gatsby "really" is. A case has

been made for worthies such as Max Fleischman, Edward Fuller, Robert Kerr, and Max Gerlach, among others. This effort to pin down Gatsby can be ludicrous, but it is not surprising, and it points to the central enigma of the novel, an enigma that made the author himself uneasy. It is well known that Edith Wharton emphasized Gatsby's "fuzziness" as a flaw in the novel, and Maxwell Perkins urged Fitzgerald to make Gatsby more distinct, more fleshed out, less mysterious. Fitzgerald's own comments on this issue are telling: "I myself didn't know what Gatsby looked like or was engaged in," he wrote to Perkins, and to John Peale Bishop he added the clincher: "Also you are right about Gatsby being blurred and patchy. I never at any one time saw him clear myself — for he started as one man I knew and then changed into myself — the amalgam was never complete in my mind." This material is cited in Piper, *Fitzgerald's "The Great Gatsby,"* pp. 106–7. There can be no question that the novel would be utterly different, not only in tone but also in meaning, if Gatsby were "clearer," less enigmatic.

11. Tanner's general view of American letters in terms of a search for freedoms that are verbal as well as moral is one that has greatly influenced my view of Fitzgerald. See Tony Tanner, *City of Words: American Fiction, 1950–1970* (New York: Harper and Row, 1971).

12. The Queensboro Bridge episode has been mentioned by several critics, usually in cautionary terms. See Richard Lehan, *F. Scott Fitzgerald and the Craft of Fiction* (Carbondale: Southern Illinois UP, 1967), p. 119, and Joan Korenman, "A View from the (Queensboro) Bridge," in *Fitzgerald/Hemingway Annual* (1975), 93–96. To be sure, this sequence does its share of foreshadowing, but its sheer verbal inventiveness and its strange lexical autonomy have not been noted.

13. The emphasis on perception is a stock item in most *Gatsby* criticism. The fun begins, however, when Fitzgerald's prose starts to look "decentered"; that is, when the various motifs such as "seeing" or the automobile begin to acquire a life of their own, a demonic kind of authority, so that one feels that events take place because the language and the metaphors "will" them. Once T. J. Eckleburg is on the scene, Owl-Eyes cannot be far behind. Perhaps all art has its subtle teleology, but when the form imperative becomes truly noticeable, when it seems more urgent than any meanings that limp afterward, then we are in the presence of a playful text that is asserting the kind of peculiar freedom I am investigating.

14. There will doubtless be some readers who think I am insane on this Biloxi, *Tennessee*, issue since their text reads "Biloxi, Mississippi." But textual reality here is as slippery as the World Series. The more recent editions of *Gatsby*, including Scribner's paperback, the current edition, and the Scribner's text used by Piper, *Fitzgerald's "The Great Gatsby,"* in 1970, all print "Biloxi, Tennessee." The older Scribner's editions carry "Biloxi, Mississippi." Scribner's has not responded to my inquiry as to *why* "Mississippi" was changed to the more interesting (to me) "Tennessee." Whatever Fitzgerald's original wording was, the book exists in the public domain, and the more modern version — one is tempted to say the more "modernist" version — does read "Tennessee." The very confusion itself gives evidence that Biloxi is alive and well, at least in the newer reprints.

15. I am indebted to James Cox for underscoring some of these parallels between Fitzgerald and Faulkner.

16. Quoted by Arthur Mizener in his "Introduction" to *F. Scott Fitzgerald: A Collection of Critical Essays*, ed. Arthur Mizener (Englewood Cliffs, N.J.: Prentice Hall, 1963), p. 10.

17. This chapter was originally written during the Reagan presidency, and the parallels between the actor-president and Biloxi as president of your class at Yale were unmistakable. The succeeding president, a nonfictional Yale graduate, perhaps displays

something of the poverty of the real thing as contrasted with the constructs of desire and the histrionic mode. And as far as ersatz logic is concerned, we can assume that Yale itself is standing in for the real castle in the air, Princeton.

Chapter 8

1. William Faulkner, *Novels, 1930–1935: "As I Lay Dying," "Sanctuary," "Light in August," "Pylon"* (New York: Library of America, 1985), p. 29. Subsequent references are to this edition and are cited in the text.

2. Needless to say, the issue of burial rites and treatment of the dead has engaged Western writers ever since *Antigone*. For the best single treatment of the existential themes at the core of *As I Lay Dying*, see the fine book-length study by André Bleikasten, *Faulkner's "As I Lay Dying"* (Bloomington: U of Indiana P, 1973), esp. pp. 115–38.

3. See the early but seminal essay by John Simon "The Scene and the Imagery of Metamorphosis in *As I Lay Dying*," *Criticism*, 7 (Winter 1965), 1–22, for a fine account of nature and consciousness in Faulkner's metamorphic scheme.

4. Charles Palliser has dealt with the philosophical and determinist dimensions of Faulkner's universe, including the "shaping" drama at work here, in "Predestination and Freedom in *As I Lay Dying*," *American Literature*, 56, no. 4 (December 1986), esp. 564–65.

5. I am indebted to William Rushton for bringing to my attention the poetry of this passage.

6. Calvin Bedient, "Pride and Nakedness: *As I Lay Dying*," *Modern Language Quarterly*, 30 (March 1968), 61–76.

7. See Bleikasten, *Faulkner's As I Lay Dying*, pp. 70–73, for a discussion of eyes in this novel.

8. For this view of Addie, I am indebted to Wesley Morris, "The Irrepressible Real: Jacques Lacan and Poststructuralism," in *American Criticism in the Poststructuralist Age*, ed. Ira Konigsberg (Ann Arbor: U of Michigan P, 1981), pp. 119, 121.

9. Richard Godden, "William Faulkner, Addie Bundren, and Language," *Studies in English*, 15 (1978), 108.

10. Olga W. Vickery, "As I Lay Dying," *Perspective*, 3 (Autumn 1950), 179–91.

11. Daniel Ferrer, "In Omnis Iam Vocabuli Mortem," *Oxford Literary Review*, 5, nos. 1 and 2 (1982), 26–27.

12. Eric J. Sundquist, "Death, Grief, Analogous Form: *As I Lay Dying*," in *Philosophical Approaches to Literature: New Essays on Nineteenth- and Twentieth-Century Texts*, ed. William E. Cain (Cranbury, N.J.: Associated University Presses, 1984), pp. 165–82.

13. See Carolyn Slaughter, *"As I Lay Dying*: Demise of Vision," *American Literature*, 61, no. 1 (March 1989), 16–30, for an insightful treatment of this theme.

14. Ferrer, "In Omnis," p. 22.

15. Bleikasten, *Faulkner's As I Lay Dying*, p. 89, proposes this Sartrean scheme as a possible way of measuring the relationship between Darl and Jewel.

16. Paul R. Lilly, "Caddy and Addie: Speakers of Faulkner's Impeccable Language," *Journal of Narrative Technique*, 3, no. 3 (September 1973), 180.

17. Wesley Morris offers a shrewd Lacanian interpretation of these matters, arguing that Faulkner's strategy is "to disguise his and his culture's obsessive belief that vaginal or virginal openness represents desire and pleasure but also sin and the threat of emasculation" ("The Irrepressible Real," p. 119).

18. Godden, "William Faulkner," p. 103.

19. Faulkner always referred to *As I Lay Dying* as a cold text, a tour de force that was executed in record time. It can hardly be accidental that the Reverend Shegog's initial flights of rhetoric are assessed as a circus act, a tightrope performance. Faulkner makes it clear that *technique* by itself (something he recommended for bricklayers and surgeons) is not enough, but we are entitled to feel, nonetheless, that he derived considerable pride from these verbal acrobatics.

20. Bleikasten, *Faulkner's As I Lay Dying*, p. 106; Sundquist, "Death, Grief," p. 176.

21. See Bleikasten, *Faulkner's As I Lay Dying*, p. 13.

22. See ibid., p. 75, for mythic references in the conception of Jewel. Nothing better captures the mythic dimensions of this novel than Jean-Louis Barrault's theatrical rendition of it in Paris in 1935, at least insofar as we can trust the remarkable commentary of Antonin Artaud, who witnessed Barrault's effort to render the coursing morphological power of Faulkner's story and saw in it a model for the theater of the future: "On n'oubliera plus la mort de la mère, avec ses cris qui reprennent à la fois dans l'espace et dans le temps, l'épique traversée de la rivière, la montée du feu dans les gorges d'hommes à laquelle sur le plan du geste répond une autre montée du feu; et surtout cette espèce d'homme-cheval [played by Barrault] qui circule à travers la pièce, comme si l'esprit même de la Fable était redescendu parmi nous" (Artaud, *Le Théâtre et son double* [Paris: Gallimard, 1964], p. 215).

23. Bedient, "Pride and Nakedness," p. 219.

Chapter 9

1. William Faulker, *Novels, 1930–1935: "As I Lay Dying," "Sanctuary," "Light in August," "Pylon"* (New York: Library of America, 1985), p. 702. Subsequent references are to this edition and are cited in the text.

2. Alfred Kazin, "The Stillness of *Light in August*," in *William Faulkner: Three Decades of Criticism*, ed. Frederick Hoffman and Olga Vickery (New York: Harcourt, Brace and World, 1960), p. 249. Kazin's position on Faulkner evolved over the years, and he is more generous to *Light in August* than he was to the Faulkner works he had written about earlier in *On Native Grounds*. Kazin's charge that Faulkner has "mulled" over and "brooded" over his materials at extraordinary length is an interesting issue in itself. He is surely right that Faulkner proceeds along these lines, taking up his donnée again and again, squeezing out all its possible meanings. But is this a weakness? This kind of "brooding" certainly characterizes criticism, and it would seem to be part of any art that works on several levels at once, or seeks to posit links between things that do not overtly cohere. It is arguable that the most interesting and meaningful connections in art (and life) are the kinds that are "mulled" through and "brooded" over.

3. The fullest critique of Faulkner along these lines remains the (rarely cited) work of Walter Slatoff, both the "The Edge of Order: The Pattern of Faulkner's Rhetoric," in Hoffman and Vickery, *Three Decades of Criticism*, pp. 173–98, and in his own *Quest for Failure* (New York: Cornell UP, 1960). Exactly how the pieces of *Light in August* were assembled and reassembled, especially in view of the burgeoning importance of Joe Christmas in Faulkner's revisions, is the subject of Regina Fadiman, *Faulkner's Light in August* (Charlottesville: U of Virginia P, 1975).

4. William Faulkner, *Absalom, Absalom!* (New York: Modern Library, 1951), p. 127. Subsequent references are to this edition and are cited in the text.

5. I am indebted here to the work of my brother, Philip Weinstein, especially as it is expressed in "Precarious Sanctuaries: Protection and Exposure in Faulkner's Fiction," *Studies in American Fiction*, 6 (1978), 173–91.

6. William Faulkner, *As I Lay Dying*, in *Novels, 1930–1935*, p. 110.

7. See, for example, the otherwise gratuitous episode of Christmas "seeking out" a car's headlights. One could imagine Sartre writing such a vignette, and it is surprising that Sartre's fine criticism of Faulkner, focused on *Sartoris* and *The Sound and the Fury*, never addresses the issue of *le regard*, so dear to French critics.

8. There is the making of a full book-length study of "man-to-man" relations in Faulkner, which has yet to be done, to my knowledge. John Irwin has delved deeply and subtly into the homosexual undertones of Faulkner's twisted relationships in his fine *Doubling and Incest/Repetition and Revenge: A Speculative Reading of Faulkner* (Baltimore: Johns Hopkins UP, 1975), passim, but the fuller connection between Faulkner's misogyny, his preference for masculine intimacy, and the freedom of the imagination still needs articulating. The team of Christmas and Burch must be seen as a (degraded) variant of Quentin and Shreve, and *Absalom* explores the profound metaphoric unity between storytelling and sexual intercourse as experienced by two young men. One thinks of the narrative situation in "The Bear" as well, especially the crucial narrative duet in the compound when Ike and McCaslin face up to the truth of the Ledgers. John Matthews's fine book *The Play of Faulkner's Language* (Ithaca: Cornell UP, 1982), is perhaps the most provocative theoretical study we have of the range of storytelling strategies operative in Faulkner, but what may be needed is a look closer to home, a more thoughtful appraisal of the speaking situations available to Faulkner. Perhaps the yarn-spinning framework which came naturally to Faulkner is a de facto male arrangement — men sitting around either in dormitories or in compounds talking together, effecting some kind of "marriage of speaking and hearing." Such creative intimacy is virtually unthinkable for Faulkner in a heterosexual grouping, and the case of the furniture dealer lying in bed "talking" to his wife at the end of *Light in August* flagrantly illustrates my point; there is nothing "joint" about this interaction, and even in this novel the scenes between Byron and Hightower are far more significantly cooperative in spirit than the laconic closing chapter that Faulkner provides.

9. T. S. Eliot, "Journey of the Magi," in *The Complete Poems and Plays* (New York: Harcourt, Brace and World, 1962), p. 69.

10. Robert Scholes, *Structuralism in Literature* (New Haven: Yale UP, 1974), pp. 80–89. Even though I take issue here (and elsewhere) with Scholes's view of Joyce's achievement, I am happy to acknowledge my debt to these observations about the morphology of character in "structuralist" fiction. I am still waiting to see a book on environmentalism and character, and I am persuaded that art teaches us a great deal about the amount of space we take up as individuals, and the extent to which our "inner life" is essentially composed of "outside" materials. The ultimate interest of this situation is located on the far side of our discovery of factitiousness, that we are made up of borrowed parts, that we are more "spread out" than commonly realized; what counts is what "we" do with this knowledge. It is in that light that I believe the willed *project* of self-making, of fashioning an identity in full knowledge of its fictionality, to be the peculiar heroism found in American letters.

11. James Joyce, *Ulysses* (New York: Vintage, 1961), p. 715.

12. William Faulkner, *Lion in the Garden: Interviews with William Faulkner, 1926–1962*, ed. James B. Meriwether and Michael Millgate (New York: Random House, 1968), p. 253.

13. Kazin, "Stillness," p. 264.

14. Faulkner himself linked this pagan dimension of the novel to the quality of August light in Mississippi: "There's a lambence, a luminous quality to the light as though it came not from just today but from back in the old classic times . . . a luminosity older than our Christian civilization" (Frederick Gwynn and Joseph Blotner, *Faulkner in the University* [Charlottesville: U of Virginia P, 1959], p. 199).

Chapter 10

1. John Updike, "The Sinister Sex," *New Yorker*, June 30, 1986, p. 86.
2. Ernest Hemingway, *The Garden of Eden* (New York: Macmillan, 1987), p. 4. Subsequent references are to this edition and are cited in the text.
3. E. L. Doctorow, "Braver than We Thought," *New York Times Book Review*, May 18, 1986; reprinted in *Ernest Hemingway: Six Decades of Criticism*, ed. Linda W. Wagner (Lansing: Michigan State UP, 1987), pp. 325–31. Doctorow expresses the pique one may feel when subjected to Hemingway's lessons in European travel and style:

> In fact so often does David Bourne perform his cultivated eating and drinking that a reader is depressed enough to wonder if Hemingway's real achievement in the early great novels was that of a travel writer who taught a provincial American audience what dishes to order, what drinks to prefer and how to deal with the European servant class. There are moments here when we feel we are not in France or Spain but in the provisional state of Yuppiedom. (329–30)

4. Updike, "Sinister Sex," p. 87.
5. For the best account of literary and biographical portraiture in *The Garden of Eden*, see Mark Spilka's superb article "Hemingway's Barbershop Quintet: *The Garden of Eden* Manuscript," *Novel* (Fall 1987), 29–55. I am pleased to acknowledge my debt to this piece, even though my reading of *The Garden* was in place before I read Spilka. Also of interest for pinpointing the people behind the characters is Gerald Kennedy, "Life as Fiction: The Lure of Hemingway's *Garden*," *Southern Review*, 24, no. 2 (Spring 1988), 451–60.
6. Robert Gajdusek, in his "Elephant Hunt in Eden: A Study of New and Old Myths and Other Strange Beasts in Hemingway's Garden," *Hemingway Quarterly*, 11, no. 1 (Fall 1987), 14–19, provides an entire roll call of Hemingway males practicing gender reversal:

> Frederic in *A Farewell*, the morning after Catherine announces her pregnancy, awakens with morning sickness and *metaphorically* takes on feminine physical attributes — his womb sack, before the chapter ends, must be stripped from him. Colonel Cantwell in *Across the River and into the Trees*, as he is considering Renata's menstrual cycle, is kissed by her hard so that he can then taste his own blood in his own mouth, which he enjoys (111). He takes the matrilineally inherited green emeralds into his own "pocket" to experience the sensation. Such metaphoric assumption of pregnancy, menstruation, and feminine fertility by the male has been covert — in other works breasts are concealed in an imagery of two stuffed upper breast pockets, and wombs in sacks attached to waists — and the sense has been that feminine attributes have been male appropriations. (14–15)

7. Kenneth Lynn, *Hemingway* (New York: Simon and Schuster, 1986).
8. Ernest Hemingway, *A Farewell to Arms* (New York: Macmillan, 1987). Subsequent references are to this edition and are cited in the text.
9. Updike, "Sinister Sex," p. 87.
10. Doctorow, "Braver than We Thought," p. 329.
11. See, for example, the sequence on p. 70, where Catherine rehearses for David the entire repertory of "girl" behavior, making it vivid for all parties just how much construct there is in it.
12. Ernest Hemingway, *For Whom the Bell Tolls* (New York: Macmillan, 1987), pp. 262–63. Subsequent references are to this edition and are cited in the text.

13. Rhoda Koenig, "Adam and Eve on a Raft," *New York* Magazine, May 12, 1986, p. 137, challenges the view of Catherine's sexual experimentation as either metaphysical or tragic, and she feels that the book is especially dated on this front: "Now it seems laughable that love shall die and the best and brightest hopes of earth depart because of some silly talk and some jiggery-pokery under the covers." If she is right, this chapter is hopelessly wrongheaded.

14. Spilka, "Hemingway's Barbershop Quintet," p. 35.

15. Ibid., p. 55.

16. Arthur Rimbaud, *Oeuvres*, ed. Suzanne Bernard (Paris: Garnier, 1962), p. 217. Subsequent references are to this edition and are cited in the text.

17. Spilka, "Hemingway's Barbershop Quintet," p. 53. Concerning Catherine's "authorship," one thinks especially of moments such as the one when she sovereignly informs David and Marita: "You look wonderful together and I'm so proud. I feel as though I'd invented you. Was he good today, Marita?" (191).

18. Ernest Hemingway, *In Our time* (New York: Scribners, 1970), p. 21.

19. In addition to the arguments made by Spilka, Kennedy, "Life as Fiction," points out how much cultural resonance, especially regarding the "physical and psychological effects of the Great War," was eradicated in the edited version (p. 455).

20. Spilka, "Hemingway's Barbershop Quintet," p. 45.

21. See Gajdusek, "Elephant Hunt," p. 15.

22. Spilka, "Hemingway's Barbershop Quintet," p. 46.

23. I disagree entirely with Doctorow's view that the elephant story is "bad Hemingway, a threadbare working of the theme of a boy's initiation rites that suggests to its own great disadvantage Faulkner's story on the same theme, 'The Bear'" ("Braver than We Thought," p. 329). As Spilka has suggested ("Hemingway's Barbershop Quintet," p. 47), Hemingway would have been especially cut by that judgmental comparison, since he was (as Doctorow himself has argued in another context) trying to do something bold and new in this book.

24. Spilka is quite suggestive on the muted presence of Hemingway's father in this text:

> Was the elephant's death, and the boy's reaction to it, a kind of breakthrough then of boyhood resentment against Dr. Clarence Hemingway for teaching his son how to kill rather than love, how to suppress rather than share his deepest feelings? If so, it provides some balance to the indictment here of Grace's androgynous ways, and indicates—perhaps for the first and only time—how much he felt his father—an obtusely sentimental if not a ruthless man—had failed to teach him how to be a friend. ("Hemingway's Barbershop Quintet," p. 48)

25. Spilka deals with the various endings Hemingway drafted in the manuscript over the years (ibid., p. 53), and he shows how essentially irreconcilable they are; for a full-scale treatment of this matter, see Robert Fleming, "The Endings of Hemingway's *Garden of Eden*," *American Literature*, 61, no. 2 (May 1989), esp. 260–70.

Chapter 11

1. Ford Madox Ford, *The Good Soldier* (New York: Vintage, 1955), p. 238.

2. Marc Chénetier has written the most serious critique of the Hawkes curve to date. In his polemical but largely on-target essay "John Jawkes contre John Hawkes: Splendeurs et misères d'une écriture," *Delta*, no. 22 (1986), 13–47, he locates the Hawkes genius in its darker, uncompromising, and largely "naive" vision, and he feels

that the move, from *Blood Oranges* on, toward a mediterranean sumptuousness with echoes of Sade and other Gallic shadows is profoundly misconceived, an effort to cover Hawthorne with Durrell.

3. John Hawkes, *Second Skin* (New York: New Directions, 1963), p. 86. Subsequent references are to this edition and are cited in the text.

4. See Tony Tanner's excellent and influential chapter on Hawkes's work in his *City of Words* (New York: Harper and Row, 1971) for a superb reading of *Second Skin*. Tanner is the first to pay adequate attention to the entire motif of stitching and sewing, and he has also helped us understand the novel as a Hawkesian metafiction. My general sense of Hawkes has been enriched by Tanner's shrewd and insightful analysis.

5. In addition to his hard-hitting critique of Hawkes's later manner, Chénetier also has to his credit an extraordinary essay on *Second Skin*, "'The Pen and the Skin': Inscription and Cryptography in John Hawkes's *Second Skin*,'" *Review of Contemporary Fiction*, 3, no. 3 (Fall 1983), 167-77, in which he offers the most brilliant and nuanced account we have of inscription as marking the body. Like all critics, he is indebted to Tanner on this front, but the subtlety and insights of his essay take Tanner's givens in wholly new and fascinating directions. Toward the end of his essay, drawing on Jean Baudrillard's notion of bodies in culture, he posits the view that the ultimate strategy of *Second Skin* is antierotic and evasive, a dream of flesh that is blank rather than "written." He cites Baudrillard's claim that the tattoo is "in primitive societies what, along with other ritual signs, makes the body what it is: a material for symbolic exchange. Without this tattoo, or without masks, the body could only be what it is: naked and inexpressive," and he goes on to argue that "Skipper sees his body as neutralizer of eroticized but worldly and therefore deadly inscriptions; witness the 'preliminary roster of persons whose love I have lost or whose poison I happily spent my life neutralizing with my unblemished flesh'" (175-76). As clever as this is, it seems to me wrongheaded in that it cancels out Skipper's song, his record of injuries and sensations, which stands, a bit like Odysseus tied to the mast, and ducks nothing whatsoever.

6. Hawkes early on likened his writing to the aims of poetry, namely, to capture the movement and life of the psyche that defies rational analysis: "Like the poem, the experimental fiction is an exclamation of psychic materials which come to the writer all readily distorted, prefigured in that nightly inner schism between the rational and the absurd" (John Hawkes, "Notes on the Wild Goose Chase," in *The American Novel Since World War II*, ed. Marcus Klein [New York: Fawcett, 1969], p. 249).

7. See G. M. Colville's fascinating "Paternités dans *Second Skin*, faits tus et perdus, foetus et pères dûs, fêtes éperdues" in *Delta*, no. 22 (1986), 69-86, for a highly sophisticated reading of the novel in terms of repressed homosexuality.

8. James Joyce, *Ulysses* (New York: Vintage, 1961), p. 469.

9. The first significant criticism that Hawkes's work received came from his mentor and friend Albert Guerard, and Guerard's essays on Hawkes are as pungent and viable today as they were several decades ago. In particular, Guerard's piece "*Second Skin*: The Light and the Dark Affirmation," in *Studies in "Second Skin,"* ed. John Graham (Columbus, Ohio: Merrill, 1971), pp. 93-102, maps out the Hawkes terrain with great insight and force. I am pleased to acknowledge my debt to Guerard's reading, and especially to his views on the bestiary in *Second Skin*; moreover, the kind of stylistic evolution, from unconscious to conscious, that Chénetier has charted in Hawkes's career is already implicitly acknowledged as a possibility at the close of Guerard's essay.

10. See Chénetier, "The Pen," and also Frederick Karl's remarks on Hawkes in *American Fictions: 1940-1980* (New York: Harper and Row, 1983).

11. John Hawkes, *Adventures in the Alaskan Skin Trade* (New York: Simon and Schuster, 1985), p. 11. Subsequent references are to this edition and are cited in the text.

12. F. Scott Fitzgerald, *The Great Gatsby* (New York: Scribners, 1980), p. 182.

13. Some of the reviews that greeted the Alaska book dwelt on the issue of the feminine narrator's mind-set. Although Hawkes was credited with trying to actualize a female perspective, Laura Marcus's parting shot in the *Times Literary Supplement*, no. 28 (1986), 216, is revelatory: "It may also be worth noting that *machismo* is not dislodged by the creation of a "new woman" who keeps lingerie catalogues among her flight manuals."

14. See Patrick O'Donnell, "Life and Art: An Interview with John Hawkes," *Review of Contemporary Fiction*, 3, no. 3 (1983), 107–26, for Hawkes's grounding of this magnificent image:

> I was talking to a few friends the other night while making *aioli*, garlic mayonnaise. It's hard to make, with a mortar and pestle, and you have to beat it for a long time. I was doing this, pouring in the olive oil drop by drop then whipping the mixture, when I suddenly found myself telling a story. I recalled two images or events from my Alaskan life that relate to my ideas about sexuality and the imagination. I remembered the one road leading out of town that went about thirty miles and then ended. Somewhere along that road there was a little cove, where the water was high, and a sunken airplane that seemed to me almost made of concrete. It was a strange object; I can't remember there being any glass in the windows. When the tide was high, the plane would be totally submerged. When the water went down, this airplane was totally uncovered, and the sea substance that was all over it—barnacles, mud, all kinds of sea life—was dead. I thought of it as very frightening and fascinating. (121)

One savors the connections in play here—eating, beating, talking, imagining—and this mythic fable of our technological world gone amok, reclaimed rhythmically by the elements. It is an anecdote; it is luminous.

Chapter 12

1. See Marc Chénetier, "Ideas of Order at Delphi," in *Facing Texts: Encounters Between Contemporary Writers and Critics*, ed. Heide Ziegler (Durham: Duke UP, 1988), for one of the best discussions of Coover's poetics to date.

2. I am indebted here, for both the information on and inspection of the hypercube, to my colleague Thomas Banchoff of the Brown University mathematics department. Banchoff's cube fits in a briefcase, and his presentations of its workings to a generation of Brown students have made it something of a legend in this community. How widespread its significance may be among mathematicians is an issue I am not competent to judge.

3. Robert Coover, *Pricksongs & Descants* (New York: New American Library, 1970), p. 39.

4. Robert Coover, *The Public Burning* (New York: Bantam, 1978), p. 488. Subsequent references are to this edition and are cited in the text.

5. Coover is worth citing on the matter of Nixon's genesis and function:

> Originally, it was the circus aspect that interested me the most. Then I developed the idea of having the Vice President at the time become the first person narrator. The world has its superheroes—figures like Uncle Sam and the Phantom—

and Richard Nixon, who wishes to be the incarnation of Uncle Sam but hasn't yet learned how to shazam himself into super-freakhood, is studying what is going on very carefully, picking up notes. (Frank Gado, *First Person: Conversations on Writers and Writing* [Schenectady: Union CP, 1973], p. 155)

It is intriguing to follow the development of Coover's concept here, and we can see the potentially Bakhtinian circus motif blend into a more patently caricatural project, one aimed at the extremist forms of authoritarian rhetoric, with Nixon left as combination witness/participant. The end result fuses both these models.

6. See David Estes, "American Folk Laughter in Robert Coover's *The Public Burning*," *Contemporary Literature*, 28, no. 2 (1987), 239–55.

7. The phrase "prairie, boondock Zeus," is Lois Gordon's (*Robert Coover: The Universal Fictionmaking Process* [Carbondale: Southern Illinois UP, 1983], p. 57). There are, of course, commentators who have not much relished Sam's style. Richard Andersen, *Robert Coover* (New York: Twayne, 1981), considers him "a composite of phony affability, insensitivity, and opportunism" (124).

8. Margaret Heckard, "Robert Coover, Metafiction, and Freedom," *Twentieth-Century Literature*, 22, no. 2 (1976), 210–27, raises these issues and refers to the important ideological critique of postmodernism formulated by Fredric Jameson. The all too prevalent view, of course, is that self-reflexive fiction is self-flaunting, navel gazing and inherently incapable of moral or historical power. For a thoughtful but typical critique in this vein, see Peter Humm, "Telling Tales on the Rosenbergs," *Literature and History*, 12, no. 1 (1986), 48–57. Others have been less kind still; the best-known put-down of the novel from this point of view was by Norman Podhoretz in "Uncle Sam and the Phantom," in *Saturday Review*, September 17, 1977, concluding that the book was "a lie. And because it hides behind the immunities of artistic freedom to protect itself from being held to the normal standards of truthful discourse, it should not only be called a lie, it should also be called a cowardly lie" (34).

9. See Jackson I. Cope's fine study *Robert Coover's Fictions* (Baltimore: Johns Hopkins UP, 1986) for a dialogical reading of *The Public Burning*. Cope is an extraordinarily canny reader of Coover, and he has a thorough grasp of the important textual history of Coover's fictions (frequently at odds with the publishing history), thereby gaining a sighting on the Coover narrational curve.

10. Geoffrey Wolff's important early essay on *The Public Burning*, "An American Epic," *New Times*, August 19, 1977, pp. 48–57, contains some further crucial Coover views on clowning:

My interest in Nixon—or my story about him—grew out of my concept of the book as a sequence of circus acts. That immediately brought to mind the notion of clown acts. . . . You have a high wire number, and then the clown comes on . . . takes a pratfall, drops his pants and exits. And then you can throw another high-wire act at them. So naturally I looked for the clownish aspects of my narrator, and you can't have an unsympathetic clown. (54)

11. The term "ontologically insecure" is taken from John Z. Guzlowski, "Coover's *The Public Burning*: Richard Nixon and the Politics of Experience," *Critique*, 39, no. 1 (1987), 58.

12. Writing this essay in 1990 with President *Bush* in the White House adds still another delicious tonality to Coover's melody and proves that truth is more shapely than fiction.

13. Cope calls Nixon's trip to Sing-Sing "a dream of pattern-breaking, of anti-generic freedom at last, a dream of personal history" (*Coover's Fictions*, p. 66). John

Ramage, in "Myth and Monomyth in Coover's *The Public Burning*," *Critique*, 23, no. 3 (1982), 52–68, has shown how Nixon's entry into Sing Sing is studded with references to his own past: Grandma Milhous, the downstairs bedroom in the house back in Whittier, his college campus, even the yellow brick road in *The Wizard of Oz*. Ramage claims that Nixon "is entering a prelapsarian realm of new beginnings where history is abolished" (59).

14. Robert Morace, "Robert Coover, the Imaginative Self, and the 'Tyrant Other,'" *Papers on Language and Literature*, 21, no. 2 (1985), 192–209, positions Coover in the American tradition much as I do, as a writer concerned with "the typically American theme of the autonomous self, or more specifically, the individual's quest to create a meaningful fictional universe" (192).

15. Gado, *First Person*, pp. 156–57. Coover is referring specifically to the impact of Durkheim's work on his notion of fiction. Yet his resulting sense of liberation, of the artist as at once anarchist and constructive, reminds one also of the paroxysmal views of theater expressed by Antonin Artaud. Thomas LeClair has pointed out, in "Robert Coover, *The Public Burning*, and the Art of Excess," *Critique*, 23, no. 3 (1982), 5–28, that Coover draws also on the work of Roger Caillois, especially in connection with his views of circus (7–8); LeClair builds an interesting reading of the novel on the notion of "extreme performances" in personal, political, religious and artistic realms.

16. Robert Scholes, in one of the earliest assessments of Coover, "Metafiction," *Iowa Review*, 1, no. 4 (1970), 100–15, first mentioned this motif, although in a rather different context: "Coover's technique is to take the motifs of folk literature and explode them into motivations and revelations, as the energy might be released from a packed atomic structure" (113).

17. Morace, "Robert Coover," p. 198.

18. For a provocative reading of the 3-D episode as the entire novel *in nuce*, see Louis Gallo, "Nixon and the 'House of Wax': An Emblematic Episode in Coover's *The Public Burning*," *Critique*, 23, no. 3 (1982), 43–51.

19. For a much more positive (and sustained) reading of *Spanking the Maid*, see Cope, *Coover's Fictions*, pp. 55–58.

20. Kathryn Hume has written a very thoughtful essay, "Robert Coover's Fiction: The Naked and the Mythic," *Novel*, 12, no. 2 (1979), 128–48, developing the view that each of these notions—naked and mythic—constitutes a deep narrative impulse in the Coover imagination. She refers quite usefully to Matthew Hodgart's distinction between "nude" and "naked": "The nude is the idealized human body, both erotic and heroic in the noble tradition begun by the Greeks: the nude is appropriate to the context of Eros (undressing for bed) or for the athletic-heroic (stripping for the games); it is the apotheosis of human anatomy. The naked, on the other hand, means undressing in a wholly inappropriate context: the naked man is caught with his trousers down, caught in the act of guilt or shame" (129). This distinction applies perfectly to the dilemmas and plights that recur with alarming frequency in Coover's work (to Nixon, Gerald, Charlie). Yet the angry charge of ubiquitous humiliation and sadism leveled by Robert Towers ("Nixon's Seventh Death," *New York Review of Books*, September 29, 1977), pp. 8–10, seems somehow overly focused, in that the Coover dynamic of freedom and entrapment is hardly limited to "bare-assed, encumbered" men (9), but extends into the larger verbal behavior of the works and succeeds in fashioning a scheme of great beauty as well as humiliation.

21. Coover has reported how reading Ovid confirmed his sense of his own scheme: "The Ovidian stories all concern transformation: now that is not a startlingly new subject—after all, fairy tales, animal fables, and the like, deal with it—but I suddenly

realized that the basic constant struggle for all of us is against metamorphosis, against giving in to the inevitability of the process" (Gado, *First Person*, p. 152).

Chapter 13

1. Mark Twain, quoted by Justin Kaplan, *Mr. Clemens and Mark Twain* (New York: Pocket Books, 1968), p. 404.

2. The expression *écriture féminine*, has been a charged and volatile critical term for several decades now. In particular, it has often been the bone of contention dividing French feminists from their Anglo-American counterparts, for it posits a special woman's *language* (rather than a particular "agenda" and so on) as the essential feature of women's writing. Ann Rosalind Jones has written very informatively about the nature and ramifications of these positions in her account of four major French practitioners—Julia Kristeva, Monique Wittig, Hélène Cixous, and Luce Irigaray—"Writing the Body: Toward an Understanding of *l'Écriture Féminine*," in *The New Feminist Criticism*, ed. Elaine Showalter (New York: Pantheon, 1985), pp. 361–77. Although these four feminists have quite varied aims, one could probably sketch some common features of the "feminine writing" itself: derived from the body, decentered, nonproprietary, libidinally charged, at war with "phallogocentric" codes of repressive order. Much of the debate on these matters has understandably focused on issues of representation and essentialism. See Margaret Homans, "'Her Very Own Howl': The Ambiguities of Representation in Recent Women's Fiction," *Signs*, 9, no. 2 (Winter 1983), 186–205, for a judicious analysis of the problems at hand in the areas of both theory and praxis.

3. Quoted by Marsha Jean Darling, "In the Realm of Responsibility: A Conversation with Toni Morrison," *Women's Review of Books* (March 1988), 5–6.

4. Toni Morrison, *Beloved* (New York: New American Library, 1988), p. 155. Subsequent references are to this edition and are cited in the text.

5. Nelly Y. McKay, "Introduction," in *Critical Essays on Toni Morrison*, ed. Nelly Y. McKay (Boston: G. K. Hall, 1988), p. 3.

6. See Toni Morrison, "Unspeakable Things Unspoken: The Afro-American Presence in American Literature," *Michigan Quarterly Review*, 28, no. 1 (1989), 1–32. In particular, Morrison explains the intent of her opening in medias res:

> It is abrupt, and should appear so. No native informant here. The reader is snatched, yanked, thrown into an environment completely foreign, and I want it as the first stroke of the shared experience that might be possible between the reader and the novel's population. Snatched just as the slaves were from one place to another, from any place to another, without preparation and without defense. No lobby, no door, no entrance—a gangplank, perhaps (but a very short one). (32)

7. Looking back at Morrison's earlier books, impressive as they are, one feels that they are far more tentative and groping than *Beloved*. *Sula*, for example, biting though it is, seems a bit tendentious and schematic when compared to the dense, beautifully textured *Beloved*, and her mythic, large-souled *Song of Solomon* appears chunky and overlong against the rich sleekness of this later book.

8. See, in addition to the articles of Ann Rosalind Jones and Margaret Homans already cited, May Gwendolyn Henderson's "Speaking in Tongues: Dialogics, Dialectics, and the Black Woman Writer's Literary Tradition," in *Changing Our Own Words: Essays on Criticism, Theory, and Writing by Black Women*, ed. Cheryl A. Wall (New

Brunswick: Rutgers UP, 1989), pp. 16–37, for an account of how the case of the black woman writer is a special one. Henderson's view of "speaking in tongues" goes back to Paul, but it has a fascinating relevance for Beloved's own discourse in Morrison's novel (which Henderson does not discuss).

9. Judith Thurman, "A House Divided," *New Yorker*, November 2, 1987, pp. 175–80, has also referred to Paul D.'s failure to grasp the magnitude of the "milk crime," but she views this moment as revelatory of Sethe's own (neurotic) fixation rather than any lack of perceptiveness on the man's part. It is clear to me that Sethe's view of milk and mothering may not be to everyone's taste—although to brand it a kind of slavery seems to me beyond the pale—but I find no evidence in the text that we as readers are *meant* to regard it as excessive or diseased. Of course, that is not to say that such responses are inappropriate; but they go, I believe (and maybe I am male-thinking this), against the grain of the novel's imperious logic.

10. Thurman, "A House Divided," p. 176.

11. Ibid., p. 179.

12. Deborah Horvitz, "Nameless Ghosts: Possession and Dispossession in *Beloved*," *Studies in American Fiction*, 17, no. 2 (1989), 157.

13. This issue of "owning" another person is deeply problematic in today's critical climate. Once again I find myself assenting to the novel's (tragic but hardly wrong-headed) view of linkage, and I cannot help feeling that Sethe and Beloved have "earned" the right to insist that each "owns" the other. "I am beloved and she is mine" seems to me the metaphoric heart of the book, but it is not likely to be seen that way by "liberationists" of any stripe whatsoever.

14. Horvitz posits that Beloved is "also" Sethe's African mother, and even suggests that she represents the African mother's mother ("Nameless Ghosts," pp. 158, 163). Horvitz offers the fullest account to date of the rich poetic suite of utterances which I regard as the emblematic *écriture féminine*.

15. Horvitz remarks in a footnote that Morrison's own trademark consists in "marking" her women:

Morrison often marks the bodies of her female characters. In *Song of Solomon*, Pilate has no navel; in *Sula*, Sula has a birthmark over her eye; in *Beloved*, Sethe's mother is branded with the cross in the circle and Sethe is permanently marked from the whipping on her back. Their bodies as well as their minds and souls are indelibly marked as different, "other," strange and witchy. As alienated women, they share being motherless. Each lost her mother to a violent death, and the marked bodies are associated with loss. Sethe's markings symbolize her separation from her mother because, in a sense, they are the "wrong" marks. She begged her mother to brand her with a cross in a circle, so she could be permanently marked as her mother's daughter. And Pilate's lack of a navel questions whether she ever had a matrilineal connection. (167)

16. I am indebted here and elsewhere to Marianne Hirsch's unpublished essay "Maternity and Rememory," which deals very fully and richly with the view of mothering put forth in *Beloved*.

17. Although I have focused my argument for an *écriture féminine* on the dark, pithy utterances of fusion and "join," one could extend this analysis to the book as a whole. Hirsch gives an eloquent account of Morrison's triumph in fashioning a multivalent textual world:

Linear and cyclical narratives of family are replaced by another shape, constructed like rememory, made possible by the 124, the gap in the sequence that opens up spaces of difference, upsets binaries, erases distinctions, reverses sequences. The trace is there and it is gone. The house burned down but it still exists, "out there." Sethe and Beloved have the same face. Beloved and Amy (Aimée), Amy/Denver and Denver, have the same name. The grandmother is baby, Baby *Suggs*. Sethe is the mother, Beloved is the child. Sethe is the child, Beloved, pregnant, combs her hair, counts her teeth, beats her up. Sethe diminishes, Beloved grows. Mr. Bodwin is schoolteacher. Mrs. Bodwin teaches Denver. ("Maternity," p. 20)

May Gwendolyn Henderson's view of black women's writing as modern-day Scripture, as instances of "speaking in tongues" in ways that at once bespeak mysteries and also unite congregations, seems marvelously apposite to the thickened oracular language at the poetic climax of *Beloved* (Henderson, "Speaking in Tongues").

Chapter 14

1. The best and fullest account of DeLillo's fiction is Thomas LeClair, *In the Loop: Don DeLillo and the Systems Novel* (Urbana: U of Illinois P, 1987). LeClair not only situates DeLillo in the company of postmodernists and deconstructionists but also invokes a galaxy of contemporary thinkers—Bateson, Wilden, Hofstader, Serres, Lyotard et al.—in articulating the notion of the "systems" novel. For a different effort to align DeLillo generically, see John Johnston, "Generic Difficulties in the Novels of Don DeLillo," *Critique*, 30, no. 4 (1989), 261–75.

2. Don DeLillo, *Great Jones Street* (New York: Vintage, 1983), p. 105.

3. DeLillo himself has characterized Wunderlich's trajectory as a move "from political involvement to extreme self-awareness to childlike babbling" (Thomas LeClair, "An Interview with Don DeLillo," *Contemporary Literature*, 23, no. 1 [1982], 22), and it is clear that this particular curve is an arresting one for the author.

4. Don DeLillo, *Libra* (New York: Penguin, 1989), p. 261. Subsequent references are to this edition and are cited in the text.

5. Don DeLillo, *The Names* (New York: Vintage, 1983), p. 6. Subsequent references are to this edition and are cited in the text.

6. LeClair, *In the Loop*, p. 194. LeClair's reading of *The Names* focuses, quite provocatively, on the tensions between orality and literacy, or intimacy and alienation. For a suggestive and alert early reading of *The Names*, see Fredric Jameson's review in *Minnesota Review*, no. 22 (1984), 118–22. Interestingly enough, Jameson finds the specific language argument itself, especially concerning the cult, at once senseless and de rigueur as postmodern trademark.

7. It is in passages such as this that we can best observe the ideological savvy of *The Names*. DeLillo is demonstrably getting his point about exploitation across, but he is content to let his plot carry it, without sinking into a political debate. This is why John Kucich's charge of racism and misogyny, in "Postmodern Politics: Don DeLillo and the Plight of the White Male Writer," *Michigan Quarterly Review*, 27, no. 2 (1988), 328–41, seems both harsh and insensitive.

8. See Matthew Morris, "Murdering Words: Language in Action in Don DeLillo's *The Names*," *Contemporary Literature*, 30, no. 1 (1989), 113–27, and Paul Bryant, "Discussing the Untellable: Don DeLillo's *The Names*," *Critique*, 39, no. 1 (1987), 16–29, for further discussion of the "Ob" language of the text.

9. DeLillo is fascinated with babbling: "Babbling can be frustrated speech or it can be a purer form, an alternative speech. I wrote a short story that ends with two babies babbling at each other in a car. This was something I'd seen and heard, and it

was a dazzling and unforgettable scene. I felt these babies *knew* something. They were talking, they were listening, they were *commenting* . . . " (LeClair, "Interview," p. 24). The episode in *White Noise* about Wilder's crying must derive from this interest.

10. This mockery of domestic fiction is DeLillo's, cited by LeClair, *In the Loop*, p. 208.

11. Don DeLillo, *White Noise* (New York: Vintage, 1985), p. 50. Subsequent references are to this edition and are cited in the text.

12. When asked about the importance of Wittgenstein to his work, DeLillo replied: "I like the way he uses the language. . . . It's like reading Martian. The language is mysteriously simple and self-assured. It suggests without the slightest arrogance that there's no alternative to these remarks. . . . Wittgenstein is the language of outer space, a very precise race of people" (LeClair, "Interview," p. 26).

13. See Michael Messmer, "Thinking It Through Completely: The Interpretation of Nuclear Culture," *Centennial Review*, 34, no. 4 (1988), 397–413, for a provocative perspective on DeLillo's book. Messmer draws suggestively on Jean Baudrillard's notion of "simulacra" and Umberto Eco's "hyperreality" in order to discuss the image-status of nuclear issues, and he turns, not surprisingly, to *White Noise*, with its airborne toxic event and its SIMUVAC (simulated evacuation) technicians, for striking textual support.

14. LeClair, *In the Loop*, p. 219.

15. I owe these definitions to LeClair, ibid., p. 230.

16. Here is the area of the novel (and of DeLillo's achievement) that LeClair very seriously misreads. His systems-analysis thesis requires that old-fashioned notions of cause and effect and so on be challenged by the newer looping models of the systems thinkers, and this in turn leads him to posit a kind of generational warfare in *White Noise*, a resistance on the part of the parents to come to terms with the "newer" thinking of the young (as embodied in the theories put forth by Heinrich). I think one has to be tone-deaf to miss the (gentle) humor and irony in DeLillo's evocation of these delicious conversational duels, and to position the author on either side of this "debate" (which it is not) is to bypass the poignancy and seriousness of the family theme altogether. See ibid., p. 209, for LeClair's version.

17. Needless to say, those who do not like DeLillo anyway may agree with Bruce Bayer, "Don DeLillo's America," *New Centurion*, 3, no. 8 (1985), 34–42, that the rendition of the human family and its secrets is utterly arid, pretentious, cerebral, clichéd, and unpersuasive. About this specific example of the Toyota Celica utterance, Bayer claims, "How does DeLillo get away with such stale gags?" (39). Bayer cites probably half the passages I hold up for praise as evidence of DeLillo's tendentiousness and failure as a writer. Anyone who agrees with him is not likely to be converted by me.

18. DeLillo arranges a perfect fusion between the German plot and the erotic plot in the lovely little scene in which Howard, the German tutor, puts his finger into Jack's mouth in order to position his tongue properly, producing thereby a moment of shocking erotic intimacy.

Conclusion

1. Oliver Sacks, "Neurology and the Soul," *New York Review of Books*, November 22, 1990, p. 49.

2. Ibid., pp. 49–50.

Index

Caillois, Roger, 338n15
Calvino, Italo, 6, 33, 256
Camus, Albert, 15
Casablanca (Curtiz), 262
Castro, Fidel, 312
Cather, Willa, 328n1
Cellini, Benvenuto, 214
Cervantes, Miguel de, 235
Chaplin, Charlie, 40, 261–62
Chardin, Teilhard de, 108
Chase, Richard, 4, 325n10
Chénetier, Marc, 221–22, 334n2, 335nn5 and 9, 336n1
Chibka, Robert, 321n6
Chinatown (Polanski), 309
Christ (Jesus), 63–64, 118–19, 124, 314
   birth of, 178
   and Christian ritual, 108
   and crucifixion, 102, 113
   dismemberment of, 121, 126
   female, 51
   and slaves, 51
   story of, 109, 177, 181
   and submission, 62
Cixous, Hélène, 339n2
The Color Purple (Walker), 280
Columbus, Christopher, 215
Colville, G. M., 335n7
Connection, 106, 127–28, 152, 184, 188, 273
   between self and Other, 253
   bodily, 54, 226, 276, 286
   of body and spirit, 178
   mother-child, 265, 278–86
   sexual, 251–52
   through art, 127
   through birth, 176–78
   through family, 52, 54, 181–83, 308
   through language, 178, 225, 252, 284–87
   through looking, 153
   through narration, 43
   through violence, 154
Conrad, Joseph, 23, 25, 67, 88, 131, 328n1
   Heart of Darkness, 33
   Lord Jim, 33
Cooper, James Fenimore, 198, 222, 230, 289
Coover, Robert, 4, 85, 146, 288, 336n5, 337nn9 and 10, 338nn14, 15, 16, 20, 21
   "The Babysitter," 216–37, 259
   "The Brother," 236
   "Charlie in the House of Rue," 261–62
   "The Elevator," 236–37, 259
   Gerald's Party, 237, 252–59, 260
   "The Magic Poker," 236, 259
   A Night at the Movies, 237, 252, 257, 260–64
   The Origin of the Brunists, 236
   Pinocchio, 260
   Pricksongs and Descants, 235–36
   The Public Burning, 5, 7–9, 26, 239–60, 264, 267, 312
   "Shootout at Gentry's Junction," 104
   Spanking the Maid, 259

The Universal Baseball Association, J. Henry Waugh Prop., 236
Whatever Happened to Gloomy Gus of the Chicago Bears?, 260
   "You Must Remember This," 262–64
Cope, Jackson, 244, 337nn9 and 13, 338n19
Cortázar, Julio, 256
Cortés, Hernando, 216
Cowley, Malcolm, 93
Cox, James, 325n12, 329n15
Crews, Frederick, 16, 20, 321n1
Criticism
   comparatist, 9
   deconstructive, 30, 38, 39, 43
   feminist, 47, 76, 339n2
   Freudian, 16
   historicist, 7–8
   New, 47
   revisionist, 47
Cyrano de Bergerac (Rostand), 93

Declaration of Independence, 4
DeLillo, Don, 4, 9, 146–47, 267, 341nn1, 3, 7 and 9, 342nn12, 16, 17, 18
   Great Jones Street, 288–89
   Libra, 5, 7–8, 245, 258, 289–90, 292, 311–15, 318–19
   The Names, 289–98, 311
   Running Dog, 288–89
   White Noise, 5, 7, 289–90, 294, 298–311
Derrida, Jacques, 39, 159, 163, 293
Descartes, René, 25, 158–59
Desire, 97, 137, 213, 262
   anarchic, 199
   and artistic creation, 197, 200
   choked, 92–93
   constructs of, 134
   and displacement, 20–21
   feminine, 196, 209
   as lack, 280
   and the past, 144
   polymorphous, 196
   and speech, 135
   woman as object of, 194
Desmond, John, 118
Dickens, Charles, 134, 181
   David Copperfield, 300, 305
Disguise, 18–19, 21, 55
   as source of freedom, 56–57, 75–78
Doctorow, E. L., 194, 333n3, 334n23
Dostoevski, Fyodor, 18, 23, 67, 78, 88
Doubles, 23, 25, 312–14. *See also* Ghosts; Twins
Douglass, Frederick, 48
Dracula, 198
Dreiser, Theodore, 48
Durand, Régis, 39
Durkheim, Emile, 338n15
Durrell, Lawrence, 335n2

Eble, Kenneth, 328n8
Eco, Umberto, 342n13
Einstein, Albert, 250, 254, 256–57